Government Budgeting a
Expenditure Managemen.

Principles and International Practice

Salvatore Schiavo-Campo

Routledge
Taylor & Francis Group

NEW YORK AND LONDON

First published 2017
by Routledge
711 Third Avenue, New York, NY 10017

and by Routledge
2 Park Square, Milton Park, Abingdon, Oxon OX14 4RN

Routledge is an imprint of the Taylor & Francis Group, an informa business

Library of Congress Cataloging in Publication Data
A catalog record for this book has been requested

ISBN: (hbk) 978-1-138-18340-7
ISBN: (pbk) 978-1-138-18341-4
ISBN: (ebk) 978-1-315-64587-2

Typeset in Sabon
by Sunrise Setting Ltd, Brixham, UK

MIX
Paper from
responsible sources
FSC
www.fsc.org   FSC® C013056

Printed and bound in Great Britain by
TJ International Ltd, Padstow, Cornwall

Government Budgeting and Expenditure Management

The government budget should be the financial mirror of society's choices. Yet most people view budgeting as the epitome of eye-glazing subjects, rarely explained in a way that is understandable to the non-specialist and too often presented without adequate consideration of a country's governance and institutional capacity. *Government Budgeting and Expenditure Management* fills a gap in the literature to redress these failings and does so in comparative international perspective.

This book provides a comprehensive but pithy and easy-to-understand treatment of public financial management, taking into account a variety of special issues including budgeting in post-conflict situations, at subnational government levels, for military/security expenditures, and in countries with large extractive revenues. Distilling the lessons of budgeting reform in countries at different levels of income and administrative capacity, each chapter gradually progresses from the basic principles to the more technical aspects and then on to implementation issues, using concrete examples and illustrations from around the globe.

Government Budgeting and Expenditure Management is ideally suited as the primary text for advanced undergraduate or graduate courses in government budgeting or public financial management, or as a supplementary text for courses in public finance, public economics, economic development, public administration or comparative politics. With its attention to practical implementation aspects, the book will also be of direct interest to practitioners, policy-makers, and government employee training organizations.

Salvatore "Rino" Schiavo-Campo is a former senior official at the World Bank and International Monetary Fund, following a full academic career that concluded as Professor and Chairman of Economics at the University of Massachusetts, Boston. He is the author of numerous scholarly articles and 14 books on topics in public financial management, governance and public administration, economic development and post-conflict reconstruction.

"Based on decades of professional experience and personal reflections, Schiavo-Campo's book provides one of the very few comprehensive accounts of how government budgets work, and why they are so important. Covering a wide range of topics, from the basics of budget classification to managing public investment, and from parliamentary approval to external audit, this volume – and the rich variety of examples and cases it draws on – has useful insights and tips for many different audiences, from public officials to policy wonks, to academics and practitioners."

Paolo de Renzio, *International Budget Partnership*

To Aaron Wildavsky, A. Premchand and Allen Schick—leaders in the resistance to technocratic delusion—and to Daniel Tommasi, who has seen it all and helped me dispel some of it in three continents.

Salvatore "Rino" Schiavo-Campo is a former senior official of the World Bank and International Monetary Fund, following an academic career that concluded as Professor and Chairman of Economics at the University of Massachusetts at Boston. He is the author of numerous articles and 14 books in public financial management, governance, public administration and economic development, and has advised governments in over 50 countries.

Contents

Preface and Acknowledgments

It is good for men to be in a situation where although their passions inspire them to do evil their interests prevent them from doing so.

(Montesquieu, *The Spirit of the Laws*)[1]

Objectives and Approach

The Montesquieu quote works equally well if we replace "their interests" with "the rules." Indeed, to the extent that the rules are enforced, compliance is generally in the long-term interest of the individual as well. In public finance, compliance with efficient rules and established norms is essential to combat the temptation to steal, misuse or abuse the public money. Institutions, in the contemporary meaning of the rules and norms that influence human behavior, are thus critical for the effectiveness of budgeting and public expenditure management. And, because those institutions differ among countries in various economic, social and political circumstances, a full understanding of the subject requires exposure to the diversity of international experience.[2] This is the first theme of the book.

The relevance of this theme has been reconfirmed recently by a roundtable convened in 2016 by the journal *Governance*, which raised the following three questions: Has public management research neglected important questions about the development of institutions of the modern state? Has it focused unduly on problems of the advanced democracies? Has it made itself irrelevant to public debates about the capacity of public institutions to deal with emerging challenges?[3] My own answers are yes, yes and in part. Institutional capacity is at the center of the book, which aims at correcting the research distortion toward advanced countries by systematic consideration of the actual experience of a variety of countries.

Second, public financial management (PFM) is too often treated in bloodless technical terms, as if budgeting systems and their functioning in practice could be divorced from the political and governance context in which they operate. Although most current treatments of PFM include a discussion of accountability and transparency, they rarely elaborate consistently on the linkages to legitimacy and governance—articulated around the four pillars of accountability, transparency, participation and the rule of law. These linkages are the other unifying theme of the book.

Based on these two core themes, the aim is to combine the conceptual foundations of PFM with the lessons of international experience, and to counter the perennial tendency to push technocratic solutions to multidimensional problems. However, the approach is positive rather than normative and the book offers a unified view, not a unified point of view. The arguments both for and against a particular approach and the diversity of international experience are presented on every topic (Chapter 13, on strengthening and reforming public financial management, is the sole exception).

The book that more than 50 years ago revolutionized the views of budgeting—Aaron Wildavsky's *Politics of the Budgetary Process* (Boston: Little Brown, 1964)—was only about 100,000 words. A lot of history has gone under the bridge since then, and a wealth of new ideas and technical contributions has been generated—especially in the past two decades. Nevertheless, one can still produce a readable and homogeneous synthesis of manageable length—although depending on instructors' and readers' interests it may need to be complemented by dipping into detailed technical material from the many journal articles and edited compilations currently available.[4]

Next to manageable length is the importance of accessibility. Most treatments of the subject presume a great deal of prior knowledge by the reader, which can make the discussion unintelligible to the non-specialist. The ivory-towerish rationalization is that public financial management is too rarefied a subject for the common folk. I know from personal teaching and technical assistance experience that this is not the case, and hope this book demonstrates that it is possible to deal with the subject in a manner that is comprehensive and conceptually sound, and yet understandable to the non-specialist.

For this reason, the language is as colloquial as the subject matter permits, and examples, illustrations and analogies are provided whenever appropriate. The most frequent analogy is to a household. And here a strong caveat is necessary. A government should not manage its finances in the same way as an individual household. What is true of an individual or a household may or may not be valid for the country as a whole. These analogies are intended solely to facilitate the reader's understanding of the technical point being made. The intended audience consists of two broad groups: university students and government officials. The book can serve as main text for advanced courses in public financial management, as complementary text for courses in public finance, public administration and economic development, as well as the basis for the hundreds of training courses in PFM conducted annually for government officials the world over.

Structure

After an introductory chapter explaining the meaning and importance of the government budget and the links to politics and society, the three chapters in Part I deal with the infrastructure of budgeting (budget systems, budget coverage, systems to cope with fiscal risk). Part II covers the "upstream" stages of the budget process—fiscal programming, preparation of the annual budget and the management of public investment. Part III explains the "downstream" stages—budget execution, public procurement and financing through debt or foreign aid. And the three chapters in Part IV address public accountability—respectively for the money and for the results of spending it—as well as the efforts to help strengthen PFM in developing countries. The final four chapters deal with special topics of major importance in today's international environment.

Although most chapters include references to the United States, the book is on the general principles and the global experience. The only exceptions are the annex to Chapter 6, which summarizes the fiscal trends and the process of budgeting in law and in practice, and the annex to Chapter 9 on procurement in the US. Readers wishing greater detail on US budgeting are advised to peruse some of the excellent books that focus entirely on American public administration. Conversely, instructors and readers from other countries may wish to skip those annexes and instead add complementary readings on the budgeting system in their country, and compare it with the general principles and international practice.

Finally, owing to the multiple audiences for the book, a special effort is needed to help students and other readers to navigate through it. For this purpose, in addition to the analytical index, the table of contents is unusually detailed.

Acknowledgments

While this book is fully current, and any earlier material that was used has been substantially revised and updated, it flows in part from my previous research and writing on public financial management and economic development. Parts of Chapters 2, 3, 6, 8 and 11 are revised and updated from material in S. Schiavo-Campo and D. Tommasi, *Managing Government Expenditure* (Manila: ADB, 1999).[5] Content from that earlier volume has been used and reproduced for years in various learning events by the World Bank and many other organizations and individual publications—almost always with proper attribution with one notable and regrettable exception. (You know who you are...) Parts of Chapters 13 and 17 come from the corresponding chapters of mine in Anwar Shah, ed., *Budgeting and Budgetary Institutions* (Washington, DC: World Bank, 2007). Chapter 15 draws in part from research done for the UN and World Bank. The second half of Chapter 5 contains material from my 2009 article "Potemkin Villages: The MTEF in Developing Countries," *Public Budgeting and Finance*, 29(2), 1–26. And the discussion of governance, institutions, and procurement draws in part from my *Public Management in Global Perspectives* (with H. McFerson; Routledge, 2008).

This book is the product of a combination of research and teaching with a 25-year engagement in technical assistance in some 50 countries. I have benefited from the ideas and experience of many academic colleagues and high government officials—as well as the feedback from hundreds of students and government employees who participated actively in the many workshops and seminars on public financial management that I have led in several countries in Asia, Africa, Latin America and the Middle East. My gratitude goes to all, but I wish to single out Alain Billon, Benoit Chevauchez, Francesco Forte, Ali Hashim, Geoffrey Lamb, Dominique Pannier, Mamadou Barry, Laura Pascua, A. Premchand, Allen Schick, Vito Tanzi, Clay Wescott and of course my old friend and associate Daniel Tommasi.

Comments and specific suggestions were offered by—and mostly accepted from—Robert Beschel and Mark Sundberg (on the book structure), Giulio de Tommaso (on state fragility), Lloyd Mitchell and P. K. Subramanian (on financial accountability), Hazel McFerson (on extractive resources and on governance), the GSA's Aretha Latimer and Chrischanda Smith (on public procurement) and Lars Jessen (on debt management).

I owe special thanks to Laura Stearns, Routledge Publisher, for her warm encouragement, Misha Kydd for editorial and production guidance, Marion Moffatt for able copy editing and John Silvester for the thorough index. Last, Jianna Schiavo-Campo made a solid contribution as research assistant, unfailingly cheerful despite my giving her no family slack.

Notes

1 The quote also heads Albert O. Hirschman's seminal *The Passions and the Interests* (Princeton, NJ: Princeton University Press, 1977).
2 I use interchangeably the terms high-income, rich and developed countries, and low-income, poor and developing countries—because, by and large, "developed" countries are also richer and possess stronger institutions. There are substantial differences within both categories—Japan is not Canada, and Nepal is not Paraguay—but the differences in wealth and institutional capacity between "developed" and "developing" countries are significantly greater than the variance within each group. Nevertheless, whenever possible, specific country examples rather than generalizations are used.
3 Brint Milward, Laura Jensen, Alasdair Roberts, Mauricio I. Dussauge-Laguna, Veronica Junjan, René Torenvlied, Arjen Boin, H. K. Colebatch, Donald Kettl, and Robert Durant, "Is Public Management Neglecting the State?" *Governance*, 29 (2016), 311–34.
4 Among the main journals are the *Journal of Public Budgeting and Finance*, *OECD Journal on Budgeting*, *Public Finance Review*, *Public Administration* (UK), *Indian Journal of Public Administration*,

Journal of Public Economics, *Journal of Public Budgeting, Accounting and Financial Management* and *Governance*. Among the books are Marco Cangiano, Teresa Curristine and Michel Lazare, *Public Financial Management and Its Emerging Architecture* (Washington, DC: IMF, 2013) and Richard Allen, Richard Hemming and Barry Potter, eds., *International Handbook of Public Financial Management* (Basingstoke: Palgrave Macmillan, 2013). On systems and practices in advanced countries, see the OECD, *Control and Management of Government Expenditure* (Paris: OECD, 2009). On various regions, see George Guess and Lance T. Leloup, *Comparative Public Budgeting: Global Perspectives on Taxing and Spending* (Albany: SUNY Press, 2010), for Latin America see Robert Beschel and Mark Ahern, *Public Financial Management Reform in the Middle East and North Africa* (Washington, DC: World Bank, 2012) and the various country case studies of different topics in budgeting in Charles Menifield, ed., *Comparative Public Budgeting* (Sudbury, MA: Jones and Bartlett, 2011).

5 ADB permission is gratefully acknowledged. The views expressed in this publication are those of the author and do not necessarily represent those of the Asian Development Bank, or its board of directors or the governments the directors represent. For information related to development in Asia and the Pacific, see www.adb.org.

1 The Government Budget
Mirror of Society's Choices

> The power of the prince . . . immediately becomes limited as soon as he establishes the plan of economy.
>
> (James Steuart, 1767, p. 277)

Introduction

The Meaning of the Budget

The government budget is often viewed as a purely technical assemblage of words and numbers, dull, opaque and best left to bureaucrats and a few powerful politicians. The reality is very different. Nothing is more fundamental to an organized society than the budget of its government. The government is expected to fulfill the various roles assigned by society to the state (see Box 1.1). Those roles are in turn articulated into policy objectives—quantitative objectives (such as reducing the rate of incidence of a disease) and qualitative objectives (such as fostering competition). A very few of these policy objectives can be met in ways that do not require significant direct expenditure, but most cannot be pursued without money. National security, law and order, transport, health, education, etc., do not materialize out of thin air from laws, decrees, resolutions, speeches or fervent wishes. Government requires resources—labor, materials, supplies, equipment, information—to perform its assigned roles. These resources are not free, and the money to obtain them must be provided in the form of taxes and fees by the people, who are collectively the presumptive beneficiaries of government services. The government budget provides the bridge between intentions and realizations, between policy and implementation.

Until comparatively recent times, the notion that the money spent by the rulers is the people's money was just as radical as the idea that government is "of the people, by the people, for the people." Indeed, the very word "budget" comes from the Middle English *budjet*—"the king's purse"—indicating that the government's financial resources were deemed to be the personal property of the ruler. Along with the political evolution from absolute monarchy to constitutional government, the meaning of the budget has changed. The government's authority to levy taxes and spend money is now anchored in its legitimacy—derived from the consent of the people—and approval of the budget is the main form of legislative economic control over the executive branch of government. (In the US, "the power of the purse" was seen as such an important protection against the risk of executive tyranny that it was entrusted to Congress and is enshrined in the very first article of the constitution.)

Unfortunately, in countries with weak institutions or authoritarian regimes, it is still a reality that some of the country's resources are handled as the personal property of the

---

Box 1.1 The Roles of the Modern State

Alexander Pope's clever but misleading ditty "for forms of Government let fools contest; whatever is best administered is best" has long since been superseded by a consensus on the major roles that any modern state is expected to perform.

These are generally understood to comprise ten areas—listed below in the historical order of public acceptance of government intervention. The first three are common to any organized society and the last three have emerged only in the twentieth century:

- Assure internal order, public safety and the rule of law
- Protect the national territory
- Manage relations with other countries and external groups
- Assure minimally adequate internal transport and communications
- Provide basic social services
- Exercise macroeconomic control, particularly for financial and monetary stability
- Protect vulnerable individuals and groups
- Preserve natural resources and the environment
- Enable/strengthen competitive markets
- Enable/foster economic growth and employment.

---

leader or of the ruling elite.[1] This reality can progressively be dispelled only as the political system evolves toward stronger representative institutions.

The bedrock principle of public financial governance is therefore that *the executive branch of government may take no moneys from the people, nor make any expenditure from those moneys, except by explicit approval of the people through the legislature as their representative*. Thus, when properly understood, the government budget should be the financial mirror of society's economic and social choices. The budget is much more than a bunch of numbers and words: It is at the very core of a country's democratic process, and public financial management should therefore reflect all four pillars of good governance—accountability, rule of law, participation and transparency—described later.

The Diversity of International Experience

The vast income, governance and capacity differences between countries demand that the analysis and recommendations on budgeting and expenditure management take into explicit consideration the country context. Forty years ago, Wildavsky (1975) stressed the major differences between formal budgeting in developed countries and the informal and patronage-based systems frequent in poor countries. Schiavo-Campo and Tommasi (1999) argued that it can never be assumed that practices suitable to rich countries with advanced institutions, strong accountability and abundant capacity are suitable to poor countries saddled with governance weaknesses and limited capacity—in particular, the only "best practice" in public financial management is that which suits the circumstances and context of the country.[2] Throughout this book, too, the discussion of every topic will bring out the distinctions between high-income, middle-income and low-income countries, and the diversity of international experience.

The Nature of the Budget

The Primacy of the Political

A valid premise of budgeting is that budgetary outcomes depend on budgetary institutions. It is important, however, to avoid the fallacy that because institutions matter, *only* institutions matter. The reality, in all countries and at all times, is that budgeting is also heavily influenced by politics—and properly so.

To budget is to choose, and such choices are inherently political.[3] Technical rules can help but cannot determine, for example, whether it is "better" to build a new school in district A or a new clinic in district B. Because in the first case the inhabitants of district B will gain nothing and in the second case the inhabitants of district A will gain nothing, the choice between a school here and a clinic there is a political one—confronting a legitimate need of one group of people against another equally legitimate need of a different group of people. Ditto for deciding "objectively" whether a necessary increase in revenue should come from one kind of tax or another: the economic and financial implications can be estimated, but the burden will fall on different groups. Money is power too, and the budget process cannot be understood without also considering its implications for the power relations in society. (This is a central aspect of the interpenetration between government and society, examined in the case of India by Premchand, 2010.) All budgetary decisions have an impact on the distribution of wealth and opportunities among individuals and groups.

In this light, two opposite views emerge from the economic and political science literature. According to the first view, because budgeting is essentially political, the use of technical methods and solutions for major expenditure decisions is mostly rationalization and pretense. According to the second view, economists, technical experts and government officials use their specialized skills to frame budget options in a manner that predetermines political choices. Both views are oversimplifications, but are useful as book-ends to the reality of the budget process, which lies somewhere in the middle.

The basic choices involved in budgeting have a time dimension, and affect the intergenerational distribution of costs and benefits as well. In aging societies, there is a bias toward services for the elderly, related to their greater propensity to vote and hence having heavier political weight than the young. This leads to a redistribution of resources toward the older generation and away from the new generation. Such an effect is found, for example, in the US, Germany and Japan—although the policy response has differed (see Kluge, 2013, for an elaboration).

In order for the budget instruments to work, there must be a political willingness *to* budget, i.e., to choose among competing expenditures and revenue sources, and a willingness to choose requires an acceptance of compromises between different priorities held by the various political groups. The best public financial management instruments avail little if the political climate is frozen in irreconcilable differences. The most accountable, transparent, rule-compliant, participatory processes are disabled if the main political actors cannot find any agreement on policies to be pursued and realistic objectives to be achieved—or, worse, if their position is determined exclusively in opposition to the other party's proposals. The quality of the stove is irrelevant if one is unwilling to cook.

The dominance of the political over the technical is illustrated by the US experience during 2011–16, when the federal budget process imploded from partisan political conflict. The two parties played repeated games of chicken in which they set short-term budget deadlines, went to the brink of defaulting on the government debt and then shut down the government for a brief time in 2013 (Meyers, 2014). No conceivable improvement in the systems and procedures of public financial management (PFM) could ameliorate this political standoff and its fiscal and economic consequences. The link between policy and budget was still manifest, but in a negative sense—in the absence of any compromise policy, the budget was financial driftwood, reflecting no policy at all.[4]

Facing Reality

One often hears the argument that taxes should be cut because they are "the people's money," or conversely, the argument that certain expenditures should be increased because they benefit some groups. Such statements are appealing. They are true. And they are meaningless. They are meaningless because, other things being equal, increased spending on "a" means that the money is no longer available to spend on "b," and reducing the tax on "x" means that tax on "y" will need to go up or that expenditure on "z" can no longer be financed. "There is no free lunch" is the first principle of economics.

In the words of US Supreme Court Justice Oliver Wendell Holmes, inscribed on the Internal Revenue Service headquarters in Washington, "taxes are the price we pay for a civilized society." We cannot get more than what we pay for. If we want a government, we have to pay for it; if we want more government we have to pay more; if we want lower taxes we have to accept fewer public services.

In principle, a country's citizens, through their votes and the actions of their elected representatives, first determine what they wish their government to do and then decide how to pay for it. (In practice, as explained in Chapter 6, the two types of decisions are made in an iterative manner and through the annual process of budget preparation.) If the taxes and other revenue collected are insufficient to pay for the desired government activities, the government will need to either cut some activities or finance the resulting fiscal deficit by printing the money, borrowing it from domestic or foreign sources, or simply not paying its bills. All these options carry economic and financial repercussions, although in diverse forms and affecting different groups.

Waste-fraud-and-abuse?

The only way out of these difficult choices is to combat the trinity of "waste, fraud and abuse." Certainly, there is waste, there is fraud, there is abuse in government operations—just as there is on Main Street and Wall Street. Depending on one's ideological predilection it is possible to argue that government is inherently more, or less, prone to these failings, but it is usually the case that problems of waste, fraud or abuse are more visible in government owing to the public transparency requirements and media scrutiny that are less applicable to private sector activity. (Box 1.2 offers some egregious examples of both public and private waste.)

But cutting wastefraudandabuse is the mantra of politicians who wish to avoid making hard budget decisions. Those who urge reducing wastefraudandabuse should be required to specify the where and the how to do so, but they rarely do. The problem is that the money wasted–defrauded–abused still ends up in someone's pocket, and the strength of the vested interests concerned makes it harder to cut wastefraudandabuse than to reduce the quantity or quality of public services or to forgo necessary operations and maintenance expenditure. Wastefraudandabuse are typically the last to go, rarely the first. Moreover, while fraud is clearly defined, whether a particular expenditure is wasteful or abused is often in the eye of the beholder. For example, a government subsidy for petroleum exploration may be viewed as a boondoggle by some or as a justifiable incentive by others. (It does seem peculiar, however, that the US Government gave in 2013 a $3 billion fossil fuel subsidy to an oil industry which had $100 billion in profits in that year.)

Box 1.2 Are waste, fraud and abuse inherent in government expenditure?

Waste, fraud and abuse can occur in all very large organizations, whether public or private.

No government bureaucrat in a developed country has ever managed to buy $16,000 umbrella stands with shareholders' money (as former Tyco CEO Dennis Kozlowsky did); or "borrow" tens of millions of dollars from their company and then have the loans "forgiven" (as Adelphia's John Rigas did); or bilk billions from thousands of savers (as Bernie Madoff did); or raise the price of a life-saving drug 5,000 percent (as Turing Pharmaceuticals' Martin Shkreli tried to do); or cause Goldman Sachs to lose $6 billion, as the unsupervised trader known as "the London Whale" did; or allow another trader to bring down Barings, one of the oldest banking firms.

But then, too, no corrupt or incompetent corporate CEO has ever paid $435 for a hammer or spent billions for weapons systems that are not needed or simply do not work (as the US defense department has done); or create a national kleptocracy (as did Mobutu Sese Seko, the late dictator of Zaire—now Democratic Republic of Congo); or steal millions from the public treasury (as did the Philippines' former President Joseph Estrada, convicted of "plunder"); or turn an entire country into an economic basket case (as Robert Mugabe has done to Zimbabwe and the Chavez–Maduro regime has done to Venezuela).

The bottom line is this: When assessing the risk of waste, fraud or abuse, the operative concepts are the *size* of the organization, the *concentration of power*, the *transparency* provisions and the strength of *accountability* mechanisms—and not whether the organization is public or private.

Governance and Public Financial Management

The budget can only reflect society's choices if the government itself is representative of society and budget decisions are made in a context of good governance. The problem of crooks and dictators in a position of political power has always been recognized, but in generic terms. After 1980, the problem was subject to detailed analysis, following the insights of the "new institutional economics" and the recognition by international organizations of the link between governance and development (Williamson, 1985; North, 1990; World Bank, 1992, 1994 and 1997; Schiavo-Campo, 1994; Ahmad and Brosio, 2015).[5]

Governance and Democracy

Although related, governance and democracy are different concepts. *Governance is the manner in which state power is exercised*—as distinct from how state power is obtained and the purposes for which it is exercised. The concept of governance is instrumental, and relates to the quality of the instruments and effectiveness of the means, not to the quality of the outcomes.

Good decisions can sometimes come from arbitrary decision-making processes, and bad ones from accountable and transparent processes. Good public management is possible in authoritarian regimes and there are many examples of badly mismanaged formal democracies. In the long run, however, good governance and democratic processes tend to go hand in hand, because sustainability is the key. Even when a decision is apparently sound but is produced in arbitrary and authoritarian ways, it cannot command the active support of the public and is thus much more likely to be ineffective or reversed. If you are concerned only with the quality of each decision and not with the quality of the decision-making process, you will get and you will deserve bad decisions—eventually.

Eventually. And here's the rub. Faced with a choice between better public services today and greater democracy tomorrow, many peoples and some countries have opted for the former and accepted authoritarianism as the price of good services. Conceptually, the way out of this dilemma is found in the critical distinction between formal democracy (as a process of government) and legitimacy (as an attribute of government), which rests on the voluntary consent of the people based on their acceptance of the validity of the laws and actions of their government.

It is true that, throughout history, the instances of well-governed authoritarian states are very few and those of well-governed totalitarian states are nonexistent. Democratic processes tend to correlate with good governance, and the absence of democratic processes does eventually erode government effectiveness and thus its legitimacy. But good governance and democratic processes go together only in the long run—and, in John Maynard Keynes' famous expression, in the long run we are all dead. In the short term, the tradeoff between democracy and good public management can be very real.

The Four Pillars of Governance

Good governance rests on four pillars—transparency, participation, the rule of law and accountability—supported by the foundation of a strong civil society (see Figure 1.1).

Transparency entails the low-cost access to relevant information on government action; participation is needed to provide a reality check and build consensus for implementation;

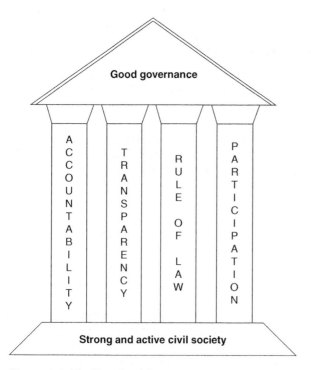

Figure 1.1 The Temple of Governance.

the rule of law calls for laws and regulations that are clear and uniformly enforced; and accountability is the capacity to call public officials to task for their behavior and actions.

Each of the four pillars is related to and necessary to support the other three. For example, accountability is hollow in the face of secrecy and is meaningless without predictable consequences. Furthermore, *all governance concepts are universal in application but relative in nature*. Accountability is not effective until one defines accountability "of whom," "for what," and "to whom"; transparency can be problematic when it infringes on necessary confidentiality or privacy; the rule of law cannot be allowed to become excessive rigidity; and, of course, it is impossible to provide for participation by everybody in everything.

The Implications for Public Financial Management

The relevance of each governance pillar for the various aspects of public financial management will be brought out throughout this book. The general implications are previewed here.

Transparency

Transparency of budget information and of financial transactions is a must for the executive branch, the legislature and the public at large—normally through the filter of capable and independent public media. It can have different meanings, however. In an elegant analogy (Heald, 2006), transparency can be compared to a car window. Outward transparency is needed for the "drivers" to see where they are going, and a fogged-up window can lead to accidents. But inward transparency is important for others to identify the driver and see who else is in the car, and tinted windows can preclude accountability.

In PFM, transparency requires public and timely communication of accurate and relevant fiscal and financial information. The information must also be in understandable form, because dumping on the public immense amounts of raw budgetary data does nothing to improve fiscal transparency. (Most countries prepare "budget in brief" or similar documents, summarizing the most important budget developments for the benefit of the media and the public. Many countries also have a portal for budget information.)

The IMF first assembled in 1998 a *Code of Good Practices on Fiscal Transparency*, revised it in 2008, and replaced it in 2014 with an updated and expanded *Fiscal Transparency Code*, accompanied by a revised *Manual of Fiscal Transparency*. The *Code* provides countries with standards on fiscal transparency and is used to prepare voluntary country reports on adherence to the standards. The *Code* underlines the importance of clear fiscal roles and responsibilities; public availability of information; open processes of budget preparation, execution and reporting; and independent reviews and assurance of the integrity of fiscal forecasts, information and accounts. Even though not all the specifics of the *Code* necessarily apply to all countries, its principles are generally applicable to developing and transition economies as well as developed countries.

The four pillars of the *Code* are:

- fiscal reporting—which should offer relevant, comprehensive, timely and reliable information on the government's financial position and performance;
- fiscal forecasting and budgeting—which should provide a clear statement of the government's budgetary objectives and policy intentions, together with comprehensive, timely and credible projections of the evolution of public finances;

- fiscal risk analysis and management—which should ensure that risks to the public finances are disclosed, analyzed and managed, and fiscal decisions across the public sector are effectively coordinated; and
- management of revenue from extractive resources—which should provide a transparent framework for the ownership, contracting, taxation and utilization of mineral resource endowments.

A detailed description of the basic, good and advanced practices under each of the principles of the *Code* is found at http://blog-pfm.imf.org/files/ft-code.pdf.

Participation

Participation in the budget process by concerned public officials and employees and by other stakeholders is required for the sound formulation of the government budget and its implementation; participation by external entities is necessary for the monitoring of operational efficiency; and feedback by the users of public services is important for the monitoring of access to and quality of the services. Appropriate public participation in the budget process is also important to gain consensus and public understanding, without which the difficult decisions made through the government budget are unlikely to be supported and implemented effectively.

Predictability through the Rule of Law

Predictability of government action occurs primarily through the consistent application of the rule of law. In PFM, the uniform application of budgetary rules underpins the legitimacy of the system and the predictability of financial resources supports the implementation of the budget and facilitates planning for the provision of services. Predictability of government spending in the various sectors is also an important signpost to guide the private sector in making its own production, marketing and investment decisions.

Accountability

Although all four pillars of governance are interrelated, accountability is at the center. It is—to again quote James Steuart—"the most effectual bridle ever was invented against the folly of despotism" (1767, p. 279). From overuse, the term "accountability" has acquired mantra-like qualities, and it is helpful to define it with some precision. Effective accountability has two components: (i) answerability and (ii) consequences. First, answerability (the original meaning of the word "respons-ibility") is the obligation of budget officials to respond periodically to questions on how they used their authority, where the money went and what was achieved with it. (As explained in Chapters 11 and 12, robust dialogue is much more effective than bean-counting or mechanistic checking of reported results.) Second, there must be meaningful consequences, without which accountability is an empty word or a mere public relations gesture.

Moreover, because government must account both for the use of financial resources and for its results, *accountability has two dimensions, internal and external.* Internal accountability of budget personnel to their superiors is necessary to protect the efficient use of resources and prevent fraud. But external accountability vis-à-vis the broader society is needed as well, to improve the efficiency and effectiveness of service delivery. (External accountability is also often referred to as "social accountability.") With the dramatic improvements in information and communication technology, feedback from service users and the citizenry at large can now be obtained at very low cost and for a greater variety of government activities. Strengthening social accountability is especially necessary in the context of initiatives to give greater budget flexibility and managerial autonomy to government departments and public servants—in order to assure that the access to and the quality of the public services are not compromised as a result of the initiative, especially for the poorer areas or segments of the population.

Corruption and PFM: A Preview

Bribery and abuse of public power have occurred from the earliest of time in all societies, and virtually every aspect of public financial management can be a source of corruption—tax administration, debt management, customs, ill-designed privatizations, large procurements and major public works projects, the payments system and so on. The subject is discussed in Chapter 16. Some general considerations are offered here.

It is essential to understand that corruption is not an independent phenomenon but an outgrowth of bad governance, and that problems of public corruption should not be addressed in isolation but as part and parcel of the broader issue of governance. Corruption is a symptom, not a cause. Lack of transparency, weak accountability mechanisms, arbitrary application of the rules and absence of relevant participation virtually guarantee corruption, and only governance improvements can lead to a lower incidence of corruption. The international recognition since the late 1990s of the "cancer of corruption" was a logical outgrowth of the understanding of the link between governance and development articulated at the beginning of the decade. (World Bank, 1996, was the first international organization official policy document on the subject.)

Definitions of corruption can be long-winded and highly legalistic, but the simplest is also the most powerful: *corruption is the misuse of public or private office for personal gain*. Misuse, unlike "abuse", covers both sins of commission (e.g., taking a bribe or other favor in exchange for an illegal action) and sins of omission (e.g., accepting a bribe for looking the other way). The inclusion of the term "private" in the definition of corruption underlines the fact that there cannot be a bribe received without a bribe given. Much corruption in government is externally driven: attention should be paid to both the corruptor and the corrupted as well as to "imported corruption" and the homegrown variety.

Well into the twentieth century, corruption was viewed as useful ("grease for the machine"), inevitable ("the way the system works") or routine ("everybody does it"). In recent years, views have changed dramatically, and for good reason. Aside from moral and legal considerations, there is solid evidence that corruption harms administrative effectiveness, diverts resource allocation away from the efficient to the dishonest, and especially hurts poor and vulnerable groups. During the past ten years, this consensus has been translated into actual policies of international organizations and governments around the world. (As shown in Chapter 16, however, the impact has been meager.)

Worldwide Trends in Governance

Because governance has to do mainly with the quality of the processes of government, most measures have focused on the attributes of governance rather than its outcomes. The worldwide governance indicators (WGI) are the most comprehensive survey, along six dimensions: voice and accountability, political stability, government effectiveness, regulatory quality, rule of law and control of corruption. Table 1.1 shows the WGI indicators for 1996, when they were first introduced, and 2014. (For details on the methodology, see www.govindicators.org.)

Table 1.1 Worldwide Governance Indicators: Percentile Rankings

Income Group/Region	Voice and Accountability		Political Stability		Government Effectiveness		Regulatory Quality		Rule of Law		Control of Corruption	
	1996	2014	1996	2014	1996	2014	1996	2014	1996	2014	1996	2014
Income												
OECD	88	87	83	77	88	88	87	87	88	88	87	85
High, non-OECD	62	59	65	77	75	76	73	73	70	75	71	74
Upper middle	48	48	45	50	49	52	51	49	45	49	47	49
Lower middle	41	42	36	37	35	33	34	34	39	34	35	37
Low income	21	25	24	22	19	17	20	22	20	20	25	20
Region												
Africa	29	33	33	31	28	26	27	30	28	31	33	30
East Asia/Pacific	57	54	60	63	57	53	58	49	59	55	57	57
Europe/Central Asia	64	66	61	64	63	70	65	70	62	68	59	64
Middle East/North Africa	30	25	35	28	47	45	41	44	46	45	47	44
Latin America/Caribbean	59	61	47	58	54	53	60	54	50	48	55	52
North America	92	88	76	80	91	88	93	88	92	81	93	90
South Asia	36	35	31	32	44	35	35	27	41	36	42	39

Source: www.govindicators.org.

Note: Individual country scores range from a worst of −2.5 standard deviations from the worldwide mean of zero to a best of +2.5 standard deviations. Based on the relative scores, countries are ranked by percentile, with higher values indicating better ratings. For example, a score of 70 on a given dimension means that 70% of countries in the world score worse and 30% score better than the country in question. Thus, the higher the number, the better the situation on that particular dimension. The income and region group scores are unweighted averages of the country percentile scores. The number of countries surveyed in 2014 was higher than in 1996, but the income group and regional averages are comparable. For the findings for individual countries, see www.govindicators.org.

Because the individual countries are scored based on the deviation of each dimension from a worldwide mean of zero, *the scores are relative*; changes between 1996 and 2014 are changes in the relative position of the income groups and regions, and do not represent absolute improvement or deterioration in governance.

Overall, the correlation between the quality of governance and country per capita income is striking and has not changed in the past 20 years—with OECD countries ranking consistently at the top and low-income countries exhibiting the lowest quality of governance. (The weight of evidence is that weak governance is the cause and slow economic growth the effect, although causality cannot be determined with certainty except through an in-depth analysis of each country's history and circumstances.) Moreover, the relative position of low-income countries has not by and large improved in the past 20 years—with small positive changes in voice and accountability and regulatory quality offset by a slight deterioration in their already weak position on the other dimensions, particularly control of corruption. Regionally, the relative position of South Asia has worsened sharply in government effectiveness and the rule of law, and Africa—which has the highest number of low-income countries—ranks consistently at the bottom of all regions across all governance dimensions in both years.

Although there are no data on absolute changes in governance worldwide, indicators of political freedoms developed by Freedom House are loosely correlated with the quality of governance and show that during 2005–15 the level of "freedom" has declined in 105 countries and improved in only 61. On the other hand, the Transparency International corruption perception indicators improved slightly worldwide. For Africa in particular, the Ibrahim Index of African Governance shows that governance improved up to 2008 but has slipped back since then. On balance, this suggests an absolute decline in governance quality in the poorer regions, where governance indicators declined in relative terms.

The income and regional averages, of course, mask a great deal of variation. For example, a severe deterioration in governance quality in countries such as Ethiopia, Malaysia, Thailand, Venezuela and Zimbabwe contrasts sharply with major improvements in countries such as Ghana, Colombia, Senegal and Indonesia. Still, the overall evidence is not encouraging, in light of the large investment of money and policy attention in the improvement of governance in developing countries. These findings may be a large part of the explanation of the equally disappointing findings concerning changes in the quality of public financial management during the past decade (see Chapter 13).

The United States was a pioneer among developed countries in prohibiting bribe-giving by US corporations through the passage of the Foreign Corrupt Practices Act in 1977 (see www.justice.gov/criminal-fraud/foreign-corrupt-practices-act). In 1999, the Organization for Economic Cooperation and Development (OECD—the "rich countries' club") promulgated the Anti-Bribery Convention, which criminalized bribery of foreign officials at par with bribery of national officials (see www.oecd.org/corruption/oecdantibribery-convention.htm). Bribes became "commissions" and other ways were found to circumvent the legislation, but the impact was significant nonetheless.

Awareness of a problem is the first prerequisite for solving it. The recognition of the costs of corruption has led to actions which have in fact somewhat reduced the global incidence of the problem (albeit with wide geographic variance). The annex to Chapter 16 shows corruption trends for various countries in the past two decades.

Capacity and Budgetary Outcomes

Next only to the primacy of politics, the capacity of the PFM system is the main determinant of budgetary effectiveness. The Nobel prize-winning economist Amartya Sen demonstrated

(Sen, 1981) that there has never been a famine in a functioning democracy, but the qualifier "functioning" is critical. Progress in governance remains fragile and easily reversible if it is not buttressed by capacity development (McFerson, 2009). Over the years, massive efforts have been made and substantial financial and technical assistance has been provided for PFM capacity building in developing countries, but more often than not with disappointing results. But what is "capacity"?

Capacity is Multidimensional

Capacity is one of those terms thrown about without precise explanation and usually associated with the availability of resources and specific skills and competencies. But capacity entails much more than human skills and has four dimensions. In logical order:

- Institutional capacity: the basic processes and "rules of the game" (both formal and informal) that influence people's behavior and the incentive framework within which organizations and people function. Historically, the term "institution" has been used as a synonym for organization, but the contemporary meaning is the complex of rules that govern human behavior, which are different from the organizations and the people that function under those rules. A football game may be played well or badly depending on the players and the size of the field, but so long as the same basic rules apply it is still a game of football. In PFM, the institutions include the hierarchy of laws on taxation and government expenditure, the regulations that flesh out those laws and the incentives framework (penalties and rewards) that underpin the prevailing financial management "culture." There are strong connections between budgetary outcomes and budgetary institutions (Campos and Pradhan, 1999). In turn, there is a correlation between the quality of budgetary institutions and national income. *Income poverty is typically accompanied by institutional poverty.* (Exceptions are many of the extractive resource-rich countries, where high income coexists with weak governance and limited institutional capacity. See Chapter 17.)
- Organizational capacity: the internal structures and organizational arrangements that administer the "rules of the game." In PFM, the most important organizations are the "core ministries" of finance, planning and economy as well as the entities responsible for monitoring public financial accountability, e.g., the auditor-general or equivalent. (These organizations and their roles are described in Chapters 6 and 11.)
- Information and communication capacity, including appropriate technology. In PFM, financial management information systems (FMIS) are essential, but must be suited to the local realities and requirements.
- Resource capacity: i.e., financial, material and, especially, human resources, that is, individuals with skills commensurate with their intended functions.

Strengthening resource capacity is often and wrongly taken as the first priority, but additional resources cannot help when inserted into an organization that lacks internal information systems and flows, has a dysfunctional structure and works according to obsolete or inefficient rules. Training, in particular, is wasted because new skills atrophy quickly if they are not actually used, and they cannot be used unless so enabled by the institutional environment and organizational structure. Providing a new skill to employees only to drop them back into the same job and work environment is not only a waste, but a source of demoralization as well.

Regarding information and communications, throwing computers and advanced software at inefficient budgetary rules and dysfunctional organizations has only resulted in suppliers' profits, devices gathering dust, waste on a large scale and plenty of bribery.

Changing organizational structures, too, is usually futile unless the institutional rules and incentive framework also change accordingly. As the Roman commentator Petronius Arbiter said 2,100 years ago: "We tend to meet difficult situations by reorganizing, which gives the illusion of progress while only creating confusion and demoralization." (For example, as discussed in Chapter 6, simply merging a ministry of finance with a ministry of planning has not improved the integration of current and capital expenditure when the officials concerned continue to work separately and were not given new incentives to cooperate.)[6]

While all four dimensions of capacity building must be addressed for sustainable improvement, institutional capacity is the logical priority and main determinant of budgetary outcomes. Logical does not necessarily mean chronological, however: human resource capacity can be augmented through appropriate training even while institutional, organizational or ICT improvements are being introduced—so long as the new skills are in fact relevant to the improved institutional and organizational environment.[7]

The Challenge of Institutional Development

Institutional development can be defined as a move from a less efficient to a more efficient set of rules and procedures, and can be measured by the reduction in "transaction costs." Think of transaction costs as the total costs of doing business (i.e., all costs associated with the time and opportunities lost in concluding the transaction in question). For example, streamlining an unnecessarily complex public financial regulation reduces the cost of compliance without adverse effects. In general, the process of institutional change is always gradual and protracted—a result of what Douglass North (1991) called "path dependence," i.e., the inertia of the accumulated stock of formal and informal norms and rules, which is massive in any society. Rapid institutional change is an oxymoron, as impossible as an oil tanker changing course as quickly as a sailboat.

The institutional challenge is complicated by the reality that many of the norms by which the public financial management system runs are informal norms (including informal incentives or penalties), which are typically not visible to the outside observer. This explains the paradox of countries where the formal budget laws, systems and processes appear sound and coherent, while in reality budgetary efficiency is poor, corruption is endemic and public services are badly inadequate. (For example, the public financial laws and regulations in the Philippines are models of good practice, even while informal norms of political patronage allow vast sums to leak out of the system.)

Many PFM innovations have failed because they were in conflict with the less-visible informal rules and incentives. For example, giving greater flexibility in personnel management in plural societies has led to managers hiring members of their ethnic groups, causing resentment and lowering productivity. Informal rules and incentives tend to be more important in low-income countries and multiethnic societies than in high-income and socially homogeneous countries. This is in part because, as institutional development progresses, the importance of formal rules and regulations increases and more and more informal norms become extinct or come to the surface and are formalized.

Capacity is Relative

Too often viewed as an absolute, *capacity is inherently relative to the tasks which the system is expected to perform.* Neglect of the relative nature of capacity has wasted efforts and resources and, in some cases, has worsened the budgetary process. A country's capacity sufficient to manage PFM systems that are simple but adequate becomes insufficient when confronted with the need to manage more demanding systems—aimed at potentially better outcomes but without consideration of the costs and risks of change. International experience over the past 50 years shows a supply-driven dynamic at work, whereby complex new PFM practices with heavier organizational, informatics and resource requirements have been pushed on to reasonably well-functioning systems, thus creating capacity constraints in countries or sectors where none may have existed. (Chapter 13 explores this theme in detail.)

Public Finance Policy and Public Financial Management

Policy versus Management

Policy concerns the question of what is to be done, management concerns the question of how it is to be done, by whom and with what resources. It is risky to draw an iron curtain between the two: lack of consideration of how policies are to be implemented or, conversely, of the purpose for which the management instruments are to be used, leads to unrealistic policies and/or ineffective implementation. Nevertheless, the distinction between ends and means, between policy and management distinction is important, particularly in public finance: policy is the domain of properly elected representatives of the people, management is the province of professionals and specialists who are charged with implementing the policy decisions. The need for a distinction and division of responsibilities surfaces in its clearest form during the process of budget execution—explained in Chapter 8.

Four Principles of PFM

Although this book uses the conventional term public financial management (PFM), administration and management are synonyms. The traditional paradigm of government "administration"—defined by the two Ps of *probity* (integrity) and *propriety* (compliance with the rules)—is associated with the proverbial green eyeshade mentality that considers it a success to comply strictly with the most trivial rules regardless of costs, delays and inefficiencies. The traditional paradigm is often set in contrast with the more recent paradigm—defined by the two different Ps of *policy* and *performance*—associated with the "new public management" (NPM), which was introduced in a few highly developed countries in the 1980s. Questions have been raised during the past 25 years or so about the shift in focus—mainly that the NPM neglects key issues of development of major institutions of the modern state, focuses unduly on problems of the advanced democracies, and has made itself irrelevant to low-income countries and to the capacity of public institutions to deal with emerging challenges (Savoie, 1995, and most recently Milward et al., 2016).

In reality, no contradiction exists. On the one hand, integrity and compliance with the rules can be not only ends in themselves, but also means to achieve certain results of government action. On the other hand, an orientation to policy and results which does not respect integrity and due process will eventually destroy both, and thus make the results unsustainable and cause the policies to fail. Good public management, including financial management, should be guided by all four Ps: probity, propriety, policy and performance. Like the legs of a chair, all four are necessary to assure the soundness, responsiveness and durability of the system. (Macaulay and Lawton, 2006, consider unsustainable the distinction between ethics and competence, because a public administrator cannot be competent without being ethical.)

Four Criteria of PFM Performance

Whatever roles may be assigned to government they must be performed well. To do so, the PFM system should meet the classic "three Es" criteria of administration: economy, efficiency and effectiveness. Economy refers to the acquisition of goods and services of a given quality at lowest cost and on a timely basis. Efficiency entails production at the lowest possible unit cost, for a given quality. (Efficiency subsumes the criterion of economy, because it cannot be achieved unless, among other things, the inputs are procured at the lowest cost. However, it is useful to retain economy as a separate criterion because it guides the important function of public procurement—see Chapter 9.) And effectiveness refers to the extent to which the ultimate objectives of the activity are achieved. For example, in a vaccination program the criterion of economy calls for purchasing quality vaccine at lowest cost and on a timely basis; the criterion of efficiency calls for performing the maximum number of vaccinations given the resources available; and criterion of effectiveness calls for the highest reduction of the disease.

Can we then conclude that a PFM system that operates economically, efficiently and effectively is *ipso facto* a good system? No. Someone must look out for the long term and for the needs of the poor and the marginalized. Thus, a fourth "E" must be added to the traditional triad: equity. Unless a government takes into fair consideration the implications of the budget for the distribution of income and the circumstances of the poorer and disadvantaged groups in society, the system will produce cumulative internal tensions and eventually lead to the withdrawal of that voluntary cooperation by the citizens that is the glue of good governance. In the short run, there may be a conflict between efficiency objectives and equity objectives; in the long run, there is none. (US President Andrew Jackson argued in the 1830s that the welfare of society must be assessed by looking at the conditions of the base, not of the top. The argument remains current in the early twenty-first-century America.)

Figure 1.2 illustrates the relationships among the principles and performance criteria of a public financial management system.

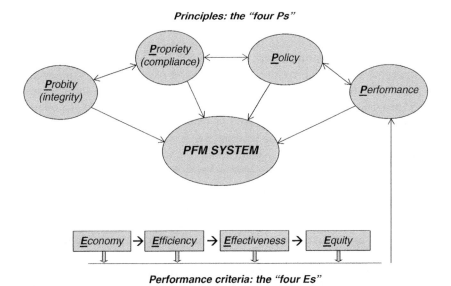

Figure 1.2 Principles and Performance Criteria of a Public Financial Management System.

Globalization and Public Finance

Finally, a word about globalization and public finance. Economic interdependence among individuals, among groups, among nations, has always been a reality—indeed, it is the basis of organized human society. Moreover, the increase in interdependence is not new. From as far back as the fourteenth century, global interdependence has been increasing because of the continuing reduction in "economic distance"—the cost of transferring goods, services, labor, capital and information from one place to another—due to improvements in transport technology, tariff cuts, creation of international organizations, etc. With that said, the acceleration witnessed in the past three decades has been spectacular. Thus, "globalization" is more than just a catchy term for an old phenomenon. There may be no difference in overall impact between, say, the invention of the railroad and that of the computer. However, the difference in degree and speed of impact is so vast as to constitute in effect a new phenomenon—particularly as it has coincided with the rapid liberalization of external financial transactions that took place in most major countries. In Thomas Friedman's expression, globalization has made the world flat (Friedman, 2005).

So, let us be clear about the key question. The genuine core of the globalization debate is not the continuing decrease in economic distance, per se, but the valid concern that in recent years *economic distance has been shrinking faster than can be reasonably managed by the international system—let alone by an individual country.* The foremost consequence of this disconnect between an integrated world economy and an un-integrated world political system is the lack of a functioning mechanism to address the problems of individuals, groups and countries at the losing end of the process.

While globalization has brought enormous benefits to the majority of the world's population, it has also caused certain groups to lose out and feel forgotten. The persistent neglect of the losers from globalization has caused a growing backlash, which found its expression in the success of the June 2016 "Brexit" referendum in Britain to leave the European Union, fueled the rise of anti-trade and anti-immigration sentiment in Europe and the US, and was a key factor in the US elections. "Globalization didn't create a lot of losers, but the ones it did were concentrated in the countries that were the driving force behind it" (O'Brien, 2016, p. A16).

This reality cuts three ways. First, globalization imposes a new constraint on many governments' capacity to sustain inefficient economic policies by persistent and structural fiscal deficits. On the other hand, ill-advised austerity forced on some countries (as in the European Union after 2010) has adverse repercussions on economic growth elsewhere, including for the strength of economic recovery in the US and for low-income countries dependent on exports to Europe. Third, the implementation of governments' independent social policies and redistributive objectives is hampered as well. (Box 1.3 summarizes the debate about the provisions on medicines in the Trans-Pacific Partnership negotiated in 2016 but now extremely unlikely to be approved by Congress.)

In addition to these three factors, globalization carries several implications of special relevance for public financial policy and management:

- Given the constraint on raising tax rates, the efficiency and equity of tax administration acquire greater importance, and so do international agreements for tax convergence.
- Given the constraint on expanding public expenditure, good expenditure management and rigorous public investment programming become critical—an issue addressed in Chapter 7.
- Given the temptation for central governments to download on to local government adverse impacts from global events, it is important to strengthen budgeting capacity at subnational government level—as discussed in Chapter 14.

Box 1.3 Global Public Health and the Trans-Pacific Partnership

The Trans-Pacific Partnership (TPP)—practically comatose after the US election—was a draft trade deal between the US, Australia, Brunei, Canada, Chile, Japan, Malaysia, Mexico, New Zealand, Peru, Singapore and Vietnam. The agreement would be one of the biggest regional trade agreements ever implemented. Although the TPP would reduce 18,000 tariffs on US goods by other countries, many health-care advocates, such as Doctors Without Borders, worry that it could raise global pharmaceutical prices, which would adversely affect the availability of medicines to people in poor countries.

There are five key issues: patentability criteria, protection of undisclosed test data, patent linkage, intellectual property and compulsory licenses and border measures. The issue of patentability is that member states would be prevented from producing and marketing lower-priced generic drugs for an average of five years. On test data, members would have to provide eight years of protection of undisclosed data—known as data exclusivity—which would further delay the release of generic drugs. A third problematic provision of the TPP is patent linkage, by which marketing approval is linked to patents, creating an additional 30-month waiting period in the US for the launch of generics. The intellectual property provision would limit governments' ability to use compulsory licensing as a negotiation tool to lower drug prices, and would encourage patent holders to engage in "forum shopping" in order to bring legal action against the government to seek monetary damages. Finally, customs authorities would be allowed to stop the trade of drugs suspected of intellectual property violations; this would severely constrain the ability of producers of generic drugs to export their product.

The TPP would thus limit the access to lower-priced drugs by poor people in developing countries, with an adverse impact on their health, and increase the cost of medical care for patients in all TPP member countries.

Sources: Shah (2015), Schiff (2016) and news reports.

- Given the importance of transparency and accountability in a globalized environment, uniform norms of budgeting, accounting and audit should be implemented—as described in Chapter 11.
- Of special importance to low-income countries are global initiatives to harmonize aid, avoid duplication and progressively foster reliance on national systems of budgeting and control—described in Chapter 10.
- Civil conflict can spill across national borders and failed states generate economic and financial implications for other countries—as analyzed in Chapter 15.

Notes

1 A trivial but telling example. When the author was resident representative of the International Monetary Fund in Somalia, he requested a receipt for his payment for the water supplied to his house by a Mogadishu municipality water truck. This was an unreasonable request, he was told, because "the truck driver is selling the President's own water."

2 More recently, Wescott (2009) noted how budget reform processes in developing countries differ from those in developed countries.

3 While the generic recognition of the political nature of the budget is long standing, the first systematic analysis was by Aaron Wildavsky (1961), later elaborated in his classic *Politics in the Budgeting Process* (1964).

4 Numerous options were formulated in the US to reduce the debt/GDP ratio in the long run—by the president's National Commission on Fiscal Responsibility, the Bipartisan Policy Center Deficit Reduction Task Force and many other think tanks and individuals. None went anywhere in Congress owing to the lack of genuine interest by elected leaders (Palmer and Penner, 2012).

5 On the New Institutional Economics see primarily Williamson and North (1990). See Eggertson, in Schiavo-Campo (1994) for an early summary, and Ahmad and Brosio (2015) for a recent elaboration with direct applicability to public finance. The link of good governance to economic growth was first analyzed systematically in 1992 by the World Bank, with early progress reported in 1994, and in 1997 a major review of the state in a changing world. A formal World Bank policy on governance was followed by a policy on combating corruption, and the other regional development banks followed suit with their own policy statements—largely along the same lines. A large literature also blossomed, with the journal *Governance* (first issued in 1987) as the flagship of the field. The World Bank's World Development Report for 2017 will focus on governance, but was not available at the time of completion of this book.

6 As another example, the creation in 2005 of the new National Intelligence Directorate in the US, superimposed on to the Central Intelligence Agency and the various other intelligence bodies, has accomplished little to improve the provision of good security information to top decision-makers, because in the absence of a concomitant change in the framework of rewards and penalties the "silo" behavior of the component agencies was not affected.

7 This is a major reason why training units in the public financial management apparatus must coordinate very closely with the operational units, and design and sequence their activities accordingly.

Bibliography

Ahmad, Ehtisham and Giorgio Brosio, eds., 2015. *Handbook of Multilevel Finance*. Northampton, MA: Edward Elgar.

Allen, Richard, Richard Hemming and Barry Potter, 2013. *International Handbook of Public Financial Management*. New York: Palgrave Macmillan.

Campos, Ed and Sanjay Pradhan, 1999. "Budgetary Institutions and Expenditure Outcomes," *Policy Research Working Papers*, Washington, DC: The World Bank.

Friedman, Thomas, 2005. *The World is Flat: A Brief History of the 21st Century*. New York: Farrar, Straus and Giroux.

Heald, David, 2006. "Varieties of Transparency," in Christopher Hood and David Heald, eds., *Transparency: The Key to Better Governance?* Oxford: Oxford University Press.

Kluge, F. A., 2013. "The Fiscal Impact of Population Aging in Germany," *Public Finance Review*, 41(1), 37–63.

Macauley, Michael and Alan Lawton, 2006. "From Virtue to Competence: Changing the Principles of Public Service," *Public Administration Review*, 66(5), 702–10.

McFerson, Hazel, 2009. "Measuring African Governance: By Attributes or by Results?" *Journal of Developing Societies*, 25(2), 253–74.

Marcel, Mario, 2014. "Budgeting for Fiscal Space and Government Performance Beyond the Great Recession," *OECD Journal on Budgeting*, 13(2), 9–47.

Meyers, Roy T., 2014. "The Implosion of the Federal Budget Process: Triggers, Commissions, Cliffs, Sequesters, Debt Ceilings and Shutdowns," *Public Budgeting and Finance*, 34(4), 1–23.

Milward, Brint, Laura Jensen, Alasdair Roberts, Mauricio I. Dussauge-Laguna, Veronica Junjan, René Torenvlied, Arjen Boin, H. K. Colebatch, Donald Kettl and Robert Durant, 2016. "Is Public Management Neglecting the State?" *Governance*, 29(3), 311–34.

North, Douglass C., 1990. *Institutions, Institutional Change and Economic Performance*. Cambridge: Cambridge University Press.

——, 1991. "Institutions," *Journal of Economic Perspectives*, 5(1), 97–112.

O'Brien, Matt, 2016. "Wonkblog," *Washington Post*, 14 September.

Palmer, J. L. and R. G. Penner, 2012. "The Hard Road to Fiscal Responsibility," *Public Budgeting and Finance*, 32(3), 4–31.

Premchand, A., 2010. *Contemporary India: Society and its Governance.* New Brunswick, NJ: Transactions Publishers.

Savoie, Donald, 1995. "What is Wrong with the New Public Management?" *Canadian Public Administration*, 38(1), 112–21.

Schiavo-Campo, S., ed., 1994. *Institutional Change and the Public Sector in Transition Economies.* Washington, DC: The World Bank.

Schiavo-Campo, S. and D. Tommasi, 1999. *Managing Government Expenditure.* Manila: Asian Development Bank.

Schiff, J., 2016. "Patently Perturbed: Trans-Pacific Partnership Trade Deal Raises Fears about Drug Patent Periods, Higher Costs," *Modern Healthcare*, June 4.

Sen, Amartya, 1981. *Poverty and Famines: An Essay on Entitlement and Deprivation.* Oxford: Oxford University Press.

Shah, D. G., 2015. "Inside Views: Impact of the TPP on the Pharma Industry," *Intellectual Property Watch*. December. Available online at www.ip-watch.org/2015/12/02 [accessed November 9, 2016].

Steuart, James, 1767. *Inquiry into the Principles of Political Oeconomy.* Reprinted by University of Chicago Press, 1966.

Tanzi, Vito, 1991. *Public Finance in Developing Countries.* Aldershot, UK: Edward Elgar.

Wescott, Clay, 2009. "World Bank Support for Public Financial Management and Procurement: From Theory to Practice," *Governance*, 22(1), 139–53.

Wildavsky, Aaron, 1961. "Political Implications of Budgetary Reform," *Public Administration Review*, 21(4), 183–90.

——, 1964. *The Politics of the Budgetary Process.* Boston, MA: Little, Brown.

——, 1975. *Budgeting: A Comparative Theory of Budgetary Processes.* Boston, MA: Little, Brown.

Williamson, Oliver, 1985. *The Economic Institutions of Capitalism.* New York: The Free Press.

World Bank, 1992. *Governance and Development.* Washington, DC: The World Bank.

——, 1994. *Governance: The World Bank Experience.* Washington, DC: The World Bank.

——, 1996. *Anticorruption Policy.* Washington, DC: The World Bank.

——, 1997. *The State in a Changing World.* Washington, DC: The World Bank.

Part I
The Budget Infrastructure

2 Budgeting Objectives, Systems, Budget Classification and the Legal Framework

Form ever follows function . . . Where function does not change, form does not change.

(Louis Sullivan)

The Objectives of Budgeting and Expenditure Management

Economic Policy Goals and Public Expenditure Management Objectives

The overall economic policy goals are stability, growth and equity. As a principal instrument of policy, public financial management (PFM) must pursue all three. Stability calls for, among other things, fiscal discipline; economic growth and equity are pursued partly through allocating the moneys to the various sectors; and all three policy goals require efficient and effective use of public money. Hence, the goals of overall policy translate into a triad of objectives of good public financial management: *fiscal discipline and expenditure control, allocation of resources consistent with policy priorities* and *good operational management.*[1] The two objectives of strategic resource allocation and good operational management parallel the distinction traditionally made in economics between allocative efficiency and use efficiency. In turn, good operational management calls for both efficiency (minimizing cost per unit of output) and effectiveness (achieving the outcome for which the output is intended). However, as stressed in Chapter 1, good budgetary outcomes cannot be sustainable without respect of proper norms and attention to distributional considerations. Thus, equity and due process are the conditions of legitimacy and sustainability of the entire system.

The first and third objectives are more amenable to technical rules than the intermediate objective of strategic allocation of resources, because the allocation of financial resources among sectors and ministries is the most political of the three objectives. As noted in Chapter 1, there are no technical guidelines to choose between expenditure programs that benefit different groups of people in different ways. As Petrei (1998) puts it:

> The allocation of funds results from a series of forces that converge at different points of the decision-making process . . . according to an imperfect perception of present and future political realities . . . The decision-making positions are occupied by politicians who, theoretically, have developed a certain intuition about what people want. In any event, the effort made at this stage of the budget process to collect and analyze information is less than at any other stage.

Yet, the composition of expenditure is economically and socially very important. One example is Uganda, where reallocation of public expenditure toward more productive sectors such as agriculture, energy, water and health led to faster economic growth and reduced poverty (Sennoga and Matovu, 2013).

Table 2.1 The Objectives of Public Financial Management

Objective	Revenue Function	Expenditure Function	Organizational Level
Fiscal discipline	Reliable forecasts	Expenditure control	Aggregate
Resource mobilization and allocation	Tax bases and incidence	Expenditure programming	Inter-ministerial
Operational efficiency a *Economy* b *Efficiency* c *Effectiveness*	Tax/revenue administration	Expenditure management	Intra-ministerial
Equity (due process)			Throughout government

There are linkages between the objectives of expenditure management and the government level at which they are operative. Fiscal discipline requires control at the aggregate level; strategic resource allocation requires appropriate cabinet-level and inter-ministerial arrangements; operational management is largely an intra-ministerial responsibility; and equity/due process must be observed throughout the system. These linkages are summarized in Table 2.1.

Complementarity and Interaction of Objectives

The scheme in Table 2.1 is a simplification. Reality is more complex. First, the objectives may be mutually conflicting in the short run and difficult compromises must be made. Second, conversely, all PFM objectives are interrelated. For example, mere fiscal discipline in the presence of arbitrary resource allocation and inefficient operations is not conducive to good budgetary outcomes. Third, good aggregate budgetary outcomes must flow from good outcomes at each level of government. In particular, expenditure control at the aggregate level should emerge as the sum total of good expenditure control in each ministry and agency of government. (As explained in Chapter 6, an initial expenditure constraint is essential for good budget preparation, but if it is *only* imposed from the top, it is as likely to starve the more efficient and worthwhile activities as to squeeze out wasted or fraudulent expenditure.[2]) Similarly, the best process for resource allocation among the ministries is worth little if the ministry's expenditure programs are inappropriate or inconsistent with overall government policy for the sector. But, in turn, operational efficiency cannot normally be improved except in an overall context of fiscal discipline and sound strategic allocation of financial resources.

In the household analogy, if spending by family members is simply cut off when the monthly money runs out, some necessary items such as food or rent are likely to be curtailed because spending on less important items or frills has been allowed to take place first. Overall, the family will not be living beyond its means, but its quality of life and cost-effectiveness of its expenditures will be adversely affected.

A Word about Sequencing

The complex issues of appropriately prioritizing and sequencing PFM reforms and improvements are addressed in Chapter 13. As a quick preview, consider the plain fact that if you cannot protect the public money nothing else follows. Therefore, expenditure control logically comes first. In those developing countries that have extremely weak control systems, efforts at improving the strategic allocation of resources and operational management should not be allowed to take attention away from this key priority. (See the discussion on reform sequencing in Chapter 13.)

By contrast, in the majority of countries where expenditure control and cash management are at least minimally acceptable, none of the three objectives of expenditure control, resource allocation and good operational management should be pursued in isolation from the others—and equity and due process must be observed at all times. Improvements in one or another area should go forward as and when permitted by circumstances, but a coherent vision of the entire reform process is needed to prevent "progress" in any one objective from getting so far out of line as to compromise progress in the other two and thus the PFM system effectiveness in its entirety. (In the household, micromanagement and excessively frequent controls on a family's cash would make it difficult to decide on a sensible spending package and to choose the most cost-effective stores.)

Budget Systems: The General Taxonomy[3]

The typology of budgeting systems sounds like an arcane and highly technical subject but is quite simple in its essence. Legitimacy always requires that the executive receive legislative approval to spend, but how and for what that approval is given can differ—and budget systems differ according to the type of legislative authorization. To begin the explanation, let us define the extremes. At one extreme, holding the executive branch accountable would be impossible if the legislature gave it a lump sum to spend however and whenever it wished; at the other extreme, good management would be impossible if the legislature had to approve the expenditure on each of the millions of different transactions carried out by the government each year. The middle ground consists, therefore, of setting limits on the type of expenditure and its purposes, but in a way to allow the executive the flexibility to implement the agreed policies.

The type of budget system depends on the *form* of legislative authorization—either to make payments *or* enter into commitments; and on the *purpose* of the expenditure—either to purchase inputs *or* to produce outputs *or* to achieve certain outcomes. In principle, therefore, as shown in Table 2.2, six budgeting systems are possible, according to both the particular form of legislative authorization and the purpose of the authorized expenditure.

The choice of budget system depends on country capabilities and circumstances but, in practice, the vast majority of countries follow budget system I—based on legislative authorization to make payments to purchase goods and services—known as a cash-based, line-item budget. A small but significant number of advanced countries use systems III or

Table 2.2 Possible Types of Budget System

Form of Authorization	Purpose of Authorization		
	To Buy Inputs	To Produce Outputs	To Achieve Outcomes
To make payments	I Line-item budgeting, cash basis	II Output budgeting, cash basis	III Program budgeting, cash basis
To enter into contracts	IV Line-item budgeting, commitment basis	V Output budgeting, commitment basis	VI Program budgeting, commitment basis

VI (program budgeting), and a handful of countries follow system V (output-budgeting). Whatever choice is made, it is essential to use *one* budget system, and avoid hybrid forms of budget systems and bases of accounting for different categories of expenditure. (For example, mixing cash and commitment budgeting would be equivalent to a store manager being told by the store owner that in the coming month he may neither exceed $20,000 in cash payments *nor* sign contracts with suppliers that exceed $20,000 in total value.)

Types of Budget System According to the Form of Legislative Authorization

The form of the authorization given by the legislature to the executive branch can be either to make payments *or* to enter into commitments (in either case, not to exceed the approved amounts). Next, the authorization can cover a specified period (normally one year) or have no time limit. The four possible options are therefore to authorize the executive to:

(i)   make payments for the approved purposes and up to an approved amount, at any time in the future;

(ii) enter into commitments for the approved purposes and up to an approved amount, at any time in the future;

(iii) enter into commitments for the approved purposes and up to an approved amount, within the budget year;

(iv) make payments for the approved purposes and up to an approved amount, within the budget year.

The first option—authorizing the executive to make payments at any time in the future would make accountability very difficult, and constitute an open invitation to theft and abuse. The last two options are discussed in turn next.[4]

Commitment Budget

In a commitment budget, the legislature gives to the executive the authority to *enter into commitments* for the approved purposes and amounts during one year, but *without limiting annual payments*.[5] For example, a ministry is authorized to sign fuel contracts of a value of no more than "x" millions within the year, but may make payments for fuel smaller or larger than "x." (Annual payments may be larger than the approved commitment limit because they can be associated with contracts of previous years.) In a commitment budget, the value of the total commitments is legally limited; the cash payments are not. Because there is no annual limit on payments, a commitment budget needs to be complemented by an annual cash plan. (In fact, a sound cash plan is necessary for good budget execution regardless of type of budget system, as explained in Chapter 8.)

In the household analogy, the designated family member would be authorized to sign contracts during the coming month for a total value not exceeding $2,000, but would not be precluded from making payments larger than $2,000 during that month.

Cash Budget

In a cash budget, the legislature gives to the executive the authority to *make payments* for the approved purposes up to specified amounts and during a year—but *without limiting annual commitments*. For example, a ministry is authorized to make payments not exceeding "y" millions for fuel within the fiscal year, but may sign fuel contracts for amounts larger than "y." In a cash budget, the cash payments are legally limited during the period;

the commitments are not. Symmetrically, because there is no annual limit on commitments, a cash-based budget needs a complementary system to monitor commitments. (Cash budgeting should not be confused with cash-based accounting. Although in practice the two normally go together, cash budgeting is compatible with accrual accounting as well, as explained in Chapter 11.)

The household analogy would be to authorize the designated family member *to spend* up to $2,000 during the coming month on the approved goods and services, but without any restriction during the month on signing contracts for a total value larger than $2,000 (e.g., for an apartment lease).

Cash budgeting is the system followed in most countries, because it is best for compliance and expenditure control, as well as for macroeconomic programming—see Chapter 5.

Types of Budget Systems According to the Purpose of Legislative Authorization

Defining the types of budget system according to the form of legislative authorization does not answer the question of what the money is authorized *for*. The money can be authorized to:

(i)   produce specific outputs;
(ii) purchase categories of inputs ("objects");
(iii) achieve certain outcomes from identified programs.

The first type of authorization entails "output budgeting"; the second entails "line-item budgeting" (where each "line" is an input or "object"); and the third entails "program budgeting." Each of these systems is described in turn, with its advantages, disadvantages and requirements. The vast majority of countries follow line-item budgeting.

Output Budgeting

In output budgeting, the money is approved for the executive to *produce outputs*—specific goods, services and works. A quasi-contract is reached before the start of the fiscal year on the outputs expected from the ministry or agency and their production cost. The money is then allocated on the basis of the contract, and the ministry is accountable for delivering the contracted products in accordance with the agreed specifications. Output budgeting produces the tightest form of executive accountability for specific results, but has heavy requirements: very high quality of governance; well-developed analytical, costing, contracting and monitoring capacities throughout the government; low or minimal corruption; and accurate and timely information. These demanding requirements are met in a few developed countries (such as New Zealand, as described in Box 2.1), but not in all other countries, particularly low-income countries. Output budgeting is therefore not discussed further in this book. The interested reader is referred to Webber (2007) and Robinson (2011).

Line-Item Budgeting

In a line-item budget, the money is allocated for the *purchase of inputs* or "objects," i.e., the various types of goods and services and works. Thus, the resources provided in the government budget to a ministry specify the amounts given to buy fuel for the ministry vehicles, furniture for its offices, services of its staff (salaries), etc., during the fiscal year. (A line-item budget is the equivalent of a household budget.) The ministry is thus

---

Box 2.1 Output/Outcome Ambivalence in New Zealand Budgeting

Key features of the system are: (i) agreement on the outputs to be produced and the resources to be supplied for this purpose; (ii) managers' freedom to use the resources allocated as they judge best; and (iii) managers' accountability for performance in producing those outputs. The first feature requires accurate and verified costing of each output; the second is limited by the need to respect due process in procuring goods and works and in managing personnel; and accountability is strongest in areas where "outputs" are clearly measurable. (For example, measuring the quantity of advice that high-level officials provide to a minister is a dubious proposition.) A technical corollary of the system is the need to move to accrual accounting, in order to account properly for the economic cost of the resources, including depreciation.

In a well-managed country such as New Zealand, with high quality of governance and capacity, strong political and personal accountability and a culture of integrity and professionalism, the central limitation of output budgeting is not found in implementation difficulties. Rather, the issue revolves around the link between outputs and outcomes—which are the true aim of government action. Ministers decide on which outputs best meet the desired outcomes, and are thus in theory accountable for outcomes, while the ministries' chief executives are accountable for the outputs themselves. Although the government is required to state how the purchased outputs are linked to its desired outcomes, parliament appropriates explicitly for outputs, and the requirement that ministers identify the links between the outputs to be purchased and the government's desired outcomes has been met in cursory fashion.

The budgeting system has been under continuous review and many improvements have been made at the margin in light of actual practice. Most notably, the high-level goals have been used to prioritize expenditures—thus introducing some outcome-orientation in the intermediate objective of strategic resource allocation. Nothing, however, can change the reality that, so long as the money is allocated to outputs, accountability will attach to outputs. Incentives are always on the side of actual money, never statements or intentions.

Source: Kibblewhite and Ussher (2002) and author.

---

accountable for the total expenditure as well as for assuring that the money is not stolen or wasted but used to purchase the items for which it was allocated. However, ministries' accountability for "performance" is limited to inputs. Therefore, line-item budgeting requires putting in place complementary mechanisms if one wishes to ascertain what results have actually been accomplished with the expenditures.

Line-item budgeting is essential for expenditure control and protection of public money. Its simplicity also makes it easily amenable to the introduction of complementary considerations related to outputs and outcomes, since the inputs can be used for a variety of purposes. However, line-item budgeting has been criticized for certain inefficiencies (discussed in Chapters 8 and 9):

- Excessive detail, with several thousand separate line-items in the budget—which makes for unnecessary red tape and tends to focus the attention of the legislature on minor expenditures rather than the major items.[6]

- Intrusive ex-ante controls on individual transactions—which are not only costly to administer, but also dilute the accountability of budget managers.
- Rigid and excessively narrow rules on transfer of expenditure between line items during the fiscal year—which make it impossible for budget managers to adjust to changes.

In the household analogy, this would be equivalent to prescribing how many apples, how many pears and how many plums may be bought during the month, with the added requirement that each day's shopping list must receive prior authorization, and without the option to shift some purchases from apples to pears to plums except by formal permission in each individual case.

Such inefficiencies are not intrinsic to line-item budgeting *as a system*, but flow from specific modalities—typically the result of an excessively detailed classification (as in India), or cumbersome rules for allotment of expenditure to tens of thousands of different items (as in Indonesia), or a confusion between administrative items and operational inputs (as in Tunisia). The appropriate response to these inefficiencies is to address them directly—reducing the number of line items, reducing ex-ante controls, providing more flexibility—and not to jettison the line-item budgeting system itself.

A valid criticism of line-item budgeting *as a system* is that it cannot assure a direct link between the budget and the government policy objectives, or the services to be delivered, or the search for the most efficient combination of inputs to deliver such services, etc. Line-item budgeting is concerned with the protection and modalities of spending the public money, but not what is achieved by it. Thus, starting in the early 1950s and continuing to this day, various "program" or "performance" budgeting reforms in both rich and poor countries attempted to address the question of the outcomes of public spending. This complex issue is discussed next.

Program/Performance Budgeting

Program budgeting (sometimes called "performance budgeting") is intended to *achieve outcomes*. In pure program budgeting, the resources are provided to a ministry to finance packages of activities aimed at defined outcomes, i.e., the purposes for which the outputs are produced. The ministry can use the money for salaries, equipment, goods, services and works in any manner it deems best—and is accountable for performance in terms of the achievement of the agreed outcomes.

The Experience with Program/Performance Budgeting

The Early Experience

The first experience with program budgeting on a wide scale was launched in 1949 in the US, following the recommendations of the Hoover Commission. The 1951 US budget included listings of the programs by budget account and narrative statements of program and performance, some of them presenting workload and full cost information. The experiment was a failure and the US abandoned it. The failed performance budgeting experiment was exported in 1954 to the Philippines: detailed line items were abandoned and the budget was presented with expenditures in blocks corresponding to programs and projects. As a result of the complexities of the system and loss of expenditure control the country soon returned to the traditional system (although some presentational changes remained).

In his pioneering 1964 book, Wildavsky recognized the appeal of program budgeting but rightly identified three problems with it: it heightens conflict, raises enormously the burden of calculation and leads to uncertain outcomes. He was wrong when he referred to it as a fad, however, because program budgeting in several variants is still very much with us. In part, this is because nobody could have predicted in 1964 that the informatics revolution would turn the immense calculation difficulties into a minor problem. As we shall see, however, the other two problems of program budgeting are just as problematic as Wildavsky saw them 50 years ago.

Planning–Programming–Budgeting System (PPBS)

An especially ambitious Planning–Programming–Budgeting System (PPBS) was launched in 1965, aimed at directly linking objectives to programs to activities and to the budget. In the planning phase, systems analysis is used to establish the objectives and identify related policy solutions. At the programming stage, means are reviewed and compared with the solutions that were identified at the planning stage. Sets of activities are then grouped into multiyear programs, which are individually appraised. Finally, these programs are costed in detail and translated into the annual budget. While the PPBS emphasis on policy–budget linkage and budgetary effectiveness is attractive, the system proved impossible to implement, not only because of (predictable) bureaucratic resistance and high transaction costs, but because reaching an indisputable "rational" organization of government objectives and activities is a fantasy. In addition, in the few countries where it was attempted, the approach muddled up ministers' responsibilities, hampered accountability and produced unintended consequences in other budgeting areas (see Box 2.2).

The PPBS embodies the pinnacle of the technocratic delusion that budgeting is a precise set of activities amenable to an engineering-type approach. The appropriate analogy is to Austria's reputed plan for the battle of Austerlitz: "4:05 a.m.—first infantry division marches to northeast; 4:30 a.m.—second and third infantry divisions march to northwest; 6:00 a.m.—cavalry attacks to the north ..." Unfortunately, Napoleon did not conform to the plan, and Austria lost the battle.[7]

As for the objective of linking policy, programs, activities and money, the research evidence indicates that very little of the vast amount of information collected on program performance has been actually used in executive decision-making or legislative oversight.

Realistic efforts at introducing into a sound line-item budgeting system a selective orientation to a few key results can produce more improvement in public services and at a much lower cost than attempts at wholesale performance budgeting. This conclusion is reprised later.

Zero-Based Budgeting (ZBB)

An especially demanding variant of program budgeting is zero-based budgeting (ZBB), which was attempted in the late 1970s in the US (and later by a handful of other countries) as reaction to the drawbacks of purely incremental budgeting, where by the pattern of expenditure continues year after year by the mechanical addition of equal percentage increases (see Chapter 6). In a pure ZBB system alternative expenditures from a base of zero are evaluated each year and must be justified from scratch. The logic is attractive: the fact that resources have been granted to a program in the past does not necessarily mean that they should continue at the same funding level or, indeed, continue at all. In practice, however, every major expenditure corresponds to a particular constituency and the assumption that it can be terminated on purely technical grounds is delusional. "If history

---

Box 2.2 PPBS and Cash Management in the Philippines

Cash authorizations were traditionally issued to government agencies each quarter through the release of cash disbursement ceilings (CDCs) which specified the maximum amounts that the agencies could withdraw from the Bureau of the Treasury to pay for their obligations. However, several agencies tended to issue checks and Treasury warrants in excess of these amounts.

In May 1990, as part of the introduction of the synchronized planning–programming–budgeting system (SPPBS), an Inter-Agency Committee on Cash Programming was created—with representation from the Department of Budget Management (DBM), the Department of Finance (DOF), the Treasury and the Central Bank. The Committee held lengthy meetings every month to assess in detail the performance of the national government for the previous month and discuss prospects for linking operations to policy during the succeeding month. On that basis, the Committee determined the monthly cash disbursement ceiling for each agency. The amount of time devoted to reporting and meetings increased substantially, but the problem of excess issue of checks and Treasury warrants worsened, even while cash releases became less timely. After one year, the system was jettisoned in favor of a system of joint decisions by DBM and DOF to release funds based simply on cash availability.

Source: Darlene Casiano, DBM, personal communication, January 1999.

---

is abolished, nothing is ever settled. Old quarrels resurface as new conflicts. Both calculation and conflict increase exponentially, the former complicating selection and the latter obstructing error correction. . ." (Wildavsky, 1988, p. 418). Life itself is incremental: we may make New Year's resolutions on making lifestyle changes at the margin, but we don't review each January 1 the costs and benefits of possible changes in our profession, our marital status, our housing arrangements, our choice of doctors, the school our kids attend ... Not surprisingly, ZBB quickly fell under its own weight, and was formally accommodated by focusing scrutiny on a few programs at the margin—thus returning in effect to traditional budgeting.[8]

The Experience with Program Budgeting in Developed Countries

In developed countries, program budgeting was attempted in the 1970s and 1980s, but not for long and was largely shelved. A 1993 study stated that ". . . the impetus for performance-based budgeting comes from those who believe it has been successfully applied in local, State, and international governments" and found "little evidence of the much-touted advances in local, state and foreign governments" (Joyce, 1993, p. 2). However, with the improvements in administrative capacity and the revolution in information technology, the persistent and legitimate concern with the results of spending rather than just the manner of spending led to a resurgence of interest, and comprehensive program budgeting has been introduced in a number of countries—e.g., France, the Netherlands and Korea (see Fouque, 2014; de Jong et al., 2013; and Park and Jang, 2015).

The Dutch case shows the importance of doing so carefully and learning from experience. Full program budgeting was introduced in 1999, but the lessons of its functioning in practice were internalized and gave rise to a major reform of the system in 2012, to strengthen internal control by the ministries as well as enable better oversight by parliament. This experience stands in contrast to the argument that program budgeting can serve to quickly reallocate resources among competing priorities (Hawkesworth and Klepsvik, 2013)—as if it were possible in the real world to cancel contracts in mid-course, fire large numbers of government employees at one go, or "reallocate" chemists to engineering jobs and carpenters to appendectomies.

The Experience in Developing Countries

In terms of developing countries, attempts at program budgeting have been pursued at various times in several Asian and Latin American countries (and a handful of African countries), but rarely taking into account the negative lessons of experience and oblivious to the heavy requirements for successful introduction of the system—listed in Box 2.3. Not surprisingly, actual experience proved uniformly unfavorable, producing vast bureaucratic activity with minimal or no benefits in terms of PFM objectives and public service effectiveness. Nevertheless, program budgeting continues to be pushed in developing

---

Box 2.3 Preconditions for Successful Introduction of Full Program Budgeting

Elements of program budgeting can be introduced selectively alongside line-item cash budgeting, but the full list of preconditions for successfully implementing program budgeting *as a system* include:

- reasonable macroeconomic stability;
- adequate revenue predictability;
- public commitment from the highest political level to specified budgetary outcomes and fiscal transparency;
- extensive cost-analysis capacity of the finance ministry and all the line ministries and central agencies;
- adequate availability of competent public accountants and auditors;
- capacity to enforce a hard budget constraint at ministries' level;
- comprehensive statistical base and good records management;
- timely and accurate financial and physical reporting;
- extensive authority given to ministries and agencies in personnel management, including hiring, reassignment, promotions and termination of staff;
- extensive flexibility given to ministries and agencies during budget execution, including moving money between wages and O&M expenditure;
- a well-established medium-term expenditure framework;
- reliable monitoring and evaluation systems in ministries and at the center;
- strong contestability by the legislature;
- strong administrative accountability, with concrete consequences;
- mechanisms of social accountability to an active civil society;
- very low aid dependence, or supportive donor behavior as well as provision of most aid as budget support.

Source: Partly based on and adapted from Robinson (2007).

countries, even countries such as Cambodia, Malawi and Zambia where few of the basic prerequisites exist. The obvious question arises of why such initiatives persist, usually with the encouragement of international donors and the enthusiastic endorsement of international consultants recruited to implement them. (Chapter 13 suggests as an answer the classic rule of investigations: "*Cui bono?*"—who benefits?)

The most aspirational of these initiatives is the 2009 decision of the council of ministers of the West Africa Economic and Monetary Union (WAEMU)[9] to *replace* the line-item, cash-based budget system in all member countries with program budgeting, *and* introduce accrual accounting—all this to be accomplished within ten years, i.e., by 2019 (see Box 2.4). Even aside from the grave governance weaknesses and civil conflict in several member countries (Burkina Faso, Guinea-Bissau, Togo and Mali), the chasm between wish and reality is shown by the absence in a majority of the countries of many of the requirements for successful program budgeting and accrual accounting. Even in developed countries where these requirements were met—for example, France, Korea—the introduction of the system has taken a massive investment and sustained effort over a long period.

Many WAEMU countries find it difficult to implement their line-item, cash-based budget well, and it is impossible to imagine that they could acquire in a few years the capacity to administer the much more complex and demanding program budgeting system. Two years before the deadline, little has happened toward implementing the WAEMU directive. Its implementation is most likely to be purely cosmetic, unless there is an attempt to actually implement it vigorously and as written—in which case it will produce a mountain of spreadsheets, platoons of consultants and cascading administrative changes, without any improvement in allocative efficiency or public services and, most assuredly, with loss of expenditure control and widespread confusion.[10]

This experience does not in the least recommend continuing neglect of the question of what results have been accomplished with public moneys. But there are realistic alternatives. Meaningful steps can be taken toward introducing *alongside the main line-item budget system* selective programmatic elements—in those countries where the capacity to do so

---

Box 2.4 The WAEMU Program Budgeting Directive

The following are the main provisions of the 2009 directive:

- Financial resources are to be allocated to programs rather than to categories and objects of expenditure.
- Medium-term budgetary and economic forecasts, including on each ministry and each program, are to accompany the draft budget.
- The authority for program implementation rests personally with the minister concerned (who, however, may delegate such authority to the program managers).
- Program managers determine the objectives of the program, allocate the resources, monitor the implementation and assure internal management and financial controls.
- A statement of expected results of each program is to be annexed to the annual budget, and a statement of actual results is to be submitted after the budget execution is completed.

Source: Directive 06/2009/CM of June 2009, available online at www.uemoa.int/Pages/ACTES/ConseildesMinistres.aspx [accessed November 5, 2016].

exists and the line-item cash budget is already implemented reasonably well. (An early example is the "modified budgeting system" of Malaysia, introduced in 1990. While preserving the main cash-based, line-item budgeting system, "controlling officers" were made responsible for monitoring the performance of their department in terms of agreed results, and given the authority to transfer resources across activities within a particular program without prior approval from the treasury.) These steps can generate needed attention to the results of public spending and strengthen accountability for performance, at a far lower cost and risk than attempts at revolutionizing the entire budget system—as discussed next.

Complementing the Line-Item Budget System with Selected Programmatic Elements

The realistic choice is not between the extremes of a line-item cash-based budgeting system that pays no attention to results, or of upsetting the apple cart by a program budgeting revolution. The disappointing record of program budgeting initiatives stems from attempts to introduce it into the whole of government, and to change the entire structure and presentation of the government budget as well as the framework of incentives for the public servants in the system. Fortunately, the line-item budget has the advantage of easily accommodating the introduction of complementary considerations. Here again is Wildavsky: "The more neutral the form of presenting appropriations, the easier to translate other changes—in program, direction, organizational structure—into the desired amounts without increasing the rigidity in categories, and thus erecting barriers to future changes" (1988, p. 420). In that spirit, during the past decade or so several countries have complemented line-item budgeting with selected programmatic elements and have achieved some positive results at acceptable cost.

Variants of Program Budgeting

Stages of Program Budgeting

Using their preferred term "performance" budgeting, Shah and Shen (2007) offer the following useful stages, in ascending order of complexity. The first three can easily be accommodated alongside a cash-based, line-item budget system:

- Performance-*reported* budgeting—which presents performance information as part of the budget documentation, but without using it for allocation of resources.
- Performance-*informed* budgeting—in which information on results is taken into some account in resource allocation, but only as a minor contributing factor.
- Performance-*based* budgeting—in which performance information plays an important role in resource allocation, along with other factors, but does not determine the amount of resources allocated.
- Performance-*determined* budgeting—whereby the allocation of budgetary resources is directly and explicitly linked to performance units (the equivalent of full program budgeting).

Piloting Ministries

In the "pilot ministry" approach, a program-based budget for an entire ministry is presented alongside the line-item budget. However, a ministry encompasses such a variety of diverse activities as to make it very difficult to attribute clear accountability for results and to learn from experience and correct mistakes. The expansive definitions of programs—for example, children's health care—associated with the pilot ministry approach have also proven problematic, as they entail very broad objectives and call for generic performance indicators. (The practical difficulties are illustrated by the troubled 2011 experiment in Rwanda's health sector—despite the comparatively good capacity in the country and extremely strong accountability of the bureaucracy to the president.)

The pilot ministry approach may be appropriate in countries with good governance and an administrative culture that allows a high degree of autonomy of the line ministries and spending agencies, adequate transparency, abundant administrative and programming capacity and strong accountability mechanisms. In such a setting, the locus of accountability is the top leadership of the ministry, and hence broad definitions of program and generic performance indicators may be actionable. In the vast majority of countries which do not have such favorable characteristics, the lesson of experience is that the pilot ministry approach is likely to cause substantial additional costs without commensurate benefit in terms of economy, efficiency or effectiveness. (A case in point is the failed experiment in 2008–9 with the education ministry in Lebanon.)

Piloting Programs

The alternative is a "pilot program" approach, focused on narrow subprograms requiring fewer activities with a specific objective—for example, pre-natal maternal care. The pilot program approach is consistent with a limited-capacity environment, and thus can be implemented gradually, with attention to unintended consequences and unnecessary red tape, learning from actual experience and gradually expanding to other programs as and when circumstances allow. The approach is particularly suitable for an administrative system that has barely enough capacity to carry on its routine business—as is the case with most ministries and agencies in developing countries. Also, the approach allows the selection of pilot programs in different ministries, thus providing the basis for comparisons and possibly triggering an emulative dynamic within the government.

Most importantly, the pilot program approach opens the door to "learning by listening" to service users and citizens in general. User feedback on service quality and access adds an element of social accountability to the administrative accountability within the executive branch. It is not helpful to try to elicit citizens' views about very broad programs and an entire ministry, because they do not have the necessary information and their views would not carry much practical impact in any event. Experience shows that users' opinions and citizens' voices are heard mainly when they relate to very specific services (Simmons, Birchall and Prout, 2012). This is especially the case in countries that lack assertive civic organizations, as with many developing countries.

The Accountability Tradeoff

An important reason why a pilot program approach is preferable to a pilot ministry approach for introducing elements of result-orientation in the budgeting system is the existence of an accountability tradeoff. There is an inverse relationship between the scope of accountability and its attribution: individuals may be held strictly accountable for results that are mainly under their control (typically, outputs of limited scope—e.g., number of vaccinations), *or* may be held loosely accountable for results that are partly beyond their control (typically, outcomes of broad scope—e.g., reduction of the rate of disease). It is not possible to hold individuals *strictly* accountable for *broad* outcomes. Accountability for results performance is thus more effectively introduced through specific activities and narrow subprograms. (This theme is picked up again in Chapter 12.)

Budget Classifications

Each budget system is associated with a particular budget classification.[11] Budget classification is another of those eye-glazing subjects that appears to be hard to understand and narrowly technical. But consider: most things in life—stamp collections, groceries, silverware, computer files—must be organized in some fashion or you are liable to waste money on duplicative or unnecessary purchases and be unable to find what you are looking for when you need it. (Public libraries "lose" books most often when they are mistakenly placed on the wrong shelf, not when they are borrowed and not returned.) In public financial management, a sound classification of government expenditures is a must—for executive accountability, budget analysis, day-to-day budget administration and protection against the theft of public resources.

The budget classification must be uniform and applicable to all types of expenditures—whatever budget system is followed. Classifying in different ways different kinds of expenditures would make it impossible to control government commitments and payments—let alone to assure that the financial resources have gone to the intended sectors and have been managed efficiently. A hybrid classification would also be an excellent way for the executive branch or individual officials to hide their activities from the legislature and the public.

The budget classification should also be consistent with international standards. These are established by the United Nations (UN) and the International Monetary Fund (IMF), and reviewed periodically to assure their continued relevance and update them as needed. The three main types of government expenditure classification are: (i) economic classification; (ii) functional classification; and (iii) program classification.[12]

Economic and Line-Item Classification

The economic classification groups expenditures according to the *type of resources* used in government activity, i.e., the various factors of production: labor (salaries), capital (interest, investment) and materials (goods and services)—in addition to transfer payments such as subsidies (see Box 2.5). Countries may use their own variant of economic classification, so long as it is fully consistent with the Government Financial Statistics (GFS) classification developed by the IMF in 2001 and most recently updated in 2014. (See the 2014 GFS Manual at www.imf.org/external/np/sta/gfsm/pdf/text14.pdf.)

An economic classification of expenditures is essential for fiscal policy and for analyzing the budget. For example, civil service compensation must be based on correct information on the wage bill and should permit comparisons with private salaries and with the share of government expenditures absorbed by wages in other countries.

Closely related to the economic classification is the line-item classification, which underpins the line-item budget system. In addition to serving as a basis for the allocation of financial resources in the budget, a classification oriented to inputs is required for management. For example, managers of spending units in the ministries need to monitor expenditure on fuel and vehicle maintenance in order to prevent "evaporation" of the fuel or inoperable vehicles. A line-item classification can easily be made compatible with the GFS economic classification.[13]

A single economic classification covering both the current budget and the development budget and consistent with the GFS is essential. Efficiency and transparency in public expenditure require the ability to compare and assess *all* expenditures against one another by common criteria—as elaborated in Chapter 6. (The economic classification is at the basis of the "economic" medium-term expenditure framework discussed in Chapter 5.)

Box 2.5 Summary Economic Classification of Expenditure

Compensation of government employees (sometimes referred to as "the wage bill")

Use of goods and services (also frequently referred to as "operations and maintenance")

Subsidies
  To public enterprises
  Other subsidies

Social benefits
  Social security and social assistance
  Employer social benefits

Interest
  To foreign creditors
  To domestic creditors

Capital
  Capital expenditure (also known as "investment" expenditure)
  Capital grants

Other (various expenditures)

Financing (lending, repayment of loan principal, sale of public assets, new borrowing, payment arrears, etc.)

Functional and Administrative Classification

A functional classification groups expenditures according to the *purpose* they serve (education, housing, etc.). A functional classification is important to permit analysis of the allocation of resources among sectors, to reorient government activity toward certain policies (e.g., for security or for poverty reduction) and to identify the historical trends in government spending.

The UN Classification of the Functions of Government (COFOG—see www.unstats.un.org) consists of 10 major groups, 69 groups, and 147 subgroups. It is expedient to simply adopt the COFOG instead of trying to develop a customized functional classification—since COFOG is well established and well documented. If a country chooses to adopt its own functional classification, it must develop a mapping table to allow going to/from COFOG, in order to permit international comparisons. The 10 major groups of COFOG are shown in Box 2.6—with group 3 broken down as an illustration. The full list of 69 groups is shown in Annex 1.

To illustrate the expenditure composition in developed countries, Table 2.3 shows the relative importance of the functional categories in the 27 countries of the European Union in 2013. The dominance of the social safety net is clearly seen in the almost 20 percent of GDP accounted for by social protection expenditure, with the basic public services of education and health accounting together for another 8.5 percent. The picture masks substantial variation between European countries. Also, the expenditure composition is quite different in other countries, where public expenditure is less than the European average of

> **Box 2.6 Classification of the Functions of Government (COFOG)**
>
> 01 – General public services
> 02 – Defense
> 03 – Public order and safety
>
> > 03.1 – Police services
> > 03.2 – Fire protection services
> > 03.3 – Law courts
> > 03.4 – Prisons
> > 03.5 – R&D public order and safety
> > 03.6 – Public order and safety not elsewhere classified
>
> 04 – Economic affairs
> 05 – Environmental protection
> 06 – Housing and community amenities
> 07 – Health
> 08 – Recreation, culture and religion
> 09 – Education
> 10 – Social protection
>
> Source: Annex 1.

Table 2.3 Percentage Share of Expenditure Categories in EU Countries' GDP, 2013

General Public Services	Defense	Public Order & Safety	Economic Affairs	Environ-mental Protection	Housing & Community Services	Health	Recre-ation, Culture, Religion	Educa-tion	Social Protection
6.7	1.4	1.9	4.1	0.9	0.9	7.4	1.1	5.1	19.9

Source: Eurostat, *Statistics in Focus*, September 2013.

50 percent of GDP. (For example, federal expenditure in the US accounts for about 20 percent of the country's $18 trillion GDP and one quarter of it is for defense—including veterans' services.)

While a functional classification groups expenditures according to their purpose, an administrative classification groups expenditures according to the government organization that is responsible for managing them—ministry, department, etc. An administrative classification is needed for accountability, delegation of responsibility and day-to-day budget management. Just as there is a kinship between economic and line-item classifications, there is a general correspondence between functional and administrative classifications, because the organizational structure of most governments is defined on the basis of the various functions to be performed—e.g., a ministry of higher education is responsible for the function of post-secondary education (COFOG 9.3).

However, administrative and functional classifications are never identical, because the functional classification is universal while the administrative classification must fit the political and social preferences of the country and the levels of responsibility and accountability in budget management. For example, while COFOG includes all tertiary education (09.4) in the education group, in some countries responsibility for research in education may be assigned to a ministry of science and technology. Or, in Islamic countries, responsibility for religious and community services (COFOG 8.4) and social protection (COFOG 10) may be in a single ministry.[14] (The administrative classification is at the basis of the simpler variant of a programmatic medium-term expenditure framework, discussed in Chapter 5.)

Program Classifications

A program classification does not replace the economic and functional classifications, but can coexist with and complement them, at least for certain types of government activity. The hierarchy of a program classification comprises, in descending order of generality:

- *function*—a broad government goal (e.g., promotion of agriculture);
- *program*—a set of interrelated activities that meet the same objective (e.g., development and production of a new crop);
- *activity*—a subdivision of a program into a homogeneous category of actions (e.g., irrigation for the new crop);[15]
- *cost element*—the expenses for the inputs required by the particular activity (e.g., sprinkler systems for the irrigation of the new crop).

There is no rule on how to define and delimit "programs" and "activities." The identification of "program" depends on the definition of the objective to be pursued, which of course can vary. As for "activity," in principle it is the level at which performance indicators can be elaborated and costs measured—but this level itself differs in part according to the result indicators themselves. (Performance indicators are discussed in Chapter 12.) And the "cost elements" obviously depend on the definition of the corresponding activity. Thus, unlike economic and functional classifications, which have been developed in standard form, a program classification can vary considerably from one government to another or even at different times. In the household analogy, if "children's education" is defined as a function, "reading proficiency" is one of the programs, activities include homework and cost elements comprise such inputs as books. In a different family or in the same family at a later time, the "program classification" for the same function could change: computer literacy might replace reading proficiency as a program, the corresponding activities would comprise lab work and the cost elements would include tablets and apps.

The hierarchy of "function," "program," and "activity" is roughly comparable to that of government structures ("ministry," "department," and "divisions"), but, again, there is no necessary correspondence between a program classification and the organizational structure of government. This raises two opposite issues. On the one hand, when the program classification differs substantially from the structure of government, problems of lack of "ownership" and loss of accountability arise. If a particular program calls for action by several government offices, it is hard to assign authority and thus accountability—if everybody is responsible, nobody is responsible. On the other hand, if the discrepancy between program classification and organization of government is "solved" by simply classifying programs, activities and cost elements along the existing organizational structure of government, the programmatic approach becomes a cosmetic relabeling exercise—the education ministry is relabeled the education function; the vocational education department is renamed the vocational education program; the technical manuals division is renamed the technical manuals activity; and the printing department is relabeled the printing cost element. This produces a plethora of meetings, paperwork, spreadsheets, new software and consultant fees, without any effective reorientation toward results. If so, it is easier, cheaper and more honest to simply stay with the administrative classification, and identify a few important specific activities for which key result indicators can be specified and monitored.

It is also possible to *supplement* the administrative classification with a *few* cross-cutting programs dealing with policy issues of special relevance to the country (e.g., HIV/AIDS, youth unemployment, etc.). For such cross-cutting issues it is essential to assign lead responsibility to one ministry or agency, have a few clear and monitorable outcome indicators and specify the cooperation obligations of the various entities concerned. Unlike "coordination," which usually consists of designating a third bureaucrat to arbitrate disagreements between two bureaucrats, genuine cooperation requires incentives—material or moral.

Combining Economic and Functional Classifications

As noted, the main classification of the budget may be complemented by elements of the other classifications, to meet special purposes and the interests of the various stakeholders. In particular, economic and functional categories are both important for budget analysis and policy-making. The simple matrix in Table 2.4 combines the major categories of the IMF GFS and the UN COFOG. The information necessary to fill all the cells with reliable figures may not be available in low-income countries (particularly in defense and capital expenditure), but reasonable approximations and estimates are usually possible and the approach provides a useful snapshot of the overall structure of the budget.

Budget Systems and Classifications: The Bottom Line

Combining the public expenditure management principles with the lessons of international experience and country circumstances (particularly capacity realities and quality of governance) leads to the following conclusion. For most countries, and virtually all developing countries, the appropriate budget system is a cash-based, line-item system, with an economic budget classification. The reform priority is therefore to improve the cash-based, line-item budgeting system—by simplifying it and strengthening the accountability mechanisms. When the system is reasonably functional, it then becomes possible and desirable to gradually

Table 2.4 A Simple Format for Budget Analysis and International Comparisons, (In Currency Units and/or Percent)

Functional Categories (COFOG)	Economic Categories (GFS)							
	Wages	Goods & Services	Subsidies	Social Benefits	Interest	Capital	Other	**TOTAL**
General services								
Defense								
Public order								
Economic affairs								
Environment								
Housing & community								
Health								
Recr., culture & religion								
Education								
Social protection								
TOTAL								

Source: Adapted from Tommasi (2010), which was in turn based on IMF (2001).

introduce selected programmatic elements, foster an orientation toward results and allow budget managers greater flexibility.

The Legal Framework for Public Financial Management

Because the budget is a fundamental legal instrument and the rule of law is a pillar of good governance, the PFM objectives, principles and modalities must be codified in formal legislation—as appropriate to the legal and administrative culture of the country concerned.

A Hierarchy of Laws

The budget principles and rules are enshrined in descending order of importance in the hierarchy of laws, in order: the constitution, a basic public financial management law, other laws and regulations, administrative instructions and circulars and—of course—the annual budget law itself. The general criterion for placing legal rules along this hierarchy is that it should be difficult to modify the basic rules but easy to modify the detailed rules.

Therefore, only the most fundamental PFM principles should find their way into the country's constitution, changes of which are deliberately designed to be very difficult. Subject to and consistent with those fundamental principles, a basic PFM law (often called "organic law" or "public finance law") contains the basic rules for managing public finances, allocating powers and accountabilities, providing financial oversight and the like. Subsidiary legislation then regulates implementation of the framework law and defines the operational parameters (e.g., the calendar for budget preparation). The next step in the legal hierarchy is administrative rules (e.g., the instructions in the budget circular that starts the budget preparation process). Finally, specific provisions and resource allocations for the coming fiscal year are incorporated in the annual budget law that is presented to the legislature, and in supplemental allocations or other budget amendments during the year.

A Basic Public Financial Management Law (PFML)

The Key Principles

The principles of good governance and objectives of public financial management should be reflected in the PFML, i.e., recapitulating the major points made in this chapter:

- No moneys collected from natural or legal persons, nor any moneys expended, nor exemptions granted, except as duly authorized by the law and other legal instruments.
- Transparency of fiscal and service information, requiring not only openness but an affirmative effort to provide budgetary information and government plans in accordance with international standards on fiscal transparency.
- Conformity of fiscal policy with macroeconomic and social objectives.
- Individual accountability of ministers, agency heads and other senior managers for the acquisition, use, accounting and reporting of public financial resources and for the taking of necessary measures to prevent abuses of such resources.
- Obligation of all government employees to comply with the rules and regulations of public financial management, and equal application of sanctions to violators of said rules.
- Participation by government employees, members of the legislature and other concerned persons in the budget preparation and execution process, as appropriate and realistic.
- Pursue expenditure control, efficient use, effective service provision and high integrity.
- Unity of the budget.

The Specific Contents

Generally, the basic budget law should contain the following:

- An introduction stating the objectives and principles of public financial management, and relevant definitions.
- Responsibilities.
- General provisions, such as the basis of accounting and financial reporting.
- Rules of budget coverage and presentation, including treatment of fiscal risks.
- Stages and rules for budget preparation, legislative debate, approval and amendments.
- Stages and rules for budget execution, including commitment and payment regulations, internal control, monitoring and evaluation.
- Principles and rules of external audit.
- Accountability provisions.
- Relations with local government.

As an illustration, Box 2.7 summarizes the development of Turkey's budget law, and Annex 2 provides the list of typical contents of a basic budget law.

Box 2.7 The Turkish Organic Budget Legislation: A Series of Legal Reforms

The legal framework governing the Turkish budget system consists mainly of the constitution of 1982 (articles 161 to 164) and a PFMC law of 2006, which revised the previous law of 2003 which in turn had replaced the venerable General Accounting Law of 1927—introduced by Ataturk and based on the French system of the time. Debt management is regulated by a special law of 2002, and a 1983 law defines the structure of the Ministry of Finance and gives it responsibility for budget preparation, execution, revenue management, accounting and reporting. External audit is regulated by a separate law on the Turkish Court of Accounts which replaced an old audit law and put external audit in line with international good practice.

The organizational arrangements include three central institutions: the Ministry of Finance for all revenue, budgetary and financial matters, the State Planning Organization for the macroeconomic framework, the public investment program and public sector statistics, and the Treasury for debt and cash management and management of state-owned enterprises.

From this sequential process of legal reforms some inconsistencies and ambiguities remain (particularly concerning the extent of the authority of the executive branch to reallocate funds between budget items without legislative approval). Also, the decision-making process is centralized and yet fragmented, and the line-item classification is excessively detailed. However, the legal framework covers all the basic requirements for sound budgeting, and enshrines the fundamental principles of PFM, including the unity of the treasury, fiscal transparency and accountabilities of ministers and heads of public administration (e.g. undersecretaries of ministries).

Source: Kraan et al. (2007).

Annex 1: UN Classification of the Functions of Government (COFOG)

01 – General public services
    01.1 – Executive and legislative organs, financial and fiscal affairs, external affairs
    01.2 – Foreign economic aid
    01.3 – General services
    01.4 – Basic research
    01.5 – R&D general public services
    01.6 – General public services not elsewhere classified (n.e.c.)
    01.7 – Public debt transactions
    01.8 – Transfers of a general character between different levels of government

02 – Defense
    02.1 – Military defense
    02.2 – Civil defense
    02.3 – Foreign military aid
    02.4 – R&D defense
    02.5 – Defense n.e.c.

03 – Public order and safety
    03.1 – Police services
    03.2 – Fire protection services
    03.3 – Law courts
    03.4 – Prisons
    03.5 – R&D public order and safety
    03.6 – Public order and safety n.e.c.

04 – Economic affairs
    04.1 – General economic, commercial and labour affairs
    04.2 – Agriculture, forestry, fishing and hunting
    04.3 – Fuel and energy
    04.4 – Mining, manufacturing and construction
    04.5 – Transport
    04.6 – Communication
    04.7 – Other industries
    04.8 – R&D economic affairs
    04.9 – Economic affairs n.e.c.

05 – Environmental protection
    05.1 – Waste management
    05.2 – Waste water management
    05.3 – Pollution abatement
    05.4 – Protection of biodiversity and landscape
    05.5 – R&D environmental protection
    05.6 – Environmental protection n.e.c.

06 – Housing and community amenities
    06.1 – Housing development
    06.2 – Community development
    06.3 – Water supply
    06.4 – Street lighting
    06.5 – R&D housing and community amenities
    06.6 – Housing and community amenities n.e.c.

07 – Health
    07.1 – Medical products, appliances and equipment
    07.2 – Outpatient services

07.3 – Hospital services
07.4 – Public health services
07.5 – R&D health
07.6 – Health n.e.c.

08 – Recreation, culture and religion
08.1 – Recreational and sporting services
08.2 – Cultural services
08.3 – Broadcasting and publishing services
08.4 – Religious and other community services
08.5 – R&D Recreation, culture and religion
08.6 – Recreation, culture and religion n.e.c.

09 – Education
09.1 – Pre-primary and primary education
09.2 – Secondary education
09.3 – Post-secondary non-tertiary education
09.4 – Tertiary education
09.5 – Education not definable by level
09.6 – Subsidiary services to education
09.7 – R&D education
09.8 – Education n.e.c.

10 – Social protection
10.1 – Sickness and disability
10.2 – Old age
10.3 – Survivors
10.4 – Family and children
10.5 – Unemployment
10.6 – Housing
10.7 – Social exclusion n.e.c.
10.8 – R&D social protection
10.9 – Social protection n.e.c.

Annex 2: Contents of a Public Financial Management Law

Part I   General Provisions

Article 1   Purpose of the Law
Article 2   Definitions
Article 3   The Scope of the Law
Article 4   General Guiding Principles
Article 5   Establishment, Coverage and Control of the Consolidated Government Fund
Article 6   Withdrawals from the Consolidated Fund

Part II   Powers for Budget Management

Article 7   Powers of the Legislature, Local Governments and Other Public Bodies.
Article 8   Powers and Responsibilities of the Council of Ministers
Article 9   General Responsibilities of the Minister of Finance
Article 10   Specific Powers of the Minister and Powers of the Minister to Delegate Authority
Article 11   Powers and General Responsibilities of the Ministry Top Leadership
Article 12   Specific Powers of the Secretary to the Treasury
Article 13   Powers and Missions of Budget Managers
Article 14   Delegation of Budget Managers' Responsibilities
Article 15   Powers and Duties of Local Government Bodies

Notes

1   This formulation differs from the classic three-part distinction by Musgrave (1959) between economic stabilization, allocation and adjustments in income distribution, but is close to the three objectives defined by Schick (1966): expenditure control, planning and resource management. The triad of expenditure control, strategic resource allocation and good management—in order—is preferable to the other formulation of objectives because it corresponds closely to the stages of the budgetary process, described in Chapters 6 and 8.
2   For a more detailed explanation of the complexities of budgeting reality, see Premchand (1998).
3   This section is a thorough reformulation of the corresponding analysis in Schiavo-Campo and Tommasi (1999).

4 The second option is known as an "obligation" budget, by which the legislature gives the executive branch the authority to enter into commitments for the approved purposes and amount and to make the related payments—but without time limit. Because there is no time limit, obligation budgeting can be used only for special programs (e.g., the Environmental Quality Incentives Program in the US). In reality, all budget systems must include adequate provisions for the authority to launch investment projects, which necessarily require long-duration contracts and making payments for many years until project completion. The key difference from obligation budgeting is that the actual payments for each project must be authorized each fiscal year.

5 In *accrual* budgeting, the legislature gives the executive the authority to cover the full costs of operations—including depreciation, changes in liabilities and all other elements of budgeting and accounting that would apply in private enterprises. This approach would account for the true economic cost of production, but is not applicable to government operations, except in less than a handful of highly advanced countries and is not discussed further.

6 Among developed countries, Australia, Canada, France, Mexico, the Netherlands and South Korea have the lowest number of individual line items in their budget (under 200), while Austria, Denmark, Italy, Norway, Switzerland and Germany have among the highest (over 500). This makes clear that a high number of line items is not in itself a hindrance to good public financial management, although when it reaches several thousand it necessarily complicates budget preparation and execution and loosens the link between broad policy and the budget.

7 The comparison is Daniel Tommasi's—personal communication, circa 2011.

8 Zero-based budgeting has a tendency to resurface, albeit in different forms, in order to send a political message of austerity or as a roundabout way to eliminate programs disliked by new leaders. In the US state of Georgia, for example, "zero-based budgeting"—originally implemented by then-Governor Jimmy Carter in the early 1970s—was reintroduced in 2012 but with the aim of shrinking state government and validating the fiscal conservatism of state government leaders, rather than of achieving greater efficiency and effectiveness. The purely symbolic effect of the ZBB process was to confirm the fiscal conservatism of state government leaders (Lauth, 2014).

9 Members of WAEMU are Benin, Burkina Faso, Côte d'Ivoire, Guinea-Bissau, Mali, Niger, Senegal and Togo. Reportedly, the reform was pushed by the IMF but with benign neglect by the World Bank.

10 A much more positive assessment can be made, instead, of the WAEMU rules to encourage fiscal "convergence" among member states, and thus facilitate the process of economic integration in West Africa. These rules are summarized in the "fiscal responsibility" section of Chapter 4.

11 For a more in-depth but still readable discussion of budget classification, see Jacobs et al. (2009).

12 A handful of advanced countries use a fourth classification, which distinguishes appropriations related to outputs from other appropriations. Thus, the New Zealand budget has seven classes of appropriation: (i) output classes (e.g., policy advice, management of contracts, policing, custodial services, etc.); (ii) benefits (e.g., unemployment, scholarships); (iii) borrowing expenses; (iv) other expenses (e.g., legal costs, overseas development aid); (v) capital contributions to ministries or public enterprises; (vi) purchase and development of highways, buildings, etc.; and (vii) debt repayment. Benefits and capital contributions are appropriated on a cash basis and borrowing expenses are on an accrual basis—as in most other countries—but all outputs are appropriated on an accrual basis.

13 For current expenditure, goods and services items can be grouped in a manner to fit the GFS categories and line-items for other current expenditures can be broken down into several sub-items to fit the GFS. The main difference is between the GFS definition of capital expenditure and the definition of "development" expenditure in several countries, which includes in capital expenditure a current expenditure component (some salaries, and goods and services).

14 *Zakat*—one of the five pillars of the Islamic faith—is the religious obligation of all Muslims (if they can afford to do so) to contribute a percentage of their income for alleviating poverty and other social purposes. In several countries the corresponding resources are managed by the government.

15 Activities can in turn be divided into sub-activities, but the required level of details is excessive in most countries.

Bibliography

Caiden, Naomi, 1985. "Comparing Budget Systems: Budgeting in ASEAN Countries," *Journal of Public Budgeting and Finance*, 5(4), 23–38.

de Jong, Maarten, Iris van Beek and Rense Posthumus, 2013. "Introducing Accountable Budgeting: Lessons from a Decade of Performance-Based Budgeting in the Netherlands," *OECD Journal on Budgeting*, 12(3), 1–34.

Fouque, Veronique, 2014. *Performance Budgeting: The French Experience.* Presentation at the Tenth OECD Annual Meeting, Paris, November.

Hawkesworth, Ian and Knut Klepsvik, 2013. *Budgeting Levers, Strategic Agility and the Use of Performance Budgeting in 2011–2012.* OECD, 8th Annual Meeting on Performance and Results November.

Jacobs, Davina, Jean-Luc Hélis and Dominique Bouley, 2009. *Budget Classification.* IMF, December.

Joyce, Philip, 1993. *Performance Measurement in Federal Budgeting.* U.S. Congressional Budget Office.

Kibblewhite, Andrew and Chris Ussher, 2002. "Outcome-focused Management in New Zealand," *OECD Journal on Budgeting*, 1(4), 85–110.

Kraan, Dirk-Jan, Daniel Bergvall and Ian Hawkesworth, 2007. "Budgeting in Turkey," *OECD Journal on Budgeting*, 7(2), 7–58.

Lauth, T. P., 2014. "Zero-based Budgeting Redux in Georgia: Efficiency or Ideology?" *Public Budgeting and Finance*, 34(1), 1–17.

Musgrave, Richard, 1959. *The Theory of Public Finance.* New York: McGraw Hill.

Park, Nowook and Joung-Jin Jang, 2015. "Performance Budgeting in Korea: Overview and assessment," *OECD Journal on Budgeting*, 14(3), 1–16.

Petrei, Humberto, 1998. *Budget and Control: Reforming the Public Sector in Latin America.* Washington, DC: Johns Hopkins University Press.

Premchand, A., 1998. "Umbrella Themes Obscure Real Problems," *Public Budgeting and Finance*, 18(3), 72–88.

Robinson, Marc, 2007. *Performance Budgeting: Linking Funding to Results.* Basingstoke: Palgrave Macmillan.

——, 2011. *Performance-based Budgeting.* Washington, DC: CLEAR/World Bank.

Schiavo-Campo, S. and Daniel Tommasi, 1999. *Managing Government Expenditure.* Manila: Asian Development Bank.

Schick, Allen, 1966. "The Road to PBB: The Stages of Budget Reform," *Public Administration Review*, 26(4), 243–58.

Scott, Graham and Peter Gorringe, 1989. "Reform of the Core Public Sector: The New Zealand Experience," *Australian Journal of Public Administration*, 48(1), 1–105.

Sennoga, Edward Batte and John Mary Matovu, 2013. "Public Spending Composition in Uganda and its Implications for Growth and Poverty Reduction," *Public Finance Review*, 41(2), 227–47.

Shah, A. and C. Shen, 2007. Eurostat, *Statistics in Focus*, September.

Simmons, Richard, Johnston Birchall and Alan Prout, 2012. "User Involvement in Public Services: 'Choice about Voice,'" *Public Policy and Administration*, 27(1), 3–29.

Sterck, Miekatrien and Bram Scheers, 2006. "Trends in Performance Budgeting in Seven OECD Countries," *Public Performance and Management Review*, 30(1), 47–72.

Tommasi, Daniel, 2010. *Gestion des Depenses Publiques dans les Pays en Developpement.* Paris: Agence Française de Developpement.

Webber, David, 2007. "Managing the Public's Money: From Outputs to Outcomes: and Beyond," *OECD Journal on Budgeting*, 4(2), 101–21.

Wildavsky, Aaron, 1964. *The Politics of the Budgetary Process.* Boston: Little, Brown.

——, 1988. *New Politics of the Budgetary Process.* Glenview: Scott, Foresman.

3 Budget Coverage, Extrabudgetary Operations and Tax Expenditures

What you don't know *will* hurt you.

The Core Requirement: Comprehensiveness of the Budget

The annual government budget cannot reflect the preferences and choices of society unless it covers as much as possible of the expected revenue and proposed expenditure. Two major issues are involved here. First, if the budget excludes major expenditures, there can be no assurance that scarce resources are allocated to priority programs and that legal controls and public accountability are properly enforced. Only if all proposed expenditures are on the table at the same time is it possible to review them in relation to one another and to choose those that have higher relative benefits for the community or command greater support. Second, the amount of expenditure that is not included is itself often uncertain and opaque. This uncertainty hampers macroeconomic and fiscal policy-making and increases the risk of corruption and waste. In both cases, the link between policy and the budget is weakened in direct proportion to the amount of expenditure that is not covered in the budget.

Imagine that, as the head of a household, you have a large income in addition to your salary but hold it separately and discuss with your family only the allocation of the salary. At best, even if the additional income is allocated well, family members cannot cooperate in making sure that it is *spent* well, nor can they feel any responsibility for mistakes in this respect. At worst, the additional income will be frittered away on frivolous expenditure, with adverse impact on the family's future finances and well-being.

Scope, Periodicity and Basic Rules of the Budget

The Scope and Geographic Coverage of the Budget

In principle, fiscal targets should cover "general government." General government includes all government entities—national as well as subnational government (SNG):

- Central government includes all governmental departments, establishments and other bodies that are instruments of the central authority, plus the extensions of central government authority that operate at the regional or local level but are not separate government units.
- The intermediate level of subnational government is state governments in federal countries (e.g., Australia, India, Nigeria, the US).[1] In unitary countries (e.g., Italy, France, Japan) the intermediate level of government is usually called a province.
- Local government consists of governmental units that exercise independent competence in the urban and rural jurisdictions of a country's territory, including counties, districts,

cities, etc. An entity is treated as local government if it is entitled to own assets and raise funds, has some discretion in its spending and is able to appoint its own staff. (These are the differences between decentralization, which entails devolution of authority and of management autonomy, and deconcentration, by which the authority of the center is exercised in part through entities acting locally but as agents of the central government.)

The criteria for deciding at which level of government a public agency belongs are the nature of the function and the source of its authority—not its physical location. For example, a hospital managed by the central ministry of health is part of the central government no matter where it is located. (Remember, the key is accountability.[2])

The basic principle of national budgeting is that *each level of the government should have its own budget* that covers its sphere of activity and responsibility. Most countries have formal revenue and expenditure assignments for the various levels of government, but in a few countries the distribution of expenditure responsibilities among levels of the government is ambiguous. Especially problematic can be long lists of "concurrent powers," where responsibility for a given activity is shared between central and provincial government, as in Sri Lanka, with a ping-pong game of blame when something goes seriously wrong. In countries with weak governance, the formal provisions for sharing revenue and expenditure responsibilities are not observed in practice, and parallel systems of revenue collection or of informal expenditure are superimposed on the formal systems (as in some central Asian countries).

A sound analysis of a country's fiscal situation and prospects calls for looking at general government rather than only the central government. Indeed, blinkered focus on central government generates the temptation to download fiscal difficulties on to subnational levels of government by reducing transfers to decentralizing expenditure responsibilities without decentralizing the revenue to go with them. (This issue is different from that of "unfunded mandates," i.e., requiring subnational governments to implement some protections or enforce certain national rules without at the same time giving them the resources to do so.) Downloading fiscal difficulties masks the underlying problem of central government finances, at the expense of public services at local level. The central government budget looks in better shape but only because the fiscal problems have been swept under the rugs of subnational government.

Conversely, closing one's eyes to mounting fiscal problems of subnational governments can lead to a national crisis when they cumulate and come to the surface unexpectedly, requiring a major intervention from the central government. A kind of "moral hazard" is at work here. If a local government can expect to be bailed out from central government, it will have no incentive to be fiscally responsible; the bailout would thus in effect enable irresponsible behavior, and the bill would be paid by the entities that have behaved responsibly which, in turn, would lose their own incentive to do so. This scenario is especially prevalent in countries where data from subnational levels of government are not available in a timely and reliable fashion—as was the case in much of Latin America in the 1980s and 1990s. (Budgeting at SNG level is discussed in Chapter 14.)

Government and Public Sector

Government expenditure is different from public expenditure. The public sector includes general government plus all entities that are majority-owned by the government, such as state-owned enterprises or state financial institutions.

In centrally planned economies, as those of the former Soviet Union and Eastern Europe, the distinction between the activities of state enterprises and those of government was fuzzy, because state enterprises were directly involved in the delivery of public services. After the fall of the Soviet Union and the regime changes in Eastern Europe, closing an inefficient state enterprise thus meant at the same time depriving the local community of basic public services. Moreover, the concomitant disappearance of central control over the managers of state enterprises gave them a free hand to strip and sell the assets of the enterprises, cutting off the income of all employees and leading to the rise of various mafias acting as intermediaries for the disposal of the assets (and then expanding abroad as a new form of cross-national organized crime). In the interest of putting a stake in the heart of communism, these realities were blithely ignored by the international organizations in the reforms they advocated in the 1990s. Consequently, without putting in place sound corporate governance arrangements to replace central control of state enterprises (which would have been feasible in the early transition years), the reforms caused severe and widespread suffering and social dislocations—producing deep resentment of the West, generating popular hostility and suspicion of the outside world and fueling the revanchist nationalism that is most evident in today's Russia.[3]

In a few countries (most importantly, China) state enterprises still act in part as agents of the state and follow central government instructions, in exchange for government support for their survival even when they are economically unviable—the so-called zombie enterprises.[4]

In market economies, state enterprises should be commercially oriented and thus need a separate legal persona and full operational autonomy. Most countries today differentiate between activities carried out by the government and those carried out by publicly owned but autonomous entities managed on commercial principles. As such, their expenditures and revenues cannot be submitted to the same scrutiny and approval mechanisms as the government budget.

The government budget should include the financial transactions between the state enterprises and the government but not their transactions with the rest of the economy, for which the government is not directly responsible. However, a coherent financial approach should be developed for the public sector as a whole—wherever data and circumstances permit—the so-called consolidated accounts of the public sector (sometimes called the *consolidated budget*, although it does not have the legal status of the government budget itself because it is not formally approved by the legislature). In any event, for accountability and transparency, the government should report regularly also on the performance and financial situation of both financial and nonfinancial state enterprises.

The Annuality of the Budget

The executive branch needs both flexibility and accountability. Again, let us dispense with the extremes. The legislature's authorization to spend cannot be required every week, which would paralyze the executive, nor just once in many years, which would in effect void executive accountability. The middle ground is a formal budget covering a "fiscal year" of 12 months: both the government's revenue-collecting authority and its authorization to spend expire at the end of the year (with some exceptions). The fiscal, or financial, year usually but not always corresponds to the calendar year, January 1 to December 31.[5]

The annual budget must not be confused with the medium-term expenditure forecasts (MTEF) used in many countries to frame the annual budget process, and sometimes wrongly called "multiyear budgets." (Much more on this in Chapter 5.) Fundamental governance principles require a distinction between the legislative authorization to spend, which covers only one fiscal year, and the multiyear expenditure forecasts. The distinction rests on a "burden of action" criterion: if the money can be spent during the multiyear period without any action by the legislature after its initial approval, the multiyear expenditure ceilings would be legally binding and a genuine multiyear budget would exist. However, *the budget is on an annual basis in every country.* Box 3.1 shows that exceptions to this in some developed countries are only apparent.

Box 3.1 Apparent Exceptions to Annual Budgeting

Multiyear Budgets?

The government budget, as fundamental legal instrument and expression of a people's choice through their legislature, is de jure annual everywhere in the world.

France has multiyear commitments which, however, do not authorize payments beyond the current fiscal year. Two documents are presented to parliament: a medium-term program which, among other things, sets expenditure ceilings for each of 33 "missions"; and the budget law for the coming year (which defines expenditures by mission and program). Both documents are approved by parliament, but no expenditure beyond the coming year can actually be made except as approved in the budget law for the year in question.

In *Germany*, the federal government and the states produce a medium-term budget scenario, presented to parliament along with the proposed annual budget but without legal standing in itself. The purpose is mainly to assure that the central and state budgets are consistent with one another and with the stability and sustainability objectives of the federal government.

In *Hungary* and *Slovenia*, a two-year budget is presented, but the appropriations for the second year require fresh approval by parliament—essentially returning to an annual budget process. Similarly, in *Russia,* the basic budget law was amended in 2008 to introduce three-year appropriations which, however, must be updated annually by parliament.

Little *Micronesia* was the one exception, with a real two-year budget, but has returned to annual budgeting.

Several *developing countries* prepare multiyear program "budgets," at the urging of the donors, with shifting coverage and little impact on the annual budget decisions (although with some utility as training tools and sources of information).

"Binding" Multiyear Expenditure Ceilings?

The expenditure ceilings for the outyears of a multiyear fiscal framework may be considered binding only for programming purposes and as political commitments. In turn, their value as political commitments is stronger in countries such as the UK, Australia, New Zealand and others, and more indicative elsewhere. In the UK and Scandinavian countries they are a public commitment of the executive which is subject to confirmation by the legislature through the annual budget process.

Expenditure figures for the outyears are not and cannot be *legally* binding unless there is a multiyear budget, which is not the case anywhere. The legal distinction is also a major de facto difference in most countries.

Source: Condensed from the author's online exchange with various colleagues, primarily Marco Cangiano, Richard Hughes, Christian Schmidt, Eivind Tandberg and Daniel Tommasi.

This is not a question of counting the number of angels on a pin. Words matter. Conceptually, a clear separation of powers between the executive and the legislature requires an equally clear distinction between budget—the legal heart of public financial governance—and projections made by the executive branch. Practically, too, the distinction matters. For example, viewing the ceilings on each ministry's expenditure in future years as legally binding may lead some ministries to consider them as entitlements—thus laying the basis for misunderstandings and tilting to the revenue side any fiscal adjustments that may become necessary.

Four Basic Budget Rules

To provide for a strong link between the policies decided by government and the budget which is intended to implement them, four basic rules apply to every expenditure financed in whole or in part by public moneys:

- Whatever the coverage of the budget, all proposed expenditures must be presented together and reviewed during the same process (as described in Chapter 6).
- All expenditures and revenues should be classified on the same basis, for accountability and to permit comparisons of relative efficiency (as explained in Chapter 2).
- All accounts must be subject to regular external audit (as discussed in Chapter 11).
- Financial reporting should consolidate the operations of autonomous funds and agencies with regular budget operations (as explained in Chapter 11).

Budget versus Budget Documentation

The budget documentation to be presented to the legislature must include important information additional to the proposed budget itself. While the budget is at the core, as the fundamental legal instrument by which the legislature authorizes the executive to collect revenues and make expenditures, other plans and information should be presented at the same time in order to provide the legislature with a full picture of government policy, the state of the public finances and the future implications. These plans are not subject to formal legislative approval. The budget plus the additional plans and information constitute the budget documentation.

Managing Off-Budget Expenditures

Although the coverage of the budget should be as extensive as possible, in almost every country two broad categories of expenditure are not included in the budget. First, some transactions are managed through special arrangements set up outside the annual budget appropriations process; these are known as "extra-budgetary" operations or "extra-budgetary funds" (EBFs). Second, other expenditures are not treated as part of government expenditure at all—even though they are identical to actual expenditure in intent and effect; these fall under the heading of "tax expenditures." (Both types of expenditure are carried out under the law, and neither should be confused with the practice in some countries of hiding revenues or setting up secret expenditure accounts, discussed in Chapter 17.)

Extrabudgetary Operations

Nature and Rationale

Usually called extrabudgetary funds,[6] these operations are not extrabudgetary in the sense that they escape approval by the legislature altogether, but in the more limited sense that they do not need to be approved *every year*. In the definition provided by the IMF Code of Fiscal Transparency, EBFs are *government operations that are set up outside the annual budget appropriations process*. The dividing line is thus clear: if transactions involving public financial resources are not subject to the *same* legislative approval process as the annual budget, they are "outside" the budget. However, they are not outside the bounds of legislative authority and oversight. The fundamental requirement of authorization by the people's representatives is still met if the legislature approves the establishment of the EBF and its governing and reporting procedures, and reviews it from time to time.

The legislative approval of the establishment of an EBF requires that (i) the delegation of revenue and spending authority is made for specific purposes and under clear criteria; (ii) the governance arrangements of the fund are satisfactory and explicit; and (iii) transparent information on the financial operations of the EBF is regularly included in the annual budget documentation (as explained earlier).

Extrabudgetary funds exist in almost every country, and extrabudgetary operations account on a worldwide average for about one-third of total government expenditure. In developed countries, pensions account for about 90 percent of non-budgeted expenditure. In low-income countries, the importance of pension EBFs is much lower, but that of other extrabudgetary expenditure is much higher: EBFs account for 20–40 percent of total spending, including spending financed from foreign aid (although for various accounting reasons the real size of transactions is probably lower than the recorded amount).

Extrabudgetary funds fall in four categories, related to: (i) the nature of the organization (e.g., a university, which requires long-term spending authority); (ii) special management requirements (e.g., projects financed by foreign aid); (iii) priority nature of the expenditure (e.g., a roads maintenance fund); or (iv) operations which generate all or a large part of their revenue.

Reasons for Creating EBFs

There are four potentially valid reasons to create an EBF:

- To bypass budgetary procedures which are too rigid or not suited to the particular category of expenditure. Although the optimal response would be to introduce greater flexibility in the budgetary procedures, setting up special arrangements may be a justified second-best response.
- To purchase goods that will be delivered at some future time, since the payments would be jeopardized by the need to seek legislative approval on an annual basis. Departmental enterprises, for example, need revolving funds to carry out their trading activities.
- For institutional reasons, such as the special status of certain professions or activities. Autonomous public entities exist in many countries and are financed partly by transfers from the budget of the central government and partly by resources they raise directly. An example is a public hospital, with its revenue partly from patient fees.
- To improve service delivery by separating it from policy formulation. A few developed countries have created autonomous "executive agencies," which establish contractual relations with the competent line ministry, committing to provide certain services of a given quality in exchange for the financial resources needed to do so.[7]

Types of EBFs

The four main types of extrabudgetary operations are sovereign wealth funds, social security funds, aid-financed expenditure and road funds.

Sovereign Wealth Funds

These are extrabudgetary funds set up to receive and manage national revenue from extractive resource exports.[8] Their financial assets worldwide are massive—totaling over $6 trillion as of the end of 2015, of which about two-thirds were in oil and gas funds. The largest sovereign wealth funds are those of Saudi Arabia, Kuwait and Norway—which together account for almost half of the total. The primary purposes of setting up a sovereign wealth fund are to conserve the revenues, smooth out their volatility and invest them for protection against unforeseen economic shocks and for the benefit of future generations.

Sovereign wealth funds are thus expected to invest prudently and with an eye to the long term, although in some countries—for example, pre-revolutionary Libya—such funds have been used as a piggybank for the regime. (Chapter 17 discusses the issues of secrecy of extractive revenues in unrepresentative regimes.)

Because they function as private sector investment vehicles, they must have full management and financial autonomy, their expenditures cannot be classified precisely along the main budget classification, and their accounting must be on full accrual. (Chapter 11 explains the bases of accounting.) Their special function and complete operational autonomy add to the imperative of sound internal governance arrangements, tight audit by the government and the fullest possible measure of transparency of operations and results.

Social Security Funds

"Social security" covers a variety of services classified into three broad categories:

- Social insurance, mainly unemployment insurance and retirement benefits for citizens, generally financed with contributions from employers and employees and yielding benefits linked to the contributions.
- Direct provision of a service or cash payment to a defined group of beneficiaries, such as family allowances, maternity grants, etc.
- Social assistance, i.e., payments or services contingent on the needs and financial status of the beneficiary (assistance to the elderly, handicapped, jobless and so on).

Although most social security expenditure constitutes entitlements that cannot be changed except by specific legislation, there is no reason why the transactions should not be included in the budget itself. A fiscal deficit is a fiscal deficit whether it arises from investment spending, civil service wages or social security expenditure. Even in countries where transactions are managed by an independent governmental agency—as the Social Security Administration in the US—a deficit must in the end be financed through the government. In reality, the social security "trust fund" is merely an accounting arrangement.

Exceptions may be made for countries in which management of social security moneys also involves employee unions and employers, as it is difficult to integrate into the budget funds that are managed by non-government entities. In those cases, at a minimum they must be consolidated in a financial report and their budget should be included in the budget documentation as an annex.

Aid-financed Expenditure

In the 1970s and 1980s, expenditures in developing countries that were financed with earmarked external aid were routinely omitted from the budget altogether. Progress has been made toward integration of foreign aid-financed expenditure in the budget, although in many countries the budgetary coverage of these expenditures remains incomplete. Aid-financed projects are often managed separately by project implementation units (PIUs) using financial management and procurement procedures ("fiduciary procedures") and personnel different from those of the recipient country government. Donors justify this practice by the need to protect the aid moneys in a context where the public financial management of the country is weak. This may indeed be necessary, but the longer that aid projects continue to be managed as institutional enclaves the less likely it is that the country's own fiduciary systems will improve. The goal of the international donor community to foster the development of fiduciary capacity in developing countries thus conflicts with the understandable reluctance of individual project managers to take risks with the aid moneys entrusted to them. (These issues are discussed in Chapter 10.)

Expenditure financed from the local currency funds generated by sales of commodity aid ("counterpart funds") also must be managed under specific procedures mandated by donor requirements (e.g., PL 480 in the US). In any case, project aid and counterpart-funded expenditure can and should be accounted for in the budget. That this goal is achievable in every aid-recipient country has been demonstrated recently by a country as conflict-damaged as Burundi. Donor agencies have a responsibility to encourage and facilitate the process.

Road Funds

Road funds are the granddaddy of extrabudgetary funds in developing countries (particularly in Africa) but are also seen in several developed countries, such as the US. The fact that road users are identifiable and that they bear some taxes (such as gasoline taxes) directly related to their road use justifies earmarking of the revenue for road maintenance and construction.

Some road funds are accounting arrangements, while others are actual organizations that finance road investments and maintenance and have managerial and financial autonomy. The objective of a road fund has been to insulate from the vagaries of annual fiscal pressures the expenditures for the maintenance and development of roads—a crucial priority, especially in Africa and South Asia, where land transport is critical and rural–urban connectivity is important for economic and social objectives.

Unfortunately, the early experience with road funds in the 1970s and 1980s was very disappointing (McCleary, 1991). Not only did those "first-generation" road funds reduce fiscal transparency, but the earmarked funds were often misappropriated or diverted to other uses. The knowledge that substantial sums were parked in a road fund account proved an irresistible temptation for well-connected officials to raid the account. Paradoxically, the existence of a road fund intended in theory to protect and preserve resources for road maintenance, rehabilitation and new investment resulted in practice in financial starvation of the sector and progressive degradation of the road network—with major negative implications for economic activity and development.

This is illustrated by Ghana's early experience (see Box 3.2), but has been a sad reality throughout much of Africa. It took the author four bone-shaking days in 2006 in a four-wheel-drive to go from Kinshasa to Bandundu in the Democratic Republic of Congo—a 200-mile trip that is known to have taken a little over four hours in 1960. In recent years, the road has been completely rebuilt with the help of foreign aid, and by 2014 the travel time by regular car has reportedly gone back to what it was a half century ago. The moral of the story is twofold: deferring necessary road maintenance and investment carries an enormous cost in terms of travel time, economic activity and opportunities lost, but

Box 3.2 Ghana: A First-Generation Road Fund

The road fund in Ghana was established in 1985, financed by a tax on fuel, as part of a program of road maintenance and rehabilitation.

Financing from the road fund was unstable, generating unpredictability that made it difficult to plan and issue contracts on a timely basis. In turn, the lack of funding predictability was used as an excuse for inaction or as a way to short-circuit the procurement procedures for the benefit of various interests. As a result, at the turn of the century, significant portions of the road network in Ghana remained in very poor condition, and the country still did not possess the basis for sustainable road-maintenance financing.

In the mid-1990s, the government decided to increase the fuel tax sufficiently to fully finance the road fund. To avoid passing to the users the proposed increase in the fuel tax, the treasury agreed to cede other excise tax revenues to the road fund, thereby keeping fuel taxes at about the same level even though the proportion earmarked for the road fund increased. After 2005, the government introduced further major changes with substantial positive impact, learning from the earlier experience.

A key lesson from the Ghanaian experience—shared by many other African countries—is that setting up a road fund is insufficient in itself to ensure financing for road maintenance. On the contrary, when the budget system works reasonably well, priority expenditures such as road maintenance can be met without a separate EBF to finance them. For example, Burkina Faso was able to finance virtually the entirety of its road maintenance through the regular budget process, without a dedicated road fund.

Source: Updated and adapted from Mwale (1997).

the transport link can be restored relatively quickly—given the financial and managerial resources to do so.

From that negative experience came the concept of "second-generation" road funds.[9] The main features of a second-generation road fund are to:

- involve road users in the management of roads;
- clearly define the responsibilities of all parties;
- set up an autonomous and independent board with private participation;
- establish clear accountability rules; and
- set up and devise a charging instrument related to road use that is easy to separate from other taxes and simple to administer (e.g., tolls).

The effectiveness of a road fund depends on several factors: good corporate governance and anti-corruption provisions; a board of directors that represents road users and the public interest rather than being captured by contractor and producer interests; the degree to which the funds are fully protected for roads rather than serve as a convenient parking place for money that can be diverted elsewhere; the effectiveness of the road fund's financial management; and robust independent audit of fund operations. Through 2015, the simulation of market discipline in second-generation road funds appears to have improved the management and maintenance of African roads, albeit not uniformly in every country: while the experience in Tanzania has been positive so far (see Box 3.3), that of other countries, such as Malawi, has not.

Interestingly, the experience with the Highway Trust Fund in the US has resembled Malawi more than Tanzania—albeit for political rather than institutional reasons. After the massive expansion of the interstate highway network in the 1950s and 1960s, and adequate provisions for maintenance until the 1990s, since then the funding of highway maintenance and investments has been haphazard, inadequate and dominated by partisan squabbles and posturing (see Box 3.4).

Risks

Regardless of the reason for their creation, EBFs pose a variety of potential problems and risks: transactions may not be subject to the same kind of fiscal discipline as budgetary

---

Box 3.3 Tanzania: A Promising Second-Generation Road Fund

Tanzania's road fund in its current form first came into operation in 2000. Its board is composed of a chairman from the private sector; the permanent secretaries of the Ministry of Works, Ministry of Finance and Prime Minister's Office for Regional Administration and Local Government (PMORALG); a senior civil servant; and several representatives of the private sector and of civil society associations, who were appointed by the minister of works. The road fund has its own dedicated secretariat.

More than 95 percent of the resources of the fund come from a fuel tax (as of 2014 about 40 US cents per imperial gallon). The fund is mandated to use at least 90 percent of its resources for maintenance and emergency repair. It allocates 63 percent of its funding to TANROADS (the Tanzania National Roads Agency) for maintenance of the national and regional roads, 7 percent to the Ministry of Works for development projects on those roads and 30 percent for local roads. The latter funds are mostly passed through to the 100 or so local councils, according to a formula agreed with PMORALG, which takes into account population, road length and division into equal shares. Of the local road funding, PMORALG itself controls directly only 1 percent for administrative expenses and 3 percent for development projects.

All these transfers are governed by performance agreements between the road fund board and the implementation agencies. The agreements specify the respective responsibilities of each party, policies, definitions, performance indicators with means of verification, agency action plans, reporting requirements and budgets, giving details of works to be undertaken during the year.

Tanzania has made good progress. The road network has improved and funding has increased from the equivalent of US$58 million in 2001 to $67 million in 2004 and over $90 million in 2012. The performance agreements between the road fund board and the implementation agencies have contributed to improved accountability. Local roads now receive significant funds for maintenance, and decentralization has been enhanced by disbursing the funds directly to the local councils.

Sources: www.roadsfund.go.tz [accessed January 2016]; Andreski (2005); Gwilliam and Kumar (2002).

Box 3.4 The Highway Trust Fund in the US

The Highway Trust Fund was established in 1956, primarily to finance the new interstate highway system, and was complemented by a smaller fund created in 1982 to support public transit. The Trust Fund is the main source of financing for highways, tunnels, bridges and public transit, and states rely heavily on it for the maintenance and repair of their transport infrastructure. It is funded by a federal fuel tax, last raised in 1993 to 18.4 cents per gallon of gasoline and 24.4 cents per gallon of fuel. Because the tax is expressed in an absolute amount rather than a percentage, and has been left unchanged from 1993, the Trust Fund financial resources have not kept pace either with the price of fuel or with the increase in road traffic occurring over the past 23 years. The resulting financial difficulties have been addressed by additional funding decided by Congress from time to time and invariably after a great deal of partisan bickering. As a result, maintenance and repair of major transport infrastructure have been delayed or neglected altogether. Among other things, in 2015 there were an estimated 80,000 functionally obsolete and 60,000 structurally deficient bridges in the US. Many of these are used by commuters every day, and if left in disarray could result in structural failure like that of the I-35W bridge which collapsed in Minneapolis in 2007, killing 13 and injuring 147.

  With federal gas taxes producing $34 billion a year and Trust Fund needs of at least $55 billion, attempting to cover the $20 billion gap with ad hoc additional financing is grossly inefficient, and its unpredictability raises the cost of infrastructural investments and repairs. Ironically, unlike road funds in many other countries, the Highway Trust Fund has worked reasonably well, with the only exception being the difficulties caused by the hand-to-mouth nature of its financing. A permanent and stable source of funding is essential. Several states have proposed to fill the funding gap by reallocating revenue from natural gas fracking into highway and bridge maintenance, but the amount would be grossly insufficient. The obvious solution would be to raise the federal gas tax, and express it in percentage terms rather than absolute amount. This would disproportionately affect low-income people, who drive older and less fuel-efficient cars—but there are efficient and administratively feasible ways to rebate the added cost to low-income drivers.

Source: Concord Coalition (2016) and various news reports.

operations, partly because they "carry their own money" and partly because they are not explicitly compared with other expenditure. Activities that would not survive the scrutiny of a regular budget process often continue because of vested interests or simple inertia.

Dealing with EBFs

When the normal budgetary procedures are unsuitable for managing certain types of transactions, the optimal policy response is to improve the budgetary procedures and/or to set up specific procedures for those particular transactions, rather than place the operations themselves outside the annual budget process. For this reason, international financial institutions strongly oppose the creation of most EBFs. In practice, separate funds or autonomous management of certain transactions may be inevitable or desirable. Thus, instead of ideological opposition to extrabudgetary funds, it is better to make and enforce provisions to manage them well and reduce their attendant fiscal and integrity risks (Schiavo-Campo and Tommasi, 1999; this position is also taken by others, e.g., Dorotinsky, 2008).

The risks mentioned earlier can be alleviated by corresponding protections—accompanied by significant penalties for violators. Note that most of these protections are the same as the provisions for good budgeting:

- The risk of waste and inefficiency can be mitigated by regular performance audits.
- For purposes of control, EBF transactions should be classified as in the main budget classification, and regularly shown in the budget documentation.
- EBF transactions must be shown in gross terms: netting out revenue and expenditure is misleading—for example, a trivial deficit of $1,000 may conceal $999,000 in revenue and $1,000,000 in expenditure giving a totally distorted picture of the importance of the fund. When the gross amounts are large, netting out impedes analysis of government activities, accurate estimates of economic costs, comparisons with other countries and prevention of abuses.
- Transparency problems can be addressed by mandatory reporting requirements.
- The risks of corruption and undue political interference can be mitigated by putting in place sound governance arrangements and strong accountability mechanisms.
- The EBFs' tendency to proliferate can be combated by placing a heavy burden of proof on to the proponents of setting up a new fund and putting in place robust gatekeeping mechanisms, both political and technical, to reduce the probability that unjustified EBFs will slip under the radar and eventually weaken the integrity of the budgeting system.

Financing Extrabudgetary Operations: Tax Earmarking and User Fees

Extrabudgetary operations can be funded in various ways, including by direct transfers from the treasury, but tax earmarking and user fees are the most common sources of financing.[10]

The three possible tax earmarking arrangements have been defined long ago:

- A specific tax or fee earmarked for a specific end use, such as gasoline taxes for highway maintenance and investments.
- A specific tax or fee earmarked for a general end use, such as a lottery whose proceeds finance general government expenditure.
- A general tax earmarked for a specific end use, such as a fixed percentage of general revenue allocated to specific programs.

In most cases, earmarking for specific uses a share of general tax revenues is inadvisable. Concerning earmarking of a specific tax or fee, the distinction is between strong earmarking, in which the link between the payment of a tax or fee and the associated expenditure is close, for example, a road toll or university tuition fees; and weak earmarking, in which the link between the benefit and the taxes is less direct, for example, the use of lottery proceeds for investments (McCleary, 1991; Hemming and Miranda, 1991).

As mentioned in the discussion of road funds, when there is a strong benefit–revenue link and the service is provided to well-identified users, tax earmarking may be desirable to induce agencies to improve performance and facilitate cost recovery. Also, some observers argue that the use of earmarked public revenue can increase taxpayers' knowledge of how the taxes they pay are used, making it more likely that they (or, more realistically, the media) will exercise vigilance over the efficiency of the services.

A user fee (or user charge) is a fee or other payment for using a public facility or service. The issue of user fees is complex. As a general rule, the expected revenue should be weighed against the administrative and transaction costs of defining and collecting the fees. In addition, there are moral and social implications when user fees risk reducing poor people's access to basic facilities or services. In the health sector, the introduction of user fees has in fact often limited access of the poor to health care.[11] Thus, in most low-income countries, it is generally not desirable to levy user fees on essential social services such as basic health care and primary education, and where they do exist their removal should be considered (see McPake et al., 2011).

In other parts of the world, governments that introduce user fees should, if practical, tailor the fee to the users' ability to pay. Also, the agencies that collect the revenue should be allowed to retain a significant portion of it—because if they cannot retain any of the revenue they have little incentive to administer the system efficiently and enforce collection of the fees. (A hospital or a university, for example, would have no interest in improving its financial efficiency if it could not use some of the revenue it receives from selling its services.)

When user fees are *both* cost-effective and socially appropriate, they must be administered transparently and efficiently, and included in the budget. The main principles governing user fees were developed by the OECD in 1998 and remain valid. They are demanding, however, and need to be adapted to the sector and country realities:

- *Clear legal authority.* The legal basis to charge for services should be clearly defined but without setting the precise amount of the fees, so that they can be adjusted without further legislative action.
- *Consultation with users.* Consultations prevent misunderstandings and improve the design and implementation of the user fee system.
- *Full costing.* The full costs of each service should be determined and made public, regardless of whether the intention is to recover them fully or partly. For partial cost recovery, this information will serve to reveal the implicit subsidy granted.
- *Appropriate pricing.* Wherever relevant, in order to allow for allow efficient allocation of the services and limit congestion, the pricing should either be based on competitive market prices, or reflect full cost recovery, or take into account variations in demand.
- *Competitive neutrality.* The costing should incorporate all cost items faced by the private sector entities operating in the same sector.
- *Equity.* Reduced or zero fees can be applied to lower-income individuals, users located in remote areas, and the like. The criteria for reduced fees must be transparent and difficult to manipulate.[12]
- *Effective collection.* The efficiency of user-fee collection can make or break the system. If the fees have been set efficiently and equitably, failures to pay should be followed up immediately.
- *Audit.* As always, regular external audits of the organization that levies and collects the charge are required.
- *Performance.* The performance of the organization should be monitored regularly to ensure appropriate levels of efficiency and service quality. User fees cannot be allowed to serve as indirect financial support for continued inefficiency.

Finally, as for all government services and regulations, public support is important for broad compliance and, in turn, broad compliance is essential for the efficiency of user-fee administration and collection. For example, enforcement of electronic road tolls would become very difficult if a majority of cars drove straight through without paying. The evidence is murky on the question of public support, and much depends on the type of service in question. While most people agree with the proposition that costs should be borne in proportion to the benefits received, in practice there is resistance to a new or increased user fee. In the case of roads, for example, replacing taxes on fuel with mileage user fees would encounter public resistance in the absence of an effort to educate voters (Duncan et al., 2014). In the US, the annual car tax levied by Virginia was hated by residents and had to be sharply curtailed, despite its strong economic and fiscal justification as linking cost and benefit directly.

Tax Expenditures

What is a Tax Expenditure?

Tax expenditures are the revenue forgone because of preferential tax provisions, such as tax exemptions, waivers or reductions. Tax expenditures aim at achieving certain public policy objectives by providing benefits to qualified individuals or entities or by encouraging particular outcomes (e.g., the mortgage interest tax deduction is intended to foster home ownership). They may also be intended to improve tax equity (e.g., exempting basic foodstuffs from a sales tax) or offset imperfections in other parts of the tax structure.

Tax expenditures must be granted through specific legislation, but are not submitted to the same internal control and legislative authorization as other expenditure. Therefore, tax expenditures are often an easier and less transparent way of granting special benefits to specific groups. In certain cases, the beneficiaries are less clearly identified than are those who would benefit from direct spending. As a result, tax expenditures often produce results that are different from the stated objectives.

Tax expenditures are for all intents and purposes equivalent to actual government expenditures—financially and economically (although not administratively or politically). Most tax expenditures produce the same quantitative impact on the public finances as an outright subsidy or other expenditure through the budget. For example, whether a corporation receives a $10 million government subsidy for research and development or a $10 million tax credit for the same purpose, $10 million is $10 million (as long as the corporation has a tax liability greater than $10 million). Thus, persons who advocate lower government spending should logically be in favor of reducing or eliminating tax expenditures as well. This is rarely the case. The main reason is that the tax credit does not show up as expenditure in the budget.

Indeed, this is a major part of the political attractiveness of tax expenditures. They are somewhat easier to introduce, and are relatively insulated from efforts to cut government spending, because they do not appear as out-of-pocket government spending. In addition to obscuring the actual expenditure and making it difficult to figure out the distributional implications of the fiscal system (let alone compare the worth of different government interventions), some tax expenditures create de facto entitlements which may compromise the ability to make necessary fiscal adjustments in the future and thus, indirectly, add to fiscal risk. (Fiscal risk is discussed in Chapter 4.) On economic and fiscal grounds an outright subsidy financed through an open tax is generally much preferable to an equivalent tax expenditure.

Tax expenditures also obscure the real size of government and the impact of its operations. For example, the budget figures show that the size of the US federal government is significantly lower than the average for rich countries. In reality, this is only apparent. When tax expenditures are added, federal spending comes up closer to the average. The difference is that the expenditure done through tax exemptions and other policies forgoing revenue is done opaquely—without comparison with alternative ways of funding, without uniformity of standards throughout the states—through a jumble of diverse programs lacking transparency, equity, efficiency and effectiveness. In a rational world, the social benefits sought through tax expenditures could be achieved by direct expenditure financed by open taxation at much lower financial and social cost, and with an honest reckoning of the impact on the various groups of beneficiaries and thus greater political legitimacy. In a rational world, that is. In the real world, progress can only come by gradually eliminating one by one the most inefficient kinds of tax expenditure and replacing other specific kinds with coherent programs, openly debated and transparently funded. Even that requires a difficult political balancing act to create public support sufficient to overcome the inevitable resistance to eliminating any benefit through the tax system. It also requires a measure of political consensus and compromise, conspicuous for its absence in the current political climate.

Types of Tax Expenditures

Tax expenditures cover the following general categories:

- Exemptions, which exclude the income of a group of taxpayers from the tax base.
- Tax deductions, which reduce the taxable base.
- Tax credits, which are deducted from the tax due as opposed to deductions, which reduce taxable income. (A $100 tax credit is worth $100, a $100 tax deduction is worth only the proportion that would be taxed.)
- Deferrals or postponements of tax deadlines, without charging interest or penalties.
- Reduced tax rates for certain categories of taxpayers or activities.

Income tax exemptions, reductions and deductions form the bulk of total tax expenditure, but the number and variety of tax expenditures are legion. The UK, for example, has over 100 different tax expenditure provisions, including income tax relief and exemptions, exemptions from capital gains tax, waivers or reduced rates of the value added tax, exemptions for energy from renewable resources and similar provisions related to climate change, and sundry provisions such as relief from stamp duty for small lotteries. And in the US there are almost 200 individual types of tax exemptions, reductions, waivers and deductions at federal level, and many more at the level of the states. Some tax expenditures are self-explanatory and easily justifiable (e.g., a waiver of sales tax on basic foodstuffs), others are difficult to justify and clumsy to administer (e.g., in the UK, an excise duty exemption for "historic cars" or for "fossil fuels used in a combined heat and power station to generate good quality electricity consumed on-site").

Impact of Tax Expenditures

To determine whether a particular tax measure generates a tax expenditure, it is necessary to identify the normal tax structure from which the measure departs. This is relatively easy when the tax expenditure corresponds to a specific exemption (for example, a special tax rate on income from agricultural activities) but when a provision affects the entire tax structure (for example, a different income tax rate for married and single persons), it is difficult to determine whether a tax expenditure is involved. Counterfactuals are too often subjective. There is also a debate about the methodology to assess the impact of tax expenditures, because it may differ from the impact of direct spending if they trigger changes in taxpayer behavior. By any measurement, however, in developed countries tax expenditures add up to massive amounts: in the US federal budget in 2015 they were $1.2 trillion, or more than the $1.1 trillion *total* discretionary expenditures (other than mandatory expenditure on social security, medicare, etc.).

In general, in addition to their lack of transparency and potential for abuse and partisan political influence, tax expenditures have a regressive impact on the after-tax distribution of income (i.e., they benefit richer people by a greater proportion of income than poor people). Thus, income tax deductions are most valuable to higher-income persons, both because their marginal tax rate is higher and because deductions must be itemized in order to be claimed—while low-income taxpayers typically only claim the standard deduction. The mortgage interest deduction, in particular, obviously benefits the most the persons who have expensive houses with large mortgages and interest payments—in effect, taxpayers in general end up subsidizing the owners of MacMansions. There are exceptions—for example, the earned income tax credit, which is targeted explicitly to low-income taxpayers—but even such broadly popular provisions as the child care tax credit benefit upper-middle income persons to a much greater extent than other groups. The impact of tax expenditures on income inequality is heavy and grows over time.

While tax expenditures are more common and larger in developed countries, they also figure prominently in some developing countries—and so do their disadvantages. In India, for example, tax expenditures are estimated to cost the government one-fourth of total revenue; the benefits are higher for higher-income groups, the provisions are scattered and frequently changed, causing diversion of savings, procedural bottlenecks, confusion and unpredictability (Jain et al., 2014). The situation described by Jain et al. is no better than the one already assessed as problematic 20 years earlier by Anand Gupta (1984b).

The Budgetary Treatment of Tax Expenditures

Ideally, tax expenditures should be subject to an explicit tradeoff against new spending initiatives, should be as transparent as possible, and their direct impact should be shown in the budget. This is only possible for tax expenditures that are easy to measure and monitor (such as tax exemptions). In general, as noted, measuring the impact of tax expenditures is difficult.

Even though explicit budgeting of tax expenditures is possible only in specific cases, an assessment of their *overall* impact should be explicitly considered during the regular process of fiscal programming and budgetary decision-making. For this purpose, at a minimum, a statement of tax expenditures should be produced, to allow a review during budget preparation and to make tradeoffs between tax expenditure and direct spending—whenever possible. In the US, a list of income tax expenditures and the associated revenue forgone is published annually by the Treasury Department. Some countries (e.g., the UK, Belgium and France) regularly include such a statement in the budget documentation. Periodic reports on tax expenditures and their fiscal and distributional impact can also be useful, along the format illustrated in Box 3.5.

Box 3.5 Guidelines for Reporting on Tax Expenditure

A report on tax expenditures, to be appended to the budget, should generally be organized as follows:

Part 1: Baseline and methodology

- Coverage of the report
- Definition of the baseline for each main category of taxes: (a) corporate income tax, (b) individual income tax, (c) sales tax, (d) customs duties and (e) other taxes/fees
- Methodology for estimating the tax expenditure

Part 2: Tax expenditure estimation

- Summary of estimated tax expenditure
- Detailed estimates of tax expenditure according to tax category
- Objective of each tax expenditure
- Beneficiary groups

Part 3: Medium- and long-term implications

- Projected evolution of total tax expenditure in the medium and long term, as percentage of GDP
- Major potential fiscal and distributional risks
- Alternatives for achieving the same objectives

Notes

1 India is a "quasi-federal" country, because the central government can, in emergencies and other special circumstances (e.g., massive corruption), remove the elected leaders of a state and replace them with its own appointees. Also, splitting states' territories and forming new states has been done frequently and with relative ease.

2 In a number of countries, managers of certain government departments assigned to local levels are loaded with dual accountability—to the ministry headquarters in the capital and to the head of the subnational government entity where they operate. Depending on the relative political power of the ministry and the subnational government entity, managers will naturally be more responsive to one or the other. In general, this practice provides both the central ministry and the subnational government entity with an easy alibi for non-performance—making the individual manager a convenient scapegoat. This is the situation, for example, in Algeria.

3 The best account of privatization in the former Soviet Union is by Nellis et al. (1995). However, they do not necessarily share the above analysis, except for the obvious neglect of corporate governance.

4 The literature on this subject is extensive. For a recent analysis, see Hsueh (2016). On China's economic model in general, see Hsueh (2011).

5 October–September for the US; April–March for the UK, India, South Africa and several other countries; July–June for Australia, Bangladesh, New Zealand; and other dates corresponding to national historical events for a few other countries—but all of 12 month duration.

6 See also the Open Budget Index entry on the subject: www.internationalbudget.org/wp-content (keyword "Extrabudgetary Funds").

7 In a few instances, setting up an executive agency improved operational efficiency, for a time, but the approach has generally has not proven effective in developed countries, and is entirely unsuitable to the institutional landscape and administrative capacity of middle-income and low-income countries.

8 See Clark et al. (2013). Although most of the book consists of case studies—Australia, Norway, China—pp. 13–30 are a good summary of the issues. For current information, see the Sovereign Wealth Fund institute—www.swfinstitute.org/fund—or the individual country websites. For the rationale for and fiscal policy implications of oil wealth funds, see Davis, Ossowsky, Fedelino et al. (2003).

9 While the focus has remained mainly on Africa (Pennant-Rae and Heggie, 1995; Potter, 2005), features of the new approach have been adopted in other countries, e.g., India's Central Road Fund and Sri Lanka's Road Maintenance Fund established in 2007.

10 The subject should not be confused with the practice of "earmarks" in the US budget process, whereby individual politicians use their power and influence to direct some public expenditure toward activities benefiting their own constituencies. (See the US section in Chapter 6.)

11 Newbrander et al. (2000) found that to be the case in all five countries they examined—Kenya, Guinea, Tanzania, Ecuador and Indonesia.

12 The OECD also argued that providing benefits directly is generally more transparent and efficient than providing benefits through reductions in user fees. In developing countries, this argument is highly doubtful, owing to the administrative costs of direct provision and the risks of weaker controls.

Bibliography

Andreski, Adam, 2005. *Case Study of Road Funds in Ghana, Malawi, and Tanzania*. Oxfordshire, UK: I.T. Transport.

Clark, Gordon, Adam Dixon and Ashby Monk, 2013. *Sovereign Wealth Funds: Legitimacy, Governance, and Global Power*. Princeton, NJ: Princeton University Press.

Concord Coalition, 2016. "Fixing the Highway Trust Fund," *Issue Brief*, February 23.

Davis, J. M., R. Ossowsky and A. Fedelino, eds., 2003. *Fiscal Policy Formulation and Implementation in Oil-Producing Countries*. Washington, DC: IMF.

Dorotinsky, William, 2008. "Extrabudgetary funds: Removing the 'Extra' and Minimizing the Risks," *PFM Blog*, IMF. March. Available online at http://blog-pfm.imf.org/pfmblog/budgetary_coverage/ [accessed November 9, 2016].

Duncan, D., J. Graham, V. Nadella, V. Bowers and S. Giroux, 2014. "Demand for Benefit Taxation: Evidence on Road Financing," *Public Budgeting and Finance*, 34(4), 120–42.

Gupta, Anand P., 1984a. *Fiscal Policy and the Poor*. New Delhi: Oxford University Press.

——, 1984b. "Management of Tax Expenditures in India," *Economic and Political Weekly*, 19(47), November.

Gwilliam, Kenneth M. and Ajay Kumar, 2002. *Road Funds Revisited: A Preliminary Appraisal of the Effectiveness of "Second Generation" Road Funds*. TWU 47. Washington, DC: The World Bank.

Hemming, Richard and K. Miranda, 1991. "Pricing and Cost Recovery," in K.-Y. Chu and Richard Hemming, eds., *Public Expenditure Handbook*. Washington, DC: IMF.

Hsueh, Roselynn, 2011. *China's Regulatory State: A New Strategy for Globalization*. Princeton, NJ: Princeton University Press.

——, 2016. "State Capitalism, Chinese-Style: Strategic Value of Sectors, Sectoral Characteristics, and Globalization," *Governance*, 29(1), 85–102.

Jain, Parul, R. K. Bhatt and A. K. Jain, 2014. "Tax Expenditures in India," *Intertax*, 42(10), 662–73.

McCleary, William, 1991. "The Earmarking of Government Revenue: A Review of Some World Bank Experience," *World Bank Research Observer*, 6(1), 81–104.

McPake, B., N. Brikci, G. Cometto, A. Schmidt and E. Araujo, 2011. "Removing User Fees," *Health Policy and Planning*, 26(2), 104–17.

Mwale, Sam, 1997. "Road Sector Reform: A Tale of Two Countries: Impact and Lessons," *Africa Transport Technical Note 8*. UNECA and The World Bank.

Nellis, John, Ira Lieberman and Enna Karlova, 1995. *Russia: Creating Private Enterprises and Efficient Markets*. Washington, DC: The World Bank.

Newbrander, William, David Collins and Lucy Gilson, 2000. *Ensuring Equal Access to Health Services: User Fee Systems and the Poor*. New York: Management Sciences Health.

Pennant-Rae, Rupert and Ian Heggie, 1995. "Commercializing Africa's Roads," *Finance and Development*, 32(4), 30–3.

Potter, Barry, ed., 2005. *Budgeting for Road Maintenance*. Washington, DC: IMF.

Schiavo-Campo, S. and D. Tommasi, 1999. *Managing Government Expenditure*. Manila: Asian Development Bank.

Wilkinson, Margaret, 1986. "Tax Expenditure and Public Expenditure in the UK," *Journal of Social Policy*, 15(1), 23–49.

4 Fiscal Risk, Fiscal Responsibility and Fiscal Rules

> A certain description of men are for getting out of debt, yet they are against all taxes for raising money to pay it off.
>
> (Alexander Hamilton, 1792)

Introduction

In theory, every government commitment that is not fulfilled immediately carries some implication for the future and—since the future is inherently uncertain—entails a degree of risk. In practice, "fiscal risk" refers to unexpected deviations from the annual revenue forecast or the budgeted expenditures, as well as to commitments with future implications—which affect budgetary outcomes, and indirectly economic activity, employment and inflation (see Cebotari et al., 2009).

Fiscal risks and uncertainties have been increasing from the end of the twentieth century. While globalization has brought vast benefits, the distribution of these benefits has been uneven both within countries, generating major political conflict and uncertainty and between countries, entailing risks of "contagion" from economic or financial problems elsewhere. The international integration of both financial markets has generated larger, more rapid, and volatile cross-border financial flows; the Great Recession of 2008–12 has obliged several governments to intervene to support the financial system and prevent an even worse economic downturn; the European debt crisis of 2010–16 has produced grave economic consequences for countries such as Greece, Italy, Spain, Ireland and Portugal; increased migratory flows have had fiscal implications and caused fears and resentment in the host countries; and the June 2016 referendum on Britain's exit from the European Union ("Brexit") has raised new political, economic and fiscal uncertainties not only for Britain and the rest of Europe but for the world economy.

The potential sources of fiscal risk are many. This chapter reviews the risks from the different types of government liability (especially loan guarantees, government lending, quasi-fiscal activity and public–private partnerships), explores the meaning of fiscal responsibility, and summarizes the pros and cons of formal fiscal rules that are designed in part to reduce fiscal risk by committing the government in advance to follow certain policies or achieve particular fiscal outcomes.

Fiscal Risk

A Typology of Government Liabilities[1]

In addition to legal commitments during the fiscal year, all governments have other explicit or implicit commitments that can have an immediate or future fiscal impact.

Government liabilities can be explicit or implicit, and actual or uncertain ("contingent"). In descending order of predictability and thus ascending order of fiscal risk, these liabilities are as follows:

- *Explicit and actual liabilities* are legally mandated and the most predictable. This category includes multiyear investment contracts, civil service salaries, pensions, debt obligations.
- *Explicit and contingent liabilities* are legal or contractual obligations that are triggered by a future event that may or may not occur. This category includes, for example, state guarantees for loans contracted by entities outside central government (subnational governments, public and private enterprises) and state insurance schemes (for banking deposits, floods, crop damage, and the like). The probability of the event that will trigger the guarantee is often high, because these guarantees are typically granted to support ailing enterprises or sectors in difficulties.
- *Implicit and actual liabilities* represent obligations or expected burdens for the government that are not contractual or prescribed by law but arise with some certainty from public expectations. For example, governments are expected to maintain public infrastructure and provide adequate public education, even when not strictly required to do so by law.
- *Implicit and contingent liabilities* are the least predictable category, representing a non-legal obligation triggered by a future event that may or may not occur. For example, the government is generally expected to intervene if the banking sector risks bankruptcy or the country faces a natural catastrophe. (The tsunami in Indonesia in 2004, the Haiti earthquake in 2010, the US banks bailout of 2008, the Ebola crisis in West Africa in 2015 are cases in point.)

Generally, budgetary decision-making focuses on the first category of liability—annual expenditure and multiyear legal commitments, such as debt service. Intra-year fiscal risk (from unanticipated changes in revenue or expenditure) is managed through budget amendments, which must be approved by the legislature, as well as provisions allowing the executive to transfer moneys from one budget category to another, within specified limits (virements). In most countries, no attention is paid to long-term obligations or to implicit or contingent liabilities.

Governments tend to overlook any fiscal risk that is not immediate, especially if they face financial difficulties or have to undergo fiscal austerity. On the contrary, when confronted with immediate fiscal problems a government is tempted to take even greater risk, replacing direct expenditure with guarantees and other contingent liabilities and kicking the fiscal can down the road. This response is politically understandable, but makes future problems worse and the cost of the eventual adjustment higher than it would have been if the problems been confronted in the first place. (In Greece, the various governments turned a blind eye for ten years to fiscal problems that had been accumulating since its adoption of the euro currency in 2001, and eventually faced a major crisis beginning in 2010, with grave damage to the economy, employment, and the welfare of the public.) Politically, however, this strategy may be the only choice, even if the decision-makers are well aware of the tradeoff. Economics counsels upfront measures and a long-term view; politics counsels short-termism and evasion of unpleasant measures.

Crisis situations aside, sound budgeting should consider the fiscal risks that government faces in the medium and long term as well as in the short term. The liabilities arising from current or new expenditure programs and policies must be assessed realistically. Strategies and methodologies to address fiscal risks are available: actuarial methods can assess the probability of default on a government loan; multiyear forecasts can ascertain the fiscal sustainability of ongoing policy commitments over the medium term; the recurrent costs of investment projects can be projected; explicit liabilities, both actual and contingent, can be disclosed in the budget documentation; and implicit contingent liabilities which, by definition, cannot be quantified or predicted accurately, can be dealt with by putting in place decision-making mechanisms to permit rapid and efficient response if and when the contingency occurs. Table 4.1 illustrates the types of direct fiscal risk and possible mitigation measures.

Loan Guarantees

The most common explicit and contingent liability is a loan guarantee. The government can guarantee loans contracted by state enterprises and other autonomous government agencies as well as loans to private corporations or individuals—whether the loan is granted by a local or a foreign entity. (International financial institutions normally require a government guarantee in order to lend to a non-governmental entity.)

Loan guarantees can have an important role in the government arsenal of policy instruments, but carry a significant risk to fiscal outcomes, sustainability and vulnerability. The temptation to address a problem or pursue an objective by guaranteeing loans is strong, since the guarantee does not require immediate expenditure. Indeed, it does not require any

Table 4.1 Dealing with Liabilities

Liabilities and Risks	Possible Measures
Explicit liabilities and commitments	
Budgetary outlays	Realistic budget (see Chapter 6)
Debt	Debt management (see Chapter 10)
Entitlements	Full information annexed to the budget (see Chapter 3)
Salaries	Multiyear expenditure projections (see Chapter 5)
Pension liabilities	Modified accrual accounting (see Chapter 11)
Explicit and contingent liabilities	
Loan guarantees	Disclosure in financial reports and the budget; assessment of risk of default
State insurance schemes (for floods, crop failure, and so forth)	Actuarial assessment of the risk of the event
Implicit liabilities	
Forward costs of ongoing programs	Multiyear expenditure programs (see Chapters 2 and 5)
Recurrent costs of investment projects	Public investment program (see Chapter 7)
Hidden liabilities (for example, pensions of public enterprise staff)	Projections and actuarial assessment
Future health and social security financing	Projections and actuarial assessment
Implicit and contingent liabilities	
Local government and public enterprise debts	Consolidated accounts and financial reports
Financial sector risks	Qualitative assessment and continuous dialogue with financial institutions
Social welfare	Qualitative assessment and continuous dialogue with main stakeholders
Environmental or natural catastrophe	Simulations of the nature and range of damage

Source: Adapted from Polackova-Brixi and Schick (2002).

Note: The list includes the major liabilities and risk-mitigation measures, but is not intended to be exhaustive.

expenditure at all . . . *if* the loan is repaid. In case of default, the government must make good on the guarantee by repaying the outstanding balance of the loan.

The risk of default on any one loan may be small but that of default on some loans rises with the number of guarantees issued. The resulting fiscal impact may be substantial, as shown by the experience of many countries in Latin America and Africa in the 1980s, where many borrowers defaulted and the governments had to assume debt servicing and repayment of those loans, thereby adding a lasting burden to already stretched budgets.

As a general proposition, a government loan guarantee is justified if the purpose of the guarantee is consistent with government objectives and policies *and* the borrower is creditworthy but lacks the formal credentials to obtain the loan from private lenders at normal market rates. When imperfect information or excessive risk avoidance gives private lenders an unjustified negative perception of a borrower's real creditworthiness, a government guarantee serves to redress the market distortion, and is appropriate from both an economic and a policy viewpoint. In practice, however, government loan guarantees are often granted without an assessment of the capacity of the beneficiary to reimburse the loan, or simply as a favor to a well-connected borrower.

Measures to cope with loan guarantee risks are discussed later in the chapter.

Quasi-fiscal Activities

Quasi-fiscal activities are financial transactions undertaken by the central bank or state-owned banks or non-financial public enterprises to achieve government policy goals.[2] These operations include interest rate subsidies, support for ailing enterprises and financial institutions and financing of exchange rate losses incurred by the government. Economically, it is better to accomplish the desired goal through transparent subsidies in the budget rather than through less transparent or hidden quasi-fiscal operations. Also, a country's central bank should concentrate on monetary policy and operations, rather than get involved in activities that substitute for fiscal operations. In general, therefore, quasi-fiscal activities should be discouraged. While they are ongoing, the quasi-fiscal operations of the central bank and other state banks or enterprises should be scrutinized as closely as if they were direct government expenditure. Estimating the cost of quasi-fiscal operations is not a simple matter but, at a minimum, a statement on quasi-fiscal activities should be annexed to the budget.

Government Lending

Direct government loans are another possible means of pursuing policy goals. These loans are normally directed to entities that cannot afford to borrow at any reasonable commercial terms, either because they need to be subsidized or because their formal creditworthiness is extremely weak. Government lending can also be used to leverage and supplement commercial lending.

Government lending is frequent in developing countries because external aid loans to finance public sector entities are granted in the first instance to the government, which then "on-lends" to the ultimate beneficiary entity. These loans are granted to the government at very low ("concessional") interest rates, but normally include a provision that the on-lending should be at commercial terms, in order to avoid creating distortions in the domestic financial market.

In principle, the fact that loans are repayable can make government lending more cost-effective than direct expenditure for achieving a public policy goal. In practice, however, government lending has sometimes been used as a way of sideslip budget discipline.

Also, the loans are often submitted to much weaker scrutiny than direct expenditure proposals, and are not always subject to legislative approval. Government loans generally have an implicit interest subsidy and carry higher risks of non-repayment than loans granted by commercial banks. Also, any exchange rate losses that may be incurred would be borne by the government.

The budgetary treatment of government lending should thus include the following:

- Because government loans substitute for direct spending, they should be reviewed together with expenditure proposals.
- All loans should be included in the budget, with full explanations of their terms and—where possible—authorized by the legislature.
- To ensure accountability and allow review of lending programs together with expenditure programs, lending must be shown in gross terms.
- In principle, the interest subsidies should be budgeted as expenditures—provided that they can be estimated with reasonable accuracy and that it is cost-effective to do so.

Export Stabilization Funds

In several developing countries in the 1970s, agencies to stabilize the price of main commodities were set up to administer separate funds which were not submitted to effective legislative review. In principle, the funds were supposed to intervene in the market to protect producers from the revenue instability generated by world price fluctuations (Erb and Schiavo-Campo, 1969). In practice, their operations were opaque and the use of the moneys unclear. In Madagascar, for example, an export stabilization fund was set up in the late 1970s, outside the formal budget. When a major financial crisis hit the country after 1982 and a decision was taken to consolidate the export stabilization fund with the formal budget, the resources that had supposedly been transferred into it during the previous years were nowhere to be found. There is no evidence that the money had been misappropriated; most probably, it had been diverted to finance other government operations. The fact remains that it was not there when it was needed.

Export stabilization funds are not, in themselves, a source of fiscal risk—rather the contrary, as they are intended to serve as a hedge against risk. In actual practice, however, the operations of such funds were opaque and carried out in parallel with regular budgetary operations. Thus, the potential risks could not be assessed. Very few of these commodity stabilization arrangements are still in existence.

Public–Private Partnerships

What sort of PPP is it?

The context for public–private partnerships (PPPs)[3] is provided by the three dimensions of public service provision: service standards (including service quality, beneficiaries and due process); service financing; and service delivery. The government must always retain responsibility for the standards, but the financing and delivery of a public service can include appropriate participation by the private sector. Public–private partnerships are in general defined as "long-term contracts between a private party and a government agency, for providing a public asset or service, in which the private party bears significant risk and management responsibility [and which] contain performance-based elements with private capital at stake" (IEG, 2014, p. 4). In practice, there can be a variety of PPPs—ranging from limited and simple contracts for the private administration of an existing facility or service to comprehensive arrangements where the private partner is responsible for all construction and subsequent management of the assets and delivery of the services. The debate on the pros and cons of PPPs is often garbled and inconclusive because the parties are not arguing about the same type of PPPs. To assess the potential advantages and risks of a particular PPP one must understand what type of arrangement it is.

Public–private partnerships are prevalent in major infrastructural projects, especially for the construction and operation of long-distance roads, ports and airports—where they are also often called build–operate–transfer (BOT) arrangements. The private partner builds and operates the asset; it recoups its investment plus a profit through charging the users of the facility or service; and after the contractually-agreed period transfers to the government the asset and its management. The attractiveness of a PPP lies in the potential to tap private financing for construction and to improve efficiency in the management of the asset or delivery of the services. In Europe, the use of PPPs has been especially extensive in the UK and France, although it is still minor compared with direct state financing and contracting.[4]

When Are PPPs Appropriate?

Whatever the type of PPP, if the arrangement is to benefit the state, the government must:

- negotiate the arrangement effectively;
- monitor it closely thereafter;
- conduct a careful assessment of the risks to the medium- and long-term fiscal position of the government, of the social impact, and of the risks of collusion and corruption; and
- frame the resulting financial obligations in the context of a multiyear fiscal perspective.

Public–private partnerships can therefore be successful only where the capacity of the public partner is very strong (as, for example, in "Partnerships UK," a joint public–private company set up in 2000 and replaced in 2010 by "Infrastructure UK"—a unit of the Treasury). Public–private partnerships are instead seriously problematic where government capacity and public accountability are insufficiently strong—not only because of the superior technical competence and negotiating experience of the private partners but also from the risk of collusion with and bribery of the government officials involved.

The overarching finding of the review of international experience is that country readiness drives PPP success (IEG, 2014). The costs and the risks of PPPs are inversely related to a country's institutional and administrative capacity. In OECD and upper-middle income countries the evidence shows some highly positive experiences with PPPs in physical infrastructure but a mixed record overall, especially in the social sectors (European Commission, 2013). In low-income, limited-capacity countries, PPPs can be useful in a few selected cases but their high risks call for placing the burden of proof squarely on to the proponents of using a PPP arrangement.

Foreign aid agencies carry a special professional and fiduciary responsibility to protect developing country governments from committing to inadvisable and risky PPPs. This is not always the case. The European Investment Bank (EIB) does meet that responsibility—providing member governments with information on both the good practices and the pitfalls of PPP initiatives they have already decided to undertake—and the African Development Bank (AfDB) advises on PPPs but without advocating. The Asian Development Bank (ADB) is generally supportive of PPPs (albeit mainly in physical infrastructure). The International Financial Corporation (IFC) of the World Bank Group is too often interested in the "sexy deal," and tends to act more as cheerleader for the PPP project than as protector of the country's interests. (See Box 4.1 for an example.)

Box 4.1 The PPP for the Queen Mamohato Memorial Hospital in Lesotho

By 2000, the old national hospital in Lesotho's capital of Maseru was deteriorating. Although the major health problems of the country—HIV/AIDS and TB—are largely in the rural areas, and the low utilization of rural health facilities is caused mainly by insufficient resources, the decision was made in principle to replace the hospital with a new state-of-the-art urban facility. Thereafter, the project dynamics took over, driven by the government determination to have a modern hospital comparable to South Africa's and by the World Bank's agreement to support it.

In 2002, the International Finance Corporation of the World Bank Group was brought in to prepare and negotiate a PPP, which it promoted as the "most innovative" in Africa. One of the only two eligible bidders was selected and, after a large upward cost revision, the PPP contract was agreed in 2008. The new hospital—the Queen Mamohato Memorial Hospital (QMMH)—opened in 2011. The government's negotiating and monitoring capacity was very low to begin with and virtually disappeared after the hospital was built.

Despite the IFC involvement, there was no analysis of the project rate of return in national economic terms, nor was there serious consideration of possible alternatives or estimates of fiscal implications and contingent liabilities. The new hospital was well built and functions very well, with highly positive health outcomes for the patients it serves. However, the weak demand-management mechanisms have led to increasing rather than reducing dependence on South Africa's hospitals; the construction cost more than double the original estimate; the debt/equity ratio became very high; and the government payments to the private operators have risen substantially above the estimates made at the contract negotiations.

By 2013 the stress on Lesotho's public finances was beginning to be apparent. The resulting opportunity cost of the expenditure in terms of the underserved rural areas and the key health needs of the population is certain to be substantial, especially in light of the country's shaky fiscal prospects. The QMMH project exemplifies the costs and risks of PPPs in a low-income, low-capacity environment. Rather than a model of "best practice," is a model of "innovation" gone wrong.

Sources: Hellowell (2014); Webster (2015); and media reports.

Assessing PPPs

Up until the mid-1990s, there was a Pollyanna view of PPPs, which rested on airy assertions that the majority of the risks would be borne by the private partner and at the end of the concession period the government would inherit a well-operated project without investing public funds and with little risk (see, for example, Menheere and Pollalis, 1996). This approach came close to a "free lunch" message, and left unanswered the obvious question of why the private partner would want to contribute all the money upfront and assume most of the risk. Actual experience during the past 20 years has shown that the picture is not quite so rosy and the situation is considerably more complex.

First, PPPs do not eliminate a fiscal constraint over the long-term; the state will eventually need to pay. Public–private partnership financing can accelerate the construction of public assets but cannot substitute for the money. Second, all PPPs carry fiscal risks. While the arrangements usually do transfer some of the risks to the private partner, the state often retains important risks. For example, in many PPPs for new schools, hospitals and prisons, the government agrees in advance to pay for building the facilities, regardless of future demand, and thus carries any excess cost of underutilized facilities. In other PPPs, as for example those for toll roads, the private company may be guaranteed a minimum revenue from users and if the actual revenue falls below the guaranteed amount the government is on the hook for the difference.[5] Fiscal risk is especially high when the PPP project is large relative to the national economy, which is normally the case only in small low-income countries.

Third, for the provision of many social services a PPP may carry substantial reputational and non-financial risks in the form of violations of due process or dilution of service quality or limits of access by the poor—especially when government monitoring is insufficiently robust. In August 2016, for example, the US government decided to phase-out all for-profit private operation of federal prisons (as well as detention centers for illegal immigrants), because of the higher cost combined with evidence of lower safety and violations of the standards of treatment of inmates, and several states are following suit with respect to state prisons. (It appears, however, that the new administration intends to move back in the opposite direction.)

Measures to mitigate the risks of PPPs are available: careful design to avoid excess capacity; fostering effective competition among public and private service providers; strong contract management; and making transparent the totality of government commitments under PPPs. (An interesting proposal to buy back PPPs has also been advanced recently.[6])

Mitigation of fiscal risk, however, is hampered because contracts are confidential, and public disclosure of analyses behind PPP investments is very limited, inconsistent and not standardized. Contingent liabilities that emerge from PPPs are rarely adequately quantified, and the data required for a full assessment of risks are simply not available. Of greatest concern is the fact that there are virtually no data on the impact of PPPs on poverty and service distribution. In any event, as noted, the prerequisite for a PPP arrangement that benefits the state is for the government to have a very strong negotiating position and monitoring capacity.

Three Lessons of International Experience

Three other lessons emerge from international experience. First, *PPPs are generally more expensive*—as shown by reports from the UK parliamentary commissions and Spain's Court of Audit. There is no generalized evidence that a PPP model is more efficient than either public provision or purely private services; on the contrary, PPPs have been costlier for the taxpayers in the long term. Specifically in the health sector, PPPs are not cost-effective compared with traditional forms of publicly financed and managed provision of health care (EC, 2013).

Second, one of the most important, yet among the least mentioned lessons, is that *the underlying project itself must be sound*. A PPP is a financing, procurement and/or a management modality, and cannot make up for weaknesses in the project to which it is attached. If the project doesn't have a sufficient rate of return in national economic terms and/or is inconsistent with country or sector needs, it should not be undertaken, regardless of what private financing or management arrangement may be available. It is possible to implement badly a well-designed and appropriate project, but even the best-designed PPP cannot compensate for bad project design or lack of fit with the strategic needs of the sector or the country.

Third and finally, *beware of innovation fascination*. The terms "innovative" and "pioneering" appear over and over in the advocacy of PPP initiatives in developing countries. The history of development assistance has demonstrated the dangers of trying to transplant practices developed in and for high-income countries into low-income countries with limited administrative capacity and a different institutional and governance environment. (Chapter 13 elaborates further.) Yet, complex PPP initiatives are constantly pushed on the governments of developing countries because of their "innovative nature," despite the absence of the essential conditions for their success and the severe risks to the country's finances and to public service access by the poor (see, for Africa, Bolosi, 2016).

Managing Fiscal Risks

The General Approach: The Fiscal Transparency Code

Unlike for private entities, where the objective is to avoid and *minimize* risk, for government the objective is to *manage* effectively those risks that only government can and should bear (Petrie, 2008). The key requirements for managing fiscal risks of all types are as follows:

- political leadership;
- awareness of the existence of fiscal risk;
- explicit consideration of major fiscal risks during the budgeting process;
- risk assessment, as appropriate to the country and the nature of the risk;
- full disclosure of risks relating to major government assets and liabilities, including loan guarantee exposure and obligations under PPPs;
- regular communication of the fiscal realities to the public.

The Fiscal Transparency Code (see Chapter 1) has a number of provisions to address direct fiscal risk. Concerning general risks to the public finances, the government should:

- publish regular summary reports on risks to their fiscal prospects;
- report on how fiscal outcomes might differ from baseline forecasts as a result of different macroeconomic assumptions;
- provide a regular summary report on the main specific risks to its fiscal forecasts;
- regularly publish projections of the evolution of the public finances over the long term.

A 2012 OECD survey of country practices yielded three other lessons: the need to coordinate closely with an independent supervisory authority to protect against systemic fiscal risk; the utility to conduct "stress testing" of government finances; and routinely incorporating risk assessment and "early warning signals" into the budgetary process (see, respectively, Kopits, 2014; Schilperoort and Wierts, 2013; Schick, 2013).[7]

But finally, a warning against too much caution. To try to protect in advance against 100 percent of all kinds of fiscal risk makes no sense. First, to do so would absorb an excessive amount of time, resources and policy-makers' attention—a certain to be much more costly than the losses from having to cope with an adverse future event. Second, complete protection against risk is an illusion—the unforeseen always comes up. It is better therefore to complement sensible protection against fiscal risk with provisions to make the budgeting system itself more adaptable—a "strategy of resilience," learning from mistakes and strengthening the system's capacity to deal with shocks, as Wildavsky (1988) put it.

Managing Loan Guarantees

Loan guarantees in particular should be managed carefully, by:

- considering the amount and implications of each proposed guarantee and allowing the risk element to be estimated, even if approximately or qualitatively;
- monitoring the financial performance of each guarantee recipient;
- providing sufficient scrutiny and accountability to prevent the misuse of loan guarantees for personal or partisan political reasons;
- assuring transparency, by at least including the information on guarantees in the budget documentation;
- putting in place a system for recording loan guarantees and the borrowers' repayment record, which would also eventually produce the database required for a solid actuarial assessment of default risk; and
- periodic reviews of the stock and status of loan guarantees, and a procedure to anticipate defaults and ways of financing them.

In several advanced countries, the government levies a fee for guaranteeing a loan. This procedure has the advantage of automatically creating the mechanism for registration and monitoring of guarantees, and also constitutes an insurance premium in case of default. If the guarantee fee is proportionate to the risk of default and the risk is assessed correctly, the fees will, in the aggregate, suffice to cover the eventual cost of defaults. (Of course, the implicit subsidy element will disappear, but the main purpose of a loan guarantee is to correct for a market imperfection, and not to subsidize credit.) When a long series of data on the frequency of loan defaults is not available, it is impossible to estimate the overall default risk and thus the expenditure equivalent of the loan guarantees. In these cases, the budget should at a minimum include a list of the loan guarantees that the government intends to grant—including information on the beneficiary and purpose of the loan. (Publicizing the names of beneficiaries is also an essential protection against corrupt or preferential treatment of influential persons.)

A ceiling on the total face value of either or both the stock or the new issue of guarantees could also be set. Such a ceiling induces more rigorous scrutiny of proposed guarantees and promotes competition among potential borrowers—channeling the guarantees to entities that are financially sounder and for priority public purposes.

Fiscal Responsibility and Fiscal Rules

Fiscal Conservatism and Fiscal Responsibility

Persons of every ideological stripe and political conviction claim to be in favor of fiscal responsibility, but define it to suit their particular outlook. Some consider that fiscal responsibility requires cutting government expenditure; others consider it fiscally irresponsible to cut basic social services; some consider that fiscal responsibility demands raising taxes on the very rich; others view any increase in taxes as fiscally irresponsible; and so on. Fiscal conservatism is often conflated with fiscal responsibility. This is politically understandable, intellectually muddled and practically misleading. Fiscal conservatism and fiscal responsibility are very different concepts.

The debate on the proper role of government is a hardy perennial in every society, and views can legitimately differ. Fiscal conservatives call for limited government and hence lower government expenditure and lower taxes to support it; fiscal progressives call for an expansive government role and hence the need for greater resources to finance it. Both can be fiscally responsible, however, because fiscal responsibility does not lie in whether government expenditure is lower or higher, or taxes are raised or reduced, or the government debt goes up or goes down, or the budget is in surplus or deficit. *Fiscal responsibility consists of confronting the short- and long-term financial implications of efficiently run government activities and finding transparent and sustainable ways to pay for them.* How much and which activity the government *should* carry out is an entirely different matter. There can be a legitimate argument for or against fiscal conservatism. There cannot be a legitimate argument against fiscal responsibility. Fiscal responsibility is a bedrock requirement of sound public finance and good governance in any society.

Fiscal responsibility tends to be loosened in crisis situations. For example, an analysis of the accounting and reporting of government interventions during the global financial crisis shows that governments no longer report all their interventions as required by accounting standards. This may jeopardize fiscal sustainability, especially since the main reporting shortcoming is in the reporting of guarantees (Bergmann, 2014).

The best contemporary illustration of lack of fiscal responsibility, however, is not found in a poor country or a country facing a fiscal crisis, but in the handling of war-related fiscal policies and budgeting practices followed by the US between 2001 and 2008. See Box 4.2.

Fiscal Rules

The issue, then, is how to foster fiscal responsibility—regardless of the prevailing views on the appropriate role of the state and size of government expenditure. The traditional approach is to foster fiscal responsibility by assuring that governance and public management *processes* are strong and effective—and otherwise leaving it to the decisions of the elected political leadership to define fiscal policies and the overall fiscal stance as it judges best under the circumstances. An alternative approach—emerging in the late 1980s—consists of legally adopting fiscal rules.

Scope and Types of Fiscal Rules

Fiscal rules can prescribe fiscal *outcomes* (e.g., a specific level of deficit) or fiscal *criteria* (e.g., a "prudent level of debt").[8]

About 25 countries, the large majority OECD members, have some type of fiscal rule. In several of these countries, the fiscal rules prescribe specific fiscal outcomes. For example, the so-called "golden rule" stipulates that government borrowing must not exceed government investment (thus in fact requiring a current budget balance or surplus, as in Germany).[9] A very few countries, for example Switzerland, require the budget as a whole to be balanced every year.[10] In the European Union, the Maastricht Treaty stipulated specific fiscal convergence criteria, concerning both the maximum ratio of fiscal deficit to GDP (3 percent) and of debt to GDP (60 percent). The former criterion has been by far the more important. EU member countries whose fiscal deficit ratio is higher than the permitted 3 percent are, supposedly, liable to substantial penalties. Similar arrangements apply in countries of the West African Economic and Monetary Union.

In contrast with rigid legal rules, other countries (e.g., New Zealand) do not mandate specific fiscal outcomes but refer to criteria such as "prudent levels" and "reasonable degrees." The government is left to specify what these criteria mean in a budget policy statement, which presents total revenues and expenses and projections for the next three years. This statement is published at least three months before the budget is presented to the parliament and is reviewed by a parliamentary committee, but is not formally

---

Box 4.2 Financing Wars by Credit Card in the US

The policy of raising revenue to finance wars was followed throughout the history of the US until this century. Federal revenue grew to finance the Civil War; increased six fold during World War I and three fold during World War II; was raised from 14 to 19 percent of GDP during the war in Korea, and from 17 to 19 percent of GDP during the heaviest Vietnam conflict years—a much smaller increase owing to President Johnson's claim that America could have both "guns" and "butter" (i.e., could fight both the Vietnam war and the War on Poverty), a claim that contributed to producing the severe inflation of the 1970s.

Compare this history with the fiscal policy followed after September 11, 2001—when the wars in Afghanistan and Iraq were accompanied by *cuts* in taxes on income, dividends, capital gains and inheritance—producing a decline in federal revenue from about 20 percent to an average of 17.5 percent of GDP. Even before the drop in revenue resulting from the Great Recession of 2008–12, the inevitable arithmetical result was a jumbo deterioration of the government accounts, from a surplus of $236 billion in 2000 to a deficit of $160 billion in 2007 (in current dollars). A deliberate policy of massive tax reduction during wartime is a first in America, and is unknown in any major country in world history. Moreover, the administration funded the war by "emergency spending" and "supplemental requests," rather than honestly including the cost in the annual budget. While this practice may be understandable at the start of the wars for 2002 and 2003, by 2004 it was obvious that the wars and their costs would continue. Elementary fiscal transparency demanded that these costs should be included in the regular budget process to prevent distorting the country's true fiscal picture.

Among the adjectives to describe such fiscal policy and budgeting practices neither the term "fiscally responsible" nor the word "conservative" come to mind. Regardless of one's views of the military actions taken against the "Islamic State" since 2014, at least the budgetary cost is being reckoned more transparently.

---

voted on. Whether in the form of outcomes or of criteria, the effective implementation of fiscal rules requires strong public financial management mechanisms (Corbacho and Ter-Minassian, 2013).

Assessing Fiscal Rules

A frequent criticism of rules that prescribe fiscal deficit outcomes is that they invite accounting gimmicks to make the deficit appear smaller by, among other means, listing one-time revenues (e.g., from privatization) as regular revenue, reclassifying government entities as private enterprises and including subsidies to public enterprises as budget financing instead of expenditure. A second criticism is that when the rules are strictly enforced, they can prevent governments from adjusting their budgets to the economic cycle, thus worsening recessions. Partly for these reasons, only Australia and the UK among developed countries currently have in place prescriptive fiscal responsibility legislation. In the US, the parameters of the 1990s Gramm–Rudman–Hollings version of fiscal responsibility law were routinely violated from the start, and quickly and quietly forgotten in actual budgeting practice.

The Achilles' heel of rules prescribing specific fiscal outcomes is that they are a government's contract *with itself*. In a presidential system of government, the system finds it extremely difficult to enforce on itself a fiscal discipline rule when the chief executive feels the need to violate it—as he or she can always claim reasons of state, national security and "emergency" needs. In a parliamentary system, where the government is a creature of the legislature, for the legislature to enforce penalties for violating a fiscal rule would be equivalent to declaring no confidence in its own government. The issue is thus the oldest issue in contract law: a contract has no legal or practical meaning unless it is enforceable, and no enforcement mechanism exists in a government's contract with itself to respect certain rules of fiscal behavior. Unenforced law is no law at all.

The driving force behind fiscal rules is a fundamental distrust of politics and government, which aims at binding the government's hands to prevent it from jeopardizing fiscal sustainability. And here is the paradox: if the government is trustworthy, legally limiting its flexibility by prescribing certain fiscal outcomes is unnecessary; if the government is untrustworthy, legally limiting its flexibility is necessary but is ineffective in practice because it will find ways to slip the rules or cook the books. For *central* government, fiscal responsibility legislation is effective where it is probably unnecessary and probably ineffective where it is necessary.

However, there are four situations in which prescribing fiscal outcomes may be useful. First, in countries with a vibrant civil society and active political contestability, breaking a major and public commitment can carry a heavy political price, which is an enforcement mechanism of sorts.

Second, in countries with fragile coalition governments, fragmented decision-making and constant bargaining over resources, setting up legally binding targets may limit the daily political bargaining and prevent "logrolling" (the reciprocal exchange of support among politicians for each other's proposals, which pushes up total spending).

Third, and most relevant, fiscal responsibility rules can be effective when applied to subnational government, because in this case the contract enforcement authority does exist: the national government. There is substantial evidence that this is in fact the case. In the US, for example, fiscal rules do affect states' fiscal outcomes—although the effect is stronger in recessions and depends on the political environment, especially if one party controls the governorship and another controls the legislature (Hong, 2015). States' expenditures are effectively constrained by three types of rules: (i) requiring submission of a balanced budget; (ii) restricting supplemental appropriations; and (iii) prohibiting the carry-over of expenditures to the next fiscal year (Smith and Hou, 2013). Chapter 14 takes up this issue in greater depth.

Fourth, and symmetrical to the argument for subnational government, fiscal rules applying to member states of an economic union can be meaningful, since the union itself has certain powers of enforcement. However, while a federal country has mechanisms for fiscal convergence and for transferring resources from surplus to deficit subnational governments, in an economic union without such mechanisms strong enforcement of the fiscal rules may produce major economic dislocation in those member countries that suffer from structural weaknesses or unforeseen problems. The experience of Greece and some other members of the European Union is the best-known contemporary example. Also, the EU rules limiting the fiscal deficit of euro-area member countries have been enforced selectively, with no penalties exacted for violations by the largest and most important EU members. The first countries to exceed the maximum permitted deficit of 3 percent of GDP were France and Germany. Moreover, Germany evaded the deficit target by highly questionable accounting. Neither France nor Germany was penalized. The same flexibility was not in evidence later vis-à-vis smaller members of the European Union.

In the developing world, too, fiscal rules intended to forge closer links and economic integration among neighboring countries need to be carefully designed and implemented with an eye to the flexibility that may be required by changing circumstances. This is the current situation in the West African Economic and Monetary Union, where the "convergence" rules are under severe stress owing in part to the emerging civil conflicts in some member countries (see Box 4.3).

Box 4.3 Fiscal Rules in the West African Economic and Monetary Union

The West African Economic and Monetary Union (WAEMU; also known as UEMOA from its name in French, *Union Économique et Monétaire Ouest-africaine*) consists of eight countries (Benin, Burkina Faso, Côte d'Ivoire, Guinea-Bissau, Mali, Niger, Senegal and Togo), which have a common central bank (the Banque Centrale des États de l'Afrique de l'Ouest) and a common convertible currency pegged to the euro (the CFA franc). To coordinate macroeconomic policies, WAEMU countries have set up convergence criteria within the framework of the Convergence, Stability, Growth, and Solidarity Pact adopted by WAEMU governments in 1999. As in the Maastricht Treaty, the convergence criteria pay special attention to the fiscal deficit and to public debt sustainability, because these factors can undermine the viability of the common currency. In addition, the pact prohibits use of the exchange rate and interest rate as policy instruments.

The following first-order criteria apply:

- Average annual inflation rate of no more than 3 percent, based on the objective of keeping a low inflation differential between the WAEMU and the euro area.
- Budget balanced or in surplus—defined as revenues (without grants) minus expenditures (excluding foreign-financed investment).
- Overall debt-to-GDP ratio lower than 70 percent.
- No change in the stock of domestic and external payment arrears.

These first-order criteria are supplemented with the following second-order criteria:

- Government wage bill less than 35 percent of tax receipts.
- Ratio of domestically financed investment to tax receipts no lower than 20 percent.
- Tax-to-GDP ratio of at least 17 percent.
- External current account deficit, excluding grants, lower than 3 percent of GDP.

In 2002, of all African regional groupings WAEMU was the farthest along in economic integration. In recent years, progress was halted and reversed owing to the civil conflict in Mali and tensions in other countries, and few of the member countries meet many of the convergence criteria. Each year the WAEMU member states prepare a three-year convergence, stability, growth and solidarity program, and every six months the WAEMU commission publishes a report to assess progress in implementing these programs.

Sources: Convergence, Stability, Growth, and Solidarity Pact; and the UEMOA official website www.uemoa.int (in French).

In sum, the strongest argument in favor of binding fiscal rules applies to subnational government entities and—to a lesser extent and with major caveats—to member states of an economic union. In all other cases, there is no meaningful alternative to careful budgeting within a medium-term perspective and responsive to changing realities. It is always important to set targets for revenue, expenditure and other macrofiscal outcomes—but targets are not straitjackets.

Tax and Expenditure Limits

Aside from the rules on fiscal outcomes at central government level, tax and expenditure limitations (TELs) have been often legislated or mandated administratively as an instrument of control of subnational budgeting.

Much of the research on tax and expenditure limitations focuses on the impact of these limits on the size of the public sector or the distribution of expenditures, but not on their impact on government budgeting. In the case of Colorado, the limits imposed by the 1992 "Taxpayer's Bill of Rights" increased volatility of both revenue and expenditure in the state (Clair, 2012). Other unexpected effects of TELs have been found. In the US, when local governments have been subject to limits on tax and/or spending, they have usually found ways to avoid the limits on revenue—by changing their revenue structure to increase reliance on those income sources that are not subject to the limits. In other countries, instead, revenue limits appear more effective in keeping taxes down, although some shifting of revenue sources does take place (see Blom-Hansen et al., 2014).

Aside from the doubts as to whether TELs are effective in keeping down taxes and containing expenditure, they may have a negative impact on income distribution and poverty. Wang (2012) analyzed the relationships between intergovernmental transfers, tax progressivity, expenditure progressivity and labor mobility, and tested whether high- or low-income residents had paid for and benefited from the tax and expenditure limits. The overall finding was that TELs significantly decreased tax progressivity and increased the poverty rate.

There is no conclusive evidence either on the overall fiscal effectiveness of tax and expenditure limits, or on their impact on the composition of expenditure and the distribution of benefits from government activity—in different countries or institutional environments. However, based on the experience so far, a healthy dose of skepticism is indicated—as well as special caution on how TELs are designed and implemented.

Notes

1 This section is based largely on the original taxonomy by Hana Polackova-Brixi, first proposed by Polackova in 1998 and then elaborated in Polackova-Brixi and Schick (2002).
2 See Mackenzie and Stella (1996) and more recently, Open Budget Index (2014; www. internationalbudget.org/wp-content/uploads/Looking-Beyond-the-Budget-3-Quasi-Fiscal-Activities.pdf [accessed November 3, 2016]).
3 For a comprehensive treatment of the issues, see IEG (2014). For a guide to the dos and don'ts of PPPs, the reader is referred to Asian Development Bank, (2008)—with special reference to infrastructure in Asian countries—and to the European PPP Expertise Centre of the European Investment Bank at www.eib.org/epec/g2g [accessed November 3, 2016].
4 The French experience during 2004–13 with these "partnership contracts" has been reviewed by Bergere (2016)—sector by sector and focusing mainly on the procurement aspects.
5 Bunch (2012) examines the need to protect the public interest in PPPs for highways in the case of Texas.
6 Sarmento and Reis (2013), in the case of Portugal, suggest that the government use some of the EU bailout funds borrowed at low interest rates to buy back the roads' concessions—estimating

that this would cut in half public payments over the next 20 years and at the same time release money into a private sector that is in urgent need of liquidity.

7 For a discussion of the risk that a government bailout of private banks may become necessary, see Draghi, Giavazzi and Merton (2003).

8 See Kopits and Symansky (1998); for a more recent treatment, see Lienert (2010) and Ter-Minassian (2010).

9 Botswana has an interesting twist on the golden rule. Instead of allowing borrowing for investment (which implies a primary balance), it earmarks all mineral revenue for development. Use of mineral revenues has followed a self-discipline fiscal rule, the Sustainable Budget Index (SBI), under which any mineral revenue is supposed to finance "development expenditure," defined as investment expenditure and recurrent spending on development projects.

10 There is some evidence that a balanced-budget rule leads to a gradual reduction in the level of public debt. However, without knowing the implications for public services and distributional impact it is not possible to infer any net impact on citizens' welfare—which depends also on the progressivity of the tax system and the composition and quality of public spending (Azzimonti, Battaglini and Coate, 2016).

Bibliography

Asian Development Bank, 2008. *Public–Private Partnership (PPP) Handbook*. Manila: ADB.

Azzimonti, M., M. Battaglini and S. Coate, (2016). "The Costs and Benefits of Balanced Budget Rules: Lessons from a Political Economy Model of Fiscal Policy," *Journal of Public Economics*, 136, 45–61.

Bergere, F., 2016. "Ten Years of PPP: An Initial Assessment," *OECD Journal on Budgeting*, 15(1), 21–123.

Bergmann, A., 2014. "The Global Financial Crisis Reveals Consolidation and Guarantees to be Key Issues for Financial Sustainability," *Journal of Public Budgeting, Accounting and Finance Management*, 26(1), 165–80.

Blom-Hansen, J., M., Baekgaard and S. Serritzlew, 2014. "Tax Limitations and Revenue Shifting Strategies in Local Government," *Public Budgeting and Finance*, 34(1), 64–84.

Bolosi, Fanwell, 2016. "PPPs as a Model for Development: An Analysis of the African Context," *Bretton Woods Observer*, Spring.

Bunch, B., 2012. "Preserving the Public Interest in Highway Public–Private Partnerships: A Case Study of the State of Texas," *Public Budgeting and Finance*, 32(1), 36–57.

Cebotari, Aliona, Jeffrey Davis, Lusine Lusinyan, Amine Mati, Paolo Mauro, Murray Petrie and Ricardo Velloso, 2009. *Fiscal Risks: Sources, Disclosure, and Management*. Washington, DC: IMF.

Clair, T. S., 2012. "The Effect of Tax and Expenditure Limitations on Revenue Volatility: Evidence from Colorado," *Public Budgeting and Finance*, 32(3), 61–78.

Corbacho, Ana and Teresa Ter-Minassian, 2013. "Public Financial Management Requirements for Effective Implementation of Fiscal Rules," in Richard Allen, Richard Hemming and Barry Potter, eds., *International Handbook of Public Financial Management*. New York: Palgrave Macmillan.

Draghi, Mario, F. Giavazzi and R. C. Merton, 2003. "Transparency, Risk Management and International Financial Fragility," *NBER Working Paper 9806*. Cambridge, MA: National Bureau of Economic Research.

Edwards, R. D., 2014. "US War Costs: Two Parts Temporary, One Part Permanent," *Journal of Public Economics*, 113, 54–66.

Erb, Guy and S. Schiavo-Campo, 1969. "Export Instability, Level of Development, and Economic Size of Less Developed Countries," *Oxford Bulletin of Economics and Statistics*, 31(4), 263–83.

European Commission (EC), 2013. *Health and Economic Analysis for an Evaluation of the Public Private Partnerships in Health Care Delivery across the European Union*. EPOS Health Management. August.

European Investment Bank, 2015. *The EPEC PPP Guide*. Available online at www.eib.org/epec/g2g/ [accessed November 9, 2016].

Hellowell, Mark, 2014. *Delivering Health Services through Public–Private Partnerships*. Edinburgh: University of Edinburgh.

Hong, Sounman, 2015. "Fiscal Rules in Recessions: Evidence from the American States," *Public Finance Review*, 43(4), 505–28.

IEG, 2014. *World Bank Group Support to Public–Private Partnerships*. Available online at ieg.worldbankgroup.org [accessed November 9, 2016].

Kopits, George, 2014. "Coping with Fiscal Risk," *OECD Journal on Budgeting*, 14(1), 47–71.

Kopits, George and Steven Symansky, 1998. "Fiscal Policy Rules," *IMF Occasional Papers, 162*. Washington, DC: IMF.

Kumar, Manmohan and Teresa Ter-Minassian, eds., 2007. *Promoting Fiscal Discipline*. Washington, DC: IMF.

Lienert, Ian, 2010. "Should Advanced Countries Adopt a Fiscal Responsibility Law?" *Working Paper 10/254*. Washington, DC: IMF.

Mackenzie, G. A. and Peter Stella, 1996. *Quasi-Fiscal Operations of Public Financial Institutions*. Washington, DC: IMF.

Menheere, Sebastian and Spiro Pollalis, eds., 1996. *Case Studies on Build-Operate-Transfer*. Delft: Delft University of Technology.

Petrie, Murray, 2008. "Controlling Fiscal Risks," in Richard Hemming, J-H. Kim and S-H. Lee, eds., *Sustainability and Efficiency in Managing Public Expenditure*. Seoul: Korean Development Institute.

Polackova-Brixi, Hana and Allen Schick, 2002. *Government at Risk: Contingent Liabilities and Fiscal Risk*. New York: Oxford University Press.

Sarmento, J. M. and R. F. Reis, 2013. "Buy Back PPPs," *OECD Journal on Budgeting*, 12(3), 1–13.

Schick, Allen, 2003. "The Role of Fiscal Rules in Budgeting," *OECD Journal of Budgeting*, 3(3), 7–34.

——, 2013. "Lessons from the Crisis," *OECD Journal on Budgeting*, 12(3), 1–31.

Schilperoort, W. and P. Wierts, P. 2013. "Illuminating Budgetary Risks: The Role of Stress Testing," *OECD Journal on Budgeting*, 12(3), 1–18.

Smith, Daniel and Yilin Hou, 2013. "Balanced Budget Requirements and State Spending: A Long-Panel Study," *Journal of Public Budgeting and Finance*, 33(2), 1–18.

Ter-Minassian, Teresa, 2010. "Preconditions for a Successful Introduction of Structural Fiscal Rules in Latin America and the Caribbean," *Discussion Paper 157*. Washington, DC: Inter-American Development Bank.

Wang, J. Q., 2012. "Who Pays and Who Benefits? The Impact of State Tax and Expenditure Limits on Tax Progressivity and Redistributive Spending," *Journal of Public Economics*, 24(4), 660–82.

Webster, Paul, 2015. "Lesotho's Controversial Public–Private Project," *The Lancet*, 386(10007), 1929–31.

Wildavsky, Aaron, 1988. *Searching for Safety*. New Brunswick, NJ: Transaction Publishers.

Part II

The Upstream Stages

Budget Preparation and Approval

5 Budgeting in Macroeconomic and Fiscal Perspective

You cannot escape the responsibility of tomorrow by evading it today.

(Abraham Lincoln)

Introduction: The Policy Context

The Goals of Economic Policy

As noted in Chapter 2, the key goals of overall economic policy are growth, stability and equity. Over the long term, these three goals are complementary: growth is necessary to accommodate a growing population and rising standards of living, but cannot last in unstable circumstances and inequitable outcomes; stability allows predictability, but stability without growth can turn into economic stagnation; equity considerations are essential, but equity without growth usually redistributes scarcity. But in the short term these goals may be mutually conflicting, and robust institutions and analytical tools are needed to balance growth, stability and equity.

The Interaction of Economic Policies

In pursuit of the key goals, four groups of policies can be used: external policy (tariffs, quotas, exchange rates); monetary policy (which regulates interest rates and the supply of money and credit); policies that affect the real sector (agriculture, subsidies, educational activities, transport, etc.); and fiscal policy (which deals primarily with taxation and government expenditure). Just as the broad economic goals are interrelated, so are the policy measures needed to implement them. These interrelated policy measures must be brought together into a consistent "policy package"—to maximize their impact and to prevent duplication, gaps and inconsistencies. For example, a higher tariff reduces imports and (usually) raises government revenue, but also pushes down private consumption, which in turn lowers sales tax collection and to that extent reduces government revenue. Or, cutting taxes may stimulate private production in certain sectors, but the resulting increase in the fiscal deficit may lead to higher interest rates in order to protect against inflationary pressures, and the interest rate increase can adversely affect investment and production in other sectors, and so on.

The complications do not end here: not only does each policy measure have an effect on other policies, but the interaction is a two-way street, with blowback on the initial policy change. Therefore, *the complex process of formulating a policy package is necessarily iterative*, with each decision affecting others, which in turn requires adjusting the initial decisions—progressing in like manner until the overall package is internally consistent, affordable and sustainable. Nor is this the end of the complexity, because almost all policy decisions entail winners and losers, and affect different groups to a different extent. The back-and-forth-and-back-again iteration is essential also to gain the social consensus necessary for the eventual policy package to be implemented effectively—and to sustain the legitimacy of the process.

Here's an analogy. In order to meet higher family expenditure from an increase in public transport fares for commuting family members, the head of household is considering taking a second job. The family income would go up. However, the head of household would now need the family car all the time, and a used second car would have to be purchased—raising family expenditure and cutting into the income increase. But in turn, the additional car would then also be available for use by the other family members, thus reducing the commuting cost of public transport for the family as a whole. To just decide to take a second job without considering the other resulting changes in revenue or expenditure would not be sensible. Finally, family peace can be maintained only if these changes and their consequences are discussed openly and solutions agreed by all concerned.

The Criteria of Good Policy-Making

For public financial management to function well as an instrument of policy, the fiscal policies themselves must be sound, and meet certain basic criteria:

- *Consistency*: Fiscal policies should not have internal contradictions—e.g., increasing government employment requires not only salaries but provision of the necessary operational expenditures.
- *Realism*: Policies should be affordable and implementable—e.g., launching a major new investment program should be accompanied by reasonable assurance of the financing and adequate capacity to implement it.
- *Stability*: Frequent policy reversals should be avoided, and a clear sense of direction for the medium term is necessary—e.g., starting a major subsidy program only to discontinue it after a couple of years wastes resources and damages the credibility of government.
- *Selectivity*: Policy-making must focus on the important issues—the budget preparation process should incorporate appropriate provisions to filter out minor matters and assure that only major disagreements are escalated to the political leadership.
- *Clarity of communications*: Goals, criteria and decisions should be explicit and appropriately disseminated—e.g., an ambiguous or badly disseminated budget decision is unlikely to be implemented effectively if it depends on private sector cooperation.

Only an effective decision-making process can yield sound policies that meet the above criteria. See Box 5.1.

The Macroeconomic and Fiscal Context

Macroeconomic Programming: The Foundation

A projections and policy framework covering the economy as a whole is necessary for the preparation of the annual budget and is especially important in poor countries. Rich countries can afford to waste resources; poor countries cannot—and without realistic programming of revenue and expenditure there is a high probability of misallocation, inefficiency and waste. Although economic development depends on an aspirational vision for the long term, without coherent and realistic programs for the short and medium term even

---

Box 5.1 Main Elements of an Effective Policy-Making Process

Based on a review of cabinet processes in Australia, Malaysia, the Philippines, Singapore, Sri Lanka and the UK, an effective policy-making process depends primarily on the following factors:

- Extensive interministerial coordination takes place when policy proposals are prepared.
- Decisions are conveyed clearly and implementation is tracked.
- Budgetary resources for implementing policies are identified at an early stage.
- The government as a whole takes and stands by decisions collectively.
- The number of cabinet ministers is small, allowing for greater policy cohesion as well as more efficient meetings.
- The cabinet agenda is limited to top-priority decisions.
- Extensive consultations have taken place before the issue is brought to the full cabinet.
- Proposals are clear and concise, with clearly stated objectives and recommendations.
- The cabinet secretariat is efficient, with highly competent staff.
- Policy proposals are presented as multiple choices for decision rather than single options.
- Mechanisms for public consultation are established.

Source: Asian Development Bank, "Case Studies on Central Mechanisms for Policy Formulation, Coordination and Implementation in the Asia Pacific Region", RETA 5685, June 1998.

---

the best development plans cannot be implemented. The challenge is to reconcile the needs and capacities of the immediate future with the long-term objectives—i.e., to resolve the short-term tradeoff among stability, growth and equity in a manner that promotes their complementarity over the long term.

A macroeconomic framework includes four sets of projections covering the main dimensions of any economy: the real sector, the balance of payments, the fiscal accounts and the monetary sector. These projections correspond to the four groups of policies mentioned earlier—on production, trade, fiscal policy and monetary aspects. The macroeconomic framework is a tool for checking that the main policy *targets* (usually, the rate of growth, inflation and employment) are consistent with the *projections* made about the main variables in each of the four sectors. As a tool, the framework must never be taken as an end in itself, nor can it ever account for the social, political and distributional complexities of policy-making in the real world—but it provides insurance against major mistakes and inconsistencies, as well as some protection of realism and common sense. (Annex 1 describes the basics of macroeconomic programming.)

Fiscal Adjustment: The New Center of Macroeconomic Programming

Adjustments in government revenues and expenditures have always been important in macroeconomic programming, partly through their influence on national production and the demand for imports and partly through their impact on domestic credit and money creation, but their role has become especially prominent during the past two decades.

In the 1970s and 1980s economic adjustment could take place either through exchange rate policy (mainly devaluation of the currency, which makes exports more competitive and raises the cost of imports) or through fiscal policies or as a combination.[1]

The IMF was a strong supporter and enforcer of fixed exchange rate in the postwar period, but changed its position in the mid-1970s and advocated flexible exchange rates until the mid-1990s. After the early 1990s, the costs of excessive fluctuations in currency exchange rates were recognized, currency devaluation was de-emphasized as an instrument of adjustment, and the IMF reverted back to regarding the exchange rate as an "anchor," which should not be changed except in response to major and permanent economic shocks (see IMF, 2006). These changes in "fundamental" IMF positions have given rise to a conspiratorial interpretation—namely, that the push for currency devaluation in most IMF lending programs for developing countries in the 1980s was deliberately designed to lower the prices of commodities exported primarily by developing countries to the advantage of rich countries, which dominate IMF policies. In fact, a relative decline in the world price of key commodities exported by developing countries did take place during that period, but mainly as a result of a variety of structural changes in the world economy. The decline did in fact arise partly from the impact of competitive exchange rate devaluations in developing countries, but there is no evidence of deliberate intent. Rather, the issue was neglect of the aggregate impact of devaluation recommendations by different IMF teams for different countries.[2]

The emphasis of economic adjustment has correspondingly shifted to the domestic economy and primarily to the fiscal side. This change in emphasis has coincided with a period of rethinking of the role of the state—toward downsizing of the state and shedding many of the functions it had acquired in earlier years. While this rethinking has taken place in most countries, it was particularly important in developing countries in order to correct the conventional wisdom of the 1970s and much of the 1980s that direct state intervention is required to generate growth.[3] In the late 1990s, a sensible consensus emerged to the effect that the private sector is the main engine for economic growth, including in developing countries, but that appropriate state action and regulation are required for the efficient functioning of the market and to produce a measure of equity, social stability and development (World Bank, 1997). This rethinking of the role of the state tilted fiscal adjustment toward reducing government expenditure rather than raising taxes.

The degree of fiscal adjustment is normally measured by the reduction in the overall government deficit relative to gross domestic product (GDP). Because the fiscal deficit is determined by both revenue and expenditure, fiscal adjustment should, in principle, incorporate a mix of revenue increases and expenditure reductions.[4] In reality, as noted, the downsizing of the role of the state has led to greater emphasis on public expenditure reductions rather than on revenue increases.[5] In turn, reducing expenditure cannot be sustained unless the expenditure *management* system is in reasonably good shape. The upshot of these shifts in economic policy posture over the past 25 years is that government budgeting and public expenditure management have acquired the central role in macroeconomic programming in both high-income and developing countries.[6]

The Composition of Expenditure Adjustment

Thus, the composition of fiscal adjustment is as important as its degree. On the expenditure side, the key issue in this regard is the essential distinction between government consumption and government investment. In the fiscal accounts, government consumption is reflected in current government expenditure and government investment in capital expenditure. Current expenditures are for all goods and services needed for the regular operations and functioning of the government during the year. Capital expenditures are associated with the production of new physical assets, which have a useful economic life extending beyond one year.[7]

Here are the main guiding rules of fiscal adjustment through expenditure changes:

- *Consider the totality of government expenditures.* All types of expenditure must be on the table, to allow comparison of the relative costs of cutting one type or another.
- *Consider the balance between current and capital expenditure* and their very different impacts on the economy.
- *No category of expenditure should be defined as a residual.* Some expenditures cannot be changed in the short term; for example, interest payments must be made, and entitlements (such as social security) are legal obligations. The "discretionary" expenditure that is left is the smaller portion of total government spending and, concerning that portion, the burden of adjustment generally falls on categories where it is politically or administratively easier to reduce expenditure. Typically, the expenditure cuts defined in such residual manner have been in operations and maintenance (O&M), and in ongoing investment projects. But cuts in O&M harm the efficiency of current operations, and cuts in investment expenditure damage the implementation of the projects. It is important therefore to look at the budget as a whole when considering expenditure reductions.

A similar approach was advocated by The Concord Coalition, an informal political group in the US that advocates fiscal responsibility. See Box 5.2.

Preparing the Fiscal Framework

Good management of expenditure begins with a good forecast of *revenue*. Because government revenue depends on various developments in the economy, preparing the fiscal program is only possible in the context of the preparation of the overall macroeconomic framework. This essential task must be performed centrally. The formation of a dedicated macrofiscal analysis unit, preferably in the ministry of finance, is therefore very important.

Setting the Fiscal Targets

The overall fiscal target is not a specific level of budget surplus or deficit in itself, but a fiscal position that implements the government policy goals and is appropriately financed and sustainable, with good management of fiscal risks. An apparently satisfactory budget situation may mask structural fiscal problems (e.g., when expenditures are dominated by rigid and mounting entitlements). Conversely, a large budget deficit may not be cause for worry if it is associated with productive investment that will add less to the country's debt than to the country's financial capacity to repay it. In virtually all developing countries, running a moderate fiscal deficit is normal and desirable. What is not acceptable in any country is a budget deficit produced by unwarranted tax exemptions or by wasteful and fraudulent expenditures.

Explicit fiscal targets are necessary to frame the formulation of the budget, and enable the legislature and the public to monitor the design and implementation of government policy—making the government politically as well as financially accountable. Fiscal targets

---

Box 5.2 Three Basic Rules for Deficit Reduction

Put everything on the table: If everyone insists on only cutting someone else's priorities, talk about deficit reduction will remain just that. The best way to end the standoff is to agree on the common goals of deficit reduction, put everything on the table—including entitlement cuts and tax increases—and negotiate the necessary tradeoffs.

Deficit reduction must be real (i.e., avoid accounting gimmicks) and the process must be legitimate and thus sustainable (i.e., confronting honestly the tough choices and make the necessary tradeoffs). One needs to identify and confront the opportunity costs of different options.

Share the sacrifice: The burden of deficit reduction should be distributed fairly. It is not fair, fiscally responsible or politically viable to make cutbacks in limited areas of the budget while exempting most areas from scrutiny. Those who can more readily shoulder the burden should be asked to do so.

Quite to the contrary, fiscal policy in this century has reduced the relative tax burden on the richest 1 percent, while altering the expenditure pattern in ways that have curtailed per capita expenditure in real terms on programs that benefit lower-income Americans.

Implement pay-as-you-go rules and budget caps: These rules, enacted in 1990 [under the Republican administration of George H. W. Bush] and extended in 1997 [under the Democratic administration of Bill Clinton], were a critical part of getting a handle on the deficit in the 1990s. The "pay-go" rule essentially requires anyone who proposes a spending increase or tax cut, including the extension of expiring tax cuts, to answer the question: "How do we pay for it?"

Source: *The Concord Coalition* (2005).

---

and indicators cover three areas: the overall fiscal position, fiscal sustainability (measured by the ratios of debt to GDP, of revenue to GDP, and of expenditure to GDP) and fiscal risk (e.g., composition of the debt, issue of loan guarantees, etc.).

The main indicator of the overall fiscal position is the *overall budget balance on a cash basis*—i.e., the difference between collected revenues on a cash basis (plus grants) and actual expenditure payments. A deficit on a cash basis corresponds (in large part) to government borrowing from domestic or foreign sources and is thus integrally linked to credit, the money supply, inflation prospects and the balance of payments. (Government borrowing does not constitute the entirety of financing of the budget, which includes other sources.) The *primary balance* is the difference between *non-interest* expenditure and revenue—thus, it is the cash deficit minus interest payments. Because interest must be paid in any case, the evolution of the primary deficit is a better measure of the government's efforts for fiscal adjustment. It is a better policy target also because it does not depend on the vagaries of interest rates.

The *current balance* is the difference between *current* expenditure and total revenue. A current fiscal surplus is by definition equal to "government saving." Thus, in a balanced budget, a current surplus shows the contribution of government to the resources available for investment and a current deficit is government *dis*-saving, subtracting of resources from those available for investment. Using the current balance as a policy target therefore helps insulate investment expenditure from cuts, and focuses the necessary fiscal adjustment on revenue and current expenditure. (However, focusing on the current deficit as indicator of the fiscal situation generates a temptation to make the fiscal situation look artificially better by reclassifying certain current expenditures as investment.)

Finally, a useful indicator is the *primary current balance*, which does not include either interest payments or investment, and thus focuses policy attention on improving the effectiveness of expenditure on salaries, subsidies and goods and services.

A good fiscal picture is provided by a combination of the overall deficit, the primary deficit and the current deficit.[8] Table 5.1 provides a numerical illustration of the various fiscal indicators.

Scope of the Fiscal Program

Ideally, as explained in Chapter 3, the fiscal program should cover "general government" (i.e., government at all municipal levels) and the fiscal targets should be broken down between central and subnational government. It is also desirable to prepare a consolidated account of the public sector, including the public enterprises. (Note, in any case, that the operations of the deconcentrated units of central government are part of central government, and must be fully included in the fiscal framework and the central government budget. The accountability of the central government does not depend on where it carries out its activities.)

Consolidated fiscal accounts are appropriate for all developed countries and many middle-income countries. In most developing countries, where reliable data on subnational government operations are not available on a timely basis, it is better not to include suspect data or guesswork and to limit the fiscal framework to central government. In such cases, the limitations of the fiscal picture should be kept in mind, and efforts should be made to progressively improve data availability and local capacity in order to eventually expand the fiscal framework to general government. In any event, measures are needed to

Table 5.1 Illustration of Fiscal Indicators (cash basis)

Revenue and grants			100
Expenditure			120
Current expenditure		100	
Of which, interest payments	10		
Capital expenditure		20	
Stock of government debt			300
Gross domestic product (GDP)			500
Indicators of fiscal position:			
Overall balance (4% of GDP)			−20
Primary balance (2% of GDP)			−10
Current balance			0
Indicators of fiscal sustainability (in percent):			
Debt/GDP			60
Revenue/GDP			20
Expenditure/GDP			24

minimize the risks that subnational budgets may be a source of instability for the country as a whole (as discussed in Chapter 14.)

A Worldwide Tendency Toward Fiscal Deficits

There is no "normal" level of government revenue or expenditure—let alone a "right" level of fiscal balance. Whether revenue, expenditure and the fiscal outturns are appropriate depends on the situation and characteristics of the individual country. Accordingly, there is a large variance in fiscal outcomes throughout the world. To show that variance, and allow the reader to make country comparisons, Annex 2 shows government revenue and expenditure in US dollar equivalent and in relation to GDP, for all 207 world countries and territories in 2014.

The figures show a clear prevalence of fiscal deficits. In 2014, of the 172 countries for which complete data are available, just 12 countries showed a fiscal surplus—a very small one for Germany, Lichtenstein and some central Asian countries, and a large one for the major oil and gas producers—Kuwait, UAE, Qatar, Norway. (With different policies than the other oil producers, Saudi Arabia's budget has been hit hard by the combination of large subsidies and the fall in oil export revenue—with a deficit of 2.2 percent of GDP in 2014, zooming to 13 percent of GDP in 2015 and doubtful prospects for containment in 2016.) As many as 32 countries show a balanced or nearly balanced budget (deficit less than 0.5 percent of GDP) in 2014. The vast majority, 128 countries, show fiscal deficits ranging from the very low single digits to 20 percent or more (with Timor-Leste an outlier with a deficit larger than GDP itself). As a broad and superficial generalization, deficits lower than 3 percent of GDP are usually not viewed as a problem. Still, 78 countries—almost half the total—experienced deficits higher than 3 percent in 2014. What explains the worldwide prevalence of fiscal deficits?

According to the theory of economic cycles, associated with John Maynard Keynes, the government budget should be in balance only incidentally, as it goes from an optimal deficit to an optimal surplus and back again depending on economic developments: in times when high "aggregate demand" (public and private) pushes against the envelope of potential production, inflationary tendencies ensue and the government should aim for a budget surplus by curtailing expenditure and/or raising taxes in order to bring aggregate demand down and prevent inflation. Conversely, in slack times, with slow or negative growth and high unemployment the government should aim for a budget deficit by raising expenditure and/or reducing taxes in order to stimulate aggregate demand and thus production and employment. This has been the case in the US and some other countries after the onset of the global recession in 2008, preventing the severe recession from turning into a full-blown economic depression. With the subsequent recovery, fiscal deficits have since come down substantially. (In Europe, by contrast, the debt crisis led to austerity measures and worsened the economic downturn in several countries.)

The worldwide reality of fiscal deficits as the norm is better explained by simple political dynamics than by macroeconomic theory. There is no good reason for a government to run a persistent fiscal surplus: if revenue largely exceeds spending, additional expenditure programs can be launched to take care of unmet needs, and/or taxes can be reduced.[9] Neither of these policies would encounter political resistance, since they produce benefits for some groups without causing losses to other groups. The opposite is not the case, of course: correcting a deficit requires expenditure cuts and/or tax increases—either of which causes tangible and immediate losses to some groups and hence encounters political resistance. Thus, surpluses are more likely to disappear and deficits to persist.

Financing the Budget

Budget financing is discussed in Chapter 10. Here's a brief preview. If the budget is in deficit, the deficit must be financed. Financing includes mainly government borrowing from domestic sources, borrowing from foreign sources, exceptional grants (recurrent grants are instead part of ordinary revenue) and net changes in payment arrears. Note that interest payments are part of current expenditure, but repayments of principal (amortization) are part of financing—negative financing, naturally.

"Payment arrears"—not paying the government bills—are also technically considered as part of "budget financing," albeit of course quite involuntary on the part of the suppliers who are not being paid. In countries where budgeting is loose and expenditure control is weak, government contractual commitments are sometimes not met in time, and payment arrears emerge (as discussed in Chapter 8). In these cases, the cash deficit *plus* the net increase of arrears is an important indicator. (The IMF Code of Fiscal Transparency requires reporting on payment arrears when the accounting system is on a cash basis, in order to avoid mistaking a fragile situation for a healthy one when the government is simply pushing off its payment obligations to subsequent years.)

The manner in which the fiscal deficit is financed and the sources of the financing are important, because different forms and sources of financing have different costs, advantages, risks and implications for the future. The nationality of the creditors makes an especially big difference. An apparently moderate debt/GDP ratio may be unsustainable if the debt is mainly to foreign creditors, whereas a much higher ratio may not be a problem if the debt is mainly domestic. For example, Argentina's 5 percent government debt/GDP ratio raises grave issues, whereas twice that rate in the UK is considered sustainable because most of the debt is owed to domestic creditors. "We owe it to ourselves" is the oversimplified way to think of this—oversimplified because high domestic debt has implications for the composition of expenditure, with some government expenditures crowded out by the interest payments.

Clearly, too, for a given level of deficit, the implications for future public finances and development are vastly different if the deficit is to be financed by aid at concessional terms and long maturities; or by domestic borrowing and credit expansion; or by expensive commercial foreign loans (see Chapter 10).

The Need for Multiyear Fiscal and Expenditure Projections

Until late in the twentieth century, government budgeting was a purely annual affair, infrequently complemented by calculations of the future implications of selected expenditures. From the 1980s, the need to reconcile short-term urgencies with longer-term policy priorities; prevent stability from degrading into economic stagnation and, conversely, foster economic growth with financial stability; and strengthen government accountability—led to recognizing the importance of adopting a medium-term perspective for the preparation of the annual budget.

The political impulse came from the emergence of fiscal crises and problems of government effectiveness in Europe and North America. In brief, by the mid-1970s, governments in developed countries had become too expensive, too big and too intrusive. A first wave of reforms followed, aiming at "less government," with public sector downsizing and privatization. After the fiscal deficits had been sharply reduced in most countries, a second phase of reform in the 1990s was aimed at "better government," by improving service delivery, deregulation, devolution of responsibilities to subnational levels of government, greater transparency and better public access to information (Bouder, 2000). Both waves of reform required substantial time to be implemented and thus, among other things, called for a fiscal and expenditure perspective longer than just a year.

Without a multiyear perspective, annual budgeting

> leads to short-sightedness, because future expenditures are not reviewed; pressures to overspend, because the future implications of current year's expenditure are considered; incrementalism that impedes major policy changes; and narrow decisions, because expenditure programs are viewed in isolation rather than in comparison to their future costs in relation to expected revenue.
>
> (Wildavsky, 1993, p. 317)

In practice, the feasibility of a multiyear fiscal perspective is greater when revenues are predictable and the mechanisms for controlling expenditure are well developed. These conditions are met in most developed economies, but not in many low-income/low-capacity countries. Nevertheless, some sort of medium-term forecast of revenue and expenditure is important, however rudimentary, to frame the annual budget preparation process. Specifically, the annual budget must reflect three multiannual factors:

- The future recurrent costs of public investment—which constitutes the largest single category of discretionary government spending in most developing countries.
- The funding needs of entitlements, where expenditures change even though the basic policy remains the same—e.g., pensions for an aging population. This is especially relevant for rich countries, with their social security and public health obligations.
- Contingencies that may result in future spending requirements, e.g., government loan guarantees that will have to be met with public moneys if the borrower defaults.

In addition, a multiyear fiscal outlook is necessary for four main reasons:

- Implementing policy changes. At the time the budget is formulated, most government expenditure is already committed. Salaries, debt-service payments, pensions, and the like cannot be changed in the short term, and other costs can be adjusted only marginally. The true discretionary margin in most countries, whether high-, middle- or low-income, is a very small proportion of total government expenditure—well under 3 percent in the US. (While "discretionary" spending is 30 percent of the overall budget, it is hard to imagine that more than 10 percent of that can in reality be reallocated on an annual basis.) Additional revenue can be mobilized, of course, but this, too, takes time and is subject to severe political constraints. As a result, a real adjustment of fiscal stance and expenditure priorities has to take place over a time span of several years. For instance, should the government set a policy to substantially expand access to technical education, the expenditure implications (building new schools, training additional teachers, etc.) would stretch over several years, and the policy can hardly be designed and implemented through a blinkered focus on each annual budget considered in isolation.
- By illuminating the future expenditure implications of a policy proposal the government can evaluate the cost-effectiveness of the proposal and determine whether it is trying to bite off more than it can chew or than can be financed in sustainable ways.
- Multiyear spending projections have a "signaling function," showing to the public the government's intentions and giving the private sector time to adjust.
- Finally, in the absence of a medium-term perspective grounded on political consensus, adjustments in expenditure either tend to be made by a hatchet across the board (as in

the case of "sequestration" in 2011 in the US), or are ad hoc and focused on those inputs and activities that can be cut in the short term. Unfortunately, the activities that can be cut more easily are often also the more important ones, such as O&M or the implementation of major public investment projects. Thus, a typical outcome of isolated annual budgeting is that O&M and investment are defined in practice as a residual—harming both the efficiency of current activities and the rate of return on investment.

Variants of Medium-Term Expenditure Projections[10]

Readers in developed countries are unlikely to have heard the term MTEF (medium-term expenditure framework), but the acronym is all too familiar to government officials, practitioners and the informed public in developing countries—because implementation of an MTEF has been a condition of most foreign aid programs in the past two decades. The basic concept entails nothing more controversial than to consider the future implications of annual budget decisions. However, the articulation and implementation of the basic concept differ widely, and some variants have been inconsistent with institutional capacity and carried substantial costs for little or no benefit.

A problem with "the" MTEF is that the term is used to refer to very different ways of stretching the time perspective of the budgeting process. The term should be unbundled into its four main variants: traditional planning, economic forecasting, functional forecasting and programmatic MTEF. These are discussed in turn below. But first, a word about appropriate forecasting methodology.

The degree of detail of the fiscal projections depends on the technical capacities within the country and the availability of data and appropriate tools. Sophisticated forecasting models can be useful, but the preparation of good fiscal projections does not necessarily require sophisticated modeling techniques. On the contrary, relying excessively on these techniques may give a sense of misplaced confidence and a "forecast illusion" which may constrain the needed adaptation to intervening changes. Moreover, in complex models an initial wrong assumption cascades throughout the model and can lead to major mistakes. As it is said, "it is better to be about right than exactly wrong."

Using simple forecasting models is both practical and, in most developing countries, desirable in view of the more fluid circumstances and the data and capacity limitations. Simple models are also friendlier to the debates on fiscal policy. The greater transparency of simple models is especially important for building trust in multi-ethnic countries, where suspicion and resentment of groups other than one's own are common.

Traditional Planning

The traditional planning approach identifies in advance all major expenditure programs and their funding over a fixed multiyear period. Some plans—such as the five-year plans of the late and unlamented command economy system of the Soviet Union and Eastern Europe—never had much to commend them. When the production targets were defined in physical terms, the outcomes were often grotesque—for example, the glass factory which easily met its plan target defined in terms of square meters, by producing such thin glass that windows broke under moderate winds; or the plant which over-fulfilled the plan target defined in terms of number of nails, by producing small nails suitable only to hang pictures. Changing the terms of the plan target—for example, defining it in terms of weight of nails produced—would produce a different kind of inefficiency. And attempting to specify from the center the exact output mix invariably produced surpluses of one type of product in one region and shortages in another region—in addition to providing strong incentives for gaming the system and cooking the books. Quality, too, took a back seat, resulting in the famously inefficient and unreliable products of the old Soviet Union.

Other plans of the 1950s and 1960s, in mixed economy countries, did provide vision, policy direction and internal coherence. However, changing circumstances make even the best fixed projections quickly obsolete. Also, because in traditional planning expenditure programs are rarely prepared under a revenue constraint, they tend to become overloaded with wishes and demands from all quarters, harming the credibility of the overall plan.

These multi-volume plans absorbed substantial capacity at the center of government, gave interesting short-term employment to hundreds of economists and other social scientists, embodied the best of economic and econometric analysis, were launched with great fanfare and disseminated widely—and then went to collect dust on thousands of government and academic shelves. The plans were technically impressive, internally consistent and complete in every detail, except for attention to the political and capacity dimensions and the question of who was to implement the plans, how, when, with what resources and under what incentives.[11]

Still, despite their failings in practice and the top-down centralizing frame of mind that produced them, the traditional plans were close in spirit to the key contemporary objective of integrating investment and current expenditure into coherent programs consistent with resource availability over the medium term:

> Plans encompass a recognition . . . that by systematic examination of both policies and investment projects as parts of a whole, one can improve their total efficiency by forming *consistent and complementary "packages"* . . . [They] increase the consistency between short-run decisions and long-run choices . . . *force a less developed country to think in terms of a balance between resources which are available, including those from foreign sources, and national economic goals* . . . Although this direct confrontation of means and ends is often evaded in actual development plans . . . an advantage of serious development planning is decreased uncertainty.
> (Schiavo-Campo and Singer, 1970, pp. 12–13; italics inserted)

The traditional fixed-term plan still exists in some countries and, for political and other reasons, cannot be replaced at one go with a rolling set of medium-term and revenue-constrained expenditure projections. However, it can be brought fairly close to it by progressive mutations. Thus, the problem of lack of revenue constraint can be addressed by starting the planning process with a reliable projection of domestic and foreign revenue; the top-down nature of the approach can be mitigated if genuine participation of the key stakeholders is obtained from the very start; and, if the old practice of one-shot mid-term review is changed to annual reviews, adaptation to changes can be made every year, thus bringing the plan close to a rolling MTEF.[12] Still missing, however, would be the core MTEF feature: a distinction between ongoing programs under existing policies and new programs—the genuinely new element in the contemporary MTEF approach.

Projecting the Economic Composition of Expenditure: A "Forecasting MTEF"[13]

The simplest type of MTEF ("medium-term fiscal framework" in the World Bank/IMF terminology) is a medium-term projection of the aggregate economic composition of expenditure (salaries, goods and services, transfers, interest payments and investment) "rolled," i.e., updated, every year prior to the start of the annual budget preparation. These projections have been done by the IMF for over 40 years, beginning with the 1974 introduction of the three-year "Extended Fund Facility" (EFF). Because the EFF was established to assist countries to deal with economic and financial problems requiring longer adjustment than the conventional one-year stand by loans, it became necessary to demonstrate balance-of-payments viability after the end of the three-year EFF period, and hence to formulate macroeconomic projections covering the entire period.[14] Moreover, given the regular IMF reviews of countries' policies and financial outturn (at least annual and more often semi-annual), the medium-term projections were regularly updated and extended forward—coming closer to the "rolling" MTEF approach.[15]

The GFS economic classification, described in Chapter 2, is the basis for this simplest variant of an MTEF. For this variant, the issue of weak institutions and implementation capacity does not arise, because the components of the projections are either straight forecasts based on actual numbers, or embody negotiated agreements on the wage bill, transfers, investment expenditure or other expenditure categories.

A "Forecasting MTEF": Projecting the Functional Composition of Expenditure

A projection of the functional composition of expenditure should in principle be made in accordance with the UN Classification of the Functions of Government (COFOG), but in practice can correspond to the organizational structure of government (as explained in Chapter 2). When the expenditure projections are articulated around aggregate estimates for each ministry and spending agency, *and* are constrained by sound forecasts of revenue, we have what may be called a "forecasting MTEF" ("medium-term budget framework" in the World Bank/IMF terminology).

A forecasting MTEF gives the line ministries a *weak indication* of future resource availability and provides the "signaling function" to help guide the private sector's own decisions. Controlling expenditure is more difficult in the absence of a medium-term expenditure perspective disaggregated by ministries and agencies. Thus, a good forecasting MTEF is a priority for all countries, and should be introduced in simple form as rapidly as possible—with foreign assistance as needed—and deepened, improved and refined over time.

A "Programmatic MTEF"

A programmatic MTEF ("medium-term performance framework", in the World Bank/IMF terminology) is the most advanced and complex form of a multiyear expenditure perspective. It is sometimes accompanied by program budgeting, i.e., the allocation of resources to programs, subprograms and activities, rather than to the economic categories (see Chapter 2). However, as a *framework*, a programmatic MTEF is compatible with any *budget* system—including of course a cash-based, line-item budget. (Nevertheless, the following should be read in conjunction with the explanation of program budgeting in Chapter 2.)

The Forerunner: Australia's Forward Estimates

Medium-term forecasting of expenditure programs was originally pioneered in the United Kingdom in the early 1980s, but the prototype of the programmatic MTEF can be traced to Australia, a leader among developed countries in reforms to control public expenditure. The core of the approach is as follows: each ministry agrees with the ministry of finance on "baseline" projections of expenditure on its *ongoing* programs, and proposes *new* programs based on projection of their full cost. This eliminates the need for bargaining about the baseline for each fiscal year, reduces funding uncertainty for ongoing programs, and focuses attention on the budgetary implications of policy changes or of strategic decisions. Australia's "forward estimates" approach is summarized in Box 5.3.

Box 5.3 Australia's "Forward Estimates" Process

In its original formulation (modified since the 1990s in a number of ways), the process works as follows. Prior to the start of the annual budget preparation, each ministry agrees with the ministry of finance on "baseline" projections of expenditure on its *ongoing* programs for three years, and the ministry of finance thereafter updates these projections according to changes in economic parameters or government decisions affecting costs. Regarding new programs, the ministry must project their full costs over the three-year period in order to have them considered for funding. This practice eliminates the time-consuming bargaining over the baseline for each fiscal year, reduces uncertainty over future funding levels for ongoing programs, and allows attention to be focused on the budgetary implications of policy changes or strategic decisions. The government then makes a *public* commitment to the forward estimates, including them in the budget documentation and publishing fresh projections of expenditure and revenue in the three months prior to an election. The role of the legislature is correspondingly enhanced, and civil society and the voters have the information and "voice" to react to the government budgetary intentions.

High-level political guidance and ownership was ensured by an expenditure review committee (ERC), consisting of the prime minister, the treasurer and minister of finance and a number of major line ministers. The ERC was responsible for approving the overall fiscal framework and managing strategic policy changes, as well as setting the expenditure ceiling for each sector ministry in the preparation of the annual budget. If the aggregate ceiling for the ministry is lower than the coming year's cost of existing programs, the ministry concerned would need to find savings or take other efficiency measures; if higher, the ministry could use the fiscal space to introduce new initiatives.

In any event, under the system it is up to the competent ministry to determine the allocation of resources among different programs in the sector, consistent with overall government policy and within a hard expenditure constraint for the current budget year. Analogously, within each ministry, line managers have flexibility with regard to both staff and money, again within the budget constraint applicable to their program.

Estimating and Allocating "Fiscal Space"

A full-fledged programmatic MTEF includes a *strong indication* of future resources for each ministry, and within such an indication it makes a distinction between ongoing and new expenditure programs, identifies measures to produce savings in low-priority programs in order to create fiscal space for new programs, and includes detailed cost estimates of any new initiative or program. The central difference between a forecasting and a programmatic MTEF is that in the latter case the ministerial expenditures are costed in detail for *each* program by the ministries themselves, whereas in a forecasting MTEF the functions are defined in broader terms and the indicative allocation is made centrally (albeit in consultation with the ministries).

Figure 5.1 illustrates a programmatic MTEF. Revenue is assumed to increase faster than expenditure under existing programs because some projects come to an end during

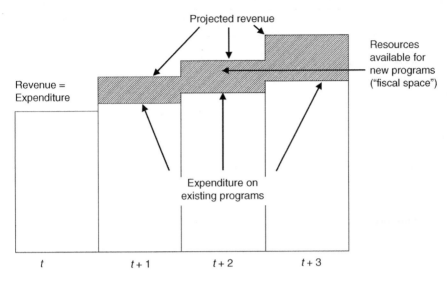

Figure 5.1 Illustration of a Four-Year Programmatic MTEF.

Note: In the current year *t*, for simplicity, revenue is assumed to incorporate the target fiscal balance. In outyears *t* + 1 through *t* + 3 the "available resources for new programs" may be partly dedicated to improving the fiscal balance or, if fiscal and political circumstances permit, be augmented by allowing a larger deficit or smaller budget surplus—as the case may be.

Source: Adapted from Tommasi (2010), p. 104.

the period (although some increase will normally take place, for demographic and other reasons).

The difference between the estimated revenue and expenditure projected under existing programs is available—*not earmarked*—to finance expenditure under new programs. (If it were earmarked, any future adjustment could only come from the revenue side, as discussed later.) The resulting "fiscal space" is then filled from the bottom up by specific expenditure programs formulated and costed in detail by the line ministries themselves—thereby giving them increased ownership along with greater predictability of funding. (The scheme in Figure 5.1 can also be used to illustrate situations where aggregate expenditure is to be cut, either because revenue prospects are unfavorable or because of the need to increase expenditure on ongoing programs. In this case, the fiscal space would be negative, providing an aggregate guideline for the expenditure reduction proposals to be required from the various ministries.)

The differences between an economic, forecasting and programmatic MTEF (to recall, respectively MTFF, MTBF and MTPF in World Bank/IMF parlance) are shown in simplified form in Table 5.2.

In reality, detailed bottom-up costing of every new program is infrequent, even in advanced systems. The ministries provide only broad cost estimates, in conformity with general guidelines set by the ministry of finance, and many of these estimates are merely incremental projections based on previous expenditure levels (see Di Francesco and Barroso, 2015). While inconsistent with the logic of a pure programmatic MTEF, this is a rational response: providing fully detailed costing of all proposed programs, subprograms and activities would entail huge administrative burdens out of line with the benefits of more precise estimates—in light of the inherently uncertain future and the need to formulate detailed spending proposals during the annual budget process anyway.

Table 5.2 Simplified Representation of Economic, Organizational and Programmatic MTEFs

	Year t	Year t + 1	Year t + 2	Year t + 3
Forecasting MTEF				
Employee compensation (wage bill)				
Goods and services				
Subsidies				
Social benefits				
Interest				
Capital expenditure				
Other expenditure				
TOTAL EXPENDITURE	110	120	140	150
Organizational (functional) MTEF[a]				
Ministry of Health				
Ministry of Transport				
Etc. . .				
TOTAL EXPENDITURE	110	120	140	150
Programmatic MTEF[b]				
FUNCTION: EDUCATION				
Program I: Primary education				
Subprogram A: Literacy				
Activity 1: School attendance				
Cost element (a): Books				
Cost element (b):. . ., etc.				
Activity 2: . . .etc.				
Activity 3: . . .etc.				
Subprogram B: Numeracy				
Activity 1: Math lab management				
Cost element (a): etc.. . .				
Activity 2:. . .etc				
Subprogram C: . . .. Etc.				
Program II: . . . etc.				
FUNCTION: HEALTH CARE				
Program I: Disease Control				
Subprogram A: Malaria				
Activity 1: Prevention				
Cost element (a): Mosquito nets				
Cost element (b):. . ., etc.				
Activity 2: . . .etc.				
Subprogram B:. . . etc.				
Program II: . . . etc.				
FUNCTION: . . . ETC.				
TOTAL EXPENDITURE	110	120	140	150

Notes:
a If the classification is functional instead of organizational, it would follow the COFOG (general public services, defense, public order and safety, etc., see Box 2.5).
b Purely illustrative; the actual programmatic classification would depend on the country and the policy objectives.

What is a "Program"?

Programmatic MTEFs in turn have two variants, revolving around the definition of "program." In the pragmatic South African and Canadian practice, a "program" is coterminous with a major division of a ministry, for example, primary health care, and only a few large "programs" are defined in each ministry. This permits defining broad objectives and very general performance indicators for each large program. Partly because the definition of programs is consistent with the organizational structure of government, this variant of a programmatic MTEF is simpler and avoids jurisdictional confusion and "turf" conflict. The more demanding variant, instead, would require introducing a full program classification of expenditure, which has been implemented only in a handful of highly advanced countries.

Either variant of a programmatic MTEF needs to be implemented gradually, with constant attention to the risk of unintended consequences and of unnecessary red tape, and with the benefit of just-in-time user feedback on service quality and access. It also requires an environment characterized by substantial technical and programming capacity within each ministry and agency, and a high degree of managerial autonomy to permit twinning authority with accountability.

Reconciling National Priorities with Sector Programs

On the one hand, national and sector strategies have little meaning in the absence of concrete programs and activities to translate them into actual services and works. On the other hand, financial resources cannot be allocated to ministries exclusively on the basis of the specific programs that appear most efficient, without regard to sector strategies and national priorities. Thus, the available fiscal space should initially be allocated to individual ministries in a manner consistent with the national priorities and broad sector strategies— and hence from the top down (albeit after consultation). But also, that fiscal space should be filled by realistic and specific expenditure programs—and hence from the bottom up by the line ministries (albeit subject to central approval). The initial inter-ministerial resource allocation can then be modified to provide sufficient resources to the best-conceived expenditure programs—thus giving the line ministries increased ownership along with incentives to develop better-quality programs and services. *Iteration is the name of the game.*

As explained in Chapter 6, this approach to an MTEF is symmetrical with the approach to annual budget preparation—whereby ministerial expenditure ceilings are decided centrally and communicated to the ministries, which are then responsible for preparing their budget requests within the assigned ceiling—following which negotiations, iteration and eventual convergence take place.

Symmetry says nothing about sequencing, however. When the annual budget process is shaky and in need of major improvements, the priority is to improve it, rather than to attempt to introduce a complex MTEF process unsuited to circumstances. Subsequently, programmatic elements can be gradually incorporated in the budgetary process through the piloting approaches discussed in Chapter 2.

Moving Toward a Programmatic MTEF

When the time is right and circumstances permit, the process of moving beyond a functional (organizational) MTEF to a programmatic MTEF consists of progressively "filling in" the aggregate expenditure projections for ministries and agencies by bottom-up estimates of the medium-term costs of *selected* specific programs. This would allow the ministries concerned and the government as a whole to learn from experience and gradually extend the practice to cover other expenditure programs—while minimizing the costs and risks. In the meantime, ministries can also be requested to begin making a distinction in their budget requests between "existing" and "new" activities. So long as the ministries are allowed to do so in general terms and not required to fill on complicated reporting templates or conduct detailed cost-analysis, the exercise can be consistent with existing capacity and the transaction costs will be kept down—while attention will begin to focus on the efficiency of existing expenditure programs the financial implications of new programs and the results of spending rather than just the manner of spending.[16] Such a gradual, organic process demands consultation and participation; the experience of countless failures demonstrates that top-down approaches simply don't work.

Evidently, the evolution of a programmatic MTEF requires substantial and sustained capacity-building over the long term. The implications for civil service employment, compensation and new flexibility in financial resources and personnel management are considerable, too. To move toward a programmatic MTEF without a concurrent capacity-building effort, stronger accountability mechanisms and adapting the rules on virements and personnel management, guarantees waste, frustration and eventual failure.

Balancing Macro-Level Flexibility and Sector-Level Predictability

A framework is not a budget. Too often, one hears an MTEF referred to as a "multiyear budget." As explained at length in Chapter 3, this is wrong on both conceptual and practical grounds. The budget is annual everywhere in the world; even when detailed multiyear programs receive legislative approval, payments (or commitments) may not be made except as authorized in the budget for the year in question (see Box 3.1). An MTEF provides the multiyear *framework* to prepare the annual budget but must not be confused with a medium-term *budget*.[17] The only legally binding expenditure ceilings are those for the current year of the MTEF, which is of course the year of the annual budget. Moreover, to stick to hard sector expenditure ceilings over the medium term would be equivalent to going back to the rigid and discredited planning approaches of yesteryear, and would in practice abandon one-half of the government's arsenal of fiscal policy and adjustment tools. Because each ministry would tend to view the expenditure ceilings as expenditure *floors*, the fiscal space would disappear and the entire burden of adjusting to changes would fall on the revenue side. With tax increases politically difficult to implement, the entire MTEF construct would in effect be made of paper, and the multiyear fiscal perspective would be inoperative.

On the other hand, sector expenditure ceilings for the out years cannot be merely casual indications to be readily discarded when the annual budget process comes around again. The line ministries and agencies would gain no added predictability from an MTEF and the exercise would be rightly ignored as a useless formality to be dumped on to peripheral offices or aid-financed consultants. (This is in fact what has happened.)

The challenge is therefore to balance the macro level flexibility needed for good budgeting with the sector-level predictability provided by a strong MTEF. The MTEF procedures should allow line ministries and spending agencies to plan on the basis of a *reasonable presumption* of availability of financial resources, while preserving the government's overall flexibility to adjust *both* revenue and expenditure in the context of the annual budget process. In effect, the objective of a programmatic MTEF is to shift the burden of proof, giving greater confidence of availability of funding to ministries which present strong expenditure programs and weakening the position of ministries which have a flimsier programmatic platform. Those who plan better do better, and those who do better get more money. Indeed, the dynamic payoff of a programmatic MTEF process consists precisely of providing the basis for constructive emulation and stimulating greater efficiency by the line ministries and agencies.

The International Experience with MTEFs

In developed countries, the evidence shows that adoption of a multiyear budget framework has improved the budget balance by about two percentage points. While there is little evidence of across-the-board improvements in expenditure efficiency or service quality, on balance functional or programmatic MTEFs have worked well in several high-income/high-capacity countries (Brumby et al., 2012).[18] The reason is the existence in these countries of a number of factors, political as well as economic and institutional—the same as those for the introduction of program budgeting (see Box 2.2). The experience of developing countries has been much less favorable.

Growing Apples in the Tropics

The overarching lesson of international experience in public administration is that systems and practices suitable to a high-income/high-capacity country cannot be transplanted to a low-income/low-capacity country, any more than apple trees can grow in tropical soils. A public management innovation cannot be imported "as is" into a different institutional environment nor can it be implemented successfully even with adaptation—except gradually and over a long period of time (McFerson, 2007). Nevertheless, from the mid-1990s the complex multiyear expenditure methodologies developed in a handful of highly advanced countries were introduced in developing countries under the same assumptions concerning accountability, transparency, public integrity and, above all, capacity. In too many cases, these unthinking attempts at transplants produced an elaborate façade of reform with nothing of substance behind it—like a Potemkin Village or Hollywood movie set.

A Scorecard in Developing Countries

The Positive

MTEF implementation had the following results (World Bank, 2011):

- a slight and temporary improvement in fiscal balance;
- some limited reallocation to priority expenditure;
- little or no improvement in budgetary predictability;
- no evidence of efficiency gains in spending.

This doesn't sound like much. One should add, however, that the very attempts at introducing a medium-term fiscal perspective have, in several countries, generated an awareness of the need to think beyond the current year. Also, when public expenditure projections have been more than purely mechanical top-down exercises, the involvement of line ministries and agencies has led in some cases to greater inter-ministerial coordination (as, for example, in Morocco). Moreover, the implicit emphasis on results, rather than solely on budgetary processes, may have contributed in some countries to an improvement in the quality of expenditure. Finally, because external validation of outputs or outcomes has become necessary, doors have been opened to user feedback and broader participation.

The positive experience with an MTEF process is exemplified by South Africa—see Box 5.4—in part owing to the substantial institutional capacity in the country, but largely by the practice of acknowledging, confronting and redressing the early failures.

Box 5.4 Learning from Experience: The Case of South Africa

In South Africa, the initial MTEF experiment launched in 1994 lasted less than two years, owing to lack of involvement by the political leadership and no clear linkage with the budget process. Learning from this experience, a new MTEF and budget preparation procedure was put in place with the 1998/9 budget, and progressively refined to include the following stages:

Initial policy review (May–September): Policy review involve the ministers' committee on the budget (MinComBud) which groups key ministers, the budget council (which includes the nine provincial members responsible for finance).

MTEF/Budget submissions (by August): Line ministries' proposals should include:

- Abaseline allocation for the medium-term.
- Identified savings and reprioritisation, within the baseline.
- Policy options which entail changes in the baseline allocation. These options should be consistent with the strategic priorities of the ministry. Estimates of investment expenditure should cover five years (two years beyond the three-year MTEF period).
- Various documents and statements (e.g., personnel numbers, analysis of risks, etc.).

Review of MTEF/budget submissions (August–October): In August–September the national and provincial medium-term expenditure committees, comprising senior officials from the MoF and other ministries, evaluate the submissions of line ministries and recommend to the MoF. In October, MinComBud discusses the outline of the medium-term budget policy statement (MTBPS); the MoF submits to the cabinet the draft MTBPS and "adjustments estimates," which are tabled in parliament at the end of October. The MTPBS includes, among other things, the three-year macroeconomic and fiscal framework, as well as medium-term expenditure aggregates for each ministry. (Of course, the MTPBS is not binding and is submitted for information and debate.)

Final Stages: In early November the cabinet approves the allocations to ministries and the conditional grants to subnational government. On this basis, the line ministries prepare their draft MTEF/budget, which includes under the same format both the estimates for the budget year and the *indicative* estimates for the second and the third years of the MTEF.

Reporting: In addition, beginning in 2005, the line ministries are required to prepare a five-year strategic plan, tabled in parliament in November, after the budget.

Source: Adapted from Fölscher (2007).

The Negative

The negative side has dominated. Most MTEFs have been pushed on to reluctant developing countries by international donor institutions. In a few cases, the host governments were influenced by the same desire for modernity that motivated donor agency staff and their managers. In several cases, they were led to believe—wrongly—that the initiative would help fix their basic budget problems. In most cases, they simply had to accept the initiative as the condition of a loan or grant. In almost all cases, the mantra of government "ownership" was a mirage. Also, the limited local capacity has meant that MTEF introduction and elaboration was done primarily by external technical experts, assisted by a few local staff. Because these initiatives were aid-financed, the net monetary cost to the recipient country has been minor. The indirect costs have been heavy—not everywhere but in many countries that could hardly afford them.

In the first place, implementation of an MTEF has absorbed scarce policy-makers' time and attention, and been a distraction from fixing the basic plumbing of the public expenditure management system. Second, the sequencing of actions has sometimes been wrong. In one African country, MTEF introduction was required for the first year of a multiyear development policy reform program, with the critical improvements in annual budget preparation left to the third year; in a South Asian country, a new macrofiscal analysis unit was supposed to be created the year *after* MTEF introduction—although expenditure projections obviously cannot be made before macroeconomic projections—which require the existence of a macrofiscal unit.

Next, MTEF introduction has placed a heavy strain on limited budgeting capacity, requiring extensive involvement of higher-level government staff, in both the ministry of finance and selected line ministries, distracting from more urgent problems.

Finally, the manner of MTEF introduction has often neglected the four conditions for successful introduction of any institutional innovation—gradualism, selectivity, simplicity and communication—causing waste, frustration and disappointment, without any improvement in expenditure control, strategic resource allocation, operational efficienc or public services.

Of Babies and Bathwater: Summing Up

The disappointing international experience has produced mounting skepticism in developing countries of *all* MTEF variants and methodologies. The prevailing view in much of the developing world is that an MTEF is an initiative pushed by aid donors and a supply-driven exercise carried out mainly by external consultants and yet taking up scarce time of local officials. This reaction is understandable, but it should not lead to abandoning the very concept of a multiyear expenditure perspective for the annual budget process.

The appropriate conclusion is not to neglect the need of a medium-term perspective, but to re-size and reformulate the approach in a manner suitable to the possibilities and capacity of the country concerned. If the right variant of a multiyear perspective is introduced, with an eye to conditions on the ground, appropriate sequencing and low transaction costs for the government, it can substantially improve the control, allocation and efficiency of government financial resources and thus, ultimately, people's access to and quality of public services.

Among those variants, an organizational (functional) MTEF is important to strengthen the link between government policy and the budget, inject into the expenditure management system some awareness of the future, and provide for a systematic dialogue on the results of public spending. However, its level of detail must be mindful of local statistical and administrative limits. In contrast, a full programmatic MTEF is quite incompatible with the circumstances of low-income countries and most middle-income economies. Nevertheless, the gradual introduction of *selected* programmatic elements in the multiyear fiscal projections, and of simple ways to foster a dialogue on results, may *in time* lead to improved fiscal outcomes and better public services.

Annex 1: The Basics of Macroeconomic and Fiscal Programming

The Model

A macroeconomic framework includes four sets of projections, on the real sector (i.e., production), the balance of payments, the fiscal accounts and the monetary sector. It is a tool for checking the consistency of the main policy *targets* (usually, the rate of economic growth, inflation and employment) with the assumptions and projections made about the main variables in each of the four sectors—government revenue and expenditure, the balance of payments, the exchange rate, inflation, credit growth, the level and composition of the domestic and internal debt, etc.

Macroeconomic programming has been dominated for more than four decades by a simple but powerful model developed by Jacques Polak and used in virtually all stabilization programs supported by the IMF. (For a readable and short summary see Polak, 1997.) The model is naturally more applicable to complex economies in relatively stable circumstances (for which the basic relationships among monetary, fiscal and real sector aggregates can be presumed to remain approximately constant), than to developing countries in fluid environments—especially fragile states just emerging from conflict. If applied mechanically and without consideration of the economic, social and political realities of the country in question, the model can lead to misleading and sometimes counterproductive policy advice. It has been refined and complemented in various ways, but even in its simplest form the basic model remains a starting point and a useful capacity-building tool—particularly in bringing out the complex interactions among the various aspects of the economy.

The simple model is based on accounting identities and a limited number of relations defined by simple ratios. The main identities are as follows:

GDP	=	private consumption + government consumption (current expenditure) + private investment + government investment + the trade balance (exports minus imports)
Quantity of money	=	domestic credit + foreign reserves
Domestic credit	=	credit to the government + credit to the private sector
Change in foreign reserves	=	balance of trade + net flow of capital (including aid)

The main relations are:

Inflation rate	=	a (change in quantity of money)
Imports	=	m (GDP), where m is the propensity to import goods and services
Quantity of money	=	$1/v$ (GDP), where v is the income velocity of money

When these identities and relations are combined with empirical estimations of the main variables and with the targets set for real GDP growth, inflation, etc., one obtains a framework that comprises the main macroeconomic variables and embodies both the policy priorities and the economic/financial realities.

The main linkages among the different macroeconomic variables are illustrated in Figure 5.2. It is worth reflecting on the nature of the complex interactions in even such a simplified scheme.

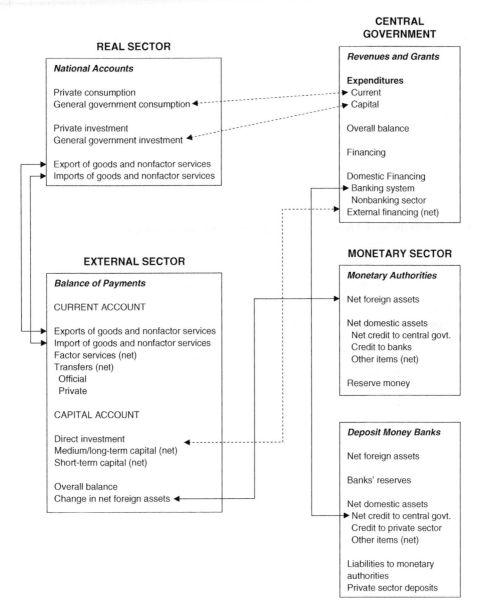

Figure 5.2 Major Linkages among Main Macroeconomic Variables.

Preparing the Macroeconomic Framework

Because of the interaction between policy measures, preparing a macroeconomic framework is an iterative exercise. A set of initial objectives must be defined to establish a preliminary scenario, but the final framework can only be reached through a progressive reconciliation and convergence of all objectives and targets. The problems revealed by the initial projections (e.g., lack of consistency between economic growth targets and external trade policy, or between developments in certain sectors and the overall GDP growth rate target) must be resolved by appropriate adjustments in the targets and/or additional policy measures, leading to revising the initial scenario. Such iterations should continue until overall consistency is achieved for the macroeconomic framework as a whole. The iteration process is also a capacity-building tool, to improve the understanding of the government staff involved—and therefore elicit their cooperation in formulating a realistic budget and implementing it correctly.

The preparation of a macroeconomic framework is not a one-shot event but a semi-permanent activity: a consistent framework is needed at the start of each budget cycle to give adequate guidelines to the line ministries, but during budget execution the macroeconomic projections require frequent updating to assess the impact of exogenous changes or slippages in budget implementation. The risks related to unexpected changes in macroeconomic parameters must be assessed and possible policy responses identified. In 2015, for example, oil-exporting countries that made timely adjustments in response to the sharp drop in the price of oil coped with the decline in revenue much better than those that stuck for too long to the initial framework, prepared on the assumption of the oil price remaining at the same level as at the end of 2014.

Making the Macroeconomic Projections Public and Credible

In addition to the assurance that the macroeconomic program is consistent, internally and with the government policy goals, the proof of the pudding remains the same: the program (and the budget within it) needs to be implemented. This calls among other things for building "ownership" by the political leadership as well as the legislature and the public. Thus, internal consultations within the executive branch are critical, and at an appropriate time before the start of the annual budget preparation the macroeconomic framework should be explained to and debated by the legislature.

The legislature and the population at large have a right to know clearly the government's policy objectives, expectations and targets, not only to increase transparency and accountability, but also to reach a modicum of consensus. Although such a consensus may take additional time and require difficult debates, it will support the effective implementation of the program.

For this, the macroeconomic and fiscal projections must be credible. In some countries, the government projections are submitted to a panel of independent and respected experts to ensure their reliability and to remove them from partisan politics, while preserving the confidentiality required for a few sensitive issues. In other countries, such as the United Kingdom, the projections are validated by the independent auditor-general. In most developing countries, the macroeconomic and fiscal projections are developed with the support of external aid organizations, which gives them a measure of credibility. In some countries, such as Tanzania, this cooperation has become close enough to make the formulation of the macroeconomic framework a virtual partnership.

Annex 2: Government Finances, Worldwide, 2014
(in billion US$ equivalent and percent)

Country	Revenue ($ billion)	Expenditure ($ billion)	Balance ($ billion)	GDP ($ billion)	Balance as % of GDP
Afghanistan	0.9	2.7	−1.8	20.0	−9.0
Albania	3.3	3.7	−0.4	13.2	−3.0
Algeria	73.7	78.6	−4.9	166.9	−2.9
Andorra	1.0	1.0	0.0	3.2	0.0
Angola	47.1	55.8	−11.7	138.4	−8.5
Antigua and Barbuda	0.1	145.9	0.0	1.2	0.0
Argentina	105.8	113.3	−7.5	548.1	−1.4
Armenia	2.3	2.6	−0.3	11.6	−2.6
Australia	487.7	519.6	−31.9	1,339.5	−2.4
Austria	217.9	228.4	−10.5	374.1	−2.8
Azerbaijan	18.5	19.5	−1.1	75.2	−1.5
Bahamas	1.0	1.0	—	—	—
Bahrain	7.5	8.4	−0.9	33.9	−2.7
Bangladesh	12.7	17.2	−4.5	172.9	−2.6
Barbados	0.8	0.9	0.0	4.4	0.0
Belarus	30.5	29.7	0.8	76.1	1.1
Belgium	276.8	293.4	−16.6	454	−3.7
Belize	0.3	0.4	0.0	1.7	0.0
Benin	1.4	1.7	−0.3	9.6	−3.1
Bermuda	—	—	—	5.6	—
Bhutan	0.3	0.4	−0.1	2.0	−5.0
Bolivia	17.0	18.1	−0.1	33.0	−0.3
Bosnia & Herzegovina	8.4	9.0	−0.6	18.5	−3.2
Botswana	5.6	6.2	−0.6	15.8	−3.8
Brazil	876.5	891.2	−14.7	1,774.7	−0.8
Brunei	5.5	5.8	−0.3	17.1	−1.8
Bulgaria	18.1	19.2	−1.1	56.7	−1.9
Burkina Faso	2.2	2.6	−0.4	12.5	−3.2
Burma	13.0	15.2	−2.3	—	—
Burundi	0.3	0.4	−0.1	3.1	−3.2
Cambodia	2.0	2.7	−0.7	16.8	−4.2
Cameroon	5.0	5.3	−0.3	32.1	−0.9
Canada	675.8	717.8	−42.0	1,550.5	−2.7
Cape Verde	0.5	0.6	−0.1	1.9	−5.3
Central African Rep.	0.3	0.3	0.0	1.7	0.0
Chad	2.5	3.5	−0.1	13.9	−0.7
Chile	58.5	61.3	−2.8	240.2	−1.2
China	2,285.0	2,469.0	−174.0	10,866.4	−1.6
Colombia	89.9	97.8	−7.9	292.1	−2.7
Comoros	—	—	—	0.6	—
Costa Rica	5.8	8.1	−2.3	49.6	−4.6
Côte d'Ivoire	4.4	6.3	−1.9	34.3	−5.5
Croatia	19.9	22.3	−2.5	57.1	−4.4
Cuba	43.6	46.2	−2.6	77.2	−3.4
Cyprus	10.4	12.0	−1.6	23.3	−6.9
Czech Republic	51.5	59.4	−8.0	181.8	−4.4
Dem. Rep. of Congo	0.7	2.0	−0.1	33.1	−0.3

(Continued)

Annex 2: (continued)

Country	Revenue ($ billion)	Expenditure ($ billion)	Balance ($ billion)	GDP ($ billion)	Balance as % of GDP
Denmark	118.3	127.5	−9.2	295.2	−3.1
Djibouti	0.1	0.2	0.0	1.6	0.0
Dominica	0.7	0.8	0.0	0.5	0.0
Dominican Republic	8.0	9.5	−1.5	64.1	−2.3
Ecuador	18.6	22.3	−3.7	100.9	−3.7
Egypt	72.7	95.7	−23.0	330.8	−6.7
El Salvador	4.4	5.3	−0.9	25.2	−3.6
Equatorial Guinea	5.2	6.3	−1.1	15.5	−3.6
Eritrea	0.2	0.5	−0.3	—	—
Estonia	9.8	9.9	−0.1	26.5	−0.4
Ethiopia	5.4	6.0	−0.6	55.6	−1.1
European Union	—	—	—	18,460.6	—
Faroe Islands	—	—	—	2.6	—
Fed. States Micronesia	—	—	—	0.3	—
Fiji	0.9	1.1	−0.2	4.5	−4.4
Finland	151.4	160.0	−8.6	272.2	−3.2
France	1,507.5	1,631.0	−124.5	2,421.7	−5.1
Gabon	5.3	5.5	−0.2	18.2	−1.1
Gambia	0.2	0.2	0.0	—	—
Georgia	5.4	10.1	−4.7	16.5	−26.7
Germany	1,721.0	1,696.0	25.0	3,355.8	0.7
Ghana	8.8	10.4	−1.6	38.6	−4.2
Greece	109.0	117.4	−8.4	235.6	−3.6
Greenland	—	—	—	2.4	—
Grenada	0.1	0.1	0.0	0.9	0.0
Guatemala	5.5	6.9	−1.4	58.8	−2.4
Guinea	0.3	0.8	−0.5	6.6	−7.6
Guinea Bissau	—	—	—	1.2	—
Guyana	0.5	0.5	−0.1	3.1	−3.2
Haiti	0.8	1.0	−0.1	8.7	−1.1
Honduras	3.0	3.7	−0.7	19.4	−3.6
Hong Kong	—	—	—	309.9	—
Hungary	65.2	68.7	−3.5	138.3	−2.5
Iceland	5.9	6.5	−0.6	17.0	−3.5
India	280.5	434.6	−154.0	2,073.5	−7.4
Indonesia	234.7	256.9	−22.3	861.9	−2.6
Iran	62.1	67.1	−5.0	425.3	−1.2
Iraq	86.0	97.6	−11.5	223.5	−5.1
Ireland	75.9	97.9	−22.0	238.0	−9.2
Israel	66.7	74.8	−8.1	296.1	−2.7
Italy	990.0	1,055.0	−65.0	1,814.8	−3.6
Jamaica	3.8	4.7	−0.9	13.9	−6.5
Japan	1,512.0	1,840.0	−328.0	4,123.3	−8.0
Jordan	5.9	9.6	−3.7	35.8	−10.3
Kazakhstan	36.6	40.5	−3.9	184.4	−2.1
Kenya	16.8	19.5	−2.7	60.9	−4.4
Kiribati	0.1	0.1	0.0	0.2	0.0
Kosovo	1.7	2.1	−0.4	7.4	−5.4
Kuwait	87.6	75.3	12.3	163.6	7.5
Kyrgyzstan	—	—	—	7.4	—

Annex 2: (continued)

Country	Revenue ($ billion)	Expenditure ($ billion)	Balance ($ billion)	GDP ($ billion)	Balance as % of GDP
Laos	0.8	1.0	−0.1	12.0	−0.8
Latvia	9.9	11.1	−1.2	31.3	−3.8
Lebanon	9.3	11.7	−2.4	45.7	−5.3
Lesotho	0.5	0.5	0.0	2.2	0.0
Liberia	—	—	—	2.0	—
Libya	18.2	32.0	−13.8	41.1	−33.6
Liechtenstein	1.0	1.0	0.1	5.5	1.8
Lithuania	14.2	16.3	−2.1	48.4	−4.3
Luxembourg	25.0	25.5	−0.5	64.9	−0.8
Macau	—	—	—	55.5	—
Macedonia	3.1	3.4	−0.3	11.3	−2.7
Madagascar	1.6	1.7	−0.1	10.6	−0.9
Malawi	1.8	1.8	0.0	4.3	0.0
Malaysia	68.1	79.6	−11.5	296.2	−3.9
Maldives	0.8	0.9	−0.1	3.1	−3.2
Mali	2.2	2.6	−0.4	12.0	−3.3
Malta	4.7	4.9	−0.2	9.6	−2.1
Marshall Islands	—	—	—	0.2	—
Mauritania	0.8	0.8	0.0	5.1	0.0
Mauritius	2.4	2.8	−0.4	12.6	−3.2
Mexico	299.6	340.6	−41.0	1,144.3	−3.6
Moldova	2.7	2.7	0.0	8.0	0.0
Monaco	0.9	0.9	−0.1	—	—
Mongolia	3.4	3.5	−0.1	12.0	−0.8
Montenegro	—	—	—	4.6	—
Morocco	25.7	31.4	−5.7	110.0	−5.2
Mozambique	3.7	4.2	−0.5	15.9	−3.1
Myanmar	—	—	—	64.3	—
Namibia	3.7	4.9	−1.2	13.0	−9.2
Nauru	0.0	0.0	0.0	—	—
Nepal	6.3	9.7	−3.4	19.8	−17.2
Netherlands	390.2	410.4	−20.2	752.5	−2.7
New Zealand	60.9	74.7	−13.8	200.0	−6.9
Nicaragua	1.4	1.6	−0.2	11.8	−1.7
Niger	0.3	0.3	0.0	8.2	0.0
Nigeria	19.3	30.0	−10.7	481.1	−22.2
North Korea	3.2	3.3	−0.1	—	—
Norway	273.9	228.4	45.5	388.3	11.7
Oman	40.1	37.7	2.4	81.8	2.9
Pakistan	48.0	51.5	−16.5	243.6	−6.8
Palau	—	—	—	0.3	—
Panama	7.8	8.5	−0.7	46.2	−1.5
Papua New Guinea	4.2	4.2	0.0	16.9	0.0
Paraguay	5.5	6.2	−0.7	30.9	−4.1
Peru	65.6	65.9	−0.3	192.1	−0.2
Philippines	31.4	36.0	−4.6	284.8	−1.6
Poland	85.3	99.9	−14.6	474.8	−3.1
Portugal	110.8	120.2	−9.4	230.1	−4.1
Puerto Rico	—	—	—	103.1	—
Qatar	92.5	58.5	33.9	166.9	20.3

(Continued)

Annex 2: (continued)

Country	Revenue ($ billion)	Expenditure ($ billion)	Balance ($ billion)	GDP ($ billion)	Balance as % of GDP
Republic of the Congo	4.8	5.9	–1.1	14.2	–7.7
Romania	59.6	67.4	–7.8	199.0	–3.9
Russia	428.6	440.1	–11.5	1,326.0	–0.9
Rwanda	2.8	—	—	7.9	—
Saint Kitts and Nevis	0.1	0.1	0.0	0.9	0.0
Saint Lucia	0.1	0.1	0.0	1.4	0.0
S.Vincent & Grenadines	0.2	0.2	0.0	0.7	0.0
Samoa	0.3	0.3	0.0	0.8	0.0
San Marino	0.7	0.7	–0.1	—	—
S.Tome and Principe	0.1	0.1	0.0	0.3	0.0
Saudi Arabia	278.9	293.3	–14.4	646	–2.2
Senegal	3.3	4.3	–1.0	15.7	–6.4
Serbia	17.6	19.6	–2.0	43.9	–4.6
Seychelles	0.3	0.3	0.0	1.4	0.0
Sierra Leone	0.1	0.4	–0.3	4.9	–6.1
Singapore	47.4	43.3	4.1	292.8	1.4
Slovakia	32.5	37.8	–5.3	100.3	–5.3
Slovenia	21.3	23.5	–2.2	49.5	–4.4
Solomon Islands	—	—	—	1.2	—
Somalia	—	—	—	5.8	—
South Africa	102.8	118.3	–15.5	312.8	–5.0
South Korea	350.7	337.9	12.8	1,377.9	0.9
South Sudan	—	—	—	13.3	—
Spain	531.7	613.2	–81.5	1,199.1	–6.8
Sri Lanka	8.5	12.6	–4.1	78.8	–5.2
Sudan	6.6	9.0	–2.5	73.8	–3.4
Suriname	—	—	—	5.2	—
Swaziland	1.0	1.5	–0.5	4.4	–11.4
Sweden	291.0	301.7	–10.7	492.6	–2.2
Switzerland	231.1	229.3	1.8	664.7	0.3
Syria	11.7	17.9	–6.2	—	—
Taiwan	75.3	90.7	–15.4	—	—
Tajikistan	1.8	1.8	0.0	9.2	0.0
Tanzania	4.6	6.1	–1.5	48.1	–3.1
Thailand	71.3	79.6	–8.3	395.3	–2.1
Timor-Leste	0.3	2.0	–1.5	1.4	–107.1
Togo	0.6	0.6	–0.1	4.5	–2.2
Tonga	0.1	0.1	0.0	0.4	0.0
Trinidad and Tobago	7.3	8.1	–0.8	28.9	–2.8
Tunisia	10.2	12.8	–1.6	48.6	–3.3
Turkey	194.5	204.9	–10.4	718.2	–1.4
Turkmenistan	4.2	4.1	0.1	47.9	0.2
Tuvalu	0.0	0.0	0.0	0.0	0.0
Uganda	2.4	3.4	–0.1	27.0	–0.4
Ukraine	38.4	44.0	–5.6	131.8	–4.2
United Arab Emirates	150.8	130.9	19.9	370.3	5.4
United Kingdom	936.2	1,106.0	–170.9	2,848.8	–6.0
United States	3,199.9	3,520.5	–491.8	17,947.0	–2.7
Uruguay	13.6	14.0	–0.4	57.5	–0.7

Annex 2: (continued)

Country	Revenue ($ billion)	Expenditure ($ billion)	Balance ($ billion)	GDP ($ billion)	Balance as % of GDP
Uzbekistan	18.3	18.2	0.1	62.6	0.2
Vanuatu	0.2	0.2	0.0	0.8	0.0
Vatican City	0.3	0.3	0.0	—	—
Venezuela	90.7	106.1	−15.4	371.3	−4.1
Vietnam	32.8	35.7	−2.9	186.2	−1.6
West Bank and Gaza	—	—	—	12.7	—
Yemen	7.3	10.6	−3.3	36.0	−9.2
Zambia	3.6	4.4	−0.8	27.1	−3.0
Zimbabwe	3.7	4.6	−0.9	14.2	−6.3

Note: — indicates data not available.

Sources: World Bank for GDP; CIA World Factbook for fiscal data; supplemented/confirmed by national government websites in certain cases.

Notes

1 In the early 1930s, competitive currency devaluations helped spread the Great Depression internationally and compounded its effects. Accordingly, a fixed exchange rate "Bretton Woods" system was devised in the postwar period and operated until 1973—with exchange rate changes taking place very infrequently.

2 In Europe, the introduction of the euro in 1999 ruled out devaluation altogether as a tool of economic adjustment, underlining the short-term tradeoff between fiscal stability and economic growth in a common-currency area.

3 This has remained the view in some countries. In Southeast and East Asia, the "Asian Tigers" (Singapore, Taiwan, Korea and Hong Kong) have continued successfully the pattern of pervasive state guidance of economic activity and interpenetration between public and private sectors. Each of these four countries, however, has unique characteristics that do not permit generalizing from their experience.

4 Measures on the revenue side should eschew short-term tax increases in favor of actions that broaden the tax base and raise the elasticity of the tax system with a view to long-term revenue expansion.

5 The extent of the downsizing can be seen, among other things, in the sharp reduction in government employment worldwide from the peaks of the early 1980s—see Schiavo-Campo, de Tommaso and Mukherjee (1997).

6 In developed countries, the fiscal consolidation that followed the 2008–12 Great Recession and the effect of demographic changes implies future shrinking of expenditure other than pensions by almost one-fifth by 2030, unless additional revenue is mobilized. The magnitude of the challenge requires planning beyond the annual budget and cooperation by many entities in addition to actions by the ministries of finance (Marcel, 2014.)

7 Gross investment is the increase in the stock of physical capital—roads, bridges, etc. Because physical assets lose value over the years, either physically from their use or economically from technological advances, the increase in productive capacity should be measured on a net basis: net investment is gross investment minus depreciation.

8 In countries experiencing very high inflation, a further indicator of fiscal position is the *operational deficit*, which is equal to the cash deficit less the inflationary portion of interest payments. Calculating the inflationary component of interest payments is not an easy matter, however, and this indicator is not generally useful.

9 The exceptions are extractive-resource exporters, whose surpluses can be salted away for a future time when the extractive resources are exhausted or when the revenue is so high relative to the country's population as to make it difficult to increase government spending in any productive way.

10 For an extensive discussion of the subject, see Schiavo-Campo (2012).

11 Albert O. Hirschman (see, for example, his *Strategy of Economic Development*, 1958) was one of the first development economists to understand that institutional factors and information

are as or more important than the conventional physical factors of production (labor, capital, materials).

12 This approach is similar to the situation in pre-revolutionary Tunisia, for example. A novel feature introduced with the 2007–11 plan was that projections are made for a longer period and then "backtracked" to the plan period for greater realism. Moreover, reviews and revisions of the plan are comparatively frequent.

13 The World Bank/IMF terminology comprises a medium-term fiscal framework (MTFF), a medium-term budget framework (MTBF), and a medium-term performance framework (MTPF). To link the discussion to the budget classifications described in Chapter 2 (and avoid drowning in acronyms), we use descriptive terms for the three main variants: MTEF is used as the umbrella term, "forecasting" MTEF corresponds to the medium-term fiscal framework, "functional" (or "organizational") MTEF" corresponds to the medium-term budget framework, and "programmatic MTEF" corresponds to the medium-term performance framework.

14 The country would commit to certain policies for the whole period of the arrangement, and agree annually on the measures to be taken. The period was usually three years, and repayments were spread over 5–10 years. The performance criteria of EFFs were comparable to the narrow criteria of standby arrangements, but, in the late 1980s, the Enhanced Structural Adjustment Facility expanded the EFF by adding structural measures, and further deepening was achieved later with the new Poverty Reduction and Growth Facility. The goal of balance-of-payments viability was replaced with the broader goal of macroeconomic sustainability, and consequently the requirement to define medium-term fiscal projections became stronger.

15 In practice, this weakened the focus on the outyears and produced a certain tolerance for rosy optimism, with viability or sustainability routinely "expected" for the year *after* the end of the IMF program. This criticism is implicit in the conclusion of the review of IMF-supported adjustment programs that such programs would benefit from consistent medium-term scenarios of economic and fiscal prospects, which would in turn permit assessing the adequacy of adjustment and realism of the investment and growth targets (Schadler et al., 1993 and 1996).

16 For technical issues not discussed here—e.g., the length of the MTEF period (current year plus two, at a minimum); the inclusion in the MTEF outyears of a contingency reserve (which should be small, in any case); the use of current or constant prices for the projections (current prices are on balance preferable); the inclusion of expected "efficiency dividends" (possible in advanced countries, but not in developing countries); and others—see Schiavo-Campo (2012).

17 Sweden had a two-stage process, under which parliament adopted in the spring spending ceilings for the next three years. Three months later, detailed estimates were presented to parliament. In 2002, the system was abandoned, as parliament no longer wanted to conduct two budget debates each year. The government presents proposals for budgetary policy in April, eight months before the start of the fiscal year, without specification of multiyear ceilings, and the full budget proposal in September (Lienert, 2010).

18 There are also indications that expenditure volatility in certain sectors was reduced (Vlaicu, Verhoeven, Grigoli and Mills, 2014).

Bibliography

Bouder, Frederic, 2000. "Public Administration Improvements in OECD Countries," in S. Schiavo-Campo and P. Sundaram, eds., *To Serve and to Preserve: Improving Public Administration in a Competitive World*. Manila: Asian Development Bank.

Brumby, Jim, et al., 2012. *Lessons on Implementing MTEFs Around the World*. Washington, DC: The World Bank.

The Concord Coalition, 2005. *New York Times Week in Review*, December 11.

Di Francesco, Michael and Rafael Barroso, 2015. "Bottom-up Costing within Medium-term Expenditure Frameworks," *Public Budgeting and Finance*, 35(3), 44–67.

Fölscher, Alta, 2007. "Country Case Study: South Africa," in Anwar Shah ed., *Budgeting and Budgetary Institutions*. Washington, DC: The World Bank.

Hemming, Richard, Jay-Hyung Kim and Sang-Hyop Lee, eds., 2012. *Sustainability and Efficiency in Managing Public Expenditures*. Seoul: Korea Development Institute.

Hirschman, Albert, 1958. *The Strategy of Economic Development*. New Haven, CT: Yale University Press.

International Monetary Fund, 2006. *Fiscal Adjustment for Stability and Growth*. Washington, DC: IMF.

Lienert, Ian, 2010. *Role of the Legislature in Budget Processes*. Washington, DC: IMF.

McFerson, Hazel, 2007. "Legal Transplants and Institutional Development in Sub-Saharan Africa," in *Encyclopedia of Law and Society American and Global Perspectives*. Thousand Oaks, CA: Sage Publications.

Marcel, Mario, 2014. "Budgeting for Fiscal Space and Government Performance Beyond the Great Recession," *OECD Journal of Budgeting*, 13(2), 9–47.

Mauro, Paolo, 2011. *Chipping Away at Public Debt: Sources of Failure and Keys to Success in Fiscal Adjustment*. Hoboken, NJ: Wiley.

Polak, Jacques, 1997. "The IMF Monetary Model: A Hardy Perennial," *Finance and Development*. *IMF Working Papers*, 97/49, December–April.

Schadler, Susan, F. Rozwadowski, Siddharth Timari and David O. Robinson, 1993. "Economic Adjustment in Low-Income Countries: Experience Under the Enhanced Structural Adjustment Facility," *IMF Occasional Papers*, 106. Washington, DC: IMF.

Schadler, Susan, Adam Bennett, S. Carkovic, María Vicenta, Louis Dicks-Mireaux, Mecagni, Mauro, John James Hubert and Miguel A. Savastano, 1996. "IMF Conditionality Review: Experience Under Stand-by and Extended Arrangements," *IMF Occasional Papers*, 128. Washington, DC: IMF.

Schiavo-Campo, S., 2012. "Of Mountains and Molehills: The Medium-term Expenditure Framework," in Richard Hemming, Jay-Hyung Kim and Sang-Hyop Lee, eds., *Sustainability and Efficiency in Managing Public Expenditures*. Seoul: Korea Development Institute.

Schiavo-Campo, S. and Hans W. Singer, 1970. *Perspectives of Economic Development*. Boston: Houghton-Mifflin.

Schiavo-Campo, S., Giulio de Tommaso and A. Mukherjee, 1997. "An International Statistical Survey of Government Employment and Wages," *Policy Research Working Paper*, 1806, Washington, DC: The World Bank, August.

Tommasi, Daniel, 2010. *Gestion des Depenses Publiques dans les Pays en Developpement*. Paris: Agence Francaise de Developpement.

Vlaicu, R., M. Verhoevenb, F. Grigolic and Z. Mills, 2014. "Multiyear Budgets and Fiscal Performance: Panel Data Evidence," *Journal of Public Economics*, 111, 79–95.

Wildavsky, Aaron, 1993. *National Budgeting for Economic and Monetary Union*. Leiden: Nijhoff.

World Bank, 1997. *The State in a Changing World*. World Development Report. Washington, DC: The World Bank.

——, 2011. *Review of Experience with Medium-Term Expenditure Frameworks*. Public Sector Governance Group, November.

6 Preparation and Approval of the Budget

Rise from a meal neither thirsty nor drunk.

(Aristotle)

Introduction

The process of budget preparation is aimed primarily at fulfilling the first two objectives of public financial management: aggregate expenditure control and strategic allocation of resources. The third objective—operational and public service efficiency—underpins budget execution and procurement (see Chapters 8 and 9, as well as Chapter 12 on performance). The budget preparation process is guided by the following three principles, flowing from basic economics and politics.

Avoid Magical Thinking

With unlimited time and resources, everything can be accomplished: anything that benefits somebody in some way deserves public money, and choices are unnecessary. This magical thinking is found every day in debates about public money. But resources are not unlimited, even in the richest countries; money spent for one purpose to benefit a particular group is not available for another purpose to benefit a different group. Choices must be made—deliberately, at lower cost and better chance of implementation, or by default, at greater cost and ineffective implementation. Budgeting must embed these realities, through systems and a process that leads to making better and more informed choices *because* they fit within the resources that are likely to be available.

Beware of Technocratic Delusions

"We" decide how much and where to spend. The problem is that within the collective "we" there are always winners and losers from any change in expenditure. In considering budget proposals the gains to some groups must be balanced against the losses to other groups—keeping in mind the national interest and long-term risks. There are no "objective" economic, financial or technical solutions to this balancing act. One hears sometimes the wish to "get the politics out of the budget process" and leave it to the experts. This wish is not only impossible but wrong, because legitimate policy decisions can only be made by the country's political leadership (hopefully a representative one). An apolitical budget preparation process is an oxymoron.

Good budget preparation does not take politics out of the process, but confines the politics to the start of the process—when the key policy decisions are made—and towards the end of the process, when coherent proposals consistent with those policy decisions are submitted to the political leadership for its consideration and disposition. In between, no partisan political interference should be allowed, precisely to allow the executive branch of government to prepare a budget that is consistent with the policy choices made by the government as a whole. Micro-interference by politicians in the midst of the budget preparation process weakens the political relevance of the budget, as it distorts it away from the policy choices made at the beginning. In practice, of course, partisan or patronage interference is all too common; the idea is to reduce it to a realistic minimum.

Don't Confuse Fiscal Problems with Budget Management Problems

Fiscal problems emerge from a mismatch between revenues and expenditure, and call for changes in *policy*—either mobilization of additional revenue or expenditure reductions or a judicious combination of both. Technical *budgeting* problems emerge from badly estimated revenue or expenditure, and call for changes in *management and methodology*. The distinction is important in order to understand that the most advanced methods and technical practices of budgeting cannot make up for inconsistent public policy or paralysis of political decision-making. Thus, rich countries can and often do have loose and incoherent budgets and, conversely, a poor country can manage its public finances well. The former case is illustrated by Greece, Italy and the US, and the latter case by Costa Rica, Bhutan and Botswana—indeed, before the discovery of large-scale deposits of diamonds Botswana was very poor, but the government budget was managed carefully and realistically. Indeed, the poorer the country the less it can afford to mismanage its public finances.

Four Requirements of Budget Preparation

Consistent with the above principles, the four interrelated requirements of good government budget preparation are: realistic estimates of revenue and aggregate expenditure; a medium-term perspective; the need for early decisions; and the setting of initial spending ceilings.

Realistic Initial Estimates

To be an effective instrument of public financial policy, the government budget must in the first place be credible; to be credible it must be realistic; and to be realistic it must be affordable. As previewed in Chapter 5, good management of public expenditure starts with a good estimate of *revenue*. "Fiscal marksmanship"—that is, the accuracy of forecasts as shown by the closeness of actual outcomes to the original estimates—is a key indicator of the quality of the budget preparation system.

On the revenue side, overestimation can come not only from technical factors, such as an incorrect appraisal of the impact of a change in tax policy, but often also from the desire of politicians or spending ministries to inflate revenue estimates in order to keep in their budget an excessive number of activities—with the intention of later requesting more money, or of using political pull to crowd out other ministries' expenditures. Overestimating revenues tends to affect adversely the effectiveness of public expenditure, since the subsequent cuts necessarily fall on the types of spending that can be curtailed more easily, rather than on the types of spending which are less important.

On the expenditure side, underestimation can come from unrealistic assessments of the cost of activities, but can also be a deliberate tactic to launch new programs. There is a natural reluctance in government to abandon a program after it has started—despite the basic rule of economics that one should never throw good money after bad. When this reluctance is combined with bureaucratic and political momentum as well as the vested interests that have been created, the expenditure program can continue for years even when there is a broad consensus that it is ineffective and wasteful.[1] No technical or methodological improvement can by itself resolve institutional and political problems of this nature. It is that much more important, therefore, to create in the system robust gatekeeping to prevent bad projects and programs from getting started in the first place. By the time they are in the budget pipeline, it is usually too late to stop them.

In the household analogy, planning the family's annual expenditure based on the vague hope of a big salary raise may mean maxing out the credit card and/or cutting wherever possible—perhaps preventive medical expenses or car maintenance. Similarly, planning to remodel the kitchen but underestimating the cost is likely to leave the new kitchen an incomplete wreck.

A Medium-Term Perspective

Chapter 5 explained why and how the process of preparing the annual budget should take place within a medium-term expenditure perspective. (In developed countries, a four- or five-year forecast is feasible; in developing countries, where the situation is more fluid and capacity more limited, a forecast covering two years beyond the coming budget year is as long as can reasonably be expected.) However, medium-term projections are neither necessary nor sufficient to improve the annual budget process and the quality of expenditure. It is quite possible—in fact it is frequent—to have some type of MTEF in place even though the annual budget preparation process is a mess. The best medium-term fiscal projections cannot remedy basic weaknesses in the annual budget process any more than a shining new faucet can fix a clogged sink. On the contrary, experience has shown that premature or ill-advised introduction of an MTEF has served in several countries to divert attention away from basic problems in their annual budgeting process, and to that extent has perpetuated those problems instead of helping resolve them.

The head of the household can design realistic long-term plans to pay for college tuition but if the annual family budgeting process is weak the annual savings required to finance those plans will not materialize and the kids are unlikely to go to college.

Timely Decisions and Political Responsibility

Budget decisions can be made, at a cost, or avoided, at greater cost. Political vacillation, partisan agendas, administrative weakness, lack of needed information, often lead to postponing these hard decisions until budget execution—which only leads to an inefficient budget process and raises fiscal risks to boot.

In the household analogy, if the monthly payments under an adjustable rate mortgage are known to go up in the near future, postponing the hard decisions to take a second job and/or curtail some spending may mean losing the home to foreclosure.

If this is so obvious, why would presumably responsible politicians postpone making necessary decisions? The answer rests in what economists call a divergence between private and social cost. Unlike the ostrich that hides its head in the sand and gets run over by the truck, the individual politician rarely pays a political price for *not* taking a position. When elected representatives know that they will bear the political cost of a controversial decision but will not reap political benefit from doing so, they tend to avoid it. This is not admirable but is rational from their individual viewpoint—the private cost of avoiding decisions is minimal even though the social cost in terms of wasted and misallocated resources is large. Each person may understand the problem quite well, but has no incentive to do anything about it except to complain about "the system." The easy answer is to raise the political cost of avoiding decisions and lower the cost of confronting them. In theory, that is. In practice, this is exceedingly difficult. Because in a democracy the framework of political incentives is set, directly and indirectly, by the people themselves, in a sense one can say that the people get the budget they deserve.

The influence of the divergence between private and social cost in the budgeting process has found one of its most extreme manifestations in the United States—where gerrymandering and political polarization mean that elected politicians have much more to fear from a primary opponent accusing them of insufficient partisanship than from the candidate of the opposing party in the general election. This makes it hard to contribute to the political compromises that are inherent in responsible budgeting. Major changes to electoral rules would be required to resolve the problem—mainly, independently determined electoral districts, automatic voter registration upon reaching voting age, and open primaries where all candidates participate regardless of political party affiliation.

Initial Spending Ceilings

The prerequisite to good budget preparation is to move the actors in the budgeting process away from a "wishlist" mentality to an "affordability" mentality. A wish-based budget preparation process starts by inviting requests from spending agencies without any indications of their financial constraints. An affordability-based process instead begins with top-down allocation of the available resources among the government agencies—spending ceilings for each agency. It is critical to emphasize that this is only the starting point of an iterative process which *must include consideration of additional taxes and not just expenditure cuts.* (Recall from Chapter 5 that the components of the macroeconomic framework and all major policy measures are interrelated.) Leaving aside for the purposes of this book on expenditure management the issue of revenue increases, a sound process of annual expenditure preparation is described next.

A Good Budget Preparation Process

Note at the outset that good practice in government budgeting is not always reflected in reality. On the contrary, violations of one or another aspect of the process are common, in rich and poor countries alike. It is important, however, to describe what good budget preparation should be, to serve as a guide for practical improvements toward the vision of the optimal process. (The following process was first articulated by Schiavo-Campo and Tommasi, 1999, then echoed in various other publications, and subsequently validated by empirical studies—e.g., Hallerberg et al., 2009.)

A good budget preparation process should flow from the elaboration of the macroeconomic and fiscal framework to the instructions by the ministry of finance on the format of budget proposals and the expenditure limits for each ministry; then the ministries' preparation of their budget proposals; negotiations on those proposals with the ministry of finance; decisions by the political leadership about major disagreements; endorsement of the draft budget by the highest level of the executive branch; and, finally, presentation to and debate and approval by the legislature. (The steps of the process are listed in Figure 6.1.) The macrofiscal framework has already been described in Chapter 5. Below we focus on the three major stages of budget preparation within the executive branch—top-down, bottom-up and negotiation/iteration—followed by a discussion of the process of legislative debate of the proposed budget and its approval.

Formulation of the draft macroeconomic and fiscal framework
V
Presentation to the legislature, for information and general discussion
V
Approval of the macrofiscal framework by the political leadership
V
Preparation of the expenditure ceilings for each ministry and spending agency
V
Approval of the ceilings by the political leadership
V
Top-down stage: Instructions for budget proposal, including the ceilings and timetable
V
Bottom-up stage: Preparation of budget proposals by each ministry and agency
V
Negotiation stage: Discussion of budget proposals between ministry of finance and each agency
V
Escalation of major disagreements to the political leadership for leadership decisions
V
Possible changes and new revenue and/or expenditure policy measures
V
Revision of the individual budget proposals and preparation of the draft budget
V
Rapid revision of the macrofiscal framework in light of the draft budget and of intervening changes
V
Approval of the revised macrofiscal framework and draft budget by the political leadership
V
Presentation to the legislature
V
Legislative hearings and debate
V
Approval of the budget

Figure 6.1 The Steps of Budget Preparation.

The Top-Down Stage

The aggregate expenditure that is consistent with the fiscal targets within a coherent macro-economic framework is disaggregated into initial allocations to each ministry and spending agency. These ceilings can be "hard" or indicative, depending on the state of advancement of the country's PFM systems and on the political landscape. The ministries' ceilings should be consistent not only with the aggregate expenditure envelope but also with the sector policies.[2] While proposed by the ministry of finance, they must be approved by higher political authority—whether the cabinet, the head of government or an appropriate inter-ministerial group.

It has become customary in the literature and in the practice of international organizations to advise giving each line ministry a "hard ceiling" at the start of budget preparation. A truly hard expenditure ceiling would mean sending back to the ministry, unread, a budget proposal that exceeds the ceiling by even the slightest amount—and requesting a revised proposal that stays within the ceiling. But in the conditions typical of developing countries it is not feasible to jump straight from a wishlist budgeting approach to a genuinely hard ceiling. Ingrained habits and informal norms will cause any such attempt to fail: exceptions are sure to be made to accept a powerful ministry's budget request that exceeds the initial ceiling, and experience shows that a cascade of other exceptions follows—undermining the entire approach and damaging the credibility of the ministry of finance and the process itself.

The logic of the argument for hard spending ceilings is unassailable. The total of budget requests should not be allowed to be in excess of available revenues, or the internal consistency of the entire macrofiscal framework would be jeopardized; also, ministries do require a clear and early indication of available resources if they are to put together realistic budget proposals. The question is how to get there. What is important is to provide at the start an indication of the resource envelope for each ministry and spending agency, even if the indication is tentative and is not expected to be enforced to the letter. Progressively, such soft indications can be grounded on better and better estimates every year and correspondingly made "harder," until the data, capacity and organizational culture have improved sufficiently to permit setting a truly "hard ceiling" at the start of the process—and then enforcing it.

The evolution from a wish list to an affordability approach could also be encouraged by giving more favorable consideration to the budget requests of ministries that come closer to the initial indicative ceiling, or comprise better quality proposals, or achieve savings in certain activities to finance expansion of others. This approach can only succeed, however, if there is a resolve by the ministry of finance—with support from the highest political levels—to continuously improve the process and reward ministries appropriately for staying within the ceilings or for better-quality proposals. This gradual approach is different from the two-step practice of a few countries, which first allow the line ministries to submit unconstrained budget proposals and then—after a brief review of the preliminary requests—to notify them of binding expenditure ceilings. This two-step approach is likely to simply default to a wishlist process because, by the time the initial budget requests have been formulated on an unconstrained basis, the chance of a disciplined budget process has gone. It is much better to have a soft ceiling at the start of the budget preparation process than no ceiling at all at the start followed by a make-believe hard ceiling weeks or months later.

Preparing the initial expenditure ceilings is largely an incremental exercise. As explained in Chapter 2, "zero-based" budgeting is a chimera. Budgets are never prepared from scratch. In fact, the true discretionary margin is very limited. Debt servicing obligations, multiyear investment commitments, pensions and other entitlements, rigidities in personnel management, the plain reality that a government cannot stop all funding for its schools, health centers, the army, etc., limit the possible annual changes. The largest portion of the sector expenditure ceilings is thus a judicious (not mechanical) projection of the financial implications of existing programs and commitments.

The question arises whether to set a single ceiling for each sector—combining current and investment expenditure—or two separate ones. Obviously, if only an overall spending ceiling is set, line ministries are enabled to make tradeoffs between their current and capital spending requests, whereas with separate subceilings the distribution between current and capital spending is set from the center.[3] The answer to that question depends on the sector concerned. In certain sectors, such as primary education, the choice of submitting a combined current/investment budget proposal may be left to the line ministry, which presumably understands better than the ministry of finance how to allocate resources most efficiently in its sector. In other cases, when the sector budget depends to a significant extent on the decision to launch a large investment project of national importance (e.g., the budget of a ministry of health would largely depend on the decision to build a large new hospital), a separate subceiling on capital expenditure would be appropriate. In general, as explained in Chapter 7, a reasonably good public investment programming process will produce a coherent capital budget, thus entailing a subceiling on capital expenditure in every ministry. (Depending on country circumstances and policy priorities, separate subceilings may also be needed for other expenditure categories—normally personnel expenditures and certain subsidies.)

Diminishing Fiscal Space in High-Income Countries: An Important Digression

Over the past 50 years, the growth in entitlement expenditure has caused in most developed countries increasing rigidity in expenditure composition, and hence a shrinkage of the discretionary margin to be allocated through the annual budget. This development can be measured by means an "Index of Fiscal Democracy," developed by Eugene Steuerle and Tim Roeper (Steuerle, 2010). The index measures fiscal flexibility by the percentage of total federal spending that is not absorbed by interest payments or expected entitlement expenditure on social security, Medicare/Medicaid and other entitlements. At one extreme, in the absence of any government debt and with no entitlement programs whatsoever, the index would be 100; at the other extreme, if all expenditure is expected to be absorbed by interest payments and entitlements, the index would be zero—meaning that there is no flexibility at all in government spending, and hence that "budgeting" is a simple technical exercise of projecting the amounts of mandatory expenditure in future years.

In 1960s America, the Steuerle–Roeper index averaged about 35 percent—meaning that almost two-thirds of federal expenditure was discretionary; in the 1980s, it had risen to over 50 percent; as of 2015 it was just over 80 percent; and, without major reforms in entitlement expenditure, on present trends by 2025 the federal government will have much less than 10 percent of its budget to allocate to everything other than interest and entitlements—repeat, *everything* other than interest and entitlements. Even this overstates the true discretionary margin, because expenditure programs cannot be eliminated from one year to the next (see Marcel, 2014, on diminishing fiscal space). In this scenario, one could hardly consider the budget to be a financial reflection of the economic and social choices of society. It would be only a reflection of historical choices encased in financial amber. It is not hard to imagine the resentment and alienation of the current generation when almost all public money is allocated based on decisions made by the previous generations.

The Bottom-Up Stage

During this stage, the ministries and spending agencies are responsible for preparing their requests, within the spending limits and other indications provided (macroeconomic assumptions and parameters, policy objectives, format instructions) but without any interference from the ministry of finance. In countries where the data and capacity exist, line ministries' budget requests should distinguish between (i) the amount necessary to continue current activities and programs, and (ii) proposals for new programs, with their approximate cost and including estimates of their impact on future budgets. These estimates also facilitate the preparation of the initial ceilings for the next year's budget.

Line ministries coordinate the preparation of the budget requests of their subordinate agencies and give them appropriate directives. The process of submission of budget proposals from these agencies to the parent ministry is symmetrical with that of line ministries' proposals to the central ministry of finance, although the budget preparation calendar is shorter and has fewer stages.

The Review, Negotiation and Iteration Stage

During this third stage, the ministry of finance reviews the conformity of ministries' budget requests with overall government policy and compliance with the spending limits or indications. The ministry then takes into account changes in the macroeconomic environment that occurred since the start of budget preparation—if any—and reviews performance issues related to the previous year's budget execution. Almost always, these reviews lead the ministry of finance to suggest modifications in the line ministries' budget requests, and negotiations follow. (On the importance and procedures of spending reviews, see Robinson, 2014.)

Three general tests are relevant during the review and negotiations stage:

- Is the proposed expenditure profile consistent with government policy for the sector? If No, discuss and adjust as necessary; if Yes →
- Is the amount requested consistent with reasonably well-designed and costed activities? If No, discuss redesign of activities and/or re-estimate of costs; if Yes →
- Are implementation capacity and complementary resources adequate? If No, recommend adjustments in the pace of implementation; if Yes, approve the expenditure request—in principle, however, as adjustments may still be needed before finalizing the overall draft budget.

The basic objective of negotiations (sometimes called "budget conferences") is to resolve as many problems as possible, and escalate to higher levels of government only the major disagreements that warrant their decision. In everyday practice, informal discussions also take place between the competent staff from the ministry of finance and their line ministry counterparts. It is a disservice to the government and the political leadership to pass the buck on minor issues instead of making every effort to resolve them directly at technical level. (Naturally, the outcome of negotiations and referral to higher authority depend largely on the relative balance of administrative and political power between the minister of finance and the line minister concerned.)

A Bad Budget Preparation Process

Unfortunately, the above guidelines and processes are violated more often than they are observed. Violation of one or more of the requirements of good budget preparation leads to one or more of a number of dysfunctional practices—seen in all types of countries and regions and described next.

Consequences of a Wishlist Approach

A wishlist budget preparation process starts by inviting requests from spending agencies without any indications of financial constraints. Because these requests reflect "needs" from the viewpoint of the individual agency, in the aggregate they invariably exceed the available resources. Spending agencies have no incentive to propose savings in ongoing programs, because they have no guarantee that the savings will come back to them, and they also include proposals for new programs as bargaining chips. Since the aggregate expenditure flowing from the macrofiscal framework is known, the process is seen as a zero-sum game and is not approached by either party in good faith. The ministry of finance assumes that the line ministry is trying to get as much money as possible and the line ministry assumes that the ministry of finance is trying to give out as little money as possible. In a wishlist environment, both sides are correct. It is irrational for a line ministry to submit a reasonable request for funds when it knows or suspects that other ministries will exaggerate theirs; consequently, it is irrational for the ministry of finance to assume that any ministry's request is reasonable. (The reader familiar with microeconomics will recognize this as a variant of the classic problem of a cartel with too many members. Since members know that a member who "cheats" by charging less than the agreed cartel price is unlikely to be discovered and would gain relative to the other members, they all have an incentive to cheat first, and the cartel falls apart.) Lacking information on the relative merits of the spending proposals, the ministry of finance is led into making arbitrary cuts across the board, or can pick and choose whatever expenditure (or minister) it wishes to favor.

Wish-based processes are sometimes justified as a way to empower the line ministries in the budget process. The opposite is true. Because the total demands by the line ministries are in excess of available resources, the ministry of finance in effect has the power to decide where cuts and reallocations are made. The less initially constrained is the process, the greater is the likely aggregate excess of ministries' request over available resources, the stronger is the role of the ministry of finance in deciding the composition of expenditure, and the more illusory is the ownership of the budget by the line ministries. And that's not all. At the end of the year, both sides have an alibi for loose expenditure control or bad service delivery—the ministry of finance points to the line ministries for their unrealistic budget requests, and the line ministries point to the arbitrary cuts by the ministry of finance. Nobody is responsible; government policy objectives are not met; strategic resource allocation suffers; efficiency in public services is harmed; and the trust and collegiality that make for effective government are undermined. This is a pretty heavy list of consequences of the simple failure of not telling people at the start how much money they have available to plan on.

Mechanical Budgeting

This practice is often referred to as "incremental" budgeting, but this is a misnomer. There is no problem with incremental budgeting, as such. As explained, the budget process must necessarily start from the current situation, continuing policies and ongoing programs, and make adjustments at the margin. The problem arises when the incremental change in expenditure is done in a *mechanical* way, multiplying every expenditure category in all ministries by "x" percent.

With mechanical budgeting, the negotiations are item by item and focus solely on inputs, without any reference to results—between a ministry of finance typically uninformed about sector realities and a sector ministry in a permanently defensive mode. Mechanical budgeting also compounds the inefficiencies of wishlist budgeting, by replicating year in and year out the distorted profile of expenditure until the budget is only a blunt tool of expenditure control and reflects society's choices as faithfully as a fun-house mirror.

Policy Volatility

At the opposite extreme of mechanical budgeting are large and frequent swings in expenditure allocations in response to purely political whims or power shifts. These swings are uncommon in developed countries, which have political checks and balances and the institutions necessary for continuity, and in any country with reasonably representative governance. In countries with strong and unaccountable elites, instead, a shift in the internal power landscape of the regime can produce a sudden massive reallocation of financial resources to newly favored clients or kinship groups—preventing the completion of ongoing projects and programs and creating fresh opportunities for corruption in the new expenditure programs.

Excessive Bargaining

An element of bargaining is always inherent in budget preparation, because compromises must be made among conflicting interests. But the bargaining should be confined to the important issues, and held at the appropriate stages. Instead, in a wishlist approach, bargaining drives the process at every stage. Negotiations take place on trivial issues. Policy focus disappears. Expenditure choices are based almost entirely on relative political weight of the various ministers, rather than also on facts or results. Bureaucratic actors have a stronger incentive to hide information, rather than to share it. And fiscal risk expands, because compromises are then reached through opaque tax expenditures, creation of earmarked funds, loan guarantees or shifting key expenditures outside the budget altogether—all of which reduce fiscal transparency and facilitate corruption.

Dual Budgeting

This issue will be discussed at greater length in Chapter 7. Here's a quick preview. While a separate *presentation* of current and investment expenditure is always needed, the problem of dual budgeting arises when the responsibility for preparing the investment budget is assigned to an entity different from the entity that prepares the current budget, *and* no effective cooperation exists between the two entities. The two separate budgets are then stapled together, producing a combined "budget" replete with inconsistencies between investment and current expenditure, and without assurance of adequate financing. The solution is not found in reshuffling organizational boxes or setting up inter-ministerial groups or other purely formal coordination mechanisms. The problem is institutional, not organizational, and requires incentives for active cooperation.

A Simple Experiment

The above discussion is bound to be somewhat abstract. Here is a simple experiment to bring it to life. Readers can conduct the experiment themselves with a small group of friends or colleagues, or instructors may assign it to their students. (If you don't have others with whom to conduct this simple experiment, use your imagination, go through the stages of the process, and you're likely to come out with the same conclusions.) Let one person act as minister of finance and each of the others as minister of a particular sector—health, education, transport, etc.

Let the "minister of finance" give out as information to the "sector ministers": (i) the targets for GDP growth rate and inflation; (ii) the previous year's expenditure for the ministry; (iii) a list of three or four ongoing activities relevant to each sector; (iv) the *total* government expenditure that can be allowed for the coming year; and (v) two or three major *national* policy priorities. Ask each sector minister to submit, separately, a written funding request to finance, respectively, its ongoing activities and any new program they may wish to propose. Put the ministers on notice that, after receiving all the individual requests, the minister of finance will adjust the resulting total request to conform to the total expenditure allowable for the year. Then give them enough time to ponder and prepare their funding requests.

When the individual expenditure requests are collected, you will invariably find that they add up to more than the allowable total expenditure. Now try to put together a coherent budget on these bases—ask each sector minister to explain the rationale for their proposals, let the dynamics of the process take over, and watch how the various dysfunctional practices emerge. At the conclusion of this exercise, it will become obvious that the root cause of the zero-sum game-playing, incoherence of the process and bad quality of the outcome is that it was unconstrained and began with a definition of needs and wishes—without any indication to the individual ministries of the expenditure ceiling which *their* request should not exceed.

Finally, a large caveat. The affordability of expenditure is a necessary condition for a good budget preparation process, but is hardly sufficient. In real life, many other factors are at work—clarity of policies, a minimum of political cohesion, a willingness to compromise and, most importantly, good governance. The point is that while it is perfectly possible to end up with a bad budget even if the process starts with a clear indication of available resources, it is rarely possible to produce a good budget if the process starts with a statement of individual needs and wishes.

Screening Expenditure Requests

As noted, the line ministries are primarily responsible for preparing their budget requests (within the available expenditure ceiling), but contestability is needed during the review and negotiations stage. Practical guidelines for reviewing the different categories of current expenditure are given below. These derive from actual international experience—although some may not be applicable in all countries, depending on the arrangements for government personnel management, compensation policy and income level. (Chapter 7 will discuss how to review funding requests for investment projects.)

Wages and Salaries

On average, spending on the wage bill absorbs around one-fifth of total spending, and pressures on wage spending will intensify over the coming decades in many countries (Gupta et al., 2016). Effective scrutiny and management of the wage bill is thus an increasingly important component of good budgeting.

The general criterion is that the wage bill request must be fully consistent with the government wage and employment policy. The three basic checks are the following:

- Is the number of employees consistent with the authorized posts for the ministry?
- Are the salaries in line with the overall government compensation policy and with compensation for comparable skills in the local private sector (including the value of benefits and adjusting for the greater security of government employment)?
- Are procedures and records sufficient to prevent "ghost employees," illicit payments, double employment or other major irregularities?

General advice for realistic wage budgeting includes the following:

- Encourage ministries to monitor labor supply and demand in their sector.
- Request from each ministry adequate proof of needs for new staff, i.e., an indication of functions, an explanation of why they cannot be filled by internal redeployment, etc.
- Do not allow too many vacant posts to be filled during the year.
- Discourage non-monetary allowances except in case of obvious need (e.g., safe housing in areas affected by violent civil conflict) as such allowances are usually distorting and tend to proliferate.
- Legally prohibit "topping up" of government personnel salaries by aid donors, and discourage moonlighting.
- Reward special job risks with a transparent and temporary salary supplement—not with promotion or a higher base salary. This is particularly important in post-conflict situations, where lack of security engenders safety concerns for personnel in particular occupations or districts.

Interest Payments

No "screening" is needed, but careful and verified calculation of amounts, creditors, terms and schedules is mandatory. (Debt management is discussed in Chapter 10.)

Non-Project Technical Assistance Services

Technical assistance directly related to investment projects is included in each project cost and should be reviewed as part of project appraisal (as explained in Chapter 7). In developing countries, free-standing technical assistance—normally for institutional development and capacity building—is a source of important potential benefits but also of serious risks of inappropriate advice, waste and bribery. The main tests are the following:

- For expatriate experts, is compensation in line with international organizations' norms?
- For local experts, is compensation in line with national fees? If national data are not available, fees in neighboring countries can be used as a norm.
- For diaspora experts, is compensation a reasonable compromise between expatriate and local salaries?
- Are there adequate provisions to facilitate knowledge transfer to local counterpart staff?
- Is there a strategy for reducing dependence on external expertise over the medium term?

Transfers

Subsidies and other transfers must be based in law and the amount determined on the basis of demographic and other developments. However, three questions should always be raised during the budget discussions, to provide a continuous dialogue on possible policy improvements:

- Is the particular subsidy likely to achieve the stated objective?
- Are there ways other than the budgetary subsidy to achieve the same objective?
- Is the administration of the subsidy cost-effective (e.g., might better targeting of beneficiaries help reduce cost or expand access)?
- Are there robust "reality checks" on the eligibility of the recipients and other provisions to minimize waste and abuse?

Operations and Maintenance

This is an area where expenditure ought normally to be encouraged, rather than compressed, because it is the area where undue cuts are most easily made: the financial savings accrue today, and the cost in terms of dilapidated infrastructure and ineffective government operations becomes visible only in the future. Here's a prime example. The subway system in metropolitan Washington, DC, once considered the best of its kind, was by 2016 in a state of thorough disrepair, from governance, funding and management problems: "The politicians who held the purse strings seemed happy to invest . . . [and] tout development at opening ceremonies. But they cared less about spending for maintenance to prevent breakdowns years later, when they might no longer be in office" (McCartney and Duggan, 2016). The eventual result was an unreliable and unsafe system, losing riders and requiring an additional $1.3 billion a year to emerge from decline—a multiple of what would have been paid for full and regular maintenance in years past. "Pay now or pay a lot more later" is one of the lessons.

The following tests may be considered in evaluating the reasonableness of ministries' requests for goods and services expenditure and the appropriate funding of maintenance:

- Ascertain that common sense has been used in addition to technical norms (e.g., that the request for fuel is consistent with the number of vehicles and their normal use).
- For durable goods, keep track of the earlier purchases, and ask for an accounting of the ones previously purchased—especially motor vehicles.

- Assure that each ministry and agency has an up-to-date register of its assets. In countries where data are not available or very difficult to obtain, focus on registering the assets that are both very valuable and at risk of misappropriation or deterioration.
- However, do not assume that because a physical asset exists it deserves to be maintained: many assets are dilapidated and may need to be disposed of.

Roles and Structure of the Core Public Financial Management Institutions

The best processes require leadership and good management. Because fiscal sustainability and economic growth are complementary, every government needs the capacity to assure that neither the long-run prospects nor the short-term needs are neglected and that the annual budget dovetails with the longer-term plans. The budget preparation process must therefore be led centrally by the ministry of finance, but with a major input from a ministry of planning (or equivalent entity) for public investment decisions. Views vary on how strong the role of the ministry of finance should be.[4] In any event, the ministry of finance depends on reliable information and good faith from the line ministries: the process demands cooperation.

The Finance Function

The main roles of the entity responsible for the budgeting process—the ministry of finance—are as follows:

- Advise the government on all domestic and international aspects of public finance.
- Propose a revenue, expenditure and budgetary policy, consistent with the government's objectives, and manage the implementation of such a policy.
- Devise and manage an efficient system for government payments.
- Mobilize internal and external financial resources (in collaboration with the planning entity).
- Ensure financial regulations to promote integrity and combat fraud and manipulation.
- Supervise activities that entail an actual or contingent financial commitment for the state.
- Supervise the corporate governance of public enterprises and other non-governmental public sector entities, and monitor their financial performance.
- Take all measures to protect major state assets, and encourage their best use.

In pursuit of these roles, the ministry of finance must do the following:

- Prepare the medium-term macroeconomic framework in consultation with the planning entity, consistent with broad objectives, for government consideration and approval.
- Prepare the medium-term fiscal framework, consistent with the macroeconomic framework and sectoral government policies, for government consideration and approval.
- Prepare the government budget, consistent with the medium-term fiscal framework, in consultation with the other government entities, but not diluting their responsibility for preparing their own budget.
- Ensure consistency between capital and current budget (consulting the planning entity).
- Monitor the financial execution of the budget (in consultation with the planning entity).

- Guide and coordinate activities in internal audit throughout the government.
- Interact with the legislature and other concerned stakeholders on all these matters.

The Planning Function

The main roles of the entity responsible for planning (and economy) are as follows:

- Prepare a medium- and long-term development strategy, for government approval.
- Prepare a poverty reduction strategy, consistent with the development strategy, for government approval.
- Coordinate and facilitate sector strategies, consistent with the above.
- Monitor implementation of these strategies, and recommend appropriate adjustments.
- Facilitate formation of a national policy on population.
- Facilitate formation of a national policy on climate change and the environment.
- Coordinate foreign aid for public investment (in consultation with the finance ministry).
- Prepare the public investment program (where appropriate).
- Monitor the physical execution of the programs (in consultation with the finance ministry).

To perform these important functions, both the finance and the planning entities must have adequate institutional capacity and physical and human resources (see World Bank, 2012).

The central finance and planning functions are shown in Box 6.1, in the assumption of a single ministry of finance and planning. In the case of separate ministries, the right and left side would be split and each deputy minister would have minister rank. In any case, the two ministers or two deputy ministers should have equal rank—even if one might carry seniority or greater political weight. The dotted lines between the deputy ministers and the respective departments indicate the need for close consultation and cooperation between the two sides.

Budget Debate and Legislative Approval

The last, and from a governance viewpoint the most important, stage is the presentation of the draft budget to the legislature for debate, possible changes, and approval. A review of innovations in developed countries is found in Posner and Park (2007) and one of worldwide practices in legislative oversight of the budget is provided by Stapenhurst et al. (2008).

The Importance of Timeliness

To permit informed debate and timely approval, the draft budget should be presented to the legislature at least two months before the start of the fiscal year, but the time allowed for debate varies considerably. The budget debate lasts about 2.5 months in India; in Germany and the Scandinavian countries, it can last up to 4 months (Lienert, 2010); in the US Congress, the law prescribes 8 months, but the process actually lasts 15 months from the day that federal departments are instructed to begin preparing their budget requests. (See the Annex to this chapter.) Instead, in much of Africa, parts of Latin America and Southeast Asia, the legislative debate tends to be much shorter, reflecting the imbalance of power in favor of the executive in most countries in these regions.

In some cases, delays in presenting the draft budget are due to special circumstances, such as political changes, pending financial negotiations with international financial institutions

Box 6.1 Structure of a Ministry of Finance, Planning and Economy

Legal counsel-----**MINISTER**-----*Secretariat*

Deputy minister (finance) ← . . . . . → Deputy minister (planning and economy)

Departments ← . . . . . → *Departments*

Macroeconomics
  Policy analysis
  Fiscal forecasting

Aid management
(in low-income countries)

Budget
  Budget systems
  Budget preparation
  Budget execution and monitoring

Treasury
  State assets register and management
  Cash planning and management
  Debt management

Revenue
  Administration
  Investigation/inspections
  Customs (often autonomous)
  Domestic taxes and other revenue
  Policy, planning, statistics
  Operations (processing, collection, etc.)
  Tax audit and taxpayer services

Accounting & reporting

Financial regulation
  (in cooperation with the central bank)

Public enterprise monitoring

Internal audit

Long-range planning
  Economic growth and employment
  Sector strategies—health, education,
    etc. (in cooperation with line ministries)
  Poverty reduction strategy

Public investment
  Large projects evaluation
  Sector coordination
  Public investment program (where
    appropriate)

National Economic Database
(joint with statistics bureau, which must
be autonomous)

Economic regulation & facilitation

External trade (if no separate ministry)

Internal audit

or other events. In several developing countries, however, delays are institutionalized, and the budget is systematically presented to the legislature just days before the beginning of the fiscal year. This puts the legislature in the impossible position of either preventing the government from operating or giving formal approval to a budget of which it knows virtually nothing. This is often a deliberate tactic to diminish the power of the legislature.

Low-income countries do not have a monopoly on such abnormal situations, however. In the US, for example, the budget for several years prior to 2014 was not approved before the start of the fiscal year (or was not approved at all), and the government functioned on the basis of successive temporary congressional authorizations for months, sometimes only weeks, at a time. (For these among other reasons, Wehner (2010), argues that legislatures do not exercise effective fiscal control.)

Systematic delays in presenting the proposed budget to the legislature are a symptom of grave governance problems or dysfunctional politics, and cause equally grave difficulties for the execution of the budget, since line ministries and spending agencies have no assurance of the amount of resources they will get and when and thus cannot plan (which, on the other hand, also gives them an easy alibi for performance problems). These delays also cause difficulties for the private sector and government suppliers. All things considered, it is less damaging to approve an imperfect budget on schedule than to present a better budget too late. There are usually incentives to amend imperfect budgets, but delays in budget presentation tend to become baked-in, and incentives usually go in the direction of continued delays. Fiscal discipline requires first and foremost compliance with the basic budget preparation rules, including the budget calendar.

To address delays justified by special circumstances, the public finance law (see Chapter 2) typically includes a provision authorizing the executive to commit expenditures before the budget is approved, under explicit conditions. This authorization is based on the budget of the previous year, rather than on the new draft budget. When the budget is not approved before the start of the fiscal year, the legislature normally authorizes the executive to spend each month up to one-twelfth of the appropriations of the previous fiscal year. However, in developing and developed countries alike, care must be taken lest these special provisions be abused and become a systematic way to sidestep the normal budget process.

The Legislative Debate

Individual members of the legislature have different personal preferences regarding the manner in which financial resources are allocated, and are subject to a variety of pressures from their constituents. The combination of these various preferences and pressures can generate a systematic tendency to increase expenditure during legislative budget debates, a phenomenon known as "logrolling." Generally worse is the practice of "pork," whereby certain expenditures (usually small investment projects) are "earmarked" into the budget by influential members of the legislature, without any scrutiny of their economic and social viability and often at the last minute and without the knowledge of members of the legislature who vote on the final package.

Accordingly, many countries have adopted procedural rules to regulate and limit pork, logrolling and other practices inimical to budget integrity and efficiency. These rules cover the sequence of voting on the budget and the legislature's powers to amend the budget. In parliamentary systems with a clear majority of one party, the budget prepared by the executive is routinely approved by the legislature; in most parliamentary systems, legislative refusal to approve the budget is equivalent to a vote of no confidence and normally results in the resignation of the government, in view of the central importance of the budget for economic management.

Approving the Budget: Legislative Powers and Limits

The powers and procedures of the legislature in amending and approving the budget vary from country to country. In some countries (e.g., France) the budget is voted in two stages: the overall amount of the budget, and next the appropriations of money among ministries. This procedure is aimed at protecting the overall fiscal target and the aggregate expenditure limit. In most countries, the budget is debated and voted on one single occasion and aggregate expenditures and revenues are reviewed together—which allows the legislature to discuss macroeconomic policy. (Recall, however, that the macroeconomic and fiscal framework should be communicated for information to the legislature before the start of the budget preparation process, in order to allow for a general debate on policy priorities.)

The legal powers of the legislature to change the proposed budget fall in three categories:

- *Unrestricted power* gives the legislature power to change both expenditure and revenue up or down, without the consent of the executive.[5] Some presidential systems (for example, in the United States and the Philippines) fit this model—although the "power of the purse" granted to the legislature is counterbalanced by a presidential veto. Unrestricted power entails substantial and direct legislative influence on the first two objectives of public expenditure management (fiscal discipline and sector allocation) as well as some indirect influence on the third (operational management).

- *Restricted power* is the power to change the budget but within limits—a maximum increase in expenditures or decrease in revenues. The extent of restricted power varies between countries. In France, the UK and the British Commonwealth countries, parliaments are not allowed to propose changes that increase expenditure, and have very restricted power to propose any other change. In effect, they can only vote the budget up or down, in which case, a political crisis is the usual result. (In India, parliamentary no-confidence can take the form of a motion to cut one nominal rupee from the government proposed budget. There is a story, certainly apocryphal, of a newly elected member of parliament who, attending his first session during the debate on a "one-rupee cut" motion, volunteered to pay the one rupee out of his own pocket to resolve the issue.) Germany allows changes, but only with the consent of the executive, which entails some limited legislative influence on resource allocation and (indirectly) on operational management.

- *Balanced power* is the ability to raise or lower expenditures or revenues as long as a counterbalancing measure maintains the same budget balance. This intermediate arrangement concentrates legislative influence on resource allocation.

It is important to keep in mind that the formal power of the legislature to change the proposed budget may be in practice inoperative if the political weight of the legislature is limited, and/or its competence and capacity are weak. Once again, the fundamental issues of governance and capacity come to the fore in the PFM agenda. Accordingly, major improvements in budgetary outcomes can result from improving the capacity of members of the legislature to understand the budget, the number and skills of the staff of legislative committees, and from enabling the participation from strengthening of key civil society stakeholders in the budget process—as discussed next.

Supporting the Capacity of the Legislature

Legislators are elected to represent their constituents and contribute to making national policies—not to become instant experts in public financial management. Technical support for the legislature is therefore essential to permit it to fulfill its constitutional responsibilities. Strong and capable committees enable the legislature to develop its understanding of public financial management and play a greater role in budget decision-making and oversight. Generally, different committees should deal with different facets of public expenditure management. For example, the finance or budget committee of parliament reviews revenues and expenditures; a public accounts committee ensures legislative oversight (the supreme audit institution normally reports to the public accounts committee); and sector or standing committees deal with sector policy and review sector budgets. In countries where the role of the legislature in modifying the proposed budget is significant, changes are usually drafted by committees rather than proposed on the floor by individual members.

The legislature and its committees should have access to independent expertise for proper budget scrutiny. In India, for example, parliamentary committees are supported with secretarial functions, and legislators have access to the parliament library and associated research and reference services; the US Congress benefits from the competent staff of the appropriations committees and the services of the large and well-equipped Congressional Budget Office, as well as assistance from the Government Accountability Office with audits and information on program compliance and performance.

Legislative committees should also have easy access to administrative information. In Germany, the Bundestag budget committee interacts quasi-permanently with government departments through regular departmental briefings. In India, the Public Accounts Committee of the Lok Sabha (the house of representatives) receives reports and departmental accounts and revenue receipts from the comptroller and auditor general. Regular executive–legislative consultation on budget policies and their implementation is a plus–plus game: strengthening the review and approval capacity of the legislature increases the legitimacy of the budget and thus the authority of the executive to implement it effectively.

Unfortunately, the record in these respects is mixed in developing countries. Although in countries such as Ghana, Senegal, the Philippines, Colombia, Tanzania and many others the appropriate legislative committees are functioning well and technical support for parliaments has been provided, much remains to be done in most low-income countries to provide the legislatures with the material, technical and human support needed to perform effectively their constitutional roles in the budgeting system.[6] Financing such support and providing practical advice should be a high priority for donors and governments alike.

Amending the Budget

The approved budget may have to be changed during the year, and most often is. Precluding any change would be quite impractical anywhere. At the other extreme, too many changes during the year would weaken the credibility of the approved budget. Thus, budget amendments are necessary, but should be limited—once or twice a year. The major changes that may need to be accommodated during budget execution include:

- Changes in major economic parameters, such as inflation, interest rate or exchange rates.
- Laws enacted after the start of the year which lead to expenditure or revenue changes.
- Major intervening policy actions which entail substantial additional expenditures.
- Exceptional expenditures required by unforeseeable events, e.g., a major earthquake.

Budget amendment procedures should be incorporated in the basic budget law. The details depend on the country but the broad principles are common. Since the budget has been approved by the legislature, revisions to it should be made by law, and any proposed budget amendment should receive legislative approval in the same way as the budget is originally approved. Amendments should be brought to the legislature as a package of proposed changes and accompanied by an updated macrofiscal framework—because requesting approval of each individual change would take up the legislature's time unnecessarily, make it impossible to compare the desirability of proposed changes against one another, and would risk compromising the overall macrofiscal stance.

To allow the executive branch to address urgent unforeseen problems on a timely basis, provisions are normally made authorizing exceptional expenditures before legislative approval. However, such provisions should be limited, the criteria should be explicit, and the government must report as soon as possible to the legislature concerning the exceptional expenditure and its reason and results, and request ex post approval.

Efficient budget execution requires that budget managers have the authority to transfer expenditure between budget items ("virements"), within specified limits and rules. (Virements are discussed in Chapter 8.) However, any reallocation *between* ministries should be included in a formal budget amendment and require approval by the legislature—because the individual ministers are theoretically accountable for the use of the resources and their budgets supposedly support sector strategies endorsed by the legislature. Reallocations between major budget categories (for example, from operations and maintenance to salaries) may or may not require prior legislative approval, depending on the country, but the legislature should be notified before the fact to have the opportunity to raise questions or objections. In developing countries, where the composition of public expenditure is critical for development and poverty reduction, reallocations between major budget categories should not be permitted except as part of a formal budget amendment.

Other Major Budget Preparation Issues

A Suitable Budget Preparation Calendar

None of the stages of budget preparation can be completed satisfactorily without providing adequate time. A pragmatic budget calendar should fit the realities of the country as well as the requirements of good budgeting. If the timetable is not long enough, one or another of the stages listed in Figure 6.1 will be unduly compressed. If the timetable is too long, changes are likely to take place during the process that may invalidate some of the initial assumptions and targets.

The most important stages to be given adequate time are the bottom-up stage and the legislative budget debate. If the bottom-up stage is too short, ministries are forced to take shortcuts and formulate their budget requests in mechanical fashion, whereas providing enough time for well-conceived and well-prepared budget proposals will make the negotiation stage shorter and more efficient and save time in the end. If the time for legislative debate and approval is too short, the legislature may be unable to approve the budget before the beginning of the fiscal year.

The overall budget preparation process, from the issue of the budget circular to legislative approval, can take as little as four months in developed countries with a parliamentary system and eight or nine months in other countries. This means that the activities to prepare the budget should begin shortly after the end of the previous fiscal year. In a real sense, good budgeting is virtually a continuous process. Box 6.2 shows an illustrative budget preparation calendar—fairly typical of well-run countries.

Contingency Reserves

Major changes require formal budget amendments. To provide in advance for unforeseen needs, a small "contingency reserve" can be introduced in the budget. Not to be confused with a contingent liability, discussed in Chapter 4, a contingency reserve is a financial cushion to permit the executive to face certain emerging needs during the year without

---

Box 6.2 Illustrative Annual Budget Preparation Calendar

Dates	Activities
January 1	Fiscal year begins.
Jan–March	The ministry of finance (MoF) prepares the macroeconomic and fiscal framework. If a "rolling" medium-term framework is prepared, as is appropriate, the framework is advanced at this stage by updating the coming year and adding a future year.
	The minister of planning (or other responsible entity) prepares the public investment program. If a "rolling" PIP is prepared, as is appropriate in most developing countries, the program is advanced by updating the coming year and adding a future year, covering the same period as the MTEF.
	Frequent and regular consultations are necessary between the two entities to assure consistency between current and capital plans.
April 1	The macrofiscal framework and medium-term projections are presented to the legislature for information and consultative debate.
April 15	The minister of finance presents to the government for approval the final macrofiscal framework, as well as the parameters for the draft budget of the following year, including the overall expenditure ceiling and the proposed ceilings or indications on the expenditure of each line ministry and agency.
May 1	The budget circular is issued to all line ministries and government agencies, including policy guidelines, the fiscal program (deficit, revenue, debt), the terms and format on which ministries must prepare their budget proposals, and the expenditure ceilings or indications within which to prepare the proposals.
May–July	Ministries/agencies prepare their budget proposals.
August 1	Budget proposals are submitted to the MoF.
August–September	Budget negotiations take place between the MoF and the line ministries and agencies.
October	Major disagreements are presented to the cabinet for resolution, following which, the MoF finalizes the draft budget.
By end Oct	The draft budget and related documentation is presented to the legislature.
Nov–Dec	Public hearings; testimony by government officials; legislative debate.
By end Dec	Vote on and promulgation of the budget law. (Should the budget law not be approved by December 31, a legislative resolution authorizes expenditure at the monthly rate of one-twelfth of the previous year's budget.)
December 31	Fiscal year ends.

having to go back to the legislature for approval. A contingency reserve is appropriate for this purpose, provided that it is small—perhaps two or three percent of the budget. If it is higher, the credibility of the budget is weakened. Also, since everyone knows that a large pot of money is held in reserve, budget execution will involve bargaining on the use of the money—which will thus quickly disappear and not be available if and when the contingency materializes.

"Efficiency Dividends" in Developed Countries

In the 1980s, Australia began to demand at the start of the budget process that each spending unit identify efficiency dividends—i.e., savings in their *ongoing* activities (about 1.5 percent annually). On the surface, this practice looks like the undesirable across-the-board cuts made by the ministry of finance in the context of a wishlist budget preparation process. However, there are three major differences:

- Efficiency dividends are notified at the start of the process and within a coherent MTEF.
- The allocation of the required savings among activities and expenditure items is entirely the responsibility of the spending agencies, which alleviates the arbitrary nature of the approach. Savings measures are much more likely to be implemented when the ministry concerned is proposing them than if they are prescribed by the ministry of finance.
- Indirectly, the total savings may be available to finance new programs by the ministry.

This approach has achieved results in Australia from the mid-1980s and in Sweden since the turn of the century. In other developed countries, the potential for fiscal savings and efficiency improvements also exists. However, the evidence is that savings are limited to the initial years, and common sense suggests that efficiency cannot be raised forever without major institutional, organizational or technological changes.

In developing countries, efficiency dividends are normally not relevant or appropriate. The current budget is often inadequate to allow ministries even to function normally, and the capital budget is determined largely by donor funding. Also, since evaluation capacity is weak, there is a real risk that "efficiency dividends" will be achieved by diminishing service quality and access—more often than not at the expense of lower-income or excluded groups.

Protecting "High-Priority" Expenditures in Developing Countries

Since the late 1990s, a peculiar form of dual budgeting has emerged in developing countries from the pressure by aid donors to track pro-poor spending and increase the allocation of funds to "high-priority expenditures," i.e., for social programs and pro-poor activities. The concern about programs important for low-income groups is entirely appropriate. The hard question, however, is how to channel more money to effective social and poverty-reduction activities without jeopardizing the fundamental objective of unity of the budget.

The answer is country-specific, but theory and experience suggest five guiding considerations:

- Ineffective expenditure management is neither pro-poor nor pro-growth—only by strengthening public expenditure management over time can countries improve the quality of expenditure in a lasting way. A pro-poor strategy is best articulated into a restructuring of expenditure over a number of years, and by setting and monitoring medium-term targets for priority programs.
- Because strengthening public expenditure management is a long-term process, it may be appropriate on a transitional basis to target and monitor priority expenditure, but any such targeting must be done within the budget to avoid creating a "poverty programs" enclave.
- Creating such an enclave within the budget would:
  - Undermine the budget as an instrument of government policy.
  - Neglect possible savings in wasteful expenditure (which can be as important as increasing spending on productive spending).

- ○ Make economic comparisons impossible, obscure the actual distribution of resources, and create coordination problems for spending agencies and local service providers.
- ○ Increase the risk of "white elephant" projects—which are not limited to roads and airports and can just as easily emerge in the social sectors. (Large, expensive and underutilized urban hospitals are a case in point.)

It has become commonplace for major aid donors to require that the government increase by a specified percentage the spending on certain categories deemed to be pro-poor. In isolation, such a requirement is inadvisable and counterproductive. First, in effect it turns an expenditure target into a floor—the very opposite of the ceilings that are conducive to good budget preparation. Second, it encourages unnecessary and wasteful spending. For example, a demand that government expenditure on primary education should increase from 18 percent to 20 percent of total expenditure can be met by hiring lots of administrators in the education ministry and building expensive schools in wealthy urban areas—which does nothing to accomplish the desired social objective of expanding access to and quality of schooling for poor children. Indeed, it is quicker and easier for the government to meet such targets in wasteful ways than by enacting the difficult complementary reforms that would be required to improve educational access and quality for lower-income groups.[7] If expenditure on certain programs is to be specified, it should be interpreted not as a mandate but as a target whose implementation is subject to review, and should be accompanied by robust expenditure tracking and monitorable indicators of the quality of expenditure, to make sure the money gets to the intended recipient and the target does not inadvertently serve to encourage inefficiency or corruption.

It is always appropriate, instead, to require tracking of actual spending to make sure that the budgeted money actually reaches the intended beneficiaries.

"Pork"

Pork—formally called "earmarks"—refers to the practice of individual politicians introducing into the draft budget specific expenditures, in order to serve their constituents (the favorable interpretation) or to curry favor with powerful local interests (the unfavorable interpretation).

The intent of an earmark may be to provide a valuable service to local citizens rather than to buy political support. Indeed, earmarks can be an important source of funding for essential services by subnational government entities, particularly in times of fiscal stress in local finance (Kunz and O'Leary, 2012). Whatever the motivation and the positive local impact, however, the expenditure being inserted into the budget by individual legislators is not subject to the same economic scrutiny as, and cannot be compared with, other expenditures included in a presumably coherent draft budget.

In every country a powerful politician can usually manage to have a favored project included in the government budget, but the practice has been especially widespread at various times in the United States, owing to the unique constitutional provision reserving to Congress the unlimited "power of the purse." While the budget as a whole is subject to presidential veto, various attempts at giving the president a "line-item veto," i.e., blocking specific expenditures while allowing the rest of the budget to become law, have failed. Earmarks had pretty much disappeared after World War II. However, they reappeared with the 1982 budget (the second budget of the Reagan administration), which included ten specific earmarks, grew to over 500 by 1991, and exploded in 2005 to a phenomenal peak of 14,000 "projects" for a total expenditure of over $27 billion—greater than the entire transport budget, and equivalent on average to 26 projects and $50 million for each member of the House (with well-connected legislators reaping a far greater booty). Earmarks declined from the 2005 peak and continued to fall to very few in 2015, but they can easily re-emerge in the future, owing to the lack of systemic safeguards.

A novel but very bad argument emerged in late 2016 in favor of reintroducing earmarks: the extreme political polarization could be attenuated if congressmen and senators could swap support for each other's "pork," as they would be forced to again interact with one another and thus reconstitute some willingness to compromise. This supremely cynical rationale for earmarks is akin to the long-discredited argument that corruption is useful "grease for the machine." Even accepting the argument, restoring the practice of unrestrained earmarks would be a huge step backward unless accompanied by a binding cap on the total amount—expressed either numerically or as percentage of discretionary spending. In addition to limiting the fiscal impact, doing so would at least provide a modicum of screening of earmarks against one another. However, it would still be a next-to-worst solution rather than second best.

The practice of earmarks is fiscally indefensible and toxic to good governance. On this score, budgeting practice in the United States has been far worse than in a developing country whose formal budgeting system is modeled after the United States—the Philippines (see Box 6.3).

Reaching Out: The Importance of Participation

Consultations and public hearings are always required during the legislative scrutiny of government strategy and the proposed budget. But the executive branch, too, should try at appropriate stages during the budget process to obtain feedback from civil society. This is fairly easy in developed countries, where an active media and a variety of organizations and think tanks of all political stripes provide regular advice and robust criticism of financial policy and major budget choices. In developing countries, an affirmative effort by the government may be needed: on crucial policy issues, the government could set up ad hoc groups comprising representatives from various parts of civil society; user surveys and meetings with key stakeholders when preparing agencies' expenditure programs can enhance program effectiveness; feedback from local citizens and service users can reveal malpractice such as "ghost schools," shoddy infrastructural works, theft and waste. Such mechanisms are generally resented by the target agency, but the political leadership should encourage them. Although these consultations must not be formalistic and should be allowed to have some influence on budget decisions, the budget preparation process needs to be insulated from undue partisan pressure and particular interests and lobbies.

When civil society participation is constructive and continuous (and not limited to one-off events such as the budget debate or the presentation of a budget amendment) a broad understanding of the reasons for budgetary decisions is generated, conflict and dissension are minimized, and the budget is more likely to be executed well.

Disseminating the Budget

When the budget is approved it must be disseminated—and in a form that is both easily accessible and understandable to the general public (usually with the help of an informed and competent media). This is mandatory for financial and political accountability, and is an important signal for private sector economic decisions. A summary should also be issued in readable form ("budget-in-brief" documents are now prepared annually by most countries).

Information and communication technology (ICT) has made the process far more efficient and transparent than used to be the case. Since the mid-1990s governments have

Box 6.3 "Pork" in the United States and the Philippines

The most egregious example of an earmark in the US budget is the "Bridge to Nowhere," from the Alaskan town of Ketchikan to an island with 50 inhabitants—i.e., $223 million of taxpayers' money to make it more convenient for local congressman Young to get to the airport and also to allow naming the bridge after him. The Bridge to Nowhere was finally deleted from the budget, but other earmarks can be equally capricious and bizarre.

It is particularly telling that a large portion of earmarks are added after the bill has already been drafted in the House of Representatives—showing the extent of under-the-table horse trading and lack of transparency of the process. Predictably, congressmen argue that their pork-barrel projects only correct the "errors" in the national agencies' budgets, which do not know the needs of their particular constituencies. But consider that:

- Neither the public nor Congress as a whole has any idea whatsoever of what projects are included in the bill before the bill is voted upon, because they are typically slipped in at the last minute and without debate.
- The only certainty about the process is that none of these projects was subject to normal cost–benefit scrutiny.
- The amount of pork at its peak was about the same as the federal government spent on food and nutrition assistance and on housing assistance, and twice as much as it spent on financial assistance to college students. (To put it differently, if pork-barrel projects were eliminated, the savings would have allowed giving financial aid to three times as many college students.)

In the Philippines, members of Congress have also traditionally drawn on pork-barrel funds to finance economic and social projects in their home districts. These funds include mainly the Congressmen's Countrywide Development Fund and the Congressional Initiative Allocations (CIAs). The CIAs are congressional changes of the budget submitted by the president and are closest in nature to US earmarks. However, the allocation per legislator depends on the budget of a particular agency rather than on the political "pull" of individual legislators. Since 2000, steps have been taken for an agreement between the legislature and the executive to limit the use of pork-barrel funds and promote greater participation and transparency in budgeting. Despite the Philippines' severe governance weaknesses, the problem has been declining since that time.

increasingly used websites and portals to disseminate budget information. From a minor proportion in 1995, 80 percent of publicly available budget documents were available online in 2006 and 96 percent by 2015. Government practice in disseminating budget information online can be assessed along four dimensions: scope, accessibility, reliability and feedback. Countries do better on scope than on accessibility and reliability, and few governments provide channels for users to submit feedback.[8]

Annex: Fiscal Trends and the Budget Process in the United States

Trends in Federal Revenues and Expenditures

The trends and composition of federal revenues and expenditure since 1940 are shown in Tables 6.1, 6.2 and 6.3—with accompanying illustrations. The reader is encouraged to

Table 6.1 Historical Revenues, Expenditures and Fiscal Balance of the US, 1940–2015 (in US$ billions at current prices and percentages of GDP)

Fiscal year	In Current US$ Billions			As Percentage of GDP		
	Revenue	Expenditure	Balance	Revenue	Expenditure	Balance
1940	7	10	−3	6.7	9.6	−3.0
1950	39	42	−3	14.1	15.3	−1.1
1960	93	92	1	17.3	17.2	0.1
1970	193	196	−3	18.4	18.6	−0.3
1980	517	591	−74	18.5	21.1	−2.6
1990	1,032	1,253	−221	17.4	21.2	−3.7
2000	2,025	1,789	236	20.0	17.6	2.3
2005	2,154	2,472	−318	16.7	19.2	−2.5
2010	2,163	3,457	−1,294	14.6	23.4	−8.7
2015	3,250	3,688	−438	18.3	20.7	−2.5

Source: Excerpted from Office of Management and Budget, Historical Tables, www.gpoaccess.gov/usbudget.

Table 6.2 Historical Composition of Revenue of the US, 1940–2015 (in percentage of total revenue)

Fiscal Year	Individual Income Tax	Corporate Tncome Tax	Social Sec & Retirement Taxes	Excise Taxes & Fees	Customs & Other Receipts
1940	13	17	26	29	15
1950	40	26	11	19	4
1960	44	23	16	13	4
1970	47	17	23	8	5
1980	47	13	31	5	4
1990	45	9	37	3	6
2000	50	10	32	3	5
2010	41	9	40	3	7
2015	47	11	33	3	6

Source: Excerpted from Office of Management and Budget, Historical Tables, www.gpoaccess.gov/usbudget.

peruse these data, as they reflect what the American people have wanted their government to do in the past 75 years and who has paid for it. Table 6.1 shows aggregate revenue, expenditure and the fiscal balance. As measured by expenditure compared with the size of the economy, the role of the federal government has about doubled from 1940 to 1970, but remained at about the same level since then. The spending increases in the first decade of this century, associated mainly with the Iraq and Afghanistan wars and—after 2009— with the need to stave off a second Great Depression, had subsided by 2015, when expenditure declined below the level of 1980. The very modest fiscal deficits of the 1950s, 60s and 70s gave way to significant deficits in the 1980s and first half of the 1990s. The federal budget moved back into balance in the late 1990s and to a historically high surplus of 2.3 percent of GDP in 2000 but, as a result of wars and recession, rose again to a peak of 8.7 percent in 2010, only to decline thereafter in 2015 to below the 1980 level. The revenue/GDP ratio and expenditure/GDP ratio in the US are only about half the average in the other OECD member countries. (One may still argue that the role of the federal government is too expansive, but it is hard to understand why a large number of Americans persist in believing that taxes are heavier than in comparable countries.)

The Revenue Side

The historical composition of federal revenue since 1940 is shown in Table 6.2 and accompanying illustrations (Figure 6.2). Currently, contrary to popular misconception, the revenue from the individual income tax makes up less than half of total federal receipts and is only one-third higher than the taxes paid for Social Security and Medicare. While individual income taxes affect higher-income persons to a greater extent, social security and

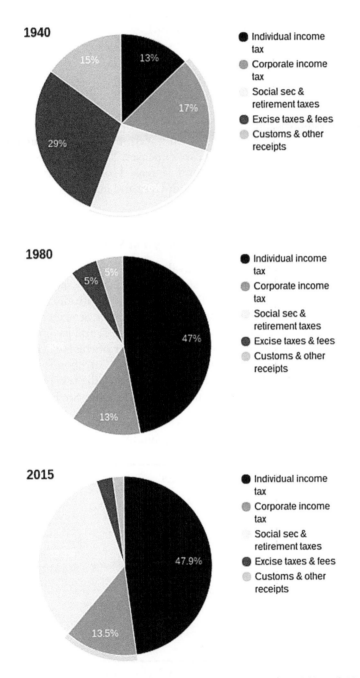

Figure 6.2 Composition of Federal Revenue, 1940, 1980 and 2015.

Medicare taxes are borne mostly by low- and middle-income persons. The relative share of total revenue accounted for by the income tax and the payroll taxes has changed slightly in this century, with the share of individual income tax declining from 50 percent to just over 40 percent, and the share of payroll taxes rising from 32 percent to 36 percent—thus shifting the overall tax burden somewhat to low- and middle-income persons. Clearly, when discussing the "tax burden" and the groups on whom it falls most heavily, it is essential to look at *all* taxes and not only income taxes. (For a complete comparison, one would also need to take into account the distribution of taxes paid at state and local levels, including state income taxes, sales taxes and real estate taxes.)

The Expenditure Side

Historical Trends

Table 6.3 shows the historical composition of federal spending. Expenditure on "human resources" has come to absorb the largest share of federal government spending, mainly owing to the entitlements of social security and Medicare expenses. The next largest category is defense expenditure, which jumped after 9/11, and decreased somewhat after 2011 in part from the winding down of the Iraq and Afghanistan wars and in part as a result of the across-the-board cut ("sequestration") legislation.

The Current Composition of Expenditure: A Visual Summary and Some Implications

Federal government expenditure ($3.7 trillion in 2015, equivalent to 21 percent of the $18 trillion GDP) consists of three broad categories: mandatory spending, discretionary spending and *net* interest payments. Two-thirds of all federal spending is mandatory, with discretionary spending less than 30 percent and net interest payments making up the rest. See Figure 6.3.

Mandatory expenditure is legislated outside the annual budget process, and its amount is determined by the eligibility criteria for each program and the number of eligible beneficiaries. By far the largest component of mandatory expenditure is the $1.3 trillion for social security and the second largest is the $870 billion for Medicare. Together, the two programs account for almost $2.2 trillion, or nearly 60 percent of total federal spending. See Figure 6.4.

Table 6.3 Historical Composition of Expenditure of the US, 1940–2015 (in percentage of total expenditure)

Fiscal year	Defense	Human resources	Physical resources	Net interest	Other functions
1940	18	44	24	10	4
1950	32	33	9	11	15
1960	52	28	9	8	3
1970	42	39	8	7	5
1980	23	53	11	7	5
1990	24	49	10	15	2
2000	17	62	5	13	3
2005	18	66	5	9	2
2010	20	67	6	6	4
2015	16	72	4	6	5

Source: Excerpted from Office of Management and Budget, Historical Tables. www. gpoaccess.gov/usbudget.

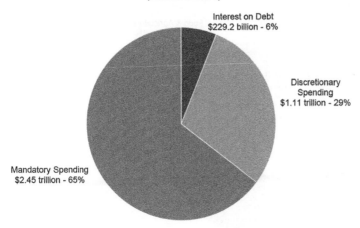

Figure 6.3 Broad Composition of Federal Expenditure, FY2015.

Source: Office of Management and Budget, www.nationalpriorities.org/budget-basics/federal-budget-101/spending/.

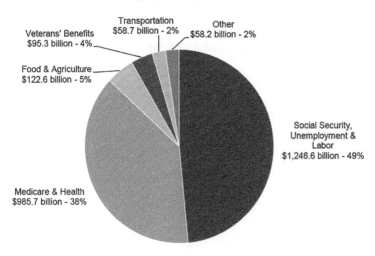

Figure 6.4 Composition of Mandatory Expenditure, FY2015.

Source: OMB, www.nationalpriorities.org/budget-basics/federal-budget-101/spending/.

Discretionary expenditure is decided through the annual budget process (as described in the next section). In 2015, discretionary spending totaled $1.1 trillion, of which $770 billion went to military-related spending (including veterans' benefits) and $330 billion were left for all civilian expenditure—housing, education, transportation, agriculture, etc., and the financing of the government itself, which was $73 billion or less than 2 percent of total expenditure. See Figure 6.5.

Finally, the overall composition of federal expenditure is shown in Figure 6.6. Readers are urged to review this information and reflect on the opportunity cost of different kinds of

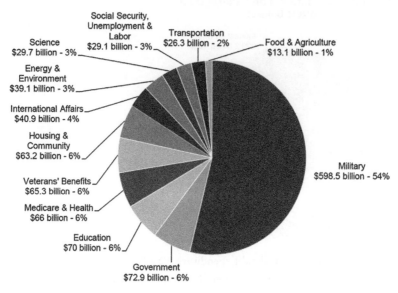

Discretionary Spending 2015: $1.11 Trillion

Social Security, Unemployment & Labor $29.1 billion - 3%

Science $29.7 billion - 3%

Transportation $26.3 billion - 2%

Food & Agriculture $13.1 billion - 1%

Energy & Environment $39.1 billion - 3%

International Affairs $40.9 billion - 4%

Housing & Community $63.2 billion - 6%

Veterans' Benefits $65.3 billion - 6%

Medicare & Health $66 billion - 6%

Education $70 billion - 6%

Government $72.9 billion - 6%

Military $598.5 billion - 54%

Figure 6.5 Composition of Discretionary Spending, FY2015.

Source: OMB, National Priorities Project, www.nationalpriorities.org/budget-basics/federal-budget-101/spending/.

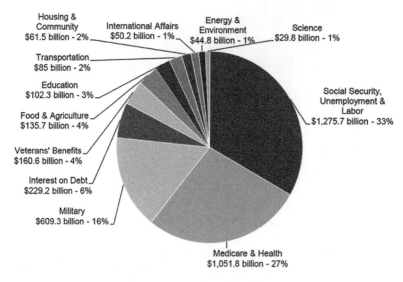

Total Federal Spending 2015: $3.8 Trillion

Housing & Community $61.5 billion - 2%

International Affairs $50.2 billion - 1%

Energy & Environment $44.8 billion - 1%

Science $29.8 billion - 1%

Transportation $85 billion - 2%

Education $102.3 billion - 3%

Food & Agriculture $135.7 billion - 4%

Veterans' Benefits $160.6 billion - 4%

Interest on Debt $229.2 billion - 6%

Military $609.3 billion - 16%

Social Security, Unemployment & Labor $1,275.7 billion - 33%

Medicare & Health $1,051.8 billion - 27%

Figure 6.6 Disaggregated Composition of Total Federal Spending, 2015.

Source: OMB, National Priorities Project, www.nationalpriorities.org/budget-basics/federal-budget-101/spending/.

expenditure. Just a few examples: a 10 percent cut in military expenditure could finance a doubling of total expenditure on science and international affairs combined; a reform in social security that produced just 5 percent in net savings could be used to double the total federal spending on education; savings of less than 10 percent of the Medicare budget would suffice to rebuild the country's transportation infrastructure. Yet, none of these reallocations and "savings" would be costless for those who now get that money (justifiably or not), and those persons and interests can be expected to fight vigorously to prevent the changes from happening. Aside from direct spending, while we're on the subject of opportunity cost consider that an elimination of tax expenditures (tax exemptions, waivers, deductions—see Chapter 2) would permit more than doubling the *entire* discretionary budget of the United States of America.

Major Fiscal Developments and their Potential Implications

Social Security and Medicare

The most significant fiscal development over the past 50 years has been the increase in social security and Medicare expenditures, which rose from under 20 percent of total spending in the late 1960s to around 25 percent in the 1980s, and over 60 percent currently. Of concern are the projections of further expenditure increases—driven mainly by the longer life expectancy of Americans and the lack of substantial government influence on the costs of health care. Nothing can be done about the former, of course, but the latter is in part the result of deliberate policy.

Despite the slowdown in health-care inflation associated with the Affordable Care Act ("Obamacare"), strong cost control remains conspicuous by its absence. Health-care inflation is a complex phenomenon with a number of causes, but two major components of health cost inflation could easily be removed. One component is the sharp increases in drug prices during the past decade. In 2003, Congress prohibited Medicare from negotiating the prices of drugs with drug companies. Take a breath and think about this: the drug companies can charge *whatever price* they wish; Medicare is legally obliged to reimburse them; and the taxpayers will bear the cost. (In 2015, Martin Shkreli, CEO of Turing Pharmaceuticals, raised the price of an essential cancer drug by 5,500 percent—from $13 to $750. There was nothing the government could do except pay—with taxpayers' money.) Combined with the associated prohibition on importing medicines (including from such safe countries as Canada), the system is a perfect way of maximizing the profits of private drug companies, for zero benefit to sick people or society. Oh, and the prohibition on negotiating drug prices was inserted during the committee chairmanship of congressman Billy Tauzin (Republican, Louisiana), who retired shortly afterwards to head PhRMA, the lobby organization for the drug industry. An alien would be justified in concluding that in the US Congress acts as an agent of the drug companies.

A second component of health-care inflation is the de facto lack of competition in the health insurance industry. Competition in the industry could be spurred by providing citizens with the option to purchase health insurance from a non-profit government entity set up for this purpose, with the private health insurance industry continuing to operate without restriction. If the government entity turned out to be inefficient, people would not use it. However, this so-called "public option" was removed from the Affordable Care bill after intense partisan opposition—by the same people who proclaim faith in free and competitive markets.

Finally, the system of fee-for-service (instead of fixed amounts paid for a bundle of services, or fees related to medical outcomes) provides an incentive to some health providers to prescribe more expensive drugs and maximize the number of medical interventions, while not prioritizing preventive health care services.

Reducing the Deficit

The fiscal deficit—in 2015 less than $100 billion or 2.5 percent of GDP—was one-fourth of its level at the peak of recession spending in 2009–10, and comparatively modest. Even so, let's try to imagine how such deficit could be eliminated without touching social security, Medicare or military spending. *All* remaining discretionary spending would need to be cut across the board by over 10 percent in nominal terms (by more, after accounting for inflation), and this on the heels of the several reductions of the previous years. Or the budget could be balanced by eliminating all federal programs in housing, community, energy and environment *combined*, as well as the corresponding government departments. Clearly, it is practically impossible and economically undesirable to achieve a balanced budget entirely from the expenditure side, and measures to raise revenue would also be required—that is, if one is serious about eliminating the deficit. The goal, however, is not so much to eliminate the deficit, which is currently small compared with other developed countries, but to prevent it from growing in the future and to improve the composition of expenditure. (Quite to the contrary, as of the time of writing, the initial plans of the incoming administration entailed further massive cuts in taxes on the wealthiest without any compensating fiscal measure or entitlement reform. If these plans are put in place, the fiscal health of the US will be compromised for a generation; fiscal space for critical social needs will disappear; and a resurgence of inflation is a near certainty.)

Keeping the Debt Under Control

Deficits, however modest, need to be financed, and most financing entails new borrowing and thus an increase in the *stock* of debt. As of end 2015, the general government debt was about $19 trillion, or about 100 percent of GDP, of which the federal government accounted for about two-thirds. This is much higher than at the start of the century—mainly from the war expenditures in Afghanistan, Iraq and elsewhere in the Middle East, and in part from the expenditures required to prevent the recession of 2008–10 from becoming a second Great Depression rivaling that of the 1930s. Although the debt ratio is still not much different from that of other developed economies—e.g., France and the UK—the central issue is *sustainability*. Unless major decisions are taken concerning the adequacy of taxation and the growth of entitlement spending on health and social security, serious deficit problems will emerge beyond the medium term. And then there is the cost of the debt.

Interest payments, currently $230 billion or 6 percent of federal spending, are determined by both the stock of debt and the interest rate. In mid-2016, the average interest rate paid by the federal government was at a historic low of 2.2 percent. Now recall that at the start of the century the average interest rate was 6.6 percent—close to the historical norm—and consider what would happen if interest rates went back to that level. Interest payments would absorb $690 billion, or 18 percent of total federal spending; the extra $460 billion would have to come from somewhere—either added to the deficit, thus kicking the (mounting) problem to the future, or increasing taxes by an average of $1,400 for every man, woman and child in the country, or cutting discretionary expenditure by more than 40 percent.

Other things being equal, that is. "Other things" are never equal (for example, an acceleration of economic growth beyond the 3 percent normally viewed as the "base rate" would more than offset the current deficit level), and a return to the earlier interest rates is extremely unlikely in the foreseeable future—but the size of these figures underlines the seriousness of the eventual debt problem if it is not addressed soon by appropriate fiscal measures. Once again, the issue is not that "the country will be broke"—in the colloquial and totally wrong expression—but that interest payments will crowd out social expenditures important for the well-being of large population groups, and that heavy and painful tax increases will become inevitable as well.

The Net Impact of Government Fiscal Operations on the Distribution of Income

A full understanding of the relative impact of government activity on people in different income groups would require taking into account the distribution of the benefits from public expenditure as well as the distribution of the tax burden. For example, certain subsidies benefit poor people disproportionately; other subsidies instead accrue largely to wealthy corporations and individuals; and the benefits of public safety are naturally most important for persons who have valuable assets to protect. Owing to these complexities, it is difficult to estimate with precision the impact of government operations on various income groups at any given time. What is clear is that, since 1980, the *net* benefit to the highest income group from government operations has increased very substantially, both in absolute terms and relative to the bulk of the population, and that fiscal policy has contributed significantly to the sharp inequality in the distribution of income and wealth.

The Federal Budget and its Preparation

The "Power of the Purse"

Unusually for presidential systems of government, Article 1 of the US Constitution prescribes specifically that

> the Congress shall have power to lay and collect taxes, duties, imposts and excises, to pay the debts . . . No money shall be drawn from the treasury, but in consequence of appropriations made by law; and a regular statement and account of receipts and expenditures of all public money shall be published from time to time.

Because of the extensive authority given to the president in other policy areas and the framers' core concern with preventing undue expansion of executive power, giving to the legislature this so-called "power of the purse" was seen as an essential component of the system of checks and balances envisaged in the constitution.

The Budget Timetable

Beyond the grant of budget authority to Congress, the constitution has no provision on how to structure the budget system. Virtually all aspects of the system have emerged through history, for practical reasons and in separate laws. The main foundations were laid with the Budget and Accounting Act of 1921, which established the Bureau of the Budget in the Treasury Department, and the 1974 Budget Act. Although the current US budgeting system has unique characteristics befitting its particular variant of a presidential system of government, it does meet the broad principles and general requirements for good budget preparation described earlier in this chapter. Whether actual budget preparation has been consistent with those sound principles and requirements is a different matter, which has depended throughout history largely on the responsibility and integrity of both the executive and the congressional leadership of the time.

The budget preparation process is formally kicked off in February by the budget proposal by the president—even though the constitution does not require the president to submit an annual budget. In a sense, budget preparation starts the previous year, with the instruction from the White House Office of Management and Budget (OMB) to the various federal agencies to submit their budget requests, which are eventually assembled in the president's budget proposal. In effect, however, the pace of budget preparation picks up only after May. The process concludes with the approval by Congress of the report of the joint House–Senate conference reconciling the differences between the House and Senate versions of the budget and producing a single bill. As all other legislation, the budget bill does not become law until signed by the president or, if vetoed, until congressional overturning of the veto by a two-thirds vote.

The budget timetable is shown in Box 6.4. The dates are flexible guidelines rather than deadlines, and allow for accommodating the legislative scheduling priorities of the House and the Senate. Also, the substantial amount of time dedicated by OMB to prepare the president's budget proposal permits resolving a number of important technical and analytical issues before the budget proposal reaches Congress. Altogether, the time available for budget preparation, consideration, debate and approval is an ample 14 months. Therefore, delays are rarely due to technical reasons, but stem from political disagreements—between the president and Congress and/or between House and Senate—that may take a long time to resolve. If the budget is not approved by the start of the fiscal year on October 1, Congress takes up a "continuing resolution," which allows the government to continue functioning by spending at the same monthly rate as in the previous year until a final budget can be approved.

The Major Stages

The process begins with the transmittal to Congress of the president's budget proposal, with a detailed outline of the executive branch's policy priorities and associated financing needs as well as a presentation of its general outlook on the economy. Although constitutionally

---

Box 6.4 Timetable of the Budget Process in the US

First Monday in February (usually the date for the State of the Union address to Congress)	*President submits the budget*
February 15	Congressional Budget Office submits report to the House and Senate budget committees
Within six weeks after president's budget submission	Budget committees submit views and estimates
April 1	Budget committees report "budget resolution"
April 15	Congress acts on the "concurrent budget resolution"
May 15	Appropriations committees consider the annual appropriations bills
June 10	Appropriations committees report appropriation bills
June 15	Congress acts on "reconciliation" legislation
June 30	House and Senate complete action on annual appropriation bills
Before October 1	Following "conference committees," House and Senate approve an identical budget bill and send to the president for approval and signature
October 1	*Fiscal year begins*

Congress is in no way bound to the president's budget, historically it took the proposal as the starting point for its own deliberations and decisions. This collegial practice changed after 2008, and political polarization reached its zenith in February 2016, with the refusal by the speaker of the House to even schedule hearings on the budget proposal submitted by the president.

The House and Senate budget committees hold *hearings* on the proposed budget, to obtain the views and advice of the administration, members of Congress, experts and the public. The "markup" phase follows, during which each budget committee makes amendments and changes in the starting budget.

On this basis, the Senate and House budget committees report their *budget resolution*, which, after approval by the full House and Senate, sets the overall spending limit for the coming fiscal year, as well as the projections of revenue, spending and fiscal deficits for the subsequent four years, and a statement on total federal debt.

The budget resolution thus corresponds to the medium-term fiscal perspective discussed in Chapter 5 and provides the framework for the detailed consideration of the expenditure and revenue legislation that is to follow. Because the budget is annual, the budget resolution is not and cannot be legally binding, and thus does not have to be signed by the president, but it is expected to provide a robust frame and set the expenditure ceilings for the annual budget decisions. If the revenue and expenditure levels in the budget resolution require changes in some laws, the resolution also contains instructions to the various committees to recommend such changes.

In May, based on the allocation in the budget resolution, the relevant committees of the House and Senate consider the 13 annual *appropriations bills* for the coming fiscal year. Each of these bills proceeds through the same hearings and markup process as for the preceding overall budget resolution. After committee approvals, the 13 bills are sent to the two budget committees, of the House and Senate, and assembled into an "omnibus" (i.e., comprehensive) package, which is then submitted to the full House and Senate for approval. By the end of June, both House and Senate are expected to have acted on the appropriations bills and thus to have assembled a complete draft budget for the coming fiscal year.

Inevitably, there are differences (sometimes major) between the House and Senate versions of the draft budget. For the purpose of ironing out those differences and to arrive at a single budget bill, *conference committees* are established, with joint House–Senate membership and (in principle) bipartisan participation. It is at this stage, which is not open to the public, that most of the horsetrading takes place—constructive compromises as well as corrupt deals, including the stealth insertion of expenditure earmarks.

The joint conference report is then submitted for formal House and Senate approval, following which it is submitted for the president's signature, upon which the budget bill becomes law and is strictly binding for the fiscal year beginning October 1.

Limited Congressional Debate and Amendments

Congress has a general rule to prohibit adding to *any* bill provisions unrelated to its subject. However, because there is no hard-and-fast criterion to decide whether a provision is or is not germane to the subject of the legislation, observance of this rule has depended on the political balance of power, and extraneous amendments are added to pending legislation all the time. The prohibition is much stronger for the budget bill, however. To prevent the budget (and thus the functioning of the entire government) from being used as hostage to push unrelated agendas, the "Byrd rule" prohibits both House and Senate from considering amendments that are not germane to the budget, that introduce "extraneous" matters, or cause the fiscal deficit to increase. Such a rule can only be waived in the Senate by a three-fifths vote. Moreover, by the Budget Act of 1974 the time for debate is limited and the budget bill cannot be "filibustered"—i.e., a vote prevented by extended debate that can only be "clotured" (cut off) by a three-fifths vote.

The Recent Reality of the US Budget Process

More than 30 years ago, Caiden (1982, quoted in Schick, 1987, p. 313) described the US budget process as "an ad hoc process preventing consistent policy making, and encouraging deadlocks, blackmail and symbolic voting. Less and less is decided with greater and greater efforts, while the really important decisions are made by default." Although her argument, along with others, paved the way for the introduction of a multiyear perspective to frame the annual budget, one could not imagine then that the US "annual" budget process would become even more dysfunctional in the first 15 years of the twenty-first century.

The reality has been quite different from what the budget legislation provides and from the budgeting practice of earlier times. In the US Congress, the systematic process of budget preparation described above is known as "regular order." Unfortunately, for the past 20 years nothing has been as irregular as regular order. In 17 of the years between fiscal 1995 and 2015, the budget process was not completed on time, and stopgap extensions of the previous year's expenditure levels were resorted to, year after year after year; and in 2013 a "sequester" hatchet cut most discretionary expenditure across the board—jaw-dropping evidence of the inability of the political system to produce acceptable compromises, let alone to do so on a timely basis. (For an in-depth discussion, see Meyers, 2014.)

At the same time, as noted earlier, the practice of "pork" grew dramatically. In 2007, Congress approved new rules requiring, among other things, identification of the members sponsoring each "earmark." Partly as a result, by 2015 earmarks almost completely disappeared.

The periodic increase in the debt ceiling also emerged as a new excuse for gridlock after 2008. Formal congressional authorization is required to increase the ceiling on the stock of federal debt. This authorization is conceptually and practically unnecessary: when Congress approves a given amount of revenue and of expenditure, by definition it approves the resulting borrowing and thus the overall level of government debt. Increasing the debt ceiling is a superfluous action, as it simply "authorizes" the administration to pay for obligations already incurred and purchases already made under the law. In fact, congressional approval of increasing the debt ceiling used to be routine, and genuine disagreements on public financial issues were voiced and resolved in the proper context of substantive discussions on government revenue and expenditure. After 2008, this useless formality turned into a script for partisan political theater and, in 2013, led to a two-week shutdown of most routine federal government operations. The whole thing would be farcical, except for the potentially disastrous consequences for the credibility of the United States and the world financial and trading system if a congressional refusal to approve the debt ceiling increase made the government unable to honor its financial commitments, domestic and foreign—commitments which, to repeat, had already been legally incurred.

The reasons for the dysfunction in the recent budget process are not technical or methodological, nor are they political in the good sense of the term; the reasons are parochial, partisan, capricious, self-serving and oblivious to the damage done to public financial management and the US economy itself. The link between government policy and the budget has been rendered largely inoperative; major fiscal and financial decisions have been systematically avoided; and budgeting has become the shadow of what an organized and effective process should be. There is no technocratic fix to this problem and nothing is seriously wrong with the mechanisms of public financial management in the United

States, but the best budget mechanisms avail little if the political system is incapable of making the policy decisions those mechanisms are expected to implement.

The dysfunction reached its peak in January 2016, when Congress refused to even hold hearings on the budget proposed by the president for fiscal 2017. It is impossible to discuss the underlying policy issues and define the corresponding budgetary choices in the absence of any dialogue between the executive and the legislative branch of government. It was not always so. Nostalgia is rarely unwarranted, but 60 years ago budgeting was simpler, more efficient, more transparent and far more collegial (see Penner, 2014).

Notes

1 Is it a coincidence that new military systems invariably end up costing much more and take much longer than initially estimated? As of end-2015, Lockheed-Martin's F-35 fighter plane was $160 billion over budget—70 percent more than the original estimate—and seven years behind schedule. And this is certainly not the end of the story. (See the discussion of military expenditure in Chapter 17.)
2 The sectoral composition of expenditure is very important, as in the case of Uganda, where reallocations led to faster economic growth and poverty reduction (Sennoga and Matovu, 2013).
3 Despite its decision to introduce program budgeting (see Chapter 2), the West Africa Economic and Monetary Union prohibits transfers between capital and current expenditures, prohibition which is inconsistent with the logic of pure program budgeting.
4 At one end, the process is seen as "monocratic," with the ministry of finance in total control (Francesco Forte, personal communication, 1999). But others note that good budgets can be prepared by several persons in various positions, when one individual emerges as the dominant figure (e.g., Sokolow and Honadle, 1984).
5 The US Congress attempts to restrict its own power (limited by the constitution only by presidential veto) through the annual budget resolution, which contains an overall spending cap as well as spending targets for congressional committees. Among other things, the so-called pay-as-you-go (or PAYGO) rule permits changes that increase expenditure or reduce revenues only if spending is cut or revenue raised elsewhere. (This budget rule should not be confused with the pay-as-you-go system of funding pensions or health funds, as contrasted to a fully funded system, whereby funds are set aside in advance to meet 100 percent of all foreseeable obligations.) The PAYGO rule and other restrictions, however, are self-imposed and can be lifted at any time by legislative action; they are thus different from a restriction imposed in the basic public finance legislation. Indeed, the PAYGO rule has been applied only sporadically after 2001. (See also the discussion of fiscal responsibility in Chapter 4.)
6 Kim (2015) compares the legislative budget institutions in different countries by means of a weighted index of the various dimensions of legislative institutional capacity, and O'Brien et al. (2016) offer a methodology for self-assessment by the legislature.
7 As concluded in an evaluation of the Chad–Cameroon oil and pipeline program: "insistence on a numerical quantum of budgeted expenditure [for pro-poor 'priority' expenditure] invited disregard for quality and cost-effectiveness, and led to surprises ex post when budget execution deviated from the approved budget" (Independent Evaluation Group, 2009, p. 37).
8 Romero León et al. (2016), drawing on research by Fundar, a Mexican civil society organization.

Bibliography

Blöndal, J. R., L. Von Trapp and E. Hammer, 2016. "Budgeting in Italy," *OECD Journal on Budgeting*, 15(3), 37–64.

Caiden, Naomi, 1982. "The Myth of the Annual Budget," *Public Administration Review*, 42(6), 516–23.

Gupta, Sanjeev, David Coady, Manal Fouad, Richard Hughes, Mercedes Garcia-Escribano, Teresa Curristine, Chadi Abdallah, Kamil Dybczak, Yehenew Endegnanew, Maura Francese, Torben Hansen, La-Bhus Fah Jirasavetakul, Masahiro Nozaki, Baoping Shang, Matthew Simmonds and Mauricio Soto, 2016. *Managing Government Compensation and Employment: Institutions, Policies, and Reform Challenges*. IMF Policy Paper, Washington DC: IMF.

Hallerberg, Mark, Rolf Strauch and Juergen van Hagen, 2009. *Fiscal Governance in Europe.* Cambridge: Cambridge University Press.

Independent Evaluation Group, 2009. *The World Bank Group's Program of Support for the Chad–Cameroon Petroleum Development and Pipeline Construction.* Washington, DC: The World Bank. October. Available online at https://ieg.worldbankgroup.org/Data/reports/PPAR_Chad-Cameroon_Petroleum_Dev_Projects.pdf [accessed November 3, 2016].

Kim, C. 2015. "A Study on Compilation and Improvement of Indices for Legislative Budgetary Institutions: With Focus on Comparative Analysis of Current Institutions in 60 Countries," *OECD Journal on Budgeting*, 14(3), 1–29.

Kunz, K. and S. O'Leary, 2012. "The Importance of Federal Earmarks to State Coffers: An Examination of Distribution Trends over the Decade," *Journal of Public Budgeting, Accounting and Finance Management*, 24(4), 579–608.

Lienert, Ian, 2010. *The Role of the Legislature in Budget Processes.* Washington, DC: IMF.

McCartney, Robert and Paul Duggan, 2016. "Metro at 40: A Mess of Its Own Making," *The Washington Post*, April 25.

Marcel, Mario, 2014. "Budgeting for Fiscal Space and Government Performance Beyond the Great Recession," *OECD Journal of Budgeting*, 13(2), 9–47.

Meyers, Roy, 2014. "The Implosion of the Federal Budget Process: Triggers, Commissions, Cliffs, Sequesters, Debt Ceilings, and Shutdowns," *Public Budgeting and Finance*, 34(4), 1–23.

O'Brien, Mitchell, Rick Stapenhurst and Lisa von Trapp, 2016. *Benchmarking and Self-Assessment for Parliaments.* Washington, DC: The World Bank.

OECD, 2015. "Budget Review: Germany," *OECD Journal on Budgeting*, 14(2), 9–79.

Penner, Rudolph, 2014. "When Budgeting was Easier: Eisenhower and the 1960 Budget," *Public Budgeting and Finance*, 34(4), 24–37.

Posner, Paul and C-K. Park, 2007. "Role of the Legislature in the Budget Process: Recent Trends and Innovations," *OECD Journal on Budgeting*, 7(3), 77–102.

Robinson, Marc, 2014. "Spending Reviews," *OECD Journal on Budgeting*, 13(2), 81–122.

Romero León, Jorge, Diego de la Mora, Liliana Ruiz and David Robins, 2016. *Digital Budgets: Improving How Fiscal Information is Disseminated Online.* International Budget Partnership. Budget Brief 34, February.

Schiavo-Campo, S. and D. Tommasi, 1999. *Managing Government Expenditure.* Manila: Asian Developmnent Bank.

Schick, Allen, 1987. *Perspectives on Budgeting.* Washington, DC: American Society of Public Administration.

——, 2007. *The Federal Budget: Politics, Policy, Process.* Washington, DC: Brookings Institution.

Sennoga, Edward B. and John Mary Matovu, 2013. "Public Spending Composition in Uganda and its Implications for Growth and Poverty Reduction," *Public Finance Review*, 41(2), 227–47.

Sokolow, A. D. and Beth W. Honadle, 1984. "How Rural Local Governments Budget: The Alternative to Executive Preparation," *Public Administration Review*, 44(5), 373–83.

Stapenhurst, Rick, Riccardo Pelizzo, David Olson and Lisa von Trapp, eds., 2008. *Legislative Oversight and Budgeting: A World Perspective.* Washington, DC: The World Bank.

Steuerle, Eugene, 2010. "The US is Broke: Here's Why," *USA Today*, January 27.

Tommasi, Daniel, 2010. *Gestion des Depenses Publiques dans les Pays en Developpement.* Paris: Agence Française de Developpement.

Wehner, Joachim, 2010. *Legislatures and the Budget Process.* New York: Palgrave Macmillan.

World Bank, 2012. *Enhancing the Capabilities of Central Finance Agencies.* Washington, DC: The World Bank.

7   Budgeting and Managing Public Investment

No matter how much you eat, save some seeds for sowing.

(Latvian proverb)

Introduction: What is Investment?

The two major divisions of government expenditure are current and capital expenditures. Current expenditure comprises the payments (or commitments) for all goods and services needed for the regular operations and functioning of the government during the fiscal year. Capital expenditure is associated with the production of assets which have a useful economic life extending beyond a year.

In everyday parlance, "investment" includes transactions such as purchasing shares of stock or buying an existing house. This is true from the individual viewpoint, but for the country as a whole these transactions only transfer the shares or the house from one entity to another, without increasing the total stock of capital. In its economic meaning, investment is an increase in the country's stock of capital—human capital as well as physical capital. Physical capital is self-explanatory. Human capital consists of the skills and information embodied in persons and organizations. It may seem inappropriate to call people "capital" but, as John Stuart Mill put it over 150 years ago: "The human being I do not class as wealth. He is the purpose for which wealth exists. But his capacities, which exist only as a means and have been called into existence by labor, fall ... within that designation" (quoted by B. F. Kiker, 1967, p. 485).[1] For budgetary purposes, however, investment in human capital is shown mainly under education in the current budget—teachers' salaries, training, books, etc.—although the physical assets such as schools, major computer systems, etc., are included as part of the capital stock.

Investment can be public or private. Public investment includes all expenditures financed by public funds—whether undertaken directly by the government or by private entities—and consists primarily of physical infrastructure for general public use—roads, bridges, hospitals, ports, airports, etc. Public investment is very low in developed countries, where private investment (factories, shops, commercial buildings, etc.) predominates. In developing countries, instead, well-designed, well-executed public investment is the main engine for economic growth and development.[2] Public investment steadily declined in developing countries between the 1970s—when the state-led model of development predominated—and 2010, but has increased in recent years, along with the new efforts dedicated to improving its management (as described later in this chapter). For this reason, as well as the fact that foreign aid to low-income countries goes mostly to finance public investment projects, the analysis in this chapter is more relevant for low-income than for high-income countries. This chapter is divided in two major sections: the budgeting treatment of public investment, and the management of public investment.

The Budgetary Treatment of Public Investment

Separate Presentation of Current and Capital Budgets

Historically, a separate presentation of capital expenditures was intended either to implement the so-called "golden rule" that government should borrow only for investment (thus requiring a balance or surplus in the current account—see Chapter 5), or to give development activities a higher profile. Logically, a separate presentation is required by the longer economic life of capital assets and their multiyear implications. Investment expenditure generates a stream of future costs and benefits and is conceptually and financially different from current expenditure whose costs and effects are extinguished within a short period. However, various current expenditures—primarily entitlements such as social security—also have multiyear fiscal implications, and the economic impact of investment depends on the future availability of the complementary current expenditures. Investment expenditure is not unique in contributing to future production—indeed, in and of themselves, physical assets contribute nothing at all. What is important for economic growth and development is the right mix of capital and current expenditure. An additional skilled nurse can have more of an influence on health outcomes than acquisition of new hospital equipment.

   Conceptual distinctions aside, the reasons to keep a distinction between the two major categories of expenditure, and thus to have a separate capital budget are eminently practical: "in the absence of properly organized capital budgets, borrowing avenues proliferate, governments resort to borrowing without due consideration of the sustainability aspects (or inter-generational equity), assets are inadequately maintained, and major projects suffer from overall poor management and performance" (Premchand, 2007, p. 89). In most countries, and virtually all low-income countries, a clear distinction between current and capital expenditure is necessary, for analytical purposes, fiscal transparency and policy-making. Indeed, the few developed countries that have not traditionally made a clear separation between capital and current expenditure in the presentation of the budget should consider doing so.[3]

   In the household analogy, imagine that a family wishes to build an addition to the home in order to provide an income-producing rental unit. To fail to keep track separately of the current expenditure necessary for the regular household purchases and the investment expenditure associated with building the rental unit, would cause confusion and lead to wrong decisions in both current and investment expenditure, and thus on borrowing and debt.

Integrating Current and Capital Expenditure

The Need for Budgetary Integration

While separating the presentation of current and capital budgets is important, it is even more important to integrate the processes of current and capital budgeting. To return to the earlier analogy, the household must also consider the impact of the rental unit on future current expenditure (utilities, maintenance, taxes), and not make the decision to build the unit based only on its construction cost. Shorn of its technicalities, the issue of integration between current and investment expenditure is an aspect of the fundamental need to reconcile the present with the future.

   Thus, the main advantage of improved integration of investment and recurrent expenditure decisions is that it permits improving the *quality* of expenditure. It does little good to select good investment projects if their future operation is hampered because the resources needed to operate them are not available. Capital-current integration is very important for raising the long-term productivity of the fixed assets created and thus the productive capacity of the economy.

Dual Budgeting: The Real Issue

The separate *presentation* of current and capital budgets should not be confused with the *process* by which those two budgets are prepared and made consistent with each other. The term dual budgeting refers to dual processes of budget preparation, whereby the responsibility for preparing the investment budget is assigned to an entity different from the entity that prepares the current budget, and insufficient coordination exist between the two entities. Because the information, knowledge and entities responsible for the current budget are different from those responsible for the capital budget, the incentive framework within which managers and technical staff operate must be conducive to coordination. Coordination is different from cooperation: coordination is a bureaucratic mechanism, put in place with the stroke of a pen; cooperation is an institutional challenge, requiring meaningful changes in incentives—rewards for demonstrated cooperation, penalties for lack of it.

Historically, in many countries the organizational corollary of a separate capital budget was to split budget responsibilities between two core ministries—the ministry of finance, responsible for preparing the recurrent budget, and a ministry of planning (and/or economy), responsible for the annual capital budget and for medium-term planning. The two entities carried out their responsibilities separately on the basis of different criteria, different staff, different bureaucratic dynamics, and (usually) different ideologies. At the end of the budget preparation period, the ministry of finance would simply collate the two budgets into a single document and call it "the budget"—thus guaranteeing inconsistency between current and capital expenditure, and inefficiency of both.

Coordination between the preparation of the recurrent budget and the investment budget can be weak not only horizontally but also vertically, between each core ministry and the line ministries. In this scenario, the ministry of finance deals with the budget departments of the line ministries, and the ministry of planning deals separately with their investment departments. This duality may even be reproduced at subnational levels of government—generalizing inconsistency and inefficiency throughout the entire public financial management apparatus. Adequate coordination is particularly difficult because the spending units responsible for implementing the recurrent budget are administrative divisions, whereas the investment budget is implemented through projects, which may or may not report regularly to their relevant administrative division. (Attempts to move to program budgeting have been motivated partly by a desire to correct these dual budgeting problems.)

In many ways, therefore, the more serious dual budgeting problem is lack of cooperation *within* each line ministry between the formulation of the current and capital budgets. (For example, if in the health ministry the hospital construction program is prepared separately from the current budget, potentially more efficient alternatives such as building fewer hospitals and buying more medicines cannot even be considered, let alone proposed.) Without integration of current and capital expenditure at the line ministry level, integration at central level cannot be fully successful. A good budget is assembled at the center, but must be grounded on good and realistic budgets proposed by each line ministry and agency.

In developing countries, pressure from aid donors has been (and remains) a major factor contributing to dual budgeting. The desire of donors to "enclave" their projects, in order to minimize risks of mismanagement of the aid and to assure sufficient complementary domestic funding, perpetuates the fragmentation of the budget system of the recipient country, reduces the government incentives to improve their investment budgeting process, and weakens domestic systems by replacing them with donor-mandated procedures. To address these problems, during the past ten years (starting with the seminal Paris Declaration on Aid Effectiveness in 2005—see oecd.org) aid donors have made formal commitments to harmonize their aid procedures as much as possible, and increase reliance on country systems and procedures. While there is evidence of some progress toward better harmonization of aid, there is little evidence of progress toward the related objective of reliance on country systems.[4]

Some have argued that the technical problem of dual budgeting was the cause of the large expansion in government expenditure during the 1970s and 1980s. But given the same governance, capacity, and political conditions prevailing in the developing world during the 1970s and 1980s (including the negative influence of superpower competition during the Cold War), the same wasteful and often corrupt expansion of government spending would have resulted even if current and investment expenditure had been ideally integrated. If only one could eliminate massive economic mismanagement by a comforting change in budgetary procedure! The bloat and corruption problems originated not from a visible dual budget, but from the black boxes and parallel budgets discussed in Chapter 4—untouchable "security" expenditures, various secret funds, misappropriation of extractive revenues, casual issue of loan guarantees to public enterprises.

There is, as usual, another side to the issue. By their larger size and more technical nature, investment projects generally offer more opportunities for corruption (Tanzi and Davoodi, 1998). In circumstances where governance and financial control institutions are weak, to integrate capital and current budgeting may simply mean concentrating power and bribery opportunities in the hands of a unified-budget entity. This would centralize rather than reduce corruption and inefficiency. In these settings, it may be desirable to focus *first* on improving the integrity of the investment preparation process—with the support and monitoring of the donors that provide the aid. The reforms to integrate investment with current expenditure can come later.

Unified or Separate Ministries of Finance and Planning?

Because the dual budgeting problem is institutional, not organizational, it cannot be solved by a simple merger of a ministry of finance and a ministry of planning. If coordination between investment and current expenditure decisions remains weak, a former minister becomes a deputy minister, organizational boxes are reshuffled, a few people are promoted and others demoted—but dual budgeting remains alive and well within the bosom of the merged ministry. In contrast, even with two separate ministries, if coordination between the two decision-making processes is close at every major stage, the capital and current budgets end up consistent with each other and with government policies, and the dual budgeting problem does not arise (see Box 6.2 in Chapter 6).

Thus, in countries where the current and investment budget processes are handled by different ministries, whether they should or should not be brought under the same roof depends on institutional factors. Where the entity responsible for investment is weak and the ministry of finance is competent, transferring responsibility for the investment budget to the ministry of finance would tend to improve budget preparation as a whole. Instead, where the investment entity is competent, merging it into the ministry of finance risks dismantling the existing team of civil servants who prepare the investment budget, without adequate replacement, and losing the government's capacity to look out for the long run.

On balance, there is an argument in favor of a single ministry responsible for both the investment and current budgets (provided that the combined ministry possesses the different skills and data required for the two tasks). Where skills are in limited supply and a single budget is difficult enough to prepare, it complicates matters unnecessarily to have two budgeting processes and two responsible entities—each protecting its turf. In developing countries, simplicity should be the organizational keynote: the more complicated the structure, the less likely it is to work well. But this argument is only a general presumption: the organizational choice must be politically and administratively sound in light of the country's specific circumstances.

It is sometimes wrongly argued that a process of programming of public investment hampers capital-current integration, and/or retards the elaboration of a medium-term expenditure framework, and/or produces fiscally unsustainable expansion of expenditure. The opposite is true on all three counts—as discussed later.

Box 7.1 gives the extreme example of dual budgeting, in India.

Box 7.1 Dual Budgeting in India

The practice of hiding a current deficit by relocating regular current expenditure into the development budget was first introduced in India by the British colonial government (see Premchand, 2007). The precedent led to the post-independence distinction between "plan" and "non-plan" expenditures—with plan expenditures including a large current expenditure component. The distinction remained as a holdover from the central planning approach of the 1950s and 1960s long after the approach was abandoned. Inertia is inherent in India's giant bureaucracy.

Because of the assumption that plan expenditures are developmental, while non-plan spending is merely government consumption, the system produced political, public relations and bureaucratic incentives to making the plan look as large as possible. After intense and well-publicized negotiations between each state and the central government, vast amounts of money would be allocated to "plan expenditure" on an excessively large number of projects, while in reality only a fraction of that money would be available. Moreover, the distinction produced an incentive to reclassify current spending (called "revenue expenditure" in India) in order to make the states' budget look more "developmental." Every party to the game knew this, but went along in order not to lose out vis-à-vis other states playing the same game. The exercise was in large measure political theater.

But it was expensive theater. First, the inclusion in the "plan" of a number of projects in excess of those which could conceivably be financed led to wasting resources on low-value projects. More damaging was the second consequence: with aggregate funds insufficient, and a failure to prioritize, most projects were starved of the funds necessary for their implementation. Consequently, even the best investment projects could not produce the intended results owing to the implementation delays and cost overruns from being constantly short of funds. The damage done over two generations by this sort of dual budgeting to economic growth and social services access and quality in India is incalculable. The situation improved after the dissolution in 2014 of the Planning Commission, which ever since 1950 was the central organ administering the convoluted process, but much more remains to be done to achieve consistency between resource availability and well-prepared expenditure programs.

Source: Author.

The Hybrid Nature of Capital Expenditure

The capital budget includes a component of current expenditures managed within the projects. There are good reasons for this. Procedures for administering the current budget are generally not suitable for managing expenditures financed by donors, which carry their own fiduciary and management requirements. It also would not make sense to include the labor costs of an investment project into the wage bill of the ministry—both because these costs will stop after project completion and because a large investment project may involve several ministries. There are bad reasons, too: in many cases shifting regular current expenditure into the capital budget is a device to cover up a deficit in the current account or to avoid accountability. (In some countries, e.g., Bangladesh, the share of current expenditures in development budgets has been as large as one-third.)

Especially harmful is the practice of entrusting regular government functions to contractual employees paid through a donor-funded investment project at much higher salaries than regular civil servants. The competition among donors to attract to their specific project the small pool of qualified locals leads to resentment and salary dualism, and induces scarce talent to leave regular government service—thus improving short-term implementation of individual projects at the cost of doing permanent damage to government capacity.

The Treatment of Individual Investment Projects

Predictability of funding is especially important for the implementation of investment projects, and it is therefore necessary to have in place budgetary provisions appropriate to the multiyear expenditure commitment required for projects. This entails:

* A legislative authorization covering the entire project cost.
* A commitment allocation setting the commitment limit during the fiscal year— allowing the carryover of unused commitments (*not payments*) to the following year.
* A payment allocation setting the cash limit for the fiscal year, without any carryover.

An especially prudent practice is to include in the budget funding for a new investment project only when the entire project is "mature," i.e., ready for launch—with all the required approvals in place, full financing assured or at least highly likely, and implementation modalities defined. Such a rule has been criticized by some as old-fashioned and by others as cumbersome, but it can be useful to protect against premature funding of projects that are not ready for implementation. Waiting a few months until a project is fully ready for implementation is sensible insurance against the risk of failure, not because of any intrinsic weakness of the project but only because it was launched too early. Delaying a good investment opportunity entails a cost, but in general a far lower cost than wasting resources by rushing its implementation. "Make haste slowly" is a pretty good slogan when committing a large amount of public money.

A bit extreme, but worth considering nonetheless, is a prohibition to even discuss a project with foreign donors for possible financing until the project has been fully appraised by the competent line ministry and then vetted first with the planning authorities and then with the finance authorities. This was the procedure followed in Tunisia from the early 1990s. Although under the pre-2011 regime the motivation was to keep tight regime control and centralize corruption opportunities, the provision did keep the government in the driver's seat—where it should be but frequently is not.[5]

The Management of Public Investment

The understanding of the link between public investment and economic growth has improved in the past two decades. The assumption of a linear and strong association between the amount of investment and the rate of economic growth dominated development analysis and policy advice from the late 1950s and 1960s (the years of the "high development economics," as Paul Krugman called it) well into the 1990s.[6] The notion that the institutions and practices of public investment *management* might have an influence on macrolevel investment efficiency was nowhere to be seen. Only the "what" was debated, never the "how."

This obliviousness was replicated at project level, via the happy assumption that if cost–benefit analysis yielded an ex ante project rate of return of "x," project implementation would miraculously occur without a hitch—thus assuring that ex post rate of return (after project completion) would still be "x." Development practitioners and government officials knew better, but the reality that productivity of public investment depends as much on good management and institutional factors as on good project design did not penetrate the development literature and reform programs until the late 1980s.[7] The importance of good management of public investment is now fully recognized. The "how" is finally at the center of the issue of the impact of public investment on development.

Public investment can be a driver of economic growth, support the delivery of basic public services, and help reduce poverty. It can do none of these things, however, if it is inefficient. On average across all countries the efficiency of public investment has been estimated at only about 70 percent of what it could be (IMF, 2015), and is significantly lower than that in developing countries. Consider what this means. Instead of investing $100 million and (other things being equal) adding $100 million to the fiscal deficit—strengthening the management of public investment to reach 100 percent of its potential efficiency would allow spending only $70 million, or spending the same but getting more in terms of economic growth and public services—year in, year out. When mismanaged or lacking close oversight, large investment projects are also an excellent source of corruption (Tanzi and Davoodi, 1997), adding strength to the case for rigorous management of public investment.

The three pillars of public investment management are: (i) the selection of good individual projects; (ii) the formulation of a coherent public investment program; and (iii) the arrangements for implementation and project management. Project selection and investment programming are discussed in the next sections. The third pillar—arrangements for implementation and project management—must be specific to the sector and the nature of the project, but in every case they must include all of the following:

- adequate budgetary provision (discussed earlier);
- a realistic procurement plan;
- a financial management and disbursement plan;
- clear assignment of responsibilities;
- concrete and rapid accountability mechanisms;
- procedures for mid-course adjustments;
- flexibility in procurement combined with close surveillance of procurement transactions, especially for computer systems and large works;[8]
- adequate financial monitoring and reporting (to the ministry of finance) and physical monitoring and reporting (to the ministry of planning or equivalent); and
- realistic provisions for seeking and receiving feedback on project execution from stakeholders and civil society.

Selecting Individual Investment Projects

The Selection Criteria

Proposed public investment projects should be screened according to four major tests, and approved for funding in the government budget only if they pass all four of these tests:

- Broad consistency with national policy (particularly the national development priorities and the strategy for the sector concerned).
- Acceptable rate of return, in national economic terms. (The uses and limitations of cost–benefit analysis are discussed next.)
- "Fit" of the project within a sound overall public investment program.
- Implementability of the project, in light of the capacity for project execution and technical/financial considerations.

The Uses, Abuses and Decline of Cost–Benefit Analysis

Cost–benefit analysis has a long pedigree and has been used for over 50 years to assess the net benefits of the project to the economy—measuring both the costs and the expected benefits in terms of the opportunity cost, i.e., the alternative uses of the resources. For development projects, it is the economic rate of return of projects that matters, not the internal financial profit. Therefore, the analysis must include appropriate consideration of the "external" effects of the project on other projects, on the sector, and on the economy as a whole. External effects may be positive (e.g., draining a malarial swamp in the process of building a road benefits the health of local residents), or negative (e.g., displacement of the population by construction of the road). Not all costs and benefits can be measured, but all significant ones must be *considered* in the appraisal of the project. Similarly, future risks should be considered—normally through simulation exercises designed mainly to make the project design more robust and resistant to failure.[9]

Cost–benefit analysis provides a useful starting point and is an excellent way to focus on the expected economic realities of the project. Its use in aid-assisted projects in developing countries has been declining, however. There are two reasons for this: the easy manipulation of the assumptions to produce the predetermined desired outcomes, and an increased recognition of the non-measurable aspects and the external costs and benefits of projects. A vicious circle has been at work: the fact that standard cost–benefit analysis is insufficient to fully appraise the development impact of public investment projects has been used as an excuse not to conduct the analysis at all or to neglect the quality of the analysis conducted—which in turn has diminished further the credibility of the methodology itself. The decline has been very sharp: between 1970 and 2010, the proportion of World Bank projects with cost–benefit analysis dropped from 70 percent to 25 percent—partly but not entirely owing to a shift toward projects in social sectors, which are less amenable to such analysis (World Bank, 2010). A similar decline has occurred in other international and national aid agencies.

In developing countries, despite the limitations of cost–benefit analysis, it should continue to be applied to large investment projects. At the same time, it is critical to assure transparency in the assumptions behind the calculation of the economic rate of return, because they can be so easily manipulated. Also, to economize on scarce capacity, simple variants of the methodology are generally preferable, and the full application of cost–benefit analysis should be limited to the largest projects. (Medium and small projects may be appraised based on their fit with sector policies and economic common sense.)

Finally, it is worth repeating that, however high the ex ante economic rate of return of a project may be, neglecting implementation requirements or failing to provide the resources necessary for project execution will inevitably cause the ex post rate of return to be lower than anticipated. Obviously, the productivity of a project depends on the actual rate of return after the project is completed and not on what has been expected before it was launched.

Providing Contestability for Project Appraisals

Concerning large projects, the experience of Korea can be applicable even to low-income countries. Korea has instituted a two-stage system, whereby "pre-feasibility studies" of project proposals are conducted by the ministry of finance independently of the line ministry concerned. This first screening reduces sharply the number of potential investment proposals, which in the second stage are then subjected to further examination by the line ministries. In effect, the second stage becomes a study of implementation modalities. Simple variants of such a system can protect countries from the risks and costs of allowing "white elephant" projects into the project pipeline (from which they are extremely difficult to extract). Equally important and especially innovative has been the "analytical hierarchy process," by which the process of selecting public investment projects reflects the "votes" of experts from different disciplines, rather than only a mechanistic application of formulas. The Korean system also includes a mid-course reassessment of the feasibility of the project, with the option to cancel it. This is a very important provision, in light of the notorious reluctance of politicians and administrators to admit mistakes and to stop pouring good money after bad.

Similar independent appraisal mechanisms have been established in other countries. In Belarus, for example, the State Appraisal Agency appraises all proposed public investment projects from the start. Funded by a fee of 5–10 percent paid by the line ministry concerned, the agency has been able to recruit a sufficient number of experts and, reportedly, provides appraisals of good technical quality and within 30 days from submission. With its central authority over all project appraisals, the procedure suits the country's authoritarian regime. In a democratic country such as Ireland, a more light-handed review is adopted, whereby line ministries have the authority to perform their own appraisals of projects in their sector, but must obtain independent review by external experts.[10] Box 7.2 proposes a comprehensive mechanism of contestability, combining independent review with central facilitation of implementation capacity in the line ministries.

Priority Ranking of Projects?

In the heyday of economic planning in the 1970s, it was common to rank projects in order of their rate of return, with the higher-ranked selected in turn until the financial envelope was filled. Aside from technical issues, comparing the social worth of activities in different sectors according to quantitative criteria is hazardous. Also, because many projects are interrelated, decisions concerning one project affect the overall composition of public investment. The ranking approach fell out of favor, but has recently re-emerged in some developing countries—partly as a rationalization for selecting a powerful minister's pet projects. However, the binary rule first set out by Squire and Van der Tak (1975) remains valid: for a given investment budget, projects are either acceptable and should be included in the investment program or are not acceptable and should be excluded. It is not unusual, of course, that a project is launched for purely political reasons—good or bad. If so, the project should still be subject to a proper feasibility study, but there is no point in wasting

---

Box 7.2 Providing Technical Contestability for Large Public Investment Proposals

To help address weaknesses in project preparation, a "technical contestability" office (TCO) could be established to provide (i) technical oversight of the preparation and execution of major projects and (ii) guidance and facilitation of capacity building in the line ministries. Such an office would be autonomous, under a board chaired by the minister of finance or planning and including other key ministers as appropriate.

For major projects, the TCO would be responsible for the following, in sequence:

- General advice on viability of project ideas before launching feasibility studies (especially important to prevent conception of potential white elephant projects).
- Confirmation that the project preparation and appraisal procedures were respected, before a project can be included in the investment budget.
- Following up on project execution.
- Leading the preparation of relevant project preparation manuals for the ministries.
- Initiating the post-completion evaluation of projects.

In its review of project preparation, the TCO would be expected to ascertain, among other things, the consistency of the proposed project with the sector strategy. It may comment on the strategy, but only to the extent that weaknesses impede the preparation of sound projects, and without any authority to review the sector strategies themselves.

The TCO would be lightly structured, with short lines of command and a small but highly competent staff. It would operate mainly by commissioning studies by external consultants, and its overhead costs would be covered by a regular budget allocation—with additional amounts allocated as needed to cover the costs of studies and other approved activities. This would permit the TCO activities to expand and contract as required. Accountability would be provided by the external auditor as for any other public entity. However, in this case, a special substantive audit of the technical quality of TCO activities would also be conducted periodically by an external firm.

The TCO could be active for a number of years, but would be inherently temporary, to transition from a system without effective quality controls to a system in which such controls exist and are exercised primarily in the line ministries themselves. Regular functions of government ought to be exercised by regular organs of government. The TCO capacity-building role would be intended for this purpose.

Source: Author.

---

time and resources in artificial rankings of projects for the sole purpose of cloaking the political decision in "technical" terms.

Rules of Thumb for Screening Project Proposals

Chapter 6 on budget preparation discussed the screening of requests for current expenditure. For investment projects, actual experience in developing countries suggests certain practical rules to screen individual project proposals. None of these rules are make-or-break, and they all admit exception, but they can provide helpful guidance.

Use the "double sense" principle: common sense and economic sense. If an economic appraisal of the project reaches a positive conclusion, but the project idea still doesn't meet the test of common sense among those with practical experience in the sector, it is worth seeking a second opinion through an independent review.

Beware of "free" money. The focus should be on project quality. If the project is selected, *then* it will be time to look for the best financing terms. And if the donor agency is genuinely interested in assisting the country's development it should be willing to re-channel its aid to finance a more viable project. Similarly, a donor agency should refuse to finance a bad project: its legitimate interest is to help the country's development, not necessarily to be nice to the government.

A good no is better than a bad yes. It is usually possible to recoup a missed opportunity but it is difficult to undo a major mistake once project implementation has begun.

External feedback. Assure appropriate external feedback, both on the project itself (particularly its design variant) and on its implementation. The farmer who still gets wet crossing the river knows better than anyone that the bridge has not been completed as reported. The form of civil society involvement will depend on the country and the type of project, but a mechanism to obtain external reality checks is essential everywhere.

Improve quality at entry. The objective of project screening is not only to reject bad proposals, but to foster lasting improvements in investment proposals. Hence, some positive incentive is needed to improve quality at entry. A "ladder approach" has proven effective in customs clearance and regulatory enforcement: importers who demonstrate compliance with customs regulations are "graduated" to the next step of lighter inspection and documentation, and so on up the regulatory simplification ladder. This approach may be useful for investment as well—namely, ministries which submit consistently better project proposals and demonstrate positive impact of investments previously undertaken could be given more favorable consideration in the next budget and/or be subject to progressively less stringent tests.

Estimating the Recurrent Cost of Investment Projects

Public investment has implications not only for economic growth and development, but for future budgets. In the positive sense, public investment leads to a future increase in revenue. At the same time, project effectiveness will depend on the provision of adequate current expenditures. To quantify the overall implications of public investment on future years' budgets is important to assess fiscal sustainability and future fiscal policy options, and reduce the risk of wastage of valuable assets for lack of sufficient operations and maintenance expenditure. This is an eminently practical challenge, but a complex one, which must be built from the ground up, major project by major project. Preaching about the need to consider recurrent costs is routine, but practical advice on how to do so is conspicuously absent.

A simple and workable sequence for estimating the future recurrent costs of investment projects includes as main steps:

- Collect standard costs from national and international experience, and technical manuals. Although the requisite information is generally available, this is a substantial exercise, which requires structuring the information clearly, and arrangements for updating it at least annually.
- Decide on the time period over which the recurrent costs are to be estimated (a minimum of five years after project completion).
- Decide on the cost elements to be considered—primarily for labor (especially the higher-level skills required, e.g., surgeons in hospitals); durable goods (especially expensive

equipment, e.g., x-ray machines) and materials; fuel and other supplies; and maintenance of buildings and other physical facilities.

- Decide on a standard simple format for preparing the estimates, and aggregate them by sector and nationally.
- Include in the terms of references for the feasibility studies of projects, the requirement to estimate future recurrent costs, on a standard format.
- Limit detailed recurrent cost estimation to large projects; for smaller projects, approximate calculations should be sufficient.
- For very large projects, examine alternative variants of project design that have different combinations of initial investment and future recurrent costs.

In the context of medium-term expenditure forecasts, the estimates of future recurrent costs of investment projects would also be rolled annually and adjusted according to changes in projections of inflation, interest rates, import prices, etc.

It must again be emphasized that such estimation affects only the expenditure side. Public investment also adds to the economy's productive capacity and thus to the tax base and government revenue. If the choice of projects is appropriate and their design, execution and financing are sound, the resulting indirect increase in government revenue should more than compensate for the associated debt service, depreciation, and operations and maintenance needs.

A Zoological Taxonomy of Public Investment Projects

Aside from the standard economic, financial and technical criteria, in screening proposals for investment projects it helps to ask: "What sort of investment animal is this?" With tongue in cheek and no pretense of analytical rigor, most public investment projects fall into one or another of five zoological categories—with a different policy approach for each.

Metaphorically:

Black Cows. Black cow projects are large and well-financed projects with a high and lasting impact on productivity. Black cows are the mainstay of good public investment. The appropriate policy vis-à-vis black cows is to make sure they are conceived properly, born in a safe environment, raised attentively, and fed everything they need. Shortchanging the gestation or the care and feeding of black cow projects will cost much more in terms of lost productivity than any savings that can possibly be achieved.

Brown Donkeys. Brown donkey projects are midsize investments—the majority of projects in most sectors—with moderate costs and benefits and limited risk. The appropriate policy vis-à-vis brown donkeys is to delegate responsibility for the design and implementation to the line ministry concerned—confining central tests to assuring that they are consistent with the sector strategy and have been adequately prepared.

Pink Pigs. Pink pigs are investment projects undertaken mainly for political patronage or regional balance. Pink pigs can be important for system maintenance, and in a fragile and conflict-affected state may be essential for the politics of reconstruction. One cannot apply cost–benefit methodology to them, because their political and/or security benefits are intangible. The appropriate policy vis-à-vis pink pigs is to set up clear criteria for "fair distribution" and to make sure that the money does go to the intended stakeholders.[11]

Gray Rabbits. Gray rabbit projects are small, geographically dispersed investments for social and humanitarian objectives, and are usually subcontracted to NGOs or local communities. Gray rabbits can make worthwhile contributions and produce visible "quick wins." Again, they may be especially important in fragile states. They are too small and heterogeneous to justify any sort of cost–benefit analysis, but they do require government clearance based on common sense and avoidance of duplication. Also, like their namesake, these small projects can reproduce very fast and can cause unexpected accountability problems and reputational risks. The appropriate policy vis-à-vis gray rabbits is to limit *total* expenditure on the group, require basic but regular reporting, and monitor implementation on a random basis.

White Elephants. White elephant projects are very large prestige projects, with exaggerated or imaginary benefits, high costs, large future expenditure requirements, and major fiscal and corruption risks. The origin of the term is attributed to the ancient Kingdom of Siam. A white elephant being extremely rare, it was considered sacred and, as such, it was gifted to the king. When the king was especially displeased with a courtier, he would re-gift the white elephant to him—and the poor man was in trouble. Being sacred, the elephant could not be made to work; being sacred, it could not be prevented from stomping on crops and destroying fences; and, being sacred, it had to be allowed to eat as much as it wanted. In a short time, the courtier would be ruined. The story may not be true, but it is the exact metaphor for a very large investment project which involves national pride, produces little or nothing of value, prevents the rise of smaller projects, and sucks up resources for a very long time. One or two white elephants can destroy the public finances of a small economy.

Developing countries have many fewer white elephants today than a generation ago—because most of them have expired of their own obesity after gobbling up large amounts of taxpayers' and aid money (state airlines head the list)—but many countries still suffer from their burdensome fiscal and corruption inheritance. As for the appropriate policy, it is very difficult to stop the gestation of a white elephant project once it is in the pipeline, and next to impossible to terminate the project after it is born—owing to the vested interests it has created and the political embarrassment it would cause to admit such a big mistake. The only workable protection against white elephants is to prevent their conception. It is critical therefore to set up political and technical gatekeeping mechanisms to prevent potential white elephant projects from even entering the project pipeline. The political gatekeeping should involve the very top of government, and require the highest-level clearance before proceeding; the technical gatekeeping must have strong political support and full operational autonomy. Finally, the answer to the question of how to tell a black cow from a potential white elephant is the same as the answer on how to define obscenity: you usually know it when you see it.

Public Investment Programming

The Objectives and Advantages of Public Investment Programming

Good projects are the bedrock of a sound public investment program (PIP), but a sound PIP is more than a collection of good projects—as it must take into account the affordability of overall investment expenditure, its consistency with the macrofiscal framework and the development strategy, the interaction among projects and the macro-externalities. A major example is the problem now emerging to affect the Mekong River Valley in Indochina, where a number of dams are envisaged to be constructed by different countries. The impact of each dam on the environment, fisheries and downstream interests can be appraised as manageable, but the adverse impact of all the dams is likely to be massive. The best appraisal of the individual projects cannot reveal the extent of the potential problem; only an investment program covering all the dams can do so. In this case, the challenge is made immensely complicated by the difficult relations between some of the countries in the region.

The main advantages of a good PIP are thus five:

- by strengthening the link between policy and the budget, it fosters growth with stability;
- by mobilizing adequate financing, it ensures the affordability of investment;
- by considering the multiyear implications of investment expenditure, it provides the core of a credible medium-term expenditure framework;
- by screening out bad project proposals and considering externalities, it raises the overall efficiency of investment and thus reduces the need for investment resources.

In the absence of a good and credible public investment program, the quality of projects is lower and implementation is hampered by insufficient or volatile funding. Moreover, without the protection of a coherent investment program, expenditure cuts are likely to fall primarily on investment, because most other categories of government expenditure are politically harder to cut in the short term. Indeed, in practice, public investment has often been defined as a mere residual: given a certain target for the fiscal deficit, the numbers can be made to add up most easily if the resources allocated in the budget to public investment are simply whatever is left over after deducting the recurrent expenditure needs from the forecast revenues. The residual character of the domestic funding of development expenditures may even be aggravated during budget execution, when expenditure is cut on ongoing investment projects—thus compromising project implementation and assuring that the actual rate of return will be lower than anticipated.

The above observations are valid only if public investment programming is rigorous. This has not always been the case: let's take a quick detour to the evolution of the focus of development assistance from the 1950s to date.

Foreign Aid: From Project to Program to Budget Support

Most developing countries—former colonial territories—became independent in the 1950s and 1960s. Throughout the first phase of development aid to those countries, aid funds were concentrated entirely on projects, almost entirely in physical infrastructure—roads, ports, etc.—and agriculture, with each project individually considered and financed separately by the various aid donor countries and organizations. In the 1970s, in keeping with the then-prevailing paradigm of state-led development, the scope of the aid was extended to industry and state enterprises, but remained centered on individual projects. Technically, this approach produced strong projects but was oblivious of the macroeconomic and institutional implications and the policy context which heavily influences the development effectiveness of the project. A classic real-life illustration is the financing of a fertilizer factory in the context of a policy of controlled low price of fertilizer. The price control is intended to subsidize local farmers and the new aid-financed factory produces quality fertilizer efficiently—but the local farmers get none of it because it is smuggled to the neighboring country where it can be sold for a higher price.

In addition to the need to consider the economic policy context, an exclusive focus on individual projects disregards the simple reality that money is fungible—a dollar is a dollar is a dollar. Suppose that an aid donor is not willing to finance a particular project A, which the recipient government wants—because it is ill-conceived, or competes with a similar project in a neighboring country, or carries risks of corruption, or any other reason. The government can request aid for a different proposed project B, which it also wants and which in the view of the donor agency is a sound investment for development—and project B goes forward with the foreign aid financing. But the aid to project B now enables the recipient government to release *its own* resources from that project to project A "which may be neither technically sound nor economically right, nor generally the kind of thing that the aid donor would want to support" (Schiavo-Campo and Singer, 1970, p. 249).[12] The aid donor has reviewed carefully the proposed project B, carried out a thorough economic analysis and assured itself that its money will go to a worthwhile development purpose, while in reality it is financing project A, which it did not want to support in the first place.

Recognition of the policy context and of the fungibility of aid moneys means that a decision to finance a specific large project requires some assurance that the sector policy is adequate and the public investment portfolio *as a whole* is sound and conducive to development. From this came the impulse to elaborate the set of tools and practices subsumed under the term of the public investment program—PIP—and the public investment reviews conducted by donors from the early 1980s.

But effective government programs require a judicious mix of investment and current expenditure, and the budget should be analyzed as an interconnected whole. The reviews of the public investment portfolio were thus expanded after the mid-1980s to reviews of the government's overall expenditure—the public expenditure reviews (PERs) conducted by the World Bank in virtually all developing and middle-income countries. In parallel, an increasing share of aid was given as "budget support" (or "program aid"), i.e., a financial contribution to the government not earmarked for any specific project but in exchange for the kind of policy reforms that would improve the efficiency and development effectiveness of all resources, foreign and domestic.

"First-Generation" Public Investment Programs

The logic was unassailable and the change in the aid paradigm was timely and appropriate. The practice, not so much. In most developing countries (especially in Africa and Southeast Asia), PIPs quickly degraded into shopping documents to attract aid money; expansionary and ill-conceived wish lists, backed up by scripts written by external consultants to be performed at international donor meetings; occasionally even "fig leaves" to cover aid given to corrupt regimes.

This was convenient both for the recipient countries' governments, which did not particularly like restrictions and conditions, and the donor agencies—whose incentives were (and remain) to get projects approved and aid disbursed. Not surprising, by the mid-1990s the credibility of these public investment "programs" was in ruins.

The problems with the first-generation PIPs of the 1980s and early 1990s were due to pervasive bad practice rather than to the concept itself. The appropriate remedy is therefore to halt those bad practices and assure that PIPs become the realistic, resource-constrained programming tools that can underpin the effectiveness of foreign and domestic resources for economic development. The proposition is a simple one: well-programmed and affordable expenditure on sound investment projects is better for development and poverty reduction than uncoordinated and unconstrained expenditure on weak investment projects. The question, as usual, is how to get there, and good public investment management provides much of the answer.

"Second-Generation" Public Investment Programs

To reiterate, a good PIP can raise investment efficiency by bringing investment allocation in line with country policies and sector priorities, assuring consistency between projects and programs, and providing the foundation for financing at favorable terms. Also, the process of PIP preparation can be important for capacity development—not only in the narrow sense of skills training but also in the sense of introducing an awareness of cost-effectiveness and a measure of social accountability. Finally, the process can serve as an instrument of coordination among donors, and thus mitigate many of the donor practices that have hampered aid effectiveness and the building of domestic capacity for public financial management (see Chapter 10).[13] The main ingredients of a second-generation PIP are as follows:

- The program should include and show all investment projects financed, in whole or in part, by public funds—foreign or domestic—with all appropriate details on size, total and annual cost, financing, estimated completion date, etc.
- It should normally cover a minimum of three years, with the current year corresponding to the budget year and two outyears, and be "rolled" annually each year by adding an outyear.
- The current year "slice" of the PIP should constitute the capital budget (with very minor differences for technical reasons).
- No project should be included in the PIP, even for the outyears, unless it has sufficient profitability in national economic terms, as demonstrated through sound economic appraisal.
- No project should be included in the current year unless financing is certain.
- No project should be included in the outyears unless financing is reasonably assured.
- For large projects, readiness for implementation should be assessed, including an adequate procurement plan.
- Financial and physical monitoring of project implementation should be frequent and reliable—and normally include feedback from local entities and civil society.
- The recurrent costs of large projects after completion should be estimated, even if approximately.
- An assessment should be made of the likely impact of the overall investment program on economic growth, relative to the future burden of servicing the debt incurred, even if tentative and generic.

When confronted with excessive investment proposals from line ministries, the ministry of planning or finance is tempted to avoid the hard decision to reject the weaker proposals by including them in the outyears of the PIP, but without any real intention of eventually financing them. Like all evasion and postponement of budgetary choices the eventual outcome is not good. In a year or two the program is cluttered with projects that everyone knows will never be completed—destroying the credibility of the programming itself. Worse still is the practice of including in the current year's program a small nominal allocation for the weak projects, as a sop to the ministry or region concerned (see Box 7.1.)

Overloading the investment program is sometimes done deliberately as a way to negotiate additional project aid. In practice, donors quickly realize that the program is deliberately overloaded, and are better able to pick and choose their preferred projects rather than the government's: the total amount of aid is the same but its allocation is distorted. Overloading can only be avoided by framing the preparation of the PIP with a binding ceiling for the coming fiscal year and strong indicative ceilings for the outyears, derived from the medium-term fiscal framework.

Assure Consistency Between the PIP and the Capital Budget

The investment decisions must be fully reflected in the capital side of the annual budget. In aid-dependent developing countries a large proportion of the funding for public investment comes from foreign aid and, except in the poorest countries and conflict-affected states, most aid-assisted projects require a local contribution from the budget.[14] Major problems arise when the amount of local currency budgeted for public investment is inconsistent with the expected foreign aid.

Problems during investment execution almost always arise anyway—from shortfalls in domestic revenue, delays in aid disbursements, unforeseen changes in costs or other reasons—even if all requisite local contributions are accurately estimated and included in the capital budget. But implementation problems are guaranteed, if the total amount of local currency in the capital budget is lower than required to cover all aid-assisted projects. Either some project will be stopped in order to shift sufficient counterpart funds to other projects—robbing Peter to pay Paul—or all projects will be delayed in implementation. And, because the local currency contribution is usually a fraction of the foreign aid, having to cut the local currency funding causes a much greater reduction in aid inflows.

Take the following illustration. The investment program consists of a hospital costing $40 million and a road costing $60 million, which are to be built with 80 percent aid money and 20 percent local funding. (Assume for simplicity that both are to be built within the fiscal year.) If the capital budget includes $20 million as the domestic contribution, and the foreign aid comes in on time, the construction of both the hospital and the road can proceed on schedule. However, if the budget includes only $12 million of local funding, either the hospital construction or the road construction or both will be delayed. (The same happens, of course, if the foreign aid disbursements don't come on time for other reasons, which occurs often.)

Implementation delays are invariably costly, both in dollar terms and in terms of absorbing the time and attention of managers and policy-makers, and the economic rate of return of both projects will be lower than had been estimated—reducing and postponing the benefits to the local populations. There's more. Since the required local contribution is 20 percent of total cost, the $12 million in local currency brings in only $60 million in aid—causing the public finances, the balance of payments, and the country itself to lose $20 million in aid. Paradoxically, the problem is worse in the poorest countries, where foreign donors are willing to cover a higher proportion of investment but the pressure to underbudget is stronger as well. In the above illustration, if the local currency contribution is only 5 percent, the "multiplier" is 20 and for every dollar-equivalent of underbudgeting the country loses 20 dollars of foreign aid.

This is not theoretical—it has been a reality in many developing countries for decades. But how can such a thing be allowed to happen in a world where donors are supposed to look after the effectiveness of their aid for development? Here's how. If the hospital is financed by donor A (who ascertains that the budget includes $8 million in local funding for investment, which would suffice for their project) and the road is financed by donor B (who ascertains, *separately*, that the budget includes $12 million in local funding for investment, which would suffice for *their* project)—both are satisfied that the local money is there to complete their project. Also, in most donor agencies, the incentives favor project approval much more than project implementation, tempting agency staff to close their eyes to insufficient local currency funding of investment. The subsequent delays in project execution and aid disbursements can then be blamed on a variety of other factors. Careers are made by getting projects approved, not by wrestling with the messy and unsexy problems of implementation in the trenches.

This is also the result when a targeted reduction in the fiscal deficit is accomplished by compressing public investment expenditure. Recall from Chapter 4 that the fiscal deficit results from transactions "above the line," while financing—including foreign aid loans at highly concessional terms—is "below the line." A target fiscal deficit can therefore be met by cutting a dollar's equivalent of local currency investment expenditure, even though this reduces concessional foreign aid by several dollars. This was the case with several IMF-supported structural adjustment programs in the 1980s and early 1990s. In those African countries that participated in IMF structural adjustment programs, the ratio of capital expenditure to total government expenditure was lower on average, indicating that the adjustment fell proportionately more heavily on public investment.[15] This kind of international financial malpractice has mostly gone with the millennial wind. Indeed, during the debt crisis in Europe in 2010, the IMF pushed for debt relief and structural reforms in the crisis countries, instead of the self-defeating expenditure cuts imposed by the European Union.

Good coordination between the IMF and the donors, as well as among donors themselves, can help assure that local currency is budgeted in an amount sufficient as counterpart of the expected foreign aid. This is only part of the development solution, however. The most important requirement is a rigorous public investment management process that assures that both the local and the aid moneys will go for good projects within a coherent program.

Annex: Assessing the Management of Public Investment

The attached list of indicators covers the four main dimensions of public investment management (PIM) (Table 7.1). The framework flows from the analysis in this chapter, but also includes some indicators from the PIM assessment matrix developed by Rajaram et al. (2014, pp. 34–7).

Not all conceivably relevant indicators are included; not all indicators are relevant to all countries; and some indicators are much more important than others. Also, the purpose of the list is diagnostic: diagnosis should never be turned into prognosis, and cannot serve as an action plan for improvements. Any choice of reform priorities and their sequencing must be specific to country context and capacity realities. Thus, *the following list should be used to produce a general assessment of strong and weak points in PIM, and not as a statutory checklist to be used prescriptively.* Because an assessment involves judgment, I do not suggest "grades" or other quantification of the status of each item. The utility of the framework lies more in comparing changes in the various indicators over time than in giving only a one-time snapshot of the public investment landscape.

The choice of indicators is largely institutional in nature: for example, there is no mention of value for money in procurement because the item is subsumed under indicators 3.2 and 3.9, or of the rate of return because it is subsumed under 2.3. The partial overlap between some indicators (for example, between 1.2 and 1.3) is deliberate, because the implications of the two indicators and the timing of the action concerned are different. Finally, the indicators in modules 2 and 3 on project selection and implementation apply only to sizeable and large projects.

Table 7.1 Public Investment Management Indicators

Dimension		Indicator
1. Budgetary integration	1.1	Aggregate actual capital expenditure as percentage of budgeted expenditure.
	1.2	Mean percentage deviation of actual projects' expenditure compared with budgeted expenditure.
	1.3	Budgeted local-currency expenditure consistent with the aggregate local-currency requirements of projects.
	1.4	Existence and enforcement of budgetary provisions for individual projects: (i) legislative authorization of entire project cost; (ii) allocation setting commitment limit during the fiscal year; (iii) allocation setting the cash payment limit for the year.
	1.5	Effectiveness of cooperation between sector ministries and the central planning entity.
	1.6	Effectiveness of cooperation between the finance entity and the planning entity.
	1.7	Reliability of estimation of foreign financing and appropriate integration into the budget.
2. Project selection and design	2.1	Consistency with national development priorities.
	2.2	Consistency with the concerned sector strategy.
	2.3	Appropriateness and quality of appraisal methodology.
	2.4	Quality of recurrent cost estimation.
	2.5	Provisions for contestability of appraisals.
	2.6	Robustness of political gatekeeping (for the largest project proposals).
	2.7	Implementability (in light of the existing capacity for project execution).
	2.8	Readiness for implementation at launch.
	2.9	Quality of provisions for ex post evaluation (large projects only).
3. Project implementation and monitoring	3.1	Adequacy of project funding in the budget (see also 1.3 and 1.7).
	3.2	Quality of the procurement plan.
	3.3	Quality of financial management provisions.
	3.4	Realism of the in-year disbursement plan in: (i) domestic resources; (ii) foreign resources.
	3.5	Clarity of responsibilities among ministry, local bodies and contractors.
	3.6	Quality of project management.
	3.7	Provisions for mid-course adjustments.
	3.8	Accountability mechanisms.
	3.9	Surveillance of large procurement transactions.
	3.10	Deviation of in-year disbursements from the disbursement plan in: (i) domestic resources; (ii) foreign resources.
	3.11	Regularity and reliability of reporting on financial implementation.
	3.12	Regularity and reliability of reporting on physical implementation.
	3.13	Enforcement of provisions for civil society feedback on project implementation.
	3.14	Process of registering the major physical assets created.
4. Public investment programming	4.1	Adequacy of coverage.
	4.2	Adequacy of information on each project.
	4.3	Correspondence between current year of the program and the proposed capital budget.
	4.4	Estimated proportion of current expenditure in the proposed capital budget.
	4.5	Verification that no sizeable project is included in the PIP unless appropriately selected (as per Section 2).
	4.6	Demonstration that financing is assured for all projects included in the current year.
	4.7	Verification that financing is highly likely for all projects included in the outyears.
	4.8	Adequate estimation of the overall likely impact of the program on economic growth.
	4.9	Adequate estimation of the overall likely impact of the program on poverty reduction and social development.
	4.10	Adequate estimation of the overall likely impact of the program on the environment.

Notes

1 Despite the extensive literature of the past 50 years on education and human capital formation, Kiker's article remains current as the best single synthesis of the evolution of the notion of human capital in the history of economic thought.

2 For example, public investment in India is planned to reach 9 percent of GDP, compared with the 2 percent OECD average, www.business-standard.com/article/economy-policy/report-claims-public-investment-as-main-fuel-for-indias-growth. The positive impact of public investment on economic growth and poverty was assessed, among others, by Anderson et al. (2006).

3 In the US, the budget process needs to move away from its focus on short-term decision-making. A recommendation advanced years ago by the General Accountability Office is especially relevant today in light of the dysfunctional budgetary politics of recent years. The recommendation is to include in the budget an explicit investment component, to help Congress and the president make better-informed decisions on consumption versus investment spending for the future—provided that such a component is set within a fiscal framework that strives to achieve a sustainable fiscal stance over the long term.

4 On these issues, see Inter-American Development Bank (2010) and Asian Development Bank (2015).

5 The popular revolution of January 2011 overthrew a repressive police state, with entrenched corruption (which increased sharply after the turn of the century). However, the administrative apparatus was and remains competent and well organized, and public financial management was prudent and comparatively efficient. These assets are of considerable help to the transition to full democracy.

6 This assumption was encapsulated in the widely used incremental capital-output ratio (ICOR), by which investment (the increment in capital) would raise GDP, and larger investment would lead to faster economic growth. While a lower ICOR by definition reflects higher investment "efficiency" in a macro sense, lower ICORs were normally assumed to result from the application of higher-level technology.

7 The earliest systematic treatment of public investment management was in Schiavo-Campo and Tommasi (1999). Various contributions followed, including recently by Rajaram et al. (2014) and IMF (2015).

8 For developed countries, see Burger and Hawkesworth (2013). Procurement is discussed extensively in Chapter 8.

9 Squire and van der Tak (1975) offer a still-current explanation of project economic analysis. See also Kohli (1993) and, more recently, ch. 4 in Rajaram et al. (2014).

10 Respectively Cho (2008) and Ferris (2009), cited in Rajaram et al. (2014).

11 The political economy priorities in post-conflict settings are to re-establish security and achieve a modicum of political accommodation. For this, an inclusive settlement is essential, and normally entails dispensing tangible economic benefits to the major stakeholders who have the power to either consolidate the peace or rekindle the conflict. (See Chapter 15.)

12 Schiavo-Campo and Singer (1970, p. 249). The fungibility of aid was first pointed out by de Vries (1967).

13 A comprehensive medium-term expenditure framework is obviously better than only a medium-term program of investments. However, to get to a comprehensive MTEF one needs to start with the category of expenditure that has the largest financial and economic implications for the future—entitlements in developed countries, and public investment in developing countries.

14 These contributions are sometimes called "counterpart funds." Confusingly, the term also refers to the local currency proceeds from selling goods or services provided by an aid donor. It is clumsier but clearer to talk of the local currency budgeted for public investment.

15 Unlike loans, grants are included above the line as part of revenue and thus contribute to a lower fiscal deficit. The perverse outcome could have been fairly easily avoided, therefore, by estimating the "grant equivalent" of foreign aid loans; including that grant equivalent as revenue; and retaining below the line the market component of the loans. The procedure for estimating grant equivalents is simple and well established, and requires only a few empirically based assumptions about the prevailing market interest rates and loan maturities. For example, a credit by the International Development Association (IDA), the concessional arm of the World Bank Group, currently carries a grant equivalent of about 70 percent. It would be easy and conceptually correct to include 70 percent of the credit as grant revenue and 30 percent as financing. The resulting picture would reflect fiscal realities far more accurately than placing the entire credit below the line, and the pressure to cut public investment for the cosmetic reason of an apparently lower deficit would be lifted. This author, among other senior IMF staff members at the time, argued unsuccessfully for such a practice.

Bibliography

Anderson, Edward, Paolo de Renzio and Stephanie Levy, 2006. *The Role of Public Investment in Poverty Reduction: Theories, Evidence and Methods.* London: Overseas Development Institute.

Asian Development Bank, 2015. *Promoting the Use of Country Systems in ADB Operations.* Manila: Asian Development Bank.

Burger, P. and Ian Hawkesworth, 2013. "Capital Budgeting and Procurement Practices," *OECD Journal on Budgeting*, 13(1), 57–104.

Cho, Junghun, 2008. *Public Investment in Belarus: A Case Study Applying the Framework for Reviewing Public Investment Efficiency.* Country study. Washington, DC: The World Bank.

Chung, I. H., 2013. "Adoption of a Separate Capital Budget in Local Governments: Empirical Evidence from Georgia," *Journal of Public Budgeting and Financial Management*, 25(4), 617–43.

De Vries, Barend, 1967. "External Aid: For Plans or Projects," *Economic Journal*, 77(307), 653–5.

Ferris, Thomas, 2009. *Public Investment Management in Ireland.* Country study. Washington, DC: The World Bank.

Inter-American Development Bank, 2010. *Strategy for Strengthening and Use of Country Systems.* Washington, DC: Inter-American Development Bank.

International Monetary Fund, 2015. *The IMF and Public Investment Management.* Washington, DC: IMF.

Kiker, B. F., 1967. "The Concept of Human Capital in the History of Economic Thought," *Indian Economic Journal*, 14 (January), 467–86.

Kim, J-H., 2013. *Public Investment in Korea.* Country study. Washington, DC: The World Bank.

Kohli, Kedar, 1993. *Economic Analysis of Investment Projects.* Oxford: Oxford University Press.

Marlowe, J., 2013. "Strategy, Priority-Setting, and Municipal Capital Budget Reform: Three Cases from the Great Recession," *Journal of Public Budgeting, Accounting and Financial Management*, 25(4), 693–718.

Premchand, A., 1998. "Umbrella Themes Obscure Real Problems: An Appraisal of Recent Financial Management Reforms," *Public Budgeting and Finance*, 18(3), 72–88.

——, 2007. "Capital Budgets: Theory and Practice," in Anwar Shah ed., *Budgeting and Budgetary Institutions.* Washington, DC: The World Bank.

Rajaram, Anand, Tuan Minh Le, Nataliya Biletska and Jim Brumby, 2010. "A Diagnostic Framework for Assessing Public Investment Management," *Policy Research Working Paper 5397.* Washington, DC: The World Bank.

Rajaram, Anand, Tuan Minh Le, Kai Kaiser, Jay-Hyung Kim and Frank Jonas, 2014. *The Power of Public Investment Management: Transforming Resources into Assets for Growth.* Washington, DC: The World Bank.

Schiavo-Campo, S. and Hans W. Singer, 1970. *Perspectives of Economic Development.* Boston, MA: Houghton-Mifflin.

Schiavo-Campo, S. and Daniel Tommasi, 1999. *Managing Government Expenditure.* Manila: Asian Development Bank.

Squire, Lyn and Herman van der Tak, 1975. *Economic Analysis of Projects.* Baltimore: Johns Hopkins University Press.

Tanzi, Vito and Hamid Davoodi, 1997. *Corruption, Public Investment and Growth.* Washington, DC: IMF.

——, 1998. *Roads to Nowhere: How Corruption in Public Investment Hurts Growth.* Washington, DC: IMF.

World Bank, 2010. *Cost–benefit Analysis in World Bank Projects.* Independent Evaluation Group. Washington, DC: The World Bank.

Part III

The Downstream Stages

Budget Execution and Control

8 Budget Execution
Compliance, Adaptability, Efficiency

> That's where the money is.
>
> (Willie Sutton, when asked why he robbed banks)

Introduction: The Framework and Objectives of Budget Execution

It doesn't do much good to have a well-prepared and realistic budget that reflects the choices and compromises of society if it is not then implemented. It is difficult to implement well a badly formulated and unrealistic budget, but quite possible to implement badly a good budget. Good budget execution follows good budget preparation, but is equally important to it.

Fiduciary Risk: The Underlying Concept

Chapter 4 explained the notion of fiscal risk—the risk to macroeconomic sustainability, arising directly from the various government liabilities and indirectly from hidden and unreported revenues and expenditures. Fiduciary risk is a different kind of risk, one more closely tied to fundamental financial governance principles. Once the budget is approved by the legislature, the executive branch of government has the obligation to execute it faithfully. Fiduciary risk is the risk of breaching this obligation, and thus the implicit contract between the government and the citizens. In law, a "fiduciary" is a person or an entity entrusted with acting in the interest of another person or entity. In public financial management, the executive branch of government is the fiduciary for acting in the interest of the population as a whole, and the interest in question is the faithful execution of the government budget.

Thus, preventing fiduciary risk in the narrow sense requires that the budget execution systems should, in order: (i) protect the money; and (ii) assure that it goes for the approved purposes. These requirements are related to the first two objectives of public expenditure management—expenditure control and strategic resource allocation (see Chapter 2). However, assuring that the money is not stolen or misallocated is not enough. In keeping with the third objective of expenditure management (operational efficiency), there is a broader construction of fiduciary risk—sometimes referred to as "development risk"—which includes also the risk that resources are not used in an efficient and effective manner.

The Objectives of Budget Execution

The three objectives of budget execution flow directly from the concept of fiduciary risk. Resources must be used to implement the approved budget. However, changes will occur during the year and flexibility is necessary to accommodate them. Finally, successful budget execution depends also on enabling efficient and effective budgetary management.

Hence, the objectives of budget execution are:

- *compliance* with the approved budget;
- *adaptability* to significant changes in environment and to implementation problems;
- *efficient management* of the budget resources.

Compliance is at the heart of traditional budget execution, and takes place through: (i) input controls; and (ii) provisions to prevent changes in the composition of expenditure. However, input controls should not be excessively detailed, nor should all changes in expenditure composition be prevented. Excessively detailed controls and rigid provisions are time-consuming and make budget management very cumbersome.

To meet the other two objectives of budget execution—adaptability and efficient management—the line ministries and agencies should be given adequate flexibility to manage their resources, within the broad categories and policy framework of the budget. Thus, *the core challenge of good budget execution systems is how to balance control with flexibility.*

The Main Cause of Budget Execution Problems: An Unrealistic Budget

The principal reason for problems in budget execution is an unrealistic budget in the first place. In most cases, execution problems "downstream" are directly related to "upstream" deficiencies in budget preparation.[1] Both overspending and underspending are related to inadequacies in budget preparation, which lead to very frequent changes in the budget during the fiscal year.[2] When facing problems in budget execution, it is always necessary to ask whether the problems are corollaries of weak budget preparation or can be addressed by strengthening the budget execution mechanisms themselves.

When revenues are overestimated and expenditures underestimated, at some point during the year the money will run out unless additional financing becomes available or, more frequently, ad hoc spending cuts are made. In this scenario, since the ministry of finance is required to control budget execution, it must decide how and to whom the money in the official budget can actually be allocated. In effect, alongside the formal budget, there is an informal budget known only to the ministry of finance and a few policy-makers. (This problem was first described by Caiden and Wildavsky, 1980.) Expenditure control may still be achieved, but at the cost of disrupting implementation of government activities and delivery of public services.

To prevent the overspending that results from an unrealistic budget, four measures can be taken, but each carries costs and risks:

- Across-the-board spending cuts lead to implementation problems in all activities.
- Selective cuts may help protect spending on priority activities—but ministries and agencies lack predictability and cannot meet their other expenditure commitments.
- Failure to make the required payments (payment arrears) creates inefficiencies and destroys government credibility (as discussed later).
- Rationing the available cash politicizes budget execution and may enable corruption.[3]

Underspending, too, is a problem, although of a different sort. Underspending is mainly found in the investment component of the budget, and is often caused by over-optimistic programming that doesn't take into account the time needed for procurement or for mobilization of external funds or for other implementation requirements. Adequate flexibility to reallocate funds from projects that are delayed to projects that are proceeding well can be helpful but is not easy. The optimal approach, as explained in Chapter 7, is a realistic public investment program in the first place combined with the practice of launching projects only when financing is assured and implementation requirements have been met.[4]

The Cycle of Expenditure

Following adoption of the budget by the legislature, the cycle of expenditure has five stages. The first four constitute the execution of the budget during the fiscal year and take place within the executive branch, and the last stage takes place after the year and is administered outside the executive branch by an independent audit entity reporting to the legislature.

- *Allocation of appropriations and release of funds to spending units.* Funds are released by the ministry of finance to the ministries and spending units concerned by notifying them of the cash limits, transferring funds to their accounts, etc. (In some countries, the release of funds includes two steps: (i) "apportionment" by the central budget office, which consists of defining which part of the appropriation the line ministries and spending decision units may use; and (ii) "allotment" by the line ministries and main spending decision units to their subordinate spending units.)
- *Commitment.* The commitment (or contract) stage is the stage at which a future obligation to pay is incurred. A commitment consists of placing an order or awarding a contract for goods or services to be received or works to be completed, respectively—after appropriate procurement procedures have been followed to get the item at the best price and a given quality. (The *procurement stage.*) Depending on the country and the nature of the expenditure, the term "commitment" may relate to the time the funds are reserved, or the time when the order is placed, or the time when the contract is awarded.
- *Acquisition/verification* (or *certification*). The commitment entails an obligation to pay but only if the other party has complied with the provisions of the order or contract. At the acquisition/verification stage, the goods are delivered and/or the services are rendered, and their conformity with the order or contract is verified.
- *Payment.* In principle, payments can be made through a variety of instruments: cash, checks, electronic transfers, vouchers, debt instruments, deduction from taxes. Payments through deduction from taxes and vouchers are problematic. Allowing tax deductions in lieu of outright payments makes future tax collection less predictable, harms competition among suppliers and creates opportunities for tax evasion. The practice was frequent in the former Soviet Union and some East European countries in the early transition years (owing to government liquidity problems), but has diminished substantially after the 1990s and as of 2016 payments through tax deductions are a rare exception. Vouchers are clumsy and prone to error when they are not paid quickly, and unnecessary when they are paid quickly. And cash payments are a recipe for corruption on a vast scale, and carry potentially disastrous implications for public service efficiency and—in the military—for national security. See Box 8.1 for actual examples. (Payment arrears are the difference between expenditures at the verification stage and payments made within the time normally allowed for payment for the type of transaction concerned.)
- *Audit.* At this final stage, the year's transactions are reviewed with an eye to identifying and reporting any fraud, irregularity or error.

Box 8.1   Government Payments: Checks versus Cash

The risks and corrupting effects of making government payments in cash are legion. To take just four examples:

- In South Vietnam in the 1960s and early 1970s, regime generals became very rich by padding the Armed Forces of the Republic of Vietnam (ARVN) payroll with "ghost" soldiers and keeping the corresponding salaries.
- In Palestine in the late 1990s, corruption in the policeforce was substantially reduced when the minister of finance forced a shift from paying police officers' salaries in cash to payments by check.
- In Cambodia, civil servants were paid in cash as late as 2010, when salaries started being paid by check.
- In Iraq some senior army officers were pocketing the salaries of soldiers. The soldiers understandably dropped their weapons and ran in June 2014 when faced with a numerically inferior ISIS force.

In country after country, a change from cash payment of salaries and suppliers to payment by check or electronic transfers has proven to be the single most powerful way to combat a major source of public corruption and of loss of state legitimacy. Moreover, by requiring the opening of bank accounts, such a change fosters the growth of retail banking even in isolated areas which previously lacked banking services—such services are now possible with information technology.

In the immediate aftermath of major civil conflict, cash payments may be inevitable owing to the extensive destruction of physical facilities and financial institutions. For example, in Afghanistan in 2002–3 paying civil servants outside Kabul and the other main cities required carrying bags of cash under heavy security. Such payments should be replaced with checks as soon as the security situation permits, as in fact was done in most of Afghanistan in 2003. In extreme conflict-affected cases, as in Somalia in 2016, what payments the formal government is able to make to its employees are necessarily in cash because there is no longer any bank in the country other than the Central Bank.

Source: Author.

In the household analogy, after the family has made a collective decision on how much and on what to spend during the month, the money is distributed to the various family members who are in charge of well-defined types of expenses—paying utility bills, expenditures for tuition or books, school lunch money, groceries, etc. (The allocation stage.) Having done that, the family needs a system to keep track of the expenditures by each family member in order to avoid surprises—buying a luxury car instead of the compact that had been budgeted for, or high-end jeans instead of school books, or whatever. (The commitment stage.) After the items have been ordered, one has to make sure that what has been purchased has in fact been delivered. (The acquisition/verification stage.) Next, the bills must be paid, and must be paid on time—to keep college credit from being withheld, or the lights from going out, etc.—and this calls for a system to keep track of the payments coming due on account of items already bought and delivered. (The payments stage.) Finally, at the end of the month, the expenditures must be reviewed to assure that the money has not been wasted, or pocketed by a "forgetful" family member, or used ineffectively. (The audit stage.)

Without procedures to assure the implementation of each of the stages of expenditure, spending would go on until the cash available runs out and then stop, which is not very conducive to an efficient use of the family's money or to building its economic future. Thus, while the responsibility for managing the money rests with the family members in their respective areas of competence, close and regular supervision by the "head of household" (the ministry of finance) is a must.

Controlling Budget Execution

Types of Controls

The types of budget execution controls track precisely the stages of the expenditure cycle. After the first stage of allocation/release of funds is completed, each stage of expenditure is associated with a specific type of control—financial, physical, accounting and audit control—with different entities responsible for each.

Financial Controls

Financial control (see Radev and Khemani, 2009) applies at the commitment stage, to assure specifically (and only) that:

- the funds have been included in the budget for the purpose specified;
- the proposed order or contract is for expenditure under the approved category;
- sufficient funds are available in the appropriate expenditure category; and
- the proposed order or contract has been formally approved by a duly authorized person.

Verification of the first three items is necessary for compliance with the approved budget; verification of the last item is essential for the validity of the contract itself and hence to protect against mistakes or corruption. (The delegation of budget authority must therefore find its correlate in the job descriptions of government officials.)

Physical Controls

At the verification stage, clear protocols are needed and specific individuals must be formally designated to attest that the goods or services have been delivered in accordance with the order or contract provisions, including quantity, quality specifications and timeliness. Authorized persons in each ministry and department must review and certify the documentary evidence that the goods have been received and that the services were actually performed.

Accounting Controls

Accounting control takes place before the payment is made. Some countries rely on accounting controls to prevent fraud and assure compliance. However, accounting control alone, while necessary, is quite insufficient to ensure compliance with the budget. Accounting controls cannot prevent payments arrears because they authorize but do not compel the actual payment, nor can they prevent an unauthorized commitment or a fake delivery because they intervene after the commitment has been made and the delivery has been certified. Accounting control is intended to assure specifically (and only) that:

- a valid contract exists;
- a duly-authorized person has certified that the goods have been received or services performed as per the contract;

- the invoice and other documents requesting payment are correct; and
- the beneficiary and their location are correctly identified.

Audit Control

Audit takes place after the expenditure cycle is completed, to examine and scrutinize the transactions and report any fraud, irregularity or error. It is mentioned here only for completion because, as a critical function external to the executive branch and with its own criteria and requirements, it is discussed at length in Chapter 11.

Organizational Arrangements for Budgetary Control

Centralized or Delegated?

There must be a separation of duties for authorizing expenditures, approving contracts and placing orders, certifying that goods have been received and that services have been provided, and authorizing payments. Except in very small government entities, such as a village, it is prudent to designate for each level of control different individuals who are accountable to different offices. In central government, this separation of duties is often associated with the distribution of responsibilities between the ministry of finance and the line ministries and spending agencies. Depending on the country, the budgetary controls may be performed by and under the responsibility of the relevant line ministry (delegated control) or by a central entity (normally the ministry of finance).

Arrangements vary. In many countries (usually low-income countries), a central office in the ministry of finance is responsible for accounting controls and effecting payments. In other countries, accounting controls are performed and payments are processed by the line ministries, but cash and bank accounts are controlled by the central treasury department, which is responsible for cash management. It is important not to confuse centralization of government *cash*, which is essential in almost all countries, with centralization of government *payments*, which may or may not be desirable depending on country circumstances. (Cash management and the treasury function are discussed later in this chapter.)

On the one hand, centralizing budgetary controls ensures that they are performed by qualified persons, and allows the central ministry to monitor that every expenditure fits the purpose stated in the budget and all payments are correct and appropriately documented. That's why centralized controls are sometimes seen as the cornerstone of fiscal discipline. On the other hand, centralized budgetary controls may not be conducive to the third objective of good public expenditure management: operational effectiveness. Delegating budgetary controls fosters the ownership of line ministries and agencies in the execution of their programs and activities and improves the opportunities for efficient management and civil society feedback. As Premchand (1995, p. 41) puts it: "government financial management can [still] be secured through . . . periodic oversight, strengthened accountability, greater citizen participation and, above all, greater transparency."

Even when payments are processed centrally under the ministry of finance, locating the accountants of the ministry of finance within the line ministries is preferable to locating them centrally, as it reduces delays in processing invoices and requests for payment.

A centralized system of budgetary control is the cost-effective solution if the government's organizational arrangements are fragmented and capacity is extremely weak. However, as line ministries' capacity improves, there should be a gradual move toward delegating financial and accounting controls. There is little logic and high cost in a system where every invoice and request for payment has to be submitted to a central office.

If the concern is with preventing corruption, centralizing controls and payments does not accomplish that, as it may simply centralize corruption opportunities rather than reduce corruption in the system as a whole. (This, of course, may very well be the real objective of proponents of centralized controls.) If the concern is with preventing excessive commitments, central control does not accomplish that either, as it may simply provide an excuse to develop "exceptional contract procedures" that go around the central system and avoid commitment controls altogether.

Concerning payments, delegating accounting controls is normal and appropriate in advanced countries (e.g., the US), but not in developing countries (e.g., Brazil, where controls are centralized). In developing countries skilled accountants are scarce: decentralized payments could increase difficulties in cash management, and the lack of strong local institutions could loosen financial discipline. Centralized controls are thus generally preferable. Both decentralized and centralized accounting controls and payment processing systems are compatible with the use of a general ledger system (GLS), into which are posted not only payment transactions but also commitments. The GLS can also be linked with the accounting and management information systems maintained at ministry and spending agency level (see Chapter 11).

Financial Control: Ex Ante or Ex Post?

In countries of the "Anglo-Saxon" administrative tradition, financial control is strictly limited to ascertaining the four items listed earlier. In countries following the French administrative tradition, financial controllers are also empowered and responsible to look into the efficiency and effectiveness of the proposed commitment—ex ante, i.e., before the contract specifications, costs and other items are finalized. In both systems, the financial controllers are normally part of the ministry of finance apparatus, but in the French-type system they are in effect financial overseers, and their view often prevails even over the wishes of the minister concerned.

The two systems have evolved under different historical circumstances and, in principle, there is no clear preference for one over the other model. Where public accountability is well developed, capacity is adequate, and administrative ethics are strong, ex ante controls by the central ministry of finance are unnecessary and inadvisable. In other circumstances, there may be a case for retaining strong financial controls in the central ministry of finance. (In countries with authoritarian regimes, ex ante central controls are the norm, but are motivated by a desire to keep a firm grip on the system and on grand corruption opportunities, rather than a concern with good public financial management.)

In some countries, the officials responsible for financial or accounting controls report to both the ministry of finance and the head of the relevant spending agency. This dual responsibility dilutes accountability and potentially submits the officials to contradictory requirements. In rare cases, however, this dual responsibility has been managed well, owing largely to the personal qualities of the officials concerned. The dual responsibility system can also serve as a vehicle for capacity-building in the line ministries, facilitator of proper reporting on budget execution and mechanism of cooperation between the ministry of finance and the line ministry.

On balance, international experience makes a strong case in favor of removing ex ante financial controls. However, to do so without prior or at least concurrent strengthening of accountability mechanisms can seriously compromise the integrity of the system. The need is for effective budget execution control *for the government as a whole*: reducing central and ex ante controls would thus create a risky vacuum unless it is done gradually and concomitantly with the development of budget execution capacity and accountability in the line ministries.

The Imperative of Clear Accountabilities

Let's close this section with an important tautology: each controller is responsible only for the type of control for which he is responsible. To try and involve a financial controller also in verifying a delivery, or an accountant in determining whether a commitment was cost-effective, or an operational manager in examining the format of payment requests—or any other confusion or duplication of roles whatsoever—does not strengthen budget control. On the contrary, unclear or multiple responsibilities weaken expenditure control, cause delays and make it difficult to assess responsibility when mistakes or illegal actions occur.

Monitoring Budget Execution

The Monitoring Approach: Close Watch, Light Hand

Budget execution must be followed closely and regularly to ensure that expenditures are appropriate and effective and to identify significant financial or policy slip-ups early enough to allow corrective action. The monitoring of budget execution should cover both financial and physical aspects: the financial implementation of the budget should be reported monthly to the ministry of finance, and the physical implementation of major investment projects should be reported to the ministry of planning (or equivalent).

In monitoring the budget, the legitimate information needs of the central authority should be weighed against the reporting costs imposed on the line ministries and agencies. Ask too little and you cannot monitor the budget; ask too much and you get junk information. The appropriate balance depends on the country and its circumstances. In general, however, ministries of finance have a tendency to impose on the spending agencies excessively detailed or too frequent reporting requirements, without really needing all the information and thus without substantive follow-up. Excessive reporting requirements are destructive all around: knowing that the ministry of finance has neither the need nor the capacity to analyze the mountain of reports—let alone to take corrective action—the spending agencies send in formalistic and sloppy reports; this pushes the ministry of finance to tighten up its reporting requirements, causing even greater waste of time and effort throughout the system for no benefit in terms of effective budget execution. In Uganda, for example, every ministry is required to submit a quarterly report on the output of every expenditure program, regardless of its nature, leading to some nonsensical reports (e.g., one-quarter of a building foundation completed), assembled at substantial costs in terms of time and data collection, and with no follow-up by the ministry of finance. (As a line ministry official said to the author: "We are required to report so much and so often on what we have accomplished that we have no time to accomplish anything.") Selectivity is as important in budget reporting as in all other areas of public sector management.

Monitoring the Different Categories of Expenditure

Monitoring of interest payments is covered under debt management in Chapter 10. The discussion next covers the monitoring of the remaining economic expenditure categories: O&M, transfers, wages and investment.

Monitoring Operations and Maintenance Expenditure

Monitoring of O&M, with its thousands of individual items, is generally limited to aggregate expenditure, but specific items should be followed individually—either because they are very expensive (e.g., fuel), or present risks of payment arrears (e.g., utilities payments), or because they are vulnerable to corruption or mismanagement (e.g., maintenance of government buildings). Also, prior experience is an excellent guide: if expenditure on a particular item has been wasted or abused in the past, it is useful to monitor it closely until regularity and efficiency have been restored.

Monitoring Transfers and Subsidies

Because the amounts and the beneficiary groups are determined by law and can only be changed by law, monitoring of transfers and subsidies is focused on assuring that the right beneficiaries are receiving the transfers, in the right amount and on a timely basis. Because it is costly and difficult to investigate each beneficiary, even on a random sample basis, the main protection of accuracy and integrity in this area is the provision of easy channels for complaints and feedback by the intended beneficiaries, along with prompt and adequate follow-up. Even so, this is an area rife with the potential for fraud and abuse.

Monitoring Personnel Expenditure

In the few countries with full program budgeting, personnel expenditure is grouped together with goods and services expenditure under the program classification, and central monitoring of the individual components of a program would be contrary to the logic of the system. In all other countries, both the total wage bill and the number of employees should be closely monitored.

In most developing countries, transfers between personnel and non-personnel expenditure are not allowed. In countries that are well managed and have a government workforce of the appropriate size and with adequate compensation, monitoring of personnel expenditure can be infrequent and light. In other countries, the number of government employees—especially contractuals and temporary—should be closely monitored throughout the year, with swift corrective measures and penalties for violating the limits established in the budget.

An effective payroll system is necessary to monitor the number and composition of employee staff limits and ensure integrity and transparency in personnel expenditures. In developing countries, the payroll must be centralized in the ministry of finance and fully integrated with the personnel management system. Experience shows that, in every case where there was not a prior or concurrent effort at strengthening the payroll system, civil service censuses aimed at identifying and removing "ghost" employees have failed and the same or new ghosts have invariably returned through various back doors. Computerization has proved to be of great help to assure full compatibility between the personnel database and the government payroll.

When the budget system has fallen into serious disrepair, rebuilding the payroll and its linkages to personnel management is one of the first priorities. However, doing so in a context of malgovernance is very difficult and is subject to heavy political constraints as in the case of Zimbabwe—see Box 8.2.

Monitoring Public Investment

Monitoring the execution of the investment budget should follow the schedules specific to each project. Financial monitoring of expenditure should be done by the ministry of finance and monitoring of the physical progress of major works by the ministry of planning or equivalent—in both cases through the line ministry concerned.

Box 8.2 The Payroll and Skills Audit in Zimbabwe

The public service in Zimbabwe was gravely affected by macroeconomic decline and the hyperinflation of 2006–9, with many government employees leaving and others demoralized, and uncertain fiscal implications of wages and pensions. In 2010, the government requested external technical support for a comprehensive audit to: (i) update and validate the government personnel database; and (ii) take stock of the existing skills based on the validated personnel data. Among the outcomes expected from the exercise were the savings from the identification and removal of a large number of "ghosts" and double dippers, and the elimination of opportunities for graft and mismanagement.

The audit, carried out by an international firm, was divided into four stages. Stage 1 built a comprehensive repository of current and past government personnel, by gathering the data maintained by the various agencies and ministries, normalizing them as needed and storing them in standardized format. In Stage 2 the employees were enumerated and personnel records verified. In Stage 3 the verified data were to be analyzed, to identify skills gaps as well as understaffed and overstaffed units. In the final Stage 4, a complete audit of the payroll and human resource management systems was to be undertaken to identify capacity-building needs as well as the infrastructure and equipment required to operate and maintain robust personnel management and payroll systems.

The completion of Stage 2 revealed, among many other problems, some 40,000 employees with weak or no qualifications, or in non-existent jobs. A large proportion of these were nominally employed in the agriculture ministry, as "advisers" or "extension agents." There were also lists of alleged but non-existent employees, with the names of new hires filled in after the fact. When confronted with the evidence that the payroll had been stuffed with large numbers of regime supporters who were either unqualified or simply no-shows, the government brought the process to a sudden halt in 2011. Nothing more has been heard of cleaning up the wage and pension bill in the budget of Zimbabwe.

Unfortunately for the regime (and for the population), the fiscal problem has not vanished along with the payroll reform. In mid-2016, the government again found itself unable to pay wages—either for the real employees in real jobs or for the ghost employees in ghost jobs, and major and widespread unrest began, threatening the very survival of the regime.

Investment execution is often beset by problems—insufficient implementation capacities, financing delays, over-optimistic construction schedules, environmental complications or difficulties in importing equipment and supplies. For the largest and most problematic projects a regular quarterly review of progress should be conducted by the line ministry concerned and complemented with a midyear review, also involving the ministries of finance and planning.

As in budget execution in general, problems in implementing investment projects are inevitable if the public investment program is weak or overambitious, or insufficient local money is included in the budget to complement foreign aid—as explained in Chapter 7.

A Few Words about Information Technology

Without pertinent, reliable and timely information, good decisions are not possible. A system to provide government budget managers with financial information (previously called an integrated financial management information system and now more realistically called a financial management information system, or FMIS) is a computerized system that tracks government expenditures and payment processing, and reports accordingly.

The topic of the uses and misuses of information and communication technology (ICT) in public financial management is much too vast to be discussed adequately here. (The interested reader is referred to Diamond and Khemani, 2005, for a first critical look at FMIS implementation in Africa; to the seminal study by Dener et al., 2011, for a comprehensive review of international experience; to Hashim, 2014, for a practical handbook on the subject; and most recently Hashim and Piatti, 2017, for an expanded and updated review of experience with FMIS.) However, a few key considerations can be mentioned here.

First, ICT is a tool, very powerful but—when misused—risky as well. As with any other tool, it must be tailored to the needs of the users and not the other way around, and designed consistently with the country's capacity and institutional realities. Second, an FMIS cannot remedy institutional or organizational weaknesses. Indeed, if adopted as a panacea, computerization has the potential to jeopardize genuine reform in public financial management. Third, if the budget coverage is limited and a large share of government transactions occurs outside the budget, by definition an FMIS for budget transactions cannot produce adequate information on government expenditure as a whole. Finally, as a practical matter, FMIS introduction typically takes at least twice as long and costs at least twice as much as originally envisaged—even when it ends up working well, which is not always the case.[5] That said, effective implementation of a well-designed and appropriate FMIS can assist the budgetary process more than any other single improvement in the technical infrastructure for public financial management.

International experience yields six lessons on FMIS design and implementation in developing countries:

- The design and implementation of a financial management information system should fit within an overall government strategy for information and communication technology. Thus, the formulation of such a strategy is a prerequisite for sustainable computerization of government financial transactions.
- If a financial management information system is to be effective, there must be assurances that all government transactions are routed through the system, and all expenditures are subject to the FMIS automated internal controls. This means among other things that no payment instructions issued outside of the system should be honored.
- Both the software and the hardware must be adequately maintained to keep the system functional and—most importantly—secure. (In May 2016, hackers managed to steal $81 million from the Bangladesh Central Bank—supposedly one of the most secure institutions in any economic system.)
- In aid-dependent countries, donor funds should also be channeled through the FMIS— even though donors may retain their own accounting system and fiduciary safeguards.
- Having a single systems platform for all government transactions is desirable for systems integration and efficiency.
- However, the single platform should be "filled" as and when data and capacity permit. Sequencing is critical, and attempts to introduce at one go a complete and integrated financial management information system have almost invariably led to expensive failures.

Several of these lessons are reflected in Box 8.3 on the experience of Malawi and Cambodia.

In addition to its uses in budget preparation and execution, the judicious application of information technology can substantially facilitate the government–citizen interaction on budgeting matters. For example, in Slovenia, a portal allows citizens to participate in government decision-making, by offering suggestions and other comments (https://joinup.ec.europa.eu/community/epractice/case/slovenia). And the Czech Republic initiated the use of open source platforms for disclosing the details of state budget performance (https://joinup.ec.europa.eu/community/epractice/case/online-click-through-budgets).

Box 8.3 FMIS in Malawi and Cambodia: Two Examples of Bad Practice

Malawi abandoned efforts to customize a financial management information system platform in the early 2000s in favor of a second-generation package that had recently come on the market. The new FMIS was rolled out quickly and with a functional core set of modules, in principle capturing the bulk of government expenditures. However, while the system itself was functional from a technical point of view, compliance was not enforced: commitment controls were frequently ignored or bypassed; spending units reportedly maintained an off-FMIS registry and uploaded funding limits on an as-needed basis; purchase orders and payment vouchers were generated simultaneously, despite directives to the contrary; key players colluded; and at least one major corruption episode took place. As noted, an FMIS cannot remedy political or institutional weaknesses. As of 2016, Malawi is again looking at investing considerable resources in yet another new FMIS, with a fresh set of problems.

In Cambodia, a comprehensive FMIS was a central component of the Public Financial Management and Accountability Project started in 2006. The project as a whole was unsatisfactory and the FMIS component was a disaster in design and thus inevitably in implementation. The risks associated with Cambodia's political and institutional environment were not adequately considered, and advanced technical solutions were pursued which gave rise to severe difficulties in procurement. In particular, the attempt at simultaneous implementation of all FMIS modules was unrealistic and placed great strains on the capacity available. Also, there was lack of participation in design by the main stakeholders. The FMIS component was finally dropped. However, the experience of the failed FMIS was used to redesign a better system in the follow-up project. There is no assurance that Cambodia's government will soon have a well-functioning FMIS system suited to its circumstances and capacities, but at least, unlike in the Malawi case, the government learned from the experience and reworked its FMIS strategy in 2012.

At the turn of the century, when the fullness of international experience with FMIS had not yet been analyzed, ambitious and unrealistic initiatives to insert a "state of the art" computerized system into a weak institutional environment with loose accountability was perhaps understandable. Now that the experience is available to all, repetitions of the fallacy of looking for "technical" solutions to political, governance and institutional problems should no longer be tolerated.

Source: Adapted from IEG (2016).

The Mechanics of Budget Execution

Managing Payments

The production of government services rests on two main pillars—procuring the necessary goods, services and works, and managing their payments. Procurement is discussed in Chapter 9. This section focuses on the management of payments.

As noted, computerization can help enormously in the management of payments, but whether the system is manual or partly or fully computerized, four rules must be followed:

- Expenditures must be verified as soon as the goods or the services have been acquired.
- Verified expenditures must be entered immediately into the accounts.
- Invoices should be paid on the due date, but not in advance.
- Payments must be accurately recorded as soon as they are made.

Overt and Covert Non-Compliance

There are two ways of violating the requirement of compliance with the approved budget. Overt non-compliance stems from excessive cash payments and cannot be hidden, because any excess of payments over the amount authorized in the budget necessarily comes to the surface sooner or later. Covert non-compliance is worse.

In a cash budget, covert non-compliance stems from lack of control over *commitments*—since the budgetary controls are on actual payments and commitments can be made even without the money to pay for them during the fiscal year. The conformity of the budget execution with the approved budget is only apparent, because certain payments due are swept under the rug, which only pushes the problem to the next fiscal years. The objective of compliance is violated under both overt and covert non-compliance but, in addition, covert non-compliance reduces fiscal transparency, harms government credibility and generates a variety of costs and problems. Therefore, in a cash budget, a separate and systematic procedure for monitoring and controlling commitments is necessary in order to prevent payment arrears and achieve genuine compliance with the budget.

The Issue of Payments Arrears

Failure to make payments on time leads to "payments arrears." An arrear is incurred when an invoice is not paid on the contractual due date. (Arrears are thus different from "float," which is the normal time after delivery that is needed to process payment invoices.) If allowed to accumulate, payment arrears are the quickest and most efficient way to damage the credibility of the government, raise government costs and distort the fiscal accounts.

Most obviously, delaying payments poses problems to the suppliers (or beneficiaries, in the case of salaries, pensions or subsidies), but also severely disrupts public financial management and raises the cost of government. When the government accumulates arrears, the private suppliers develop defensive strategies—demanding payment before delivery, overbilling or bribing the officials responsible for managing the waiting list of payment arrears.

Arrears have many causes. Improved monitoring of commitments is generally required, but other measures are needed as well: realistic budget estimates, internal management controls and good personnel management. Arrears in payments to public utilities for their services are especially common: state-owned utility companies cannot afford politically to stop providing services to government agencies even when they are not paid (imagine cutting off the electricity of the office of the minister who appoints your CEO), and they cope with the problem by demanding larger and larger government subsidies to cover the resulting losses. Conveniently, the payment arrears also provide the utilities with an alibi for their own mismanagement or bad performance. Preventing payment arrears thus improves fiscal transparency at the same time as it brings to light the deficiencies in the utilities themselves and facilitates reforms. Limiting payments arrears to public utilities requires (among other things) good estimates of annual consumption as well as management measures (such as installing meters). All such measures should be identified during budget preparation, as it is normally too late to introduce them during budget execution.

In cases of severe fiscal stress, the government may simply be unable to meet all its payment obligations on time. As soon as the crisis is over, however, arrangements should be made for a negotiated settlement with all creditors—instead of simply burying one's head in the sand and allowing the problem to keep growing in an uncontrolled, inefficient, costly and inequitable fashion.

The process of settlement of payments arrears can be as problematic as the initial accumulation of arrears, and is a major source of bribe opportunities. In principle, payments of past due bills should be prioritized according to the date on which the invoices were due, and, if full payment is financially impossible, an equitable system of pro-rated payments should be implemented. In practice, unpaid invoices can be included, or "accidentally" excluded; can be paid sooner, or later; payment can be authorized although the goods were defective and the invoice was originally rejected; the supplier and the government official can collude to modify invoices or manufacture them altogether; the interest accrued since the due date can be calculated conservatively, or generously;[6] and so on. Any of these can occur depending on the soundness of the program for settlement of payment arrears and the "consideration" received by the government officials who are in charge of settling the overdue payments. It is critical therefore to have a program of arrears settlement that is: (i) fully comprehensive and simultaneous; (ii) governed by strict rules without exception; (iii) monitored by an independent external entity; and (iv) subject to a special audit by the external audit office.

Balancing Control and Flexibility in Budget Execution

As emphasized in Chapter 2, none of the three interrelated objectives of public expenditure management—expenditure control, strategic resource allocation and operational efficiency—should be pursued in isolation. Central control alone may assure aggregate expenditure control but cannot facilitate resource allocation, let alone the efficient use of the money. At the other extreme, giving excessive flexibility to the spending agencies in the name of operational efficiency would likely lead to uncontrolled expenditure and fiscal risk. The challenge is to find that balance between control and flexibility that enables good management while assuring control, in light of the specific country circumstances. The control/flexibility balance revolves mainly around the questions of (i) when and how funds are released to the line ministries and spending agencies, and (ii) the extent to which the line ministries are empowered to shift funds from one item to another during budget execution.

Release of Funds: Provide Predictability of Resources

Ideally, funds should be released to line ministries and spending agencies in accordance with a detailed budget implementation plan, prepared at the start of the fiscal year.[7] Consistent with the budget implementation plan, a cash plan should be prepared and adjusted subsequently as needed. The preparation of a cash plan is discussed in the last section of the chapter. In any event, the authority to spend must be given to line ministries and spending agencies in useful time. Predictability is the watchword, and the system should meet the following main criteria:

- Inform spending agencies of the amounts they will be authorized to spend, and when.
- Release the funds in time. (In case of unforeseen liquidity problems, the schedule for releasing funds will need to be revised, but the revised schedule should be communicated to the line ministries instead of just delaying the release of funds compared with the agreed schedule.)
- Pay special attention to government agencies located in remote areas. (Cooperation is needed between the ministry of finance and the line ministry concerned, and between the line ministry and its regional offices.[8])

When the budget is particularly unrealistic or major unforeseen fiscal problems arise, cash rationing ensues, and funds are released to ministries only as and when cash is available. Under cash rationing, the ad hoc release of funds is vulnerable to political pressure and personalistic considerations. Cash rationing thus produces a de facto budget that is quite different from the budget approved by the legislature. Moreover, although cash rationing is intended to control expenditure, it cannot actually do so because the line ministries and spending agencies are legally entitled to continue to make commitments according to the formal budget, and will thus accumulate arrears—adding to government liabilities and burdening future budgets.

Such situations were frequent, particularly in transition economies (in Ukraine in 1996, cash was rationed daily, making it virtually impossible for government to perform normal activity), but have lessened substantially everywhere as the economic situation has stabilized. In conflict-affected states, however, cash rationing remains common.

Virements: Provide Management Flexibility

Next to compliance with the approved budget, adapting to change and enabling managerial flexibility are the other two objectives of good budget execution. Minor changes can be handled through a small contingency reserve in the budget itself, and formal budget amendments deal with major changes during the fiscal year and with expenditure reallocations between ministries. However, adequate flexibility must be built into the budget execution rules themselves, to adapt to frequent changes and enable budget managers to take advantage of new opportunities and make efficient choices in performing their functions. This flexibility is provided by rules that permit transfers of money from one line item of the budget to another—called virements (transfers in French).

Virement rules must be established in the basic budget law or the financial regulations. Within the budget appropriation to a ministry, the executive branch should be generally free to reallocate as it judges best—within certain limits. Such reallocations are effected under rules that define the level of authority required for different types of expenditure:

- virements that may be made freely by the individual budget managers within their own authority, e.g., between different kinds of current supplies;
- virements that require approval by the head of department or the minister (depending on the amount involved), e.g., between current supplies and durable goods; and
- virements that require approval by the ministry of finance (e.g., between major expenditure categories, or for amounts that go beyond a certain percentage of budgeted expenditure).

Obviously, virements cannot be permitted for categories of expenditure the amount of which is determined by law, such as government employee pensions or certain subsidies. But other types of virement may also need to be restricted. Thus, where a bloated wage bill has substantial fiscal implications, reallocations into personnel expenditure from other expenditure categories should not be allowed. Conversely, certain expenditure categories may need to be protected. For example, the frequent problem of government delays to pay for the utilities it consumes may justify prohibiting virements out of the budget appropriation for utility services. (In program budgeting, within a program the line ministry must have full authority to shift resources between activities—possibly in consultation with the ministry of finance if the reallocation goes beyond a certain percentage of authorized expenditure.)

The situation is different for investment projects. Their multiannual nature and uncertainties of implementation and funding necessarily call for giving the executive branch more flexibility in the timing of commitments and payments within the year. Also, it should be permitted, within certain limits, to reallocate funds from projects whose execution is delayed to projects that are proceeding well. Instead, reallocation of funds between very large projects or between major programs—e.g., from primary to technical education—would normally call for consultation with the legislature. At the other extreme, microvirements, within a project, should be left entirely to the authority of the project manager and not be nickel-and-dimed by the line minister—let alone by the ministry of finance or planning.

Controlling and keeping track of all virements is time consuming and absorbs substantial resources. Thus, the opportunity to make virements during budget execution should not be used as an excuse for sloppy estimation of costs and of inputs during budget preparation: again, good execution of the budget largely depends on the quality of its preparation.

The Treasury Function and Cash Management

The Treasury Function

The treasury function includes:

- providing spending agencies with the funds needed to implement their activities in a timely fashion;
- managing government cash to minimize the cost of government borrowing;
- managing public debt;
- managing the *financial* assets and liabilities of the government; and
- handling all government bank accounts (for all the above).

Whatever the budgeting system, control of government cash is a key element of macroeconomic and fiscal management, to ensure that: claims are paid according to the contract terms and due dates; revenues are collected on time; and government borrows at the lowest available interest rate and maximizes returns by investing in liquid interest-yielding instruments.

This is well established in high-income countries, and the treasury function is routinely performed in satisfactory fashion. In developing countries, governments often do not pay sufficient attention to cash management: budget execution focuses on compliance issues; daily cash needs are met by the central bank; and ministries and agencies are allowed to keep large idle balances in their accounts. Experience has shown that very large savings can be made by improving the management of government cash to minimize borrowing costs and maximize short-term returns. (In Sri Lanka at the start of the century it was estimated that efficient central control and better management of government cash could yield at least $20 million annually.)

Managing Cash Flows

Concerning cash inflows, it is important to minimize the delay between the time when cash is received and the time when it becomes available to finance expenditure. Collected tax revenues need to be processed and made available promptly. For this, commercial banks are better placed than tax offices to receive the revenues—which also frees up tax offices to focus on tax enforcement. The banks need to be remunerated, but through explicit fees and not by allowing them to keep the money for longer than necessary.[9]

The control of cash outflows poses more difficulties. The objective is to ensure that there will be enough cash at the due date of payments. Cash payments are not only cumbersome, but, as noted earlier, are an open invitation to theft and discrimination in circumstances where oversight and accountability mechanisms are weak. This is especially the case for payment of government employee salaries and other monetary allowances: major and rapid reductions in corruption have been achieved by the simple device of requiring all employees to have a bank account and depositing their salaries directly into the account (see Box 8.1). Cash payments should be avoided if at all possible, and the promotion of even rudimentary banking facilities in outlying areas can serve important social objectives as well. Here, too, information technology comes to the rescue. Mobile money in East Africa—M-Pesa, where pesa means money in Swahili—was introduced ten years ago by private telecom companies as a system of money transfers through cell phones, and has grown rapidly to form an important medium of exchange, including in areas where banks are non-existent.

Centralizing Cash and Treasury Single Accounts

To minimize borrowing costs and maximize interest-bearing deposits, cash balances should be kept to a minimum. When ministries and agencies have their own bank accounts, idle cash balances accumulate—earning nothing and causing the government to borrow in order to finance ongoing expenditures even though the necessary cash is available somewhere in the system. As noted, the payments can be centralized or decentralized to the agencies, but cash must always be centralized.

Cash balances can be efficiently centralized through a treasury single account (TSA). A TSA is an account, or set of linked accounts, through which the government receives all revenues and transacts all payments.[10] A standard treasury single account is organized along the following lines:

- The treasury has a single account at the central bank.
- Ministries and agencies hold accounts for daily pass-through operational purposes, either at the central bank or, for convenience, with commercial banks, but in both cases the accounts are subsidiary accounts of the single treasury account.
- The ministries' and agencies' accounts are "zero-balance" accounts, with money being transferred by the treasury to these accounts as approved payments are to be made.
- The accounts are automatically "swept" (cleared) at the end of each day and the balances are transferred automatically to the central treasury.
- The central bank consolidates the government cash position at the end of each day.

Under the general notion of a treasury single account, there are various ways to centralize transactions and cash flows, which can be grouped in two broad categories:

- *Active treasury single account* with centralized accounting controls (as in francophone African countries—see Tommasi, 2010). Requests for payment are sent to the treasury which verifies them, effects the payment, and manages the float of outstanding invoices.
- *Passive treasury single account.* Payments are made directly by each spending agency, but through the treasury single account system. The treasury sets cash limits for the total amount of transactions, but does not control individual transactions. The banks accept the payment orders sent by the spending agency up to the limit defined by the treasury, and settlement is made at the end of each business day with the central bank.

From a cash management point of view, either of these arrangements produces the same result. The passive variant of TSA has the advantage of making the spending agency responsible for internal management. Its feasibility depends on the level of technological development of the banking sector and of the government. Modern technology allows electronic links between spending agencies, the banks and the offices of the treasury, but poor banking and IT infrastructure in some developing countries make it hard to combine centralization of cash balances with decentralization of payment processing.

In several countries, cash management arrangements have been designed implicitly to prop up ailing banks—either by allowing them to keep revenues for a period of time or by holding government accounts in the banks. Risk can flow in the opposite direction as well. Entrusting to commercial banks the management of the government's accounts could burden them with the government's own liquidity problems, if the treasury is not able to meet its obligations.

The above discussion of treasury single accounts—like most of the literature on the subject—glosses over the political and financial difficulties of establishing the system in practice. To establish a treasury single account on paper is easy: just issue a decision that all revenues and expenditures are to be deposited in a single government account at the central bank and that ministries are to close all of their separate accounts, and provide the technical instructions for these purposes. It is not quite so easy in reality to make sure that all separate accounts of all government entities are identified; that most of them are closed; that the balances are actually transferred into the TSA; that a reliable procedure and IT system are put in place to sweep all those accounts daily to centralize the entirety of government cash; and that several other practical steps are taken to permit efficient cash management and eliminate this particular source of inefficiency and corruption.

In the real world, reforms are never easy where large sums of money are concerned, especially where governance is defective. In Nigeria, for example, a federal TSA was finally brought close to full completion only after years and years of attempts—genuine under some governments, half-hearted under others. Ministries and spending agencies were understandably loath to give up control over their separate bank accounts. More than 700 spending government agencies (out of the total of 900), accounting for 98 percent of the federal budget, were finally brought into the system as of December 2015. This led to the "discovery" of more than $11 billion equivalent in federal government cash that has been squirreled away in the individual agencies' accounts. Ironically, this is about the same amount as the projected federal budget deficit for 2016. Even in Russia, where central control is far stronger and more effective that in Nigeria, TSA implementation took more than five years (see Box 8.4).[11]

Box 8.4 Treasury Single Account in the Russian Federation

Establishment of a treasury single account for all federal budget revenues and expenditures was approved by the government of the Russian Federation in 2000, but it took over five years to complete the migration of all federal treasury offices to the new system. In light of the vastness of the territory, the Russian treasury is administratively deconcentrated and the system works through the regional treasury offices. Also, unlike in many other countries, there is no involvement by commercial banks, and everything takes place through the central bank. In all other respects the system is consistent with the basic TSA characteristics:

- The federal treasury has a single account at the central bank for the federal treasury at the ministry of finance.
- Each regional treasury office (RTO) maintains an account at the central bank for tax and other revenue collections in its jurisdiction.
- Each RTO also maintains an operational account at the central bank for expenditures made under the federal budget.
- In addition, accounts for expenditures financed from special sources are opened in accordance with the federal government orders, in foreign or domestic currency.

As a result:

- All federal budget resources are accumulated in the TSA.
- All revenues, as shared between the federal and subnational budgets, and the execution of federal budget expenditures are processed via the accounts maintained at the central bank by the relevant RTOs.
- All federal budget revenues and expenditures (as received and incurred at the RTO level) are recorded in the general ledger on a daily basis.

Source: Adapted from Dener (2007).

Cash Planning

Annual cash plans, consistent with the budget implementation plan, set out projected monthly cash inflows, cash outflows and the resulting borrowing requirements, and the projections should be updated every month to take into account, among other things, changes in exchange rates and interest rates, changes in the payment schedule of large investment projects, and outstanding commitments. The preparation and updating of the cash plan requires close coordination between the treasury department, the budget department, the tax and customs department and the macrofiscal unit.

Concerning cash inflows, forecasts of revenue should be prepared and updated monthly, by the tax and customs offices. Concerning outflows, the seasonality of expenditures in different sectors is a critical consideration, and forecasts should include both payments and commitments. Obviously, the government borrowing plans flow directly from the difference in forecast cash inflows and outflows—underlying the importance of a realistic and timely cash plan consistent with the approved budget.

The End-of-Year Spending Rush: A Perennial Issue

Even with the best budget implementation plan and cash plan, and provisions for adapting to intervening changes, in most countries one sees a rush to spend at the close of the fiscal year. Data show that, in virtually every country, expenditures in the fourth quarter are significantly higher than the quarterly average and substantially higher than expenditures in the first quarter. The proportionately lower expenditures in the first trimester are due to a variety of delays experienced at the start of the fiscal year, even in well-managed systems, usually from a delay in the legislative approval of the budget. But the spending spree that is common towards the end of the year calls for more explanation.

This end-of-year spending rush—called *shturmovschina*, "the storming," in the former Soviet Union—was typical of centrally planned economies, but it occurs in market economies as well. The most common reason to spend more money at the end of the fiscal year is to make sure that the following year's budget allocation will be made on a higher base. However, a spending bulge at the end of the year may reflect a ministry's commendable prudence to keep its expenditures down throughout most of the year, as protection against unexpected cuts in appropriations. Still, rushing expenditures almost invariably requires avoiding or bending of the procurement rules—which is not a practice to be encouraged. (In countries with weak governance, instead, a ministry may have an incentive to spend as fast as possible whatever funds it gets—lest its budget be raided by a more powerful ministry closer to the ruling elite. Prudent financial management would not be rational in these circumstances.)

By now the reader is probably tired of hearing it, but here again the importance of a sound and realistic budget is brought into focus. Because a good budget preparation process would not decide allocations merely on the basis of the previous year's expenditure, the line ministries' incentive to waste money at the end of the year would be much weaker. Also, with a good budget and budget implementation plan, ministries could count on receiving the funds on the established release schedule and would not need to artificially compress expenditures in the first half of the year to protect against cuts in the latter half. The optimal response to end-of-year spending sprees is therefore to tighten up and improve budget preparation.

Nevertheless, unforeseen events do happen during the year and, especially in developing countries, it may indeed be wise for a line ministry to be prudent with spending in the first eight or nine months of the year, which will lead to a slight spending bulge in the last few months. In this case, a provision authorizing a proportion of budgeted expenditures to be "carried over" to the following fiscal year may serve as a second-best mechanism to remove the temptation to spend leftover funds before the spending authority comes to an end. The additional flexibility would entail negligible cost in terms of the integrity of budget execution or of fiscal discipline—because expenditures carried over from the previous year would be offset by expenditures carried over from the current year to the following year. Moreover, a carryover would tidy up line ministries during the first weeks of the year, while the implementation wrinkles of the new budget are being ironed out.[12]

However, carryover provisions can be easily abused. When a carryover is justified, the provisions should be clearly spelled out and incorporated in the basic budget law, rather than being authorized every year "as needed." Also, any carryover should be quite small—experience suggests a *maximum* of about three percent of total expenditure in developing countries and five percent in high-income countries.

Notes

1 In particular, controlling commitments is not likely to be successful if the root cause is unrealistic budget preparation (Diamond, 2006).

2 This problem has been called "repetitive budgeting" by Caiden and Wildavsky (1980).

3 Cash rationing has sometimes been called cash budgeting. This is highly misleading, because the budget system is on a cash basis in most countries. Cash rationing is not "budgeting"; it reflects the *absence* of good budgeting.

4 Wondering why in China money cannot be spent as budgeted, Ma and You (2012) concluded that the budgetary controls installed beginning in 1999 did not succeed in preventing underspending—not because the new controls were too tight but because they aren't yet effective.

5 In the US in the 1990s, for example, the Internal Revenue Service spent upwards of $6 billion to introduce a new computer system, the functioning of which was described as equivalent to turning on the porch light and hearing the toilet flush.

6 In Burundi after the end of the civil war it was discovered that large and unwarranted interest charges had been added to some past-due bills at the suggestion of a government official who was involved in managing the payments arrears settlement process—for a price, of course.

7 In some Commonwealth countries, "warrants" are issued at the start of the year to authorize the government to implement the budget. This practice is a historical remnant and is mainly ceremonial, since these warrants only relate to the allocation of funds that has already been decided.

8 Before computers, spending agencies had to make repeated visits to the controller's office to get their money, particularly in the districts which claimed that authorization had not reached them from the ministry of finance or the line ministry.

9 For a description of how the challenge of cash management has been faced in a transition economy see section 4 in Kraan et al. (2013).

10 The system applies to the government, not to the public sector as a whole. State enterprises are outside any TSA arrangement. Also, difficult practical questions arise when attempting to cover general government, and the TSA system may be limited to central government in most countries. Finally, some special accounts are not suitable for incorporation into the system, e.g., aid donor accounts or the accounts of extrabudgetary entities that have legal status and full operational autonomy. (If the extrabudgetary funds have satisfactory governance arrangements, the financial and integrity issues can be appropriately addressed—see Chapter 3.) For additional technical details on treasury single accounts see Pattanayak and Fainboim (2010).

11 A description of improvements in TSA and cash management in Vietnam is available at: http://documents.worldbank.org/curated/en/2014/01/20431619/implementation-treasury-single-account-strengthening-cash-management-vietnam.

12 Owing to its multiyear nature, capital expenditure should be subject to much more flexible rules for carryover, requiring only approval by the ministry of finance rather than legislative action.

Bibliography

Caiden, Naomi, 1996. *Public Budgeting and Financial Administration*. Stamford, CT: JAI Press.

Caiden, Naomi and Aaron Wildavsky, 1980. *Planning and Budgeting in Poor Countries*. New Brunswick, NJ: Transaction Press.

Dener, Cem, 2007. *Implementation Methodology of the Integrated Public Financial Management Systems in Europe and Central Asia*. Washington, DC: The World Bank.

Dener, Cem, Joanna Watkins and William Dorotinsk, 2011. *Financial Management Information Systems: 25 Years of World Bank Experience on What Works and What Doesn't*. Washington, DC: The World Bank.

Diamond, Jack, 2006. *Budget System Reform in Emerging Economies*. Washington DC: IMF.

Diamond, Jack and Pokar Khemani, 2005. *Introducing Financial Management Information Systems in Developing Countries*. Washington, DC: IMF.

Hashim, Ali, 2014. *Handbook on Financial Management Information Systems for Government: A Practitioners Guide for Setting Reform Priorities, Systems Design and Implementation*. Washington, DC: The World Bank.

Hashim, Ali and Moritz Piatti, 2017. *Learning from World Bank FMIS Engagement: Critical Success Factors and Key Failure Points in Design and Implementation*. Washington, DC: The World Bank.

Independent Evaluation Group, 2016. *Malawi: Financial Management, Transparency, and Accountability Project*. Washington, DC: The World Bank.

Kraan, Dirk-Jan, Lisa von Trapp, Valentina Kostyleva, Jan van Tuinen and Matthias Morgner, 2013. "Budgeting in Ukraine," *OECD Journal on Budgeting*, 12(2), 69–140.

Ma, J. and L. You, 2012. "Why Money Cannot Be Spent as Budgeted? Lessons from China's Recent Budget Reforms," *Journal of Budgeting and Financial Management*, 24, 83–113.

Pattanayak, S. and Israel Fainboim, 2010. *Treasury Single Account: An Essential Tool for Government Cash Management*. Washington, DC: IMF.

Premchand, A., 1995. *Effective Government Accounting*. Washington, DC: IMF.

Radev, Dimitar and Pokar Khemani, 2009. "Commitment Controls," Fiscal Affairs Department Technical Note 09/04. Washington, DC: IMF.

Schiavo-Campo, S. and Hazel McFerson, 2008. *Public Management in Global Perspective*. Armonk NY: M. E. Sharpe.

Schiavo-Campo, S. and Daniel Tommasi, 1999. *Managing Government Expenditure*. Manila: Asian Development Bank.

Tommasi, Daniel, 2010. *Gestion des Depenses Publiques dans les Pays en Developpement*. Paris: Agence Française de Developpement.

9 Public Procurement

> Just as it is impossible not to taste honey or poison that one may find at the tip of one's tongue, so is it impossible for one dealing with government funds not to taste, at least a little bit, of the King's wealth.
>
> (Kautilya, Indian administrator, in *Arthasastra, c.* 100 BCE)

Introduction[1]

Good budget execution passes through good government procurement. Government can execute no budget, perform no function, provide no protection to the citizens, implement no laws, deliver no social services—without the materials, equipment, goods, and services necessary to do so, all of which must be purchased (procured) by the government. Few reforms can expand the provision of services, reduce taxes or curtail corruption as much as improvements in procurement. At the same time, no other aspect of public expenditure offers the same potential for inefficiency, bribery and waste. Procurement is not an exciting subject, but if readers feel their eyes beginning to glaze they are urged to remember the importance of the subject for the process of budget execution and the very functioning of government.

Wherever there has been government, there has been purchasing of goods and services to perform government functions or to make the rulers happy. Contemporary procurement has its roots in the purchasing of goods and services for the military (see Box 9.1). Procurement activities gradually expanded along with the expansion in the roles of government, and became a core function of budget execution. The range of government contracting and purchasing is vast, from weapons systems and large industrial plants to paper, milk, vaccination needles, custodial services, construction, and so on. A substantial proportion of expenditure at every level of government goes toward acquisition of goods and services and for construction activity ("works"); it accounts for about one-fifth of expenditure in developed countries, and about one-half in developing countries, where it is the largest single expenditure category. (The average masks large variance between countries, ranging from a low of one-fourth to a high of three-fourths.)

There are important differences between the procurement process in government and in private companies. A private company places less emphasis on formal competitive bidding, documented procedures and conflicts of interest. This is because private managers have a built-in incentive to purchase goods that provide high value for money and to hire contractors who will do high-quality jobs at competitive prices. Their accountability is related to results, not process, and private procurement inefficiencies will show up in their impact on overall company profit.

In contrast, public procurement is subject to special constraints, and must follow prescribed procedures that give a major weight to fairness and equity, and government

---

Box 9.1 Procurement in Seventeenth-Century England

Samuel Pepys was appointed in the seventeenth century to look into the reasons why the quality of ships and supplies for the Royal Navy was so unreliable and their prices so high.

His diary gives a striking description of the procurement function in seventeenth-century England and the uncontrolled scope for self-enrichment by government officials and contractors in those times. Pepys did manage to clean up the defense procurement process by delving into administration as a professional, learning what was required by the navy and why, negotiating fiercely on quality and price, and following up to see that contracts were properly fulfilled. He was troubled by the ease with which he (like many others before him in his position) could receive "tokens" of appreciation from successful contractors. On occasion, Pepys himself yielded to the temptation. The diary also speaks about the required reporting on procurement to an increasingly assertive parliament in its watchdog role and the type of detailed documentation that is needed to justify the conduct of the executive.

His progress notwithstanding, Pepys' conclusion was a resigned acknowledgment in 1662 that "it is impossible for the King to have things done as cheap as other men."

Source: Adapted from Latham (1978).

---

procurement is subject to oversight by the legislature and public audit (in addition to internal administrative accountability mechanisms). Also, government procurement is often used as a tool for public policy goals (e.g., fostering the growth of local industry, benefiting disadvantaged ethnic groups, etc.). Moreover, unlike private procurement, mistakes or malfeasance in public procurement can have political repercussions owing to their greater visibility and the attention of the media and the citizens. Finally, private companies and non-government organizations prefer stable relationships with suppliers and long-term contracts for certainty and easier business planning, but public agencies are committed to fostering competition and prevented from developing such long-term relationships by other factors, such as the fear of collusion with contractors (with the signal exception of military procurement).

Contracting for works and construction (roads, bridges, ports, buildings, etc.) is handled differently from purchase of goods and services. Unlike goods and services that are consumed in short order or serve as intermediate inputs, public works are long-lasting final outputs. The standards and specifications for bids and contracts are different, and the qualifications of bidders are paramount. Also, the contracting process for works lends itself to unbundling into separate contracts for each component (e.g., design, technical services and actual construction). The process of contracting therefore stretches over a much longer period than the acquisition of goods and services and calls for closer and continuous supervision.

Objectives of Government Procurement

As previewed in Chapter 1, the four Es criteria of performance in public administration are economy, efficiency, effectiveness and equity. Efficiency relates to producing an output at lowest cost per unit, effectiveness is the achievement of the purpose—outcome—for which the output is produced, and equity is observance of due process. The basic criterion of public procurement is economy.

Economy

The primary objective of government procurement is to acquire goods and services and works in an economical manner, i.e., providing the best value to the government and the people. The criterion of economy is thus not only the acquisition at the lowest price but also on a timely basis and without sacrificing quality. From an economist's point of view, economy is subsumed under efficiency because the output cannot be produced at lowest unit cost unless the inputs needed to produce it are themselves obtained at lowest cost. However, economy remains a very useful separate criterion, as it is the main basis on which to assess the performance of the public procurement function. Also, poor procurement management has an impact beyond raising the direct production cost: it reduces the benefits of government programs, hampers private sector activity and enables corruption.

Wasteful procurement can arise from duplication and overlap in government operations, from lack of funding predictability, and from lack of incentives for employees to make the best use of supplies. Economical procurement, therefore, depends on a variety of organizational and incentive factors within government, well beyond the control of the individuals in charge of procurement itself. The objective of economy is pretty much the only one applicable in private procurement. In public procurement, instead, it is complemented by, and often balanced with, several other objectives.

Other Objectives of Public Procurement

Fostering Competition

Competition in procurement is defined as equality of opportunity for qualified suppliers to compete for government contracts. Competition and impartiality are needed not only to ensure a beneficial outcome in price and quality, but also to promote public accountability for the process. Fostering the growth of competition in public procurement is a goal of most governments and is supported by international organizations as well. In the US, for example, the Competition in Contracting Act of 1984 aimed at increasing competitive efforts within departments and to narrow the justification for "sole-source" contracting (also called "no-bid" or "direct selection" contracts). Several European countries require their local governments to use competitive bidding for all purchases and services (partly to conform to EU directives), and many also require their governments to try to attract more firms to compete for government business.

Because the degree of competition is partly related to the number of qualified suppliers, many countries and most aid agencies support the provision of information and technical assistance to potential bidders, in order to better understand the rules of procurement, become qualified to compete and expand the pool of potential suppliers.

Import Substitution and Domestic Preference

Public procurement may encourage the growth of local industry, by giving preferences to local suppliers, or restricting purchases from foreign firms (which is equivalent). These preferences are different in motivation and impact from the regulations to offset market imperfections that prevent domestic suppliers from competing on an equal basis. Unlike those justified regulations, domestic preference is suspect from both an efficiency and a development viewpoint.

In developing countries, however, giving some preference in public procurement to domestic firms has traditionally been accepted by donor agencies as a means to stimulate the growth of local competitors to large multinational suppliers. Similarly, while the World Trade Organization (WTO) prescribes uniform treatment of domestic and foreign suppliers in procurement, it provides for special treatment of developing countries in order to safeguard their balance-of-payments position and promote the development of domestic industry. (The EU also allowed central and eastern European countries applying for membership to keep domestic preference provisions, but only for a limited time.)

While political interference and corruption are a reality in public procurement, competition is often restricted by market imperfections as well, such as barriers to entry and information gaps for small and less-experienced suppliers. These barriers are sometimes put up by the government itself, such as the tendency to float very large bids in order to save time with a single decision, or the formalistic overspecification of requirements that small and less-experienced firms find very costly to fulfill. In some areas, for example, emerging technology, specialized services or complex equipment (as in military procurement), developing countries may be obliged to deal with only one or two suppliers because the aid is "tied" to purchases from the donor country's firms. In all these cases, the long-term strategy consists of:

- encouraging the development of the domestic contracting industry;
- lowering the barriers to entry for small business and non-profit organizations; and
- pushing to untie aid as much as possible through better cooperation among donors.

In developed countries, competition is usually restricted by political interference, corruption, emergency—or a combination of all three, as is typical in wartime. The solution in such cases is essentially political, via pressure from the public or from opposition parties to clean up the operation of the system and enable more vigorous competition.

Protecting Public Service Provision

When service delivery is outsourced, government retains the basic responsibility to protect the standards and ensure that the services reach the citizens. In procurement, this responsibility implies monitoring contract execution, providing reliable information to citizens about the service providers, and opening complaint channels. Without these protections, outsourcing to the private sector the delivery of public services can lead to inefficiency, inequity and violation of service standards. (An interesting illustration of these problems in the context of private prison management is provided by the Netflix series "Orange is the New Black.")

Protecting the Environment

Since the mid-1990s, the preservation of environmental quality and the reduction of waste are recognized factors in public procurement, and policies are reviewed to reduce any adverse environmental impact. However, the potential of public procurement as an active instrument of environmental objectives is limited and can occasionally be counterproductive (see Lundberg et al., 2016).

Fostering Equity and Offsetting Past Discrimination

Last but not least, and especially important in ethnically plural countries, the procurement system can be designed to include preferences for ethnic or regional minorities previously excluded or discriminated against. There is a risk that such preferences may persist long after the underlying impact of past discrimination has been corrected. Also, they can be circumvented or abused by putting up "front companies" created exclusively to take advantage of the procurement preference regime. These risks exist and must be addressed, but do not at all mean that minority group preferences are impractical or inadvisable. South Africa offers a good illustration of how to move from a discriminatory system to one with an explicit equity component—see Box 9.2.

The Legal and Regulatory Framework

The emphasis in developed countries has been on adopting a uniform procurement framework, supplemented by rules promulgated by each ministry for its specific needs. For example, in Australia, the procurement framework is contained in the *Commonwealth Procurement Guidelines*, with the states allowed to issue complementary regulations. At subnational level, the *Model Procurement Code for State and Local Governments* in the US has been the most comprehensive attempt to adapt good procurement practice to particular state and local circumstances. The EU requires from prospective member countries, among other things, certain uniform procurement reforms as a precondition for EU membership. (Procurement issues at subnational government levels are discussed in Chapter 14.)

The most widely used model for public procurement law is the one adopted in 1994 by the United Nations Commission on International Trade Law (UNCITRAL), which

---

Box 9.2 Procurement Reform in South Africa after Apartheid

Procurement reform in South Africa was an aspect of the imperative of dismantling the discriminatory structure of the apartheid regime. The old procurement system not only reflected extreme racial discrimination, but was also fragmented, hard to use, and biased toward large, established businesses. All contracts had to be approved by ten tender boards (one national and nine provincial), and there were separate boards or committees for public enterprises and local authorities.

Owing to this background, South Africa is among the few countries whose constitution contains a special provision on government procurement. Section 187 of the 1994 constitution provides for "fair, equitable, transparent, competitive and cost-effective" bidding, and the constitutional provision is articulated in the 1996 Public Financial Management Act. Public procurement reform in South Africa was therefore aimed at three main objectives: good governance, uniformity and the achievement of socioeconomic goals—balancing the objective of economy with the encouragement of broader participation and the overcoming of discrimination.

The Preferential Procurement Policy Framework Act of 2000 is a key piece of legislation and aims at enabling small contractors to bid for lower-value contracts and obtain some redress for past discrimination. (A penalty clause is included to discourage established firms from establishing front companies in order to qualify for the preference.)

The system has generally worked well and the South African legislative framework for public procurement is a model for other multiethnic countries that must reconcile cost-effectiveness with long-term sustainability and equity.

For details, see: www.bowman.co.za/FileBrowser/ArticleDocuments/Public-Procurement-in-South-Africa.pdf.

consolidated previous laws and was updated in 2011 to incorporate new practices such as e-procurement and framework agreements.[2] The law is intended to be a model for developing and transition countries, but is also expected to improve the procurement laws of middle-income and some high-income developed countries, and to make their laws more compatible with international trade practices. The UNCITRAL model law has formed the basis for national procurement reform in many developing countries, with support from international donor agencies.

Although as a framework law the UNCITRAL model law does not set forth all the necessary regulations, it recommends open competitive bidding as the most effective method to promote competition, economy and efficiency in procurement. This recommendation has been supported by the evidence—both before and after the promulgation of the model law. For example, publicizing a public procurement auction has been shown to reduce the costs of procurement and induce more bidders to enter. The evidence suggests that publicity affects rebates and discounts by increasing the number of bidders (Coviello and Mariniello, 2014).

To the extent compatible with general contract law, most countries regulate public procurement by internal rules that prescribe the formal process of bidding, the evaluation of bids, the awarding and conclusion of contracts and contract management (see the UK guidelines in Box 9.3).[3] The rules also include procedures for dealing with court challenges from unsuccessful bidders and for contract interpretation, breach of contract and dispute resolution and arbitration. Matters of policy (e.g., giving preference to domestic suppliers in international competitive bidding) are generally issued as binding instructions for all ministries and agencies, but different countries allow departmental discretion in devising procurement regulations. In Singapore, for example, all government entities must strictly follow the administrative procurement procedure laid down by the ministry of finance. By contrast, the UK, New Zealand and most other developed countries issue central guidelines but allow individual departments to issue regulations specific to their own needs. There are advantages to issuing a single set of procurement guidelines for common guidance while allowing individual agencies to supplement and vary these according to their needs and those of their clients—provided that the overall governance climate is satisfactory and channels of protest and feedback are functioning.

Government agencies tend to feel that the procurement process has become an end in itself, stressing literal compliance with rules to the neglect of economy or efficiency. Before the streamlining of 1994, the United States had 889 laws on defense procurement alone, causing a product to be on average 50 percent more expensive simply because it was purchased by the defense department. Indeed, in regulating procurement too much oversight may in practice mean too little oversight. The proper response is not to violate or avoid the rules, but to revise them and make them less burdensome and more effective. In the interim, it is understandable that dedicated civil servants may be tempted to take shortcuts around cumbersome rules in order to facilitate government activity.

Several countries have moved to streamline and consolidate existing laws and regulations on procurement. Success has been varied: regulations are hardy weeds—some have returned by the back door and others have been deleted only to be replaced by new rules. In the US, the Federal Acquisition Streamlining Act of 1994 repealed or modified 225 provisions and raised the value thresholds requiring full compliance with the regulations, thus exempting 95 percent of the transactions. Nevertheless, and despite a massive "reinventing government" effort in the late 1990s, aimed at simplifying regulations of all sorts, as of 2016 the Federal Acquisitions Regulation still listed 310 separate chapters and provisions, and was nearly 1,800 pages—supplemented by agency-specific regulations, supplemented in turn by instructions and case law.

Box 9.3 Procurement Guidelines in the United Kingdom

The procurement practice and development team is the central unit in the UK treasury that promotes best practices and the development of procurement by government departments. The key criteria of good procurement are:

- value for money;
- compliance with national and international legal obligations;
- cost-effective fulfillment of users' needs;
- appropriate level of competition; and
- honest and impartial relationships with suppliers.

The procurement process is also intended to ensure:

- fairness, efficiency, courtesy and firm dealings;
- high professional standards;
- wide and easy access to information on the procurement process and documentation;
- prompt notification of the outcome of the bidding;
- efficiency and integrity in contract management; and
- prompt response to suggestions and complaints.

In the selection of bidders, undue emphasis should not be placed on size, and the standards of financial and technical capacity should be proportionate to the nature and value of the contract in question. The criteria for the award should not consist of price alone, but should also consider lifetime cost (including operations and maintenance), quality and terms of delivery. Lifetime cost is especially relevant in complex procurements, including large supply and service contracts and construction projects, to compare the higher initial price of better quality assets against the lower maintenance costs over the asset life.

For details, see: www.directgov.uk.

The Management of Public Procurement

Organizational Arrangements

The main organizational issue in procurement is very similar to that of accounting controls, addressed in Chapter 8—i.e., whether procurement transactions should be carried out by one central purchasing agency or decentralized to the spending ministries and agencies concerned.[4] Conflict between central procurement offices and the spending agencies is a typical feature of public administration, with the central office complaining that the agencies don't respect the rules and the agencies complaining that the central office is picky and dilatory and doesn't understand the agencies' needs. The main advantage of a central procurement office is that the staff become familiar with the law, policies, and procedures and build up the institutional memory to gain the best value for money. The main advantage of decentralized procurement is that it speeds up the process and facilitates the suitability of the goods and services for the ministry concerned. Once again, the answer depends largely on the country's institutional capacity and quality of governance:

in authoritarian regimes, centralizing procurement means in effect centralizing corruption; in circumstances of good governance but limited administrative capacity, it makes sense to centralize the procurement process (while progressively building up procurement capacity in the line ministries).

The issue hinges on the right balance between efficiency and risk. Typically, line ministries and spending agencies always push for delegation of procurement, on the grounds that they are the best judge of their own requirements and can meet them faster and at less cost than going through a central procurement agency. This would be almost always true, except that senior agency managers tend to neglect the procurement process—as discussed later. The disinterest of senior managers means that once procurement is delegated to the spending agency, it is no longer given the prudential attention it deserves. In such cases, the risks of corruption and violation of national policy are probably greater than when procurement is administered centrally.

Instead of debating whether procurement should be central or decentralized, it is more constructive to ask *which* of the procurement functions are best performed by a central agency. The general answer from international experience is that a central entity is essential to: (i) set policy, (ii) define uniform procurement rules and standards, (iii) exercise oversight, and (iv) handle appeals. However, the actual purchasing, contracting and contract management should be left to the spending ministry and agency directly concerned. (Subnational government units should have the autonomy and flexibility to procure their own goods and services—see Chapter 14.)

Regardless of the organizational arrangements for procurement, consultation between the center of government and the line ministries is important. Building a consultation mechanism into the procurement process serve not only to give the spending agencies the benefit of expert advice but also to alert them to an imprudent procurement transaction before it takes place. As an outgrowth of such consultation, spending agencies may be exempt from the normal bidding requirements if the purchases are made from an approved contractor preselected by the central procurement agency. Or, agencies may be required to consult specialized entities when acquiring computer systems and scientific services. Interagency committees may be set up for the procurement of supplies involving several agencies, and various other mechanisms may be established for effective consultation between the central procurement entity and the spending agencies. Box 9.4 gives examples of procurement organization in several developed countries.

The Procurement Process

The forms of procurement depend mainly on the nature of the goods, services and works, the size and complexity of the contract, the administrative level and the market structure. In order of complexity, the main forms of procurement are: competitive bidding (international, national, limited); "shopping"; sole-source contracting (aka "direct selection," "no-bid," or "single-tender"); "force accounts"; and consulting services.

They are discussed in turn next, in descending order of contract value, with the priciest items requiring full international competitive bidding and the simplest procurement modality used for low-value purchases.[5]

Competitive Bidding

Also known as open tendering, competitive bidding is by far the preferred form of procurement, and aims at providing all eligible bidders with timely and adequate notification of

---

Box 9.4 Procurement Arrangements in Different Developed Countries

While the objectives of public procurement are generally the same everywhere (albeit assigned different relative importance), the organizational arrangements can vary considerably:

- In Slovakia, procurement is the sole responsibility of the ministry of construction and public works.
- In Singapore, with some exceptions (e.g., pharmaceuticals) the government has decentralized the bulk of purchasing to the ministries, departments and statutory boards, but under detailed and binding central rules.
- In the UK, a procurement policy team, joint between the treasury and the Department of International Trade, advises the ministers on procurement policy.
- Australia's procurement structure is a good example of strategic coherence in procurement, combining central agencies and decentralized departments. In the federal government, procurement management is substantially delegated, with each department responsible for its own procurement within a centrally prescribed framework of procurement policy and advisory guidance by the Department of Administrative Services.

Other countries (e.g., Canada, and a number of Asian and European countries) have set up a specialized purchasing agency to provide certain common services and materials for several government ministries. In the Australian state of Victoria (which has pioneered many public management innovations), the agency "Procurement Australia" was established in 1985 and has been operating for 30 years to aggregate the buying power of local government entities and negotiate contracts for local government, public sector organizations and non-profit groups.

Sources: Government websites.

---

requirements and with an equal opportunity to bid for the required goods, services or works.

International competitive bidding is required for very large works or goods contracts. *National* competitive bidding is normally used for lower-value contracts and when foreign bidders are unlikely to be interested, either because of the nature of the works or goods or when the contract is not large enough. *Limited* competitive bidding without public advertisement is indicated when the purchase is small or there are only very few qualified suppliers: bids are sought from a number of potential suppliers that is limited and yet broad enough to assure competitive pricing. Many local governments float such limited competitive bids on an annual basis for repetitive purchases (e.g., construction materials) and place repeat orders with one or more contractors.

The specific modalities of competitive bidding depend on the country, but the main requirements are similar in all cases: a clear and accurate description of what is to be purchased, a publicized opportunity to bid and fair criteria for selection and decision-making. In accordance with these requirements, competitive bidding has five stages:

- pre-bid (defining specs and bidding modalities);
- issue of public notice and invitation to bid;

- bids evaluation;
- contract award; and
- resolution of complaints.

Shopping

Like anything else, competitive procurement is subject to the law of diminishing returns: pushing competitive modalities too far results in higher transaction costs and thus violates the principle of economy in procurement. Shopping is the procurement modality used for readily available off-the-shelf goods of small value, such as standard office equipment and supplies, medicines, books and educational materials. Shopping involves obtaining price quotations from at least three suppliers, comparing them, and choosing the best one in terms of both price and quality. The contract is simple and often consists of a mere exchange of letters. Some countries permit the registration of authorized vendors and the placing of orders with these vendors on a rotation basis during the year. Also, many countries allow the award of contracts at a negotiated price to labor unions and community associations, after ascertaining their competence and experience. None of these procedures present a problem unless they are administered dishonestly. For example, a registered-vendor list can become a tool for government employees to extort money from vendors who wish to be placed on the list, or avoid being dumped from it.

Procurement thresholds can be gamed by breaking up the purchase into several smaller contracts, each below the value that requires national or international competitive bidding, a practice known as "contract-splitting." There may be good reasons for this, however. The practice may be forced on an agency by fluctuations in the availability of funds during the fiscal year owing to a badly prepared budget or unrealistic cash plan (see Chapter 8). Also, splitting up a large purchase may be the only way for an agency to get around the roadblock of an inefficient central procurement office. In these cases, the optimal solution is to improve the budget execution process, reform the central procurement entity or streamline the procurement rules, but in the interim contract-splitting is a rational and efficient response. When contract-splitting is instead used as a way to evade otherwise sound rules, appropriate penalties should be levied on the individuals responsible *and their manager*. The main safeguards against unwarranted contract-splitting are vigilant senior managers and robust sample audits of contracts.

Sole-Source Procurement

Sole-source procurement is cost effective for small contracts and the procurement of specialized consultant services, when a track record of technical expertise is essential. It is also appropriate in emergencies; or for the purchase of highly complex systems and equipment; or when the standardization of equipment or spare parts justifies additional purchases from the same supplier. Combining all three elements, war provides the strongest rationale for sole-source procurement, as well as the best excuse for corrupt procurement and large-scale profiteering.[6]

All countries limit sole-source procurement to specific circumstances, normally when one or more of the following conditions obtain:

- the value of the purchase is low (thresholds vary between countries);
- there is one qualified supplier, *and* there are no close substitutes for the good or service;
- it is required by international treaty or by national law in specific cases;

- it is justified by national security considerations; or
- in emergencies or other unusual urgency.

Because several of these conditions entail a judgment call, very often "sole-source selection" becomes "sole source of abuse." Fake emergencies are used to justify sweetheart contracts to a favored supplier; after contracts are split to stay below the sole-source threshold all the pieces are quietly awarded to the same company; or the regulations are simply disregarded—trusting that the sheer mass of government transactions will hide the violation. Special care must be exercised in evaluating the bids in spot purchases of commodities like crude petroleum and armaments, as these typically involve very large sums and have been the subject of scandals (e.g., the Food for Oil program in Iraq between the two Gulf Wars).

Frequently, unwarranted sole sourcing does not occur as deliberate abuse, but from plain laziness on the part of the procurement staff. The easiest way for a procurement employee to avoid the homework and careful processes of competitive bidding is to award repeat contracts to the same individual or firm. Some excess cost is bound to be the result. It may not involve bribery but, in time, such laziness risks leading to corruption, when the relationship between government buyer and private seller loses its arm's length distance and becomes a cozy affair between friends.

Force Accounts

A force account is the provision to a ministry of goods, services or works produced by the government's own personnel and with its own equipment. (The practice should more properly be called "command procurement," as it consists of a central administrative instruction to a government agency to deliver certain goods or perform certain functions for another government agency.) It is justified where the works are both small and scattered, or the amount of work cannot be specified in advance, or in emergencies. In all other cases, procurement by force accounts has tended to be less economical owing to the lack of any competition. Force accounts were the standard method of procurement in the former Soviet Union and other centrally planned economies, and their use has dropped drastically with the end of the USSR and the transition to a market-oriented economic system.

Procurement of Consulting Services

The term "consultant" includes a wide variety of private and public entities—individuals, management firms, engineering firms, non-profit organizations, banks and universities. Consultants may help in a wide range of activities, from policy advice to engineering services and project supervision. The use of foreign consultants is especially widespread in developing countries, and in a variety of core government functions—including budgeting and public expenditure management. Because the wrong advice can do much more, and more lasting, damage than buying the wrong goods, selecting the right advisory expertise is a very important procurement decision. However, selection of the right consultants is not easy, because:

- Advice is intangible, and thus its value is difficult to assess in advance.
- Impressive paper qualifications may not reflect the real competence of the consultant, and show only the consultant's successes, not the failures and mistakes.
- A consultancy cannot be realistically tested before contracting.
- The government employee cannot have the same specialized competence as the consultants, and thus finds it difficult to choose among different candidates.

In general, the overriding consideration in consultants' procurement is the quality of the advice, rather than the price, as in most cases the consulting fees are a small fraction of the total project cost, while good technical advice is key to its success. But price does matter. Accordingly:

- Both quality and cost should be considered when the nature of the assignment, time required and associated costs can be defined with reasonable precision (e.g., for a detailed feasibility study of a project when the main technical solutions are already known).
- Quality-based selection is appropriate for specialized assignments for which it is difficult to define *precise* terms of reference.
- Cost-based selection is appropriate for assignments of a standard or routine nature.
- Sole-source selection is appropriate for small contracts with individual consultants (normally, below $100,000). However, repeat contracts to the same consultant for work flowing from the initial contract should generally not be awarded on a sole-source basis. In some cases, consultants should be made ineligible to compete for follow-up work to avoid giving them any temptation to slant the advice in order to obtain such work. This is especially the case for consulting on institutional development, where the process of improvement is usually sequential.

For all these reasons, selection of consultants must rely heavily on their *demonstrated* qualifications, prior experience and actual track record in similar assignments. Because even the weakest experience can be manipulated and embellished into a beautiful resume, confidential references and direct feedback by the consultant's former clients are a must.

Other Forms of Procurement

Other forms of procurement include procurement by agents, requests for proposals (RFPs), and indefinite-quantity contracts (IQCs). Interested readers are referred to Baily et al. (2015).

Contract Management and Monitoring

Importance of Contract Management

Chapter 7 explained the importance of good project implementation to assure that the expected rate of return on a project is matched by the rate of return after project completion. But projects are implemented largely through contracts: just as good project implementation is essential for project success, good contract management is essential for good project implementation.

Choosing the winning bid and awarding the contract is not the end of the procurement process. The goods and services still must be delivered as ordered, and the works begun and completed as per the contractual agreement. As for the government budget itself, it is possible to execute badly a good and clear contract but it is difficult to execute well a badly formulated contract. In the first place, therefore, the effectiveness of contract management is strongly influenced by decisions made prior to contract signature. Ambiguous, unrealistic or conflicting agreements make it very difficult for the public manager to oversee their execution. Also, many contracts do not have clear performance standards, which permit the contractors' work to be assessed and also protect them from arbitrary interference. Procurement managers should be encouraged to draft contracts that emphasize appropriate *key* results, provide for close but selective monitoring, and are easily under-standable to field staff and contractors alike.

It is important to note that while government activities cover the entire country, the procurement for very large contracts is concentrated at the center. Consequently, the government units in the field responsible for managing a contract often have no idea of the basis for the award of the contract and are in a difficult position to manage it effectively. Coordination between the central line ministry and its field offices is critical for effective contract management.

Contract Monitoring and Quality Assurance

Even when the contract is clear to begin with, it is unlikely to be executed well without supervision and monitoring. This is a critical but often neglected area in many developing countries and even some developed countries—reflecting either weak supervision capacity or inattention by senior government managers, or both. No amount of careful preparation of the contract or detailed specifications will ensure adequate performance if the actual performance is not monitored. Experience the world over is rife with examples not only of delays and excessive costs of implementation, but also of abuse, waste and fraud in contract execution. Indeed, unscrupulous suppliers count on administrative lack of interest in the nuts and bolts of contract execution to take shortcuts in quality or justify supplemental payments for "unforeseen" changes.

Monitoring should continue through the life of the contract. Monitoring contract execution is especially important for large works, and should include careful review of contractor reports, inspections, audits and users' and citizens' feedback. The relationship between the public official and the contractor should not be adversarial—on the contrary, establishing good professional relations with the contractor can do much to assure good contract execution—but the two parties have different interests. Direct inspection of the physical progress of the work remains the most important element. Financial audits, while necessary, come too late to remedy problems of execution—though they can provide evidence of wrongdoing, which can be used to sue or disqualify the contractor from future work.

Quality is a component of "economy," and quality assurance is thus a critical aspect of contract monitoring. Quality depends in the first place on the clear drafting of the technical and other specifications of the goods, services or works to be provided under the contract. That aside, the modality of quality assurance depends on the nature of the output. Inspectors of construction works, for example, must demand compliance with building codes and similar legal mandates, in addition to compliance with the contract specifications. (Most countries have established quality control units in their ministries of public works.)

The four principal requirements for robust contract monitoring are as follows:

- The central procurement office should disseminate guidelines for the inspection and testing of goods, services and works under different types of contracts, including quality assurance (e.g., a requirement to obtain certificates of compliance or certified test results to accompany deliveries).
- There should be a formal system for reporting complaints against vendors by user agencies and the public; for taking action on deficiencies noted during inspection; and for dealing with product warranties and latent defects in goods.
- The payment schedule should be tied to satisfactory inspections, so that payments can be withheld when problems occur and until they are resolved satisfactorily.

- Citizen associations and local non-government organizations should be systematically consulted, not only because of their involvement as stakeholders, but also because feedback from informed citizens is a highly reliable and cost-effective way of monitoring contracts and ensuring the integrity of public officials.

Some developed countries have a policy of making the contractors themselves responsible for verifying and certifying product quality prior to delivery. This self-policing requires a high degree of contractor professionalism, contract management skills and swift dispute resolution. In developing countries, all three factors may be deficient, and contractors' self-policing is risky. Also, governments should not rely too much on physical output indicators, as they could mask deterioration in output quality. (See Chapter 12 for a full discussion of performance indicators.)

A final word. It is easy for the long list of requirements to become a monster of red tape, with all parties in the process protecting themselves by redundant, duplicative or cosmetic requirements. *Regulatory restraint is essential for efficient public procurement.* Less is more in this area. Without trust and strong accountability, no regulatory framework, no matter how demanding, can assure integrity and efficiency in public procurement; with trust and strong accountability, a reasonable minimum of essential rules will be enough.

Major Issues in Public Procurement

Systematic Neglect by Senior Management

A fundamental problem in public procurement is the disinterest and neglect by policy-makers and senior managers, who tend to leave procurement to the specialists. The reasons are several. Top managers are typically more interested in policy and find the purchasing function dull by comparison. Also, they rarely have enough time to understand the intricacies of product quality, pricing structures and technical specifications. Moreover, keeping some distance from purchasing operations insulates them to some degree from scandals or potential charges of corruption. Finally, senior managers' distance from procurement decisions is encouraged by the procurement specialists themselves—usually because they view managers' involvement as interference with little value added, but occasionally to keep them away from underhanded dealings. (A time-honored defensive response to a sudden interest by senior managers is to provide them with a large mass of indigestible technical material.)

The general disinterest of policy-makers and senior managers in procurement matters finds its expression, among other things, in the cursory treatment of the subject in public financial management books and training programs—a neglect which this book aims to correct. (By contrast, business and management schools normally offer one or more courses in purchasing and in contract monitoring.)

This is not a healthy state of affairs. In the first place, as noted earlier, the entire field of public financial management has its historical origin in the concern with a malfunctioning procurement system. Second, as stressed throughout this book, the effectiveness of budgeting and expenditure management depends largely on achieving a good balance between control and flexibility; between protection of equity and provision of individual incentives for performance; and between short-term results and long-term sustainability. These are all vital considerations in procurement and deserve adequate attention from the top of government—particularly for large civil works and informatics contracts.[7]

Unfortunately, along with neglect by senior management there is an aversion to risk on the part of the rank-and-file procurement staff. This is understandable, in view of the imbalance between the lack of rewards for a correct decision and the potentially heavy penalties to which public servants are exposed in the event that something goes wrong. Only a climate of trust and strong higher-level support for the actions of procurement specialists can prevent such risk aversion from turning into operational paralysis.

Accordingly, while top managers are certainly not supposed to become procurement specialists, they must be fully aware of the process and its risks, and accept a responsibility to become much more involved in the oversight of procurement than is currently the case, especially for large contracts. Greater attention to procurement by senior public managers would find a loose parallel in the evolution in the private sector from product orientation to client orientation. As a result of this evolution, beginning in the 1970s, the separate purchasing activities of companies were merged and brought more and more under top management.

A failure to do so can have heavy financial and political repercussions, as illustrated in the United States by the Air Force tanker aircraft scandal described later in Chapter 17 (Box 17.4). (When questioned about that scandal, then Defense Secretary Donald Rumsfeld disclaimed any responsibility for overseeing the department's procurement of almost $100 billion a year: "I have got fifty million things on my desk and this isn't one of them" *Washington Post*, June 20, 2006.)

The Abuse of "Emergencies"

As part of the overall process of managing government expenditure, the procurement function cannot be exercised efficiently without good advance planning. You cannot decide what to buy and when, unless you have previously decided what you want to accomplish and how. True emergencies justify the use of special procedures but, if the needs can be anticipated, advance planning would avoid recourse to special procurement procedures. If the government agency is able to do its planning in good time but doesn't, it cannot then use the "urgency" of the situation as an excuse to short-circuit the procedures that protect against abuse and misuse of the taxpayers' money. When the emergency is unanticipated and is sufficient to justify deviations from established practices, the use of emergency procurement procedures then demands much tighter supervision and scrutiny by top managers and the political leadership. Box 9.5 provides an illustration of what happens when prior planning is deficient or non-existent.

The Role of Buyer's Discretion

As a general proposition, the greater the discretionary margin given to the buyer the worse the procurement outcomes—in terms of price either or of quality or of corruption or all three combined. The one exception may be in bidding for public works of a value lower than a certain threshold, which may be carried out through a restricted auction. An analysis of a large database for public works in Italy found that when the buyer had some discretion in terms of who *not* to invite to bid, the observed procurement outcomes did not deteriorate and in many cases improved (Coviello et al., 2016).[8] The advantage of excluding bidders who are known to the experienced buyer to be unreliable or less competent offsets the disadvantage of a smaller number of bidders. That exception aside, restricting the role of buyer discretion generally leads to better procurement outcomes and a more credible and acceptable process.

Corruption in Procurement

Corruption in public financial management is discussed in Chapter 16. The specific issues of corruption in procurement are addressed next.

Box 9.5 Good Procurement Requires Good Planning

According to the US General Accountability Office (GAO), a "gross error" was committed in late 2004 by the Air Force in its $45 million award of contracts to Operational Support Services (OSS), a private translation company, on a sole-source (no-bid) basis. The contracts were for identifying and paying bilingual English–Arabic speakers to act as translators in the preparation of Iraq's constitution and the holding of elections.

There are reports that political pressure was exerted by the Defense Department to use the contracts to pay "friendly" Iraqi exiles. Be that as it may, competing firms that had not been allowed to bid for the contracts protested the sole-source award to OSS. The Air Force argued that the no-bid procedure was required by the urgency of the situation, with only a short time remaining before the Iraqi elections in January 2005. The GAO didn't buy it. Not only did the Air Force issue a second sole-source contract several months after the elections, but the first contract could easily have been put up to competitive bid if the Air Force had done its planning in time. With the invasion of Iraq occurring more than 18 months earlier, the need for Arabic translators should have been obvious long before.

Aside from partisan political pressure and favoritism, the lesson from this episode is that good procurement requires good advance planning—which specifies in useful time the nature of the services, their quality, the qualifications required of the service provider, and all other matters needed to proceed to normal competitive bidding.

Source: General Accountability Office, Report B-296984, November 14, 2005.

Overt Corruption

Public procurement is a notorious source of corruption the world over. The most direct route to bribery is to avoid competitive bidding altogether and have the contract awarded to the desired party through direct contact. Other than that, to extract bribes the public procurement staff can:

- tailor the specifications to benefit particular suppliers or contractors;
- restrict information about bidding opportunities only to some potential bidders;
- claim urgency as an excuse to award the contract on a sole-source basis;
- give "preferred" bidders confidential information on offers from other bidders;
- disqualify potential suppliers by improper prequalification or excessive bidding costs; or
- act directly in collusion with the bidders or outside influences to influence the process.

The private suppliers, too, can take actions to distort the bidding process to their advantage:

- collude to fix bid prices;
- collude to establish a "rotation" or other system by which bidders take turns in bidding or in deliberately submitting unacceptable offers—thus favoring the supplier whose turn it is to "win" the contract. Even the most careful scrutiny of *individual* transactions will not reveal this tactic, because every rule will appear to have been strictly followed. It is thus necessary from time to time to review all the procurement *results* for a given period and see if suspicious patterns emerge;

- promote discriminatory technical standards; or
- use their influence or bribes to push political leaders or senior public officials to interfere improperly in the evaluation of bids.

After the bids are submitted, other opportunities for misbehavior arise. When the rules do not require that all bidders be present when the bids are opened, it is easy for the procurement officer to reveal the lowest bid to the desired bidder and enable the latter to submit an even lower bid, which is then included in the bid evaluation process. Corruption opportunities exist also after the award of contract and during the contract execution phase, through:

- failing to enforce quality standards, quantities or other specifications of the contract (it can be "understood" in advance that enforcement will be superficial or nil);
- agreeing to pay for shoddy construction or delivery of unacceptable goods and services, or fictitious claims of transit losses or false deductions for material losses in construction;
- allowing "lowballing" (artificially low bids, subsequently jacked up by mutual consent);
- delaying payment of invoices to extort a bribe; or
- giving individual legislators influence over the award of contracts in their constituencies.

It should not be assumed, however, that corruption in procurement is exclusively associated with budget execution. Collusion can begin with the process of budget preparation. For example, a favored supplier can be told in advance that the budget will include a particular item, the item specifications and the cost estimate. After the budget is approved, the bid announcement can specify a very limited time for submissions—which allows the favored supplier to submit the bid in time before the deadline owing to his prior knowledge of the specifications and the contract amount. The collusion is especially difficult to detect because an ex post audit of the bidding process and contract award will not show any violation of procurement rules.

By far the easiest and most profitable form of corruption in public procurement or works is simply to not deliver the goods or build the works. In countries with weak accountability systems, very low administrative capacity or widespread systemic corruption, it is not difficult to falsify delivery documents or certificates of work completion. It is in this area that civil society can help reduce the incidence and weight of corruption in procurement. Citizens' feedback can be a particularly powerful weapon against corruption. The peasant who still gets wet feet crossing the stream is best placed to know that the government bridge was not completed—regardless of what the paperwork says. Organizations can also be created to help improve procedures and facilitate blowing the whistle on bribery and other types of corruption. An example is Procurement Watch Incorporated, a non-profit organization in the Philippines.[9]

Let's conclude with a minor but most elegant instance of official corruption. Government money allocated for a village well in rural Odisha in India was pocketed by the village chief. When the activity was randomly selected for inspection, the visiting inspector told the chief to give him the money and he would fix the problem. He reported that the well had been dug but mosquitos were breeding in the stagnant water, and he thus instructed the village chief to have the well filled in. He further recommended a new inspection to verify that the well had been filled in properly—along with a reimbursement to the village chief for the added expense. (The scheme was foolproof except that a villager accidentally overheard part of the conversation and informed the district authorities.)

Covert Corruption: The Risk of Cozy Relationships

Corruption can also occur in covert and roundabout ways that do not formally violate laws or regulations. In virtually every developed country, after leaving government service government officials are prohibited from working in an industry they oversaw or for a corporation they did business with while in government—at least for a significant period of time. Among the peculiarities of the American administrative system is the extraordinarily permissive attitude to the revolving door from public service to private employment and back again. In the US, a public official responsible for purchasing and contracting with a private entity, or overseeing regulations affecting it, can go to work for *the same* private entity after leaving government employment—albeit with minor restrictions that do nothing to alleviate the incestuous nature of the relationship.

Such looseness is extreme even by the standards of Japan, where the symbiosis of government and business is legendary (the so-called "Japan, Inc."). The practice of *amakudari* ("descent from heaven") allows high-ranking civil servants to cash in upon retirement by going to work for private corporations. In Japan, however, they cannot work in the same industry which they used to regulate. In America, the door has been revolving under Democratic as well as Republican administrations, and for elected legislators as well as members of their staff. That such practices are technically legal demonstrates the weakness of the federal conflict-of-interest laws.

For years, the necessary reforms have been as obvious as their chances of approval were non-existent. As is done in most countries, after leaving government all members of the legislature and staff of the legislative and the executive branch should be prohibited for a minimum of two years from private employment in the area of their direct responsibility, and should *never* be permitted to work for private entities on which they had direct oversight or allocative authority. A timid but meaningful first step was implemented in 2006, prohibiting former members of Congress from lobbying for at least two years after leaving office. This will prevent future occurrences of extreme cases such as the one described in Box 9.6, but will not eliminate the grave potential for conflicts of interest.

Flexibility Without Accountability

In budget execution, to assign greater managerial discretion and autonomy without the robust oversight that such autonomy demands is to ask for big trouble. More autonomy can lead to greater efficiency but only if accountability is strengthened along with it. When public spending is stable or grows at a slow and steady rate, flexibility is less risky, as abuses are more visible and thus less frequent. When spending increases rapidly, or transactions are very large and complex, it is difficult for supervision to keep pace and, unless special oversight measures are taken, procurement waste and fraud have a tendency to grow.[10]

Managing Risk in Public Procurement

The Determinants of Procurement Risk

Procurement risks include corruption, inefficiency and unsuitability. The degree of risk of any sort differs in different sectors, agencies and transactions. Three variables determine the risk: (i) specificity; (ii) market structure; (iii) size of the transaction; and (iv) level of management.

Box 9.6 Hiring the Overseer: Two Examples

Congressman Billy Tauzin (Republican, Louisiana) was until 2005 the chair of the House committee that oversees the pharmaceutical industry. In that capacity, he had the lead in initiating and clearing new legislation affecting the industry:

- In 2003, he sponsored the prescription drug bill that, among other things, prohibited the government from negotiating with drug companies the price of the drugs the taxpayer would ultimately have to subsidize, and kept the ban on importing from Canada the identical drugs at a much lower price.
- In 2004, he resigned his chairmanship and did not run for re-election.
- In January 2005, immediately after the expiration of his term in Congress, Tauzin started working as the head of PhRMA—the pharmaceutical industry lobby—for a reported $2 million a year (which increased to $11 million by the time he left the job in 2010). Incredibly, he had been having private discussions about the terms of this job as chief lobbyist for the drug industry while he was still in Congress chairing the committee overseeing the selfsame industry. Even more incredibly, none of this was illegal.

Mrs. Letitia White was a senior staffer of the House Appropriations Committee, which is responsible for funding all federal programs. Unlike members of Congress, congressional staffers must wait a year before lobbying the committee on which they served. This prohibition is extraordinarily mild. (Most developed countries have a "cooling off" period of at least two years for former staff and a lifetime prohibition to do any work on issues of which they had been in charge.) Moreover, it applies only to staff with a salary above a certain amount—at the time $120,000 a year. Exactly one year before resigning from the committee staff in January 2003, Mrs. White took a pay cut that brought her $80 under the annual salary cap. One day after resigning she joined a lobbying firm (as reported by Paul Kane in *Roll Call*, July 27, 2006; www.rollcall.com). The reader should be able to connect the following dots:

- At the House Appropriations Committee, Mrs. White oversaw the award of "earmarks" (see Chapter 6), of which $22 million worth went to 16 defense companies.
- The lobbying firm she joined was partly owned by a former congressman, a very close friend of congressman Jerry Lewis, the chair of the committee.
- In her first year at the lobbying firm, Mrs. White was paid $670,000.
- She attracted to the firm 16 new clients.
- The new clients were the same defense contractors who had received the earmarks.
- She was, and remains, free to lobby the committee she used to work for, on behalf of the firm owned by the friend of the committee chairman.

All this, too, perfectly legal. . .

Sources: Various reports and other news accounts.

Specificity is inversely related to risk: the more specific the product or contract, the fewer the opportunities for manipulating the procurement process. It's easier to rig the procurement of pencils and paper than the procurement of electron microscopes. (However, greater specificity is also generally associated with less competition.) The market structure in the sector is important, with a smaller and less competitive market associated with greater risk. Large transactions are normally also more complex technically, which offers greater openings for manipulation and makes oversight more difficult. And the level of management at which procurement decisions are made also affects risk, with middle management the riskiest level: middle managers' operational discretion combined with neglect by senior management can produce corruption opportunities. (The sector that combines all four elements of procurement risk, and to the highest degree, is the military—as explained in Chapter 17.)

To illustrate, information and communication technology is an especially sensitive area in terms of procurement risk. This is because it entails the purchase of expensive equipment and requires a level of buyer expertise that is not normally found in government; there is little competition among the few suppliers. Also, it is frequently supply-driven or donor-driven or both—irrespective of the real needs of the users in the company or the government—and decisions are usually made at middle management level. In this and similarly risky sectors for procurement, it is essential to set up a mechanism to obtain independent technical advice, as well as assure participation by the final users of the equipment or the software from the very beginning of the process.

Thus, any delegation of procurement transactions should begin first in the less risky sectors or agencies and gradually expand to other sectors. Also, government should delegate the least risky phases in the procurement cycle first, keeping close tabs on their functioning and maintaining strong central control on the other phases—progressively delegating more and more procurement phases as experience permits and performance warrants.

Quantifying Procurement Risk

The main phases of procurement—standard setting and invitation to bid, bid evaluation, contract negotiations and award, and contract monitoring—are of course interrelated, but each individual phase is associated with a different degree of risk. The simple matrix in Table 9.1 helps guide decisions to delegate different phases of procurement to sectors with different degrees of risk. In the table, the degree of risk of delegating a specific stage of procurement is on a scale of 1 to 10 (with 10 the highest risk); and the procurement risk in sectors A through E is assessed based on the first three risk factors discussed earlier (specificity, market structure and size of transactions).

Table 9.1 Risk Matrix for Delegating Procurement Functions

Sector	Phase of Procurement and Risk Rating (1=lowest risk; 10=highest risk)			
	Criteria and Standards	Bidding and Bid Evaluation	Contract Negotiations	Contract Monitoring
A	1	1	2	2
B	3	3	3	9
C	9	2	2	2
D	2	8	7	1
E	8	8	8	9

In this hypothetical illustration, in the safest sector A the entirety of the procurement process can be safely delegated; in the riskiest sector E no phase of procurement should be delegated at all; strong central control should be kept in the monitoring phase for sector B, in the standard-setting phase for sector C, and in both the bid evaluation and negotiations phases for sector D. In practice, it is difficult to assign realistic ratings of risk to the various phases of procurement and in the different sectors of the economy—but the scheme in Table 9.1 is useful to frame the situation and facilitate decision-making.

Annex: Procurement in the United States

Purchasing and contracting by the US federal government dates back to the earliest days of the republic and, as in Britain and many other countries, began as a way to assure reliable supplies for the armed forces. As observed in 1781 by Robert Morris, then-superintendent of finance and major financier of the American Revolution: "In all countries engaged in war, experience has sooner or later pointed out that contracts with private men of substance and understanding are necessary for the subsistence, covering, clothing, and manning of an army."

The federal government acquires most of its goods, services and works from private entities. In 2000, federal agencies bought about $235 billion in goods and services, reflecting an 11 percent increase over the amount spent five years earlier. Additional growth since then has taken place primarily from increased spending on defense and homeland security. Although a bit down from its peak in 2009, federal contracting in 2014 was $447 billion—a 50 percent increase (in real terms) from the beginning of the century. The Defense Department is the largest agency in terms of contracting dollars spent, accounting for about two-thirds of the total and more than twice the amount spent by the next nine largest federal agencies combined. (The Air Force, Army and Navy each spend more than the largest civilian agency, the Department of Energy.)

Federal contracts are spread around 175,000 companies, for an average contract value of about $2.5 million. However, almost one-fourth goes to six companies—the big five defense contractors (Lockheed-Martin, General Dynamics, Raytheon, Northrop Grumman and Boeing) plus Halliburton's KBR—for an average yearly contract value of over $15 billion. (Oh, and of the money going to the Big Six, more than half was contracted without full competitive bidding.)

Policies, Regulations and Organization

Federal Procurement Policy

The foundation of modern federal procurement was built shortly after World War II, with the Federal Property and Administrative Services Act of 1949 and the Armed Services Procurement Act also of 1949. Subsequently, the Federal Procurement Policy Act of 1974 (related to the Budget Reform Act of the same year—see Chapter 6) created the Office of Federal Procurement Policy and placed it under the Office of Management and Budget (OMB).[11] The Competition for Contracting Act of 1984 set the main government-wide procurement policies and principles, and the Federal Acquisition Streamlining Act of 1994 articulated the operational aspects of federal procurement.

The Federal Acquisition Regulations System

The Federal Acquisition Regulation (FAR) system is established for the codification and publication of uniform policies and procedures for acquisition by all executive agencies.

The system consists of the FAR, which is the primary document, and agency-specific regulations that implement or supplement the FAR. The FAR is issued jointly by the General Service Administration (GSA), and the Department of Defense (DOD) and National Aeronautics and Space Administration (NASA) under their separate statutory authorities. Consistent with the requirements of the 1974 Federal Procurement Policy Act, the bedrock principle of the FAR is that government business shall be conducted in a manner above reproach and, except as expressly authorized by statute or regulation, with complete impartiality and no preferential treatment. The practice often differs.

Organizational Arrangements

As noted earlier, a central question in procurement is whether responsibility should rest with the agency that requires the goods and services or with a central purchasing agency. In most countries, standards and rules are set by a central agency, but actual purchasing is done by the individual agencies in conformity with these standards and rules. This is the case in the United States as well, albeit with certain differences.

In addition to the standard-setting responsibility of the OMB Office of Federal Procurement Policy, the General Services Administration is the central office for administering the procurement regulations. (The Department of Defense and NASA have their own procurement approaches, to fit their special missions.[12]) The general mandate of GSA is to "help federal agencies better serve the public by offering, at best value, superior workplaces, expert solutions, acquisition services and management policies." Prior to 1994, the GSA included the Federal Technology Service (FTS), the Federal Supply Service (FSS), the Public Buildings Service and various staff offices. The FTS and FSS were merged into a single new organization, the Federal Acquisition Service, which is organized into four major offices, each with multiple business lines: General Supplies and Services; Travel, Motor Vehicle and Card Services; Integrated Technology Services; and Assisted Acquisition Services (www. gsa.gov/portal/content/105080).

Conforming to good international practice, actual procurement is done by each federal department and agency on its own account. For this, many US agencies have been relying increasingly on outside intermediaries to do their purchasing and contracting, a practice with advantages and risks discussed in Chapter 11. The past decade has seen the emergence of several changes in the way in which the government buys goods and services, as Congress and the administration have sought to simplify the acquisition process and contract negotiation, to shorten procurement delays, reduce administrative costs and improve results. The Defense Department is the glaring exception, with a study in 2015 uncovering $125 billion in administrative waste annually (although not all from bloated procurement).

Improving the Procurement Workforce

Based on the Services Acquisition Reform Act of 2003, which covered the definition of acquisition requirements, the measurement of contract performance, and technical and management direction, the federal government established in 2005 a government-wide framework for creating a federal acquisition workforce with the skills necessary to deliver best-value supplies and services, find the optimal business solutions, and provide strategic business advice to accomplish the agency procurement objectives.[13] Building on the previous efforts of 1992 and 1997 to improve the skills of procurement personnel, this framework recognizes the need for a professional workforce and sets the education, training and experience requirements for entry and advancement in the acquisition career.

The Past Decade: Spend More, Manage Worse

The rapid increase in federal contracting, noted earlier, has been associated with a rise in the incidence of contract mismanagement. The primary areas of mismanagement have been in:

- award of non-competitive contracts;
- reliance on types of contracts known to be risky;
- abuse of contracting flexibility;
- poor procurement planning;
- inadequate contract oversight;
- unjustified fees; and
- straight bribery.

The worst instances have occurred in contracting for homeland security, the wars in Iraq and Afghanistan (primarily the former), and Hurricane Katrina recovery. (While procurement problems were also experienced in contracting under the anti-recession American Recovery and Reinvestment Act of 2009, they were trivial compared with the abuses of contracting in connection with Iraq and Afghanistan war expenditures.)

In the Department of Homeland Security (DHS) alone, a weak control environment has enabled wasting over $20 billion on ill-conceived purchases and misuse of credit cards. The GAO and the Department of Homeland Security's own Office of Inspector General estimated that almost half of DHS purchase-card transactions were not properly authorized; more than half did not give priority to designated sources, and for an astonishing two-thirds—$14 billion—there is no evidence that the goods or services were ever received. The review also found frequent failures to dispute incorrect transactions; improper use of the purchase card (e.g., $460,000 for prepackaged meals); abusive transactions (e.g., purchase of a beer-brewing kit and a 63-inch plasma TV costing $8,000 and found unused in its box six months after purchase); and tens of thousands of dollars for golf and tennis lessons at resorts.[14]

But the main driver of waste, fraud and abuse has been the award of contracts without full competition. While it is understandable that no-bid contracts may be needed in the early days of a new agency, the value of non-competitive contracts at DHS *increased* from under $800 million (25 percent of total contracts) in 2003, when DHS was created, to a peak of $5.5 billion in 2005, seven times the initial amount and more than 50 percent of the total value of DHS contracts. The charitable explanations of this phenomenon are a remarkable lack of procurement planning and a failure of elementary oversight and monitoring responsibility.

Although there are no precise estimates of waste and fraud in war contracting and for Iraq and Afghanistan reconstruction activities, the amount is certainly much higher than that of the no-bid contracts for homeland security. The issue in this context is not the wisdom of the activities or the underlying policy decisions, but the collusion between business leaders and senior government officials and the other risks that led to stupendous waste and grand theft of taxpayers' money.

The hopeful lesson is that such problems can be fixed: in fiscal 2014, DHS awarded non-competitive contracts of a total value of only $306 million (9 percent of the total value), and barely 1.5 percent of the $8.7 billion grants were awarded on a non-competitive basis. Good management works.

Notes

1 This chapter can only provide a summary of the vast agenda of government procurement. Moreover, it is focused primarily on the links to budgeting and public expenditure management. Readers interested in a comprehensive treatment of procurement are referred to Baily et al.

(2015), geared primarily to developed countries, and to de Mariz et al. (2014) for procurement issues in developing countries. Other sources used in the chapter include Schiavo-Campo and McFerson (2008); Pope (1996); Hauck and Leighland (1989); Stockholm International Peace Research Institute (www.sipri.org); Perry (1989); Cooper and Newland (1997); Rehfuss (1993); and other sources individually cited. Other sources are the official procurement guidelines issued by the World Bank, the African Development Bank and the Asian Development Bank; WTO statistics; OECD; Commonwealth Secretariat; and information in country governments' websites, current as of early 2016.

2 The UN Commission on International Trade Law was set up in 1968 to promote the harmonization of international laws relating to trade. In addition to the procurement law, UNCITRAL has formulated other model laws, on international commercial arbitration and conciliation, international sale of goods and related transactions, cross-border insolvency, international payments, international transport of goods, electronic commerce and international construction contracts. (See www.uncitral.org.)

3 The procurement criteria and rules are normally incorporated in three documents: (i) a policy manual, with the purchasing criteria and main rules; (ii) an operations manual of internal practices and procedures; and (iii) a vendor manual, often in the form of a booklet entitled something like *Doing Business with the Government*.

4 In countries where autonomous "executive agencies" or "delivery units" are set up for operational government functions, they are given autonomy in procurement, subject to certain features of national procurement policy. Similarly, extrabudgetary funds (see Chapter 3) normally have management autonomy and full authority to carry out their own procurement—again, as consistent with national policy requirements.

5 For example, the World Bank sets value thresholds for each borrowing country, based on its Country Procurement Assessment Reviews, with a view to maximizing competition and efficiency in procurement. The value thresholds are specific to each country, but typically the Bank requires international competitive bidding for works contracts greater than $5 million and goods contracts greater than $500,000; national competitive bidding for works contracts up to $5 million and goods contracts between $200,000 and $500,000; and allows "shopping" for goods contracts of a value lower than $100,000. Thresholds are set higher in good governance countries, and lower in countries with known corruption problems. (In rare cases, such as a World Bank project to strengthen public financial management in Cambodia, the threshold for prior review of contracts was set at an extremely low $50,000, making project implementation unusually cumbersome and ineffective.) The Inter-American Development Bank ICB thresholds are similar, averaging $4.4 million for works and $530,000 for goods.

6 The Iraq war has provided surreal instances of corrupt procurement and war profiteering (see Chandrasekaran, 2007). Somewhat less surreal, but no less wasteful, has been US procurement during the war in Afghanistan.

7 For an analysis of procurement in investment projects see Burger and Hawkesworth (2013).

8 The findings are robust even when controlling for the location, corruption, social capital and judicial efficiency in the region of the public buyers running the auctions

9 See Sanchez (2013); Bohorquez et al. (2012), for other examples of citizens' initiatives; de Simone and Shah (2013), on the broader subject of citizen monitoring of procurement, and *Transparency International* (2014), for a practical guide on combating corruption in procurement.

10 The new flexibility in procurement, which was partly responsible for these problems, was extolled by an anonymous official source in "Emergency Procurement Flexibilities: A Framework for Responsive Contracting & Guidelines for Using Simplified Acquisition Procedures," *Journal of Public Procurement*, 2004, 4(1), 116–32.

11 The 1974 act also provides for the training of professional procurement staff. Subsequently, in 1990 an interagency group developed a plan for procurement professionalism. (Relevant courses are offered by the General Services Administration Interagency Training Center.) In the 1990s, OMB established career management, education and training requirements for acquisition personnel in civilian executive agencies

12 To disseminate regulations appropriate to its special mission, the DOD has established the Defense Acquisition University, partly to integrate operations and contracting for support of operations. The Civilian Faculty Plan establishes opportunities for a pre-eminent faculty in support of acquisition education. There are approximately 235 civilian faculty and 70 military positions in DAU. The NASA Procurement Management System is part of the NASA Acquisition Information System and includes the Simplified Acquisition Process for the Goddard Space Flight Center; the Industry Assistance/Small Business Office, for contracts of $25,000 or more; and the Offices for Earth Sciences, for Mission Enabling, and for Space Sciences Support.

13 Policy Letter 05–01, April 15, 2005, of the Office of Federal Procurement Policy .
14 *Purchase Cards: Control Weaknesses Leave DHS Highly Vulnerable to Fraudulent, Improper, and Abusive Activity,* GAO-06–957T, July 19, 2006.

Bibliography

Baily, Peter, David Farmer, Barry Crocker, David Jessop and David Jones, 2015. *Procurement Principles and Management,* 11th Edition. Edinburgh: Pearson.

Bohorquez, E. and Deniz Devrim, eds., 2012. *A New Role for Citizens in Public Procurement.* Mexico City: Transparencia Mexicana. Available online at http://corruptionresearchnetwork.org/marketplace/resources [accessed November 5 2016].

Burger, Philippe and Ian Hawkesworth, 2013. "Capital Budgeting and Procurement Practices," *OECD Journal on Budgeting,* 13(1), 57–104.

Chandrasekaran, Rajiv, 2007. *Imperial Life in the Emerald City: Life Inside Iraq's Green Zone.* New York: Vintage Books.

Cooper, Phillip and Chester A. Newland, eds., 1997. *Handbook of Public Law and Administration.* San Francisco: Jossey-Bass.

Coviello, Decio and Mario Mariniello, 2014. "Publicity Requirements in Public Procurement: Evidence from a Regression Discontinuity Design," *Journal of Public Economics,* 109, 76–100.

Coviello, Decio, Andrea Guglielmo and Giancarlo Spagnolo, 2016. "The Effect of Discretion on Procurement Performance," *Management Science,* 62(7).

Davenport, Christian, 2016. "Watson to Take on the Federal Morass," *The Washington Post,* March 21.

de Mariz, Leon, Christine Menard and Bernard Abeillé, 2014. *Public Procurement Reforms in Africa: Challenges in Institutions and Governance.* Oxford: Oxford University Press.

de Simone, Francesco and Shruti Shah, 2013. *Civil Society Procurement Monitoring: Challenges and Opportunities.* Mexico City: transparencia Mexicana. Available online at www: transparency.org [accessed November 9, 2016].

Hauck Walsh, Annemarie and James Leighland, 1989. "Designing and Managing the Procurement Process," in James Perry, ed., *Handbook of Public Administration.* San Francisco: Jossey-Bass.

Klitgaard, Robert, 1998. *Controlling Corruption.* Berkeley: University of California Press.

Latham, Richard, 1978. *The Illustrated Pepys.* London: Bell and Lyman.

Lundberg, Sofia, Per-Olov Marklund and Elon Stromback, 2016. "Is Environmental Policy by Public Procurement Effective?" *Public Finance Review,* 44(4), 478–99.

Perry, James L., ed., 1989. *Handbook of Public Administration.* San Francisco: Jossey-Bass.

Pope, Jeremy, 1996. *National Integrity Systems: The Transparency International Sourcebook.* Berlin: Transparency International.

Rehfuss, John, 1993. *Designing an Effective Bidding and Monitoring System to Minimize Problems in Competitive Contracting.* Available online at www.reason.org/htg03.pdf [accessed November 9, 2016].

Sanchez, Alfonso, 2013. "The Role of Procurement," in R. Allen, R. Hemming and B. Potter, eds., *International Handbook of Public Financial Management.* New York: Palgrave Macmillan.

Schiavo-Campo, S. and Hazel McFerson, 2008. *Public Management in Global Perspective.* Armonk, NY: M. E. Sharpe.

Transparency International, 2014. *Curbing Corruption in Public Procurement.* Available online at www.transparency.org/whatwedo/activity/curbing_corruption_in_public_procurement [accessed November 9, 2016].

10 Financing the Budget
Debt and Aid Management

> Annual income twenty pounds, annual expenditure nineteen pounds nineteen shillings and six pence, result happiness. Annual income twenty pounds, annual expenditure twenty pounds and six pence, result misery.
>
> (Mr. Micawber in Charles Dickens' *David Copperfield*)

Introduction

For a household, Mr. Micawber had a point. For a government as a whole, he was wrong. A budget in surplus can mask severe underlying fiscal weakness (especially when the cost of new entitlements comes due in the future, or budget coverage is inadequate and substantial off-budget expenditure programs exist). And an apparently large deficit may not be a problem if the budget is sound and well-executed and the deficit is sustainable. To be sustainable, among other things, the deficit must be financed in appropriate ways and at favorable terms. Recall from Chapter 4 that fiscal responsibility does not lie in whether the budget deficit is higher or lower, per se, but in confronting realistically the expenditure implications of government activities and finding sustainable ways to mobilize revenue to pay for them and finance the deficit.

This chapter explains the modalities of financing the budget, and the principles of good management of the resulting debt. In low-income countries, where foreign aid is a major source of financing, the efficient management of external aid is a major priority for the government and the effectiveness of the aid is a prime consideration for the aid donors. The chapter will also review the issues of aid management and its organizational architecture, and conclude with a capsule analysis of the mixed record of efforts made since 2005 to improve the effectiveness of aid.

Financing the Budget: The Overall View

Autonomous and Compensatory Transactions

Please refer back to Box 2.4 and Table 5.2. There is a conceptual distinction between government transactions that are undertaken for their own "autonomous" reasons (e.g., salaries are paid in order to obtain the services of the employees), and financing transactions that are undertaken only as "compensatory" of the autonomous transactions (e.g., governments take out a loan in order to finance the budget outcome and not as an end in itself). The expression "above the line" and "below the line" delineates the distinction and defines the boundary between the autonomous government transactions and the compensatory ones undertaken to finance the budget deficit.

The "bottom line" of the budget is a fiscal surplus if revenues and ordinary grants add up to more than total expenditure, and is a fiscal deficit if expenditure exceeds revenue and grants. If the budget is persistently in surplus, the question is whether to use the surplus to

reduce the outstanding stock of government debt, or invest the money for future generations, or expand government activities, or reduce taxes—or a combination. The normal
issues of budget financing thus arise only in the context of a budget deficit.

To recapitulate, the deficit can be financed by grants or loans, and from domestic and
foreign sources. Grants considered as part of financing are the "exceptional" grants which
cannot be counted on to continue. (Recurrent grants are part of ordinary revenue and are
thus shown above the line.) Loans include government borrowing from the domestic
banking system or other domestic sources, and government borrowing from foreign
sources. The budget can also be financed by the simple (and destructive) device of not
paying for some goods and services and works: net changes in payment arrears are below
the line as part of financing ("negative financing" if arrears are being reduced on a net
basis). Finally, just as new debt is part of positive financing, repayment of loan principal
(amortization), which reduces the stock of government debt, is part of negative financing.

Each type of financing and each source of financing carries its own advantages, disadvantages, costs and risks—all of which should be carefully assessed and managed. In general, it is clear that, other things being equal, grants are better than loans and borrowing
at concessional terms is better than borrowing at commercial terms. Good debt management and aid management are key components of a sound public financial management
system. Debt management is important everywhere, but especially in countries where debt
on commercial terms constitutes the majority of financing. Foreign aid constitutes by far
the bulk of financing of the budget of developing countries, and good aid management is
therefore especially important for them.

Financing versus Adjustment: Liquidity versus Solvency

Fiscal problems can be temporary and caused by transitory factors, or permanent and
caused by a structural imbalance between expenditure commitments and revenue. In a
household, a temporary financial difficulty (such as, for example, an unexpected car repair)
calls for resorting to the credit card or dipping into savings, while a permanent financial
problem (such as, for example, loss of job) calls for a major adjustment in the household
expenditure pattern or raising regular revenue from other sources. Temporary problems
give rise to lack of liquidity, and can be addressed by *financing* until the normal fiscal
situation has returned; permanent problems give rise to insolvency, and call for *adjustment*
in expenditure and/or revenue and/or structural reforms. Misjudging an insolvency problem as a liquidity problem leads to providing a temporary remedy without a solution and
to postponing the necessary permanent adjustment that the situation requires—mopping
up the floor over and over again without fixing the leaking faucet. (The best recent case in
point is the early misdiagnosis of the Greek debt crisis as one of liquidity instead of basic
insolvency.) In a household, a temporary financial difficulty (such as, for example, an
unexpected car repair) calls for resorting to the credit card or dipping into savings, while
a permanent financial problem (such as, for example, loss of job), calls for a major adjustment in the household expenditure pattern or raising regular revenue from other sources.

But lack of liquidity can itself lead to major permanent difficulties unless the requisite
temporary financing is provided. (Indeed, bank failures are historically linked more to
liquidity problems, which affected depositors' confidence and hence caused them to
demand their money back all at once. In the old saying: if everyone thinks the bank is no
good, the bank is no good—regardless of how solid its investments or how sound its management may be.) The distinction between financing and adjustment, between liquidity
and solvency, is at the heart of the post-World War II international financial system, which
was set up largely to prevent temporary liquidity crises from turning into permanent financial problems for the country concerned and everyone else.

Coming Down from Abstractions

Trusting that the readers remember that the analogy between a family and a country's economy is often fallacious, it is time for another quick dip into the household analogy. The autonomous transactions of a household include rent *in exchange for* the use of the apartment, payments to the supermarket *in exchange for* groceries, tuition payments *in exchange for* education services, etc. If the overall family budget is in balance or surplus—total spending equal to or less than income—there is no need for financing. But if spending exceeds income, the gap must be filled somehow: borrowing, dipping into previous savings, etc. You don't do this in exchange for anything and surely not for the thrill of it; you do it in order to *compensate for* the net result of all of your other transactions.

In turn, as your deficits continue, you necessarily accumulate more and more debt. The interest payments on the debt then become part of your regular expenditure, because they are payments *in exchange for* the use of the loan money; the repayments of the loans' principal are instead part of financing because they reduce your indebtedness. Finally, if the deficits come from a temporary shortfall in income or a one-time expenditure, the problem is one of insufficient liquidity, and can be addressed with financing. But if the income decline or the expenditure excess result from structural factors in the family's financial situation, the problem is one of insolvency, and requires timely "structural adjustment"— getting a second job, cutting out some recurring expenditure, or a combination. Continued financing of an unsustainable situation causes the debt to go up and up until a point where further borrowing becomes impossible and drastic measures become inevitable: getting evicted, dropping out of grad school, and such. (The macroeconomic reality is far more complex, but the above should help to understand the basics.)

Debt Sustainability

What is the Sustainable Level of Public Debt?

In most countries, a modest fiscal deficit is normal, and in developing countries (except those with abundant extractive revenues) a deficit is positively desirable, *provided* that the corresponding expenditures are efficient, growth-promoting and poverty-reducing. Obviously, unless it is financed exclusively by grants, the deficit requires borrowing and thus—other things being equal—adds to the stock of government debt. The issue is debt sustainability, and not a specific amount of government debt. There is no easy answer to the question of how much debt is too much (for a general analysis, see Kraay and Nehru, 2006). An instructive example is India, whose public debt has been increasing rapidly in absolute value during the past decade. On this partial and superficial basis, it has been viewed as unsustainable by some (Mathur, 2014). But this is clearly not the case: from about 90 percent of GDP in 2004, India's debt has declined to 74 percent of GDP in 2008 and to 65 percent in 2015—back to the level of 20 years ago. This is because the economy has grown faster than the stock of debt, the cost of debt to the government has fallen, and the currency composition and maturity profile have both improved (Pradhan, 2014). It would not have been good policy ten years ago to compress public expenditure or raise taxes in order to keep the debt from rising in absolute value, since doing so would have kept the economy from growing. Be careful, though. Sustainability of aggregate expenditure says nothing about the composition of public expenditure. For example, a lot of productive expenditure in India has been crowded out by the mounting government wage bill.[1]

What Factors Matter for Debt Sustainability?

While the answer to how much debt is country-specific, four factors determine its sustainability. In the first place, if the government borrowing finances activities that will add more to the country's productive capacity than the cost of borrowing, the country's capacity to service the debt will rise by more than the added cost of the loans. (Borrowing beyond your means to buy a luxury car is very different from borrowing for graduate school tuition.) Second, a given stock of debt is obviously easier to service if interest rates are low.

Third, the currency denomination matters greatly. If the debt is in domestic currency and owed to domestic creditors, the economy as a whole is not significantly affected, because what the government pays out to service the public debt is equal to what the domestic private creditors receive and there are no balance-of-payments repercussions—in a real sense, we owe the debt to ourselves. But if the debt is denominated in foreign currency and owed to external entities, to pay it off requires a real transfer of resources from the national economy to the foreign creditors—with the specter of a major financial crisis if the resources become insufficient to repay the loans and the country defaults. This explains the apparent paradox that a country, such as Spain, where public debt is lower than GDP, is in financial difficulties while another country, such as Japan, can cruise along (so far . . .) with a debt of two and a half times GDP. That said, whatever the stock of public debt may be, it must be managed carefully, to minimize borrowing costs and protect against risk.

Fourth, the nationality of the creditor matters, too.[2] All debt owed to non-residents is defined as "foreign debt" regardless of the currency. In Denmark, more than 75 percent of domestic 10-year government bonds are held by foreigners. Given the country's very low fiscal deficits or slight surpluses, any possible risk from an investor sell-off of government bonds is to the reserves of foreign currency rather than to the sustainability of the debt. (The same is not true in other countries in a less favorable fiscal situation.) But domestic entities can also borrow foreign-currency denominated government debt. For example, in 2015 and 2016 Egypt issued treasury bills denominated in dollars and euros, and in Lebanon the government typically issues eurobonds, to make lending to government more attractive to the local banks. The real-life difference is that the government can treat domestic holders of foreign-currency denominated government securities much less favorably, if it wished, than foreign creditors. Stiffing your own nationals is much less costly than stiffing foreign creditors.

Depending on the country's economic system, private sector debt may be a concern as well. Twenty years ago, the 1997 Asian financial crisis (especially in Thailand and Indonesia) was triggered by the inability of the private sector to repay high debts to foreign creditors. Currently, while China's official debt is only about 50 percent of GDP, its total indebtedness is approaching 280 percent. This is worrisome not only because of the very high level but also because it has been rising fast. Compared with 2010, China's total public and private debt doubled in 2016, to a gigantic 25 trillion US dollars. Unless reforms are adopted, with the slowdown in Chinese economic growth the ratio is likely to rise further and lead to a major crisis even though almost all the debt is domestic. Worse, much of the debt has been incurred to prop up zombie state enterprises and to build vast infrastructure (particularly housing and "new cities") where demand is weak to non-existent and the cities sit empty.

How to Assess Debt Sustainability

Whether a given level of debt is or is not sustainable depends on the factors noted above, to which must be added the intangible factor of confidence in the country's ability to repay. Ratios and formulas can provide a sound starting point, but to depend exclusively on formulas becomes a straitjacket for intelligent fiscal and debt policy. With that caveat in mind, the basis for assessing the sustainability of debt is provided in relatively simple arithmetic flowing directly from the definitions of the fiscal deficit. Let's see how.

In the first place, a large economy can carry a larger debt than a small economy—hence, what matters is not the absolute amount of debt but the country's ability to handle the debt, which is measured by the ratio of debt to the country's GDP. Second, the dynamics of the debt ratio depend on both the fiscal outturn as well as the relation between the interest rate on the debt and the growth rate of GDP.

The primary deficit is the fiscal deficit less interest payments, and interest payments are the average interest rate multiplied by the stock of debt. Intuitively, if the primary account is in balance and GDP grows faster than the interest payments, the debt-servicing capacity rises by more than the debt itself, some of the debt can be repaid and the stock of debt will come down—and vice versa. Therefore:

Change in debt = Primary deficit + [(Interest rate – GDP growth rate) × Debt].

Dividing everything by GDP gives:

Change in debt/GDP = Primary deficit/GDP + [(Interest rate – GDP growth rate) × Debt]/GDP

Readers should go through the formula and find the variety of combinations by which the debt/GDP ratio can increase or decrease—*including* the interaction among the terms of the formula itself. For example, a primary deficit does not in itself mean that the debt ratio will increase: if the deficit is associated with an increase in productive investment, the future rate of growth of GDP will rise and debt sustainability may well improve. Or, in view of the critical role of confidence in financial markets, a change in government may increase credibility and lead to lower interest rates charged on its debt. On the contrary, election of a new government known for opposing necessary structural changes may cause creditors to charge a higher interest rate and worsen the debt sustainability prospects even though nothing else has yet changed.

Finally, a government facing unsustainable debt obligations may still be able to reschedule the debt or negotiate some form of debt forgiveness—as discussed later in this chapter. If those options are not available, there remains the possibility of simply not paying—relieving the debt service burden but at the cost of being shut out of the international credit market for decades and suffering many other unpleasant consequences. The costs of this "nuclear option" are far heavier than those of maintaining a sustainable fiscal policy and making timely adjustments in the first place—thus retaining the international confidence that allows financing of deficits at favorable terms.

Debt Management

Coping with Debt Risk

Debt management must identify, manage and mitigate a variety of different risks. A primary objective is to minimize the overall risk exposure of the public debt portfolio. In general, the riskiest forms of debt are short-term debt, debt at variable interest rates and debt denominated in foreign currency. Therefore, the risk exposure of a debt portfolio is determined primarily by its composition—the shares of short-term debt, of variable interest rate debt, and of debt denominated in foreign currency. A relatively large debt portfolio dominated by long-term fixed-rate loans denominated in domestic currencies is much less risky than a smaller portfolio of short-term debt at adjustable rates—as millions of home mortgage borrowers found to their chagrin during the Great Recession of 2008–11. Unlike homes, countries cannot be foreclosed on, but high exposure to risk can lead to a debt crisis, with ensuing massive economic, social and political repercussions—as several European countries found to *their* chagrin during the post-2010 European crisis. The types of risk faced in debt management are listed in Box 10.1.

Pillars of Debt Management

The four pillars of sound debt management are a debt management strategy; centralized control; an annual borrowing and repayment plan; and proper accounting—as summarized next.[3]

Box 10.1 Debt Risks

The types of risk to be addressed by debt management fall in three broad categories: market risk, commercial risk and operational risk.

Market risk

- *Interest rate risk and refinancing risk* refer to the increase in the cost of servicing variable-rate loans, and fixed-rate loans when they are refinanced, when interest rates rise. (Refinancing risk may be considered separately because inability to refinance or a very high increase in borrowing costs can cause a major debt crisis in a country.)
- *Exchange rate risk* refers to the increase in the cost of debt denominated in foreign currency when the foreign currency becomes more expensive relative to the domestic currency. Such changes occur all the time and can reduce as well as increase the cost of debt, but the exchange rate volatility itself has an adverse effect on predictability and calls for careful management.
- *Liquidity risk* refers to a situation where the volume of liquid assets drops sharply because of unanticipated cash flow problems (e.g., an internal conflict that stops tax revenue collection in the affected region and also causes a spike in expenditure).

Commercial risk

- *Credit risk* refers mainly to the risk of non-performance by borrowers on government loans.
- *Settlement risk* refers to the risk that a counterpart to an agreement does not meet its obligations after the country has already made the payment according to the agreement.

Operational risk

- Comprises the variety of difficulties encountered by debt managers in their day-to-day work—including errors in executing and recording transactions, failures in internal controls or systems, security breaches, etc.

Source: Condensed and adapted from IMF/World Bank (2014).

A Debt Management Strategy

The government needs a strategy that focuses on public debt and the risk to the public finances, covering at least the same period as the medium-term fiscal perspective, and also updated annually. The absence of such a strategy almost invariably leads to higher borrowing costs than necessary and to higher risk. Developing a strategy essentially means identifying the preferred composition of the debt domestic versus external, fixed versus variable interest rate, redemption profile, etc. The composition will define the degree of risk exposure of the debt (Jessen, 2016). The content, level of detail and format of the debt management strategy depend on the circumstances and needs of the specific country, but the strategy should be public. In low-income countries with limited capacity a debt strategy is still needed, but can be expressed in the form of broad guidelines (e.g., more domestic debt, preference for long-term debt), rather than target ranges for specific risk exposure indicators (e.g., share of debt maturing in one year, share of external debt).

Central Control

Centralized control of government borrowing is essential. The autonomous expenditure decisions should be made by the line ministries and agencies concerned, but individual ministries or spending agencies should not be allowed to make financing decisions, and under no circumstances to contract debt. Conceptually, this is because the borrowing requirements of the government are not associated with one or another specific sector of the economy or category of expenditure, but flow from the budget as a whole. Borrowing must be addressed in an integrated manner to assure that the budget is financed at least cost to the economy and that financing needs are met for the entire government. Practically, to allow decentralized authority to borrow is a source of major fiscal risk, hampers transparency, and opens up opportunities for corruption and favoritism. (In one African country in the early 1980s, for example, the officially recorded external debt doubled in a single morning, after the president directed all ministers to provide current information on the loans they had actually contracted during the previous years.) Accordingly, the basic budget law (or even the constitution) should prescribe that only one government entity has the authority to contract debt obligations for the government. (Normally, that entity should be the ministry of finance.)

The central control of borrowing by subnational government entities—states in federal systems, provinces, districts, municipalities—is a critical component of the management of general government expenditure, and is discussed at some length in Chapter 14 on expenditure management at subnational government levels. Concerning fiscal risk in particular, relevant recent analyses are by Luby and Kravchuk (2013), Pérez and Prieto (2015) and Zhang (2015).

Annual Financing and Borrowing Plan

As discussed in Chapter 9, as soon as the budget is approved by the legislature, a budget implementation plan and a cash plan should be issued to assure that the resources will be available for the approved expenditures on a timely basis—taking into account the seasonality of revenue and of different kinds of expenditure. If a fiscal deficit is expected, there will obviously be financing requirements for the year as a whole, and part of those requirements will be met through borrowing. The annual budget documentation should therefore outline the government financing and borrowing plan, consistent with both the annual targets and the necessity to fill the monthly gap between revenue and expenditure.

(A publicly available borrowing plan can also be useful for the development of a market for government securities, particularly in middle-income countries.) Formal approval of the financing and borrowing plan by the legislature is neither required nor advisable, in light of the fluid nature of capital markets and frequent changes in loan terms, but the legislature must be informed and is also entitled to know from whom the government expects to contract new loans and at what terms. (Moreover, in many developing countries, certain types of external loans must be specifically approved by the legislature.)

Proper Recording

Each loan transaction must be individually recorded, both for fiscal transparency and to assure that the individual loan repayments will be made on schedule. Reports on the stock of debt and on repayments and new borrowing should be produced by the government, on a regular basis and in standard format, and adequately publicized. Note that, even in the cash-based system of accounting that is normal and appropriate in most governments (see Chapter 11), debt is the only expenditure category that should be recorded when due, rather than on the date when the payment is made. Among other reasons, if government debts are not repaid on the contractual due dates, government credibility will be gravely compromised. (For a household, the "savings" from skipping a couple of mortgage payments are trivial compared with the damage to your credit record and the risk of losing the home to foreclosure.) An-up-to date and comprehensive database of all government loans outstanding and of the exact schedule of repayments of each loan is therefore mandatory. (In aid-dependent developing countries, preparation and maintenance of such a database requires the active cooperation and support of the donors.)

Organizational Arrangements for Debt Management

A dedicated department facilitates sound management of government debt. Normally, the debt management department is located in the ministry of finance, but in a few countries (e.g., Denmark) can be located in the central bank. The mandate of the department, its responsibilities and organizational structure must be clearly defined, and cannot be left to administrative decisions subject to frequent change. However, especially in developing countries, the organizational structure should be allowed to develop with a changing debt management environment—expanding from the basic functions of debt recording, timely payment and reporting to stronger roles, as circumstances permit. Whatever the organizational details, the debt management structure generally includes three main components: a "front office," a "middle office," and a "back office."

The Front Office

The core responsibility of the front office is to implement the medium-term debt management strategy. The portfolio of loans must be managed and regularly adjusted to keep it within the parameters set by the strategy—including the average maturity of loans, the foreign exchange composition and the exposure to interest rate changes. The front office decides when to contract new loans, from which source, and at what interest rate and maturity. This requires among other things that the front office staff must keep up with the market for foreign currencies and for bonds, and be in continuous contact with participants in the domestic financial market. In general, the balance between risks and returns in government debt management should lean heavily in favor of safety and risk minimization, especially in developing countries.[4]

The Back Office

The actual transactions decided by the front office are handled and settled in the back office. Accordingly, the back office is responsible for maintaining the public debt database of the government, and for the accounting of the debt transactions (on accrual, as noted). In the absence of an ironclad separation between the front office, which makes decisions on the loan portfolio, and the back office, which handles the transactions, conflicts of interest and corruption opportunities would be rife. Hence the name of the third office, which is literally "in the middle" between the front and the back office.

The Middle Office

The core responsibility of the middle office is to provide policy analysis and advice on debt management. The middle office is the interface between fiscal policy and the decisions on budget financing. As such, it is responsible for formulating the medium-term debt management strategy consistent with the macroeconomic and fiscal parameters. As part of its debt policy advice function, the middle office is responsible for monitoring the activities of the front office, in order to keep the loan portfolio consistent with the public debt management strategy.

In some circumstances, the middle office may contribute to the monitoring of fiscal risk—interacting with and overseeing the borrowing by subnational government, which in several countries—especially in Latin America in the 1990s—has been a major source of fiscal risk (see Chapter 14). Also, it is in the middle office that a register of contingent liabilities and other fiscal risks associated with government borrowing should be compiled. (The government contingent liabilities stemming from the foreign-exchange exposure of commercial banks were a major trigger of the Asian financial crisis of 1997–2000.)

Finally, as noted, the middle office is the watchdog against conflicts of interest and corruption and other operational risks in debt management. Critical in this respect is for the middle office to serve as a "Chinese wall" between the front and back offices.

Locating the Debt Management Function

In principle, having one debt management entity reduces operational risks and facilitates coordination of the different debt management functions. The entity is located in the ministry of finance almost everywhere, but it is not uncommon for the central bank to undertake some of the debt management functions (typically the primary issuance of domestic debt) as well as some other back-office functions. In these cases the respective roles and responsibilities should be clearly set out in a formal memorandum of understanding between the central bank and the ministry of finance. (In the immediate aftermath of violent internal conflict, however, the central bank may be the only institution capable of handling debt management functions.)

If the responsibility for debt policy and debt management is shared in some fashion among the ministry of finance, the central bank and the ministry of planning, the closest possible cooperation and dialogue must be assured between these key institutions—and preferably formalized through some appropriate arrangement, for example a high-level debt management committee.

What is imperative, under any organizational arrangement, is to consolidate the operational and transactional dimensions of debt management into a single administrative unit under one roof, with clear authority and—therefore—accountability. Fragmenting these functions between different offices in the ministry of finance or, worse, among the ministry of finance, ministry of planning and central bank, leads to incoherent procedures, high transaction costs and unnecessary risks of errors.

Debt and Developing Countries

Although not a permanent feature of the debt management function, the relief of an unsustainable debt burden is of special importance for highly indebted poor countries. A sovereign country cannot be obliged to pay its debts. In theory, that is. In olden times, military attack or invasion served as a pretty effective enforcement instrument—for example, Egypt became a de facto British protectorate when it was invaded in 1882 to force it to pay the debts incurred in the construction of the Suez Canal. Today, the main penalty for default is exclusion from the international financial market, for middle- and high-income countries, and a halt in most forms of aid, for low-income countries. Simply not paying can be very tempting, but is not a feasible solution of a high debt burden.

For poor and highly-indebted developing countries, therefore, the international community had to devise acceptable solutions. In the first place, when the debt service becomes so large as to be in effect unpayable, keeping it on the books is only an accounting requirement and practical ways must be found to reduce it to an affordable level. Moreover, in poor countries the issue of debt also has a moral and governance dimension. On the moral side, the question is the one asked by Tanzania's late President Julius Nyerere: "Must we starve our children in order to pay our debts?" On the governance side, the question is: "Should a country repay debt contracted by a former dictator to enrich himself and his cronies, especially when the dictator has been actively supported by the creditor countries?" (The term for such debt is "odious debt.") Take the example of Zaire, now Democratic Republic of Congo. In 1990, the external debt of Zaire to western creditors was about $4 billion. This was the same amount as the estimated personal wealth of Joseph-Désiré Mobutu, the president of Zaire—who had been placed in power with western help in 1965 and was supported for the following 30 years. You connect the dots.

Debt Rescheduling and Debt Forgiveness[5]

Both debt rescheduling (or "restructuring") and debt forgiveness lower the annual cost of servicing the country's external debt. However, debt rescheduling does so by stretching out the maturity of the existing loans (and in some cases lowering the average interest rate), but does not reduce the stock of debt. Debt forgiveness does so by reducing the stock of debt itself and thus permanently reducing the future flow of debt service payments. Thus, rescheduling kicks the debt can down the road (sometimes over and over for years) to a time when, somehow, the country's debt-servicing capacity will become sufficient to repay interest and principal. Because all creditors should receive equal treatment, debt rescheduling requires a collective agreement between the creditors and the debtor government. For debt owed to private creditors, such an agreement is reached in the context of the so-called London Club; rescheduling official debt, owed to other governments or to public international institutions, is handled in the context of the so-called Paris Club.[6]

The Rescheduling Merry-Go-Round

Beginning in the early 1980s, the practice emerged to require for debt rescheduling that the IMF and/or World Bank attest that the debtor country was engaged in a process of reform that would put it on a sounder financial footing and was implementing a budgetary policy oriented to development and poverty reduction. This gave the two institutions—especially the IMF—enormous influence on the process and the outcome of the negotiations. Consider the following example. In the US, since 1979 the "Brooke amendment" prohibited the administration from extending additional aid to any country that was more than a year late on repaying loans from the US.[7] Since debt rescheduling calls for agreement by all major creditors, and the IMF seal of approval was required for such an agreement, the IMF in effect had the power not only to deny the debtor country its own financial assistance but also to make financial assistance from the US legally impossible.

Moreover, debt owed to the international financial institutions was legally non-reschedulable, according to their charters. This created a neat merry-go-round: unless the country was current in its payments to the IMF, World Bank and the regional development banks (African, Asian, Inter-American) none of these institutions could resume its assistance; a reform program sufficient to endorse a rescheduling of the country's debt could not be negotiated; the rescheduling discussions couldn't take place; some major bilateral donors could not legally extend aid if the country owed them money; and the loans from the IMF, World Bank and other international organizations couldn't be repaid. A poor country with no ability to repay was thus in an absurd situation. Fortunately, in international practice, when a particular outcome would be absurd, solutions are usually found to circle around the problem. Thus, when faced with a poor country that just had no capacity to repay anybody, the IMF and/or World Bank would informally arrange for a short-term bridge loan from a friendly commercial bank. This would permit the country to make the past-due payments to them and thus reopen the door to additional official assistance—assistance which would then go right back to repay the commercial bank that had made the bridge loan. The bridge loan proceeds would in fact go to the IMF or World Bank, albeit officially passing through the debtor government, and the process would be completed within weeks or days. In reality, the international financial institutions were rescheduling their own debt, without having to say so. And why not? The arrangements worked, with a minimum of transaction costs and no legal fuss.

Debt Forgiveness

The troublesome experience of the 1980s and early 1990s with repeated reschedulings of the debt of poor countries helped trigger the Highly Indebted Poor Countries initiative (HIPC) taken by the World Bank in 1996 to forgive part of the debt of poor countries faced with an unsustainable debt burden—provided that they would undertake certain policy reforms to improve their long-term prospects and reduce poverty. Subsequently, the World Bank, IMF and African Development Fund agreed to forgive the *totality* of debt owed to them by countries that had successfully completed the HIPC program.[8] As of early 2016, 36 countries (all but six of them in Africa) had completed the HIPC requirements and received the associated debt relief. The sums involved are substantial, with total debt relief estimated at about $80 billion.[9]

Beyond resolving the financial problem of an unsustainable (and unpayable) debt, the development objective of these debt relief initiatives is to release funds that will be used for development and poverty reduction. In this context, it is logical and appropriate to require the beneficiary country to commit to use the funds for these purposes. The commitment must be articulated in specific understandings about the composition of public expenditure and needs to be underpinned by various mechanisms to monitor the actual expenditure. The question is how to best formulate these understandings. Some arrangements are more effective than others, and carry different implications for budgeting and sound public expenditure management.

The Budgetary Treatment of Debt Relief in Developing Countries

The resources from debt relief can be reflected in the budget in a variety of ways. At one extreme, the resources can be segregated into a special account earmarked for agreed expenditures considered important for development and poverty reduction. At the other extreme, the resources can be commingled with other domestic and external resources and be used as any other funds for an agreed program of public expenditure. Intermediate arrangements are also possible. The differences in budgetary treatment of debt relief are exemplified by the experience of five African countries, summarized below and described in detail by De Groot et al. (2003).

In Burkina Faso and Cameroon, donors' worries about the appropriate use of the HIPC savings led to setting up an Institutional Fund Mechanism, with strict "ring-fencing" of the money. The HIPC savings were lodged in special accounts at the Central Bank of West African States (BCEAO), and were kept separate from the general budget expenditures and managed by HIPC implementation units established especially for this purpose. This diverted attention from the review of overall public spending and the analysis of its impact on poverty reduction. It also complicated budget execution and strained the already weak capacity of the ministry of finance in the two countries—indeed, both countries experienced longer execution delays for the expenditures financed from HIPC funds than for the other expenditures. Moreover, such ring-fencing could not even ensure that the *additional* public resources are allocated to poverty reduction, because they might have simply replaced regular expenditures without any increase in the total allocation for poverty reduction. (As a Cameroonian high government official said to the author in 2009: "We could not very well paint the HIPC money a different color."[10])

By contrast, Benin, Ghana and Tanzania channelled the savings from the HIPC debt relief through the normal budget procedures, and presented the expenditures in the budget in the same manner as the other expenditures.[11] However, Benin and Ghana introduced a *virtual* fund mechanism—whereby certain budget line items agreed with the donors are tagged as "HIPC-related expenditures," but only for reporting purposes and without formal earmarking or ring-fencing in a separate account. Tanzania neither established a separate HIPC account nor implemented a special tracking system for HIPC-related expenditures, but chose instead to stay with its unitary budget and adopt a tracking mechanism for *all* expenditures.

The experience of Burkina Faso and Cameroon shows how enclaving expenditure is clumsy and inefficient, weakens the country's budget process and may not even achieve the intended purpose of spending more on the priority programs. The experience of Benin and Ghana shows that a virtual fund mechanism may succeed in meeting donor concerns about the developmental use of the money without fragmenting the unity of the budget. However, even a virtual mechanism should be temporary, because it focuses attention on only a few activities rather than on the overall strategic allocation of resources for development and poverty reduction. The experience of Tanzania demonstrates that comprehensive expenditure monitoring is adequate to track the developmental use of HIPC debt relief—when the quality of overall expenditure management is good enough to make donors comfortable with endorsing the use of the country's own system for allocating the HIPC savings—along with all its other resources.[12]

One can see how important are institutional capacity and the quality of public financial governance for engendering trust in the international community. Unlike the debt rescheduling merry-go-round, a virtuous circle is at work here: improvements in public financial management produce greater trust that allows donors to rely more on country systems, thereby strengthening local capacity and in turn facilitating further progress in public financial management.

Aid Management

Aid *management*, as a key government function in an aid-dependent country, is different from aid coordination, which relates primarily to donors' efforts to prevent inconsistencies and duplication in their respective aid programs. The actual record of aid management is mixed, with problems on both the donor and the recipient side. Government ownership and effectiveness of aid have improved in several developing countries (particularly those where significant progress has been made in the quality of governance), but in too many developing countries the framework for aid management is still weak and the government attitude is passive, with external donors de facto determining budgetary priorities. International experience suggests that four basic principles should govern aid management.

Principles of Aid Management

Put the Government in the Driver's Seat

Foreign aid should support the recipient country's development, and thus should help finance the priorities, programs and activities decided by the recipient country's government in the exercise of its sovereignty. Therefore, effective government supervision over the aid process is essential, and aid management is a core function of government. The problem arises when government legitimacy is in doubt and major governance weaknesses exist, for in such case it can no longer be assumed that the priorities of the regime in power in fact correspond to those of the population and for the development of the country.

Assuming acceptable quality of governance, the economic reason why aid should be driven by the recipient government is the need for policy coherence and integration of aid within overall financial resource availability. It is impossible for a government to implement coherent economic policy if decisions on the allocation of a big slice of financial resources are made elsewhere. However, the primacy of the recipient government in the management of external aid does not at all exclude the need for donor participation in supervising the use of the aid money and the implementation of aid-financed activities—especially when PFM systems are weak or corruption is a problem. Donor agency staff are accountable to their superiors and the agencies themselves are accountable to their own government constituencies and have a fiduciary responsibility for the resources entrusted to them.

Focus on the Activity to be Financed, not on the Financing Terms

It is a common temptation to focus first on the terms of aid rather than on the project or the activity the aid is expected to finance. The attention should be on the quality of the expenditure and its contribution to development, and not on the compensatory transaction that finances the expenditure. Understandably, it is especially hard to refuse a grant, which does not add to the government debt. But the grant may be intended to build a facility that is not priority for the country and will require scarce domestic funds for its future operations and maintenance. The grant itself is "free money," but its economic consequences can be costly. Contrary to the old proverb, one should look a gift horse in the mouth. The projects to be financed by aid should be assessed for their development impact on the same criteria and in the same way as any other spending, regardless of the aid terms. Having decided that a particular project is priority, it is obviously best to finance it at the most favorable terms, but ask first what should be done, and only then look for the best way to pay for it.[13]

Show all Economic and Financial Aid in the Budget

As Chapter 2 explained, the budget should be as comprehensive as possible and the budget documentation should include all types of government expenditures, even if they have to be managed by special arrangements. The exception is expenditures financed by humanitarian and emergency assistance. Such assistance responds to special needs and follows criteria that are not necessarily economic or financial in nature. Moreover, much humanitarian assistance is in-kind and to try and include it in the budget would require questionable valuations and calculations, for little benefit in terms of public financial management.[14] However, accountability and transparency apply to humanitarian and emergency aid as they are for financial resources, appropriate oversight is necessary, and the legislature should be regularly informed.

But all economic and financial aid—whether grants or loans, and from whatever source—must be integrated into the government budget or at least reflected in the budget documentation to provide a full picture of the public finances.[15]

Handle Counterpart Funds Transparently

Also shown in the budget should be the so-called "counterpart funds," i.e., the local currency proceeds from selling goods or services provided by aid donors—regardless of the conditions the donor may pose on their utilization. In the past, counterpart funds have been a source of duplication of expenditure and have compromised fiscal transparency. The responsibility for oversight of counterpart funds should be placed in the treasury, along with all other government expenditures, and the accounts set up for counterpart funds by agreement with the donors concerned should be monitored and audited in the same way as any other government accounts.

Organizational Arrangements for Aid Management

The high profile of aid means that organizational arrangements in this area are particularly visible and have a significant influence on the credibility of the government vis-à-vis the international community. The details of the organizational structure for aid management should be country-specific, but international experience over the past three decades points to certain criteria—which are not always applied.

One Aid Management Entity

There should be one aid management entity, in central government, as a focal point for all external economic assistance, including technical assistance. In theory, splitting responsibility among different ministries for different aspects of aid management should be manageable if inter-ministerial coordination is strong. In practice, this has never worked and split aid management responsibilities have proven to be a recipe for confusion, waste and conflict. The frequent two-way split of aid responsibilities between a ministry of finance and a ministry of planning is problematic enough (see Chapter 7 for a discussion of "dual budgeting"). The occasional three-way split which includes a role for the ministry of foreign affairs is next to impossible to administer. The result is that the government loses control altogether, and aid decisions are driven by competing donor agendas.

Aid Management Located in a Core Ministry

Aid is money and is usually for investment. Thus, the aid management unit should be located in the ministry of finance or the ministry of planning—preferably the ministry of finance, which is responsible for developing a coherent budget covering all available financing. (Ministers of foreign affairs sometimes argue that because the aid is foreign its management belongs in their ministry. This is the worst location for aid management, although the foreign ministry does have the important role of negotiating broad framework agreements with donors, which govern the diplomatic aspects of the relationship.) As a transitional measure in some countries, an aid management entity could be placed outside the regular structure of government—reporting to the prime minister or the president. However, as soon as time and capacity permit, the aid management function should devolve to the ministry of finance. As a regular function of government, it should be exercised by a regular organ of government.

Organization Along Donor Lines

An aid management unit should be organized along donor lines (e.g., a "World Bank desk," a "UN desk," etc.) to build expertise on the procedural requirements of different donors, match the various terms of aid with different projects, and help keep all donors "inside the tent"—collaborating with a single government organization on an equal footing with one another. The alternative of organizing aid management along sector lines (e.g., an "agriculture desk," a "social sectors desk," etc.) appears logical, but has not worked in practice because it hasn't created the local expertise to negotiate effectively with the different donor agencies, each with its own requirements.

Focal Point for Donor Contacts

The aid management entity should be the focal point in the government for contacts with donors, and must be systematically informed of ongoing activities by both donors and end-users. Beyond traffic control, the aid management entity must have all information needed to look for the most favorable terms and to advise on integrating aid proposals into the budget. To act as focal point does not mean that the aid management entity has a monopoly on information and contacts. On the contrary, as discussed next, the purpose of a single focal point in government for aid management is to support, not substitute for, the decision-making process of sector ministries, and to make their daily life easier by not having to entertain overlapping donor delegations at the most inconvenient times.

Function to Facilitate

The aid management entity must function to facilitate. This prescription has two parts. The entity should function well (and thus needs adequate capacity and human resources), but it must function to facilitate and not obstruct relations between donors and their counterpart ministries (and thus clear limits must be placed on its mandate). Its first job is to regulate "traffic." Each donor country and donor delegation tends to act as if it were the only one with a claim on local officials' time and attention. With half a dozen donors supporting the country, each sending several delegations a year, if the timing of these visits is not regulated the country's ministers and officials would spend most of their time interacting with visiting donor missions. However, while the aid management entity must be invariably informed of donor missions and of ministries' aid requests, it may but need not have the authority to clear donor missions.

On the other hand, it is also necessary to stop individual donors from end runs around central aid management to make their own separate deals with specific line ministries—which has been shown to fragment the budget process, create unhealthy clientelism and enable corruption. This is also for the protection of the line ministries themselves, who would otherwise be besieged by donors pushing their pet projects through the back door when they don't fit the government priorities or the investment program.

The existence of a central aid management entity does not preclude the formation of aid coordination units in individual ministries. On the contrary, the effectiveness of central aid management depends crucially on knowledgeable decision-making in each sector ministry. Thus, the central entity should help build complementary aid management capacity in the sector ministries. Helping to build capacity in the ministries also creates goodwill for the aid management entity and defuses suspicions that it will monopolize foreign aid management.

Non-interference in the Budget Process

Similarly, the aid management entity should never be allowed to interfere in budget proposals and project selection. It does have to be regularly informed of such decisions; have authority to approach the right donor for financing the various projects; and routinely participate in budget discussions in order to help ensure the adequate provision of local funding complementary to aid resources. But sector budget proposals and project selection decisions are the responsibility of the line ministry concerned; the overall investment program is the responsibility of the competent core ministry—either finance or planning; and budget formulation, of course, is the responsibility of the ministry of finance.

The Architecture of Aid Management

The provisions discussed earlier are reflected in the architecture of the aid management function shown in Figure 10.1. It is worth examining the figure with some attention, as it includes the essential informational and prescriptive linkages to and from other agencies of government and, by implication, to the main functions of public expenditure management. Figure 10.1 shows the optimal structure of a mature system, but variants are possible and parts of it may be too heavy for a limited-capacity developing country. At the start, the aid management entity can be very small and interact only with the main counterparts, gradually moving toward the mature structure as government needs require and capacity permits.

Aid Effectiveness and Capacity Development

Three strategic factors help determine the effectiveness of aid to developing countries: national ownership, harmonization of aid and capacity development. In fact, the focus should not be on improving aid effectiveness, but on improving development effectiveness— to which aid makes an important contribution.

The critical importance of ownership and the role of foreign aid to complement and support national priorities have always been acknowledged by the donors, although mostly at lip-service level. On the other hand, only a government with substantial legitimacy, clarity of vision, realistic programs and credible public management systems has a strong claim to asserting its "ownership" rights fully vis-à-vis the donors and the international community.

Harmonizing Aid Procedures and Fostering Capacity Development

Aside from ownership itself, the two factors most relevant for the development effectiveness of aid are the harmonization of donor practices and donor reliance on country systems (especially procurement and financial management). Diverse donor practices have

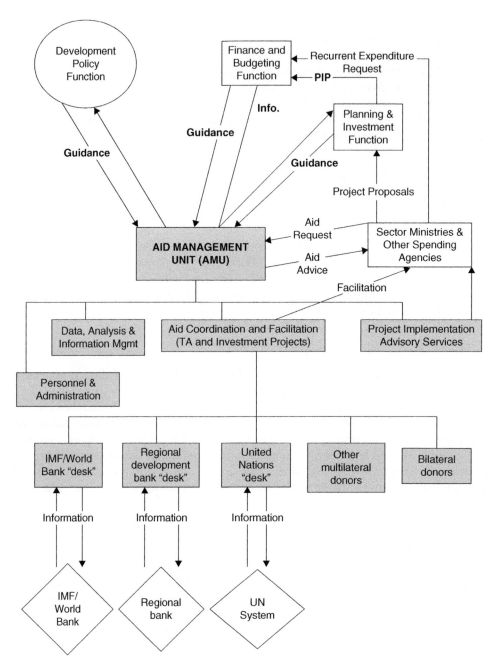

Figure 10.1 Organizational Architecture of Aid Management.

been a perennial source of confusion and the large transaction costs of trying to cope with conflicting requirements. A call for harmonization of aid rather than simple coordination was first made 45 years ago, and took 35 years to be answered:

> Just like aid resources are complementary with domestic resources, so ... different sources and forms of aid are complementary with one another [suggesting] the

formation of a common set of ground rules of the aid game and of criteria ... which all participating countries commit themselves to apply.

(Schiavo-Campo and Singer, 1970, p. 294)

Recognizing the inefficiency of uncoordinated development assistance and diverse procedures, since 2004 there have been declarations by donors to focus on aid results, avoid duplication, and foster capacity development by greater reliance on national systems of public financial management and control. Box 10.2 summarizes the major international events that have addressed the aid effectiveness agenda, starting with the fundamental Paris Declaration of 2005.

The Results So Far

Actual results have been mixed. In several countries, "basket fund" mechanisms have been put in place to support an agreed agenda of public financial management reform (notably in the Tanzania Public Financial Management Reform Programme). Other mechanisms for pooled aid in support of a particular sector have prevented duplication of aid and limited synergy has been achieved by "sector-wide approaches." Even when positive

---

Box 10.2 The International Debate on Aid Effectiveness

Key milestones of the debate during the past decade were as follows:

- The Paris Declaration on Aid Effectiveness (March 2005) set indicators and targets to improve the delivery and management of aid based on five principles: ownership (country-led development strategies), donor alignment with country strategies, harmonization (use of common procedures by donors), managing for results and mutual accountability by donors and countries.
- The first High Level Forum on Aid Effectiveness (Accra, 2008) concluded that progress on implementation of the Paris Declaration was too slow, and adopted the "Accra Agenda for Action" aimed at strengthening country ownership, building more effective partnerships and delivering and accounting for development results.
- The fourth High Level Forum on Aid Effectiveness (Busan, South Korea, 2011) reiterated pretty much the same points but also generated a political momentum for a long-overdue shift from aid effectiveness to development effectiveness. It launched the Global Partnership for Effective Development Cooperation, and decided to strengthen the indicators for global monitoring and accountability.
- The Post-Busan Interim Group (July 2012) approved a proposal to strengthen the monitoring indicators, retaining those from the Paris Declaration framework that developing countries had identified as particularly important and supplementing them with indicators of transparency, gender equality, private sector engagement and an enabling environment for civil society organizations. The Busan process also gave a stronger push to the country systems agenda than was contained in the weak provisions of the Paris Declaration.
- The High-Level Meeting of the Global Partnership for Effective Development Cooperation (Mexico City, 2014) "reviewed progress" and "exchanged experiences," but essentially marked time on the entire agenda.

overall, sector-wide approaches have experienced difficulties ranging from disbursement delays to weak integration between the aid to the sector and the general budget—as exemplified in Box 10.3 on the experience of the education sector in Burkina Faso.

There has been some slight improvement toward the goal of fostering greater reliance on countries' own procurement and financial management systems. In the early years after the 2005 Paris Declaration, reliance on country systems did not increase at all, but the process picked up somewhat and by 2015 the situation was slightly better than in 2006. Reviewing the data on the 41 countries which had a Public Expenditure and Financial Accountability (PEFA) assessment during both 2007–10 and 2012–15 shows an increase in the score for "Proportion of aid that is managed by use of national procedures" from an abysmal 1.18 to 1.50. (The scores, translated from the letter "grades" in the PEFA assessment, go from a low of 1.0 to a high of 4.00.) Experience differs greatly between the major regions. Latin America and the Caribbean had the largest average improvement, from 1.20 to a still low but minimally adequate 2.00—followed by Eastern Europe and Central Asia (from the lowest possible score of 1.00 to an average of 1.60), and East Asia and Pacific (from 1.25 to 1.75). Africa and South Asia—the regions with the largest number of poor countries—remained at an extremely low average of 1.3 in both periods. (See Table 13.1 for details on this and other selected PEFA indicators.)

Box 10.3 Pooling Aid for Sector Support: Education in Burkina Faso

Several donors pooled their funding in support of primary education in Burkina Faso, based on four pillars: a ten-year sector strategy; a budget framework to support the strategy; gradual orientation toward results; and a monitoring mechanism.

The donor partnership has four main elements: a formal partnership framework; designation of a "lead donor"; a mechanism of coordinated financing; and the associated special treasury account. The pooled fund is complemented by budget support from the EU and projects financed by other donors—all consistent with the agreed sector strategy (at least formally).

Central to the arrangement is the leadership role of the Ministry of Primary Education in coordination with donors, using a joint biannual review of progress—in addition to several thematic groups and monthly coordination meetings. The cascade of meetings to coordinate with donors, however, has interfered with the need for internal coordination within the ministry itself—a major problem in light of the ministry's responsibility for leadership of the program.

Other problems were weak predictability of financial resources (which usually fell short of the announced amounts); systematic delays in disbursements which interfered with timely implementation of the activities; and inadequate assessment of progress and insufficient recommendations for improvements.

Finally, three issues typical of sector-wide assistance and pooled funding are clearly visible in the Burkina education experience: lack of integration between general budget support and the aid to the sector; weak linkage between financial management in the education ministry as a whole and the conduct of the specific program of support for primary education; and lack of clarity on whether the pooled funds were in fact additional to the financial resources allocated to primary education, or replaced other financial resources.

Source: Adapted from Cafferini and Pierrel (2009).

On balance, it does not appear that the international community as a whole has yet tackled in earnest the transition to a better balance between the fiduciary responsibility of donors and the commitment to foster capacity development in developing countries.

It is easy to scoff at international meetings producing high-sounding declarations that do not bear quick operational fruit, but the Paris Declaration did set out fundamental principles, and the subsequent series of international debates on aid effectiveness during the past decade have had an initial positive impact. Some harmonization of aid practices has occurred, and the increased pooling of technical assistance from different donors has helped reduce red tape and the transaction costs imposed on developing country officials. It is certainly true, however, that most of the aid harmonization and capacity-building agenda is yet to be achieved; how much can be accomplished will depend heavily on political considerations and international developments.

It is also true that the route to sustainable capacity development goes through actual practice in expenditure programming, financial management, procurement, etc.—confirming the Inter-American Development Bank approach to help create capacity in country systems *in order to use* the country systems. Confucius is reputed to have said: "If I hear, I forget; if I read, I remember; if I do, I understand."

Notes

1 As a result of the Sixth Pay Commission report, the government's expenditure on salary and allowances sharply increased in 2008, causing the wage bill to rise from 16 percent of revenue to over 25 percent—even while the top government employees remained underpaid and the bureaucracy retained its proverbial inefficiency. The bloated government workforce, heavily weighted toward lower-level staff, remains the single largest constraint on the efficiency of government expenditure in India, as it has been for generations.

2 Actually, by the IMF definition of external debt, it is the residence—the usual place of business—of the creditor that matters, not the nationality per se.

3 Readers interested in an in-depth treatment of the subject are referred primarily to Wheeler (2004), and to the IMF/World Bank guidelines (2014). The guidelines update those first issued in 2001 and amended in 2003, and reflect in part the lessons of the severe debt crisis experienced by several European countries after 2010.

4 In some developed countries, the front office is allowed under certain circumstances to take advantage of interest rate differentials by arbitrage—assuming that it has the capacity and competence to do so. Arbitrage is not speculation. Arbitrage is the taking advantage of a difference in price for the same commodity in two (or more) different markets, by simultaneously buying and selling it in the two markets. If the price on a particular debt instrument is higher in country A than in country B, a profit can be made by committing to buy the debt instrument in country B and *at the same time* committing to sell it in country A. In theory, arbitrage is risk-free. In practice, because such price discrepancies are tiny and inherently short-lived, timing is of the essence and the game is won by the slightly faster, slightly better informed, slightly better "wired" player. However, as an assertive debt management posture debt buybacks and debt swaps are much more common than arbitrage.

5 This section relates mainly to low-income countries. The issues of debt relief for middle- or high-income countries, problems of sovereign default, "hold-out" creditors, "vulture funds," etc. are too complex to be discussed here. From the extensive literature on the subject, interested readers are referred to Beers and Nadeau (2015), for a comprehensive database of sovereign defaults, and to Wong (2012), for an analysis of the difficult issues at stake. For Argentina, one of the most complicated cases in recent times, see "Gauchos and Gadflies," *The Economist*, October 22, 2011.

6 The names originate, respectively, from the first private debt rescheduling meeting, which took place in London, and from the venue for discussion of rescheduling official debt, usually the Paris office of the World Bank.

7 For a description of US foreign aid policy and programs, see Tarnoff and Lawson (2009).

8 This is known as the Multilateral Debt Relief Initiative (MDRI). In 2007, the Inter-American Development Bank also decided to provide additional debt relief to the five HIPC countries in Latin America and the Caribbean.

9 Some relief of debt owed to commercial creditors has also been provided, through a few large debt buyback operations supported by the World Bank's Debt Reduction Facility.

10 On the fungibility of money and its implications for budgeting, see the section on *Foreign Aid: From Project to Program to Budget Support* in Chapter 7.

11 The government of Benin resisted the initial donor request to enclave the HIPC savings in a special account at the BCEAO, on the reasonable argument that doing so would contradict its ongoing budget reform, which was aimed at better unifying the different budget components.

12 This conclusion was supported by the joint government–donors external evaluation of the Public Financial Management Reform Program in Tanzania (unpublished report by Schiavo-Campo, et al. (2006)—confidential to the Government of Tanzania).

13 This reasoning applies only to economic and financial aid and technical assistance. Emergency and humanitarian assistance is subject to different considerations as it is not understood to be part of the government's ordinary financial resources.

14 The IMF Code of Fiscal Transparency calls for aid in kind to be recognized, reported and incorporated into the budget process. While this is correct in principle, in most developing countries it is doubtful that the benefits in terms of budgetary outcomes would justify the substantial estimating and administrative cost. Providing adequate information to the legislature should suffice.

15 One of the most significant benefits that aid-dependent developing countries receive from the "second-generation" public investment programs described in Chapter 7 is that the process of PIP preparation itself gives an opportunity to review, and then integrate into the budget, aid-financed expenditures that were previously not budgeted.

Bibliography

Beers, David and J-S. Nadeau, 2015. *Database of Sovereign Defaults*. Ottawa: Bank of Canada.

Cafferini, L. and H. Pierrel, 2009. *Sector Program Support: Lessons and Perspectives*. Paris: Agence Française de Developpement.

De Groot, Albert, Geert Jennes and Danny Cassimon, 2003. *The Management of HIPC Funds in Recipient Countries: A Comparative Study of Five African Countries*. Rotterdam: ECORYS.

IMF and World Bank, 2014. *Revised Guidelines for Public Debt Management*. Washington, DC: The World Bank.

Jessen, Lars, ed., 2016. *Government Debt Management: Designing Debt Management Strategies*. Washington, DC: The World Bank.

Kim, E. M. and Lee, J. E., 2013. "Busan and Beyond: South Korea and the Transition from Aid Effectiveness to Development Effectiveness," *Journal of International Development*, 25(6), 787–801.

Kraay, Aart and Vikram Nehru, 2006. "When is External Debt Sustainable?" *World Bank Economic Review*, 20(3), 1–35.

Luby, M. J. and R. S. Kravchuk, 2013. "An Historical Analysis of the Use of Debt-Related Derivatives by State Governments in the Context of the Great Recession," *Journal of Budgeting and Financial Management*, 25(2), 276–310.

Mathur, B. P., 2014. "India's Financial Crisis and Mounting Public Debt: Need to Restore Fiscal Balance," *Indian Journal of Public Finance*, 14(4).

Pérez, J. J. and R. Prieto, 2015. "Risk Factors and the Maturity of Subnational Debt: An Empirical Investigation for the Case of Spain," *Public Finance Review*, 43(6), 786–815.

Pradhan, K. 2014. "Is India's Public Debt Sustainable?" *South Asian Journal of Macroeconomics and Public Finance*, 3(2), 241–66.

Schiavo-Campo, S. and Hans W. Singer, 1970. *Perspectives of Economic Development*. Boston, MA: Houghton-Mifflin.

Tarnoff, Curt and Marian Leonardo Lawson, 2009. *Foreign Aid: An Introduction to US Programs and Policy*. Washington, DC: Congressional Research Service.

Wheeler, G., 2004. *Sound Practice in Government Debt Management*. Washington, DC: The World Bank.

Wong, Yvonne, 2012. *Sovereign Finance and the Poverty of Nations*. Cheltenham, UK: Edward Elgar.

Zhang, P., 2015. "Facing Fiscal Crisis: Managing Counter-Cyclical Debt Financing of the State and Local Governments," *Journal of Budgeting and Financial Management*, 27(4), 523.

Part IV
Fostering Accountability
For Money and for Results

11 Accountability for the Money
Accounting, Reporting and Audit

> When offices handle public money, there must necessarily be another office that examines and audits them.
>
> (Aristotle)

Introduction: Public Financial Accountability

The public money cannot be protected unless it is accounted for; the money cannot be accounted for unless the expenditures are reported accurately; and assurance is needed that the money has gone for the purposes for which it was authorized and that has been used efficiently. Hence, a good accounting system, reliable financial reporting and robust audit are essential for the management of public expenditure.

Public financial accountability is the responsibility of the executive branch to render to the people an account of what it has done with the people's money. The Russian proverb "trust, but verify" underlines that trust and verification are interdependent. If you mistrust everything you are forced to verify everything—which is impossibly inefficient. But if you never verify anything it is very tempting for most persons to skip the rules and use their position for personal gain. Public financial accountability therefore depends on *robust but selective* verification of government financial transactions. Naturally, no verification is possible without reliable financial information; this, in turn, calls for the production of such information along a uniform classification and for the regular reporting of transactions. The connection to governance is evident: accurate and timely financial information, verification and assessment of results are crucial for transparency, accountability and the rule of law.

This chapter reviews the different bases of accounting (cash, accrual and variants of each) and the features of a good accounting system for the government; describes the requirements of reliable reporting of expenditure to fit the needs of the various users; and covers both internal audit (a management support function to assess risk) and external audit (the ex post verification of the correctness and effectiveness of expenditure). External audit in particular is critical for public financial accountability.[1]

Accounting[2]

Main Accounting Systems

Accounting systems are generally classified in the two broad types of cash accounting and accrual accounting—depending on the rules that determine when the transactions or events should be "recognized." Variants can exist (modified cash, modified accrual), and elements of one accounting system can coexist with elements of another. The main differences between cash and accrual accounting for government operations are summarized next. (For a detailed comparison, see Gnanarajah, 2014.)

The standards applicable to the different bases of accounting for preparation of financial statements by governments and other public sector entities are set by the International Public Sector Accounting Standards Board (www.ifac.org/public-sector). The accounting system that is appropriate to public enterprises, which are supposed to be autonomous and run on a commercial basis, is not usually applicable to public goods provision and governmental activity. Note also that defining the standards appropriate to the different accounting systems does not imply a preference for one or another system, the choice of which depends heavily on country characteristics and circumstances, and on the proposed uses of the information.

Cash Accounting

Cash-based accounting "recognizes" transactions and events when cash is received or paid. Financial statements produced under cash accounting cover cash receipts, cash payments and the opening and closing cash balances. For example, if $1 billion in taxes are due for the year, but only $800 million are actually collected before the last day of year, cash accounting recognizes the actual revenue of $800 million. Simplicity is the advantage of cash accounting, which requires only limited capacity and enables greater transparency. Also, cash accounting in government allows a direct link between the fiscal accounts and monetary developments (see Chapter 5).[3]

Accrual Accounting

Accrual accounting recognizes transactions and events as of the time they are concluded regardless of when the cash is paid or received.[4] Thus, revenues reflect the amounts due during the year, whether they have been collected or not, and expenses reflect the value of goods and services consumed during the year, whether they have been paid or not. Moreover, the costs of durable physical assets are recognized across their lifetime—which requires calculating the depreciation of each asset every year.[5] It is economically inappropriate to lump the entire cost of a durable physical asset in the year in which it is acquired, rather than spreading it across all the years of its useful economic life. Accrual accounting is normally used in private enterprises and commercial operations of public entities although, as noted in Chapter 2, several developed countries use accrual accounting for government transactions as well.

A Simple Illustration

You own a business which is expected to sell a total of $270,000 worth of products in 2017 and in subsequent years. Of this, it is estimated that $220,000 will be received during each year and the remaining $50,000 in the following year. You expect to incur current expenditure of $200,000, of which you will need to pay 95 percent (or $190,000) during each year and the remaining 5 percent (or $10,000) in the following year. At the start of 2017 you also need to invest $50,000 in a facility which will last two years before having to be replaced. The accounts for 2017 and 2018 look as follows:

	Cash		Accrual	
	2017	*2018*	*2017*	*2018*
Income from sales	220,000	270,000	270,000	270,000
Current expenditure	−190,000	−200,000	−200,000	−200,000
Capital expenditure	−50,000	—	−25,000	−25,000
Net	−20,000	70,000	45,000	45,000

The difference in bottom line for the first year is stark. If you don't have an adequate financial cushion available at the beginning, the 2017 cash deficit would force you to borrow $20,000 at possibly unfavorable terms, or to incur payment arrears which will compromise your credibility vis-à-vis suppliers and thus the results for 2018—and you might well conclude not to start the business in the first place. The accrual basis of accounting gives a much more faithful reflection of the economic status of your business: if the initial liquidity difficulty is overcome, the business would show a healthy pre-tax return of about 17 percent of sales. Thus, you should rely on the accrual account for your economic decisions, but also need a cash and financing plan for 2017 to avoid getting into trouble over a temporary liquidity problem. (Indeed, the single most frequent cause of the failure of small business start-ups is a lack of liquidity, which is temporary but makes your business disappear permanently.)

Government Accounting in Practice

In government, cash and accrual accounting produce a significant difference primarily on the expenditure side. As noted, accrual accounting would provide an economically more accurate picture of the true costs of government *if* data, skill and institutions permitted its implementation. However, many government transactions are far more complex and the cost estimation is less precise than in the private sector, where market prices provide a firm reference point. Moreover, there is no clear consensus on how, or even whether, to depreciate national public assets such as defense equipment, cultural patrimony, national parks, and the like. Most importantly, the requirements for the effective implementation of accrual accounting include fully reliable and timely information on all government activities; an adequate supply of competent public accountants; strong control systems; close cooperation within government; and a culture of rule compliance. Accrual accounting is therefore appropriate for government in highly developed countries, but cannot be implemented in low-income countries and in most middle-income countries. Unreliable accrual accounting is much worse than reliable cash accounting. (Also, the impact of government operations on the financial markets can only be assessed on a cash basis.)

A somewhat less demanding system is *limited accrual accounting*, which recognizes all liabilities and all *financial* assets, but accounts for the entirety of physical assets in the year when they are acquired. Thus, limited accrual accounting does not require calculating the depreciation of physical assets—which is a complex challenge in the public sector—and provides upper middle-income countries a realistic stepping stone from cash accounting to full accrual accounting.[6]

Requirements of any Government Accounting System

Whatever the basis of accounting, any accounting system must have the following features:

- adequate procedures for checking budget compliance and cash availability, systematic recording of transactions, compliance data security and systematic comparison with banking statements;
- recording of all expenditures and revenues according to the same methodology;
- a uniform classification of expenditure and revenue;
- regular production of financial statements.

Relationship Between the Accounting and Budget Systems

As explained in Chapter 2, budget systems are classified according to the form of the legislative authorization. To recall, the two main types of budget systems are: cash-based budgets, by which the executive is authorized to make payments during the fiscal year; and commitment-based budgets, by which the executive is authorized to enter into commitments during the year. A cash-based budget is in principle consistent with any accounting system (although mixing a cash budget with accrual accounting causes confusion in practice), but an accrual-based budget requires accrual accounting. Debt must be on an accrual basis even under a cash-based budgeting system, since all governments must honor debt obligations at or before the time they fall due.

Chart of Accounts and General Ledger

A chart of accounts is a classification of transactions and events (payments, revenues, depreciation, losses, etc.) according to their economic, administrative, functional or accounting nature. The chart of accounts is organized according to the way transactions or events are defined (e.g., commitment, liability, payment, depreciation) as well as by administrative category (for accounts covering internal operations). The budget classification used defines the structure of the subaccounts of the chart of account that are related to budgetary operations. It is good practice to have the budget classification and the accounting codes aligned.

The set of books or the database where all the transactions are recorded along the chart of accounts (including the budget classification system) is called the general ledger. With a computerized financial management system, every transaction and its attributes can be recorded in the general ledger. These attributes cover both the budget classification categories (function, organization, etc.) and the other chart-of-account categories (liabilities, increase of assets, etc.). In a manual system, commitments are generally recorded in ancillary books, which are linked (often badly) with the general ledger. In a computerized ledger system, a single entry of the transaction posts the identical details to both the main ledger and the ancillary books for tracking the uses of appropriations.

A computerized financial ledger system permits financial reporting to be tailored to the needs of the different users, and can perform budgetary execution controls, such as commitment and payment controls. A computerized ledger fits a system with centralized ex-ante controls (e.g., Brazil or France) just as well as a system where budget execution is controlled by each spending agency. Instead, in a manual system (which is increasingly uncommon), accounting should be centralized, because decentralized accounts are inconvenient for disseminating information.

Administrative Organization of Government Accounting

In the traditional centralized model, the government accounts are prepared at central level, either by the treasury department or by a separate central accounting office (such as the accountant general in anglophone African countries—see Box 11.1). In the decentralized model, ministries and other spending agencies prepare their own accounts, for subsequent consolidation at the central level. Unlike the institutional issues raised by the choice of centralized or delegated payments, whether or not to centralize the preparation of government accounts revolves around eminently practical concerns and the proposed use of the information.

Centralized accounting is cost-effective in countries with a scarcity of public accountants, but cannot function well if line ministries and spending agencies report the commitments they have made only when they request the funds to make the actual payments. In the centralized model, therefore, appropriate administrative sanctions are needed to assure timely reporting of commitments by ministries and spending agencies. In large

---

Box 11.1 Tanzania's Accountant General's Department

The Accountant General Department is a major department within the Tanzania Ministry of Finance, and has a number of key functions—somewhat broader than in most other countries. Core functions include: financial management of the treasury accounts; monitoring the preparation of ministry and agency accounts, and of special funds; accounting for development revenue; responsibility for accounting and financial agreements; and a lead role in developing the government accounting system as well as accountancy legislation.

In addition, the Accountant General Department manages the central payment system; monitors and controls the decentralized subtreasuries; and manages the payroll system.

Tanzania entrusts to the accountant general the responsibility for maintaining the database for both domestic and external debt, and to ensure that debt obligations are met when due. Responsibility for borrowing policy and debt strategy, however, is entrusted to the separate Policy Analysis Department. Although, as noted in Chapter 10, it is in principle preferable for all debt management functions to be entrusted to a separate department set up for this purpose, it does not appear that Tanzania's division of responsibility for debt policy and debt transactions has created any difficulty. However, the arrangement whereby the accountant general shares with the treasury the responsibility for internal audit is ambiguous and problematic.

Source: Based in part on www.mof.go.tz.

---

countries, decentralized accounting is generally preferable. However, without a good computerized financial information system, it may be difficult to transmit the accounts to the center in a timely manner—and consolidation of the government accounts cannot be completed if even just one spending agency fails to transmit its accounts on time. Because the transmittal problem is fast disappearing with the expansion of functioning financial management information systems, one can expect that most countries will move to decentralized accounting, as and when competent public accountants become available in the line ministries and spending agencies.

Improving Government Accounting in Developing Countries

In most high-income countries, the government accounting system is on a solid basis and improvements consist of refinements at the margin and of implementation of new informatics systems. In some middle-income countries and most developing countries, instead, major improvements in public accounting are central to the process of strengthening the public financial management apparatus.

These improvements do not entail an accounting revolution, however. Even in rich countries, the introduction of accrual accounting in government has absorbed vast amounts of money and taken a decade or more to be completed. In developing countries, where many of the basic institutional and capacity prerequisites for accrual accounting do not exist, the clear priority is to gradually improve weak cash accounting and unreliable reporting. In a few upper middle-income countries where circumstances permit, the progressive introduction of limited accrual accounting might be considered after cash accounting has been placed on a solid basis, but the benefits to be gained against the costs of moving to the new accounting system should be carefully assessed. (However, as noted, all public enterprises in any country, as well as public agencies that deliver commercial services or consume a large quantity of capital goods, should assess their full costs and adopt full accrual accounting.)

Improving an accounting system requires addressing its major current weaknesses. In developing countries, these include one or more of the following:

- Some payments are not recorded in accordance with the uniform expenditure classification.
- Budget execution is reported on the basis of requests for payment. In principle, these requests should correspond to the delivery/verification stage, but when a government has lost credibility from previous accumulation of payment arrears, private suppliers require payment before delivery. In this case, payment orders are usually based on proforma invoices, and are entered into a liability account, where they stay for months or years. This liability account is a perfect mess of true invoices, proforma invoices, old vouchers for transfers to government entities and subsidies that were budgeted but never paid.
- Moreover, while the budget execution reports show the requests for payments along the budget classification, and everything appears in good order, the *real* budget execution lies in the discretionary selection of the vouchers to be paid among all those parked in the liability account. The true "budget" being executed is therefore unknown, and the power to decide which vouchers will be paid and when generates corruption risks.
- Sometimes, internal payments (i.e., transfers of funds between government agencies) and payments to external suppliers get mixed up, requiring time-consuming line-by-line reconciliation.
- Scarcity of trained accountants in government and lack of clear accounting procedures create a variety of difficulties: comparisons with bank statements are rarely made, forms are coded haphazardly, different accounts are commingled, etc.
- Management of assets is weak, with valuable assets deteriorating for lack of maintenance, transport and other equipment left idle for lack of fuel, and other durable goods unaccounted for. Yet, line ministries continually include requests for additional purchases in their budget proposals. (See Chapter 6 on the screening of expenditure requests.)

Reporting[7]

Principles of Fiscal and Financial Reporting

The principles and types of public financial reports have been well established for many years and are applicable to all countries—albeit with practical modifications to take into account local needs and capacities. In general, reporting on budget operations should provide the basis for assessing how well the government is managing the public finances. In practice, compliance remains the priority, and financial reporting should first and foremost be sufficient to assess budgetary integrity and rule compliance.

Maximally, financial reports should meet the following criteria:

- *Completeness.* The report should cover the main aspects of the entity's operations.
- *User friendliness.* Reports should be understandable to a reasonably informed and interested user. Where possible, illustrations should be used to improve readability.
- *Reliability.* The information presented should be verifiable and free of bias. Reliability is different from precision or certainty, however. For certain items, a properly explained estimate is better, even if rough, than no estimate at all (e.g., on contingent liabilities).

- *Consistency.* Consistency is required not only internally, but also over time. Once an accounting method and reporting format are adopted, they should be used unless there is good cause for change—in which case the report should show the impact of the change.
- *Timeliness.* Delays diminish the usefulness of information. A timely approximate estimate may be more useful than precise information that takes longer to surface.
- *Comparability.* Financial reporting should help users to make relevant comparisons between reporting units, such as comparisons of the costs of specific functions or activities.
- *Usefulness.* Reports should contribute to understanding the current and future activities of the entity, its sources and uses of funds, and the diligence shown in the use of funds.
- *Relevance.* Information should meet a recognized need. Reports should be relevant for different users (political leadership, ministries and agencies, parliament, the private sector and civil society), but consistent with accepted standards of form and content. A frequent criticism of government financial reports is that they are at the same time overloaded and useless.

Reporting on Budget Execution

For managing budget execution the following reports are needed. The first three are submitted to the ministry of finance; the last is submitted to the ministry of planning or equivalent entity:

- Daily flash reports on cash inflows and outflows.
- Weekly breakdown of expenditure and revenue by broad economic categories.
- Monthly reports on financial budget execution based on the budget classification system, specifying the initial appropriation (and any revision), commitments, expenditures at the verification stage and payments.
- Quarterly reports on physical progress of large investment projects.

Reporting on Public Sector Entities

While the budget itself is limited to the government, financial reporting should encompass the entire public sector, including financial reports produced by entities controlled or owned by the government. The information is needed for fiscal transparency as well as for policies on subsidies, financing of public enterprise investments, etc. As noted, the accounts of public sector entities carrying out business activities should be on an accrual basis, and their financial statements should meet accrual accounting standards. Rules for identifying which public entities must produce annual financial statements are established either via legislation (as in France) or through accounting regulations (as in Australia).

Reporting on Public Investment

In parallel with the requirements for good public investment programming (see Chapter 8), reports on investment are usually presented by project, indicating (i) the expenditure during the year; (ii) total project costs; and (iii) the balance required to complete the project.

In addition, accrual-based information on the progress of projects is important, especially in transport, communication, energy and public works, where payment schedules do not necessarily coincide with physical implementation. For large infrastructure projects, the increase in asset value should be presented, along with the indicators of physical progress of the works.

Reporting on External Aid

In principle, aid should be reported at the time it is received. However, in the procedures of many donors the aid is accounted for as of the time the disbursement is approved. Discrepancies in information from the two sources are therefore pretty much inevitable, and the major ones should be identified and explained. No matter how efficient the data collection system may be, there is invariably a time lag between drawings from foreign loans and verified expenditures, the length of the lag depending largely on the procedures of the lender. In practice, many aid-dependent countries rely entirely on information from donors to estimate aid-financed expenditures. This often leads to mixing up cash-based information from some donors with commitments or even mere "pledges" from other donors. Because of the importance of aid as a component of budget financing, clarity in this matter is important.

Better monitoring of aid is needed in most developing countries, with the active cooperation of donors, whose procedures are responsible for many of the discrepancies. This monitoring should generally be done at the project level, which is the only level at which expenditures financed with external aid can be reliably estimated. Even then, data from donors must be collected and compared with the data from the project. However, it is very hard for the recipient country's government to resolve this problem on its own. The solution lies in the first place in harmonizing the aid procedures of all donors—a challenge as old as foreign aid itself and still far from being met, despite all the international conferences to address it.

The Annual Budget Report

After the end of the fiscal year, an annual budget report is generally submitted to the external audit office and to the legislature. In many countries, its production and publication takes a year or more, making it practically useless. Preliminary information on budget execution should be compiled and published no later than two months after the end of the fiscal year.

The annual report should cover the consolidated financial operations of the government, over a period of at least two fiscal years in order to allow for comparisons. The report should be prepared in accordance with the IMF government financial statistics (GFS) standards; complemented with accrual information on debt as well as information on expenditures at the verification stage, and payment arrears if any; and include three tables for central government, local governments and general government. Financial information for extrabudgetary funds should be consolidated into the accounts of the relevant level of government (see Chapter 3).[8]

Management Controls and Internal Audit

Much confusion has arisen from a misunderstanding of the word "control" in English and French usage. In English, the term carries prescriptive and enforcement connotation, while in French and other Latin languages it is much closer to verification or monitoring. In both meanings of the term, effective controls by budget managers are critical for protecting the public's resources and achieving operational efficiency, and require a combination of enforcement and monitoring. The key budget execution controls were described in Chapter 8. This section recapitulates the basic principles of management control systems, and of the internal audit that advises the responsible officials on the strengths and weaknesses of those systems.

Objectives and Types of Management Controls

Management controls are defined as the complex of systems and procedures put in place by a public or private entity to pursue the following objectives:

- the efficient and effective achievement of the entity's objectives;
- production of timely and reliable financial and management information;
- compliance with relevant laws and regulations;
- safeguarding of assets and information; and
- prevention and detection of fraud and error.

In all countries, management's first priority must be the protection of the organization's financial resources against theft or improper use. This entails a variety of management controls:

- Physical and cyber controls are the security procedures intended to restrict unauthorized access—access to inventories of high-value items, access to particular rooms or buildings, or access to electronic databases and other records.
- Accounting controls, discussed earlier, include the procedures by which transactions are recorded in the accounting system—for example, a requirement that all cash receipts be deposited daily in exchange for a written receipt.
- Process controls are the procedures designed to assure that actions are taken only with proper authorization and, for large transactions, require approval from higher levels.

Standards for Management Controls: Balancing Protection with Effectiveness

Ideally, the standards can be summarized as follows:

- Management control structures should provide reasonable assurance that the objectives of the organization will be accomplished.
- Specific control objectives should be developed for each line ministry or agency and should be appropriate, reasonable and integrated into the overall organizational structure.
- Managers should monitor their operations and take prompt action on major findings of irregular, inefficient or ineffective operations.
- To the extent possible, at least two persons should be involved in risky transactions. In cash collections, for example, one person collects the cash, a second makes the bank deposit, and a third reconciles the cash receipts and enters the data in the records.

A balance is necessary between the procedures intended to foster the achievement of the entity's objectives and the protective systems designed to assure compliance with the rules and prevent fraud and abuse. Lack of adequate protections entails risks, but an excess of protective measures is costly and hampers efficiency. The objective of the control system should be to provide "reasonable assurance" that significant improprieties will not occur or will be revealed when they do occur. Whistleblower protection is an essential component of the system.

The formulation and implementation of management controls are the responsibility of the top leadership of the organization. Management controls are designed to help the top managers control the organization—not to control the top managers themselves, who can easily circumvent the systems, bypassing the controls directly or instructing or authorizing others to do so.

The first obvious requirement for effective management controls is therefore the personal integrity and professionalism of the top leadership. Next comes the need to assess the risks facing the organization and to identify useful risk-mitigating measures. Third, whatever control systems are put in place must be ones that the management will actually use, and will require to be used throughout the organization. Accordingly, the controls must be cost-effective and not so detailed and onerous as to hamper organizational effectiveness. The tendency to introduce redundant or burdensome controls is especially strong in government and public organizations, where even minor misuse or abuse of financial resources is likely to generate a public scandal or a political problem—one of the many important distinctions between public and private management and an unavoidable source of public sector inefficiency.

Internal Audit

The risks in any organization change with changes in the nature of operations, the external rules or the economic environment. It is therefore important to keep under regular review the systems of management controls—strengthening some and eliminating others that are no longer needed or have become too costly. This is where internal audit comes in. According to the definition by the Institute of Internal Auditors (www.theiia.org), internal audit is an independent and objective assurance and consulting activity designed to add value and improve the organization's operations, by evaluating and improving risk management, control and governance processes.

Internal audit is thus not to be confused with internal *inspection,* which is designed to detect specific fraud, abuse and individual responsibility for major errors, in order to take appropriate disciplinary or other action. Internal audit is instead intended to keep under review *the system* of management controls, and advise the senior officials responsible on how to plug gaps, strengthen internal accountability or improve efficiency of operations by lightening burdensome regulations. Unlike inspection, the internal audit function is not adversarial: "Beware the inspector, befriend the internal auditor," is the motto of the wise manager. The internal auditor should not only review the soundness of the control systems, but also conduct such tests as may be necessary to assure that the systems are operating properly in actual practice.

Internal audit is established *within* an executive branch entity as a service to its top management to assess the effectiveness of management controls. Despite the similarity of names, the role of internal audit is thus very different from that of the external auditor (although good internal audit facilitates external audit). As discussed next, the external auditor is independent of the government organization and reports to an external entity—usually the legislature. The internal auditor, on the other hand, is part of the organization and is accountable to its management for a continuing assessment of the control system and to recommend measures to reduce risk. Consequently, internal audit is effective not only when its recommendations are valid, but when they are followed up by management. Internal auditors can support managers, but cannot substitute for them.

Because internal audit is a management support function, a central office for internal audit (usually in the finance ministry) should not dictate to ministries and government agencies how to conduct this function, but should aim at guiding and facilitating internal audit development throughout government—as in the example of the Internal Audit Agency of Ghana (see Box 11.2).

A final word: in some countries, internal audit is being developed (usually at the urging of aid donors) even where management control systems are weak or lacking altogether. Because the primary function of internal audit is to evaluate and recommend concerning the adequacy of the control system, it makes no sense to put in place an internal audit apparatus to advise the management on the strengths and weaknesses of management control systems that do not exist. The establishment of adequate management controls comes first. Guidance and facilitation should be provided centrally, based on uniform standards but only as and when requested by the individual ministries and agencies.

External Audit[9]

The Centrality of External Audit in Public Financial Accountability

Robust review and scrutiny of government financial transactions after the end of the fiscal year is critical to close the public financial management loop and provide assurance of financial integrity and compliance with the rules. Recalling that the legitimacy of the initial budget depends crucially on its approval by the legislature as representatives of the citizenry, it follows that the execution of that budget must also be reviewed by the legislature. Owing to the complex nature of financial transactions and the technical issues involved, the legislature needs the intervention of a competent and capable auditing entity.

Box 11.2 Ghana's Internal Audit Agency

A major PFM reform in Ghana has consisted of gradually transferring budgetary authority and responsibility for expenditure control to the line ministries and other government agencies. (Recall from Chapter 2 that the foundations of a sound overall budget and aggregate fiscal discipline are good budget proposals and expenditure control by each spending agency of government.) As part of this transfer of responsibility and control, it became necessary to develop the internal capacity in each agency to review and recommend concerning the robustness and efficiency of its control systems. Accordingly, the Internal Audit Agency (IAA) was established by the 2003 Internal Audit Act, and put in place from 2005—governed by a board of nine members including from the private sector.

In keeping with the basic vision of the reform, the IAA's mandate is not to prescribe actions to the line ministries and agencies, but to set standards and procedures for the conduct of internal audit work in the ministries and agencies; facilitate the creation of internal audit units in each ministry or agency; coordinate their internal audit activities; and evaluate and provide quality assurance—to strengthen the ministries' and agencies' systems for the protection of resources and enhancement of efficiency, accountability and transparency in the management of public financial resources.

Source: Based in part on Ghana's Internal Audit Agency; www.iia.gov.gh.

This audit entity should ideally be "external" to the executive branch of government that executed the budget, but must be independent in all cases.

Reversing the proverb *trust, but verify*, "by institutionalizing mistrust of public finances, government auditing creates trust in public administration" (*The Economist*, 2015). In countries with official corruption and weak governance, the importance of external audit is matched by the personal risks to the individuals responsible for it. External audit can be a very dangerous job if performed well; for example, Heidi Mendoza, the head of the Court of Audit in the Philippines, has a permanent security detail.

The fundamental requirement for effective external audit is the independence of the external audit entity. This requirement was set out 40 years ago by the Lima Declaration of Guidelines on Auditing Precepts, unanimously approved in 1977, which opens with the following statement:

> The concept and establishment of audit is inherent in public financial administration as the management of public funds represents a trust. Audit is not an end in itself but an indispensable part of a regulatory system whose aim is to reveal deviations from accepted standards and violations of the principles of legality, efficiency, effectiveness and economy of financial management early enough to make it possible to take corrective action in individual cases, to make those accountable accept responsibility, to obtain compensation, or to take steps to prevent—or at least render more difficult—such breaches.

Effective external auditing is intended to:

- Detect irregularities involving the misuse of public funds and identify related weaknesses in management controls that may imperil the integrity of the organization and the effective implementation of budgetary and other policy decisions.
- Determine the reliability of reports on budget execution and other financial data.
- Identify instances and patterns of waste and inefficiency that, if corrected, will permit more economical use of available budget resources.
- Provide reliable data about results as a basis for future adjustments in budget allocations.

Organizational Arrangements

The organizations responsible for external audit of the government have different names in different countries but are collectively referred to as supreme audit institutions—SAIs. Most English-speaking countries follow an "office model," with the SAI an independent national office headed by an auditor-general. Examples include the General Accountability Office in the US, the National Audit Office in the UK, the Office of the Comptroller and Auditor-General in India and the Auditor-General of South Africa (see Box 11.3).

Most countries following the continental European traditions follow the "judicial model," with the SAI as a judicial or quasi-judicial institution—composed of magistrates and headed by a presiding judge—as the Cour des Comptes in France, the Corte dei Conti in Italy, the Tribunal de Cuentas in Spain, the majority of SAIs in South America and the SAIs in francophone Africa, as for example the member states of the West African Economic and Monetary Union (see Box 11.4).

There are several variations of these two basic models. Thus, the external audit entity in Germany, Austria, Holland and several Central and Eastern European countries combine characteristics of both the "office" and "judicial" models—as also does the SAI of the European Union, the European Court of Auditors.

Box 11.3 South Africa's Auditor-General's Office

The Auditor-General of South Africa (AGSA) was established under the 1996 constitution as one of the state institutions supporting constitutional democracy. The independence of the auditor-general is explicitly recognized and guaranteed, as the
auditor-general must be impartial and exercise its functions "without fear, favour or
prejudice."

The constitution describes in general terms the functions of AGSA, which are
articulated in the subsequent Public Audit Act of 2004. The act, among other things,
makes a distinction between the mandatory functions which the auditor-general
must perform to comply with the mission described in the constitution, and other
audits left to the discretion of the auditor-general.

In keeping with good international practice, the auditor-general is accountable to
the South African legislature, to which it reports concerning performance of its functions and their results. A standing committee of the legislature oversees the performance of the auditor-general, based on the two main accountability instruments: the
budget and strategic plan, and the annual report.

Ex-post audit reports are produced annually on all government departments,
public entities, municipalities and public institutions. In addition, reports on
discretionary audits, performance audit and other special audits are also produced, and then used by the national legislature, provincial legislatures
and municipal councils, as appropriate, in accordance with their own rules and
procedures.

Source: www.AGSA.co.za.

Box 11.4 Developing External Audit in the West Africa Economic and Monetary Union

The member countries of WAEMU have adopted the quasi-judicial "court of
audit" model of external audit. The WAEMU treaty requires that the presidents
of the courts of audit of the member countries meet once a year to take stock of
the systems of control and the results of the external audits during the previous
year.

A number of measures have been enacted by the presidents of the WAEMU member states to harmonize public financial management and establish a set of common
rules around the code of transparency first established by the WAEMU authorities in
2000.

In particular, the code of transparency envisages that every member country
should have in place a functioning court of audit, meeting the international standards of ex-post audit, which must be efficient, entrusted to an independent entity
and given extensive investigative authority and the necessary capacity. This has been
done in member countries, although in some of them the independence and effectiveness of the new external audit entity leave much to be desired.

Source: www.primature.gov.ml.

Standards of External Audit

The International Organization of Supreme Audit Institutions (INTOSAI) has promulgated standards for the external audit of government organizations and operations. These standards have been adopted by government audit organizations around the world, including virtually all SAIs. (Interested readers can obtain a copy of the standards from the INTOSAI Secretariat in Vienna—www.intosai/org.) The most important standards are statutory independence, managerial autonomy and resources.

The independence of the auditing organization is essential to assure that its work will not be biased by any relationship to the entity being audited. Independence is typically accomplished by creating the SAI as a separate organization apart from the executive branch of government, and usually responsible only to the national legislature. This is the arrangement in the US, UK, most of the Commonwealth countries, most members of the European Union and a majority of all other countries. An additional way of securing independence is to make the appointment of the auditor-general or the members of the court of audit joint between the executive and the legislature, or contingent on legislative approval (as in Spain, Germany and the Netherlands). In other countries, e.g., Italy, France and Portugal, appointment of the members of the court of audit is made by the executive, but the independence of the court is assured by the permanent status of the court members, who cannot be dismissed except for grave cause and even then only with the consent of the legislature.

Not only should the SAI be independent, but so must be the individual auditors with respect to the audits for which they are responsible. This is usually handled through internal regulations promulgated by the SAI, but may also be covered in various laws, including those that are generally applicable to the civil service, which also address potential conflicts of interest. (As an obvious example, an auditor may not be an investor in an entity that might be affected by the results of the audit.)

The SAI must have managerial and financial autonomy and sufficient resources to exercise its functions. The SAI should have statutory authority to determine the scope of its audits, obtain any documents and records relevant to the audit, and exercise its judgment as to the audit results to be reported. But legal authority is hollow without management autonomy and resources. Statutory independence from the executive branch of government means little if the executive branch can limit at will the budget and other resources of the external audit entity, or interfere in the internal management of the organization.

Integrity and professional credibility are the key assets of any SAI. Among the necessary resources are the technical skills necessary to conduct the types of audits that the SAI conducts. However, while a strong internal core capacity is essential, it is not necessary for the SAI to have a large permanent staff sufficient to meet its entire work program. For specialized audits or for major audits the SAI can hire specialized consultants or contract a private firm to carry out all or part of an audit for which it lacks the necessary resources or specialized skills—provided that it retains full authority and responsibility for overseeing the work, certifying the findings and handling the audit.

Types of Audits

As specified in the appropriate legislation, SAIs are required to perform certain audits, and are allowed to perform additional ones.

Ex-ante Audit

Most external audit is ex post. In several countries, however, there is a form of ex-ante audit (also called "pre-audit" or "a priori auditing"), by which individual transactions are examined for propriety and regularity *before* they are completed—for example, a commitment may not be entered into until an auditor has approved. In francophone systems, financial controllers are detached from the ministry of finance to serve in each ministry and agency to exercise this ex-ante audit function. (In France itself, however, the system has been changed in major ways during recent years.)

As a general principle of good public financial management, ex-ante audit by entities external to the ministry or agency should be avoided, since the ministry or agency must itself have the responsibility and authority to assure that the transaction is consistent with the approved budget and other applicable rules. (See the discussion of financial control in Chapter 8.) However, where accountability systems are in serious disrepair, it would be seriously imprudent to eliminate ex-ante external controls, until and unless these systems have been sufficiently reinforced. In a very few countries, e.g., Lebanon, the court of audit exercises *both* ex-ante and ex-post audit. While such arrangements might be understandable in light of the particular circumstances and fraught history of this particular country, it is evidently risky and inefficient: there is an inherent conflict of interest if the entity responsible for the ex-post audit of government financial transactions also has a role in approving those transactions before they have occurred.[10]

Regularity (Compliance) Audits

This form of external audit aims at determining the legal propriety of the transaction, by checking after the fact that government financial transactions have been conducted consistent with the appropriate authorizations and with the rules applicable to the transaction (including particularly whether the moneys were spent for the authorized purpose in the budget). Because it is impossible to audit every government transaction, compliance auditing must be very selective. However, the selectivity should be strategic, not random, in order to allow the SAI to identify the control system weaknesses that allowed the irregularities to occur and to demonstrate the consequences of failing to correct those weaknesses.

One approach to implementing such strategic selectivity is to concentrate the auditing on areas where *frequent* irregularities are known to occur. The individual irregularities in such areas may be small but their total amount may be large. Furthermore, they may create a climate of tolerance that, over time, can undermine the integrity of the entire organization. Another approach is to focus on specific areas of government activity where there is a high risk of *large* irregularities—for example, large procurements. The two approaches are of course not mutually exclusive.

The purpose of a strategic approach to regularity auditing should be to strengthen the prevention systems, and not just to detect past errors. International experience shows that unless compliance audits are part of a broader strategy to deal with the sources of the irregularities, detecting errors or malfeasance is unlikely to prevent the same error or malfeasance from arising again and again. If the source of the leakage is not identified and corrected, plugging the individual leaks as they occur does not strengthen the vessel.

Financial Audit

Most SAIs are required by the constitution or the law to perform annual audits of budget execution and of government financial reports. The review of government financial statements focuses on whether they are accurate, complete and presented in accordance with the budget classification and other relevant rules. The findings of the review are presented in a report that is made public and—usually—tabled in the legislature (to which the external auditor normally reports). The executive branch of government is then expected to respond to those findings. However, any action to be taken on the SAI findings depends entirely on the legislature and/or the executive. The function of the external auditor is to audit and report, not to sanction or correct.

Value-for-Money (Performance) Audits

This type of audit has become increasingly common among SAIs. A value-for-money audit (VFM—frequently also called "performance audit") examines an entire entity, activity or program in order to suggest ways of improving the efficiency and effectiveness of those operations. The VFM auditor searches for areas of waste and mismanagement that, if eliminated, would permit the same purposes to be achieved at less expense, as well as areas where the same resources, used differently, would produce greater value for the same cost. This type of auditing can make a major contribution to increasing the efficiency of government— provided that the necessary information exists and is reliable and that the government agency has sufficient authority and flexibility to manage its resources to make good use of the recommendations.

However, value-for-money audits should themselves demonstrate that they produce value for money.[11] Particularly because of capacity limitations of SAI and the institutional constraints existing in many developing countries, it is essential to give careful thought to relative priorities. The highest priority must be assigned to building and maintaining the integrity of the public financial systems, especially where the risk of corruption is high. In countries where PFM systems are weak and management controls are unreliable, as is typically the case in developing countries, the emphasis must be on compliance and financial audits. Value-for-money audits should generally await the time when the basic PFM systems have become strong and the SAI has established its capacity and credibility to carry out the essential compliance and financial audits. (Small experiments in VFM, however, can still take place as a way to learn-by-doing and set the bases for more extensive performance audits at a future time when circumstances permit.)

Reporting the Audit Results

Requirements for distribution of external audit reports are often specified in the basic public financial management law or a separate law establishing an SAI. In most countries, all audit results must be reported to the legislature. However, during transitional periods in fragile states, the external auditor may report to the head of state. Usually, reports to the legislature are delivered to a special committee with responsibility for overseeing the work of the SAI, such as a Public Accounts Committee. Formal reporting relationships aside, most SAIs enjoy considerable discretion to distribute additional copies of their reports as they deem appropriate.

The general rule is to distribute audit reports to those with an interest in the topic and especially to those who are expected to act on the findings and recommendations contained in the report. For example, the audited entity should always be informed of the audit results and the ministry of finance should be routinely informed of reports that have implications for the budget. If the audit shows the need for new or amended legislation, the SAI may bring this to the attention of the parliamentary committees that would consider such legislation as well as to the ministry that would be responsible for proposing or implementing it.

The general public has a legitimate interest in the results of the audits of government and public entities—since the expenditures are financed with public money. Thus, all SAI reports should be made available to the public unless restricted for specific and overriding national interests, for example for national security or ongoing criminal investigations. Indeed, the media are very important for the effective follow-up of audit results, as the public at large is most unlikely to be interested or directly competent to interpret the audits. (Box 11.5 illustrates specific audit findings.)

Acting on Audit Findings

As noted, for the most part, auditors are authorized only to report their findings. It is for other authorities to take action to correct the problems. However, the auditor bears considerable responsibility for eliciting an appropriate response to audit findings and issuing

---

Box 11.5 Some Examples of Concrete Audit Findings

Audit can uncover a variety of deviations from compliance, regularity or performance:

- Japanese auditors found improprieties in the House Purchasing Loan Program, designed to facilitate home ownership, as several borrowers rented out the houses they had purchased, violating program requirements. Most of the improperly borrowed funds were recouped.
- New Zealand auditors examined the procedures used to prevent and detect improper payments for medical and pharmaceutical services. They found that existing procedures detected some irregularities and probably deterred others. However, some types of transactions, representing considerable risk, were not adequately covered by existing procedures. The auditors recommended procedural improvements to reduce this risk.
- Indian auditors found that machinery for a state enterprise was purchased at an unnecessarily high price, installation of the machinery was delayed beyond the warranty period, defects subsequently developed and the machinery was lying unused.
- Auditors in Hong Kong, China, examined the General Post Office facilities occupying a very valuable waterfront site, and concluded that considerable savings could be realized by relocating the facility. The relocation, however, was delayed by lack of proper planning and coordination and by unnecessarily restrictive specifications for the new site.
- In an assessment of a new drug evaluation and approval process, Australian auditors found that there had been great improvement in the speed with which drug applications were approved, but that the reporting of adverse reactions to drugs was inadequate.
- In auditing the execution of the budget, auditors of the People's Republic of China found that some departments violated public financial management laws, some financial reports were untruthful, and some entities failed to collect or surrender the proper amount of revenues. The imposition of sanctions by the National Audit Office stimulated remedial actions.

Source: Author.

reminders when necessary. To facilitate action, the audit reports themselves must meet certain requirements:

- Clear findings: General observations that "money was wasted in program X" are not helpful. The nature of the problems and their consequences should be stated clearly.
- Convincing evidence: The evidence supporting the findings must be relevant and credible and must be presented in a clear and persuasive fashion.
- Cost-effective recommendations: If a problem is identified, it is incumbent upon the auditor to suggest a reasonable and concrete solution. If changes are needed in laws, regulations or procedures, they should be described with as much precision as possible. The costs of implementing recommendations should be proportionate to the problem.
- Effective communications strategy: The best-written audit report serves no purpose unless its contents are made known to those who can act on its findings and recommendations. A brief, well-written executive summary accompanying the report can help, as can follow-up conversations with the officials or with key members of their staff.
- Open dialogue: The audited entity must have a full opportunity to respond to a draft report before it is finalized and have its comments and corrections taken into proper consideration. Effective external audit should also be viewed as a critical part of the long-term development of the country's public financial management capacity. As stressed in the discussion on accountability in Chapter 1, dialogue is often more effective than fault-finding or bean-counting, and is far more conducive to the development of institutional capacity.

Trends in Audit Capacity and Effectiveness in Developing Countries

In part, the effectiveness of external audit depends on the extent of active participation and involvement by citizens. Like law enforcement, robust audit requires cooperation by civil society. The Philippines Court of Audit introduced the concept of "citizen audits" in which regular government employees are encouraged to contribute their inputs to the audits of public services, including by interviewing service users. As for audit capacity, it has increased during this century. In the developing world, the example of West Africa was already mentioned in Box 11.4. The region where recent improvements have been most significant is Latin America and the Caribbean. As late as 1990, external audit mechanisms in Latin America and the Caribbean were extremely weak or non-existent; control was in many countries the sole prerogative of the executive branch; and external audit was inoperative throughout much of the continent. By 2012, all but one of the countries in the region had an institutional audit strategy plan in place; most countries had adopted international norms for external audit; and almost all countries published audit reports and provided freer access to information as well as communication of audit results—compared with fewer than half just ten years before. Citizen participation in the external audit function was still lagging—which is understandable, since this is a dimension of external audit that has particularly long gestation.

Capacity, too, shows substantial improvements. In Latin America, the staff of supreme audit institutions increased by 40 percent, twice as fast as population. Especially noteworthy is the professionalization of the organizations, with the internal composition of staff changing markedly toward professional auditors—who constituted more than half of total personnel in 2012 compared with about 40 percent in 2002. The increase in financial resources, too, was substantial, with SAI budgets on average three times larger in 2012 than in 2002—more than keeping pace with the large growth in total government expenditure. Nevertheless, SAI operations absorbed just one tenth of one percent of the overall national budget—indirect but clear evidence of the cost-effectiveness of external audit.[12]

Table 11.1 External Audit Indicators in Latin America and
Caribbean, 2002–12 (number of countries
exhibiting the indicators shown)

	2002	2012
Areas and Indicators		
Regulatory support		
Institutional strategy plan	13	25
Dissemination of norms plan	12	19
Adoption of international norms		
External audit	13	20
Internal audit	9	13
Transparency		
Publication of audit reports	9	19
Follow-up mechanisms	12	17
Accountability		
Free access to information	16	22
Communication of results	18	23
Citizen participation		
In audit and control activities	7	11
In publication of information	8	14

Source: Schiavo-Campo (2013).

Table 11.2 Capacity of Supreme Audit Institutions in Latin America and Caribbean, 2002–12
(in number of staff and millions of US$)

Subregion	*Total Staff*			*Number of Auditors*			*SAI Budget*		
	2002	*2012*	*Percent Change*	*2002*	*2012*	*Percent Change*	*2002*	*2012*	*Percent Change*
Average Fourteen Latin-American Countries	1115	1477	32	476	761	60	39	116	197
Average Seven Caribbean Countries	153	174	14	114	123	8	5	8	60

Source: Schiavo-Campo (2013).

Table 11.1 shows the increase in the number of countries in the region which met the indicators of audit performance in the ten years between 2002 and 2012, and Table 11.2 shows the improvement in staff and financial resources.

Comparing the current state of affairs to the situation before the 1990s reveals a remarkable improvement in public financial accountability—which paralleled and in many ways consolidated the far-reaching democratic changes that have taken place in Latin America since then.

Notes

1 The reader interested in a more detailed explanation of several of these subjects is referred to Wang (2014).
2 See Label (2013) for an accessible explanation of the basic principles of accounting, albeit one focused on the private sector.

3 *Extended cash accounting* recognizes also transactions and events expected to result in cash payments within a specified period after the end of the year. The accounting period thus includes a "complementary period" for payments (but not receipts) after the close of the fiscal year. Payments made during the complementary period, which are related to transactions and events of the previous fiscal year, are reported as expenditure of the previous fiscal year. This provision was necessary in some countries in earlier years, when certain types of payments or payments in certain areas of the country would take a long time. With current information technology, a complementary period is no longer necessary in most countries and causes unnecessary confusion: keeping open the books of the previous year leads to the overlapping execution of two budgets, and requires adjusting the budget data to chronological time to allow comparison of fiscal and monetary statistics. Moreover, if the complementary period is longer than a month or so it provides an easy opening for corruption.

4 See Premchand (1995) and Das (2006) for the policy and practice of accrual accounting in government, and Boothe (2007) for lessons for developing countries.

5 From the cash/accrual distinction comes the distinction between *expenditure* (under cash accounting) and *expense* (under accrual accounting).

6 The formal standards are only for cash and accrual accounting, although intermediate steps are shown to progress to accrual accounting.

7 Drawn in part from Office of Management and Budget, Objectives of Federal Financial Reporting Statement of Federal Financial Accounting Concepts, Statements no. 1 and 2, 1993; and Henley (1993a,b).

8 The quality of the annual reports can be improved by appropriate recognition of the best reports, as in Canada, which established in 1945 the Certificate of Achievement for Excellence in Financial Reporting Program to encourage and assist state and local governments to go beyond the minimum requirements of generally accepted accounting principles to prepare comprehensive annual financial reports.

9 Interested readers are also referred to Santiso (2009) and Shand (2013).

10 In the case of Lebanon, however, the problem is not really one of conflict of interest, but the extreme weakness of the court of audit, which is unable to carry out either ex-ante or ex-post audits in a minimally effective way. This, too, is a reflection of the balkanized nature of Lebanon's government and society.

11 To credit an old article published in the 1970s ("Is there value for money in value-for-money audit?")—which the author has been unable to track down.

12 The corresponding increases in Caribbean countries were much less marked, but the staff and financial resources of Caribbean SAIs was already comparatively ample in 2002.

Bibliography

Aikins, S. K., 2012. "Determinants of Auditee Adoption of Audit Recommendations: Local Government Auditors' Perspectives," *Journal of Public Economics and Financial Management*, 24(2), 195–220.

Aristotle, *Politics*, Book 6, Chapter 8, p. 38. (B. Jowett translation, available online at www.classics.mit.edu/Aristotle/politics.html [accessed November 9, 2016].)

Boothe, P., 2007. "Accrual Accounting in the Public Sector: Lessons for Developing Countries," in Anwar Shah, ed., *Budgeting and Budgetary Institutions*. Washington, DC: The World Bank.

Das, S. K., 2006. *Rethinking Public Accounting: Policy and Practice of Accrual Accounting in Government*. New Delhi: Oxford University Press.

Economist, The, 2015. "Government Auditors: The Wisdom of Watchdogs," July 4, p. 73.

Gnanarajah, Raj, 2014. *Cash Versus Accrual Basis of Accounting: An Introduction*. Washington, DC: Congressional Research Service.

Henley, Douglas, 1993a. "What are the Rules for Financial Reporting?" in Douglas Henley, Clive Holtham, Andrew Likierman and John Perrin, eds., *Public Sector Accounting and Financial Control*. London: Chapman and Hall.

Henley, Douglas, 1993b. "What are the Rules for Financial Reporting?" in Douglas Henley, Clive Holtham, Andrew Likierman and John Perrin, eds., *Public Accounting and Financial Control*. London: Chapman and Hall.

Hudspeth, N. W., D. F. Merriman, R. F. Dye and A. W. Crosby, 2015. "Do Troubled Times Invite Cloudy Budget Reporting? The Determinants of General Fund Expenditure Share in US States," *Journal of Public Budgeting and Finance*, 35(4), 68–89.

Janssen, Roel, 2015. *The Art of Audit: Eight Remarkable Government Auditors on Stage.* Amsterdam: Amsterdam University Press.

Label, Wayne, 2013. *Accounting for Non-Accountants.* Naperville, IL: Sourcebooks.

Modlin, S., 2012. "County Government Finance Practices: What Independent Auditors Are Finding and What Makes Local Government Susceptible," *Journal of Public Economics and Financial Management,* 24(4), 558–78.

Premchand, A., 1995. *Effective Government Accounting.* Washington, DC: IMF.

Santiso, Carlos, 2009. *The Political Economy of Government Auditing.* New York: Routledge.

Schiavo-Campo, S., 2013. *External Audit in Latin America and the Caribbean: Improvements in the Institutional, Organizational, Human and Financial Capacity of Supreme Audit Institutions, 2002–2012.* Operations Financial Management and Procurement Services Office. Washington, DC: Inter-American Development Bank.

Schiavo-Campo, S. and D. Tommasi, 1999. *Managing Government Expenditure.* Manila: Asian Development Bank.

Shand, David, 2013. "External audit," in R. Allen Richard Hemming and Barry Potter, *The International Handbook of Public Financial Management.* New York: Palgrave Macmillan.

Wang, Xiao Hu, 2014. *Financial Management in the Public Sector: Tools, Applications and Cases,* 3rd Edition. New York: Routledge.

World Bank, 2004. *Overview of the ROSC Accounting and Auditing Program.* Washington, DC: The World Bank.

Wynne, A., 2004. *Is the Move to Accrual-Based Accounting a Real Priority for Public Sector Accounting?* London: Association of Chartered Certified Accountants.

12 Accountability for the Results
Performance, Monitoring and Evaluation

Not all that can be counted counts, nor all that counts can be counted.

(Albert Einstein)

Introduction

A supportive governance environment, good fiscal policy, sound macroeconomic and fiscal framework, orderly budget preparation process and strong control of resources during budget execution ... none of these can do much good if the money is spent badly. The people's money must be spent to provide government services to the people—security, transportation, justice, education, health, etc. Just making sure that it isn't stolen and that the rules are obeyed is not enough. The *results* of public expenditure must be considered; the government must be judged not only for the quality of its processes and compliance with the laws, but also for its performance in actually delivering the services for which it collects the people's money in the first place.

This chapter reviews the concept of performance and its various indicators, and how to gradually introduce in the budgeting system an effective orientation toward the results of public spending—in light of the lessons of international experience in a variety of different countries. Also, monitoring and evaluation (M&E) systems are needed, by which improvements can be introduced and systematically built upon and weaknesses corrected. Monitoring deals with what is happening, while evaluation deals with what has happened and why. The chapter describes how good M&E can close the expenditure management loop, and summarizes the approaches to evaluation suitable to countries with different capacity.

The Concept of Performance

Why Focus on Performance?

Since the early 1990s, and building in part on the pioneering conceptual work of Mancur Olson (1973), increasing attention has been paid to introducing consideration of "performance" in public sector management. Several factors have led to this: pervasive dissatisfaction with government employees' unresponsiveness to the public; increase in size of government, which puts pressure on the public finances; recognition of the obvious but often forgotten fact that the purpose of public expenditure is to bring concrete benefits to the population and the country; and the influence of the so-called "new public management" (NPM) paradigm still popular around the end of the last century.[1]

The accumulated experience of three decades now permits making distinctions between the useful innovations and the useless or counterproductive changes. With reference to performance, it is important to understand the complexity of the issue; if performance is viewed as a simple notion, the chance of effective performance-oriented reforms is virtually nil. Indeed, experience shows that it is the introduction of performance-based systems as if they were easy and simple that has led to failures and damaged the credibility of the performance concept itself. That said, for a government to forget the real purpose of spending the public money eventually generates a culture of means rather than ends, disregard for the public and the legendary bureaucratic mentality that views it a success to insist on strict and literal observance of tight and internally consistent controls—regardless of whether they are necessary or even helpful in executing the functions assigned to the state. Thus, an orientation toward the results of government spending rather than only the manner of spending should be encouraged.

However, "performance" must be defined in a manner appropriate to the country and its circumstances. In Greek legend, a local kinglet named Procrustes had the unpleasant hobby of either cutting off part of his unsuspecting guests' legs or forcibly stretching them to make them fit his bed. Such a one-size-fits-all approach is ill-suited to institutional reforms, which by definition cannot be effective unless they match local realities. Because "performance" is such a seductive and misleadingly simple term, the first order of business is to analyze it closely.

What Sort of Performance?

By Effort or by Results

Dictionary definitions of "performance" include such alternative terms as "accomplishment," "achievement," "realization," "fulfillment." Most of these terms have to do with the *objective* results; but some relate to the *subjective* sense of satisfaction from one's efforts. Accordingly, performance may be defined in terms of effort or in terms of results. To recognize individual effort is important not only to avoid hurting people's feelings, but also to motivate efficiency.

Consider what happens if you, as the manager of a unit, choose to define performance *only* in terms of objective results. The smarter/more capable members of the unit will almost always achieve better results, and will thus be rewarded; the less capable employees will usually achieve lesser results even if they work hard, and will thus be unrewarded or penalized. By tailoring the reward system only to results, you are sending two messages, as clearly as if they were emails in bold face and all caps: you are telling the former group of employees that they will be rewarded even when they don't put out their best effort, and you are telling the latter group that they will receive no reward no matter how hard they work. Now, some employees are smarter or more capable and others less so, but they are all equally rational and capable of understanding that in effect they are being told that effort makes no difference. Neither the more capable nor the less capable employees will continue to exert their best effort. The level of effort will therefore decline across the board and, in a short time, your entire unit will be populated by cynical or demoralized underachievers. Then you are likely to be fired as a manager, and will wonder why—since you applied a rigorous objective test of staff performance only in terms of results. Yes, the test was rigorous; but it wasn't smart.

Recognizing (even if not actually rewarding) genuine individual effort can do much for morale, and also serve as a demonstrator for others, thus fostering the effectiveness of the organizational unit as a whole. More fundamentally, in the ancient adage: "man does not live by bread alone." For most human beings, a sense of accomplishment in their work— what Thorstein Veblen (1899) called the "instinct of workmanship"—is a strong motivator of their action, independent of salaries, penalties or other material incentives. This is true of private employees and even truer of government employees—many of whom are in government because of a spirit of public service. If public management reforms inadvertently remove that motivation, the efficiency of personnel is likely to decline, and the effectiveness of public action along with it. A reductionist view of human nature risks, in time, reducing effectiveness and increasing the risk of corruption. To reiterate: defining performance exclusively in terms of results is likely to diminish the results themselves and their quality.

Nevertheless, claiming "effort" is an excellent alibi for lack of results. If you as a manager recognize only effort, and accept as valid on its face an employee assurance that "I am doing my very best," you are sending the opposite message that *results* don't really matter, and end up with an even more inefficient organization (in addition to losing your best employees to another unit where their results are recognized and rewarded). The bottom line is this: to introduce a stronger performance orientation in the budgeting system one should *rely mainly on results but never neglect the effort dimension.*

Performance in Terms of What?

In one sense or another, all budgeting is "performance" budgeting. But performance in terms of what? *Performance is a relative and culture-specific concept.* The world offers a variety of institutional contexts, in which performance has different meanings. In a context where rule-compliance is the dominant criterion, good performance consists of sticking to the rules and accounting for every cent of public funds; but in a context where what matters is the outcome, good performance consists of achieving positive results, even in unorthodox ways. In a strictly hierarchical system, government employees are considered to be performing well if they obey to the letter their superiors' legitimate instruction, no matter how stupid the instruction may be; but in a system where initiative is viewed positively, employees are seen as good performers if they exercise their own judgment and initiative. In a system where conflict is discouraged, good performance is defined as harmonious cooperation for group influence and cohesion; but in a system where individual competition is the accepted norm, individuals are good performers if they compete vigorously for individual influence and resources. Finally, in a system devoid of accountability and transparency, government employees are considered good performers if they implement without question any and all orders of the political leadership; but in a system where the rule of law and norms of integrity prevail, good performance entails refusal to obey an illegal order or to be silent in the face of high-level corruption and misbehavior. You get the idea: the same individual behaving in the same fashion can be seen as an excellent performer in one administrative culture and a disaster in a different administrative culture. Being rational, the individuals will adapt their behavior to the definitions and incentive frameworks of the dominant culture—moreover, if young enough to adapt, they will rapidly change behavior when moving from one administrative culture to a different one.

This does not at all mean that all the diverse administrative cultures should be considered as equally efficient. Indeed, the very definition of institutional development is to move from a less efficient to a more efficient set of norms and rules. The point of this discussion is to emphasize that the notion of performance is relative and in part culture-specific, and to recognize that administrative cultures do not just happen but evolve in response to man-made incentives and concrete problems. Thus, even when an administrative culture has become demonstrably obsolete or dysfunctional, it is still necessary to understand its institutional roots if one wishes to help improve it in a durable way.

For example, the practice of advancement by seniority has been criticized for preventing the recognition of individual merit. This is generally true, today, but one must remember that the seniority principle was originally introduced in the public sector *as a reform* to insulate the system from political pressures on government employees. (In the British Royal Navy of the eighteenth century, for example, promotions up to the rank of captain depended in part on seamanship and command ability but also on political and family connections. Once included in the captains' list, however, seniority was the one and unbreakable rule for further promotion—precisely in order to preclude the advancement of well-connected incompetents to admiral positions.) Correspondingly, depending on the quality of governance and social structure in a country, a change to a "merit-based" system may carry the risk of reopening the door to such pressures. For example, if promotion by seniority is replaced with promotion by "merit," in an ethnically plural society you are liable to find that employees belonging to the same ethnic group as the boss are somehow always rated as more meritorious than the others.

The Complete Definition of Performance

Summing up, *performance is the achievement of agreed results within the resources and time provided, without diluting quality and respecting the prevailing norms of due process.* It is worth considering on every word, because most of the mistakes and failures of attempts at introducing in PFM an orientation toward performance stem from neglecting one or another of the clauses of that definition. Thus, performance has to do with achievement—not promises—of results that have been agreed—not imposed. A resource and time constraint is inherent in any notion of performance, because with unlimited resources and time almost anyone can produce almost any result. Finally, quality and integrity are the Achilles' heel of result orientation, because there is an understandable temptation to achieve results by cutting corners in quality or by breaking the rules. The impact of lower quality and rule violation is not visible in the short run and only becomes apparent when the system has fallen in complete disrepair and requires a major investment—far most costly than if the protection of quality and prevailing norms had been assured in the first place.

Performance Indicators

Types of Performance Indicators

Four aspects of performance can be identified, in terms of inputs, outputs, outcomes and process. Using law enforcement as an illustration, inputs are the resources used to produce the good or service, in this case the police officers, prisons, police cars, handcuffs, etc.; the social value of inputs is measured by their cost; and the performance criterion corresponding to inputs is economy, i.e., the timely acquisition of inputs at lowest cost for a given quality. (Recall that economy is the criterion of the performance of public procurement.) Output is the good or service itself, for example, the number of arrests; the social value of outputs is approximated by the market price for the same or the closest equivalent service (or in its absence by production cost); and the performance criterion corresponding to outputs is efficiency, i.e., minimizing cost per unit of output. Outcome is the purpose that is achieved by producing the good or service, in this case, reduction in the crime rate; the social value of outcomes is difficult to assess, except as may be revealed by public reaction in the political arena; and the performance criterion corresponding to outcomes is effectiveness, i.e., maximizing outcomes in relation to the outputs produced.[2]

Finally, process is the manner in which inputs are procured, outputs produced or outcomes achieved. The value of good process is undetermined. In most areas of public activity, "due process" has its own independent validity and is a key element of good governance. For example, an increase in arrests achieved by violating civil rights does not constitute "good performance" by the police. In other areas, process indicators are a useful proxy for performance when outputs or outcomes cannot be defined with clarity. ("Bedside manner" in health care, rules for free debate in policy formulation, etc., are examples of process indicators.) Process indicators can be quantitative (e.g., the percentage of class time dedicated to student questions) but are usually qualitative. Even then, they can be transformed into quantitative indicators by feedback from users: for example, hospital patient satisfaction can be assessed through a survey and translated numerically. In any case, all indicators must be defined clearly—numerical when quantitative, in precise language when qualitative.

In the public sector several important functions are simply not amenable to intelligent use of formal performance indicators—let alone of quantitative indicators. Also, not all valuable data concerning a public service are necessarily performance indicators. For example, the percentage of arrests made as a result of citizens' direct complaints is a useful statistic for law enforcement and provides evidence of citizen involvement, but does not necessarily say anything about the performance of the law enforcement apparatus. Figure 12.1 shows the performance hierarchy and Table 12.1 provides examples of input, output, outcome and process indicators in various sectors. Deliberately, some indicators in Table 12.1 are good indicators, while the use of others reduces or distorts performance rather than improves it. Readers should peruse the table and decide for themselves which is which—asking themselves the question: "what is likely to happen *in practice* if this indicator is used to determine rewards and penalties?"

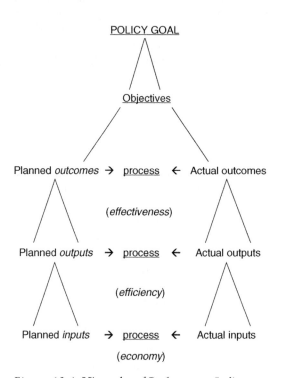

Figure 12.1 Hierarchy of Performance Indicators and Criteria.

Table 12.1 Examples of Performance Indicators: the Good, the Bad and the Ugly

Sector	Type of Indicator			
	Input	*Output*	*Outcome*	*Process*
General administration	Number of staff	Number of policy papers	Better decisions	Openness of debate
Education	Student/ teacher ratio	Retention rates	Higher literacy	Encouraging student expression
Judicial system	Budget	Cases heard	Low appeal rate	Assistance for indigent defendants
Police	Number of police cars	Number of arrests	Decline in crime rate	Respect for citizen rights
Corrections	Cost per prisoner	Number of prisoners	Recidivism rate	Preventing abuse of prisoners
Health	Nurses/ population	Number of vaccinations	Lower morbidity	Good "bedside manner"
Social welfare	Number of social workers	Number of persons assisted	Exits from welfare system	Dignified treatment

Different Indicators for Different Organizations

In the taxonomy developed by Wilson (1989), public organizations fall in four categories: production organizations, procedural organizations, craft organizations and "coping" organizations. An example of a production organization is tax administration—whose role it is to "produce" tax revenue (given legal parameters and certain process constraints). An example of a procedural organization is hospital administration—whose role is to assure the optimal functioning of the hospital. An example of a craft organization is the police—whose role is to use certain skills and authority to implement law enforcement. And an example of a "coping" organization is the foreign service—whose role it is to interact with foreign countries in pursuit of the government goals. The boundaries are not sharp, there are overlaps between different categories of organizations, and all four organizational dimensions can coexist within the same government entity—but the distinctions are important to define the scope of accountability, and hence the mechanisms to monitor and improve the performance of different government entities:

- In *production organizations*, outputs and outcomes can *both* be useful. For example, the performance of tax administration can be assessed by both the revenue collected (the output) and the impact on the fiscal situation (the outcome), the performance of the primary education department can be assessed both by the number of students enrolled (the output) and the improvement in literacy (the outcome), etc.
- In *procedural organizations*, output measures are useful but not outcomes. For example, the performance of hospital administrators can be meaningfully assessed by the number of patients served (given the resource and other constraints) but not by the outcomes of improved quality of medical care or reduction in disease—for which the administrators themselves are not directly responsible.
- In *craft organizations*, the reverse is true: output indicators are not useful but outcomes are. For example, it is a mistake to judge the performance of police officers only by the output indicator of the number of arrests, without considering how the arrests are made or the gravity of the crime. However, given sufficient time, the outcome of a

reduction in crime rate could be a meaningful indicator of the performance of the system as a whole.

- Finally, in *coping organizations*, *neither* outputs *nor* outcomes are meaningful indicators of performance, and only process or qualitative assessments are appropriate. It is obvious that measuring the performance of ambassadors by the number of diplomatic receptions they hold (an output of sorts) or the number of treaties they negotiate (an outcome of sorts) would make no sense: in the first instance, an incompetent ambassador who holds a lot of parties would be judged favorably; in the second instance, a major diplomatic success would weigh less than a number of trivial agreements. In these cases, performance is assessed mainly by asking the confidential views of a number of knowledgeable interlocutors.

Performance Assessment and Accountability

Assessing performance should not be an end in itself. Performance assessment must be viewed as part of the management of the organization and thus directly linked to the accountability of individual managers. In turn, as explained in Chapter 1, accountability means answerability *plus* consequences. Without consequences, "accountability" is hollow, and without a link to accountability, performance assessment is a waste of time or an alibi for arbitrary decisions.

"What Gets Measured Gets Managed"?

This maxim is often viewed as the epitome of contemporary management wisdom. In fact, it is almost five centuries old, and attributed to sixteenth-century mathematician Georg Rheticus. Origin aside, this appealing maxim is easy to prescribe and to follow—provided that you don't care about the results and long-term implications. Even in private companies it is risky to follow this principle unquestioningly; in the public sector, the "tyranny of the measurable" is lethal for good public administration and budgeting. Let's see why.

In the first place, "what gets measured gets managed" works only if the right things are measured. Measuring the wrong things results in managing the wrong things, to the exclusion of the important ones—hardly something to be desired. Table 12.1 showed how easy it is to apply the wrong performance indicator: great care is needed to identify the relevant aspects of the activity that are to be measured (and thus managed). Second, the right things have to be measured *in the right way*. The methodological challenges of performance measurement are very complex, and incorrect measurement necessarily leads to inefficient management.

By far the most important caveat, however, rests in the corollary to that maxim. Even if the right things are measured, and are measured in the right way, it necessarily follows that "what does not get measured does not get managed." Yet, the main reason why certain activities are in the public sector in the first place is because their social importance, external effects, or long-term consequences make them unsuitable to be carried out by private entities. Almost by definition, these are activities of which the most important aspects are precisely those that *cannot* be measured. Applying the management consulting performance principle to the public sector would distort the assessment of the most critical functions of government. (For example, if you were to assess a program of housing subsidies only by the measurable benefits to the low-income residents, you would totally miss the unquantifiable social benefit of preserving urban diversity.)

This is not meant to argue against the measurement of results, when it is meaningful and possible, but to emphasize the need to be sure that quantitative indicators are appropriate to assess the activity in question. Indeed, most of the wrong advice given in the area of performance management stems from neglecting the qualitative dimensions of government functions.[3]

Let's again take the example of law enforcement. It is impossible to measure police courtesy and respect for the citizen and yet they are very important for the effectiveness of law enforcement. Beyond the civic and moral duty of the police to respect all citizens, due process and courteous professionalism engender trust between the citizens and the police. In turn, such trust leads to public cooperation with law enforcement personnel in the reporting of crimes and in support for their actions. Running roughshod over individual rights and dignity leads to the opposite outcome, making any short-term crime-fighting achievement temporary, raising the long-term incidence of crime in the community, and—not incidentally—imperiling the safety of the police officers themselves. Voluntary rule compliance by the large majority is the essential requirement for effective pursuit of the small minority of rule violators—in this as in all public domains.

The Accountability Chain

There is a hierarchy of results in the complex production function of public services, whereby the out*come* of one stage is an out*put* of the next, higher, stage. In this "accountability chain," accountability is clearest and most immediate by the narrowest performance criterion (economy use of inputs), and most ambiguous and diffuse by the broadest performance criterion (net impact). For example, village nurses can be held strictly accountable for the output (the number of vaccinations), and rewarded or penalized accordingly; but it is difficult to hold them responsible for the outcome of improving the health of village children. Yet, their affirmative involvement in household sanitary conditions, or nutrition or family counseling may have more influence on the outcome of improving village children's health than a greater number of vaccinations.

Moreover, without close supervision it is difficult to prevent immunizations from being performed with less than the recommended quantity of vaccine (the remaining vaccine "leaking" out of the public health system). Therefore, abandoning input and quality controls in favor of only output indicators carries substantial practical risks. Input and quality controls must be retained alongside the output indicators.

The above means that the choice of appropriate indicator depends on the stage of the aggregate production function of public services. Other things being equal, the closer the activity is to the final user, the more direct is the link of outputs to the desired outcomes. In "downstream" activities that are close to the ultimate user (e.g., trash collection), the output–outcome link is clear and immediate enough to permit using output indicators as a good proxy for outcomes. In trash collection, a failure to collect the garbage is immediately visible and is directly linked to the risks to public health in the neighborhood. In "upstream" activities this is not so: in the regulatory area, for example, the number of rules produced is hardly a desirable measure of public performance.

Defining Outcomes

There is an inverse relationship between precision and relevance, and the definition of outcomes is inherently ambiguous. Smith (1996) defines outcome as "a personal valuation of quality-adjusted output," expressed in the identity:

Outcome = Valuation (Output × Quality).

This formulation is useful because it calls attention both to the oft-forgotten dimension of quality and to the issue of *whose* valuation should be considered. Even when it is feasible to ask the beneficiaries' opinion, it is not clear how one should aggregate the subjective valuations of the same outcome by different persons in different personal circumstances. It is even less clear how one should take into account the different distribution of benefits from activities with the same "average" outcome. A proxy measure of outcome value is the users' willingness to pay, which reflects the weighted subjective valuation of the outcome. This works operationally, but for many public services (such as basic medical care), valuing the outcome only by the prospective users' ability to pay is morally and socially unacceptable in most societies today. Even less simple is the utilization of outcome measures for performance assessment, because of the variety of influences on outcomes that are outside the control of the person or agency responsible. This leads to an accountability tradeoff.

There is no great methodological difficulty in defining and measuring outputs: the issue with output indicators is their relevance. Similarly, the interpretation of outcomes is rarely in doubt: the issue with outcome indicators is their feasibility. Outcome indicators are almost always more meaningful and output indicators almost always more feasible. Combining these two considerations yields the general presumption that measuring performance by results is most appropriate for those government activities where there is a direct and immediate relationship between the government agency's outputs and the desired public outcomes.

The Accountability Tradeoff

It is possible, in the earlier example, to hold the trash collectors strictly accountable for a failure to collect garbage in a neighborhood, but the failure affects mainly that neighborhood. Conversely, the failure to achieve a general public health outcome affects the country as a whole, but is associated with a variety of factors and thus cannot be directly attributed to specific individuals. The accountability tradeoff is this: *accountability can be either tight and narrow, or broad and loose—but can never be* both *tight in application and broad in relevance.*

This means that as one proceeds up along the accountability chain, precise measurement of performance and tight accountability for outputs become less and less meaningful, and need to be replaced by a focus on outcomes—particularly in the area of public financial management. Because it is difficult to attribute outcomes to individual managers, the accountability mechanism should consist of a robust dialogue on all aspects of performance. Indeed, when such a dialogue is led by persons knowledgeable about the activity and the management systems, it can yield more and far more meaningful information on performance than any number of quantitative measures.

The Role of Social Accountability

Participation (one of the four pillars of governance) is not limited to feedback on service provision, but must include upstream involvement in decision-making, the design of expenditure programs and the identification of beneficiaries. During budget preparation, social accountability entails systematic consideration of citizens' "voice" through budget hearings and similar measures. During and after budget execution, the objective of operational efficiency requires open channels of communications to and from civil society.

When assessing the delivery of services to the public, the public itself is an obvious main source of relevant information and feedback on government performance. Assessing the results of a public activity from around a conference table in the capital and based only on official reports from government offices in the field is akin to Scott Adams' "Dilbert" character of the pointy-haired boss who believes he is managing the office with a toy computer unconnected to anything.

Active involvement by service users, however, does not occur spontaneously. Affirmative support is needed. One powerful means to elicit user views is the "citizen report card" survey, pioneered by Samuel Paul (2002). Citizen report cards are participatory surveys that provide user perceptions of the quality, adequacy and efficiency of different public services and the government agencies delivering them—and use publicity to identify problems and spur improvements. Among other initiatives, civil society organizations can be supported in their monitoring of public services and advocacy of better governance. A recent example is the Citizen Action for Results, Transparency, and Accountability (CARTA) program. Between 2011 and 2015 CARTA financed a number of small-scale projects in various sectors in Nepal and Bangladesh for local organizations to carry out awareness-raising, monitoring, capacity-building, and empowerment activities. (See Partnership for Transparency Fund, 2016; www.ptfund.org.)

Moving to the Right Performance Framework

The General Rule

The general rule for introducing formal performance assessment in public sector management is the following: *when results measurement is both appropriate and cost-effective, performance should be assessed according to that combination of key output, outcome and process indicators that is realistic and suitable for the specific activity, sector, country and time.* This principle is very general and doesn't provide specific guidance, but it does have actionable implications:

- Unless it is demonstrated that results measurement is appropriate to the activity *and* that its expected benefits outweigh the costs, it should not be introduced in the first place. It is too often the case that performance-based systems have been advocated based on a simple argument that they would improve results; this may be true, but very rarely is the question asked of how much improvement, and at what cost.
- No single indicator can suffice for performance assessment—a combination is necessary—and the right combination differs for different countries, sectors and activities.
- One cannot just "set and forget" the performance indicators. Because it is impossible to foresee all the real-life consequences of introducing performance assessment, the performance framework itself needs to be monitored and adjusted according to actual experience. For this process of adaptation, nothing is more important than to listen to the actual experience of both the service providers and the beneficiaries.

How Many Indicators?

A single indicator cannot adequately capture performance, but an excessive number of indicators is unworkable and inefficient. Practically, it is costly: not only do the relevant data have to be collected and maintained, but each indicator then requires adequate monitoring. Conceptually, it is impossible to assign a weight to each indicator, and inaccurate to give them all equal weight. Thus, too many indicators produce "assessment ambiguity"—which is the enemy of strong accountability. There is no right number of performance indicators between one and too many, but a practical rule of thumb is to use a minimum of two and a maximum of four. Of course, only key performance indicators (KPI) should be considered. Because to identify the indicators that are truly "key" requires considerable knowledge of the activity in question, performance indicators cannot be selected from an armchair at the top of a ministry but require the participation of people directly knowledgeable about that activity.

The selection of result indicators is heavily influenced by data availability and information technology. In high-income countries, a supply-driven dynamic is at work: because lots of data sources exist and ICT is widespread, extensive performance information is collected regardless of its relevance, and result indicators have a tendency to proliferate. "Measurement creep" has affected particularly the basic social services. Performance indicators in health care, for example, have grown to the point of diluting the concept of performance itself. In the US, "the measurement fad has spun out of control . . . there are so many different hospital ratings that more than 1,600 medical centers can now claim to be included on a . . . 'best hospitals' list" (Wachter, 2016, p. 8). Measurement creep has not occurred in developing countries owing to the scarcity of reliable data (a rare instance where limited information has served as protection), but the experience in several high-income countries is a clear warning to low-income countries not to follow the same path—by respecting the principle of diminishing returns in the collection of information and the need to *assess* performance and to do so with a *few key* indicators.

The "CREAM Rule"

Management consultants usually say that a key performance indicator must be SMART: specific, measurable, achievable, relevant and time-bound.[4] This may be appropriate in the private sector. In the public sector, however, a good indicator need not be "measurable" if the function in question is not suited to meaningful quantification, but must always be precise and thus *monitorable*. The acronym SMART also misses that a performance indicator must be cost-effective, i.e., economical, to avoid generating data collection costs out of proportion with the presumed benefits from assessing performance. Finally, it is incorrect to refer to "achievable," which relates to the *target* to be set, and not to the nature of the indicator itself. A better rule, particularly for public financial management, is the "CREAM" rule, by which a good performance indicator should be:

- Clear—because ambiguity is the enemy of accountability.
- Relevant—it must capture a key dimension of the activity.
- Economical—collection of the requisite data should be cost-effective.
- Adequate—when in conjunction with the other KPIs.
- Monitorable—taking into consideration capacity, geographic difficulties, etc.

Picking Targets: Metric and Process Benchmarking

Having chosen the right combination of a few key indicators, the target values must be set. As a general rule, targets must be challenging but achievable. Both overambitious and easy targets lead to underachievement: overambitious targets discourage effort, and easy ones do not stimulate better performance. In any case, targets must be related to something meaningful, either the previous achievements of the individual or the unit, or the norms and standards prevailing elsewhere—"benchmarking."[5]

The two main approaches to benchmarking are metrics and process benchmarking. Metrics benchmarking focuses on comparing performance targets within a unit with similar data from other units in the same area of activity. Metrics benchmarking is a useful diagnostic tool, but cannot tell you what improvements can be made and how. For that purpose one has to turn to process benchmarking, which focuses on the comparison of the processes underlying the performance of a given function. In brief, metrics benchmarking helps to identify the problem areas, and process benchmarking helps to find ways to deal with the problem areas.

The first steps in process benchmarking involve the preparation of process "maps" for the activities in the selected focus areas, collection of information on resources consumed by those activities, and an analysis of the procedures and working methods that determine the performance of those activities. At this stage many obvious inefficiencies in the existing processes are revealed, the elimination of which can already yield significant performance improvements. The next stage is to obtain comparator data for other organizations, compare the processes, develop recommendations and implement changes. The new values of the performance indicators provide a measure of the improvements achieved and the basis for starting the next round of benchmarking—the reason why the literature often refers to the process as "benchmarking and continuous improvement."

Comparators can be either internal or external. Internal comparators are between divisions of the same organization where similar processes are performed (e.g., comparing the performance of public hospitals in different cities). External comparators can be direct competitors (e.g., public schools could be benchmarked against private schools in the same area) or can be other organizations, public or private, for similar business processes—such as accounting, procurement, customer service, etc. It is usually best to start with internal benchmarking—comparing performance between different offices and understanding the reasons for the differences—before going to outside comparators.

Benchmarking can introduce a form of competition in the public sector. If the results are publicized, they can be a force for change and help raise the organization's attention to the service users—as the "citizen report cards". The so-called "league table" approach places a unit's performance in relation to the others, as in the ranking of sports teams in their league. It is catchy, but can demoralize those at the bottom of the league and often does not adequately consider the different circumstances. For example, the lower ranking of a public school in a low-income area lacking transport and other services cannot be fairly compared to the higher ranking of another public school in a rich neighbourhood. The alternative to the league table approach is to focus on the changes over time in the performance gap between a unit and the best-performing unit.

It is clear from the above that process benchmarking is highly demanding in terms of resources, data, time and assessment capacity. Its utilization should therefore be limited to the few key areas which have the largest costs and where performance measurement is most feasible—as in urban transport (see the example in Box 12.1). Also, there is little evidence that benchmarking has actually improved budgetary outcomes. In the words of Eugene Rotberg (2013): "We never measure or report opportunities lost ... We design performance measures to cover-up error. We call them 'benchmarks'."

Fostering Results-Orientation in the Budgeting System

Understanding the complexity and pitfalls of the measurement of performance has deflated the simplistic and risky assumptions of earlier years. Introducing into the budgeting system an orientation to results must be done gradually, realistically and consistent with the methodological challenge and the country realities. International experience, and particularly the many mistakes, suggests the three guiding principles described next.

Box 12.1   An Example of Benchmarking: The Hong Kong Mass Transit Railway

The Hong Kong Mass Transit Railway Corporation (MTRC) is an independent corporation with the government as majority shareholder. For over 20 years, MTRC has used both metric and process benchmarking to ensure that it became and remained among the most reliable urban transportation systems.

The MTRC performance benchmarking originates from a "Community of Metros" project begun in 1995. The benchmarking group spent considerable time defining the 18 key performance indicators to compare one metro system with others. In half of the categories, MTRC was initially classified as "best in class" but weak in "staff efficiency" and "incident management." To improve these areas, MTRC set up special task forces that met regularly and visited sites of the best performers. Improvements were partly due to the recognition and consideration of social and cultural factors.

The corporation is consistently rated as one of the best in the world—possibly the best—in both efficiency and customer service, carrying more than five million people a day with a 99.96 percent on-time record, and generating substantial profits.

Source: MTRC, www.mtr.com; and *The Atlantic* (2013).

Respect the Law of Unintended Consequences

At the very moment when a performance indicator is promulgated a signal is thereby sent to all persons in the organization of what will determine their rewards or penalties. Consequently, they will adapt their behavior accordingly, which may lead to outcomes very different from those intended. For example, if police performance is assessed by number of arrests, an incentive is immediately created for capricious arrests; if the indicator is changed to "arrests resulting in convictions," an incentive is created to pursue the minor misdemeanors that are easy to prove and process through the courts, avoiding the lengthy investigations of major crimes; if the indicator is then changed to "arrests resulting in convictions for felonies," an incentive is created to neglect misdemeanors altogether. The point here is not to criticize one or another indicator, but simply to underline that the choice of performance indicators has an impact on human behavior and that there is a need to assess the major risks and identify the appropriate mitigation measures.

Much can be achieved by simply asking oneself: "How would I personally react in response/defense to this new performance indicator?" The *process* of choosing the performance indicators must include front-line staff and service users. Both groups are best able to say how their behavior would change in response to the new incentives, and should contribute to the process of definition of the appropriate KPIs. Regrettably, this is almost never done, and performance indicators are typically chosen by government officials and consultants sitting in a central ministry office—which explains much of the disappointing record of attempts at introducing results orientation in the budgeting system.

Assuring Independent Setting of Result Indicators and Targets

If you allow me to define the options and results, I will gladly allow you to judge my performance. While the input of stakeholders is always necessary for realistic and effective indicators, performance indicators should never be defined by those directly affected by the performance measure. As rational beings they would naturally select the indicators of their preferred results and the most easily achieved targets. In Friedrich Nietzsche's words, "success can be a great liar."

Linking to the Budget Process: The "KISS Rule"

Developing greater result orientation in budgeting calls for giving more responsibility to managers, measuring costs, and setting up KPIs. It does *not* call for major changes in the budget system. Expenditure control remains the basic requirement; inputs must continue as the major basis of budget allocation; and any link between performance and the budget should be assessed intelligently and as a complementary activity. Indeed, the confusion often caused by introducing a performance orientation into the budgeting system and replacing line-item budgeting system with "performance budgeting" has led to costly failures without any positive impact on performance orientation itself.

To be avoided in all cases is a mechanistic approach whereby various performance measures are given "points" that are then aggregated and used to determine budget allocations. Not only is this antithetical to good budgeting and common sense, but any experienced bureaucrat can run rings around it and manipulate the system to produce favorable results. On the other hand, there is no purpose in monitoring budget performance unless there is some link to the subsequent budget preparation process. What is essential, as noted earlier, is to build into the budget preparation process a requirement for a robust dialogue on the results of the previous year's expenditure—dialogue between budget managers and their minister, and between the line ministries and the ministry of finance. (Such a dialogue would best take place at the negotiations stage—see Chapter 6.)

Finally, a word of caution about detailed "contracts" within the budget process. An explicit (and therefore written) understanding of the key expected results is important for accountability, but must not be allowed to expand into a formal fine-print contract. Experience shows that if the budget system is straitjacketed into such detailed contracts—cascading from the ministry of finance to the line ministries to the directorates to the division chiefs to the office managers to the district chiefs to the heads of deconcentrated services, and so on—the chance for genuine accountability is gone, and all that is left is a monumental paper chase. The exercise of judgment is essential. The guiding rule for performance monitoring in the budget system remains the "KISS" principle: *Keep It Simple, Stupid.*[6]

The Ten Commandments of Performance

This section offers analogies, metaphors and anecdotes to illustrate the issues described earlier. The intent is not to add analytical content, but to provide memory aids to anchor these issues, and to take some of the dryness out of the discussion.

The Patton Premise ("Know where you're going before you get going")

In the movie *Patton* (1970), the actor playing General George Patton stumbles on a sleeping soldier while inspecting the state of the US Army after the disastrous defeat in their first battle against the Germans at Kasserine Pass in Tunisia in 1942. The soldier says: "Hey! I am trying to sleep!" then, realizing it's the commanding general, mumbles some apology. Patton replies: "Don't worry, son, you're the only s.o.b. in this army who knows what he's trying to do."

The first requirement for strengthening performance is to be clear about the objective of the activity being performed. Yet, often because of the force of fashion and to imitate "cutting edge" practices, many countries introduced performance indicators without well-defined goals, which resulted in weakening control and accountability systems that had been working acceptably well.

The Stepsisters' Predicament ("If the shoe doesn't fit, get another")

In the original version of the Cinderella story, one stepsister cut off her toe to fit in the glass shoe; the other cut off part of her heel. Both ended up with mutilated feet and neither got the prince.

This book has stressed throughout that improvements in the budgeting and expenditure management process must be tailored to country circumstances. Too often, instead, the approach to results orientation has ignored administrative capacity limitations and institutional constraints. Predictably, the only results have been failure of the reform and loss of credibility of the approach itself.

The Accountability Tradeoff ("There's no free lunch here, either")

In statistical inference, there is an inverse correlation between precision and probability (given the size of the sample). A point estimate is highly precise but carries near-zero probability of being right (i.e., corresponding to the true value of the variable). Conversely, a very wide band estimate is highly likely to comprise the true value but is too broad to be useful. Similarly, as explained earlier, in the domain of performance there is an "accountability tradeoff": *accountability can be broad or tight, but not both*. Tight and immediate accountability is by definition narrow; conversely, the link between action and results becomes more ambiguous the broader the results.

We can either measure very accurately the performance of specific things (and then hold those in charge strictly accountable for those specific things), or resign ourselves to a rough idea of the important results (and then tolerate the resulting vagueness in attributing responsibility).

The Titanic Warning ("It's what you can't see that sinks you")

The great ship *Titanic*, which was considered unsinkable, went to the bottom on its maiden voyage in 1912 after its below-water compartments struck an iceberg in the North Atlantic. There are two lessons here. The first is never to believe that any institutional reform is unsinkable; the second is that the *Titanic* was sunk by the unexposed portion of the iceberg.

The total stock of institutional rules in any society is always much greater than the portion visible as formal rules. Indeed, sometimes the visible formal rules are simply inoperative. The Soviet Constitution of 1936 was a model document, with strong protection of individual rights—but anyone foolish enough to act as if this were really so found themselves in serious trouble. In reforms intended to encourage stronger performance orientation, a failure to recognize and take into account the key informal rules (which are generally below the surface) is likely to lead to a failure of the reform itself. This does not mean that reformers or external advisers are supposed to acquire their own expertise in the inner workings of society, which would be presumptuous and unrealistic. It does mean that they have a responsibility to identify those who do know and understand the local informal rules, and to get them to participate in the design of the reform.

The Observer Dilemma ("Beware the law of unintended consequences")

In physics, the observer effect means that certain systems cannot be measured without being affected. In the context of performance measurement, as noted earlier, one can never be sure that the actions undertaken will have the effects intended and only the effects intended. Introducing new ways of evaluating results leads to changes in behavior that may be at odds with the desired objective, or even worsen the initial situation.

Some examples, all from real life, follow:

- When agricultural subsidies are given with the intention to preserve small family farms, the increase in the price of land—now more profitable because of the agricultural subsidies—puts small farmers at a competitive disadvantage vis-à-vis large agribusiness.
- If hospital subsidies are based on the number of patients waiting for treatment, hospital administrators have an incentive to keep the number who are waiting as high as possible, by focusing entirely on critical care; if the subsidies are based on the number of patients treated, an incentive is created to process patients as fast as possible, letting them out of the hospital much too early, etc.
- When the 2002 "No Child Left Behind" legislation in the United States provided education grants linked to state spending on poor children, the richest states, which spent more anyway, ended up with the lion's share of the grants.
- When an aboriginal tribe in Australia was informed that its sanitation subsidies from the government would depend on their performance in keeping the sanitary facilities clean, they did so by thoroughly cleaning the toilets, and then closing them to the public.

The Turkish Evasion ("If it ain't worth doing, it ain't worth doing well")

A traditional Turkish folk story tells of a man who searched for his purse under a lamp on the main street because, he said, it was too dark in the back alley where he had lost it. The fact that assessing performance in meaningful ways is difficult cannot justify assessing it in easy but meaningless ways.

The Dreedle Illusion ("Better about right than exactly wrong")

In Joseph Heller's classic antiwar satirical novel, *Catch-22* (1961), the Air Force general Dreedle, enamored of "tight bombing patterns," praises a pilot whose raid produced an orderly set of bomb craters in an empty field and scolds another who destroyed the assigned target with bomb hits scattered all over it.

Spreadsheets and flow charts with neat indicators of results and timely monitoring do nothing to stimulate performance if the indicators are not relevant to the outcome sought or the data themselves are phony. In fact, this false accuracy can channel civil servants' energies away from their real work of providing public services and into presenting the data better, or even manipulating the data to make them fit the desired pattern.

The Mechanic's Principle ("If it ain't broke, don't fix it")

If the public expenditure management aspect under consideration is performing tolerably well, there is a possible risk that changes may inadvertently worsen the situation. Even if this doesn't happen, resources and attention may be diverted from more serious problems in other aspects. (However, if the process is dysfunctional or thoroughly corrupt, radical changes may be the only way to improve it.)

The Gardener's Principle ("Start with the low-hanging fruit")

In basic economics, the "production possibilities" concept makes a distinction between getting actual production closer to the ceiling which is set by resource and technological constraints, and raising the production ceiling itself. By analogy, it is advisable to first stimulate what improvements are possible under the existing regulatory and incentive framework, before introducing new results-based performance indicators and incentives.

The Missouri Test ("He who lives by the sword must be willing to duel")

The motto of the state of Missouri is: "Show me." It is inherent in the logic of any performance-based system that the system, too, must be subject to a reality test.

It is important to build into performance reforms specific provisions to *assess the performance of the performance reform itself.* But even before the reform is introduced, the political leadership, the public, and the media should demand that the proponents take the Missouri test. The test calls for a demonstration (not a mere assertion) that the concrete benefits of the reform are likely to outweigh the costs and for a good answer to the question of how and when one can know whether the reform has performed as expected. If the proposed reform cannot pass the Missouri test, the only sensible course of action is: "Just Don't Do It."

Monitoring and Evaluation in the Budgeting Process

Monitoring ascertains what is happening as it is happening; evaluation aims at understanding how and why it has happened and at drawing useful lessons for the future. Physical and financial monitoring has been covered in Chapters 7 and 8. Here we focus on evaluation.

Objectives of Evaluation

As external audit closes the legitimacy loop, so good evaluation closes the effectiveness loop—by feeding into the preparation of the next budget relevant information concerning the execution of the previous budget. The objective of evaluation is to provide decision-makers with information to decide whether to continue or change a policy or program, by *assessing* (not necessarily measuring) the effects of government policies and programs and ascribing those effects with confidence to the policy or program under examination. Evaluation is the key function that connects the past to the future—the vehicle for continuous improvements in public financial management systems—feeding lessons from actual experiences back into the programming and the decisions for future actions.

Approaches to Evaluation: By Objectives or by Results

The classic approach to evaluation is to assess the degree to which the objectives set at the inception of the task have been achieved. The pragmatic approach is to assess the results actually achieved, whether or not they match the initial objectives. The two approaches do not necessarily lead to the same conclusions, and each has disadvantages. The classic evaluation approach can be criticized for excessive formalism, giving no weight to positive results if they do not match exactly the ones defined at the outset, and often enabling simple ideas to turn into monsters of red tape. A case in point is the abuse of the "logical framework" concept: initially a simple and valid tool to connect objectives, means, processes and results, it has mutated into lengthy and garbled matrices produced largely for cosmetic purposes. Also, it is not hard for a budget manager to define targets that appear ambitious but are in reality easy to achieve, thus virtually guaranteeing a favorable evaluation. On the other hand, the pragmatic approach can encourage sloppy initial definition of objectives, degrade into an alibi for perennial postponement of reckoning with the key issues, and reward budget managers for lucky results caused by events outside their control. On balance, it is preferable to adopt the classic approach of evaluation by objectives but, whenever possible, complement it with some form of mid-course fact-based assessments. (By this combined approach, evaluation shades into supervision.)

Appropriate Stakeholder Involvement

Successful evaluations require agreement among the parties, especially between the evaluator and the requester, as to the question being evaluated, the resources (both money and time) available to answer the question, the evaluation method to be used in the light of the resources that are available, and the level of confidence that one can expect to have in the answer.

For evaluations to be effective, there must be cooperation among the key participants in the evaluation process. Those who request the evaluation must work with those who perform the evaluation and with those who will be affected by the results. The views of those with an interest in the findings of the evaluation, such as the managers of the program being evaluated, must be considered in defining the questions and planning the evaluation, as they are expected to supply data to the evaluator and often play a major role in implementing any recommendations that emerge from the evaluation. However, when stakeholders fail to cooperate because they believe their interests to be threatened, higher authority needs to intervene to encourage or if necessary compel production of the requisite data and information.

In-house or External M&E Capacity?

The standard assumption is that the M&E capacity should be created within the government itself. However, it is a fallacy to assume that because evaluation *of* government activities is important it must necessarily be conducted *by* government. In-house evaluation has the advantage of inside expertise, savvy and operational knowledge of the programs being evaluated. The disadvantage is a natural tendency to overstate results, and, where accountability systems are weak or non-existent, even to whitewash failures.[7] The advantages of external evaluation are, first, its stronger independence and, second, the probability that the evaluators are familiar with similar programs in other sectors or other countries. The disadvantages may be unfamiliarity with the circumstances of the country and lack of understanding of the local context. Chile is one of the few countries that rely largely on commissioning independent external evaluations, although the process is managed by the government ministry concerned. In contrast with the US "self-rating" approach, the cost-effectiveness of the Chilean approach may make it replicable in some developing countries.

The advantages are not exclusive, however. In-house evaluation organs can also be assured of a degree of independence close to that enjoyed by external entities. And if external evaluators contribute on a regular basis, they will develop the intimate understanding of operations and of country context that is needed for an informed evaluation. The disadvantages, too, are not exclusive. In particular, if the governance climate is not conducive to candid evaluations, even the best external evaluations will be suppressed or distorted to produce the desired findings. (A major study that identified $125 bilion in possible savings over five years for the US Defense Department was buried until it surfaced in the press two years later.)

The choice is thus entirely pragmatic and cost-driven. A thorough evaluation requires a substantial input by economists, researchers and auditors—skills that are in limited supply in all developing countries and are best employed in designing and running sound programs, not in evaluating them. In developing countries, therefore, evaluation should be conducted largely on the basis of expertise and inputs external to the government and, in many cases, external to the country. At the same time, an organic link to the regular administrative apparatus needs to be created. The approach to creating M&E capacity in developing countries should therefore rest on two complementary efforts: relying on external evaluations, especially for major expenditure programs, and creating a small but strong in-house capacity to design, guide, contract and monitor the external evaluators. Such in-house evaluation capacity must not then be confined to a small "evaluation ghetto" but be systematically connected to the public finance management apparatus and to the line ministries.

Finally, appropriate civil society participation can augment the limited governmental capacity for M&E, and at much lower cost than that of permanently expanding in-house capacity. The role of non-governmental organizations (NGOs) is especially relevant here. The experience of Uganda, among others, has shown both the contribution of NGOs to effective M&E as well as their concern with the risk of being co-opted. The issues of involving NGOs in evaluating government programs are delicate, but a balance between cooperation and independence can be struck.

Other lessons of international experience in M&E are summarized in Box 12.2.

Box 12.2 Selected Lessons of Experience of Monitoring and Evaluation

International experience with M&E programs yields several important lessons:

- Simply placing M&E on the government agenda is in itself a significant accomplishment (as in Sri Lanka).
- Also a significant accomplishment is to help build a common M&E conceptual understanding among ministries (as in Egypt).
- Cross-fertilization of ideas and country comparisons can be helpful, as in the effective use of Chile's experience of Chile by other Latin American countries.
- An excessive focus on "macro" evaluation of public sector management issues detracts from robust M&E of individual services. Better linkages of evaluation activities with the responsible ministry staff and service providers are important.
- The mere availability of funding for M&E is insufficient to advance the M&E agenda if it is not targeted on capacity-building in the country itself.
- Excessive monitoring, through a large number of indicators, produces little effective monitoring (as in Uganda).
- Overreliance on one-off evaluation workshops or similar events is not productive. Although these events can be important to put M&E on the map, sustained capacity-building efforts are required to improve the performance of the public sector on a lasting basis.

Source: Author's experiences and Independent Evaluation Group.

Notes

1 The genesis of the NPM can be traced to the early 1980s (essentially starting from the Thatcher reforms in the United Kingdom), and its heyday was marked by the completion in the early 1990s of the public sector management revolution implemented in New Zealand and Australia. For an exposition of the NPM, see Hood (1991). For a summary of the arguments for and against the

NPM see, respectively, Borins (1995) and Savoie (1995). By 2015, many of the valuable aspects of the NPM have been incorporated in countries where national income, governance and institutional capacity allowed; some of the excesses have been pulled back; and the more fanciful innovations have been abandoned. Attempts to introduce NPM approaches in developing countries, where neither economic nor institutional capacity was available, produced only frustration, high trans-action costs, and, in some cases, actual damage to budgetary outcomes. In Madagascar, for example, the Public Expenditure and Financial Accountability (PEFA) assessment found that the introduction of program budgeting in 2005 resulted in confusion and weaker ability to control the budget. By 2009, the initiative had been dropped. Ironically, Madagascar is also the country where one of the earliest attempts at program budgeting was made in 1987, at World Bank urging, for the agriculture budget; one year later, the ministry of agriculture was the only one incapable of producing coherent accounts, and the government returned the ministry to normal line-item budgeting. Until 2005, that is . . . only to give up on program budgeting again four years later. The resilience of failure is remarkable: an explanation is provided in Chapter 13 on PFM reform.

2 "Impact," often wrongly used as a synonym for outcome, is the *value added* from the activity, i.e., the "gross" outcome minus the contribution from other entities or activities. The notion is important but, in the correct meaning of value added, impact is nearly impossible to measure and thus to use as a performance criterion.

3 Every now and then, a new fashion emerges on how to "measure" performance of individual employees—and slowly dies in the face of futility or counterproductive results. One of these is the system of "forced rankings," which obliges unit managers to rank a specified percentage of their employees in the lowest performance category regardless of their judgment on actual employee performance. The practice was advocated at the end of the nineteenth century by the *then*-admired head of General Electric, Jack Welch, spread to many large corporations in North America and some in Europe, and has persisted long past the point where it was demonstrably detrimental to employee motivation and company productivity. In addition to devaluing the role of managers' judgment and limiting their flexibility, the system creates an antagonistic climate within organizational units, turns the coaching and mentoring function into a zero-sum game, and is a strong disincentive to the cooperative team approach that is essential for innovation in any large organization: help your colleagues, and you may end up in a performance bracket lower than theirs. (Fortunately, this particular "best practice" did not spread to the management of government personnel.)

4 The genesis of the acronym has been variously attributed to different authors (G.T. Doran being the most likely).

5 In budgeting, Hood (2006) notes that explicit targets can be useful to stimulate budgetary performance. This is not likely in developing countries, and not even in all developed countries: Joyce (2003) notes that, for example, the achievement of budget targets in the US is routinely compromised by interference from individual politicians.

6 An operational guide to measure and monitor performance in public expenditure management has been produced for Morocco by Collange et al. (2006).

7 The most sophisticated framework for internal performance monitoring and evaluation has been created by the Auditor-General of the Australian state of Victoria (see the AG report for 2014.) In the United States, departments are required to rate the performance of all their programs, but these self-ratings are reviewed, and often overridden, by the Office of Management and Budget (OMB), which assesses the reliability of the agencies' findings and constitutes in effect a critique of their M&E methods. These approaches are much too demanding in terms of data, capacity and resources to be of value in developing countries—except possibly for a few major selected programs.

Bibliography

Atlantic, The, 2013. "The Unique Genius of Hong Kong's Public Transportation System." Available online at www.theatlantic.com/china/archive/2013/09/the-unique-genius-of-hong-kongs-public-transportation-system/279528/ [accessed November 9, 2016].

Borins, Sanford, 1995. "The New Public Management Is Here to Stay," *Canadian Public Administration*, 38(1), 122–32.

Collange, Gerard, Pierre Demangel and Robert Poinsard, 2006. *Methodological Guide for Performance Monitoring.* (Prepared for the Government of Morocco.) Rabat: World Bank.

Goodhart, Charles, 1975. "Problems of Monetary Management: The UK Experience," *Papers in Monetary Economics*. Sydney: Reserve Bank of Australia.

Heller, Joseph, 1961. *Catch 22*. New York: Simon and Schuster.

Hood, Christopher, 1991. "A Public Management for all Seasons," *Public Management and Development*, 69(2), 3–19.

——, 2006. "Gaming in Targetworld: The Targets Approach to Managing British Public Services," *Public Administration Review*, 66(4), 515–21.

Jones, David S., 2000. "Uses and Limitations of Performance Measurement in the Civil Service: An Assessment from the Singapore and New Zealand Experiences," *Asian Journal of Political Science*, 8(2), 109–36.

Joyce, Philip, 2003. *Linking Performance and Budgeting: Opportunities in the Federal Budget Process*. Arlington, VA: IBM Center.

Olson, Mancur, 1973. "Evaluating Performance in the Public Sector," in Milton Moss, ed., *The Measurement of Economic and Social Performance*. Cambridge, MA: National Bureau of Economic Research.

Partnership for Transparency Fund, 2016. *Lessons from the CARTA Program in Nepal and Bangladesh,* November. Available online at http://ptfund.org/wp-content/uploads/2016/03 [accessed November 9, 2016].

Patton, 1970. Directed by F. J Schaffner [Film], USA: 20th Century Fox.

Paul, Samuel, 2002. *Holding the State to Account: Citizen Monitoring in Action*. Bangalore: Books for Change.

Rotberg, Eugene, 2013. *Remarks on the Occasion of the 50th Anniversary of the Eurobond Market,* London, June 24, available online at www.icmagroup.org/assets/documents/About-ICMA/Eurobond-anniversary/Eurobond%20dinner%20speech%20Eugene%20Rotberg%20June%202013.pdf [accessed November 5, 2016].

Savoie, Donald, 1995. "What Is Wrong with the New Public Management?" *Canadian Public Administration*, 38(1), 112–21.

Schiavo-Campo, S., 1999. "'Performance' in the Public Sector," *Asian Journal of Political Science*, 7(2), 75–87.

——, 2004. *External Review of the Operations Evaluation Department's Work in Egypt and Uganda*. Operations Evaluation Department. Washington, DC: The World Bank, March.

Shand, David, 1998. "The Role of Performance Indicators in Public Expenditure Management," *Staff Working Papers*. Washington, DC: IMF.

Smith, Peter, ed., 1996. *Measuring Outcome In The Public Sector*. Abingdon: Taylor & Francis.

Veblen, Thorstein, 1899. "The Instinct of Workmanship and the Irksomeness of Labor," *American Journal of Sociology*, 4(2), 187–201.

Victoria, Auditor-General, 2014. *Public Sector Performance Measurement and Reporting*. Melbourne: Government Printer.

Wachter, Robert, 2015. *The Digital Doctor: Hope, Hype and Harm at the Dawn of Medicine's Computer Age*. New York: McGraw Hill.

——, 2016. "How Measurement Fails Us," *The New York Times,* January 17.

Wilson, J. Q., 1989. *Bureaucracy: What Government Agencies Do and Why They Do It*. New York: Basic Books.

13 Reforming and Strengthening Public Financial Management

It ain't what you don't know that gets you into trouble. It's what you know for sure that just ain't so.

(Mark Twain)

Introduction

This chapter reviews the international experience in public financial management (PFM) reform and assesses the approaches to be taken to improve PFM, in light of the governance and institutional context of each country. The focus is primarily on developing countries.

What Do We Mean By "Reform"?

Literally, to reform means to reshape, but if you look up the synonyms you'll find humble verbs (improve, amend, revise) along with ambitious ones (rebuild, reorganize, transform). "Improvement" is a better umbrella term, as no country is constantly "reforming" its public management systems. However, semantic battles are rarely worth the effort, and we may as well stick to the commonly used umbrella term "reform," provided that we recognize that: "reform" covers a wide range of changes, from minor procedural improvements to extensive institutional reengineering; consistent small improvements can add up over time to a major reform; and any significant change has political and distributional implications, which must be considered in its design and implementation.

It also helps to beware of the value-laden terms used to neutralize pesky doubters—reinvent, reengineer, empower, synergy, holistic, etc. (Savoie, 1995). Beware, too, of seductive analogies. The most attractive and most misleading such analogy is that between the PFM reform process and the construction of a building—as if in the real world institutional reforms could ever proceed neatly, from site preparation to foundation through ground floor and successive upper floors and up to attic and roof, and without any reversals.

How, Not Just What

Unimplemented reform is no reform at all. Without the political will and the capacity to implement it, the best reform program is hardly worth the paper it's written on. In itself, a PFM reform strategy paper is not a strategy and it reforms nothing—it is just a paper, unless it addresses realistically the questions of how the reforms are to be implemented, with what resources, when and, most importantly, by whom they are to be implemented. Political will and capacity stand at the center of the PFM reform agenda. Yet, budgeting reforms have often been designed and pushed on to developing countries' governments with no attention to implementation requirements or consideration of the red tape and transaction costs that are imposed on the public administration. As elaborated below, it is critical to tailor the reforms to local realities, and build capacity alongside the gradual implementation of the reforms.

Country Context and the Central Lessons of Experience

Developing countries have different characteristics than middle- or high-income countries. First, in developed countries the major part of the institutional framework is composed of formal and explicit rules, whereas in developing countries informal rules and customary norms are more important, and are rarely visible to the outsider (McFerson, 2007). Second, developed countries possess complex organizations, reliable flows of information and greater availability of money and professional talent, whereas developing countries have weaker organizations, inadequate information and scarcity of both financial resources and skilled personnel. Third, most developed countries are comparatively homogeneous economically, socially and ethnically, whereas in a majority of developing countries heterogeneity is the norm and government decisions must carefully balance the interests of different groups. Finally, most developed countries have evolved state legitimacy and government representativeness over a long period of time, whereas with the comparatively recent independence of most developing countries, political accountability remains shaky and civil society is not yet strong.

So, let's ask a few rhetorical questions. Is it conceivable that a complex administrative practice of a developed country can be transplanted "as is" to a poor country with limited capacity, dominated by customs invisible to outsiders, with many transactions running on personal favors, weak rule of law and loose accountability? Is it sensible, for example, to approach financial management information systems in a country like, say, Yemen, as if it were the same as Iceland—except a lot warmer and populated by tribal Arabs? Or to push budget managers' flexibility and "performance" bonuses in a system like, say, Malaysia—with a delicate balance between the two major ethnic groups where every exercise of management discretion triggers suspicion and conflict? Or to encourage public–private partnerships in a country like, say, pre-revolution Tunisia—when the "private" firm is controlled by the president's wife? Or to replace rudimentary but functioning padlocks protecting public moneys in a country like, say, Madagascar, with a budgeting system focused on ex-post results, leaving the front door wide open for misallocation and abuse?

Well, no. Allen Schick (1998) outlined almost 20 years ago some of the reasons why such ambitious reforms are unsuitable to developing countries, and international experience since then has demonstrated that they have caused useless commotion and waste of resources, at best, or, at worst, counterproductive consequences—consequences which were borne not by the reform proponents but by the people of the host country, who could hardly afford them. The cemeteries of PFM reform are full of the bones of innovations pushed in disregard of country realities.

All this is not in the least intended to suggest that PFM reforms are not desirable in poor countries. Quite the contrary: *sustainable and sustained improvements in PFM systems and practices are critical for poverty reduction and economic growth.* Historically, it is through such gradual improvements that poor countries have acquired the capacity to absorb and make good use of the more complex systems and practices in public financial management. Indeed, the other side of the experience coin is positive: PFM reforms have been successful in cases when they were carefully suited to the country's governance, economic, institutional and cultural context. As Mark Twain (1897) put it:

> we must take from an experience only the wisdom that is in it, and stop there; lest we be like the cat that sits down on a hot stove-lid. She will never sit down on a hot stove-lid again—and that is well; but also she will never sit down on a cold one anymore.

Assessing Public Financial Management

One cannot very well formulate recommendations without assessing the situation. As explained in Chapter 8, the fact that all financial resources are fungible means that the development effectiveness of aid requires assessing the entire PFM system of the beneficiary country. However, until early in this century, a consensus methodology to assess PFM systems was lacking.

From Assessment Recognition to Assessment Indigestion

Because donor agencies are accountable to their own constituency, each major agency developed its own assessment instrument and administered it individually. At the turn of this century, the main such assessments included the following:

- The World Bank's Public Expenditure Reviews (PER). When the World Bank moved to budget support from the late 1980s, it needed to analyze the budget being supported, and the public investment reviews were replaced by broader public expenditure review covering also current expenditure. The PER covered mainly "upstream" PFM issues up to and including budget approval, but generally not budget execution.
- The World Bank's Country Financial Accountability Assessment (CFAA) was introduced to assess fiduciary risk and thus covered mainly "downstream" issues of budget execution—except for those relating to procurement.
- The Country Procurement Assessment Review (CPAR) complemented the triad of assessment instruments by focusing on economy, efficiency and integrity of procurement.
- The International Monetary Fund Fiscal Report on Observance of Standards and Codes (Fiscal ROSC) was developed in response to the 1997–9 Asian financial crisis, mainly to examine the countries' observance of the provisions of the Code of Fiscal Transparency.
- The joint IMF/World Bank Public Expenditure Tracking Assessments and Action Plans for Heavily-Indebted Poor Countries (HIPC AAP) followed the introduction of the HIPC debt-reduction initiative to assure that the resources released by the debt reduction would be devoted to poverty reduction and other priority development expenditures.
- European Commission "audits" were periodic ex-post assessments of whether EU budget support was used in line with prior agreements, and formed part of the basis for subsequent decisions on whether to extend additional budget support.
- The UN Development Program developed its own instrument—"CONTACT"—a comprehensive checklist/questionnaire comprising over 600 individual items.
- The UK Department for International Development (DFID) implemented its own approach to assessing fiduciary risk in the broad sense.

The Emergence of the "PEFA Approach"

The dizzying assortment of assessment instruments, with different requirements for information and meetings, carried heavy disadvantages for both the donors and the recipient countries. It:

- led to superficial and overlapping analyses, providing neither donor nor recipient with a clear picture of fiduciary risk or the basis on which to make PFM improvement efforts;
- precluded clear consensus among donors and confused the reform picture;

- was costly for the donors themselves; and, most troubling;
- generated huge transaction costs for the host countries, straining their already limited administrative capacity for little or no good purpose.

Donor missions followed one after another and sometimes overlapped—with everyone requesting similar but not identical information, taking up an inordinate amount of time of busy policy-makers, interfering with the everyday work of local officials (sometimes, ironically, even during the intense budget preparation period) and, in the final analysis, making much more difficult the already challenging job of managing the budget, let alone improving the PFM systems. A variety of ad hoc coordination attempts (e.g., joint donor missions) didn't help, as each donor agency was still obliged to follow its own methodology, and the transaction costs of separate donor missions were thus replicated in giant joint missions taking up a month or more in the field. This was the untenable situation which gave rise to the Public Expenditure and Financial Accountability (PEFA) initiative.

Genesis and Evolution

The PEFA Performance Management Framework is managed by the PEFA Secretariat, a joint entity located at the World Bank but supported by the World Bank, European Commission (EC), IMF, DFID, France, Switzerland, Norway and the Strategic Partnership for Africa. Based on the approach formulated by Allen et al. (2004), the PEFA Secretariat developed a detailed assessment methodology, comprising ratings on 28 indicators (from A for best through D for worst—PEFA does not give F grades) covering the entire range of issues—from budget reliability to fiscal transparency, management of assets and liabilities, fiscal strategy and budget preparation, budget execution, accounting and reporting, external scrutiny and audit. (Three additional indicators address donor practices.) In addition, the PEFA reports contain a qualitative narrative, based on the ratings but providing broad context. (See www.pefa.org for the details of the methodology, which can be seen "in action" by perusing any of the country reports.)

From the June 2005 launch through mid-2016, over 500 PEFA assessments have been conducted, including repeat assessments and assessments at national and subnational government level. Of these, about one half have received the permission of the concerned government to be published.[1] Although the assessments are conducted jointly among several donors, until mid-2010 the World Bank took the lead in most cases. Since then, the European Commission has taken a more active leading role, focusing on leading PEFA assessments at subnational government level. Africa has had by far the largest coverage, with only a handful of countries declining to conduct PEFA assessments and several countries with repeat assessments—which are particularly important to obtain a sense of changes over time in the various PEFA indicators. In February 2016, PEFA released a revised framework with new and updated benchmarks, based on experience but essentially preserving the structure and methodology of the assessments and the reports.

Assessing the Assessment

The PEFA performance measurement framework is not intended to address issues of fiscal policy or to identify reform priorities. The PEFA assessment is a *diagnostic*, intended to provide a "map" of the strengths and weaknesses in the PFM systems. Such a map is an important starting point from which to carry out in-depth analysis and dialogue on which aspect of the system to improve and how best to do so, but it is only a starting point. The fact that a particular indicator is rated D and another B does not dictate—or even suggest—that improvement efforts should focus on the former indicator. Each indicator carries a different weight of importance; several ought to be viewed jointly as part of the same strength or weakness of the system; implementing changes can be much harder for one indicator than another; and the payoff from further improving a positively rated indicator could be higher than that of improving a poorly rated one. Numerical ratings are no substitute for country-based analysis, judgment and dialogue.

If understood correctly and within its limitations, the PEFA initiative has succeeded. To begin with the most practical aspect, the initiative has drastically cut down on the multiplication and overlaps of uncoordinated donor assessments, and on the resulting transaction costs borne by the host countries. Depending largely on the quality of the assessment teams, PEFA has also produced sound PFM diagnostics of a large number of countries and, simply by providing the venue and the occasion for reflection by the host government authorities themselves, it has enabled better understanding of their own PFM systems and, in some cases, a reform stimulus. The PEFA assessments have thus become the starting point for discussion of reform programs, and the dataset is helpful to researchers worldwide. However, the temptation to use the assessments in mechanical fashion is problematic, and has reinforced the tendency to exceed on the side of fiduciary caution instead of moving toward greater reliance on using country systems for the implementation of aid-financed projects.

There are some criticisms of the PEFA methodology and of its application in certain cases, but these criticisms can be addressed and remedied. (The principal concern is with the diverse competence of the assessment teams. Also, despite the uniform methodology, it is difficult to be sure of the reliability of changes in ratings when the assessments have been conducted by different teams.) But the main problem with PEFA is neither with its methodology nor with what it has achieved. The main problem is the grave risk from the users' propensity to misinterpret the ratings as if they provided a reform platform. The PEFA assessment is a tool, and as any tool it should be used for the purpose for which it is intended, and stop there.

Changes in PFM During the Past Decade

For three decades loans and technical assistance have been provided to improve PFM and since the 1990s PFM reforms were incorporated in policy programs supported by external aid (when it was recognized that effective budget support requires an agreement on the overall expenditure program as well as financial management systems adequate for its implementation; see Chapter 8). The focus on PFM intensified in this century, along with rapid growth in innovation and a burgeoning literature (focused largely on advanced countries). PFM reforms have been included in virtually every major budget support program, and have been financed by a large number of specific lending operations in almost a hundred countries. What has been achieved with all this money and effort?

Because of the absence of a common methodology, changes can only be identified since 2005, from the evidentiary basis provided by the PEFA assessments. It would not make sense to average all the ratings into a single aggregate "PEFA score"—because this would implicitly give equal weight to different aspects of PFM that carry vastly different importance depending on country circumstances. However, to try and formulate some meaningful conclusions worldwide, I have selected six main indicators—the first three related to budget preparation and the second three to budget execution. Table 13.1 shows rating changes for these indicators in all 41 countries where a PEFA assessment was conducted during 2007–10 and 2012–15.

Table 13.1 Average Scores on Selected PEFA Indicators (41 countries, 2007–10 and 2012–15)

Indicator		2007–10	2012–15	Average
PI-2	Composition of expenditure outturn compared with original budget	2.27	2.20	2.24
PI-3	Aggregate revenue outturn compared with original approved budget	3.45	2.71	3.08
PI-7	Extent of unreported government operations	2.39	2.13	2.26
PI-16	Predictability in the availability of funds for expenditure commitments	2.23	2.35	2.29
PI-19	Competition, value for money and controls in procurement	2.18	2.32	2.25
D-3	Proportion of aid that is managed by use of national procedures	1.18	1.50	1.34

Source: PEFA.org. See the text for explanation of the scores.

The numerical scores in Table 13.1 correspond to the A, B, C and D grades of the PEFA methodology—respectively 4, 3, 2 and 1. PEFA gives a "plus" for the intermediate value, for example, C+ is a 2.5. However, to be consistent with usual student grading practice, in assembling the table D+ was assigned a value of 1.25, C+ of 2.25 and B+ of 3.25. The scores are the weighted averages of the scores for each region, and the corresponding tables for each region are in Annex 1.[2]

The scores on the budget preparation indicators did not improve; on the contrary, revenue marksmanship dropped from satisfactory to marginally satisfactory. While a discrepancy of actual from estimated revenue can be caused by unforeseen events during budget execution, the more likely explanation is that the initial estimates of revenue worsened. The scores on the budget execution indicators remained about the same. Of the selected indicators, only the proportion of aid managed by national procedures increased. The proportion remains very low overall—proof of initial progress of the international policy for greater reliance on country systems but also of the very long road ahead.

The PEFA assessments provide no evidence of improvement in PFM in low- and middle-income countries. Individually, some countries have seen substantial progress, for example Nepal—from marginally satisfactory to satisfactory; and other countries have experienced major setbacks, for example Madagascar—from a fairly positive assessment in 2008 to a very poor one in 2014 (possibly because of the intervening attempt to introduce program budgeting). Among the main regions, only Europe and Central Asia showed a slight improvement, suggesting further consolidation from the transition of the 1990s. It is especially discouraging that the poorest region—Africa— showed a decline in the scores on the selected indicators, despite the massive investment in PFM reform. Perhaps the PFM reforms financed during the past decade were unsuited to country circumstances?

The significance of the comparison is limited by four factors. First, only published PEFA assessments could be included in the comparison. While it is reasonable to infer that unpublished assessments would show a less favourable PFM picture than the published ones, one can assume nothing concerning changes between the two periods in the unpublished assessments. Second, only countries on which an assessment was conducted during both 2007–10 and 2012–15 could be included. Combined, these two limitations bring the total number of countries to 41, less than one-third of the total national-level PEFA assessments. Third, the assessment teams were different for most countries in the two assessments. Finally, the selection of the indicators in Table 13.1 is arbitrary to some extent and may not be representative of the changes in all PEFA indicators. (However, a cursory analysis suggests that the findings summarized above are consistent with the entire set of indicators. See www.pefa.org, for details on all indicators in the 256 published assessments.)

The evidence from the changes in governance in the past 20 years (see Chapter 1) is consistent with the findings from the PEFA assessments: the poorest regions of Africa and South Asia also lost ground in governance quality. However, there has been a slight improvement in corruption perception (see Chapter 16). Also, budget transparency increased for the countries that provide sufficient information to be rated along the Open Budget Index. Thus, more and more systematic research would be needed for robust conclusions on the net impact on developing countries' PFM of the technical assistance and PFM innovations of the past two decades. But what evidence exists suggests that the vast investment in money and advice has not produced a remotely commensurate improvement in budgetary processes.

Why the Disappointing Record of PFM Reform in Developing Countries?

Focus on the Experience of Developed Countries

The literature on public financial management has bloomed in the past two decades, with important intellectual and operational contributions. The vast bulk of it, however, has focused on the problems of interest to highly advanced countries and on improving their already complex and sophisticated systems. The result has been twofold: no comparable contributions have been made with direct relevance to the PFM problems of low-income countries and, partly because of that, there has been a tendency to try to transplant the new PFM concepts and innovations to the very different circumstances of those countries.

Insufficient Attention to Governance and Social Accountability

First, the attention given to the governance context of PFM has been insufficient. Many problems of budgeting in poor countries stem not from technical difficulties, but from governance weaknesses and lack of political-level mechanisms to make expenditure choices and stick to them during budget preparation and execution. Improved technical gatekeeping to screen out ineffective or unaffordable expenditure proposals cannot accomplish much without stronger political gatekeeping.

Second, more attention should be paid to the interaction between government and civil society on public expenditure issues. Especially in subnational government, appropriate public participation can make an important contribution to the design of expenditure programs, the effectiveness of their implementation, and, indirectly, fiscal transparency and integrity. However, while lip-service to participation is commonplace, meaningful actions to increase participation in budgeting are few and far between. Aid agencies find it easier and quicker to deal with one friendly minister than to push for involvement by non-governmental organizations.

Third, as previously noted, the comparative neglect of capacity issues is problematic. PFM improvements are inherently capacity-intensive. If the focus of attention is on aid disbursements and on meeting formal conditions, rather than on capacity-building, effective reform implementation is unlikely. (Because countries usually prefer—rightly so—not to borrow for technical assistance, the capacity-building requirements of PFM reforms are a powerful argument in favor of financing technical assistance on a grant basis and not through lending.)

Weak Accountability for the Quality of Advice

The aid agencies' teams carrying out the diagnostic work and formulating the recommendations do not always have the right mix of technical skills and country-specific knowledge. Aid teams have frequently engaged the recipient government in a dialogue on complex technical issues of budgeting or accounting without any team member with adequate technical competence and familiarity with international experience in these areas. Not surprisingly, recommendations have often been either wrong on the merits, or correct in principle but advanced without a sense of proper sequencing and practical requirements.

Regrettably, accountability for the quality of technical assistance in PFM has been weak to non-existent in donor agencies (including the World Bank), and advice provided by the IMF is too often of the cookie-cutting sort. Make a big mistake in procurement and your career may be over; give the government wrong advice in important PFM issues and hardly anyone will notice. Because host country governments understandably believe that donor agency experts have the right solutions, the actual damage has been substantial. International financial institutions have a responsibility to select competent persons capable of careful and nuanced assessments and then to monitor their advice and provide independent quality assurance.

The Pressures to Lend

Governance weaknesses can dilute or cut the normal link between money and impact.[3] In PFM, the correlation between the amount of financial assistance and its impact is especially weak, and in some cases is even negative. Let's explain this perverse effect. The critical component of PFM reform is good advice, but the provision of advice is comparatively inexpensive and is not conducive to meeting agency aid-disbursement targets. Technical assistance projects are therefore typically loaded with by expensive works, hardware and large-scale training programs. During project implementation, supervisory attention is naturally focused on disbursements under the big-ticket components, and oversight of the advice—which is the central component—takes a back seat.

How to disable this perverse effect is as easy to prescribe as it is unlikely to be implemented: aid agencies should reward their staff not only for project design and successful negotiation but for its effective implementation; host governments should give at least as much attention to the advisory dimension of the project as to the procurement of expensive equipment and works; both sides should refocus project supervision on the institutional aspects of the project. Regrettably, most of the individual incentives pull in the opposite direction.

The Challenge of PFM Reform

Approaches to Reform

In general, reforms should be advanced as fast as possible when circumstances permit, and as slowly as necessary to permit accountability to catch up, capacity to grow, resistance to be overcome, and public consensus to be built. Thus, both "big bang" and "gradualism" fail as strategies when they are followed regardless of circumstances (Schiavo-Campo and McFerson, 2008). The motto of the reformer should be "torto-hare" from the slogan *tarta-lepre*—combining tortoise (*tartaruga*) and hare (*lepre*)—coined by the Italian traffic police in the 1960s to describe optimal driver behavior: drive fast or slow but always adapting to conditions (see the strange creature in Figure 13.1). The worst approach to driving in erratic traffic and poor visibility is to set the cruise control, whether at high or at low speed. This is the history of many PFM reforms in developing countries—failing to adapt to the

Figure 13.1 "Torto-hare,": The Public Sector Management Mascot.

fluid circumstances and opaque institutional context. The reform challenge is thus to identify the areas where and when it is feasible to move fast, and the areas where it is essential to build slowly a solid foundation—and even occasionally to effect tactical retreats.

The Need for Sequencing

Since it is impossible to reform all aspects of a complex system at once, PFM reforms must be "sequenced" in some fashion in every country. The question is whether it is possible to identify a sequence of improvements that is valid in all situations, albeit still adapted to each country. Some say no—arguing that sequencing is necessary, but that almost everything about it is contingent on the specific characteristics and circumstances (including political) of the individual country, and there is no point in chasing the elusive holy grail of a generalizable reform sequence. Others say yes—but differ as to the approach to be taken in the sequencing of PFM reforms.

The Basics First

The most intuitive approach to sequencing is to tackle the "basics first" (Schick, 1997; see Schick, 2012 for a brief recent summary). However, there is no consensus on what the basics are, in every country. (Much more on this later.) Indeed, Schick himself (1966) had earlier argued that in the United States budgeting reforms had taken place as targets of opportunity surfacing at different times, and not as deliberate sequencing of related actions.[4]

The Platform Approach

In most cases, an isolated reform is unlikely to carry lasting benefits because of the lack of the complementary steps required for its effective implementation.[5] From this recognition came the "platform approach," which advocates implementing a set of interrelated measures which, *once completed*, can serve as platform for a next, higher set of also-interrelated improvements, and so on (Brooke, 2003).

The platform concept underlines the complementarity among PFM processes, and may also help inform the reform efforts by providing a "vision" of the end result and of the intermediate stages. The approach was innovative and appeared initially promising (aided by the seductive analogy of constructing a building—blueprint, foundations, ground floor, etc.). However, it has lost credibility in recent years and after 2010 it has been attempted in only a handful of countries (e.g., Kyrgyz Republic and the Indian state of Odisha), owing to mounting criticism of both the approach itself and how it has been implemented. Primarily, in the platform approach:

- There is no guidance on how strong the complementarity among different PFM processes should be in order to include them in the same platform.
- There is no single sequence of reform "packages" any more than there is a single sequence of individual reform measures. In fact, there isn't a platform approach—there are as many platform approaches as there are public finance economists and ministers of finance, sequenced in as many different ways as there are countries with different problems. This makes the platform approach functionally equivalent to the view that there cannot be any common reform sequencing at all.
- Overlaps between platforms compromise the very logic of the platform approach: "The important thing is that each platform establishes a clear basis for launching to the next"(Brooke, 2003, p. 2.) But in reality these overlaps are common. In Uganda, with three platforms, some actions in platform two and three were implemented while some actions of platform one were still incomplete. In Tanzania, there was significant overlap of actions between the six platforms adopted.
- Finally, although not a weakness of the approach itself, in practice the platform approach has been overloaded in design and actions—hence, hard to manage and prone to reform fatigue and failure. It is very difficult to monitor implementation of each of a large number of activities, and thus to decide whether the platform goals have been achieved and it's time to move to a higher platform. (See Box 13.1 on the experience of Cambodia.)

Combining the Valid Elements

A realistic approach to reform sequencing should build on the valid kernels of all three views. The PFM reform must indeed begin with the basics, but should attempt to introduce a package of improvements that complement one another. However, after the basics have been consolidated, further PFM reforms can only be decided and sequenced based on the economic, political, social and institutional context of the individual country.

Naturally, this combined approach still assumes that a common list of "basics" can be identified in most low-income, limited-capacity countries. In turn, identifying the basics depends on which among the three objectives of expenditure control, strategic allocation and operational efficiency is viewed as priority. While none of the three objectives is more important than the others, expenditure control is the logical prerequisite. (This is also consistent with the priorities suggested by Diamond, 2013.) Preventing public resources from being misappropriated is the paramount fiduciary duty of public managers. If you cannot protect the public money, you cannot control it; if you cannot control it, you cannot allocate it; and if you cannot allocate it, you obviously cannot manage it well—it just isn't there.

The subject of protecting the money by combating corruption is addressed in Chapter 16, and basic anti-corruption measures can be gleaned from that analysis. Concerning expenditure control, it is unlikely that any specific set of basic measures will command universal agreement. For any list, some will undoubtedly view one or more of the items as being beyond the "basics" and others will argue for including additional items. Nevertheless, Annex 2 shows the list of the measures I consider likely to be essential for controlling expenditure in every developing country.

Box 13.1 Implementing the Platform Approach in Cambodia

The platform approach was used by the World Bank in its Public Financial Management and Accountability Project for Cambodia (2006–13). The project established four platforms—respectively for the objectives of "More credible budget," "Effective financial accountability," "Fully affordable policy agenda through policy-budget linkage," and "Effective program performance accountability." The hierarchy of objectives appears reasonable. The main problem was the gross overloading of the reform program: platform one alone called for 27 activities and 250 specific actions. This would be enough to overwhelm implementation and monitoring capacity in a highly developed country—let alone a country like Cambodia where, as the project itself emphasized, institutions were dilapidated and capacity was extremely weak.

The Bank argued that although the project covered so many activities, selecting fewer activities would have resulted in less impact. But selecting activities produces no impact; only implementing them can do so, and the evidence shows the absence of positive impact—rather the reverse. The post-project PEFA assessment in 2015 found that the only significant PFM improvement during the project period was in accounting/reporting—while strategic budgeting, resource management and external accountability all deteriorated. Fully 12 of the 31 indicators were given the lowest rating of D (with only four indicators scoring B or higher). Of these findings, the most telling are the D rating for the composition of expenditure outturn compared with the original budget, which is critical for the objective of a credible budget; and the NR ("not rated") for external audit, implying lack of any effective audit, which is key for sustainable efficiency and integrity in any PFM system. (The external audit component was dropped entirely during project implementation.)

The Bank's Independent Evaluation Group ranked the project in its next-to-lowest category of Unsatisfactory. It would be hard to argue not to accept that this particular variant of the platform approach had a lot to do with the failure of the project.

Beyond Sequencing

A central theme of this book is to anchor PFM on the bedrock of the principles of good governance and on economic fundamentals. These call for careful consideration of the costs as well as the benefits of proposed changes; recognition that the impacts of reform are unevenly distributed; and that actions are needed to generate a measure of consensus, which is in turn needed for effective implementation of the reform. Reform attempts should also rest on two lessons of experience: (i) selectivity and realism are always critical—when too much is crammed on to the reform plate, capacity limits and political resistance intervene to doom the reform; and (ii) the sequence is neither linear nor unidirectional—progress moves in ellipses, fits and starts, slippages and occasional reversals.

The above approach implies, among other things, the following guidance for PFM reform:

- *Make your own mistakes.* It is unavoidable that the process of change entails the risk of making mistakes, but it is avoidable to repeat mistakes made previously or in similar countries. Preserving institutional memory and reviewing the relevant international experience can identify common mistakes and help avoid them.
- *If it's broke, fix it, but if it ain't broke, at least don't* break *it.* If an aspect of the PFM system is performing adequately, changes may actually make the situation worse.

But conversely, if the budget process is extremely weak and corrupt, radical changes may be the only way to improve it.

- *Provide for the appropriate incentives.* Nothing causes reforms to fail faster than the realization that the individual officials and staff involved in the reform will be required to make greater efforts and take risks, but will receive no reward for success and no penalty for failure.
- *Ensure systematic feedback* from front-line staff, service users and the public, in both the design and the implementation of the reform.

The Iron Triangle of Technical Assistance for Public Financial Management Reform

Yet, the push to introduce PFM practices incompatible with the country context has continued unabated, with the same "reform" moving from unsuitable country to unsuitable country and sometimes replicated within a few years in the same country where it failed in the first place—even when the circumstances had not changed. What explains this persistence in attempts at stuffing square pegs into round holes?

In international assistance to public sector management, and especially government budgeting, an "iron triangle" has been at work, joining the international consulting industry with the aid organizations financing their services and with the officials of the country receiving the advice. Consulting firms have a propensity to advocate "state of the art" systems rather than simpler improvements that are appropriate to the country's realities and politically implementable. The staff of aid agencies tend to rely on large international consulting firms—reinforced by a desire to be associated with the "modern." And officials in developing countries have little choice but to try to implement the external advice. In time, all concerned become invested in the "reform," emotionally and professionally, and the triangle becomes self-perpetuating.

There is nothing necessarily conspiratorial about this dynamic. Indeed, in many cases the consulting firms counsel reforms they believe to be desirable; the aid agency staff finance the provision of the advice because they view it as consistent with the objectives of the aid; and the local officials accept it either because they believe it is in the interest of their country's development, or because they wish for reasons of national pride to import the latest thing.

As usual, the core of the problem is found in the incentives framework. Understandably, consulting firms look to the next contract and thus lean toward recommending the kind of complex systems that can only be implemented with their continuing involvement. Aid staff are subject to their agency pressure to lend and have little incentive to do the extensive homework needed to identify the right consultants and to monitor their advice. And country officials depend on cooperation with the aid agencies to gain bureaucratic influence or, in many cases, receive additional compensation in a variety of ways.

But the damage is still done. When the "reform" fails to produce the expected results, the consultants blame their local counterparts, aid agency staff blame the consultants and the government's "lack of ownership," the government blames the aid agency and the consultants; and everyone blames the limited local capacity—with nary a thought to the plausible explanation that the capacity problems were caused by the overambitious reform itself. Because capacity is inherently relative to the complexity of the tasks the system is asked to perform, pushing complex new budgeting practices on to a simpler but tolerably functioning system creates capacity constraints where none may have existed. (In some cases, this is a deliberate tactic to assure that the reform cannot be carried out without the continued participation of its proponents. Scott Adams' cartoon *Dilbert* has a "consultick" character, who gives advice that cannot be implemented without him, burrows into the client's wallet, sucks the cash and never leaves.) This is not development assistance; it is development sabotage.

The dynamic is difficult to resist, owing to the strength and convergence of the interests involved, but it is possible to contain the damage by improving consultants' selection and creating contestability. For example:

- Consulting firms should be chosen for their familiarity with different PFM systems and practices in countries in diverse circumstances—the outcomes of their previous assignments should be checked, and references should be requested from other governments or organizations for which they have worked.
- A government can set up a pool of experts "on call" to take a look at major innovations suggested and give their advice, for which they can be held accountable in due course.
- The internal quality assurance mechanisms in the major international organizations should be given real muscle and systematically include independent outsiders.
- Foreign consultants and aid staff should be handcuffed to knowledgeable local persons who can explain to them the facts of local politics and society.
- A developing country government could declare a "reform timeout," to analyze the actual benefits and costs brought about by each of the major PFM reforms attempted during the previous years, and then adjust as the evidence suggests.

A Concluding Word

The juggernaut of technocratic delusion is still chugging along in the developing world. Many observers and most participants individually agree on the waste it can cause, but none seem to have the power to stop it.

If all the technocratic-oriented PFM reforms had produced demonstrable significant improvements in budgetary processes and outcomes of low-income countries, we would be having a different debate. But the only extant reliable assessments offer scant evidence of such improvements, rather the reverse. And so, the best conclusion for this chapter is a simple piece of advice I have been giving for three decades to governments of developing countries:

When you hear "best practice," run.

Annex 1: Average Scores on Selected PEFA Indicators, Major Regions, 2007–10 and 2012–15

	Africa			
Indicator		*2007–10*	*2012–15*	*Average 2007–15*
PI-2	Composition of expenditure outturn compared with original budget	2.13	1.83	1.98
PI-3	Aggregate revenue outturn compared with original approved budget	3.06	2.31	2.69
PI-7	Extent of unreported government operations	2.36	1.79	2.07
PI-16	Predictability in the availability of funds for expenditure commitments	2.11	1.94	2.02
PI-19	Competition, value for money, and controls in procurement	2.20	2.24	2.22
D-3	Proportion of aid that is managed by use of national procedures	1.21	1.29	1.25
No. of countries 17				

(Continued)

Annex 1: (continued)

East Asia and Pacific		2007–10	2012–15	Average 2007–15
Indicator		*2007–10*	*2012–15*	*Average 2007–15*
PI-2	Composition of expenditure outturn compared with original budget	1.75	1.98	1.86
PI-3	Aggregate revenue outturn compared with original approved budget	3.75	3.00	3.38
PI-7	Extent of unreported government operations	2.43	1.98	2.20
PI-16	Predictability in the availability of funds for expenditure commitments	1.80	2.55	2.18
PI-19	Competition, value for money, and controls in procurement	2.08	1.73	1.90
D-3	Proportion of aid that is managed by use of national procedures	1.25	1.75	1.50

No. of countries   4

Europe and Central Asia		2007–10	2012–15	Average 2007–15
Indicator		*2007–10*	*2012–15*	*Average 2007–15*
PI-2	Composition of expenditure outturn compared with original budget	2.73	2.79	2.76
PI-3	Aggregate revenue outturn compared with original approved budget	4.00	3.00	3.50
PI-7	Extent of unreported government operations	2.44	2.61	2.53
PI-16	Predictability in the availability of funds for expenditure commitments	2.65	2.89	2.77
PI-19	Competition, value for money, and controls in procurement	2.10	2.75	2.42
D-3	Proportion of aid that is managed by use of national procedures	1.00	1.60	1.30

No. of countries   11

Latin America and Caribbean		2007–10	2012–15	Average 2007–15
Indicator		*2007–10*	*2012–15*	*Average 2007–15*
PI-2	Composition of expenditure outturn compared with original budget	2.4	2.44	2.42
PI-3	Aggregate revenue outturn compared with original approved budget	3.06	3.00	3.03
PI-7	Extent of unreported government operations	2.48	2.48	2.48
PI-16	Predictability in the availability of funds for expenditure commitments	2.10	2.50	2.30
PI-19	Competition, value for money, and controls in procurement	2.23	1.98	2.10
D-3	Proportion of aid that is managed by use of national procedures	1.20	2.00	1.60

No. of countries   5

Annex 1: (continued)

Indicator		South Asia		
		2007–10	2012–15	Average 2007–15
PI-2	Composition of expenditure outturn compared with original budget	2.00	1.97	1.98
PI-3	Aggregate revenue outturn compared with original approved budget	4.00	3.00	3.50
PI-7	Extent of unreported government operations	2.20	1.80	2.25
PI-16	Predictability in the availability of funds for expenditure commitments	2.53	2.63	2.58
PI-19	Competition, value for money, and controls in procurement	2.43	2.53	2.48
D-3	Proportion of aid that is managed by use of national procedures	1.33	1.33	1.33
No of countries 3				

Annex 2: List of "Basic" Requirements of Expenditure Management

Budget Coverage

- At least half of all government expenditure included in the annual budget.
- Inclusion in the budget documentation of all revenues and expenditures of extrabudgetary operations.
- A uniform expenditure classification system covering all government expenditures.

Multiyear Perspective

- A set of medium-term macroeconomic projections, even if highly aggregated, showing the interrelationships among the balance of payments, the fiscal accounts, real sector developments and the monetary accounts.
- Within the above, a medium-term fiscal framework with aggregate estimates of economic categories of expenditure.
- An estimate of the total medium-term cost of completing the major investment projects.

Public Investment

- Put in place procedures against the conception of "white elephant" projects, with early involvement of high-level policy-makers.
- Assure that very large projects are appraised in reasonable detail.
- Provisions to prevent launching a large project unless financing is reasonably assured and it is ready for implementation.

Budget Preparation

- Build good budgeting habits, by issuing timely budget instructions, enforcing the budget preparation timetable and providing adequate time for debate in legislature.
- Include in the budget instructions aggregate and ministerial spending "ceilings," even if soft and only indicative at first.

- Assure that the ministry of finance has clear authority and adequate capacity.
- Assure some budgeting capacity in the largest spending ministries.
- Assure that subsidies and transfers have clear legal basis.
- Assure the correctness of the payroll, establish an employee database and provisions for its maintenance and build strong safeguards against fraud and error.

Budget Execution

Given a realistic budget to begin with, the following measures are basic to ensure conformity with the budget and control of expenditure:

- Formulate a cash plan, even if rudimentary, consistent with the budget.
- Centralize cash balances, and close separate ministries' bank accounts.
- Introduce controls at each stage of expenditure (commitment, verification and payment), at first with direct oversight by the ministry of finance.
- Centralize monitoring of financial transactions.
- Minimize sole-source procurement and progressively move to competitive bidding, beginning with limited national competitive bidding.
- Prohibit all government borrowing without ministry of finance approval.
- Establish and maintain an accurate debt database, and a system for timely tracking of borrowings and repayments.
- Introduce an inspection function (not internal audit) in the main spending ministries.

Accounting and Reporting

- Assure that cash-based accounts are prepared on a timely basis.
- Prepare regular reports on debt.
- Require extrabudgetary funds to report their transactions on the basis of the uniform expenditure classification.
- Record loan guarantees individually, including amounts and beneficiaries.
- Prepare and publish the basic financial statements.

External audit

Assure that the external audit entity has:

- Freedom of access to public financial information.
- Predictable funding and adequate minimum internal capacity.
- Full management and operational autonomy. (The external auditor should report to the legislature. Initially, however, external audit might still function well even if it is within the executive branch.)

Relations with subnational governments

Chapter 14 discusses in detail the issues of budgeting at subnational government level. The basic measures at central level include:

- Ensure clear and legally grounded assignment of expenditure responsibilities.
- Require central ministry of finance approval for SNG borrowing.
- Allow flexibility to local government in implementing central mandates.

- Assure the effective audit of subnational government activity.
- Assure respect for governance and at least minimum representativeness of the organs of subnational government.

Notes

1 When a country has significant disagreements with the PEFA assessment, it can refuse to agree to publication and the report remains confidential. However, this generates a presumption that serious problems have been identified—which creates a negative image with adverse consequences. Countries are therefore under practical pressure to give ground and allow publication, even when the government considers that the report is incorrect in material ways.
2 The Middle East and North Africa region is not included. While PEFA assessments were done in most countries of the region, only two countries had published assessments for both periods.
3 For example, more public spending on health reduces child mortality only where governance is good (Wagstaff and Claeson, 2004). Similarly, investing in roads in Africa does not *in itself* reduce transport costs in a lasting manner in the presence of governance and regulatory problems. Instead, the elimination of barriers to entry in road transport, by closing corruption opportunities, can lead to major reductions in transport costs without additional investment in maintenance or construction, as in Rwanda (Teravaninthron and Raballand, 2008).
4 Andrews (2006) criticizes the "basics first" approach in his treatment of performance budgeting. The critique is correct but superfluous, because performance budgeting is way beyond a "basic" reform.
5 There are a few exceptions, for example a move from cash payment to payment by check is almost invariably beneficial in and of itself—see Chapter 8.

Bibliography

Allen, R., S. Schiavo-Campo and T. C. Garrity, 2004. *Assessing and Reforming Public Financial Management: A New Approach*. Washington, DC: The World Bank.

Andrews, Matt, 2006. "Beyond 'Best Practice' and 'Basics First' in Adopting Performance Budgeting Reforms," *Public Administration and Development*, 26(2), 147–61.

——, 2013. *The Limits of Institutional Reform in Development: Changing Rules for Realistic Solutions*. New York: Cambridge University Press.

Beschel, Robert and Mark Ahern, 2012. *Public Financial Management Reform in the Middle East and North Africa*. Washington, DC: The World Bank.

Brooke, Peter, 2003. *Study of Measures Used to Address Weaknesses in Public Financial Management Systems in the Context of Policy Based Support*. London: Bannock Consulting.

Cady, S. H., J. Jacobs, R. Koller and J. Spalding, 2014. "The Change Formula: Myth, Legend, or Lore," *OD Practitioner*, 46(3), 32–9.

Diamond, Jack, 2006. "Budget System Reform in Emerging Economies," *Occasional Paper No. 245*. Washington, DC: IMF.

——, 2013. *Good Practice Note on Sequencing PFM Reforms*. IMF and European Commission. Washington, DC: PEFA.

McFerson, Hazel, 2007. "Transplants as Legal Colonization," in David S. Clark, ed., *Encyclopedia of Law and Society: American and Global Perspectives*. Thousand Oaks, CA: Sage.

Peterson, Stephen, 2015. *Public Finance and Economic Growth in Developing Countries: Lessons from Ethiopia's Reforms*. New York: Routledge.

Savoie, Donald, 1995. "What is Wrong with the New Public Management?" *Canadian Public Administration*, 38(1), 112–21.

Schiavo-Campo, S. and Hazel McFerson, 2008. *Public Management in Global Perspective*. Armonk, NY: M. E. Sharpe.

Schick, Allen, 1966. "The Road to PBB: the Stages of Budget Reform," *Public Administration Review*, 26(4), 243–58.

——, 1998. "Why Most Developing Countries Should Not Try New Zealand Reforms," *World Bank Research Observer*, 13(1), 123–31.

——, 2012. "Basics First is Best Practice!" Available online at blog-pfm.imf.org/pfmblog/2012/07 [accessed November 9, 2016].

Teravaninthron, S. and G. Raballand, 2008. *Transport Process and Costs in Africa: A Review of the Main International Corridors*. Washington, DC: The World Bank.

Twain, Mark, 1897 [1968]. *Following the Equator*. New York: Harper Collins.

Wagstaff, A. and M. Claeson, 2004. *The Millennium Development Goals for Health: Rising to the Challenges*. Washington, DC: The World Bank.

Wong, C., 2016. "Budget Reform in China: Progress and Prospects in the Xi Jinping Era," *OECD Journal on Budgeting*, 15(3), 27–36.

World Bank, 1989. *Madagascar: Public Expenditure, Adjustment and Growth*. Washington, DC: The World Bank.

Part V

Selected Special Topics in Public Financial Management

14 Fiscal Decentralization and Budgeting at Subnational Government Level

Unity to be real must stand strain without breaking.

(Gandhi)

Introduction

The geographic articulation of the powers of the state has been a central issue throughout history—in the African empires of Songhai and Great Zimbabwe as in the days of the Ch'in Dynasty in China, of Ramses the Great in Egypt or of Octavian Augustus in Rome. A major aspect of the issue is the territorial distribution of the tax burden and of the benefits from public expenditure. For large states, success in managing the collection of revenues and controlling expenditure in the provinces and localities has been a key to their prosperity and survival. For example, the weakening of the Ottoman Empire from the eighteenth century was associated largely with the increasing reliance on "tax farming" (subcontracting the collection of taxes to private companies), which caused an erosion of state legitimacy and a loss of central executive power.

After providing a bird's eye view of decentralization, this chapter reviews the major public expenditure management issues at levels of subnational government (SNG); how SNG budgeting is influenced by the features and timing of the national budget process; the fiscal relationship between central and subnational governments; and the methods of controlling SNG borrowing and mitigating fiscal risk from SNG operations. The overarching lesson of experience is that budgeting reforms in SNG should not take place in isolation, but should be designed as part and parcel of the objective of strengthening public expenditure management in the country as a whole.

Levels of Government

Three levels of government normally exist in any country: the "first tier" of central government; the "second tier" of intermediate government—state (in a federal system) or provincial governments; and the "third tier" of local government—county, district and municipalities. In several countries there is also a "fourth tier," composed of various forms of village government in rural areas and submunicipal organizations in cities, such as neighborhood associations. This fourth tier can be especially important in developing countries, as it is directly related to the delivery of the most basic services and to the informal resolution of disputes and conflict management. (The "village courts" set up for local reconciliation in the aftermath of the genocide in Rwanda are an excellent example.) The resources of the fourth tier are mostly in-kind and the management arrangements are very simple. Although the fourth tier will not be discussed further, national or state actions should take care not to harm its effectiveness. The most important contribution of formal government entities to the fourth-tier organizations is to provide physical protection against external threats and otherwise leave them to manage their own affairs (subject to human rights and minority protections).[1]

The design and content of the public financial management system depends largely on the structure of the country. In a federal country, such as Australia, the legal framework enables the federal government to achieve national goals while preserving a great deal of subnational government autonomy. In a unitary government, such as Japan, SNGs are integral parts of the national system and their role is subordinate to the central government. In quasi-federal countries such as India, the states have substantial economic and fiscal autonomy but in emergencies their management can be taken over by the central government. Whatever the structure of the state, the objective is the effectiveness of PFM for the country as a whole. (Recall that the Code of Fiscal Transparency calls for fiscal targets to be defined for "general government," that is, for all levels of government.) To place in context the discussion of expenditure management in SNG, the main issues of decentralization are addressed next.

Degrees of Decentralization: Deconcentration, Delegation, Devolution

The degrees of "decentralization" differ according to the extent of autonomy of the SNG entities, ranging from simple relocation of a few central government employees all the way to permanent assignment of power and authority to the subnational government level:

- *Deconcentration* partly shifts the management workload from central government to subordinate field staff in the regions, provinces or districts. Deconcentration is an efficiency measure internal to central government, and does not involve a downward transfer of decision-making authority from the national level. It can improve efficiency, but also creates a double responsibility of the employees to the local government as well as to their bosses in the capital. Thus, for deconcentration to be effective, responsibilities should be clear and the central government should give its staff in the field some latitude to make adjustments to suit local conditions.
- Through *delegation*, central government gives the SNG entity broad authority to implement decisions in specified areas without the direct supervision of central ministries. (As implicit in the term, delegation is revocable.)
- *Devolution* carries the highest decision-making independence and involves permanent assignment of certain functions to SNGs, which can recruit their own staff, raise revenues and interact reciprocally with other units in the overall government system of which they are a part. Devolution transfers to the SNG both policy formulation and decision-making authority, subject only to basic national standards (e.g., non-discrimination).

The Weight of History and the Legacy of Colonialism

To understand why subnational levels of government have greater or lesser power and institutional capacity one needs to consider the country's history. In some countries, for example Italy with its city-states, local government units were sovereign for centuries and the local habits of government and administration were well-rooted long before the country in its present form was constituted in 1860. Not surprisingly, local governance regionally tends to be much better than in the country as a whole. In France, the historical drive to bring and keep together the various components of the state led to a heavily centralized system, and institutions are weaker in the periphery. Most developed countries have a long historical experience of gradual evolution of internal spatial change. Not so ex-colonized developing countries, where the spatial divisions were determined largely by the economic interests of the former colonizing power.

The historical experience differs in different regions. In Africa, colonialism imposed artificial state boundaries—set externally by the scramble for territory among western powers, and internally by the colonial objectives of resource exploitation and maintenance of control. After independence, this heritage made it difficult to establish links among economic activities and ethnic groups, and has been inimical to the formation of a national identity. The urban elites who had acted as intermediaries for the former colonial power dominated the political landscape in the post-colonial era and thus, in general, post-independence policies had a strong anti-rural and centralizing bias. Even in countries where the original post-independence leaders were replaced—by military coups and other means—the urban orientation persisted and economic policies were strongly pro-industry and pro-city. The centralization of political and economic power was intensified by the central planning prevalent in the 1960s and 1970s. As one consequence, subnational government has remained extremely weak in most of the continent.

There are exceptions. There were no local intermediaries in the former Portuguese colonies of Angola and Mozambique, where virtually every formal job was filled by Portuguese. When most of them departed suddenly in 1975, following the revolution in Portugal that deposed the dictatorship of Antonio Salazar, they left behind not a local elite but a total administrative vacuum. (It was a remarkable achievement in both countries, and especially in Mozambique, to have built a post-colonial local administration in a short time and virtually from scratch.[2])

Similarly, at independence in 1960 the former Belgian Congo had a grand total of three Congolese university graduates, since the Belgians fully expected to continue controlling the territory by indirect means. The murder of the elected Prime Minister Patrice Lumumba was followed by 30 years of kleptocracy and 25 years of chaos and violent conflict. (The Congolese tragedy extends all the way back to the brutal private regime of Belgian King Leopold II in the late 1800s. Paradoxically known as the "Congo Free State," Leopold's immense personal domain was set on a foundation of systematic atrocity and deliberate terrorizing of the population in order to force it to collect ivory and, later, rubber for the world market.[3])

There are positive exceptions, as well. Tanzania's President Julius Nyerere—who was educated first at Makerere University in Uganda (then a first-rate institution, viewed by the Imperial College in London as its equal in quality), and then at the University of Edinburgh where he earned a Master's degree (only the second African to obtain a university degree outside Africa)—developed policies that were deliberately inclusive of the countryside, with substantial autonomy given to local governments.[4] Such policies, as well as his insistence on Kiswahili as the unifying national language, were a key factor of Nyerere's success in turning Tanzania from an assemblage of ethnic groups into a nation—one of the few exceptions in Africa in this respect.

The situation was different in Asia, where the end of colonialism generally led to the emergence of political leaders from the more populated rural areas. Some national political theorists in the 1960s also fueled rural fears about falling prices for agricultural products, identified rural life with tradition and genuine nationalism, and created the myth of the parasitic role of cities. (The murderous pathology of the Khmer Rouge regime in 1970s Cambodia is the most extreme example.[5]) Consequently, the intermediate and local levels of government acquired greater responsibility and authority and economic policies were slanted toward rural interests.

In Latin America, the centralized system of colonial exploitation of minerals coexisted with the power of large colonial planters in outlying areas of the colonies, while vast tracts of the continent were untouched owing to their geographic remoteness. In the latter part of the twentieth century, fiscal and administrative decentralization grew out of democratization movements, by which elected governments operating under new constitutions replaced autocratic central regimes in most countries of the continent. The stronger democratic processes at intermediate and municipal levels brought new power to indigenous groups which, in turn, fed back into contributing to more accountable national government.

Rationale, Advantages and Costs of Decentralization

The Political Rationale

Much decentralization was associated with broader political developments. In Latin America, as noted, decentralization grew out of democratization movements in the 1980s and 1990s. In parts of Africa, regionalism and ethnicity gave rise to somewhat greater local participation. (Regrettably, regionalism, whether ethnic or religious, has also led to persistent civil conflict in many countries.) In continental Europe, the growing unresponsiveness of the central government apparatus fueled a widespread push in many countries toward greater regional and local control of service delivery and, at Europe-wide level, strong centripetal forces are shaking the European Union, bolstered by the referendum on Britain's exit ("Brexit") from the Union.

In some cases, decentralization has been a strategy to keep the country united. For example, political and ethnic cleavages and the long civil wars in Mozambique or Uganda paved the way for the granting of greater autonomy to all localities, or the forging of "asymmetrical federations" (by which some SNGs have more powers and autonomy than the others.) Ethnic conflicts have also exerted strong pressure for decentralization in Sri Lanka, Indonesia and the Philippines. In Indonesia, previously governed by autocratic central regimes, decentralization came to be seen as the natural alternative to repressive central authority.

Other countries have broken up. The breakup of Czechoslovakia was peaceful and that of the former Soviet Union almost so, but national divorces are more often bloody and messy, as shown by the civil wars in the former Yugoslavia and Sudan.[6]

The Economic Rationale: Oates' Theorem and the Subsidiarity Principle

The literature sets out a clear economic rationale for decentralization. It is argued that the allocative efficiency of public resources can be raised if expenditure decisions are made at lower government levels, which are supposedly more responsive to local demands than a remote central administration. This closer nexus between expenditure decisions and their beneficiaries also provides opportunities for more efficient use of public resources. From a pure efficiency standpoint, the rule governing the geographic articulation of government services is provided by Oates' "decentralization theorem": a public service should be provided by the government jurisdiction that controls the smallest geographic area that would internalize both the benefits and the costs of providing the service (Oates, 1972). The theorem has a strong proof but is intuitive as well: if residents of a particular area receive all the benefits from a particular service they should pay for all the costs of providing it. For example, trash collection in a mountain village should be provided and paid for by the village authorities because only the inhabitants benefit if the trash is collected and suffer if it is not. In reality, this test is tough to set up and satisfy, in part because technology changes and people's consumption habits are not static, and in part because people move around. While Oates' decentralization theorem remains the conceptual anchor, a more practical criterion is needed.

Such a practical criterion is found in the principle of "subsidiarity." According to this principle, spending, taxing and regulatory functions should be exercised by lower levels of government unless a convincing case can be made for assigning them to higher levels of government.[7] This turns the cumbersome analytical challenge of the Oates theorem into a simple burden-of-proof test—which is better suited to decisions that are inherently political.

The principle of subsidiarity is embedded in the US Constitution, which gives states all powers not reserved for the federal government (except for the federal power to regulate any state action which can be construed to materially affect interstate commerce). However, subsidiarity does not apply *within* states, which operate on the opposite *ultra vires* principle, i.e., reserving all powers except those explicitly delegated to counties and other local government. (This is referred to as the Dillon Rule, formulated in 1872 by federal judge John F. Dillon.) The logic of this differentiated approach is that the founding blocks of the US political system are the individual states. Thus, just as the United States was formed by the individual states (the former separate colonies), which freely decided to cede specific powers *up* to the federal government, substate government units are also creatures of each state, which consequently decides what specific powers to delegate *down* to them.

Subsidiarity was also introduced in the Catholic Church by Pope Leo XIII in 1891, in response to a plea for expanding the authority of bishops and parish priests. In contemporary times, the principle of subsidiarity has been adopted by the European Union, incorporated as "fiscal decentralization" in the Single Europe Act of 1987, and formally adopted in 1993.

The Potential Advantages of Decentralization

Decentralization can bring major political and economic benefits, but is never a panacea and can neither remedy governance problems nor quickly improve PFM systems. The early optimistic view by Rondinelli and Nellis (1986) was rebalanced later by Prud'homme (1995) and Tanzi (2001)—among many others. In any case, the choice is not binary: the right question is not whether to decentralize, but what to decentralize, to whom, how, when and with what resources.

Subnational government expenditures as a percentage of total public expenditures have increased over the past two decades. In principle, decentralization of both expenditure authority and revenues can strengthen accountability to its citizens, and reduce the "democracy deficit" that exists in many countries. In practice, the situation differs in different countries. The potential gains of decentralization are:

* Decentralization may create opportunities for more accountable government. Residents who participate in decisions can more easily monitor and evaluate government's compliance with the decisions made.
* Decentralization may lead to greater transparency. Policy-making and implementation of projects can be known even to the residents in the remotest areas.
* Decentralizing fiscal powers to SNGs can ease the financial strain on the central government since subnational governments can more readily mobilize funds by collecting fees and charges for the services they provide. (Unfortunately, this also generates the temptation to download expenditure responsibilities to subnational governments without giving them the authority or capacity to raise the required resources.)
* Greater closeness to service users may open up public participation in government decision-making, resulting in: more flexible administration, since the government can tailor its services to the needs of the various groups; more effective administration, as local leaders can better locate services and facilities within communities; and greater political stability and national unity, as civil society organizations are given a stake in maintaining the political system. For an illustration of the latter, see Box 14.1.

Box 14.1 Rural Community Participation: Northeast Brazil in the 1990s

The chronic poverty in northeast Brazil was caused partly by the weak resource base in the region and the virtual absence of a functioning rural financial system for the poor. Efforts to reduce rural poverty in the 1980s cost the central government large sums with little impact. In mid-1993, the Brazilian federal and state governments reformulated the poverty intervention programs and made the projects community-based, with funds going directly to community associations to finance small-scale subprojects they had identified themselves. Unlike previous rural development programs, the reformulated program also addressed institutional issues such as community organization and participation, transparency in decision-making and training and technical assistance to municipalities.

   The results were a general improvement in the living conditions of the rural poor and an increase in productivity and employment in the region. In addition to improved project design, what contributed to these positive outcomes were the increased participation by residents in subproject selection and execution, the transparency in project design and implementation, and the decentralization of fiscal and investment decision-making to state and local governments.

Source: Parker et al. (1995).

The Potential Costs and Risks of Decentralization

Decentralization can also carry costs and risks, which are almost the mirror image of the advantages (see Ter-Minassian, 1997, and Bahl, 1999):

- It can entail the loss of scale economies and generate unnecessary duplication and underemployment of staff and equipment.
- It can create coordination problems and conflict where none existed, and may subvert the overall macroeconomic objectives of the central government. More importantly, decentralization can jeopardize the civil and social rights of certain minorities, and, in time, contribute to national disintegration.[8] Where resource endowments and capacities are uneven, decentralization may deepen regional inequalities.
- The potential efficiency gains from decentralization can be undermined by institutional constraints: when subnational governments have weaker capacity than central government, services may be delivered less efficiently.
- Most importantly, decentralization can worsen governance in the country as a whole, in cases where the quality of governance is lower and corruption higher at local levels than at national level. Local autocrats are worse than central bureaucrats.

The Legal Framework for Decentralization

International Diversity of Structures

Normally, the country's constitution embodies the outline of decentralization, i.e., the territorial divisions, the broad responsibilities of different levels of government, the major institutions at central and subnational levels and the process by which these can be amended. The powers of each level of subnational government should be specified by law. It is highly inadvisable, however, to codify into law the local informal norms and customs: *when codified, custom loses its natural capacity to adapt to change.* Some functions are amenable to shared responsibility between national and subnational government, but the number of these functions should be limited, to avoid turf fights and loose accountability.

In developing countries, legal provisions on SNGs differ substantially between regions. In Africa, they cover the entire range from strong centralization to substantial devolution. South Africa, Uganda and Tanzania exemplify a legal framework that empowers local government and encourages and in some cases prescribes civic participation. In South Africa, the post-apartheid constitution defines the powers of local government, and calls on local governments to give priority to the basic needs of the community. Tanzania was among the first countries to recognize the role of subnational government and the importance of civic participation, which has been instrumental in forging a civic attachment to the Tanzanian state. In Kenya, a major change took place in 2010 following the communal violence during the 2007 presidential elections, with the approval of the new constitution which specifically sets out the fundamental principles of local self-governance and public participation. At the other extreme are Ethiopia's centralized system and Zimbabwe, where the constitution does not even recognize local government and all bylaws of local councils must be approved by the central minister.

In Asia, although most countries do not carry the handicap of arbitrary colonial boundaries, severe tensions continue between the aspirations for local autonomy and the drive to preserve central control. In Myanmar, ethnic differences have been repressed for decades by a brutal and corrupt military oligarchy, and it is not yet clear that the democratic opening of 2011 will lead to a permanent end to the repression. In Indonesia, hopeful signs have emerged with the settlement of the autonomy claims of the people of Aceh province (tragically, it took the devastating tsunami of 2005 to produce such a settlement), and in the Philippines with a halting process for greater autonomy in the Muslim parts of the island of Mindanao (see Schiavo-Campo and Judd, 2005). However, new conflicts have surfaced in Thailand with the Muslim population of the south of the country, and Sri Lanka's centralized state has been unable to manage ethnic and religious tensions which produced civil conflict for two decades, followed by an intense war and even more centralization. In India, the unique combination of central interventionism and extreme localism is overlaid by the underlying tension between Hindus and Muslims, and among Hindus between higher and lower castes.

The accommodation of ethnic pluralism within a unified state will remain the core challenge in multiethnic societies for years to come. In countries affected by internal conflict or where central government has failed to meet its responsibilities to the entire population, there is no practical alternative to channeling some power and resources directly to the local communities.

Intergovernmental Coordination

The challenge of effective intergovernmental relations is to achieve balance: balance between the autonomy of subnational units and necessary central control; balance between promoting efficiency and protecting equity; and balance between ensuring responsiveness and assuring sustainability. In Australia, for instance, the Council of Australian Governments gathers together federal and state ministers, as well as presidents of local government associations; central governments in Scandinavian countries regularly consult local associations on fiscal and other legislation affecting local authorities. Again, post-apartheid South Africa is an encouraging example of good vertical coordination, enshrined as a constitutional principle (see Box 14.2).

Box 14.2 Cooperative Intergovernmental Relations in South Africa

The principle of cooperative governance is articulated in chapter 3 of the South African Constitution and has proven to be a cornerstone of intergovernmental relations. Where government functions are a shared responsibility of national and provincial government, as in the social services, the national government provides the policy framework while the provinces are responsible for delivery of services. This division of responsibilities, combined with the considerable economic disparities across provinces, requires strong coordination to ensure that expenditure planning is aligned with policy goals and to promote equity in social services access.

To facilitate this coordination, each of the major government sectors has a policy forum comprising the competent national and provincial ministers. Joint meetings are also held between the finance forum and individual sector forums to review the policy issues in light of the budget constraints. These joint meetings enhance the understanding of the cost of policy choices and encourage the development of alternative methods of delivering services.

The policy forums for finance, education, health, welfare and transport are supported by technical committees composed of national and provincial officials. These committees deal with policy implementation, developing coherent policy within sectors, setting norms and standards for service delivery, evaluating the affordability of policy choices and evaluating other issues of a technical nature. A key task of the technical committees is to develop service delivery indicators against which to measure government performance.

Source: Laura Walker, personal communication, 2000.

Conversely, lack of constructive interaction can damage well-designed national policies, as in Indonesia where the central ministries formulated and implemented their own decentralization policies with very little discussion among themselves or with local governments, leading to conflict, inefficiency and duplication (see Box 14.3).

Approaches to Defining Subnational Territory

There are several approaches to subdividing the territory of the country into subnational government entities—with different implications for budgeting at SNG levels.

Physical Approach

The intuitive approach to dividing the national territory is on the basis of the physical features of regions within the country—especially concerning such matters as water supply, land drainage, erosion control, irrigation, recreation, etc. In the UK, for example, each of ten water authorities is responsible in its area for the entire range of functions connected with water usage—and the geographic boundaries of each water authority are determined by the natural water catchment areas. Another example of an administrative structure based on geographical features is the Tennessee Valley Authority in the United States, probably the best instance of a multipurpose development authority based on a watershed area. Physical geography can also offer an appropriate basis for economic and social planning, especially if the lives of the inhabitants are tied closely to the exploitation

---

Box 14.3 Poorly Coordinated Decentralization in Post-Dictatorship Indonesia

The federal constitution of Indonesia at independence was quickly replaced by a unitary and strongly centralized system. A legal framework for decentralization established in 1979 was in fact a dead letter and the Indonesian state remained highly centralized. In 1999, after the fall of the Suharto regime, the Indonesian Parliament passed two laws to replace the earlier legal framework. The Regional Law revised the assignment of functions and roles of institutions at all levels of government, and the Fiscal Law defined the financing for devolution, deconcentration and co-administration of government functions. These laws have improved the statutory framework, although there were initial implementation problems that hampered the transition from a centralized to a decentralized administration.

Working groups were formed to draft implementing regulations and to plan and monitor the implementation process. However, the activities of the groups were not coordinated because of lack of interaction among the ministries, and duplication of regulations and unnecessary competition among the concerned ministries resulted. The Ministry of Home Affairs claimed that 30 additional decrees were needed to support the Regional Law, and drafted several, while the Ministry of Finance separately drafted implementing regulations to support the Fiscal Law. Much progress has been made since then, but much remains to be done for Indonesia to work as a fully decentralized system, and a live debate continues on whether the country should return to a fully federal system. (As of 2016, the province of Aceh is the only fully autonomous one.)

Source: Claudia Buentjen, personal communication (1999) and author.

---

of natural resources—for example, in the case of tribal people living in a specific forest area, as in the Indian state of Odisha. When the natural characteristics are dominant, as a valley or a defined coastal area or a mountain range, geography can provide a good basis for administrative divisions. However, space is a continuum and any division of it is inherently arbitrary. Other criteria are also needed.

Management Approach

The management approach aims at dividing territory into "manageable" parts according to how government work can best be handled. The number and location of field offices are decided based on an optimum span of control by headquarters or on the workload appropriate for a field office. In the assignment of responsibilities to subnational government entities, management and capacity constraints are taken into account as much as geographic features.

Community Approach

By the community approach, subnational government boundaries should correspond to the areas whose inhabitants manifest common needs interdependence. This approach involves identifying urban centers and their "natural" hinterlands, with the interdependence between city and hinterland indicated mainly by the number of regional inhabitants employed in the city's banks, shops, schools, hospitals, newspapers, and so on. Sometimes also known as the "central town" concept, the approach has been applied notably in Belgium, Germany, Sweden and France, where strong links were built between urban centers and the corresponding hinterlands.

The community approach is useful for the design of traffic management, highway development and public transport. If done well, the definition of subnational government boundaries on this basis not only "internalizes" the costs and benefits of local government, but also produces a more equitable distribution of services in the (interdependent) community. The approach can be very useful when it grows organically from the bottom up, but is likely to lead only to substantial waste when it is misapplied as a top-down government attempt at creating regional "growth poles" from scratch—as in the approach of the French economist François Perroux, popular in the 1950s.[9] The message is simple: do take into account the existing interdependence between city and surrounding area, but do not try to manufacture it by government policy.

Social and Ethnic Approach

The territorial structure of government may include socially distinct regions based on history, ethnicity, culture, religion, language or some combination. The social/ethnic approach is especially useful when some of the constituent regions of the country have a sense of separate identity. In extreme cases, when faced with centrifugal tendencies, redrawing subnational boundaries and reshuffling the distribution of powers to reflect ethnic identities may become necessary for the survival of the unified state. Iraq offers the most dramatic contemporary illustration. For centuries comprising different provinces within the vast Ottoman Empire, "Iraq" was in large measure an artificial creation of Franco-British colonialism in 1920 and was kept together after independence mainly by repression from successive central governments in Baghdad. After the American invasion in 2003 and the fall of the Saddam Hussein regime, the country faced the extremely delicate challenge of accommodating within a single state the previously repressed aspirations of the three very different Kurdish, Sunni and Shi'a communities (all three in turn segmented among different sects, tribes or clans). With the war in Syria, the extreme and ultra-violent ISIS, the proxy conflict throughout the region between Iran and Saudi Arabia, and the geopolitical complications from Turkish, Russian and American involvement, the shape of an eventual settlement is wholly unclear. The only certainty is protracted conflict and vast human suffering in most of the Middle East.

Functional Approach: What Belongs Where?

The functional approach matches area to function by identifying the government functions and delimiting the geographic boundaries within which the functions are to be performed. In this approach, the hierarchy of geographic areas corresponds to the scale of operations necessary for the optimum performance of the general government. Here, too, there are difficulties. Aside from the problem that the different functions may produce overlapping boundaries, it is impossible to objectively restrict the "natural" geographic area of certain functions such as health, housing or the environment. The functional assignment remains the primary approach, but needs to be complemented by other considerations.[10]

Moreover, although many Western European countries (e.g., Denmark, Germany and Sweden) have reduced the number of their municipalities through mergers, there is no conclusive evidence that operating in larger jurisdictions is necessarily more efficient than operating in smaller ones. Scale economies constantly change with changes in technology, and exploiting scale economies does not necessarily require an administrative entity of "optimum" size, because they can also be achieved by joint service agreements and by subcontracting to the larger entities.

Functions such as defense, foreign affairs, external trade and finance and monetary policy are almost exclusively the responsibility of central government; others, such as water supply, waste management, firefighting, are performed almost exclusively at local level; and responsibility for all other normal state functions is shared in some fashion among the central, intermediate and local levels of government. Policy and standard-setting are done at central level for most services except only for police and municipal services, and are shared with state and local levels for education, roads and parks and recreation. Conversely, local governments are usually responsible for the actual delivery of public services, either on their own or in cooperation with the private sector.

Public Financial Management at Subnational Government Level

General Considerations[11]

Regardless of the political structure of the country, the machinery of public financial management in most SNGs is generally a microcosm of the central or federal machinery, and tends to reflect changes at national level. During the past decades, improvements made in the public expenditure management systems at the central level have found their way, slowly, to the SNG level. The reverse has also occurred on occasion. In the UK and the US, for example, local governments have shown considerable imagination in introducing budgetary innovations.

Size Matters

It is not unusual to see the same analysis applied to SNGs in different countries and circumstances, and there is a striking similarity in the PFM reform prescriptions supported by external aid at SNG level. Yet, the size of the entity and its population are important determinants of the nature of the expenditure management problems. Consider that the smallest state in federal Nigeria has a much larger population than several of the neighboring countries, and the entire population of the Seychelles could easily fit into a residential neighborhood in Manila. It makes no sense to address the budgeting problems of one small archipelago in the Indian Ocean in the same manner as those of the Philippines—yet, analysts and policymakers frequently yield to the temptation to look at all SNG units through the same lens. That said, there are common elements that do not depend on territorial size or population.

The Common Elements

Whether the country is large or small or unitary or federal, all intergovernmental arrangements must define three elements: fiscal assignments (i.e., which level of government collects or distributes what revenues); the division of revenues among levels of government; and rules for negotiated settlements between the various levels of government. Both analysis and policy advice must recognize the distinction between: components of the system that are within the control of the SNG concerned; components over which the SNG has no control; and components over which control is shared between the SNG and the central government.

Fiscal Decentralization

Fiscal decentralization (sometimes called "fiscal federalism") involves the transfer of expenditure and revenue responsibilities from central government to SNGs, and can consist of: tax sharing; joint provision of public services; expansion of local tax revenue; intergovernmental transfers; and local borrowing authority. In addition to controlling SNG borrowing (discussed later), the main principles of effective fiscal decentralization are as follows:

- Each level of government should have clear assigned responsibilities; overlaps and long "concurrent lists" of shared responsibilities should be avoided.[12]
- Fiscal and revenue-sharing arrangements between the central and local governments should be stable. They may be amended from time to time, but renewed bargaining each year should be avoided at all costs.
- Revenue assignment should be fully consistent with expenditure assignment. When new responsibilities are transferred to SNGs, compensatory revenues should be provided (of course, if some responsibilities are removed, transfers to SNGs should be reduced).
- SNGs must receive an early estimate of revenues and grants from the center before preparing their budgets, instead of having to wait for the final central government budget.
- Incentives for efficiency are needed. Central governments often reduce transfers to SNGs when they economize in spending or improve tax collection, thus eliminating all incentive to do so. SNGs must be allowed to benefit from improvements, at least in part.
- "Downloading" the deficit should be avoided, and central government should not pass its problems to SNGs through cuts in transfers or new unfunded expenditure mandates.
- In case of SNG budget overruns or accumulation of arrears, legal sanctions or adjustment measures should be considered, e.g., mandatory expenditure cuts or, in extreme cases, temporarily placing the SNG budgets under the authority of the central government.
- Accounting and financial reporting standards are critical, and SNG budget classification and systems for budget execution and audit should be as in the central government.
- Finally, issues of administrative and financial management capacity at SNG and local level are crucial. Mere lip-service paid to their importance is insufficient, however. Sustainable PFM improvements require an assessment of the realities of administrative and PFM capacity, and should be accompanied by remedial measures (see Box 14.4).

The Special Budgeting Problems of SNGs

In both developed and developing countries fiscal arrangements reflect a growing dependence of subnational governments on the central government. In the United Kingdom, 75 percent of SNG funds are transfers from the central government; in India, central transfers have increased to about 60 percent of the financial resources of the states. The fiscal dependence on the center causes a separation between the funding entity and the entity responsible for providing services, which dilutes accountability for service provision.

The SNG dependence on the center engenders three major budgeting problems: timing, risk and administrative cost. These problems are especially difficult to manage because subnational government entities are normally obliged to balance their budget.[13]

Timing

Budgeting in SNGs is subject to a special timing problem which does not affect central government budgeting. As noted in Chapter 6, good expenditure programming starts with a a reliable forecast of revenue, and budget preparation requires enough time for ministries

Box 14.4 Local Government Capacity

One of the classic objections to decentralization is that local governments are incompetent. Citing statistics on illiterate mayors, crude accounting systems, inadequate facilities and widespread nepotism, critics of decentralization argue that subnational governments are incapable of taking on expanded functions. Even when such criticisms are well-founded, this argument is not as compelling as it may appear at first glance. As a practical matter, when a major public service is decentralized, existing resources and personnel are normally decentralized with it. Thus, when primary education was decentralized in Colombia and Mexico, central government teachers were decentralized at the same time. They became no less or more competent than they had been when employed by the central government. Moreover, capacity can grow over time, and if a function is suitable to be performed at lower government levels efforts should be made to strengthen the local capacity to perform it well—rather than keep the function centralized until a never-arriving future when local capacity will magically become sufficient. Often, capacity limitations are used as political excuses to retain central power and not to decentralize.

However, real problems have emerged when central government employees have refused to move. In Peru, for example, after a decision to decentralize road construction and maintenance, many central government highway engineers chose to retire rather than work in local government. Local staff then proved incapable of taking up the job, which eventually led to the collapse of the initiative and recentralization of road construction and maintenance. Governments can make it somewhat easier for central government employees to transfer to local level by requiring local governments to offer them the same wages and benefits they received as central government employees. But this makes it difficult for local government to adapt wages and benefits to local conditions or to introduce management and personnel reforms, and may generate resentment among less well-paid local personnel. Also, it is never easy to convince or induce people to move with their families from the capital to a peripheral location. Training of local personnel thus emerges as an essential complement of decentralization efforts.

Source: Author.

and spending agencies to prepare their proposed expenditure programs, for the negotiations to follow, and for the legislature to engage in an informed and meaningful debate on the proposed budget. Because a large portion of SNG revenue consists of transfers from the central government, SNG budgeting is subject to special uncertainty in this respect. Even when the transfers are not discretionary but largely rule-based, their actual amount depends on macroeconomic developments and on aggregate resource availability at national level. Hence, the amount of transfers is normally not determined with finality until after the central government budget has been drafted, delaying the preparation of the SNG budget.

When the budget is not approved by the legislature until just before or even after the start of the fiscal year, subnational governments cannot begin the final phase of their own budget preparation until that time and their fiscal "year" is in effect reduced to nine months or less—with adverse effects on efficiency and service delivery. Moreover, when intergovernmental transfers are used as a mechanism of macroeconomic stabilization—increasing them during recessions and reducing them during boom periods—a further element of uncertainty is added to budgeting in SNGs.

The SNG budget preparation process is thus subject to a Hobson's choice of whether to start without a clear picture of available resources, or to compress the time period available for it. Both options weaken the budget preparation process, albeit in different ways. The first option produces "need-based" budget proposals adding up to an unaffordable amount. The second option means either rushing the preparation of expenditure proposals, or short-circuiting the negotiation phase, or preventing informed legislative debate.

The governance implications, too, are significant, for under these circumstances the power of the finance department of the SNG entity vis-à-vis the spending agencies becomes greater than it should be; the same is true of the power of the executive branch vis-à-vis the local legislature; and fiscal transparency itself (which requires time as well as resources) is compromised.

The timing problem cannot be fully resolved, but its impact may be reduced by a pragmatic combination of a conservative revenue estimate and a two-stage SNG budget calendar. When the amount of transfers becomes known with certainty, upward expenditure adjustments can be made to an already well-prepared preliminary budget. This means that, at the start of budget preparation, only "core" expenditure proposals would be requested, with additional expenditure programs in certain sectors prepared on a contingency basis in case the revenues turn out to be greater than the initial conservative forecast. Normally, such a distinction between "core" and "non-core" expenditures is inimical to the effectiveness of the budget process (especially in public investment), and should be avoided in budgeting at central government level. However, it may provide a second-best solution to the special timing problem of SNGs, at lower cost than either lack of sector budget constraints or a compressed budget preparation calendar.[14]

Risk

Subnational government finance can be a major source of fiscal risk (see Chapter 5). The impact of honoring guarantees given by an SNG may be heavy, and contribute to fiscal crisis in the country. At the municipal level, court judgments or debtor failures may contribute to municipal bankruptcies.[15] Addressing the fiscal risk from SNG loan guarantees has two elements: data should be compiled on outstanding loan guarantees—amounts, purposes, beneficiaries, etc.; and SNGs can be required to enact legislation governing the issue of loan guarantees, and to take them into account during budget preparation.

Other mechanisms can also be used to evaluate the quality of SNG public finances and the resulting degree of systemic fiscal risk. These include mainly the rating of SNG debt by independent credit-rating agencies, and self-evaluation in terms of criteria set by central government. The recommendations of credit-rating agencies, however, have proven to be much less than reliable—let alone timely—as the Asian crisis of 1997–9 and the global financial crisis of 2008–11 have shown once again; and self-evaluation carries obvious limitations unless it is validated by an independent external entity.

Administrative Cost

Most issues of budget execution, discussed in Chapter 10, apply equally to SNGs and to central government. One important issue, however, applies specifically to PFM at subnational government level: the costs of administering grants from the center—from inception to final utilization. Many of the conditional grants extended by central government are released only after receipt of required reports. Experience shows that central governments tend, in their zeal to control lower-level government, to prescribe too many detailed reports, which add to costs and lead to reporting delays. Reducing the coverage and complexity of these reports would be a positive step.

The conditions attached to specific-purpose grants should be relevant and not unnecessarily burdensome. Too often, instead, they are driven by bureaucratic self-protectiveness rather than fostering the objective of the grant, are unnecessarily intrusive, and hamper operational flexibility with redundant controls. (The superfluity of conditions may even be counterproductive in terms of achievement of the objective for which the grant was designed.)

Procurement in Subnational Government

Subnational government procurement becomes more important with increasing decentralization and the greater range of functions performed by provincial and local governments. In developed countries, there are advantages in combining centralized procurement policy with decentralized procurement operations. In developing countries, instead, with scarce skills in local governments and greater scope for questionable expenditure, delegation of authority for procurement transactions should proceed carefully and be accompanied by appropriate oversight. In countries where the central government is especially corrupt, to decentralize procurement is likely to improve matters in and of itself, even without special safeguards or capacity-building technical assistance (but then, in those countries central government is unlikely to wish to move in that direction).

Once purchasing authority is delegated, the higher government level should retain the power to monitor and conduct audits, but should not intervene in the award or administration of any specific contract. To remedy the problem of limited capacity, the state or provincial government could encourage joint procurement by a number of jurisdictions, as is done in France. Also, the intermediate level of government (state or province) could help by removing barriers to entry for small contractors in local jurisdictions, organizing training programs for contractors and construction firms, and providing support services. Some countries have set up public sector consulting organizations to assist local governments in planning and managing large construction works and procuring supplies and services. Finally, SNG units could also take advantage of central rate contracts with reputable suppliers (as in India).

Although not subject to the same rules and constraints, a good deal of procurement takes place between levels of government. Contracting with another government agency may provide small local government units with a stable level of assured services. However, local government should not become a captive client of higher-level government agencies— the choice of whether to purchase from higher-level government agencies or from private suppliers should be left to the local government concerned, except in specified instances.

Model procurement codes for local governments envisage a procurement policy unit reporting to the city manager or the district or county commissioner, as the case may be. Such a unit has no operational responsibility, but provides research support, maintains a contractor database and monitors complaints. This system is suitable for small towns, with limited staff and skills.

There is no clear evidence one way or the other that procurement has become more efficient in SNG in general. In developed countries, however, major improvements have taken place in large cities as a direct result of stronger transparency and accountability provisions—as exemplified by the experience of New York City summarized in Box 14.5.

Box 14.5 Improving Local Government: The Case of New York City

The dynamics of improvement in local government are illustrated by developments in New York City. Beginning in the late 1800s with the attack on the political spoils system through the "progressive era" of the 1930s, the main obstacle was voter opposition to raising taxes. To square that circle, city officials began in the 1970s to contract out the delivery of work or services. As a defensive reaction to the negative publicity generated by three major scandals, however, the city began to saddle the contracting process with an ever-increasing plethora of rules, procedures and reviews by different oversight bodies.

In 1987, Governor Mario Cuomo created the New York State Commission on Government Integrity, known as the Feerick Commission, to investigate New York City's procurement practices and make recommendations. The Commission's blunt report concluded that: "the city's labyrinthine contracting system wastes millions of dollars, . . . is mired in red tape, scares away vendors, and remains vulnerable to corruption" and made recommendations to simplify the process. As a result, the New York City charter was completely revised in 1989. Among the changes, the most important were placing the procurement function directly under the mayor, requiring competitive bidding, including private sector members into the new Procurement Policy Board, mandating ex-post audit, and establishing a vendor database (VENDEX) with information on contractors' qualifications and background. In addition, all procurement staff are required to divulge their personal finances and the Department of Investigation is given broad powers to investigate the finances of city employees and of contractors eligible for a city contract.

As of 2015, about $18 billion worth of goods, services and works (of which one-third is for human services) are contracted out annually in New York City using the Procurement Policy Board rules (which are only a couple of hundred pages, compared with the thousands of pages of federal regulations). Although public procurement problems have certainly not disappeared from New York City, the state of public procurement is a far cry from its disrepair of 25 years ago. The inefficiencies in the services still provided directly by city government—particularly in the morass of residential housing and construction regulations—remain to be addressed, however.

Sources: Anechiarico and Jacobs (1996), Hondale et al. (2004) and author.

Financing SNGs and Controlling SNG Debt

Borrowing is a normal source of funds for the capital requirements of subnational governments, especially if large public investment responsibilities are decentralized to SNGs. Borrowing may also serve as a useful stopgap for deficits caused by a temporary imbalance between SNG government revenue and expenditure assignments. However, the debt crisis in the 1990s in SNGs in federal Brazil, the inflationary impact of subnational financing in Argentina, city-level bankruptcies in the United States, cumulative payments arrears in several Russian regions, and other developments have made controlling SNG debt a major concern of central governments. Even when formal borrowing controls are strict, a weak central government may give the impression that when push comes to shove it will pay for SNG deficits in order to maintain basic service provision—especially when its credibility has been damaged by previous bailouts or by political dependence on alliances with local politicians. (In Brazil in the 1990s, for example, the expectation of federal bailout of states in financial difficulties weakened SNG fiscal discipline.)

Subnational governments may obtain financing in four ways: borrowing through the central government; borrowing through a public financial intermediary; borrowing from the capital markets; or financing through private participation in the delivery of public services. (Financing through private participation has a very limited scope, as discussed in Chapter 4.) Of the three financing sources, borrowing through the central government is likely to become enmeshed with politics, possibly resulting in fiscal risk for general government or enabling politically motivated expenditures. To a lesser extent, the same risk applies to borrowing through a public financial intermediary, with the additional disadvantage that the debt of a financial intermediary is an *implicit* liability of the central government and is thus less transparent. In contrast, subnational governments' direct access to capital markets allows for the development of a more transparent and market-based relationship with lenders, and a greater chance for the central government to control the borrowing effectively.

Accordingly, subject to the core requirement of proper design of fiscal decentralization in general and clear definition of SNG borrowing authority, subnational borrowing can be controlled in four ways (Ter-Minassian, 1997):

- *Control through market discipline* (e.g., in Canada and the US). This works where the capital market functions reasonably well, credit-rating agencies are reliable and timely, and the government lets the credit market operate freely without favoring subnational government entities. In the US, for example, the federal government has typically refused to come to the rescue of a state or locality in financial trouble. In 1975, when virtually bankrupt New York City applied to President Gerald Ford for federal help, the response was, in a celebrated *Daily News* headline: "Ford to City: Drop Dead." The response was unjustified, as the city's financial crisis was to a large extent due to its carrying many national responsibilities, and the federal response led to years of unnecessary service deterioration and human suffering. Yet, in part from having to cope with its own problems, New York City today is in many respects an example of good megacity governance. (See Box 14.5.)
- *Cooperation among different levels of government* (as for example in Australia's earlier practice of the Australian Loan Council, a forum for the negotiation of state debts, comprising representatives from the states and the central government). For the cooperative model to work, subnational governments should be consulted during the formulation of the macroeconomic and fiscal framework, in order to become aware of the fiscal implications of their actions and improve fiscal discipline. The cooperative approach works best where local officials are reasonably competent and representative, and where there is strong national leadership in economic and fiscal management.
- *Controls based on administrative rules* and/or formal "fiscal responsibility" legislation (as, for example, in Brazil).
- *Direct controls by the central government* (as, for example, in Mexico, where subnational governments may not borrow at all without explicit authorization by the central government). Direct controls include setting limits on subnational debt; authorizing individual borrowing; or centralizing all government borrowing, with on-lending to SNGs. Controls must be more stringent for foreign than for domestic borrowing. Indeed, experience has demonstrated that only fully centralized control of foreign borrowing by SNGs can prevent the contagion effect of a deterioration of the credit ratings of one borrower on the ratings of other borrowers, and on the country as a whole.

In most developing countries, it is not possible to rely on market discipline to control SNG borrowing, because the financial market is weak, central government intervention to prevent SNG default is widespread, and local politicians are less responsive to market warnings. Direct central control of subnational borrowing is, on balance, preferable but must not be too intrusive and the central government should not attempt to micromanage SNGs with the excuse of controlling their debt. As time and circumstances permit, the system should gradually evolve toward rule-based or market controls. However, experience has shown the high risks of moving too fast in that direction, and an evolution toward indirect control of SNG borrowing must be very cautious and monitored closely.

Notes

1 The United States offers a striking example of variety and profusion of local authorities, all delivering different public services and managing their affairs in their own way. As of 2015, there were about 90,000 local government units in the 50 states of the Union. These comprised about 3,000 counties, 19,000 municipalities, 20,000 townships, 15,000 school districts and 30,000 special districts. With such variety, useful generalizations are difficult. Moreover, the core principle of subsidiarity enshrined in the US Constitution—that powers not explicitly assigned to the federal government are reserved to the states—means that those vast non-enumerated powers are exercised in very different manner in the different states. The interested reader is referred to Andrisani et al. (2006).

2 When the author expressed surprise during a visit to Maputo in 1984 that the highly competent director-general of the ministry of agriculture was only 31 years old, her reply was: "I was a lot younger nine years ago when they gave me the job." The contrast with the extremely corrupt authoritarian regime in Angola is sharp, demonstrating that a common colonial experience does not necessarily determine subsequent developments.

3 An estimated 10 million Congolese lives were lost during that period, and nobody can guess at the number of amputations of children's limbs as punishment for their parents' failure to collect enough of the desired commodities. Hochschild (1999) gives a carefully researched and vivid account of what ranks at the top of the long history of colonial brutalities. In contemporary times, the armed conflict of the past 25 years has caused an estimated five million Congolese deaths, mainly in the eastern parts of the country—again, basically driven by control and exploitation of the country's extractive resources.

4 It was at Edinburgh, partly through his encounter with Fabian theory, that Nyerere began to develop his vision of connecting socialism with African communal living—the later *ujamaa* villages. (See Nyerere, 1962.)

5 The regime viewed the capital of Phnom Penh as "The Great Whore by the Mekong River," and forcibly emptied it, as well as the other cities, systematically butchering over a million people, including virtually all educated individuals.

6 In Sudan, the centuries-old conflict between the Muslim and Arab North and the largely Christian and Nilotic South produced an agreement for full autonomy in 2005 and independence of South Sudan in 2011. Less than three years later, the new state disintegrated into violent internal conflict, this time on an ethnic basis between the two main Nilotic groups—Dinka and Nuer—in part fueled by personal rivalry between the two leaders of the two groups. The three million victims of the old North–South conflict have been succeeded by an estimated million (so far) new victims of the Dinka–Nuer conflict within the South itself—confirming once again the old African saying: "When elephants fight, the grass gets trampled." A peace agreement reached in April 2016 unraveled within two months, and a regional peace-keeping force was deployed in the capital of Juba in August. Stay tuned.

7 In its most extreme formulation, subsidiarity entails that no level of government should undertake activities except those which demonstrably exceed the capacity of individuals or private groups.

8 For example, the argument of states' rights was used in the American South in the twentieth century to preclude federal interference with "Jim Crow" discrimination against African Americans.

9 Originally published in 1949—see *Concept of a Growth Pole,* www.applet-magic.com/poles. htm. See also Darwent (1969).

10 A variant of the functional approach is the "efficiency approach" aimed at achieving the highest efficiency (lowest unit cost) in government service provision. This approach tends to produce large jurisdictions with large populations, permitting subnational governments to widen their range of activity to serve more people, benefit from a larger tax base, and optimize their workloads. The efficiency approach is most appropriate for local public services such as urban planning, housing, water, sewerage and transportation. However, unlike these services, whose output is quantifiable, it is a lot harder to set appropriate boundaries based on measuring the "output" of services of teachers, social workers and police officers.

11 This section relies in part on Fischer (2016) as well as the pioneering review by Rondinelli et al. (1983), many of the concepts and findings of which remain current after more than 30 years, although the understanding of the risks and limits of decentralization has much improved since then.

12 Until recent years, budgetary control in China has been weakened by the lack of clarity in expenditure assignments, which made it difficult to define tax assignment and revenue-sharing mechanisms. Local governments were often forced to accept unfunded responsibilities that properly belonged to higher-level government, thus adversely affecting the quantity and quality of the public goods and services they supplied, and indirectly encouraging local corruption. (See Ahmad et al., 1995.) In the Russian Federation, considerable overlap in the tasks of regional (*oblast*), county (*rayon*) and municipal governments emerged after the dissolution of the Soviet Union and continues to exist to this day.

13 Aside from constitutional provisions and applicable federal laws, the only major institutional feature that US states have in common is the requirement to live within their means. Unlike the federal government, a state does not have the power to print money and a balanced budget is required, explicitly or implicitly. This requirement can be avoided for a time, with accounting gimmicks or "special" financing, but sooner or later expenditure cuts and/or tax increases become inevitable to bring the budget back into balance.

14 A similar timing and uncertainty problem applies to municipal and local government in relation to the provincial levels. In most cases, however, transfers from provincial to local government are to finance investment projects, and it is possible to advance or delay certain projects depending on resources becoming available. Current expenditure is usually financed from local revenues that are more easily estimated in advance.

15 The US bankruptcy code provides that in these cases only the municipalities (not the creditors) may commence proceedings and that the bankruptcy court may not interfere with the local government. There are similar procedures in other countries (e.g., South Africa) where municipalities are allowed to borrow from the market.

Bibliography

Ahmad, Etisham, Qiang Gao and Vito Tanzi, 1995. *Reforming China's Public Finances.* Washington, DC: IMF.

Andrisani, Paul J., Simon Hakim and E. S. Savas, eds., 2006. *The New Public Management: Lessons from Innovating Governors and Mayors.* Norwell, MA: Kluwer.

Anechiarico, Frank and James Jacobs, 1996. *The Pursuit of Absolute Integrity: How Corruption Control Makes Government Ineffective.* Chicago: University of Chicago Press.

Bahl, Roy, 1999. Implementation Rules for Fiscal Decentralization. Paper presented at the International Seminar on Land Policy and Economic Development. Land Reform Training Institute: Taiwan.

Bahl, Roy and George Martinez-Vazquez, 2006. "Sequencing Fiscal Decentralization," *Policy Research Working Paper 3914.* Washington, DC: The World Bank.

Baicker, K., J. Clemens and M. Singhal, 2012. "The Rise of the States: US Fiscal Decentralization in the Postwar Period," *Journal of Public Economics*, 96(11–12), 1079–91.

Baskaran, Thushyanthan and Lars Feld, 2013. "Fiscal Decentralization and Economic Growth in OECD Countries: Is There a Relationship?" *Public Finance Review*, 41(4), 421–45.

Bos, F., (2013). "Economic Theory and Four Centuries of Fiscal Decentralization in the Netherlands," *OECD Journal on Budgeting*, 12(2), 9–60.

Canuto, Otaviano and Lili Liu, 2013. *Until Debt Do Us Part: Subnational Debt, Insolvency and Markets.* Washington, DC: The World Bank.

Corrigan, Paul, Mike Hayes and Paul Joyce, 1999. *Managing in the Local Government*. San Francisco: Jossey-Bass.

Darwent, David, 1969. "Growth Poles and Growth Centers in Regional Planning: A Review," *Environment and Planning*, 1(1), 5–32.

Edwards, Ryan, 2010. "US War Costs: Two Parts Temporary, One Part Permanent," Working Paper 16108, *National Bureau of Economic Research*, 113, 54–66.

Fischer, Ronald, 2016. *State and Local Public Finance*. New York: Routledge.

Gold, Joseph, 1981. *Conditionality*. Washington, DC: IMF.

Hochschild, Adam, 1999. *King Leopold's Ghost*. Cambridge MA: Houghton-Mifflin.

Hondale, Beth, Beverly Cigler and James Costa, 2004. *Fiscal Health for Local Government*. San Diego: Elsevier.

Jha, G., 2013. "Fiscal Decentralisation for Strengthening Urban Local Government in India: Lessons from Practices in Developing and Transitional Economies," *Indian Journal of Public Administration*, April–June.

Lewis, B., 2013. "Local Government Capital Spending in Indonesia: Impact of Intergovernmental Fiscal Transfers," *Journal of Public Budgeting and Finance*, 33(1), 76–94.

Luby, M. J., 2013. "The Impact of the Great Recession on the Financial Management Practices of State and Local Governments," *Journal of Public Budgeting, Accounting and Financial Management*, 25(1), 158–234.

Nyerere, Julius K., 1962. *Ujaama: The Basis of African Socialism*. Dar es Salaam: Tanzania Government Printer.

Oates, Wallace E., 1972. *Fiscal Federalism*. New York: Harcourt Brace Jovanovich.

——, 2006. "On the Theory and Practice of Fiscal Decentralization," CREI Working Paper 1/2007, Rome: Institute for Federalism and Intergovernmental Relations.

Parker, Andrew N., Johan van Zyl, Tulio Barbosa and Loretta Sonn, 1995. "Decentralized Rural Development and Enhanced Community Participation: A Case Study from Northeast Brazil," *Policy Research Working Paper 1498*. Washington, DC: The World Bank.

Prud'homme, R., 1995. "On the Dangers of Decentralization," *World Bank Economic Review*, 10(2), 201–20.

Rondinelli, D. and John Nellis, 1986. "Assessing Decentralization Policies in Developing Countries: The Case For Cautious Optimism," *Development Policy Review*, 4(1), 3–23.

Rondinelli, D., John Nellis and G. Cheema, 1983. "Decentralization in Developing Countries: A Review of Recent Experience," *Working Paper 581*. Washington, DC: The World Bank.

Saunoris, J. W. and R. K., Goel, 2014. "Government Decentralization and Prevalence of the Shadow Economy," *Public Finance Review*, 44(2), 263–88.

Schiavo-Campo, S. and Mary Judd, 2005. "The Mindanao Conflict in the Philippines: Roots, Costs and Potential Peace Dividend," *Social Development Papers 24*. Washington, DC: The World Bank.

Schiavo-Campo, S. and Hazel McFerson, 2008. *Public Management in Global Perspective*. Armonk, NY: M. E. Sharpe.

Shah, A., 1998. "Balance, Accountability, and Responsiveness," *Policy Research Working Paper 2021*. Washington, DC: World Bank.

Shah, A., ed., 2007a. *Intergovernmental Fiscal Transfers: Principles and Practice*. Washington, DC: The World Bank.

——, ed., 2007b. *Local Public Financial Management*. Washington, DC: The World Bank.

Tanzi, Vito, 2001. "Pitfalls on the Road to Fiscal Decentralization," *Working Paper 19*. Washington, DC: Carnegie.

Ter-Minassian, Teresa, ed., 1997. *Fiscal Federalism in Theory and Practice*. Washington, DC: IMF.

15 Reconstructing Public Financial Institutions in Fragile and Conflict-Affected States

When weapons talk, laws are mute.

(Roman proverb)

Introduction

Internal conflicts have occurred from the beginning of organized society, and have been either peacefully managed or "resolved" through conflict and the prevalence of one or another party. In Europe and elsewhere, the nation-state grew slowly but organically, albeit usually accompanied by war and violence. In Africa and parts of Asia, colonialism repressed internal conflicts in the interest of exploiting the colonies' mineral and natural resources. Moreover, the arbitrary country boundaries resulting from the "Scramble for Africa" sanctioned by the major European powers at the Berlin Conference of 1885 threw together diverse ethnic groups that historically had their own culture, governance and separate territories. After the independence of most former colonies in the late 1950s and 1960s, the Cold War served to continue to repress those conflicts, this time in the interest of "East–West" superpower competition.

With the end of the Cold War in 1989 and the dissolution of the Soviet Union in 1991, the lid came off the pot and many of the repressed internal conflicts bubbled up to the surface, aggravated by the artificial boundaries. Inter-state conflicts gave way to intra-state conflicts (about 80 percent of total conflicts), often culminating in extremely violent and destructive civil wars. Many of these were in Africa, but the same phenomenon took place elsewhere as well—for example, in the Balkans after the dissolution of the former Yugoslavia, Sri Lanka and Timor-Leste in Southeast Asia and, of course, in the Middle East after 2010.

In addition to the increased incidence of violent internal conflicts, the manner in which the conflict ended differed markedly after the 1980s. From the end of World War II to 1990, 58 percent of civil conflicts concluded with a decisive victory by one party, and only 32 percent ended without either a victory or a formal agreement. Between 1990 and 2005, just 14 percent of conflicts ended with a decisive victory and almost half ended without either a clear victory or a formal agreement (Walter, 2002; Kreuz, 2010). It remains to be seen how many of the latter have in fact ended. The most important single factor in preventing a resurgence of conflict has been the degree of inclusiveness of the post-conflict power-sharing arrangements—across political, economic, territorial or military lines (Cammett and Malesky, 2012).

Severe internal conflict, especially its most virulent ethnic or religious forms, destroys much more than buildings and power plants. It short-circuits the rules that keep human interaction constructive and predictable, targets primarily the organizations and individuals who administer those rules, and wipes out most positive forms of social capital. Thus, post-conflict reconstruction is first and foremost an institutional challenge

(Schiavo-Campo, 2003; Schiavo-Campo and Judd, 2005). In turn, the challenge of institutional reconstruction affects the entirety of state functions and, among these, the management of the public finances occupies a central place.

Drawing on the lessons of 25 years of international experience in post-conflict reconstruction (see, among others, World Bank, 2011; UN, 2014), this chapter will deal first with the strategic criteria for reconstruction and recovery, then discuss the budgeting process in fragile and conflict-affected situations, outline the public financial management reform priorities, and conclude with a review of the arrangements for financing reconstruction and recovery—primarily the experience with multi-donor trust funds.

Searching for Clarity

What is Fragility?

Fragility is an elusive concept which is given different meanings. The OECD defines a state of fragility as encompassing five dimensions: violence; lack of access to justice; unaccountable and discriminatory institutions; weak economic base; and inability to adapt to shock and adverse events. The IMF identifies as "fragile states" those in which the government is unable to deliver basic services and security to the population. And the international development institutions define a fragile state as one where the policy and institutional framework is especially weak and/or a peace-keeping mission has been in place during the previous three years.

By any definition, the core feature of a fragile state is the existence of stress factors (ethnic, religious or regional; discrimination and exclusion; severe population pressure over land, etc.) which erode the fabric of society and lead to inability to cope with major economic, social or environmental shocks. Think of the factors of fragility as termites in a table, constantly working to weaken it but not easily visible until a sudden impact on the table causes it to collapse.

Often, the symptoms of fragility are confused with its causes. For example, Pakistan is generally viewed as a "failing state," with the rise of Islamic militancy as the main cause of state failure. On the contrary, Islamic militancy is a result of state failure. It was the Zia ul-Haq regime that fostered fundamentalism in the 1980s in order to maintain political control and it is the state's corruption and inability to provide minimally adequate public services that caused the delegitimization of the state and the rise of Islamist insurgency (Khan, 2007).

Fragility and Conflict

Both fragility and conflicts are a continuum. No country is entirely free of internal stresses and no country is so thoroughly conflict-ridden as to make a degree of reconciliation impossible. "Post-conflict" is an especially nebulous category. Some countries are still considered post-conflict long after the end of major civil violence (e.g., Cambodia, Ivory Coast), and some are classed as post-conflict even though violence remains widespread and central authority is weak. In any event, persistent fragility is almost always associated with eventual civil conflict. Of the 40 states that were considered fragile for five or more years between 1978 and 1990, 17 were still fragile as of 2012 and 16 of those had experienced violent internal conflict (De Tommaso, 2016). It is preferable therefore to refer to "fragile and conflict-affected" states (FCS). Even so, the dividing line between these and other countries is necessarily arbitrary.

The best-known list of FCS is that formulated by the World Bank, African Development Bank and Asian Development Bank, based on weak policy and institutional capacity or the presence of an international peace-keeping force.[1] Table 15.1 lists the 32 countries considered as FCS as of 2015, with a combined population of about 1.5 billion; 17 countries

Table 15.1 Fragile and Conflict-Affected States, 2015

Afghanistan	Kiribati	Solomon Islands
Bosnia	Kosovo	Somalia
Burundi	Liberia	South Sudan
Central African Republic	Libya	Sudan
Chad	Madagascar	Syria
Congo, Dem. Republic	Mali	Timor-Leste
Côte d'Ivoire	Marshall Islands	Togo
Eritrea	Micronesia	Tuvalu
Guinea-Bissau	Myanmar	Yemen
Haiti	Palestine	Zimbabwe
Iraq	Sierra Leone	

Source: worldbank.org

are outside Africa and 26 are low-income, with a poverty rate double the 22 percent average in low-income countries in general.

Common Challenges and Strategic Guidelines

The principal challenge of reconstruction is to restore the legitimacy and credibility of the state—primarily by re-establishing order and security; rebuilding the social capital destroyed during the conflict; and addressing the urgent needs of the moment without compromising long-term goals. And the key requirement for restoring the legitimacy and credibility of the state is an inclusive political settlement. The concept of inclusive settlements emerges from contributions in politics, economics and history, which examine the links between political stability, the exercise of power and the economic outcomes (for an early statement, see Khan, 1995).

External interventions must therefore be designed to support an inclusive settlement and the consolidation of physical security or—at a minimum—not undermine them. Taxation and government expenditure policies, in particular, should take care not to aggravate the factors of fragility, while also advancing a long-term vision of economic and financial progress.

Common Challenges

While each situation has its own genesis and unique features, most FCS countries share a number of challenges that influence heavily the task of rebuilding core government functionality:

- Low state capacity to carry out the core functions of governing a population and its territory. This is compounded by often inadequate transportation and communication links, which result in the isolation and insecurity of geographic areas and communities.
- Low levels of positive social capital. Truth and trust are the first casualties of conflict, and the low level of trust among individuals and groups generates among other things a breakdown of voluntary compliance with all norms, including those of PFM.
- High fear and uncertainty, arising from the sense that the normal rules of human interaction have ceased to operate and violence could re-emerge at any moment. This uncertainty, in turn, contributes to pervasive insecurity, inability to think beyond the immediate future, and a risk that small problems—which could otherwise be easily managed—escalate into something much bigger.

- A dearth of timely and accurate information. Fiscal records are missing or destroyed; statistical agencies have ceased functioning; access to parts of the country is hazardous; and public financial management staff may have died or emigrated, taking important institutional knowledge with them.

Strategic Guidelines

Several lessons of actual experience can help meet these challenges. These lessons are generic, but most mistakes of the past can be traced to neglecting one or more of them:

- *Avoid the tabula rasa fallacy.* Almost all post-conflict countries possessed central institutions prior to the conflict. It is important to build on what institutional legacy remains, albeit without replicating inefficient or illegitimate past practices. However, the destruction of dysfunctional systems may allow the selective introduction of more efficient institutional practices. The basic decision is thus among the "three Rs"— replace, repair or reconstruct (Diamond, 2013; Box 8.1).
- *Manage the "outsider vs. insider" tension.* The diaspora can be an important source of expertise and knowledge, but also brings its own challenges. Diaspora returnees are mistrustful of local insiders and their possible complicity in the conflict, and insiders resent persons returning from comfortable exile without personal exposure to the conflict.
- *Provide assistance without creating distortions and chronic dependence.* In most cases, recovery requires substantial aid. Yet the presence of numerous competing donors risks distorting the local economy and crowding out local initiative and organizations. Aid has often become part of the problem rather than the solution—fostering permanent dependence and creating a new source of conflict over the flow of aid money.
- *Re-establish confidence in government* through the provision of security for the citizens, basic justice and key essential public services. The need to restore state legitimacy demands some "quick wins" and visible benefits on the ground. However, the services must be allocated and delivered in a manner viewed as legitimate. Not only is it essential to prevent capture by local elites or accidental exclusion of certain groups, but in a post-conflict setting resentment that another group gets more government service than your group can overcome the goodwill resulting from your group getting more government service than before.
- *Reduce or eliminate abuse and harassment of citizens by government agents*, which can contribute to trust in the new government as much or more than the provision of actual services.
- *Accept the inevitability of temporary reversals.* Historically, recovery and institutional reconstruction have been characterized by setbacks as well as progress. It is important to manage public expectations.
- *Support the right state.* In the absence of an agreed-upon structure of the state and its geographic articulation, quasi-state informal structures tend to emerge that have neither the backing of the relevant powerful groups nor the potential for efficient administration. Supporting these informal structures for the sake of short-term stability may re-ignite conflict and solidify their disruptive power—which would not otherwise last.
- *Pay attention to sequencing*, which differs substantially in different post-conflict situations. For example, the diagnosis and sequence of reforms differed substantially between Bosnia (where functioning administration and many skilled personnel were present after the 1995 Dayton Agreement) and South Sudan (where administrative capacity was virtually non-existent in the wake of the 2005 Peace Agreement).

- *Address the immediate needs without compromising long-term objectives.* To be able to navigate between the urgencies of now and the long-run needs one should identify and implement those variants of urgent interventions which *also* facilitate the building of durable local institutions, and avoid taking measures which will solve immediate problems but jeopardize institutional development.

The Public Financial Management Dimension of Institutional Reconstruction

Remedying key weaknesses in the basic structures and systems of public financial management (PFM) is urgent in every post-conflict situation, especially because government revenues fall sharply during civil conflict, and any misuse of public money undermines the credibility of the new government as well as the economic recovery. Thus, a first generalization is that, of the three objectives of PFM—expenditure control, resource allocation, operational efficiency—achieving a measure of expenditure control is the critical priority in post-conflict settings.

A second important generalization is the need, already noted, for public financial decisions to support the political settlement and the consolidation of security. This requires a close dialogue between the government's finance authorities and the international organizations (primarily the UN) responsible for supporting a political settlement and restoring order and security.

Third, and related to the need to support the political and security consolidation, is the disagreeable reality that tolerating some corruption and forswearing punishment of powerful criminals may be part of the price to be paid for peace. (This dilemma has bedeviled all attempts at a resolution of the conflict between the government and the FARC rebels in Colombia, until the compromise agreed in late 2016.) This reality, however, must not be used as an all-purpose excuse to allow unchecked bribery or close one's eyes to gross violations of human rights. Also, to navigate between the risk of triggering a resurgence of the conflict and that of allowing corruption to compromise long-term recovery, when resources must be allocated for political reasons to powerful individuals or groups ways should be found by which the allocation can *also* contribute to the economy and society. George Washington Plunkitt, an early twentieth-century political boss in New York City, made a distinction between "dirty graft" and his "clean graft," which consisted of taking bribes only for projects that would also benefit the city (see Riordon, 1993[1905]). This is a slippery and risky distinction but, in the immediate aftermath of civil conflict in a country with very limited capacity, it provides part of the answer.

Fourth, despite the inevitable compromises, revenue and expenditure policy and management should be broadly consistent with a vision owned by the government and supported by the international community. This does not require a full-fledged development plan—the prerequisites for which do not exist until after the immediate post-conflict period—but a general sense of economic and financial direction which must flow from a genuine dialogue between the new government, the main donors and the principal community and regional groups.

Budgetary Principles in FCS

While the conditions for a normal budgeting process may not be present in a conflict-affected situation, *a formal and public budget, even if rudimentary, is essential*:

- to reflect the financial implications of the reconstruction program;
- to signal basic policy directions;

- as a vehicle for government–donors dialogue;
- to make clear and transparent the resource allocation among groups and regions; and
- to create a *process* through which the practice of open debate and the habits of peaceful compromise can begin to be rebuilt.

In FCS, four principles emerge from experience, on both the revenue and the expenditure side:

- *Selectivity.* Owing to the low-information, high-uncertainty environment, trying to enact too many PFM reforms at once risks backlash and loss of credibility (World Bank, 2011).
- *Maximum simplicity.* The limited capacity precludes the introduction of complex budgeting practices. Also, simple systems are more conducive to transparency—which is especially important in a post-conflict situation, where every shadow can be perceived as a threat and every private meeting as a potential conspiracy.
- *Combination of pragmatism and efficiency.* The choice of public finance institution-building measures should be largely dictated by conditions on the ground, but must also be consistent with good practice lest state fragility be perpetuated. There are efficient ways to meet political or security goals, if one looks for them.
- *Transitional means transitional.* When the situation demands emergency fiscal, procurement and financial management measures that are not necessarily consistent with efficiency and integrity, they should be designed and understood as strictly transitional, and a robust mechanism must be put in place to assure that they lapse after they have served their emergency purpose.

Likely Legal and Organizational Priorities

In very low-capacity countries, these actions may entail creation of new entities; in countries with adequate capacity, measures targeted to specific gaps may suffice:

- *Rapid review of the legacy legal and regulatory framework for PFM.* Using this legacy as the starting platform helps rebuild the organizations and reduces the need for changes. Revisions, if any, should be targeted and limited, with tax and customs legislation and regulations taking priority. This review should be kept to the barest minimum necessary to assure a legal foundation for restoring state legitimacy in PFM. Any in-depth modernization should be left to a much later time.
- *Create or strengthen the central public finance and planning authority.* There must be a functioning focal point for the government in all public finance and planning matters.
- *Establish or strengthen the revenue agency.* Four actions are priority: put in place the basic infrastructure for tax administration; appoint the key staff; establish registration and taxpayer identification; and set up basic tax filing and payment procedures.
- *Establish or restore the supreme audit institution.* In the typical FCS situation of very limited capacity and few qualified auditors, the actual audits may be outsourced, so long as they remain under the authority of the SAI itself. What is fundamental is to embed in government and the public the early acceptance of independent audit.
- *A medium-term fiscal perspective is important also in FCS.* However rudimentary and tentative, such perspective can provide the underpinning for donor pledges over a

period of several years, thus improving the predictability of aid and the timing of disbursements *pari passu* with increases in local absorptive capacity. (See the "Collier Paradox" at the end of the chapter.) The practice of medium-term forecasts should be introduced only to obtain a realistic sense of the range of revenues and expenditures beyond the current year, and not to build a complex MTEF, which may be possible only years down the line.

Likely Revenue Priorities

On the Government Side

International experience suggests the following likely priorities in FCS:

* *Rely on taxes suited to conditions.* Indirect taxes (especially customs), although regressive, are the most feasible source of early revenue.
* *Prevent the growth of exemptions and limit fraud and evasion*, particularly in customs.
* *Do not attempt to tax agriculture or the informal sector*—it is likely to be disruptive to security, inequitable and cost-ineffective.
* *Do not view extractive revenues as a substitute for taxes.* Even when the government obtains sufficient revenues from natural resources, domestic taxes are necessary to counteract the tendency of extractive resource revenues to crowd out institution building.

On the Donors' Side

Donor agencies can exert both a positive and a negative influence on tax policy and administration in FCS. Positive contributions include support for revenue mobilization. Aid for revenue mobilization has been minimal, however, at less than one-tenth of one percent of all aid, or just around $37 million for all FCS states (OECD, 2014). There has been a noticeable increase in the tax/GDP ratio, on average, in the first years after conflict settlement (IEG, 2013). Nevertheless, greater donor investment in revenue mobilization would have high returns in terms of integrity, efficiency and political consolidation in fragile and conflict-affected countries.

Also positive would be other actions by donor countries, primarily to be more transparent about their own aid procedures and associated tax exemptions, and to avoid practices that distort the pattern and efficiency of government fiscal operations (see Chapter 10).

Likely Expenditure Management Priorities: Budget Preparation

The paths and pitfalls of reconstructing public expenditure institutions differ in different post-conflict settings, depending on political and security conditions and the initial capacity. Box 15.1 illustrates four country cases.

General Measures

The first critical requirement, noted earlier, is for one central authority—the ministry of finance—to be responsible for the preparation of the budget. The other following

Box 15.1 Public Expenditure Management Improvements in Four Post-Conflict Cases

After initial halting PFM reforms, a renewed effort was made in Cambodia from 2004. A medium-term fiscal framework was established and significant improvements in cash management were made—producing a major reduction in use of cash and consolidation of myriad government accounts into a treasury single account. However, the medium-term fiscal framework remained on paper, major intended improvements (e.g., a well-functioning FMIS) did not materialize and PEFA assessments continued to reveal basic problems in PFM, directly related to the governance weaknesses of the country.

In the DR Congo, PFM reforms have proceeded intermittently since 2003, with limited traction provided by the incentive of debt relief (in 2010). PFM capabilities remain limited and concentrated in the central finance and budget ministries, with very weak capacity in the line ministries. There have been some improvements in recording and reporting of expenditures, but formal PFM systems are frequently undermined by informal practices driven by short-term political needs, and official corruption is endemic.

In Kosovo, the progress toward internationally recognized statehood (achieved in 2008) and the "shared sovereignty" in place for several years have facilitated PFM improvements. The once dominant role of international agencies has been gradually declining. Reforms were most successful in budget execution, especially the treasury functions, while budget planning and annual budget preparation remain problematic.

In Sierra Leone, the PFM system has seen major donor involvement and external technical assistance. The country has received direct budget support and completed the conditions for debt relief in 2007. Reforms have covered all areas of the budget process, including fiscal decentralization, although challenges in central–local relations remain. However, PFM reforms remain over-dependent on externally-funded local consultants in the ministry of finance and in line ministries and agencies. Sustainable government capacity is a thing for the future.

Source: Adapted from World Bank (2012).

priority measures should be considered in most FCS, albeit at suitable levels of complexity and depth:

- *Prepare various budget scenarios and formulate a procedure for frequent in-year budget amendments.* Single scenarios are not compatible with the special uncertainties of the post-conflict period, in part because more aid may become available if new and justified expenditure proposals emerge. At the same time, without a clear and agreed procedure for frequently amending the budget, erratic and opaque changes can compromise the credibility of the initial budget itself and provide corruption opportunities.
- *Initiate selective efforts for budgeting capacity in the major line ministries*, and gradually scale up to other ministries. In the early post-conflict period, the normal iteration in the budget preparation process between each line ministry and the ministries of finance and planning is replaced by dialogue between the government and the donors.

- *Establish a simple and practical system for collection and dissemination of basic financial information*—not a formal financial management information system (FMIS), which is not feasible in post-conflict settings.
- *Put in place procedures for legislative consideration and approval of the budget.* The initial quality of the legislative debate is almost certain to be very low, but the habits of formal legislative consideration and timely approval should be established early.

Current Expenditure

For budgeting current expenditure, among the screening criteria advanced in Chapter 6, the most important in a post-conflict environment are: careful review of the wage bill (to prevent the strong pressures to hire new government employees from compromising fiscal prospects for years and years to come); adequate funding of operations and maintenance expenditure, essential to get the government functioning again; and assurance that any subsidies are transparent and public—especially if they are designed to support political consolidation and the restoration of order and security.

Investment Expenditure

Investment is the category of expenditure where both the risks and the opportunities for supporting a durable political settlement are especially high. Investment priorities in an FCS setting are determined in part by security and political circumstances, and the profile of public investment will depend on the evolution of the political process (e.g., if elections are imminent). This does not at all imply a free-for-all abandonment of investment rules and criteria, but does require making distinctions between projects responding to political or security objectives; projects tailored to humanitarian or damage-control goals; and projects that must meet the standard rules of economic appraisal, readiness for implementation, monitoring, execution and evaluation.

It is inevitable in the immediate aftermath of conflict that major investment projects are largely designed by the aid donor agencies, and their implementation is entrusted to special project implementation units. However, it is important to begin to rebuild the public investment management capacity:

- establish a small unit for preparation and clearance of investment projects;
- formulate simple rules of investment programming and project appraisal and selection;
- formulate an action plan to gradually strengthen the investment proposal and execution capacity of the major line ministries;
- put in place early safeguards to prevent the emergence of enclave-type arrangements whereby a donor agrees with a ministry on investments in the sector without reference to the overall reconstruction program or development and fiscal sustainability objectives;
- conduct a rapid review of the overhang of incomplete investment projects launched before the conflict—placing the burden of proof on restarting a project rather than on excluding it, and discontinuing projects not selected for completion; and
- selectively open initial channels of systematic feedback from civil society on investment needs and project implementation (as security and other circumstances permit).

Special Post-Conflict Expenditure Programs

In the aftermath of civil conflict, a variety of special programs are needed to address the needs of particular groups—internally displaced persons, child soldiers, rape victims, etc.

For these programs, evaluation on economic grounds is neither possible nor appropriate. However, budgeting for these special expenditure programs should still meet certain standards— particularly: correct identification of the beneficiaries; realistic estimate of expenditures on the basis of the actual activities envisaged; costs broadly consistent with prior experience in similar cases; adequate monitoring and reasonable accountability for outcomes.

The Difficult Challenge of Security Sector Expenditures

Military expenditure will be discussed in Chapter 17. In fragile and conflict-affected states, security expenditures are at once especially necessary, especially risky, and especially delicate—due to the intimate connection between security and political consolidation. Many post-conflict states have displayed high tolerance for inefficient spending in the security sector—tolerance which can become culturally entrenched and has been over-looked by the donors of aid for civilian purposes. Some security activities in a post-conflict setting will by their very nature remain secret and the corresponding expenditures totally off-budget. However, a quite unnecessary problem has been the lack of constructive inter-action between the security and the development agencies, and the ensuing lack of coordi-nation of security and development expenditure. In several cases, including but not limited to Iraq and Afghanistan, some development activities were carried out by the military without any consultation with or oversight by the civilian authorities, and conversely, development programs in insecure areas or risky sectors did not seek the advice and coop-eration of security personnel—in both cases with huge waste of resources and few results.

Likely Expenditure Management Priorities: Budget Execution

Whatever measures are assessed as priority for budget execution in the country in ques-tion, their design and implementation modalities should be as simple as possible, and should in all cases be designed to encourage a culture of oversight, integrity and account-ability. The first objective of budget execution systems is to foster compliance with the approved budget—to avoid both budget under-runs (inimical to the recovery), and over-runs (inimical to fiscal discipline and sustainability). In post-conflict situations, the main risk is underspending. (A case in point is Timor-Leste, which for years after independence and the end of conflict was only able to spend half the approved budget.) That aside, the following measures (from among those described in Chapter 8) are likely to be priority in post-conflict circumstances:

- As soon as possible, replace cash payments with payments by check to close off easy corruption opportunities and prevent a resurgence of conflict.
- In cash management, take care that separate banking operations by individual govern-ment ministries and agencies are fully transparent and are periodically re-authorized to avoid their becoming permanent.
- Introduce simple controls at each of the three stages of expenditure (commitment, verification and payment). In the immediate aftermath of conflict, these controls can be directly administered by the ministry of finance. Later, progressively greater reli-ance can be placed on internal controls in the line ministries themselves.
- Introduce internal inspection (not internal audit, which is premature in the absence of internal controls) in the largest spending ministries.
- Establish a simple cash-based bookkeeping system. The reliability and timeliness of accounts are the critical need. Even single-entry bookkeeping may suffice at the

beginning, although it should be expanded as soon as possible to double-entry book-keeping. (Any move beyond cash accounting should be left to a very distant future.)

- Assure financial reports on budget execution, only the key ones and equally simple, but issued on a regular schedule. (Periodic reports on the physical execution of large investment projects can be issued by the dedicated project implementation unit.)
- Assure the maximum feasible flexibility in the application of procurement and financial management procedures. (The consequences of a rigid application of standard rules are illustrated in Box 15.2.) This is a slippery slope, however, and normal standards should be met as soon as security and market conditions allow—especially regarding sole-source procurement.

Aid Management

Aid management in general was discussed in Chapter 11. Special considerations relevant to fragile and conflict-affected states are addressed in this section.

The Setting

First, it is critical to keep in mind that when international assistance is given in the context of a violent conflict, it becomes part of that context and thus also of the conflict (Anderson 1999). Without an understanding of the social environment and the genesis of the conflict, the security situation and the nature of the political settlement, aid can inadvertently exacerbate social divisions, open up opportunities for corruption and abuse, and possibly rekindle the conflict itself. That said, well-designed aid, tailored to the characteristics and circumstances of the country and delivered in realistic modalities, can make an invaluable contribution.

Box 15.2 Procurement Rigidities in Post-Conflict Timor-Leste

The application of standard World Bank and Asian Development Bank procurement rules was a source of delays and complications in project management during 2000–2 after the end of the conflict. The demanding procedures for bidding, prior review, etc., were quite unsuited to the emergency requirements of a very small country with a virtually non-existent domestic market. The only major concession to reality was the option to use simpler procedures for community participation and local activities, but this did not help large reconstruction projects, which were implemented much more slowly than they could have been.

The World Bank concluded later that better results could have been achieved by greater use of pre-qualification, faster deployment of procurement staff, better use of technology and simplified project documentation and processing. However, in the institutional vacuum of Timor-Leste at that time, there was also a risk that excessive procurement flexibility might have generated serious corruption and reputational costs. In hindsight, in this special case the right approach would have been to hire an international procurement firm as agent—since very little national procurement capacity could have been built anyway owing to the strong expatriate tilt of the UN entity that administered the reconstruction program in the early years.

Source: Schiavo-Campo (2003).

In fragile and conflict-affected states in general, aid accounts for about 23 percent of GDP and taxes for about 14 percent. In post-conflict countries in particular, aid dependence is even higher because as a result of the conflict both GDP and tax revenues are very depressed. Unless large extractive resources exist and can be mobilized rapidly, domestic revenue consists mainly of customs duties and some other indirect taxes. In the long-term, the objective is to foster economic growth while raising the domestic revenue/GDP ratio—which reduces aid dependence while strengthening the mutual accountabilities between the citizens and the state (OECD, 2014)—but in the immediate post-conflict period high aid dependence is inevitable. It is therefore especially important that aid be effectively managed by the government and donors coordinate their assistance closely.

In a conflict-affected setting, the aid management unit set up to provide the government–donors interface (discussed in Chapter 10) can initially be very small and link only with the central finance and planning entities (and of course the main donors). In some countries, the aid management architecture was not seriously affected during the conflict and there may be significant continuity. In others, an aid management entity may need to be created from scratch. Diaspora personnel can be useful for this purpose, provided that they are twinned with locals.

Transitional Governmental Arrangements

In conflict-affected situations where regular government agencies have virtually ceased to operate, a transitional government body may have to be established to manage aid and the aid-financed programs while the rebuilding of the regular agencies proceeds. The structure and modalities of such a transitional agency must necessarily be specific to the country and situation, but in general it can play the following roles:

- Function as the primary source of initial government ownership and the bridge between donors and government.
- Be the government's focal point to formulate the reconstruction program, and in some cases directly implement a number of projects and activities.
- In extreme cases, when government institutions have been destroyed by the conflict, serve as a proto-government to incubate initial capacity in the various sectors that will eventually transform into regular ministries of government.

These roles should be relinquished as the regular organs of government begin to function, but in practice a "sunset dilemma" has emerged. When the transitional aid and program management agency functions too well, donors prefer to engage with it; the agency hangs on to its roles instead of gradually devolving them to the new line ministries; and the development of capacity in the regular organs of government to exercise the regular functions of government is thwarted. A case in point is the Palestinian Economic Council for Development and Reconstruction (PECDAR). Created in late 1993, the organization which was supposed to devolve its functions to the regular ministries and go out of business by 1998 (Palestinian Authority and World Bank, 2004). However, PECDAR was so effective that donors kept relying on it and it is still operating 20 years later—while many of the Palestinian line ministries remain very weak.

The key lesson is that government and donors should agree from the outset on a clear sunset clause, by which the special entity will be closed and its functions absorbed into the regular structure of government at a specified time. To do so meaningfully, however, institutional capacity must be built during the transition within the regular organs of government in order to create a sound alternative. One cannot transition to nothing.

Financing Reconstruction

Options

The largest investment projects, as well as humanitarian aid and security-related programs (such as de-mining), can be financed individually. In all other respects a *unified* budget reflecting a *unified* agreed program requires a *unified* financing mechanism. Effective donor financing of the budget in FCS requires: (i) prior agreement between the government and the donors on a broad program of activities; (ii) a systematic interface between government and the donors; (iii) an administrative mechanism that minimizes transaction costs and delays; and, most importantly, (iv) a robust system that provides fungible budget support while also assuring that expenditures are reported to the contributing donors.

A variety of aid sources are available to countries in the aftermath of conflict. In cases of a special political relationship with a foreign country (usually the former colonial power), the bulk of the untied aid to finance the budget may come from a single donor partner. In other cases, "parallel" or "joint" financing may be provided by a number of donors. However, parallel financing is hard to program and disburse appropriately, and joint financing presents other transactional difficulties. In many post-conflict countries, therefore, untied budget financing has been channeled through an "umbrella" multi-donor trust fund (MDTF), usually administered by the United Nations or the World Bank.

Multi-Donor Trust Funds (MDTF): Combining Fungibility and Predictability

An umbrella trust fund can avoid aid fragmentation and duplication; helps the predictability of aid flows; builds a close link with the budget; protects against fiduciary risk; and provides the basis for a robust government–donor dialogue on recovery, peace-building and development policy. A well-designed and well-run MDTF can also significantly reduce transaction costs for both donors and the government.

Some MDTFs have functioned well; some have not. Substantial experience now exists to identify and avoid past mistakes and to apply good practices. Based on the principle of a unified financing mechanism, experience has been generally negative where several trust funds were established (as in South Sudan), and positive in cases where one single MDTF was set up to finance the bulk of donor-financed government expenditures (such as the Holst Fund in West Bank and Gaza set up in 1993 or the Afghanistan Reconstruction Trust Fund set up in 2002). Separate trust funds can of course be dedicated for specific purposes (e.g., de-mining), or for assistance targeted to special groups (e.g., reintegration of child soldiers), but care should be taken to avoid proliferation of funding mechanisms, which would lead to fragmentation of the government budget and dispersal of donor efforts.

The key features of an effective MDTF are as follows:

- It fulfils both a fiduciary and an executive function—legal custodian of the money as well as manager of its efficient use.
- It covers both investment and current expenditure (including a portion of the wage bill, subject to understandings on the size and compensation of the government workforce).
- It includes incentives for individual donors to contribute. This is the tricky part: each donor must be provided with a degree of comfort that its money goes for its preferred purposes; yet, earmarking the aid to specific expenditures would defeat the purpose of

an untied budget financing mechanism. The solution is provided by the fungibility of money: all contributions are commingled in a common pool; the general preferences of donors are formally acknowledged; and expenditures from the fund are reported back to the donor but *along broad categories*. This approach avoids financing rigidities while allows each donor agency to infer—and attest to its public—that its resources have gone to finance its preferred uses.

- The MDTF governance arrangements include a steering committee composed of the principal donors and chaired by an "administrator" (usually the UN or World Bank). The steering committee meets frequently and regularly to review funding proposals *endorsed by the government*. Once approved, the project is managed by and under the responsibility of the administrator, based on rules for procurement and financial management that have been pre-agreed with the government and the participating donors.
- The steering committee reports periodically to the larger group of all contributing donors, and the trust fund resources are replenished from time to time as previously negotiated.

Major Issues: Fiduciary Systems, Technical Assistance, Donor-Generated Distortions

Fiduciary Systems

The subject of fostering local capacity for procurement, financial management and monitoring was discussed in Chapter 10. In the aftermath of conflict, there is no practical alternative to donors using their own fiduciary systems, as local capacity is by definition inadequate and no donor agency can accept the high risk of misallocation or theft of the money that it is responsible for. The country systems agenda can become relevant only after security has been fully restored, the political settlement has been consolidated, and the line ministries have acquired minimally adequate capacity to carry out their regular functions.

Subject to that reality, it is important to:

- Assure that the procurement and financial management systems used by donors are themselves based on sound principles and good practice, and are thus reasonably uniform among donors.
- Implement the donor fiduciary systems in a manner consistent with the realities on the ground and with the maximum possible flexibility.
- "Twin" investment assistance with appropriate technical assistance to transfer knowledge about sound procurement and financial management.
- To the extent possible, design the project implementation units also as incubators of local capacity and training of national civil servants.

Dealing with Technical Assistance

A technical assistance component—engineering, architecture, environment, etc.—is included in most physical investment projects. Self-standing technical assistance, not associated with investment projects, is normally for institutional development. Non-project technical assistance has made significant contributions to some countries in post-conflict situations, but has much too often been the source of conflicting advice, inappropriate solutions, and, in some cases, conflicts of interest and corruption. The issues of recruitment and compensation of technical experts were discussed in Chapter 5. Other lessons of experience to maximize the potential benefits of technical assistance while mitigating the risks are to:

- avoid duplication of advice;
- arrange for independent assurance of the quality of the technical advice and its suitability to the local context;
- find cost-effective ways to mobilize experts of demonstrated competence and experience;
- insist on contractual provisions to assure the transfer of knowledge, rather than merely the provision of one-off advice. Transfer of knowledge calls, among other things, for assigning to the external consultant local counterparts capable of absorbing the knowledge, and making the last payment to the consultants contingent on a demonstration that their counterparts have in fact done so;
- be aware of the tendency of external consultants insufficiently familiar with local realities to recommend the introduction of PFM practices unsuited to circumstances and carrying potential risks for the restoration of security and the consolidation of the political settlement.

Timeliness of interventions is especially important in post-conflict settings, where delays are inherently dangerous. Unfortunately, most donor agencies have excessively lengthy processes. In the UN, the recruitment and fielding of experts takes a minimum of nine months. Aid procedures should be expedited—or special ones created—to provide sound just-in-time technical advice.

Finally, while core government functions cannot be re-established without some external advice and direct involvement by a few competent individuals or firms, persistent dependence on resident external technical assistance is lethal to long-term capacity development. As soon as the immediate post-conflict urgencies have been surmounted, the government should formulate a strategy for gradual exit from external technical assistance and its replacement with national expertise—with support from the donor community.

Donor-Generated Distortions

The time perspective and objectives of individual staff of donor agencies are not necessarily congruent with the needs of post-conflict recovery and overall development. A major disconnect is evident in the practices relating to the hiring of national government staff. Individual donor representatives, staff or project managers have an understandable incentive to do everything possible to make their own project succeed, and to do so in a timeframe relevant to their career. Thus, among other things, they try to attract the best local staff by paying whatever salaries are required—salaries which are almost always in excess of what the government can pay within a sustainable salary structure. One particularly destructive practice is to pay salary "top-ups" to government officials and staff who are involved in managing aid-assisted projects. This practice twists government officials' efforts toward the aid-assisted projects and away from other government activities—which may be equally or more important. The already-limited capacity of the government is thus weakened, compromising both short-term recovery and the long-term effectiveness of the aid itself.

The converging incentives of the individual donor staff and the local government officials involved in the aid project are strong. The moral issue is complex as well, pitting the rights of local individuals to better their economic position against the interests of the government as a whole. However, certain measures help substantially to minimize the distortions:

- Provisions to avoid creating incentives for government employees to leave government service (or to treat government service as secondary to their work on aid projects) should be embedded in formal multi-donor agreements. These provisions should include public guidelines for compensation of local staff, to make it roughly comparable to the compensation of permanent government employees.
- "Topping up" of civil servants' salaries by donors should be strictly prohibited, with appropriate sanctions on both the donor agency and the individual civil servant concerned. It is essential that the government issue a formal declaration that this practice is illegal.
- The risks that individual donor practices weaken government capacity can be mitigated, in part, by channeling as much external aid as possible through a multi-donor trust fund that is managed in accordance with standards agreed to by all major donors.

Beyond Post-Conflict: Three Paradoxes

The challenge of transitioning from emergency to normal aid modalities has not been met adequately in fragile and conflict-affected states. Three aid paradoxes have been in evidence:

- The "*Collier paradox*." Conflict is continuing news. Peace is news once. International interest in assisting a country is at its peak in the immediate aftermath of conflict, precisely at the time when the country's capacity to absorb it is at its lowest. By the time the country has become capable of using substantial amounts of aid well, some donors have moved on to the next crisis hotspot and the available aid is reduced (paraphrasing Collier, 2002).
- The "*discontinuity paradox*." As the political situation is consolidated and recovery takes root, there ought to be a gradual move toward normal types of assistance. Instead, there is a tendency to either continue the kinds of projects appropriate to the immediate aftermath of conflict or "a rush to move toward financing projects in every possible sector . . . driven partly from internal pressures" (IEG, 2013, p. 24).
- The "*fiduciary paradox*." Special and accelerated emergency aid procedures ought to give way to regular norms and processes, but donor staff as well as the government have an interest in continuing to stick with the simpler and quicker emergency procedures. (This becomes a problem when the shortcuts necessary in the immediate aftermath of conflict become a black check for violating important protections of integrity and efficiency.)

Therefore, in the immediate post-conflict period it is important to firm up donor pledges for the medium term, through an appropriate expenditure forecast. And, beyond the immediate period, a review should be held between the government and all major donors on when and how to begin transitioning out of emergency projects implemented through emergency modalities.

Note

1 Various indicators form a "Country Policy and Institutional Assessment" (CPIA) score. FCS countries are defined as those with a CPIA score of 3.2 or below, or the presence of a UN and/or regional peace-keeping or peace-building mission in the previous three years. However, the CPIA is a highly generic indicator: countries with scores below 3.2 may not exhibit significant fragility

and countries with scores above 3.2 may have grave fragility issues. Moreover, the CPIA score is sticky, and does not change appreciably except in response to major events. Alternative measures are currently under consideration.

Bibliography

Anderson, M. B. (1999). *Do No Harm: How Aid Can Support Peace or War*. Boulder, CO: Lynne Rienner.

Cammett, Melani and E. Malesky, 2012. "Power Sharing in Post-Conflict Societies: Implications for Peace and Governance," *Journal of Conflict Resolution*, 56(6), 982–1016.

Collier, Paul, 2002. *Globalization, Growth and Poverty: Building and Inclusive World Economy*. Washington, DC: The World Bank.

De Tommaso, Giulio and Rohullah Osmani, 2016. "Rebuilding State Institutions, Post-Conflict: Reform Experiences from Afghanistan and Somalia," *SAIS Review of International Affairs*, 36(1).

Diamond, Jack, 2013. *Sequencing PFM Reforms*. Washington, DC: IMF. January.

Fitz-Gerald, Ann, 2012. *Thematic Review of Security Sector Reform to Peacebuilding and the Role of the Peacebuilding Fund*. New York: United Nations.

IEG, 2013. *World Bank Group Assistance to Low-Income Fragile and Conflict-Affected States*. Washington, DC: The World Bank.

Khan, Feisal, 2007. "Corruption and the Decline of the State in Pakistan," *Asian Journal of Political Science*, 15(2), 219–47.

Khan, M. H., 1995. "State Failure in Weak States: A Critique of New Institutionalist Explanations," in J. Harris., J. Hunter and C. M. Lewis, eds., *The New Institutional Economics and Third World Development*. London: Routledge.

Kreutz, Joakim, 2010. "How and When Armed Conflicts End: Introducing the UCDP Conflict Termination Dataset," *Journal of Peace Research*, 47(2), 243–50.

Leong Swee, E., 2015. "Together or Separate? Post-Conflict Partition, Ethnic Homogenization, and the Provision of Public Schooling," *Journal of Public Economics*, 128, 1–15.

OECD, 2014. *Domestic Revenue Mobilization in Fragile States*. Paris: OECD.

Palestinian Authority and World Bank, 2004. *Handbook for the Palestinian Economic Council for Development and Reconstruction (PECDAR)*. Ramallah and Washington, DC: Palestinian Authority and World Bank.

Riordon, William, 1993. *Plunkitt of Tammany Hall: A Series of Very Plain Talks on Very Practical Politics*. New York: St. Martin's Press. (Originally published in 1905.)

Schiavo-Campo, S., 2003. "Financing and Aid Management Arrangements in Post-Conflict Situations," *Social Development Papers 6*. Washington, DC: The World Bank.

Schiavo-Campo, S. and Mary Judd, 2005. "The Mindanao Conflict in the Philippines: Roots, Costs and Potential Peace Dividend," *Social Development Papers 24*. Washington, DC: The World Bank.

United Nations, 2014. *Lessons Learned: Review on UN Support to Core Government Functions*. New York: United Nations.

Walter, Barbara, 2002. *Committing to Peace: The Successful Settlement of Civil Wars*. Princeton: Princeton University Press.

World Bank, 2011. *Conflict, Security and Development*. World Development Report. Washington, DC: The World Bank.

——, 2012. *Public Financial Management Reforms in Post-Conflict Countries*. Washington, DC: The World Bank.

16 Corruption and Public Financial Management

> Physicians say of consumption that in the early stages . . . it is easy to cure but difficult to diagnose; whereas later on . . . it becomes easy to diagnose and difficult to cure. The same thing happens in affairs of state.
>
> (Niccolò Machiavelli)

Introduction

Problems of corruption in government are hardly new. Official corruption is known as the second oldest profession, and most government corruption takes place in public finance, where the money is. Corruption is also found within the private sector, of course. Indeed, with the Enron and other major corporate scandals of the early twenty-first century, the linkage between public and private sector corruption has re-emerged as an area of special concern—particularly in the US, Europe and East Asia.

Most definitions of corruption emphasize the abuse of public power or position for personal advantage. The succinct definition by the World Bank (1997, p. 8) is "the abuse of public office for private gain." The OECD defines it similarly as "the misuse of public office, roles or resources for private benefit" (OECD, 1999, p. 13). These simple statements are elaborated in the definition employed by Transparency International (TI): "Corruption involves behavior on the part of officials in the public sector . . . in which they improperly and unlawfully enrich themselves, or those close to them, by the misuse of the public power entrusted to them" (Pope, 1996). In the area of procurement, the World Bank (1997) defines a corrupt practice as "the offering, giving, receiving, or soliciting of anything of value to influence the action of a public official in the procurement process or in contract execution." These definitions do not cover the problem of corruption within the private sector nor the role of private individuals in fostering corruption in government. It takes two to tango. Better, therefore, is the pithy definition of the Asian Development Bank (1998): "Corruption is the misuse of public or private office for personal gain."

Types of Corruption

General Distinctions

The Inuit people have several different words for "snow," depending on its specific characteristics. Corruption, too, takes different forms, not all of which are equally important or costly. The appropriate policy response depends on the type of corruption being addressed:

- Bribes given to induce public officials to deviate from their duties must be distinguished from bribes given to get them to do what they are supposed to do or to do it faster. The corrupting effect is the same, but in the former case the allocation of resources and services is distorted as well.

- "Syndicated" corruption, in which elaborate systems are devised for receiving and disseminating bribes, is different from non-syndicated corruption, in which individual officials seek or compete for bribes in ad hoc and uncoordinated fashion.
- A third important distinction has been made by Transparency International between "grand corruption" and "petty corruption." Grand corruption typically involves senior officials, major decisions or contracts and large sums of money. Petty corruption involves low-level officials, the provision of routine services and goods and small sums of money.
- A related distinction is between systemic corruption, which permeates an entire government or ministry, and individual corruption, which is more isolated and sporadic. Systemic corruption is a major governance and public management problem; isolated corruption is a run-of-the-mill law enforcement problem.

Although grand corruption either starts from or is tolerated by the top political levels, petty corruption itself can in time destroy the integrity of public administration—in addition to imposing significant transaction costs on businesspeople and citizens. Moreover, corruption rarely stands still, and shows a tendency to increase over time. The analogy with cancer is apt—since the disease only gets worse through time, by a competitive dynamic that leads otherwise honest employees and officials to conform to a culture of corruption. When corruption becomes accepted as normal ("everybody does it"), the non-corrupt minority of government officials are viewed as fools rather than honest; bribery becomes a necessary "lubricant for the machine"—efficiency and effectiveness in government are undermined and the poor and powerless suffer the most.

"Corruption" is short-hand for a wide variety of illegal and illicit behaviors, ranging from outright theft or pilfering of state assets, to collusion in procurement, exchange of favors for recruitment and promotions, bribes to obtain basic services, and so on. A list of the kinds of behavior typically viewed as corruption is in Box 16.1. The list shows that some types of corruption are internal—interfering with the ability of a government agency to manage its financial and human resources—and other forms of corruption are external—involving efforts to manipulate or extort money from clients or suppliers, or to benefit from inside information. Still other types consist of unwarranted interference in market operations, for example, the use of official power to artificially restrict competition and generate monopoly rents.

Corruption in Public Financial Management

In PFM, corruption is associated primarily with ghost government employees and phantom jobs, large investment projects, cash payments, procurement and artificially controlled exchange rates. Corruption in the government wage bill, public investment, cash payments and procurement was discussed in Chapters 6, 7, 8 and 9, respectively. The single most efficient, safe and profitable form of corruption comes from having privileged access to undervalued foreign currency, which can then be resold at a premium on the black market for a virtually instantaneous profit. In Somalia in the 1980s, for example, the black market foreign exchange traders were operating two blocks from the Central Bank.

Political Corruption

Political corruption differs in intent and outcomes from economic corruption, described above. Political corruption includes such practices as the financing of political parties in exchange for contracts or official posts, or the co-optation of legislators by giving them influence over the award of contracts in their constituencies. Illicit political financing or

---

Box 16.1 An Illustrative List of Corrupt Behaviors

Corruption includes any of the following actions:

- Theft or embezzlement of public property and moneys.
- Design or selection of uneconomical projects because of opportunities for financial kickbacks and political patronage.
- Procurement fraud, including collusion, overcharging or the selection of contractors, suppliers and consultants on criteria other than the legal procurement criteria.
- Illicit payments of "speed money" to public officials to facilitate delivery of goods, services and information to which the public is legally entitled (e.g., permits).
- Illicit payments to public officials to facilitate access to goods, services or information to which the public is not entitled, or to deny others access to goods, services, or information to which they are entitled.
- Illicit payments to public officials to prevent the application of regulations in a fair and consistent manner, particularly in public safety, law enforcement or revenue collection.
- Payments to public officials to foster or sustain monopolistic access to markets in the absence of a compelling economic rationale for restricting public access.
- Misappropriation of confidential information for personal gain (e.g., using knowledge about intended public transportation routes to buy real estate that is likely to appreciate).
- Deliberate disclosure of false or misleading information on the financial status of corporations that would prevent potential investors from accurately valuing their worth (e.g., non-disclosure of large liabilities or the overvaluing of assets).
- Sale of official posts or promotions, nepotism or other actions contrary to the civil service regulations.
- Abuse of public office (e.g., using the threat of a tax audit to extract personal gain).
- Obstruction of justice and interference in the duties of agencies tasked with detecting, investigating and prosecuting illicit behavior.

---

pork-barrel politics are a blight on the integrity, efficiency and effectiveness of public management, but the problem is essentially political and is not amenable to technical or administrative remedies. (This is a major reason why illicit political financing is not included in the international anti-corruption agreements, such as the OECD Anti-Bribery Treaty and the UN Convention Against Corruption.) However, the boundary between political corruption and outright bribery is very fuzzy, as illustrated in Box 16.2.

The Semantics of Corruption

In keeping with the different forms of corruption, an extensive terminology has emerged throughout the world. The semantics of corruption can be catchy and very creative. (See Box 16.3.) The most sophisticated term is the Italian *tangente* (tangent) which replaced the humble "little envelope" as corruption became an integral component of the political financing system. Taking its inspiration from the circular flow of money and production that characterizes economic activity, tangente refers to the portion of money spun out of the circular flow by the centrifugal forces of influence and patronage. The massive corruption scandal that led to the replacement of virtually the entire political class in Italy in the early 1990s—a bloodless revolution that has not received as much credit as it deserved—was called *tangentopoli*.

Box 16.2 Lobbying and Political Corruption in the United States

The top three industries paying the most lobbyist fees are banking, defense and education. The following are only a few among the myriad illustrations of "pay-to-play" politics:

- In January 2004, a group of lobbyists met with the then-House Majority Leader Tom DeLay at a restaurant owned by convicted felon lobbyist Jack Abramoff, reportedly to discuss ways to increase contributions to Republican lawmakers.
- Kenneth Kies, former chief of staff of the Joint Committee on Taxation from 1995 to 1998, contributed almost $300,000 to preserve the "synfuel" tax credit, through which $1 billion to $4 billion per year were paid to companies that sprayed coal with diesel fuel or other substances and thereby claimed a tax credit for creating a "synthetic" fuel. The firms for which Kies worked took in nearly $2.4 million in lobbying fees from the Council for Energy Independence and nearly $5.4 million from General Electric since 1998. The top recipient of Kies' contributions was Jim McCrery (Republican, LA), who intervened with the IRS and the treasury on behalf of "synfuel" makers.
- In 1996, lobbyists Denny and Sandra Miller hosted two fundraisers for Senator Ted Stevens (Republican, AK), aka the "King of Pork," raising $160,000. Miller was one of two lobbyists who helped negotiate language calling for $30 billion in military spending to lease air refueling tankers from Boeing, one of his clients. (The tanker deal did not go through, and it would have cost the government much more to lease the planes than to buy them outright—see Box 17.4.)
- Four lobbyists were convicted of felonies in 2005 and 2006: Jack Abramoff; Tony Rudy, former deputy chief of staff to Tom DeLay; Michael Scanlon, DeLay's former spokesman; and Neil Volz, former chief of staff to Bob Ney (Republican, OH).

Box 16.3 The International Lexicon of Bribery

Different countries have come up with different terms—some very elegant—for bribery, either as a euphemism or for deniability. Most of these terms have to do with petty corruption. Grand corruption usually goes under the more pedestrian all-purpose term of "commission" or "agency fees," which of course also cover legal payments for real services. Aside from fiddling expense statements and the common "instant fine" payable on the spot and in cash to traffic police or other minor officials, an international sampling of the semantics of bribery includes:

- *Bustarella*: Italian for "little envelope"—sometimes quite large—either to perform a service to which the citizen is entitled, or to avoid a legal obligation, or to gain an advantage over a less generous or less dishonest competitor. (The term "envelope" is also used in other European countries to refer to bribes.)
- *Expediting fee*: used pretty much everywhere as a euphemism to refer to bribes to get goods out of customs or obtain a license or simply to make sure your application for anything doesn't accidentally get lost or stay at the bottom of a tall pile for years.

- *Speed money* or *grease money*: similar to the "expediting fee," but used for minor transactions throughout most of Asia and elsewhere. Both terms carry the same connotation of lubricating the system to make it work without squealing.
- *Dash*: common in anglophone West Africa, and used as both noun and verb— e.g., "I'll have to dash him."
- *Chai* (tea): common in anglophone East Africa and parts of Asia. (Note that "tea" can also refer to dinner.)
- *Fanta* or *Coca-cola*: common in francophone Central Africa.
- *Pot de vin*: French for glass of wine—common in North Africa, francophone West Africa and other francophone countries, including parts of Indochina.
- *Pourcentage*: French for percentage, normally referring to bribes for large contracts.
- *Refresco*: Spanish for "refreshment"—used through most of Latin America.
- *Pasalubong*: in the Philippines (but also used to refer to normal gifts to friends and family when returning from a trip).
- *Baksheesh:* ubiquitous as a term for "bribe" throughout the Middle East and Central Asia (but also meaning ordinary gifts or normal tips for service).

Corruption: Arguments and Costs

The Cancer of Corruption

Corruption has not always been seen as having a negative impact on the economy or society. On the contrary, in earlier decades it was argued that corruption could advance efficiency by helping to restore government-controlled prices to their market levels. Others maintained that corruption plays a useful redistributive role from wealthy individuals and corporations to those of more modest means, or that it could serve as a tool of national integration by allowing ruling elites to co-opt fractious political, ethnic or religious groups. Next, it was argued that corruption can channel resources to those who can use them most effectively. Finally, some scholars argued that corruption is a natural stage of development, widespread in many advanced countries until the early twentieth century, when it was reduced through the enactment of public sector reforms.

These arguments fail on several grounds (Klitgaard, 1993):

- They focus on the alleged benefits of specific illicit acts, and do not consider the systemic impact of corruption. A bribe may have a positive result (it certainly does for the person who receives it), but also generate negative externalities for the system as a whole.
- The effects of corruption only appear beneficial against the background of public sector failure. The experience of countries such as Singapore and Hong Kong shows that persistent efforts to improve public management result in far greater benefits than tolerating corruption to compensate for public sector deficiencies.
- Corruption encourages people to avoid compliance with both good and bad rules. Importers who bribe a customs official to clear a badly needed medicine one day will bribe the official to clear illegal narcotics the next day.

Most importantly, the arguments that corruption is harmless fail the test of simple common sense. Corruption does not channel resources to those who produce most efficiently, but to those who bribe most efficiently. Corruption can help the poor only if you believe that the poor and the powerless are better "connected" than the rich and the powerful. Bribing government employees does not compensate for inadequate salaries, but undermines merit and destroys morale. Corruption is not even an efficient means to cement political loyalties; on the contrary, it breeds public cynicism toward the political process and all who are associated with it, and turns loyalty into a commodity for sale to the highest bidder.

A Cautionary Tale

In June 1997, everything looked good in Southeast and East Asia—rapid economic growth, progress in human indicators, social peace, apparent financial stability. There was tolerance of the closed circles of influence and privilege; obliviousness to the mounting economic costs from lack of transparency and accountability; and shrugging acceptance of corruption—indeed, even a benevolent view that public–private collusion was a necessary lubricant for the system. These attitudes were not limited to the government, but included lax supervision of the banking system and severe problems of corporate governance in the private sector itself—stemming from lack of transparency and absence of strong competitive checks and balances. Merit and competition were secondary to personal relations of kinship, networks and collusion. And yet, the system had been humming along for many years, Asia seemed to be an exception to the nexus between development and good governance and "Asian values" were alleged to be at the root of the success of the system. Some observers had raised doubts about the sustainability of such a system, but were dismissed as nay-sayers. A few Cassandras had even predicted collapse, but, like all Cassandras, were ignored.

Then, seemingly out of the blue, the Asian financial crisis struck, first in Thailand on July 2, 1997, and then in Indonesia, Korea, Philippines and, to a lesser extent, other Asian countries—with the shockwave spreading through much of the rest of Asia, then to Russia and the rest of the world. The worm in the apple was indeed the corruption in the system. The "Asian exception" was no more. Corruption was indeed a key impediment to sustainable development in Asia as everywhere else in the world, and the new generation is no longer willing to accept "the old way" of running things—as shown in South Korea by the political upheaval caused in 2016 by a corruption scandal involving the President herself.

The Costs of Corruption

Direct Costs

The direct costs of corruption are both huge and diverse, as the following examples show:

- During 1980–2000, Indonesia lost an estimated $48 billion in corrupt resource transfers abroad, surpassing its entire stock of foreign debt of $41 billion.
- In the Italian city of Milan, anti-corruption initiatives reduced the cost of infrastructure outlays by more than one-third. In Italy as a whole, official corruption had earlier added at least 15 percent, or $200 billion, to government debt.
- If Bangladesh had been as successful as Singapore in reducing corruption, its annual per capita GDP growth between 1960 and 2000 would have 1.5 percent higher, leading to a per capita GDP in the year 2015 about double its actual level, and taking at least 40 million Bangladeshis out of poverty.[1]

- When customs officials in Bolivia were allowed to retain a percentage of what they collected, customs revenue jumped by 60 percent within one year.
- In New York City, businesses were able to cut $330 million from an annual waste disposal bill of $1.5 billion by ridding the garbage industry of mafia domination.
- Twice the annual GDP of Ghana, Kenya and Uganda combined has ended up in private foreign bank accounts (Pedersen, 1996).
- The foreign debt of Zaire (now Democratic Republic of Congo) under the dictator Mobutu Sese Seko was equal in 1989 to Mobutu's estimated private wealth—held abroad.
- In countries where corruption is endemic, senior enterprise managers spend as much as a third of their time dealing with government officials, as opposed to less than 5 percent of their time in countries where corruption is not a major problem.
- Studies of procurement in several Asian countries reveal that corruption has caused governments to pay from 20 percent to 100 percent more for goods and services.

Indirect Costs

Even more damaging can be the indirect costs of corruption, which cannot be measured with precision. Corruption can skew investment decisions to favor expensive and unnecessary projects over smaller and more productive ones and over necessary maintenance and rehabilitation expenditure—lowering investment productivity and reducing asset life. At times, quality is compromised and public safety is endangered, such as when building code violations contribute to widespread structural failure during earthquakes and other natural disasters. Morale can be eroded and productivity decline across the civil service. In extreme cases, political stability can be threatened (Khan, 2007). Finally, corruption is especially costly for the poor and the vulnerable. (Serious anti-corruption efforts are among the most effective measures to reduce poverty and exclusion.) Although these costs may not become apparent for a time, in the long term corruption has a heavy negative impact on both poverty and growth.

A Variable Impact

The net weight of evidence suggests that corruption increases income inequality in every type of country but does not appear to affect significantly economic growth in high-income democracies (Drury et al., 2006). On balance, however, correcting for other variables, countries that tolerate relatively high levels of corruption tend to perform less well economically. Study after study has demonstrated that corruption is strongly and negatively correlated with the rate of investment, and thus with economic growth (Mauro, 1995).

Other factors affect the costs of corruption. In some countries corruption is highly routinized, and payoffs are generally known in advance and concentrated at the top in a "one-stop" fashion. This may reduce transaction costs and add a measure of predictability to investment decisions—making the country inherently less risky than other countries where many different officials can demand unspecified and unanticipated payments, or even countries with honest officials but haphazard application of petty regulations.[2] From the investor's viewpoint, it is the added cost of doing business that matters, and not necessarily the source of that cost. Also, the extent to which the profits remain in the country and are invested in productive economic activity, rather than flowing abroad into foreign bank accounts, will also have an impact upon a nation's ability to tolerate relatively high levels of corruption and still enjoy decent rates of economic growth.

Finally, recall once more that the damage done by corruption is often not visible except in the long term. The surface of the administrative and economic apparatus appears intact while growing corruption eats away at the foundations of public administration until the damage is permanent and irreversible, the administrative apparatus disintegrates and a thorough rebuilding of public management becomes inevitable.

Among the protections against the spreading of official corruption, measures to foster ethics and integrity in the public service rank high. The subject is too complex to be addressed here, and the interested reader is referred to Schiavo-Campo and McFerson (2008). Suffice it to recall from Chapter 2 that good budgetary outcomes cannot be sustainable without the respect of norms and due process. An implicit message that "we don't care how you get it done, just get it done" encourages cutting corners, selective rule compliance, and accepting the risk of conflicts of interest. The same questionable act will receive far closer scrutiny in public financial management than if it took place in private companies. Better therefore for government budget managers to be especially circumspect—in the spirit of a saying of the Prophet Mohammad: "That which is lawful is clear and that which is unlawful likewise, but there are certain dicey things between the two from which it is well to abstain."

Fighting Corruption

Historically, concern about corruption has run in cycles: revelations of official abuses prompt anti-corruption campaigns and administrative countermeasures that subsequently fade from view, until the next round of scandals provides further impetus for ad hoc reform. However, the desire to reduce or eliminate corruption has been at the core of all initiatives for good governance.

Evolution of an International Consensus

The US was a pioneer in global anti-corruption efforts, with the 1977 Foreign Corrupt Practices Act that prohibited American corporations from bribing foreign government officials. However, without concomitant action by other countries, the act could not be truly effective. Also, American corporations complained, with some justification, that the act placed them at a disadvantage vis-à-vis other countries' companies. Moreover, at the time, official corruption was frequently viewed either as inevitable or as a "lubricant" for economic activity.

In the late 1980s and early 1990s, as noted earlier, a variety of analytical findings came together to underscore the importance of effective institutions in fostering growth, and the pernicious impact that weak governance and corruption can have upon economic growth and development. In parallel, a national and international consensus gradually evolved on the need to combat official corruption, as the chronology in Box 16.4 shows.

A General Anti-Corruption Approach

The general approach to fighting corruption rests on three pillars. First, because corruption is a symptom of malgovernance, not a cause, anti-corruption efforts should be made not in isolation but as part and parcel of the good governance agenda and through specific reforms in each area of public sector management. Second, it is necessary to expose and penalize misbehavior at the top of an organization or of the political system, rather than just catch a few "small fish" for public relations purposes. Third, success in anti-corruption

Box 16.4 Milestones in International Anti-Corruption Legislation

Among the many international measures enacted since the end of the Cold War to combat public corruption, the following are most notable:

- In 1992, the World Bank produced the first policy on "governance and development."
- In 1994, the Organization of American States (OAS) pledged to outlaw cross-border bribery and the "illicit enrichment" of officials in the hemisphere.
- In 1996, the taboo on mentioning and tackling corruption was lifted by former World Bank President James D. Wolfensohn's speech on the "cancer of corruption."
- In 1996, 21 member states of the OAS signed the Caracas Convention, calling for collective action in preventive measures and international cooperation, transnational bribery, illicit enrichment and extradition. (However, the Caracas Convention was ratified only by Bolivia, Costa Rica, Ecuador, Mexico, Paraguay, Peru and Venezuela.)
- In May 1996, the OECD approved a resolution encouraging its member states to end the tax deductibility of foreign bribes and "commissions" paid by their national corporations.
- In December 1996, the United Nations General Assembly passed the Declaration Against Corruption and Bribery in International Commercial Transactions.
- In 1997, the OECD approved recommendations for criminalizing transnational bribery, enacting stricter accounting requirements, external audit and tighter public procurement.
- In September 1997, the World Bank introduced a formal anti-corruption policy, and the regional development banks—the Asian Development Bank, African Development Bank and Inter-American Development Bank—followed suit shortly thereafter.
- In 1999, an OECD convention entered in force making the bribery of foreign officials a criminal offense on a par with the bribery of local government officials in the country where the corporation is based.
- In 2000, the International Chamber of Commerce approved tighter rules of conduct that prohibited bribes and recommended adoption of these rules by its member associations.
- In December 2005, the UN Convention Against Corruption entered into force.
- In September 2006, all international development and financial institutions reached an unprecedented common agreement on a Framework for Preventing and Combating Fraud and Corruption—standardizing the definition of corruption, improving the coherence of their investigative procedures, sharing information and assuring that enforcement actions taken by one institution are supported by all others.

requires that the expected cost of a corrupt action is raised and the benefit expected from it is lowered. The expected cost of a corrupt action is the severity of the penalty multiplied by the probability of getting caught swiftly: raising the cost of corruption thus requires robust and uniform enforcement. The expected benefit of a corrupt action is the amount of the gain multiplied by the probability of obtaining it: lowering the benefit thus calls for reducing the opportunities for corruption.

Improvements can be achieved by national government action. However, the trans-border nature of much official corruption calls for a global approach grounded on international cooperation and centered on four basic objectives:

- supporting competitive markets and efficient, effective, accountable and transparent public administration;
- supporting promising anti-corruption efforts on a case-by-case basis;
- ensuring that all projects and programs financed with public moneys receive adequate scrutiny—or at least are fully transparent before legislative approval; and
- vigorously pursuing the "supply side" of corruption, that is, bribes and influence-peddling done by large corporations and their pressure on public officials.

As part of this global anti-corruption approach, one must also confront the role of the enabling intermediaries, i.e., the banks, through which the illicit gains are channeled and which usually get off scot free. Regrettably, this agenda is yet to be aggressively pursued. A healthy warning was provided in 2006 with a heavy penalty imposed on the Riggs Bank for facilitating the corrupt transactions of Chile's former dictator Augusto Pinochet and "parking" the proceeds of his bribery. However, penalties on the corporation affect the shareholders and not the individuals responsible. The financial crisis that caused the Great Recession of 2008–10 did not result in any criminal prosecution of senior Wall Street managers—the sole exception was a low-ranking trader. In another instance, three bankers were indicted in connection with the Swiss bank UBS helping wealthy Americans to evade taxes: UBS paid a large fine; the three were given probation and fined from $100 to $7,500; the only criminal penalty was to … the whistleblower who broke the scandal, who was sentenced to 40 months in prison. The message is clear. Accountability is individual or is nothing.

The Experience in Developed Countries

The international consensus is that combating corruption should rely on a combination of mechanisms rather than on any one single measure (OECD, 1999). Mechanisms reported as most effective include law enforcement and independent investigation techniques; preventive methods and financial controls; transparency mechanisms (e.g., declarations of assets, open administration, public exposure); raising the awareness and the skills of officials; and adequate remuneration of public officials. It is very important, however, to assure that the anti-corruption measures do not result in paralyzing the administration, but achieve a reasonable combination of anti-corruption and efficiency, and avoid "the pursuit of absolute integrity" (Anechiarico and Jacobs, 1998).

Targeting Financial Improprieties

Most initiatives in developed countries target the openings for financial impropriety, mainly through requiring asset registers, public listing of corrupt firms, asset declaration requirements, registers of lobbyists, etc. But corruption prevention is more complex than just passing laws or creating new anti-corruption institutions. Increasingly, countries have looked at how systems provide conditions that encourage or restrain the growth of corruption. Switzerland, for example, has improved the effectiveness of existing provisions such as criminal, taxation and competition law—and loosened its banking secrecy (albeit only after scandals and international pressure). Germany and other countries have introduced risk analysis to identify the areas of the public sector most susceptible to corruption. (See also the procurement risk analysis in Chapter 9.)

Transparency Mechanisms

These mechanisms fall into three groups: measures that guarantee the openness of systems and standardization of public processes; measures that provide scrutiny of public sector processes; and measures that facilitate reporting and exposure of wrongdoing. A recent innovation is the creation of monitoring bodies with special responsibility for administering transparency legislation: Greece established a special parliamentary committee; Italy established the office of "guarantor of legality and transparency"; Belgium established a parliamentary commission to oversee the transparency of election campaign funding; the US Federal Elections Commission monitors compliance with political financing rules. So far, the effectiveness of these mechanisms ranges from modest to nil. It is the non-profit non-governmental organization Transparency International that has made a major contribution with its surveys of corruption perception in various countries and other information.

Citizens' Responsibility

It is a mistake to conceive of anti-corruption as exclusively a governmental challenge. Individual citizens have a central role. As in every area of public management, active participation and support by civil society are needed for successful anti-corruption efforts. Recall that it is impossible for a public official to receive a bribe unless a bribe is given. Even when the corrupt transaction is initiated by the public official and the citizens and private firms are the victim, they should consider the implications of giving in. Bribes are like potato chips: you cannot have just one. If the first bribe demand is satisfied, it will be followed by others. Take a tax audit as an example: if you give in to a crooked tax auditor's first demand for a bribe, you are signaling your ability and willingness to pay bribes, and can expect the same auditor at your front door for years to come. Much better to take your lumps and pay the additional tax and penalty (and report the auditor to the authorities).

Institutions for Anti-Corruption

Investigation and prosecution of misconduct should normally take place through a well-functioning law enforcement and judicial system. But the legislature also has a role. Permanent parliamentary bodies to investigate corruption exist in Germany, Greece, Ireland, Mexico, Poland and Sweden. In Belgium, Ireland, the Czech Republic, Germany, Hungary, Italy, Korea and Mexico, provisions exist for setting up an ad hoc anti-corruption committee at any time. In some countries, special anti-corruption bodies have been set up, for example the Italian Special Commission for the Prevention and Repression of Corruption. On the healthy principle that integrity begins at home, some legislatures have established a mechanism to review their own ethics, for example in Sweden through a parliamentary oversight committee, or in Japan through deliberative councils in both houses of parliament, or in the US through the House and Senate Ethics Committees. Again, the effectiveness of all these mechanisms has generally not been impressive.

Investigative power for detecting corruption has also been given to the traditional control bodies internal within ministries or agencies, for example the inspectors-general in each federal department of the US. In addition, some countries have specialized units within the police to investigate corruption (France, Belgium), while in Italy a specialized "anti-Mafia" judiciary has been set up to coordinate all activities to combat organized crime, with signal success. To be effective in the long term, internal controls need to be combined with external independent controls: there is no substitute for robust external audit.

The Experience in Developing Countries

Most of the anti-corruption measures adopted in developed countries are potentially applicable to developing countries as well—taking into account the different availability of resources and of administrative capacity. In most developing countries, however, there is a specific prerequisite of anti-corruption activities: get them out of the police departments or the interior ministry—which are often the foxes guarding the chicken coop.

That aside, effective approaches to anti-corruption should follow the model of the Hong Kong Independent Commission Against Corruption (ICAC), which was highly successful after the 1970s and turned Hong Kong from a corrupt public administration to one of the most honest—in Asia second only to Singapore. The Hong Kong approach emphasizes three concurrent efforts—awareness-raising, prevention and enforcement (de Speville, 1998). Like the three legs of a stool, each is necessary, and none is sufficient: prevention and enforcement cannot succeed if corruption is viewed as normal or inevitable; awareness and enforcement cannot be effective if corruption opportunities are too many and too easy; and limiting corruption opportunities combined with awareness is equally ineffective if enforcement is lax or non-existent. There are exceptions: "stroke-of-the-pen" reforms abolishing key controls (e.g., on prices and exchange rates) can instantly eliminate a major opportunity for corruption. Or, there are times when enforcement is clearly the urgent priority. Beyond the immediate impact of individual reforms, however, concerted action on all three fronts is necessary if official corruption is to be reduced across the board in a lasting manner.

Trends in Worldwide Corruption: Cause for Optimism?

The Annex shows the Transparency International corruption perception indicator (CPI) scores and rankings for all countries worldwide in 2000 and 2014. The TI indicators are based on perceptions. Objective result-based corruption indicators do not exist (although a growing body of research points to the links between corruption and the outcomes of state activity) but corruption perceptions have been widely validated as excellent proxies for the incidence of actual corruption.

Corruption worldwide has diminished slightly during this century. As the Annex shows, the average score for the 90 countries for which the CPI was available in both 2000 and 2014 rose from 47.6 to 49.4—indicating a small decline in corruption by about 4 percent. For all countries, instead, the score fell—indicating worse corruption—but only because the "new" countries for which the CPI was not available in 2000 had on average far more corruption than the rest of the world, with an average score of 37.9 compared with 49.4. (It is impossible to know whether these countries were less corrupt in 2000 or experienced some improvement as well.)

The five Nordic countries and Canada, the Netherlands, New Zealand and Singapore rank consistently highest in public integrity. At the other end of the corruption scale are found many African countries, some former Soviet republics (including Russia itself) and several Asian countries (Indonesia, the Philippines). Some of these countries showed a significant improvement between 2000 and 2014 (e.g., Armenia, Ghana, Indonesia, Nigeria, the Philippines), and others a further deterioration (e.g., Belarus, Zimbabwe). In general, Eastern and Central European countries have done better than the republics of the former Soviet Union, with Central Asia in particular in worse shape than in the early 1990s (Anderson and Gray, 2006).

The sectoral picture shows the most improvement in the area of customs. Customs is the public function where the incidence of corruption has historically been among the highest, and there is still a long way to go before it can be considered relatively clean in most countries. However, the improvement in many countries has been real and significant, and is proof that reforms can be effective even in areas where corruption is most entrenched (De Wulf, 2005).

The most serious corruption is found in the sectors where it is to be expected—tax collection, public works, procurement and police—but grave corruption problems have also emerged in the judiciary, which is especially damaging for the economy because contract enforcement, bankruptcies, etc., depend crucially on independent and honest judges. Most often, the problem arises from a combination of inadequate compensation of judges and lack of accountability for the exercise of their substantial discretionary powers. Occasionally, the root governance problem is found in the prosecutorial function. In Bulgaria, for example, after the fall of the communist regime the desire to get away from politically driven prosecutions led to the creation of a wholly independent office of prosecutor-general, with total authority over initiating prosecutions and practically impossible to remove during their term of office. In a perfect example of the law of unintended consequences, in Bulgaria's weak governance environment of the time the appointment of the prosecutor-general could be heavily influenced by mafia interests—interests that would naturally be protected after the individual's appointment. Political capture was replaced by private capture.

So, despite the very slight improvement in the indicators, there is no cause for optimism on a global scale. Considering the substantial efforts made against official corruption, one would expect to see much greater improvement. Still, let's conclude on a positive note: the demonstrated possibility of rapid progress in anti-corruption. Until the 1960s, Singapore was commonly known as one of the most corrupt places on Earth—with most public services for sale, police, judges and legislators for rent, and ad hoc laws available for private drafting at a reasonable market price. In a comparatively short time, Singapore became a model of administrative integrity and has remained so ever since. The recipe was a combination of public education, extremely generous incentives for competent and honest behavior of public officials, and ferocious enforcement of the rules—with very harsh penalties for illicit actions. For these reasons, Singapore is very often brought up as a model of this or that good practice. It is true that, outcomes achieved by an authoritarian government in a city-state at the crossroads of international commerce cannot easily be replicated elsewhere. And yet, this example demonstrates how a "deep-seated culture" of rule violation and lack of integrity can change rapidly if the rules are vigorously enforced and the incentive framework is rotated toward honesty rather than public theft. One good generation will do.

Annex: Corruption Perception Scores and Rankings, 2000–14

Country	2000		2014	
	Score	*Rank (out of 90 countries)*	*Score*	*Rank (out of 167 countries)*
Afghanistan			12	166
Albania			33	88
Algeria			36	88
Angola	17	85	19	163
Argentina	35	52	34	107
Armenia	25	76	37	95
Australia	83	13	80	13
Austria	77	15	72	16
Azerbaijan	15	87	29	119
Bahrain			49	50
Bangladesh			25	139
Belarus	41	43	31	107
Belgium	61	25	76	15
Benin			39	83
Bhutan			65	27
Bolivia	27	71	35	99
Bosnia and Herzegovina			39	76
Botswana	60	26	63	28
Brazil	39	49	43	76
Bulgaria	35	52	43	69
Burkina Faso	30	65	38	76
Burundi			20	150
Cambodia				
Cameroon	20	84	27	130
Canada	94	5	81	9
Cape Verde			57	40
Central African Republic			24	145
Chad			22	147
Chile	74	18	73	23
China	31	63	36	83
Colombia	32	60	37	83
Comoros			26	136
Congo Republic			23	146
Costa Rica	54	30	54	40
Côte d'Ivoire	27	71	32	107
Croatia	37	51	48	50
Cuba			46	56
Cyprus			63	32
Czech Republic	43	42	51	37
Democratic Republic of the Congo			22	147
Denmark	98	2	92	1
Djibouti			34	99
Dominican Republic			32	103
Ecuador	26	74	33	107
Egypt	31	63	37	88
El Salvador	41	43	39	72

(Continued)

Annex: (continued)

Country	2000		2014	
	Score	Rank (out of 90 countries)	Score	Rank (out of 167 countries)
Eritrea			18	154
Estonia	57	27	69	23
Ethiopia	32	60	33	103
Finland	100	1	89	2
France	67	21	69	23
Gabon			37	99
Gambia			29	123
Georgia			52	48
Germany	76	17	79	10
Ghana	35	52	48	56
Greece	49	35	43	58
Guatemala			32	123
Guinea			25	139
Guinea-Bissau			19	158
Guyana			30	119
Haiti			19	158
Honduras			29	112
Hong Kong	77	15	74	18
Hungary	52	32	54	50
Iceland	91	6	79	13
India	28	69	38	76
Indonesia	17	85	34	88
Iran			27	130
Iraq			16	161
Ireland	72	19	74	18
Israel	66	22	60	32
Italy	46	39	43	61
Jamaica			38	69
Japan	64	23	76	18
Jordan	46	39	49	45
Kazakhstan	30	65	29	123
Kenya	21	82	25	139
Korea (North)			8	167
Korea (South)	40	48	55	37
Kosovo			33	103
Kuwait			44	55
Kyrgyzstan			27	123
Laos			25	139
Latvia	34	57	55	40
Lebanon			27	123
Lesotho			49	61
Liberia			37	83
Libya			18	161
Lithuania	41	43	58	32
Luxembourg	86	11	82	10
Macedonia (FYR)			45	66
Madagascar			28	123
Malawi	41	43	33	112
Malaysia	48	36	52	54

Annex: (continued)

Country	2000		2014	
	Score	*Rank (out of 90 countries)*	*Score*	*Rank (out of 167 countries)*
Mali			32	95
Malta			55	37
Mauritania			30	112
Mauritius	47	37	54	45
Mexico	33	59	35	95
Moldova	26	74	35	103
Mongolia			39	72
Montenegro			42	61
Morocco	47	37	39	88
Mozambique	22	81	31	112
Myanmar			21	147
Namibia	54	30	49	45
Nepal			29	130
Netherlands	89	9	83	5
New Zealand	94	3	91	4
Nicaragua			28	130
Niger			35	99
Nigeria	12	90	27	136
Norway	91	6	86	5
Oman			45	60
Pakistan			29	117
Panama			37	72
Papua New Guinea			25	139
Paraguay			24	130
Peru	44	41	38	88
Philippines	28	69	38	95
Poland	41	43	61	30
Portugal	64	23	63	28
Qatar			69	22
Romania	29	68	43	58
Russia	21	82	27	119
Rwanda			49	44
Sao Tome and Principe			42	66
Saudi Arabia			49	48
Senegal	35	52	43	61
Serbia			41	71
Seychelles			55	40
Sierra Leone			31	119
Singapore	91	6	84	8
Slovakia	35	52	50	50
Slovenia	55	28	58	35
Somalia			8	167
South Africa	50	34	44	61
South Sudan			15	163
Spain	70	20	60	36
Sri Lanka			38	83
Sudan			11	165
Suriname			36	88

(Continued)

Annex: (continued)

Country	2000		2014	
	Score	Rank (out of 90 countries)	Score	Rank (out of 167 countries)
Sweden	94	3	87	3
Switzerland	86	11	86	7
Syria			20	154
Taiwan	55	28	61	30
Tajikistan			23	136
Tanzania	25	76	31	117
Thailand	32	60	38	76
Timor-Leste			28	123
Togo			29	107
Trinidad and Tobago			38	72
Tunisia	52	32	40	76
Turkey	38	50	45	66
Turkmenistan			17	154
Uganda	23	80	26	139
Ukraine	15	87	26	130
United Arab Emirates			70	23
United Kingdom	87	10	78	10
United States	78	14	74	16
Uruguay			73	21
Uzbekistan	24	79	18	123
Venezuela	27	71	19	158
Vietnam	25	76	31	112
Yemen			19	154
Yugoslavia	13	89		
Zambia	34	57	38	76
Zimbabwe	30	65	21	150
Averages:				
Overall score	**47.6**		**43.1**	
Countries for which CPI in both 2000 and 2014	**47.6**		**49.4**	
Countries for which CPI only in 2014			**37.9**	

Note: Scores range from 0 (totally corrupt) to 100 (totally clean). Conversely, higher rankings (out of 90 countries in 2000, out of 167 countries in 2014) indicate *worse* corruption. TI indicators were not available prior to 2000 for many of the countries listed. Average scores are unweighted.

Source: Transparency International www.transparency.org

Notes

1 Extrapolated from a comparison made by Sheng-Jin Wei (1985).
2 In the late-1980s the anteroom of the office of the Director of Customs in Mogadishu sported a table taped to the wall with the list of informal payments expected for clearances and other import transactions. The practice meant that everyone knew exactly how much they would have to pay in bribes and—to that extent—was less damaging to the functioning of the economy than opaque and shifting bribery.

Bibliography

Anderson, James and Cheryl Gray, 2006. *Anticorruption in Transition: Who Is Succeeding and Why?* Washington, DC: The World Bank.

Anechiarico, Frank and James B. Jacobs, 1998. *The Pursuit of Absolute Integrity: How Corruption Control Makes Government Ineffective*. Chicago: University of Chicago Press.

Asian Development Bank, 1998. *Anticorruption: Policies and Strategies*. Manila: ADB.

Beekmana, G., E. Bultea and E. Nillesenb, 2014. "Corruption, Investments and Contributions to Public Goods: Experimental Evidence from Rural Liberia," *Journal of Public Economics*, 115, 37–47.

Cordis, A. S. and P. L. Warren, 2014. "Sunshine as Disinfectant: The Effect of State Freedom of Information Act Laws on Public Corruption," *Journal of Public Economics*, 115, 18–36.

De Speville, Bertrand, 1998. *Hong Kong Policy Initiatives Against Corruption*, Development Centre Studies. Paris: OECD.

De Wulf, Luc, 2005. *Customs Modernization Handbook*, Washington, DC: The World Bank.

Drury, A. Cooper, Jonathan Krieckhaus and Michael Lusztig, 2006. "Corruption, Democracy, and Economic Growth," *International Political Science Review*, 27(2), 121–36.

Ferraz, C., F. Finanand and D. B. Moreira, 2012. "Corrupting Learning: Evidence from Missing Federal Education Funds in Brazil," *Journal of Public Economics*, 96(9–10), 712–26.

Khan, Feisal, 2007. "Corruption and the Decline of the State in Pakistan," *Asian Journal of Political Science*, 15(2), 219–47.

Klitgaard, Robert, 1993. *Controlling Corruption*. Berkeley, CA: University of California Press.

Kumar, Datta, 2013. "Combating Corruption for Ethical Governance in India," *Indian Journal of Public Administration*, July–September.

Mauro, Paolo, 1995. "Corruption and Growth," *Quarterly Journal of Economics*, 110(3), 681–712.

Niehausa, P. and S. Sukhtankarb, 2013. "The Marginal Rate of Corruption in Public Programs: Evidence from India," *Journal of Public Economics*, 104, 52–64.

OECD, 1999. *Public Sector Corruption: An International Survey of Prevention Measures*. Paris: OECD.

Pedersen, P. E., 1996. "The Search for the Smoking Gun," *Euromoney*, 49, September.

Pope, Jeremy, ed., 1996. *National Integrity Systems: The Transparency International Sourcebook*. Berlin: Transparency International.

Schiavo-Campo, Salvatore and Hazel M. McFerson, 2008. *Public Management in Global Perspective*. New York: Routledge.

Sheng-Jin Wei, 1985. "Corruption in Economic Development: Beneficial Grease, Minor Annoyance, or Major Obstacle?" *World Bank Policy Research Working Paper 2048*. Washington, DC: The World Bank.

World Bank, 1997. *Helping Countries Combat Corruption*. Washington, DC: The World Bank.

17 "Black Boxes"

The Special Issues of Extractive Revenue and Military Expenditure

Oil is not black gold; it is the devil's excrement.

(Juan Pablo Pérez Alfonso)

Every gun that is made, every warship launched, every rocket fired, signifies in the final sense a theft from those who hunger and are not fed, those who are cold and are not clothed.

(Dwight D. Eisenhower)

Introduction

As discussed in Chapter 3, certain categories of expenditure—"extrabudgetary funds"—are not included in the annual budget process but their creation is approved by the legislature and their governance and operations are subject to legislative and public scrutiny. Not so for the "black boxes" of secret revenue and hidden expenditures which exist in several countries. While there may be good reasons for setting up an extrabudgetary fund, there are no good reasons for secrecy concerning revenues or for hiding expenditures, with a very few exceptions (e.g., for covert security operations). The motivation for secrecy is not necessarily nefarious.[1] In any event, whatever the motivation, such secrecy is economically and fiscally indefensible.

Revenue secrecy and opaque expenditure are prima facie evidence of weaknesses in governance or of outright corruption, and constitute an important source of long-term fiscal risk. Pushing them to the surface and including them in the budget—or at least showing them in the budget documentation—is a prerequisite to improving fiscal transparency. The two major "black boxes" are the revenue from extractive resources such as oil or precious gems (and the associated expenditure), and military and security spending.

Extractive Revenue

The "Resource Curse"[2]

This book started by telling readers that government budgeting has major implication for democracy and human welfare. The combination of bad governance with vast revenue from mineral wealth disables the public financial management systems. Until the late 1970s, abundance of mineral riches was generally viewed as an unqualified advantage. Indeed, it does sound counterintuitive that it should turn out to be a curse. However, evidence accumulating since the late 1970s demonstrates a strong empirical link between dependence on extractive resources and unrepresentative governance (mostly but not exclusively in developing countries). In many countries the revenue from abundant mineral resources (export, royalties, dividends) is a contribution to the purse of the president or political slush fund rather than part of the official government budget. Both the revenue and the associated spending are a black box, inaccessible to anyone but a select elite, and budgeting is a mere paper exercise—because the real allocation of the largest financial resources occurs behind closed doors. Partly as a consequence, institutions are very weak, poverty is widespread and economic growth is slow—and zero in the sectors other than the extractive resources.

While abundance of extractive resources and malgovernance reinforce each other, the evidence suggests that malgovernance comes first: if governance is initially weak the discovery of large extractive revenues precludes any improvement. However, if governance is sound to begin with, the subsequent extractive revenues are likely to be budgeted transparently and used for public purposes.

The "curse" is most visible in African and Middle Eastern countries, but is not inevitable in these regions nor is it confined there—for example, authoritarian governance in Kazakhstan has been associated with large hydrocarbon resources, and control over gemstones has enabled the ruling military elite to remain in power in Myanmar for decades (until the political opening in late 2011). Consider, too, that the only countries in North Africa and the Middle East where governance has been improving are Morocco, Tunisia, Jordan and Lebanon—the only ones that do not have substantial amounts of oil and gas. Friedman (2009) has pointed out that in the Middle East power grows out of the barrel of a gun and out of a barrel of oil. Juan Pablo Pérez Alfonso, Venezuela's oil minister in the 1960s and one of the founders of the Organization of Petroleum Exporting Countries (OPEC), was indeed prescient in his early statement quoted at the start of this chapter.

The Paradox of Plenty

Although the resource curse is not exclusive to Africa, many cases are found there. In these countries there is a "paradox of plenty": abundant resources and thus high average income per capita coexist with high poverty and low levels of human development.[3] In sub-Saharan Africa as a whole, the incidence of poverty is very high, with almost half of the one billion people living below the poverty line ($1.90 a day as of end-2015). Yet, African countries own almost 8 percent of global oil reserves, receive at least $300 billion in oil revenue annually, and have in addition large deposits of gems and other very valuable minerals, with large revenue from their export. The resource curse provides the explanation of the paradox of plenty.

Corruption is the handmaiden of the resource curse. Corruption losses in Africa have been estimated by the African Union at around $150 billion a year—several times the total foreign aid, and equivalent to one quarter of Africa's GDP. All but one of the seven countries richest in mineral resources have very unfavorable governance indicators and low human development indicators. As shown in Table 17.1, corruption is highest and regulatory control is weakest in countries with abundant extractive resources, with Equatorial Guinea as the worst (Box 17.1) and Botswana the only exception (Box 17.2).

Explaining the Resource Curse

But why do mineral riches tend to produce such unfavorable outcomes? The major explanations of the resource curse are three—economic, financial and political:

- "Dutch disease" is the discouragement of domestic production of goods and services that arises from the abundance of revenue from exports of valuable minerals.[4]

The export revenue raises the value of the currency, which makes the country's domestic production less competitive. In time, the dependence on natural resource revenue makes most domestic production disappear, with major implications for unemployment. (Eventually, when the resource is exhausted, the country is left without any economic base.)

- Revenue volatility, from the vulnerability to price changes. The greater the volatility of revenue, the harder it is to budget effectively, and the sharper the internal conflict over the lower revenue. This has been especially evident in 2015 with the sharp fall in the world price of oil.[5]

- The "rentier state": when government receives most of its revenue from a foreign company which conducts all extraction and sales of extractive resources, it doesn't need to make any effort to mobilize domestic resources. The link between government and the citizens is replaced by a link between the government and the foreign company. Accountability to the citizens is lost and governance is weakened. Reversing the familiar maxim: "no representation without taxation."

Table 17.1 Scores and Rankings of Corruption Perception and of Economic Regulation (seven extractive resource-rich African countries, 2014)

Country	Corruption Perception[a] (out of 167 countries worldwide)		Regulation[b] (out of 47 African countries)
	Score	Rank	Rank
Angola	1.9	161	42
Botswana	6.3	36	3
Congo Republic	2.3	152	38
Democratic Rep. of Congo	2.2	154	44
Equatorial Guinea[c]	1.7	171	41
Gabon	3.7	94	31
Nigeria	2.7	136	36

Sources: Transparency International for corruption perception; World Bank, *Doing Business* survey for regulatory ranking.

Notes:
[a] Low score (1–10) and high rank indicate worse corruption.
[b] Rank is a composite of 10 indicators of ease of doing business; low rank indicates lighter regulation.
[c] 2008 for CPI, out of 174 countries. No recent corruption surveys conducted.

Box 17.1 Equatorial Guinea: The Worst of the Worst

Since independence in 1968, Equatorial Guinea—one of only two former Spanish colonies in Africa—has been ruled by two men from the same family: Francisco Macias Nguema, a mass-murdering psychopath, was overthrown and executed in 1979 by his nephew Teodoro Obiang Nguema Mbasogo ("The Liberator"), the current president. At independence, the Fang people from the mainland Rio Muni, as the larger group, won the first (and only) elections and ever since then the Mongomo clan of the Fang (and the Nguema family within it) has totally dominated the country. Repression and malgovernance were extreme long before the discovery of offshore oil reserves, but oil and gas have further consolidated the position of the ruling elite and made it hugely wealthy.

Equatorial Guinea is the most glaring example of the paradox of plenty. The estimated $6–7 billion a year from oil exports would suffice to finance development for the entire population of 800,000—even if the elite took the lion's share. Instead, the elite has taken almost the whole revenue. While average per capita income is $15,000, 75 percent of the people live on $2 a day, half of the people don't have access to clean water, and life expectancy is under 50 years.

> Equatorial Guinea sometimes seems a parody of an oil kleptocracy—a Blazing Saddles of the world of petroleum. Yet it has emerged as an all-too-real example of how a dictator, awash in petrodollars, enriches himself and his family while starving his people.
>
> (Maass, 1990)

The situation today remains as described 25 years ago. The ruling elite owns most businesses; potential competitors disappeared long ago—economically or physically; three-fourths of *recurrent* expenditures are off-budget, and nobody knows how much "investment" spending takes place; the budget director is a relative of the president; oil revenues are a state secret and the president has placed them in foreign bank accounts of which he is the sole signatory, "to protect the government revenue from corruption." The president is also the chief auditor, and personally signs off on any but the smallest expenditures. Corruption is therefore impossible in Equatorial Guinea.

Forestry is the country's second export sector and is as opaque as the oil sector—in addition to the environmental damage from logging of exotic hardwoods. The president's son "Teodorin" (little Teodoro) is Minister of Agriculture and Forestry; in 2006, he bought his third mansion abroad, in Malibu, California, for $35 million (Ljungaeus, 2007)—in cash, presumably saved from his salary of $5,000 a month.

The oil companies are complicit. They have invested more than $10 billion since oil was discovered. When their payments to the regime were scrutinized by the US Securities and Exchange Commission under the Foreign Corrupt Practices Act, they revealed among other things a payment of $500,000 to a 14-year-old relative of the president; payments for the children of government officials to study in the US; and payments for luxury apartments in Paris, free flights, mansions in Corsica, etc., etc., etc. (Shaxson, 2007; Black, 2007).

Source: Condensed and adapted from McFerson (2009); with additional references.

Box 17.2 Botswana: The Hopeful Exception

Botswana exports over $2 billion a year worth of diamonds, nickel, copper, gold and other minerals—more than 80 percent of its total exports. It is the eighteenth largest resource exporter out of 161 countries, and ranks highest on extractive resource integrity in the continent, largely because of sound institutions and good governance. An electoral democracy, the country is Africa's most stable, and is the exception to the repression and corruption pervasive in other mineral-rich countries. As a result, Botswana has a good record of human development, and has maintained one of the world's highest economic growth rates since independence, rising from one of the poorest countries to middle-income status and a per capita income of almost $17,000 in 2015.

How did Botswana manage to exorcise the resource curse?

Acemoglu et al. (2003) attribute Botswana's political legitimacy, good public sector management and protection of property rights to four factors:

- inheritance of pre-colonial political institutions;
- limited British colonialism;
- strong and accountable political leadership since independence; and
- the political elite's motivation to reinforce institutions.

The first two are enabling factors, but are hardly sufficient to ensure coexistence of good governance with resource abundance—as shown by the fact that several other African countries (notably, Nigeria) inherited the same well-functioning institutions and local autonomy and yet developed a culture of corruption facilitated by resource rents. More distinctive to Botswana are the latter two factors: political leadership and reinforcement of institutions.

However, there is an even more important fifth factor: the ethnic and cultural homogeneity of Botswana society—in sharp contrast with the ethnic pluralism and internal tensions characteristic of most African states as a result of artificial colonial boundaries. This fifth dimension rounds out the picture of why Botswana is the happy exception to the resource curse in Africa. But, although an exception, Botswana also points the way that African countries can follow in order to shake off the resource curse: support for building institutions; gradual strengthening of public management (especially fiscal transparency and accountability organizations); and encouraging the growth of "bridging networks" among different groups, that can partly defuse conflict and manage it when it arises.

What Has Been Done? Standards and Initiatives

The Fiscal Transparency Code

Standards for extractive resource management are found in the Fiscal Transparency Code developed by the IMF in 2014. The main ones require that:

- There is an open and competitive process for the allocation of rights.
- Assessment and collection of resource revenues is accurate and timely.
- All resource companies regularly disclose information on their resource extraction and trading activities.
- The government regularly publishes its resource revenue collections.
- The allocation of resource revenue for public spending and saving is legally authorized, and is disclosed in the annual budget.
- There are clear mechanisms and rules for the establishment and operation of natural resource funds, aligned with international principles of good practice.
- Governments disclose, analyze and manage social, environmental and operational risks associated with natural resource exploitation.

The problem is that, with the possible exception of Norway, no resource-rich country fully meets all the standards listed in the *Fiscal Transparency Code*. (Norway also has the best designed sovereign wealth fund to invest and protect oil revenue for the next generation.) *The Code* would be more useful if it included some guidance on the main priorities. It is impossible for any resource-rich country with governance problems and weak institutions to attempt to meet all the standards at once. Although the standards are complementary, a systematic analysis of the relative importance of each and of the possible sequencing options would be important. Also, while clear standards are necessary as guideposts, they must be made real through the implementation of concrete initiatives—described next.

Various international initiatives have been undertaken from the start of this century to improve transparency in the extraction and sale of mineral resources, to allocate the revenues, and to contain corruption. None of these initiatives has had a major impact, and the extractive sector has the highest bribery of any sector—at an average of over 20 percent of the total value of transactions—but some positive initial improvements have been generated. The three best-known initiatives are the Extractive Industries Transparency Initiative (EITI), the Kimberley Process and "Publish What You Pay."

The Extractive Industries Transparency Initiative

Based on principles adopted in 2003, the EITI is a coalition of governments, companies, civil society groups, investors and international organizations, governed by a board with representation from those constituencies. It aims to improve transparency and accountability in the extractive resources sector, and sets global standards for companies to publish what they pay to governments and for governments to disclose what they receive. The EITI has a well-defined implementation process in which countries are evaluated on the basis of certain progress indicators—at the conclusion of which the country is certified as EITI compliant. As of end-2014, 41 countries were considered as "implementing" EITI, and 31 countries were certified as "EITI compliant." The inclusion of such countries as Chad and the Congo Republic—precisely the two countries showing the sharpest deterioration in governance and corruption indicators since 2004—casts grave doubt on the realism of the certification. (Even Equatorial Guinea was initially accepted as an EITI candidate, before being delisted in 2009!) Nevertheless, the EITI initiative has had some modest positive impact on the transparency of extractive revenues and—to that limited extent—on the integrity and effectiveness of public financial management.[6]

The Kimberley Process

The Kimberley Process (named after the South African city where it was agreed) was spurred by the civil war in West Africa and introduced in 2003 to certify that rough diamonds being sold in international markets do not originate from conflict areas. The process requires member states to set up an import and export control system to prevent "blood diamonds" from entering the international market, and thus presumably assure buyers that they do not indirectly finance war and human rights abuses. Although 75 diamond-producing, trading and manufacturing countries participate in the process, its limitations are severe. As listed by the international anti-corruption organization Global Witness, the Kimberley Process:

- Defines conflict diamonds very narrowly as rough diamonds used by rebel movements to finance wars against legitimate governments, and thus does nothing to limit the use of diamond revenue to finance human rights abuses by a government, for example in Zimbabwe.[7]
- Has been plagued by persistent enforcement issues—for example, despite its embargo in 2013 on diamonds from the Central African Republic, conflict diamonds from

areas controlled by armed groups in that country still easily reach international markets.

- Because it applies only to rough diamonds, the stones are no longer covered once they are cut (see www.globalwitness.org/en/campaigns/conflict-diamonds/kimberley-process).

Despite the initial promise of the scheme, it has been a failure within its current organization and limits. The woman who gets a diamond engagement ring still has no assurance whatever that the gem on her finger is not directly associated with oppression, torture, suffering and murder.

"Publish What You Pay"

The Publish What You Pay initiative originated in 2002 in a call by a coalition of NGOs worldwide for mandatory disclosure of the payments made by oil, gas and mining companies to all governments for the extraction of natural resources—in order to help citizens of resource-rich countries to hold their own governments accountable for the management of the revenues. The initiative found its most important success in June 2016—when the US Securities and Exchange Commission promulgated a rule requiring oil, gas and mining companies listed on US stock exchanges to publicly disclose the billions of dollars in payments they make to governments around the world in exchange for natural resources. "Promoting Revenue Transparency" is a related initiative calling on the international oil and gas companies to make regular reports in all areas relevant to revenue transparency, on a country-by-country basis, and to discourage governments from including confidentiality clauses in contracts with them.

What Else Can Be Done?

The EITI Global Conference in Lima in February 2016 recognized the extensive violations of its founding principle of independent, equal and full participation by civil society, violations which have gravely weakened the initiative (Westenberg, 2016). It is not clear that the EITI will address this problem forcefully in the future. A hopeful development, however, was the adoption of a new standard. The new standard significantly broadens the reporting by implementing countries, and its most significant provision is the requirement to disclose the identity of those who own and profit from extractive activities. Because secret ownership structures can enable extractive companies to evade taxes or hide improper relationships with government officials, all countries are expected to ensure that the companies that bid for, operate or invest in extractive projects declare who their beneficial owners are. Inexplicably, the requirement is scheduled to take effect only in 2020 "to give countries time to undertake the necessary preparations," but it is potentially important. Only time will tell.[8]

The Kimberley Process could regain some effectiveness if: (i) its provisions applied to diamonds in all forms; (ii) it considered the implications for *all* human rights abuses, including internal, before giving its approval to exporting the stones; and (iii) it was administered by a permanent independent organization instead of the current system of rotating country chairs. (In 2011, the Kimberley organization chair was from the Democratic Republic of the Congo, despite the fact that diamonds and other precious minerals in the east of the country have been the basis for a major regional conflict with millions of casualties.)

Approaches similar to a (strengthened) Kimberley Process should be devised and applied to other conflict minerals, the exploitation of which has been associated with severe conflict and human tragedy on a massive scale, for example the columbite and tantalite that are essential for electronic devices.

Much would be accomplished, too, if all countries adopted the US Securities and Exchange Commission requirement that oil, gas and mining companies listed on stock exchanges must publicly disclose the payments they make to governments in exchange for natural resources.

An especially promising alternative to complicated arrangements to use the extractive revenue for investment projects, targeted public expenditure and other schemes is to simply make cash transfers from the revenue to local communities or individuals (see Moss et al., 2015). The Independent Evaluation Group evaluation of the Chad–Cameroon oil development and pipeline construction noted that direct cash transfers to low-income people would have been far preferable to the complicated budgetary arrangements to allocate a portion of the oil revenue to pro-poor activities—arrangements which fell apart after a short time of implementation. At least there would be assurance that the money is received by those who need it.

Botswana has a very simple and effective way to protect extractive revenues. In a twist on the "golden rule" (by which borrowing can only be for investment, thus implying a primary balance), all mineral revenue is destined for investment. Use of mineral revenues has followed a self-discipline fiscal rule, the Sustainable Budget Index (SBI), under which any mineral revenue is supposed to finance "development expenditure," defined as investment expenditure and recurrent spending on development projects.

Other steps may also be taken within the affected countries themselves, by gradually and selectively increasing the capacity of citizens to exert influence over their government. In the same context, well-designed international initiatives to support and give voice to local communities in the mining regions and to small-scale and artisanal miners may be realistic, and could help make the sharing of extractive revenues less inequitable and alleviate some of the conflict and human costs of mineral exploitation.

In the final analysis, however, the road to exorcising the resource curse goes through a lasting improvement in governance in the concerned countries, which would open the door to a variety of measures to use extractive resource revenue for the benefit of the majority of the population.

Improving governance in extractive resource-rich countries is a delicate and long-term agenda, but the international community can at least abstain from strengthening the position of ruling elites in unrepresentative regimes in resource-rich countries. Unfortunately, but not surprisingly, the opposite takes place and the local populations of resource-rich countries pay a heavy price for the appetite for extractive resources of both western and Asian countries.[9] (It was particularly jarring to see President Barack Obama and his wife, Michelle, in 2010 beaming out of a *Washington Post* photo next to the president of Equatorial Guinea and his wife—in sharp contrast with the speech on good governance that Obama himself had delivered in Ghana a few months earlier.)

Military and Security Expenditure[10]

Three General Considerations

First, there is no necessary connection between military expenditure and the security of the nation or of its people. It is often argued that military unpreparedness invites attack, and thus that military expenditures preserve peace. This may be true under some circumstances, but the opposite can be true as well. The Greek historian Thucydides identified 2,500 years ago what later came to be called the *security dilemma*: "What made war inevitable was the growth of Athenian power and the fear which this caused in Sparta" (Blanco and Roberts, 1998). When a state feels threatened by the higher military spending of another state to enhance its security, it may follow suit and the resulting arms race actually ends up diminishing security for both states. It is not a paradox that Costa Rica is the most secure (and most democratic) country in Central America. As former Costa Rican president and 1989 Nobel Peace laureate Oscar Arias put it: "Costa Rica enjoys greater external security *because* it has had no army for 60 years." (Personal communication, February 1999.) And, concerning internal security, consider the reality that in much of the developing world the worst threats to the security of the ordinary citizens come from their own police and soldiers.

Second, in countries where a military apparatus is considered justified on grounds of genuine national security, it does not necessarily follow that further *increases* in military expenditure bring about an improvement in security. The relationship of military spending to national security is not linear: it depends on the composition of expenditure, the extent of wasteful spending, the suitability of military hardware and the nature of the expected conflicts. Intangible motivational factors are important as well. For example, the huge military and security apparatus of the Shah of Iran gave the regime no protection against the 1979 revolution. (Even his personal guard, "The Immortals," melted away, giving rise to the quip that the name was explained by their ability to avoid danger.) And, in June 2014, the Iraqi military in the city of Mosul—unpaid, untrained, unled—simply ran when confronted with a far smaller number of ISIS fighters.

Third, when it is determined that a military apparatus is necessary, the overall amount of spending is appropriate, and its composition is suitable—the opportunity cost must still be reckoned with. Opportunity cost is the real measure of cost, i.e., the goods or services or assets that could have been produced by the same resources. As in the Eisenhower quote at the start of the chapter, military expenditure inevitably crowds out civilian expenditure (and/or requires tax increases, and/or destabilizes the public finances). Low-income countries spend on average about 50 cents on the military for every government dollar they spend on health and education combined. The opportunity cost is high in rich countries as well. In the US, for example, it is a matter of simple arithmetic that the money spent on the wars in Iraq and Afghanistan alone could have assured the financial sustainability of the social security system, or extended financial aid to all college students in the country, or paid off a large part of the public debt, etc. Economic activity is affected adversely as well: there is evidence that a high share of GDP dedicated to military spending is associated with lower economic growth in the long run (Shieh et al., 2002). Returning to the example of Costa Rica, that country's good economic performance for 60 years and excellent human development indicators are unquestionably related to the higher government spending on social services permitted by not having to spend the money for military purposes.

The Size of Military Spending

After its reduction in the 1990s following the end of the Cold War, military expenditure has bounced back, amounting in 2015 to $1.8 trillion worldwide (on average $250 per year per person), of which over one-third, $610 billion, was spent by the United States (on average $1,900 per year per person). Moreover, the true size of the military sector should include the sales of arms-producing companies. The top 100 arms-producing companies combined sold in 2015 over $400 billion worth of arms, with the United States, France and Russia as the major producers. Some 45 countries produce some type of arms, and many of them (including, in addition to the major producers, Israel, Korea, Brazil, South Africa and Singapore) undertake military exports. The size of the military sector worldwide is larger than the GDP of France.

Moreover, official military expenditure figures understate the actual amounts, and are opaque. Military expenditure is rarely disaggregated, and intelligence expenditure is usually secret altogether. (In the US, the "black budget" of the civilian and military intelligence agencies is debated and decided behind closed doors, although the total spending is known—about $85 billion in 2015, substantially more than total federal expenditure on education.) The income from arms exports and the earnings from the business activities of the military are not fully shown on the revenue side. Off-budget items, such as expenditure on paramilitary forces, food or housing subsidies to army personnel, military R&D, and subsidies for arms production, are often not shown separately in the budget at all. Even when the secrecy and opaqueness are justified on national security grounds, they make it difficult for oversight agencies to exercise audit and vigilance; military and security spending thus carries an inherent potential for waste and abuse. Sunshine is the best disinfectant.

A major source of fiscal risk is that the financial repercussions of a war last long after its conclusion and are not properly considered in the budget process. In addition to the overt costs of war, the costs borne by combatants, their families, and the country are life-long. Edwards (2010) shows that the benefits distributed over the remaining life spans of veterans and their dependants account for between one-third and one-half of the historical war costs. The private financial burden of war borne by survivors, primarily the uncompensated costs of a service-related injuries, are also large and long-lasting.

Analyzing Security Sector Expenditures

In principle, expenditure in the security sector (military, paramilitary, intelligence and police) should be guided by the same criteria of good governance and public financial management that apply to civilian expenditure—accountability, transparency, rule of law and participation—but in this sector the criteria have special meaning and clear limits. Conceptually, it is much harder to assess the benefits of military expenditure than those of expenditure on civilian activities, such as transport or education; quantifying costs is easier for some expenditure categories (e.g., military salaries) than for others (e.g., alternative weapons systems which rest on different strategic assumptions); and certain concepts are simply inapplicable to the military (e.g., "depreciation" of a Tomahawk missile). Practically, of course, the subject is highly sensitive, and governments have an understandable resistance to external scrutiny.

There has also been a disconnect between the economic and the political. Attempts have been made at designing reviews of expenditure in the security sector—see the initiative in the African Security Sector Network (2016) as an example—but with little success. The knowledge gap is large. Public expenditure reviews (mainly by the World Bank) have traditionally avoided military and security issues, as being beyond their mandate to support economic development; and reviews of the security sector (mainly by the UN) have neglected issues of public expenditure and financial management. The challenge is to join the political to the economic, the civilian with the military, and—possibly the hardest aspect—induce the World Bank and the UN to cooperate closely.

The main requirement for a meaningful security sector expenditure review is strong commitment by the national leadership, supported by active cooperation from the key officials of the concerned ministries—primarily defense, interior and, of course, finance. This is clearly out of the question in countries ruled by unrepresentative regimes relying on the military or police to stay in power. When circumstances permit, however, it can be very important for the country to have an independent and fact-based analysis of the level of security spending compared with civilian expenditure, its composition and sustainability, the efficiency of military procurement, and the institutional framework which governs relations between the security apparatus and the civilian government. This is especially true of countries emerging from dictatorships, that wish to reassert civilian control within a representative political structure. Guinea after the transition to (still shaky) democratic government in 2010 is a case in point (see Box 17.3).

Box 17.3 Revenue and Expenditure in the Security Sector of Guinea

Recognizing the potential threats from the security apparatus, after the exit from 50 years of dictatorship, the new government launched in 2011 a Security Sector Reform National Action Plan to reform and modernize the internal security and defense forces. Under UN leadership, various international partners are defining their roles in support of the strategic reorientation of the security sector; the UN itself is providing technical support to implement the security reorientation; and the World Bank is addressing the public financial implications.

The central challenge is to strengthen the control of the civilian authorities over the finances of the security sector. Neither the revenue accruing to the internal security and defense organizations nor their expenditures were known, as a result of their totally off-budget nature. As a consequence, fiscal transparency was nil, integrity was highly suspect, and the real costs of maintaining the security apparatus were unknown. The immediate priorities were to undertake a comprehensive audit of military expenditure; establish basic fiduciary controls (including procurement and financial management); and ensure a link between the eventual national security policy and the fiscal capacity of the Guinean state. Accordingly, the World Bank provided support to strengthen transparency and civilian oversight of budget preparation, budget execution and monitoring in the security sector, and specifically to:

- Identify the sources and estimate the revenue accruing to the security institutions, and recommend measures to assure transparency, integrity and appropriate allocation.
- Quantify the total expenditure of the security and defense organizations (particularly wage and pension expenditure), in order to establish a baseline for the potential savings expected from the strategic reorientation as well as evaluating future budget requests from those organizations.
- Formulate a realistic approach to integrate all security sector expenditures into the annual government budget; associate the security organizations with the preparation of the budget, at par with the other organs of central government; assure that the classification of security and defense expenditure conforms to the uniform budgetary classification; and produce scenarios of expenditure needs over the medium term, as an input into the overall medium-term fiscal and expenditure forecasts.
- Define provisions for financial reporting and external audit that are appropriate to the specific aspects of the security and defense organizations while also consistent with overall reporting and audit standards applicable to civilian revenue and expenditure.

Sources: Government of Guinea; World Bank reports.

The Special Issues of Military Procurement

The Nature of the Market: A Bilateral Monopoly

Military procurement differs from civilian procurement, as it is affected by considerations of national security and is thus politically sensitive and conducted in a less transparent manner than other forms of procurement. Equally important is the bilateral monopoly structure of the market for military equipment and weapons. On the supply side, the number of suppliers is limited to less than a handful due to the barriers to entry generated by the high investment in research and development (R&D) and the enormous fixed costs in the production of costly defense equipment. On the demand side, the government has a monopsony (is the sole buyer) on the equipment and spare parts produced by the defense industry.

The special problems of military procurement arise from both sides of this bilateral monopoly. Indeed, the "demand" and "supply" sides become intertwined as part of a single Gordian knot, extremely difficult to unravel and politically impossible to cut. The label "military–industrial complex" (from President Eisenhower's farewell speech on leaving the presidency in 1960) sums up the nexus between domestic industry and the defense establishment. Military hardware (aerospace equipment, telecommunications and electronics, explosives, shipbuilding equipment, etc.) accounts for the single largest share of total equipment expenditure in the US, and contracts for defense equipment and R&D can give suppliers a competitive advantage in technological, commercial and financial terms.

The Situation in Developed Countries

A distinction should be drawn between special military equipment that has a specific defense use and commercial off-the-shelf defense supplies—for both civilian and defense use. The purchase of special military equipment cannot be subject to the normal procurement processes, and the sums involved can be enormous: just the pilot's helmet for the F-35 joint strike fighter costs $400,000. However, there is no justification for not applying the principles of public procurement to purchases of foodstuff, transport and civilian supplies. Even in such ordinary purchases there are stories of grotesque overpricing—$5,000 coffeepots, $200 pliers and similar absurdities (Gregory, 1989). In part, these "prices" are only an accounting quirk—the result of spreading vast overhead expenses across the entire range of products. But only in part—because overpricing arises more often from excessive specifications in military contracts even for everyday items and from grossly inadequate cost-consciousness of the responsible government authorities. In defense of high prices, contractors argue that they must recover the entire overhead cost of production from the items supplied to the military (as opposed to spreading the cost across millions of items in a production run for civilian sales). This is quite unconvincing in large countries, where the scale of the military purchases of ordinary supplies is more than ample to absorb production at lowest unit cost. We are talking of raincoats here, not aircraft carriers.

In the case of military equipment and supplies, many countries prefer to buy from home producers, even at additional cost. Regional procurement agreements, such as those of the EU, eliminate preferences for locally produced civilian goods but exempt military equipment.

In developed countries, the process of military procurement is complex, normally including a protracted itinerary through various levels of approval, from contracting officers to their superiors, then the treasury, and finally a ministerial committee. The process is further complicated by unnecessarily detailed requirements and specifications, compelling the industry to prepare costly and voluminous proposals, which then have to be analyzed in great detail by a large team of evaluators. Not surprisingly, all this red tape is then used by suppliers to justify their overpricing. Much of the military waste and delay that has been publicized in the US can be attributed to the vicious circle of over specification; excessive paperwork and compliance requirements; too many layers of authority and supervision within the executive; and micromanagement by the Defense Department and the Congress (Gregory, 1989). These complicated requirements were introduced partly to combat corruption, but have not even succeeded in doing so (see Box 17.4 for an example).

Box 17.4 Buying the Buyer: Boeing and Air Force Procurement

As the number two procurement executive for the Air Force, Darleen Druyun negotiated a bizarre deal by which the Air Force would spend billions to lease from Boeing tanker planes that the department's own experts said were not needed—at a
higher cost, when properly calculated, than the cost of buying the planes outright.
Not only did she agree to a $100 million lease price per aircraft, much higher than
appropriate, but she also gave Boeing confidential information about a competitor.
This was no isolated billion-dollar peccadillo, however. Among Ms. Druyun's many
other favors to Boeing, in chronological order:

*   In 2000, she agreed to pay $412 million to Boeing as settlement over a clause in
    an aircraft contract...
*   Boeing hired her son-in-law.
*   In 2001, she was the lead procurement official in awarding Boeing, over four
    competing firms, a $4 billion contract to modernize the C-130 plane...
*   Boeing hired her daughter.
*   In 2002 she awarded $100 million to Boeing as part of the "restructuring" of a
    NATO AWACS contract. Then came the tanker plane deal, and, right after
    Druyun retired from the Air Force...
*   Boeing hired *her*.

The General Accountability Office received protests alleging Druyun's exercise of
improper influence on contracts awarded to Boeing. The GAO sustained the protests: the C-130 contract was resubmitted to competition and the tanker leasing deal
was stopped altogether. Darleen Druyun was sentenced to less than a year in jail and
fined $5,000. The real issue is not her behavior, however, but the colossal failure of
oversight in the system. Nobody in Air Force senior management was penalized for
such failure of oversight, and no employee of Boeing was prosecuted (although the
CEO was eased out, with all his perks and golden parachute intact).

   Aside from all other considerations, what is curious is how cheap it can be in America
to buy your government buyer. For the price of three jobs, adding up to perhaps a
measly half million dollars a year, Boeing got preferential treatment in the award of
contracts worth billions of dollars—a return on investment of over 10,000 to one.

Sources: GAO, *Air Force Procurement: Protests Challenging Role of Biased Official Sustained*,
Report GAO-05-436T, April 14, 2005, and various news accounts.

The complications arising from the demand side are complemented by various suppliers'
practices. The three most frequent ones are:

*   An unrealistically low bid is made in order to gain a contract, only to claim larger
    expenses after the contract has been awarded. This is facilitated by the "cost-plus"
    provisions frequent in military procurement contracts, by which the supplier is reim-
    bursed all of its costs plus a profit—removing all incentive to economy and efficiency.
    (The alternative is a fixed-price contract, which military suppliers resist, alleging the
    greater uncertainties of production for the military.)
*   Another tactic is to "get the camel's nose in the tent," used for exceptionally costly pro-
    grams. When the sticker shock of the total cost of the entire program would raise ques-
    tions about objectives, means and cost-effectiveness, the program is fragmented into

separate pieces, the costs of which are revealed piece by piece so that the total amount of money never appears at any one time. After large sums have been spent, and vested interests have been created, it is much harder for the legislature and the public to resist spending whatever is needed to actually complete the program.

- Political and financial opposition can be neutralized by distributing bits of the production of major weapons programs in dozens of different electoral districts throughout the country—generating support by local elected politicians. (This is a double-edged tactic, however, because it also makes it very hard to terminate programs or close unneeded military bases.)

Finally, the secrecy inherent in the security sector, the specialized authority exercised by a few individuals and the high cost of military equipment are a perfect recipe for corruption. This corruption can take the form of outright bribes as in the case described in Box 17.4, but normally takes the safer and more insidious form of post-retirement million-dollar jobs for procurement officials in the same defense firms from which they had authorized the purchases made. (The topic of corruption in procurement is addressed in Chapter 16.)

The Situation in Developing Countries

The situation is very different for developing countries, most of which have no defense industry and depend entirely on imports, where the balance of bargaining power is with the suppliers. Where purchase evaluation capacity is weak, the potential for bribery is aggravated by the danger of purchasing inefficient equipment—guns that do not fire or planes that do not fly. At the same time, building a domestic defense production capability is neither possible nor desirable; apart from problems of patents and secrecy, the R&D costs are unaffordable for most developing countries. And when they can be afforded, as in the largest countries such as Brazil and India, the large investment required would add far more to the country's well-being and long-term security if it were spent on improving basic health care and education and lifting millions of citizens out of poverty. (The exception is North Korea, where vast expenditures are made on weapons production in the midst of deprivation of most of the population and starvation of a large segment of it.)

Where military aid loans are tied to purchases from the lending country, the recipient country has little control over the cost and quality of the equipment, and merely watches as its foreign debt rises along with its defense spending. Locked into the use of particular equipment and transport, the country also becomes vulnerable to a cutoff in supply of spare parts and replacements. Military procurement thus becomes the handmaiden of the vagaries of foreign policy. Conversely, countries seeking to buy locally the foodstuffs, spares and supplies needed in connection with their military assistance are often confronted with collusion and corruption. (South Korea in the 1960s is a case in point—see Klitgaard, 1991. The situation in that country is quite different today.)

Unlike in arms-producing developed countries, the administrative challenge in developing countries is not to reduce overregulation and complexity, as in developed countries, but to move toward transparent and consistent practices for military procurement, adequate legislative oversight and audit, and the reduction of individual discretion by institutionalizing decisions relating to the acquisition of costly equipment from foreign suppliers.

Military procurement is permeated by the interplay of international and local companies, liaison agents, arms bazaars, bribes and contributions to political parties, and is punctuated by the outbreak of scandals and media exposés. The best cover for corruption in international defense procurement is the "commission" paid by the foreign company to a local agent. The agent is given enough money to land the contract by any means necessary, without the company having to know the details, creating a comfortable distance between the company and the bribe and enabling all parties to disclaim any knowledge of the unsavory details of the deal—should these be exposed. The corruptive influence of military equipment imports in a developing country is next only to that from large extractive resources such as oil.

Are Improvements in Military Procurement Possible?

It is certainly possible to apply sound procurement principles to military purchases while fully protecting confidentiality and secrecy for national security. For example, while protecting the confidentiality of transactions, Singapore has declared and implemented a transparent policy for defense procurement based on open bidding. The approach is to plug up the openings for corruption by selecting the best source that meets Singapore's military requirements and gives best value for money. The government does so by dealing directly with overseas and domestic suppliers and avoiding intermediary agents in contract negotiations. Canada has devised a "Smart Procurement Initiative" in consultation with the defense industry—including incremental acquisition, greater flexibility and delegation of procurement for small-value and off-the-shelf items, and streamlined decision-making. At a minimum, even military procurement must be subject to oversight by the supreme audit institution, as in the US with the publication of General Accountability Office audit reports for the benefit of the legislature and the public.

These good practices are unlikely to be adopted in most countries: in developing countries accountability is weak, and in developed countries the domestic arms industry holds great sway over the government. If, as Samuel Johnson said in 1775, patriotism is the last refuge of scoundrels, national security is the best cover for crooked procurement deals. Moreover, in countries where the survival of civilian government depends on the support of the military, touching military procurement is like touching the electrified third rail of the subway.

Partial solutions can be found in the application of ICT. By putting to work the computing power of today's technology, the choices to be made under the complicated regulations of military procurement can be rationalized and expedited. An initiative to that effect was launched in the US in 2016 (see Box 17.5) and similar efforts are just beyond the horizon in other developed countries with substantial military spending.

Box 17.5 Tackling the Military Procurement Monster in the US

Lost in trying to navigate the 1,900 pages of the acquisition process, and rebuffed in their attempts to defeat the procurement bureaucracy, humans are now looking for deliverance to Watson—IBM's cognitive learning supercomputer. Suppliers and the Air Force are developing software to harness artificial intelligence to digest the immense documentation and requirements of military procurement. If successful, the initiative would be a plus–plus: government procurement staff could have all their specific queries answered easily; the suppliers would be able to identify quickly programs and equipment they may be interested in bidding on; both sides could track the stages of the process in real time; transparency would increase; and, possibly, the space for collusion and favoritism would be reduced. The first step is to feed Watson all the relevant rules and documents. After it has digested them, it will receive thousands of specific questions to enable it to understand context and nuance and provide feedback that will lead to transactions that are rapid and effective as well as legal.

On a different track, Congress is being urged to allow procurement of military packages, giving the responsible manager in the Pentagon the flexibility to replace, change or adjust one or another component of the package without having to go back to Congress each time for permission.

Source: Adapted from Davenport (2016).

Notes

1   In Cameroon, for example, oil revenue was considered a state secret, ostensibly to avoid the public pressures to expand government expenditure that would ensue from widespread knowledge of the large revenue; the argument sounds suspect, but in fact government expenditure from independence through the early 1980s was well contained and fiscal policy was prudent. The motivation of the secrecy and the use of the revenue changed for the worse after the removal of former President Ahidjo in 1982 (Schiavo-Campo et al., 1982).

2   The term "resource curse"—credited to Alan Gelb (1988)—refers to the negative impact of excessive reliance on revenue from extractive resources, which in many countries has led to pervasive corruption, economic stagnation and lack of representative institutions. For a summary of the main issues, see Gelb (1988), whose findings were first confirmed by Auty (1993), and later by many others, including Karl (1997) and McFerson (2010).

3   The term "paradox of plenty" was coined by Karl (1997).

4   The word was coined in the late 1970s by *The Economist* magazine to explain the consequences of the discovery of North Sea natural gas near Holland.

5   The implications have been widespread throughout the world. Contrasting examples are Venezuela, where the decline in oil rents that have been propping up the increasingly inefficient economic model caused it to totter, and Nigeria, where a peaceful democratic transition in 2014 has been threatened by the sharp drop in revenue and thus social spending.

6   Revenue transparency is necessary but not sufficient to improve the use of extractive revenues for growth and poverty reduction. In 2006 the World Bank launched the "EITI++" initiative, which aims at addressing problems throughout the entire value chain—extraction, exploitation, revenue and utilization (see Alba, 2009, for details). Unlike the EITI, which is a standard-setting and rule-compliance initiative, the EITI++ is intended to provide technical support to governments that wish to use the extractive revenue for development and poverty reduction, and thus require real government ownership—hardly to be expected in the likes of Angola and Equatorial Guinea.

7   The Kimberley organization approved export of the diamonds in Zimbabwe's Marange region (where mining activities were forcibly taken over by the army in 2008)—despite evidence that the revenue was used to finance the secret police and government repression. The regime's Central Intelligence Organization has its own parallel budget, financed by a Hong Kong businessman in exchange for diamond concessions.

8   For details on the new EITI standard see https://eiti.org/news/2016-eiti-standard-reports-results [accessed November 9, 2016].

9   Cf. *US Foreign Policy Saps Human Rights Improvements in Ethiopia and Equatorial Guinea.* Testimony by Lynn Fredriksson to the House Committee on Foreign Affairs, Washington, DC, 2007.

10 This section relies in part on Stockholm International Peace Research Institute (SIPRI) (2014); Gregory (1989); Brzoska (1999); and Jones (1999).

Bibliography

Acemoglu, Daron, Simon Johnson and James Robinson, 2003. "Botswana: an African Success Story," in Dani Rodrick, ed., *In Search of Prosperity: Analytic Narratives on Economic Growth.* Princeton, NJ: Princeton University Press.

African Security Sector Network. 2016. Available online at www.africansecuritynetwork.org [accessed November 9, 2016].

Alba, Eleodoro Mayorga, 2009. *Extractive Industries Value Chain: A Comprehensive Integrated Approach to Developing Extractive Industries.* Washington, DC: The World Bank.

Auty, Richard M. 1993. *Sustaining Development in the Mineral Economies: The Resource Curse Thesis.* London: Routledge.

Black, Lambert, 2007. "Oil Money Remains a Poisonous Influence in International Politics," *World Politics Review Exclusive*, September 7.

Blanco, Walter and Jennifer Roberts, eds. 1998. *Thucydides: The Peloponnesian War.* New York; London: W. W. Norton.

Brzoska, Michael, 1999. "Military Conversion: The Balance Sheet," *Journal of Peace Research*, 36(2), 131–40.

Clark, Gordon L., Adam Dixon and Ashby Monk, 2013. *Sovereign Wealth Funds: Legitimacy, Governance, and Global Power.* Princeton, NJ: Princeton University Press.

Davenport, Christian, 2016. "Watson to Take on the Federal Morass," *Washington Post*, March 21.

Davis, Jeffrey, Rolando Ossowski, James Daniel and Steven Barnett, 2001. "Oil Funds: Problems Posing as Solutions," *Finance and Development*, 38(4).

Edwards, Ryan, 2010. "A Review of War Costs in Iraq and Afghanistan," Working Paper 16163. National Bureau of Economic Research.

Friedman, Thomas, 2009. "Bullets and Barrels," *The New York Times*, June 20.

Gelb, Alan, 1988. *Oil Windfalls: Blessing or Curse?* New York: Oxford University Press.

Gregory, W. H., 1989. *The Defense Procurement Mess*. Lanhan, MA: Lexington Books.

Jones, Philip, 1999. "Rent-Seeking and Defense Expenditure," *Defense and Peace Economics*, 10(1), 171–90.

Karl, Terry Linn, 1997. *The Paradox of Plenty: Oil Booms and Petro-States*. Berkeley, CA: University of California Press.

Klitgaard, Robert, 1990. *Tropical Gangsters*. New York: Tauris.

Klitgaard, Robert, 1991. *Controlling Corruption*. Berkeley, CA: University of California Press.

Lissakers, Karin and Peter Rosenblum, 2009. "Secrecy Fuels Suspicion About Mining Contracts," *Financial Times*, October 16.

Ljungaeus, Diana, 2007. "Malibu Bad Neighbor," *LA Weekly*, January 17, available online at www. laweekly.com/2007-01-18/news/malibu-bad-neighbor/ [accessed November 9, 2016].

Maass, Peter, 1990. "A Touch of Crude," available online at www.petermaass.com/articles/a_touch_ of_crude/ [accessed November 9, 2016].

McFerson, Hazel, 2009. "Governance and Hyper-Corruption in Resource-rich African Countries," *Third World Quarterly*, 30(8), 1529–47.

——, 2010. "Extractive Industries and African Democracies: Can the 'Resource Curse' Be Exorcised?" *International Studies Perspectives*, 11(4), 335–53.

Moss, Todd, Caroline Lambert and Stephanie Majerowicz, 2015. *Oil to Cash: Fighting the Resource Curse Through Cash Transfers*. Washington, DC: Center for Global Development.

Naim, Moises, 2009. "The Devil's Excrement: Can Oil Rich Countries Avoid the Resource Curse?" *Foreign Policy*, September/October.

Schiavo-Campo, S., J. Roush, A. Lemelin and M. McLinden, 1982. *The Tortoise Walk: Public Policy and Private Activity in the Economic Development of Cameroon*. Washington, DC: USAID.

Shaxson, Nicholas, 2007. *Poisoned Wells: The Dirty Politics of African Oil*. New York; Basingstoke, UK: Palgrave Macmillan.

Shieh, J., C. Lai and W. Chang, 2002. "The Impact of Military Burden on Long-Run Growth and Welfare," *Journal of Development Economics*, 68(2), 443–54.

Stockholm International Peace Research Institute, 2014. *Year Book 2014: Armaments, Disarmaments and International Security*. Oxford: Oxford University Press.

Westenberg, Erica, 2016. "What You Didn't Hear about EITI," available online at www. resourcegovernance.org [accessed November 9, 2016].

Index

Figures and tables are given in *italics*